The Digital Filmmaking Handbook

Presents

Premiere Pro for Filmmakers

Sonja Schenk

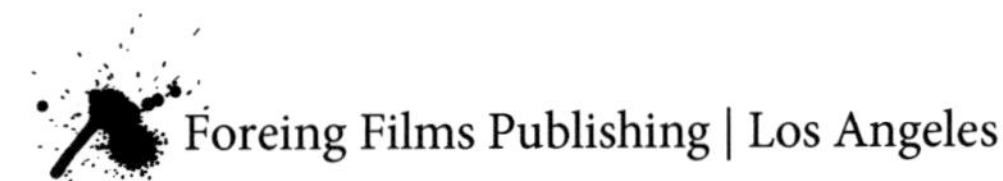

The Digital Filmmaking Handbook Presents (series)
Premiere Pro for Filmmakers
Sonja Schenk

Foreing Films Publishing

General Manager: Rainer Plain

Project and Copy Editor: Diego Harper

Technical Reviewer: Lauren Atchison

Interior Layout Tech: FF Inc.

Media credits:
Adobe product screenshot(s) reprinted with permission from Adobe; *The Olivia Experiment*, courtesy of Mansfield Films; *Jackson's Hole,* courtesy of Juri Koll; mural art media courtesy of Shutterstock; Artemis Program images courtesy of NASA, *Mural Art Today* footage courtesy of Foreing Films; Sapphire effects image courtesy of Boris FX; green screen images courtesy of Red Giant; *Brewmance* courtesy of Christo Brock; *Hell CA* courtesy of Bonné Barton; all other uncredited images and media, Sonja Schenk

Library of Congress Control Number: 2019957930
ISBN-13: 978-1-7331502-0-0
ISSN 2690-0424

Foreing Films Publishing 3751 Motor Avenue, #1885, Los Angeles, CA 90034 USA

For product information and technology assistance, contact us at: publisher@thedigitalfilmmakinghandbook.com
For permission to use material from this text or product, submit all requests via email to publisher@thedigitalfilmmakinghandbook.com

Visit our website at **thedigitalfilmmakinghandbook.com**

ACKNOWLEDGMENTS

There are many people to thank. Our publisher, Rainer Plain, for dedication and support, technical editor, Lauren Atchison, for offering exceptional expertise and sharing her passion for filmmaking, and a special thank you to Ben Long, co-author of The Digital Filmmaking Handbook and writing partner of many years.

Last, but not least, we'd like to thank the filmmakers, writers, and producers who gave us their photos, their film clips and, most importantly, their stories: Alexandra Komisaruk, Juri Koll, Bonné Bartron, Christo Brock, Sean Wagstaff, Eugene Rosow, Regina Saisi, Dawn Dagucon, William MacCollum, Paquita Parks, and Jason Hampton.

ABOUT THE AUTHOR

Sonja Schenk is a Los Angeles-based filmmaker and artist. Her first short film premiered at the AFI festival when she was a student. She has an MFA in film from the University of Southern California. She directed the theatrically-released, independent feature comedy, *The Olivia Experiment,* and has written several screenplays. Her showrunner credits include several prominent television series, including *The Bachelor, The Bachelorette,* and *High School Reunion.* She has edited over 15 feature films, both scripted and docs, including premieres at the Sundance Film Festival, Rotterdam International Film Festival, and many others. Having started out as a video artist, she continues to make and exhibit art that shows internationally and is a member of the video collective *Paper Tiger TV*, a retrospective of which was included in the 2019 Whitney Biennial. She has contributed many articles on filmmaking and video technology to various publications, is the co-author of *The Digital Filmmaking Handbook* and the editor of the companion book series *The Digital Filmmaking Handbook Presents.* She is currently in development on a new feature film.

The Digital Filmmaking Handbook Presents

Premiere Pro for Filmmakers is the first book in our new, single-topic, companion series, *The Digital Filmmaking Handbook Presents.*

Many readers have been asking for more in-depth discussion of topics like cinematography, editing applications, color grading, and screenwriting. This series picks up where *The Digital Filmmaking Handbook* leaves off, tackling each topic exclusively, and as always, from the perspective of working filmmakers.

CONTENTS

Introduction

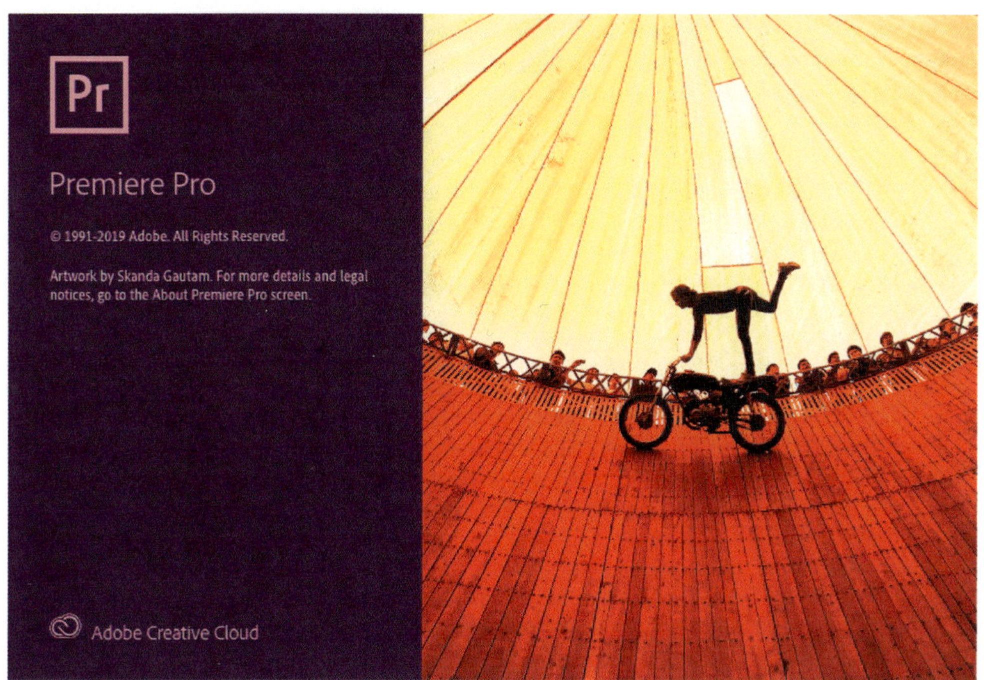

Editing for Filmmakers

EVERYONE EDITS VIDEO, at least a little bit. But there's a huge difference between trimming a clip for social media and truly making a film, whether it's short, long, or episodic. During the film editing process, filmmakers work with many different shots, often from multiple cameras, and combine them with other key elements such as music, graphics, and effects, to tell a story that builds from beginning to end.

Storytelling is the ultimate goal of all filmmakers. As a result, everything you do while editing your film serves this goal. Shot choices, tone, and pacing are all part of the storyteller's palette. As for the editing software, it's just a tool to help you get there.

Filmmakers—even beginners—use tools like Premiere Pro to their fullest capacity.

This book was written to help you learn how to use Premiere Pro to edit your film so that you can tell the story you want to tell.

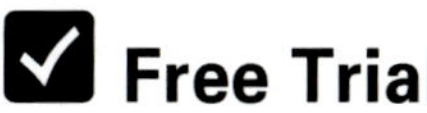

Free Trial

Adobe offers a 30-day free trial version of Premiere Pro, which is long enough to work your way through this book. And they offer reduced subscription rates for students.

Why Premiere Pro?

Adobe Premiere has been around for a long time. It's one of the original digital editing applications, launched way back in 1991. A couple years ago, it got a significant update from Adobe and is now part of their Creative Cloud suite of visual design applications. That means a lot of people use it, from filmmakers to designers to just about anyone who needs video.

From a very practical perspective, Premiere plays nice with others. Not only does it feature seamless integration with related apps like After Effects and Media Encoder, it also lets you work with all kinds of media, even 360-degree VR footage. And it doesn't force you to suffer through long conversion or transcoding processes to do this. Add to this, the very tight integration of plugins, such as the many popular audio and special effects packages, and you have a full-featured, extensible editing system. Best of all, if you have a Creative Cloud subscription, it's included. So, if you're thinking of trying to learn how to edit or put a short film together, you can likely have Premiere up and running on your computer in a matter of minutes.

Adobe Premiere comes in three flavors:

> **Premiere Pro**, as you might guess, is the professional version of Premiere, aimed at filmmakers, episodic series producers, and serious students. It is designed to compete with other professional editing applications like Avid Media Composer and Apple Final Cut Pro. It offers a complex array of editing, media management, audio, graphics and special effects capabilities. If you're making a dramatic film, TV pilot, or documentary, this is the version of Premiere you want.
>
> **Premiere Elements** is a scaled-down version of Premiere aimed at entry-level users and people who may only need to use Premiere occasionally and for shorter projects. If you use Premiere once or twice a year to make a video for your family or a class project, Premiere Elements may be all you need and the learning curve will be less steep. Think of it as Adobe's answer to iMovie.
>
> **Premiere Rush** is a sort of baby Premiere aimed at quickly creating clips or movies for the web on your phone or your computer. Premiere Rush is particularly useful for editing video that you shot on your phone. If your project is a web series or even if you just have a bunch of clips you want to put together for something like a crowd funding campaign, Premiere Rush could be a great choice for you.

In this book, we focus on Premiere Pro.

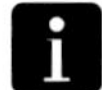 The Latest Version

Adobe tends to do frequent updates of Premiere Pro. The most current version at the time of this writing is Premiere Pro 14, aka Premiere Pro 2020 The examples in this book are from that version, but they will generally work with other versions as well. You should also make sure you have the right version of Media Encoder installed, since Premiere and Media Encoder need to work together. In addition, when you get to the sections on Audition and After Effects, you'll need to make sure that you have compatible versions of these applications and Premiere in order for Adobe Dynamic Link to work.

The Adobe Creative Cloud

In addition to Premiere, the Adobe Creative Cloud Suite offers a large selection of applications that are included in the subscription cost and there are many that you might use for your film. In reality, filmmakers use many apps during the course of making a movie so this book also includes discussions of the following apps when appropriate:

After Effects is probably the most popular motion graphics application for filmmakers. It offers very sophisticated tools for creating titles, adding motion to still images, and compositing. Sure you can do most of these things in Premiere but After Effects does them better. That doesn't mean you have to use it, but if you do use it, know that it works seamlessly with Premiere thanks to Adobe's Dynamic Link technology.

Audition is Adobe's audio editing companion to Premiere. Like After Effects and Media Encoder, it works seamlessly from within Premiere thanks to Dynamic Link. Most filmmakers will do the majority of their audio work in Premiere itself, but every now and then there will be an audio clip that has special needs. In those cases, Audition really comes in handy. And for those with sound editing backgrounds, Audition will be faster and better than the sound editing tools in Premiere.

Media Encoder This is a useful tool that lets you transcode media before you bring it into Premiere and export edited sequences from Premiere based on your settings. Media Encoder primarily functions as a background application, invisibly serving your media conversion needs while you edit in Premiere.

Prelude is a scaled-down logging application designed to let producers ingest, log, and make rough cuts of video. If you already have one of the three versions of Premiere, you probably won't need this app.

Photoshop or Lightroom If you have a lot of still images in your film, you'll want to pre-process them in one of Adobe's photography apps, Photoshop or Lightroom. It's much easier to make adjustments and corrections in these apps, which are designed specifically to work with still images, before you start editing with them in Premiere.

Bridge is a media cataloguing application that builds a database based on the contents of your computer and your hard drives. If you only have standard video and audio files, you really won't need Bridge. But if you have lot of other elements, like photographs and archival video clips, Bridge can be very useful. It lets you build smart folders (called Collections) and quickly scroll through thumbnails of your media.

Portfolio is an online web site service that comes free with your Creative Cloud subscription, similar to Weebly or Wix. It has a handful of templates and is aimed at visually-oriented websites. You can build a site that Adobe hosts for free or register a domain name for about $20 a year and link your site to that web address. It's a simple way to create a website for your film or production company. The only limitation is that they do not, at present, offer any form of "shopping" integration. So if you need a website in order to self-distribute your film with pay-per-view downloads, you'll have to go elsewhere.

Illustrator is the granddaddy of line-based, vector graphics. It's great for designing with text for titles and for creating scalable animation. Originally designed for very detailed, line-based work, Illustrator is usually used for print (like the diagrams in this book), but it's also frequently used to create elements for motion graphics.

Other stuff that the Creative Cloud subscription includes are access to hundreds of Adobe Typekit fonts, access to stock media at an additional price (including film clips, photos, and vector-graphics), cloud storage, and Adobe Color, which is just a fun app to play with.

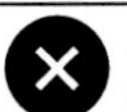

Bug Watch!

Premiere Pro is a big program and occasionally you'll encounter a bug. We'll use this icon to let you know about the ones that are important and offer some fixes or workarounds whenever possible.

Who This Book Is For

When Ben Long and I decided to write *The Digital Filmmaking Handbook*, our goal was to write a book we would want to read. We were both interested in making low-budget indie feature films. We looked for filmmaking books that integrated digital technology with traditional filmmaking tasks at the time and couldn't find anything. So we wrote it ourselves.

The same is true for this book. Adobe makes great software, but they are notoriously skimpy on documentation. At the time of this writing, their online manual for Premiere Pro doesn't even cover the current version of the software, which has been available for months. Half the time, if you try to search for help topics, you end up in a forum of fellow Premiere users who are just as confused as you are.

Lately, I've been finding myself using Premiere Pro more and more. In fact, I recently edited a feature documentary with it. With hundreds of hours of footage, shot over four years, using several different cameras, not mention archival materials from the 1970s and beyond, I can assure you that I've learned a lot about Premiere Pro.

This is the book that I wish I had when I started editing that movie.

So in a way, I wrote this book for me. But that doesn't mean it's only for pros, because like most filmmakers, I really enjoy digging into the basics of how Premiere works. I want to understand how to work with Premiere and not against it, and to avoid the pitfalls and technical challenges that could set me back days or weeks.

You May Need to Install Codecs

Premiere Pro needs to have the right codecs installed in order to playback and export video properly. To do the tutorials in this book, you should have the Apple ProRes and h.264 codecs installed. Video codecs work in a way that's very similar to printer drivers: they add functionality to your computer. You'll need to search for them in your web browser, download, and follow instructions to install. (They are free.)

What You'll Find in This Book

There are other books about Premiere Pro, but they focus more on what the software offers and less on how to make it work for you, as a filmmaker. In this book, we try to keep our eyes on the prize: making a movie. Aspiring filmmakers, serious students, and seasoned editorial professionals will find that this book covers everything they need to know. It starts out with the simple nuts and bolts of editing and works its way up to the highly specialized processes that every filmmaker needs to truly make their film with Premiere Pro.

This book is organized into four sections:

Editing in Premiere Chapters 1-3 are designed to quickly introduce you to all of the basic tools and techniques for editing films in Premiere Pro. Not only will you learn the Premiere Pro application, you can also learn to edit from these three chapters.

Organization and media management Chapter 4-6 take you through the technical side of working in Premiere—setting up a custom project, importing and playing media, media management, and troubleshooting technical issues. You can skip these chapters if you just want to work through the editing tools, but they provide an important background for those planning to edit their own films with Premiere.

Advanced editing Chapters 7-9 dive into more challenging editorial processes available in Premiere—advanced trimming tools, working with multicam footage, mixing different types of media in a sequence, and an introduction to workaday visual effects for editors.

Post-post Chapters 10-14 cover the topics you need to understand as your film gets closer to finished: sound editing, titles and graphics, more advanced visual effects like compositing, working with color, and last but not least, finishing and exporting your film.

About the Tutorials

This book is filled with tutorials that help you experience the information presented first hand. If you're an old pro, you may find that you can skip them. But for everyone else, we have gathered footage from real movies so that you can edit and learn the features of Premiere Pro in a meaningful and memorable way.

Scenes from four feature films comprise the bulk of the tutorials in this book. You'll get to edit a visual montage set to music, a comedic dialogue scene, an action scene, a horror scene, a multicam scene, and a scene from a documentary. These scenes run the gamut of creative and technical challenges for the filmmaker. It's actual footage, not cleaned up for you, so you'll get to work through many common real-world situations using Premiere Pro.

Problems to Solve

At the end of each chapter, we've added questions that are relevant to all filmmakers, not just students, to help you assess the topics covered in the chapter and apply them to real world situations that have nothing to do with Premiere and everything to do with making a movie.

Tutorial Media Downloads

The tutorial media for this book can be found at *thedigitalfilmmakinghandbook.com*, under the "Book Resources" menu, in the *Premiere Pro for Filmmakers* section. Video clips are encoded as 1920 x 1080 HD using the h.264 codec, a highly compressed format that makes downloading faster. The media is gathered into a single folder and organized within that folder by topic. I recommend downloading all of the tutorial media at the outset.

What Kind of Computer Do I Need?

Editing applications need a lot of processing power now that video that can be 4K (per frame) or larger. So we recommend using a newer, full-featured, desktop computer. Some laptops are up to the job and they're great for shorter projects. But if your project is big enough to require external hard drives, then you'll appreciate the additional connectivity that desktop computers offer, the increased processing speed, and the expanded screen real estate.

At minimum, you should use a computer that has an Intel 6thGen or newer CPU with 8 GB of RAM and 2 GB of GPU VRAM. If your project requires more space than you have on your internal hard drive, you'll need 7200 RPM external hard drives. A set of RAIDs is often recommended but not required. If you are planning on using shared footage on a Cloud-based project, you'll need fast and reliable wifi or a hardwired internet connection. Last, but not least, most filmmakers prefer two monitors because editing takes up a lot of screen space.

You'll find the latest system requirements on the Adobe web site, so always be sure to check there before you buy new gear.

What Can You Get Away With?

I edited a multicam web series, shot in 2K, with half-hour episodes on a 2013 MacBook Air running Premiere Pro 2017—clearly this doesn't live up to the minimum hardware requirements. But it worked fine, so it might be worth just trying it out on whatever computer you have and seeing if it works for you. I used a fast, external drive (G-Tech, 8TB USB-C) and found that rendering sequences really helped with playback. Adobe makes older versions of the software available for download so that might help if you don't have the current operating system available on your older computer.

➡ More in *The Digital Filmmaking Handbook*

This book can stand alone but it was designed to work in tandem with *The Digital Filmmaking Handbook*. While this book sticks to tools and concepts related to Premiere Pro, there's a lot of related material in the DFH that covers basic concepts of editing, sound design, and so on. So if you're using the two books in tandem, look for this pointer to find references to related topics in the DFH.

➡ All About Editing Hardware

The Digital Filmmaking Handbook, Chapter 11 is devoted to video hardware and building an editing workstation.

1

Cut to the Chase

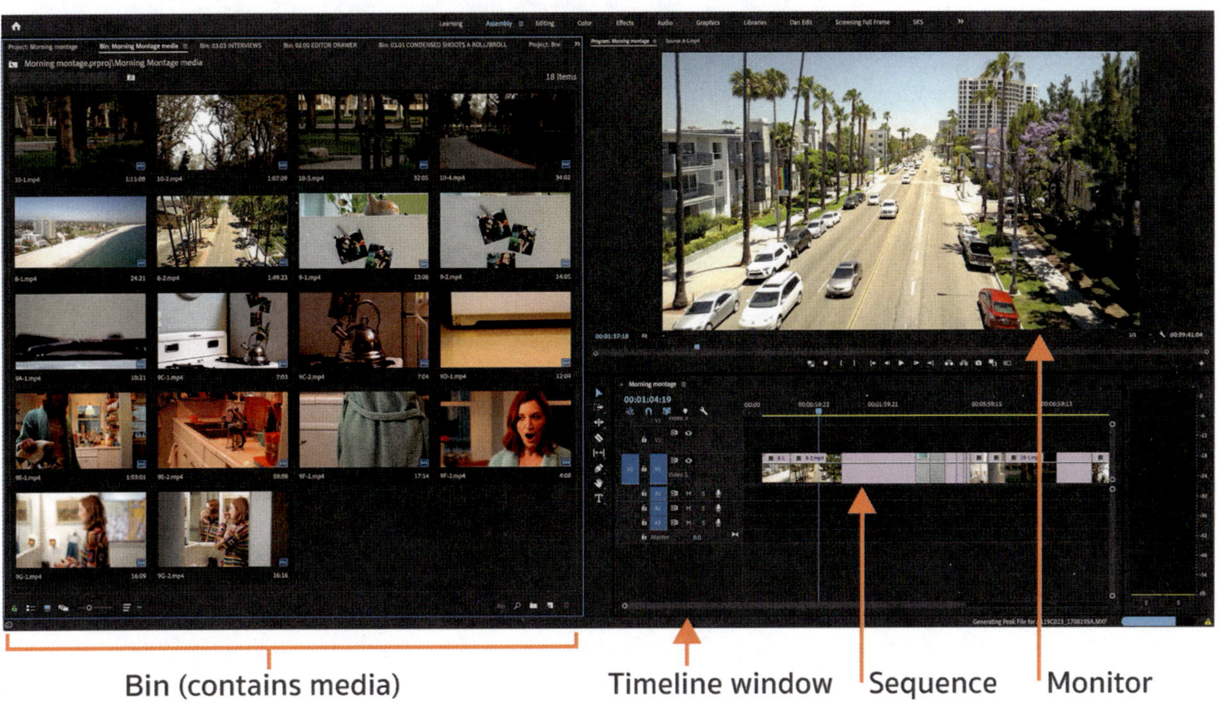

Figure 1.1

The Premiere Pro interface, shown here in Assembly mode.

EDITING IS REALLY FUN AND CREATIVE. It's where your shots get turned into a movie. Nothing about that sucks. But there are also parts of editing that require intricate control, highly technical knowledge, and many challenging decisions. For now, we're going to skip all that and go right to the fun part.

In this chapter you get to jump into the creative work of editing a music-driven montage in Premiere Pro (Figure 1.1). But don't worry, we're going to cover all the other stuff too, later in the book. And hopefully you'll appreciate that the intricate, technical, and challenging side of editing is cool too.

So let's cut to the chase.

☑ Tips for Pros

If you're an experienced editor, this chapter might be a little basic for you. Then again, if you're like me you dive in head-first and then have to backtrack to figure out how things actually work. A quick skim might be worth your while. There will also be more tutorials that build on the ones in this chapter later in the book.

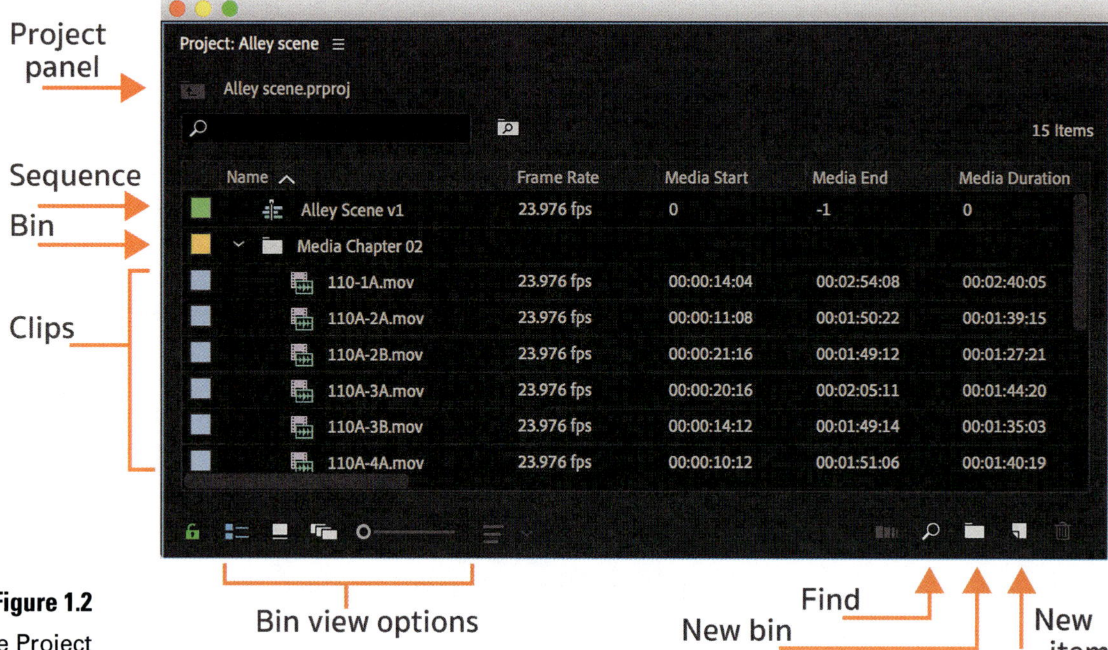

Figure 1.2

The Project panel is the main directory that contains bins, sequences, and clips. At the bottom of the panel are the bin view controls. This window is shown in List view.

The Organizational Interface

Premiere Pro is a complex application, but it can be broken down into two primary functions: organizing media and editing it.

The organizational interface in Premiere is very simple and easily understood by anyone who uses a computer. Special windows called *panels* contain sub-folders known as *bins* which are used to hold media files, or *clips* (Figure 1.2). When you're using Premiere, you rarely need to go out to your desktop and file folders. Instead, you'll build a mirror-world of your computer within Premiere that allows you to work using the files on your hard drives without changing them directly. (More on that in a bit.)

Projects

The main document that holds all your media and cuts is called a *project* and each project has a special window called the Project panel (Figure 1.2). The Project panel in Premiere is the heart of the application and it opens automatically when you create a new project. At first, the Project panel is empty, but as you start to create bins, import media, and organize, it becomes a top-level directory for all the elements in your film. Since you can have more than one project open at once, you can also have more than one Project panel.

 Panel or Window?

Adobe likes to invent their own words for things. What they call "panels" are what the rest of us call "windows." In this book, these terms are used interchangeably.

Bins

If the Project panel is a directory, bins are the folders. It's up to you to create the bins you think you will need (File > New > Bin). Depending on how you choose to import your media, Premiere may automatically create bins that correspond to the folders on your hard drive containing your media. But rearranging the contents of your bins in Premiere won't change the contents of the folders on your hard drives.

You can view the contents of a bin three ways: List view (Figure 1.2), Icon view (Figure 1.3), and Freeform view (Figure 1.13). List view is self-explanatory, but Icon and Freeform views offer additional capabilities. You can move the clips around and arrange them in whatever order you choose, much like a storyboard. You can also playback each clip within the bin itself, by clicking on the clip and activating the playback bar on the bottom of the clip icon. Freeform view takes Icon view a step further and lets you vary the size of each icon and move them around without conforming to a grid.

Media

Premiere can handle many types of media: digital video, multicam sequences, still graphics, music, audio, motion graphics, 360-degree video, and more. These pieces of media are referred to as *clips*. Clips live in bins and can be moved around, renamed, and organized as needed. Clips—aka shots—are the building blocks of your film.

When you import raw media from your hard drive into Premiere, the original files on your hard drives remain untouched. Instead, Premiere creates a set of pointer files that reference the original files on your drive without ever changing them. That means that if you move a shot from one bin to another in Premiere, the files on your hard drive won't move.

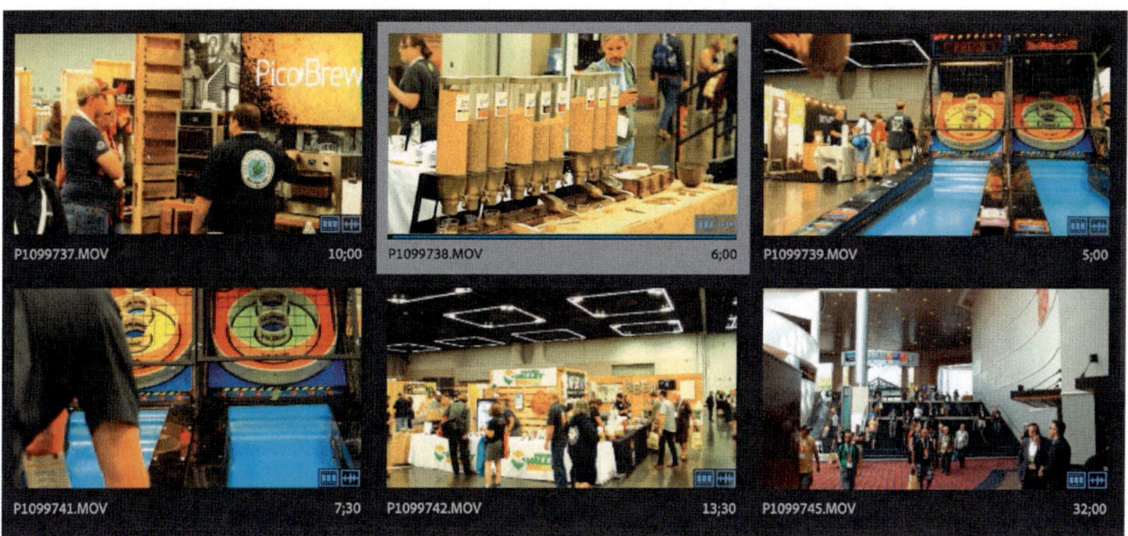

Figure 1.3

Icon view makes it easy to identify shots at a glance.

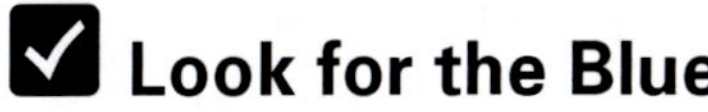

Look for the Blue

Blue is an important color in the Premiere interface—it indicates active windows, buttons, and selected items. If you're used to "green means go" or bright white highlighting, in Premiere you'll see blue instead. If you're in an unfamiliar panel, anything blue is probably worth exploring further to see what it does.

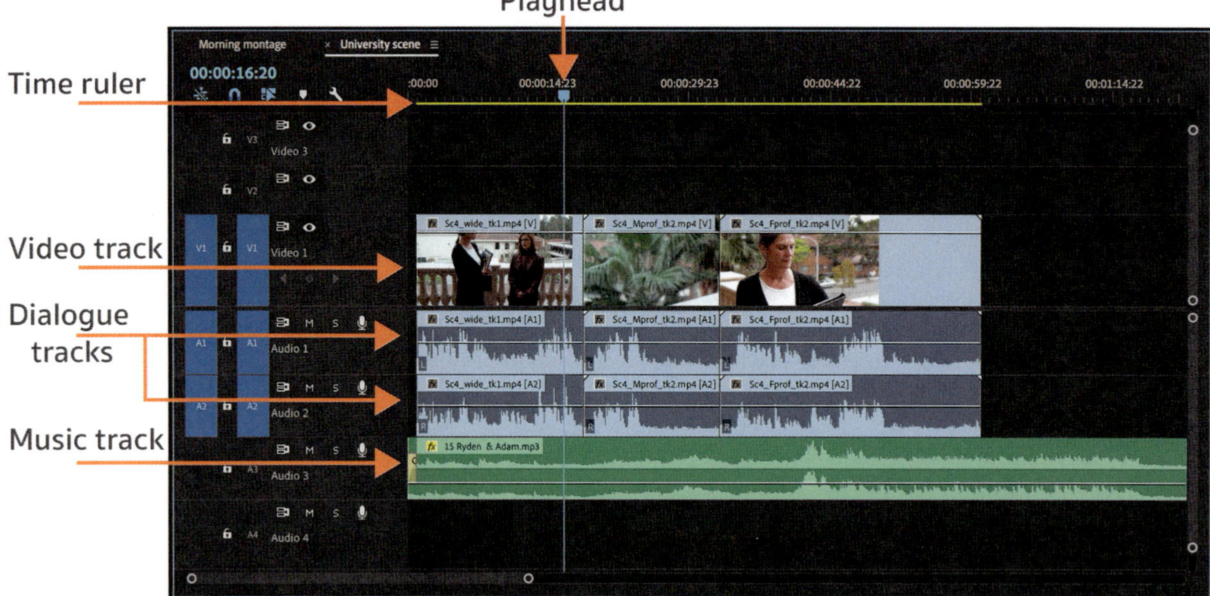

Figure 1.4

A simple sequence in the Timeline window, consisting of video, dialogue, and music.

The Editing Interface

The editorial interface will be very recognizable to anyone with previous editing experience. Clips are built into chronological *sequences*, which are displayed in a *timeline* that is divided into *tracks*. Software-based *monitors* display source media and edited sequences (Figures 1.1 and 1.18).

Sequences

A sequence is a string of shots arranged in chronological order—in other words, it's your film. Like clips, sequences live in bins and have their own icon in List view. When you double-click on a sequence, it opens in both the Program and Timeline windows. When you play the sequence, you can watch its progress through the Timeline as the video plays in the Program monitor. This is where you'll spend the majority of your time when you edit with Premiere Pro.

Timeline

The thing that's unique to editing applications is that they need to display the way that your edited movie plays out over time. And yet, you want to be able to take it in at a single glance to get an overview of your work in progress. That is the most basic purpose of the Timeline. It's a graphical display of an edited sequence in chronological order (Figure 1.4).

When you drag shots into the Timeline, they'll show up as pieces of video and audio that start at the left and the end at the right. As you're working in the Timeline, your mouse will change from the standard arrow to various other cursors, depending on where in the Timeline you are hovering. The most important cursor in the Timeline is the *playhead*, which is a blue vertical bar that crosses the entire Timeline (Figure 1.4). It indicates where you "are" in your film. To move the playhead, click and drag in the *time ruler* along the top of the Timeline. Because the

Timeline actually measures time itself, you can zoom the Timeline view all the way in until you see every single frame of video. When you zoom out, you'll see a larger portion of your sequence, which is also a larger portion of time. The increments of time in the time ruler change to reflect this as you zoom.

Tracks

The building blocks of the Timeline are called *tracks* (Figure 1.4). It might help to think of them as layers, streams, or channels. Video tracks fill the upper portion of the Timeline and contain video, animation, titles, graphics, adjustment layers, and any other type of visual media that Premiere accepts. Below them, audio tracks contain all the sound—dialogue, music, sound effects, voice-over and so on.

Monitors

Playing media is one of the most basic functions in editing and like most editing apps, Premiere has two software-based monitors that have different purposes: the Source monitor plays raw media, so that you can prepare to add it to a sequence, and the Program monitor plays the sequence itself. If you choose to work with a single-viewer workspace (Figure 1.1), the Source and Program monitors will share a window and you'll use tabs to switch from one to the other. Two-monitor workspaces are the more traditional way to work—the Source monitor is on the left and the Program monitor is on the right (Figure 1.18), allowing you to see both your footage and your cut at a glance. We'll be using both in this chapter.

☑ Preferences

Premiere Pro preferences are found under the Edit menu for Windows and under the Premiere Pro window for Macs.

Basic Settings

Before your start the tutorials, there are a handful of settings that you should check to make sure Premiere works smoothly:

Nothing is more frustrating than losing your work because of a crash. Luckily, you can turn on **Auto-save** (Preferences > Auto-save). The default saves every 15 minutes and the last five versions of the project are retained in a special Auto-Save folder. It also saves your project at its current location if you check that box in the preferences.

Under **Memory** preferences (Preferences > Memory), change the RAM settings to match your computer's configuration. It is recommended to have at leave 16 GB of RAM reserved for Premiere Pro. For example, on my computer I have 32 GB total and I reserve 6 GB for other applications. Rendering should be optimized for "performance."

Select **Show Tool Tips** (Preferences > General) so that Premiere displays names and other info about various elements of the interface as you hover the mouse over them.

You will want to **Show Video Thumbnails** and **Show Audio Waveforms** in the Timeline as you work your way through this chapter. Use the menu under the wrench icon in the upper left corner of the Timeline (Figure 1.5) to turn them on.

The video track needs to be fairly large in order to see thumbnails, so adjust the track height by selecting **Expand All Tracks** from that same wrench menu.

Figure 1.5

This innocuous wrench icon in the Timeline contains a Display Settings menu where you can tell Premiere to display thumbnails, waveforms, and expand or minimize all tracks. The Source and Program monitors also have Settings menus under a wrench icon.

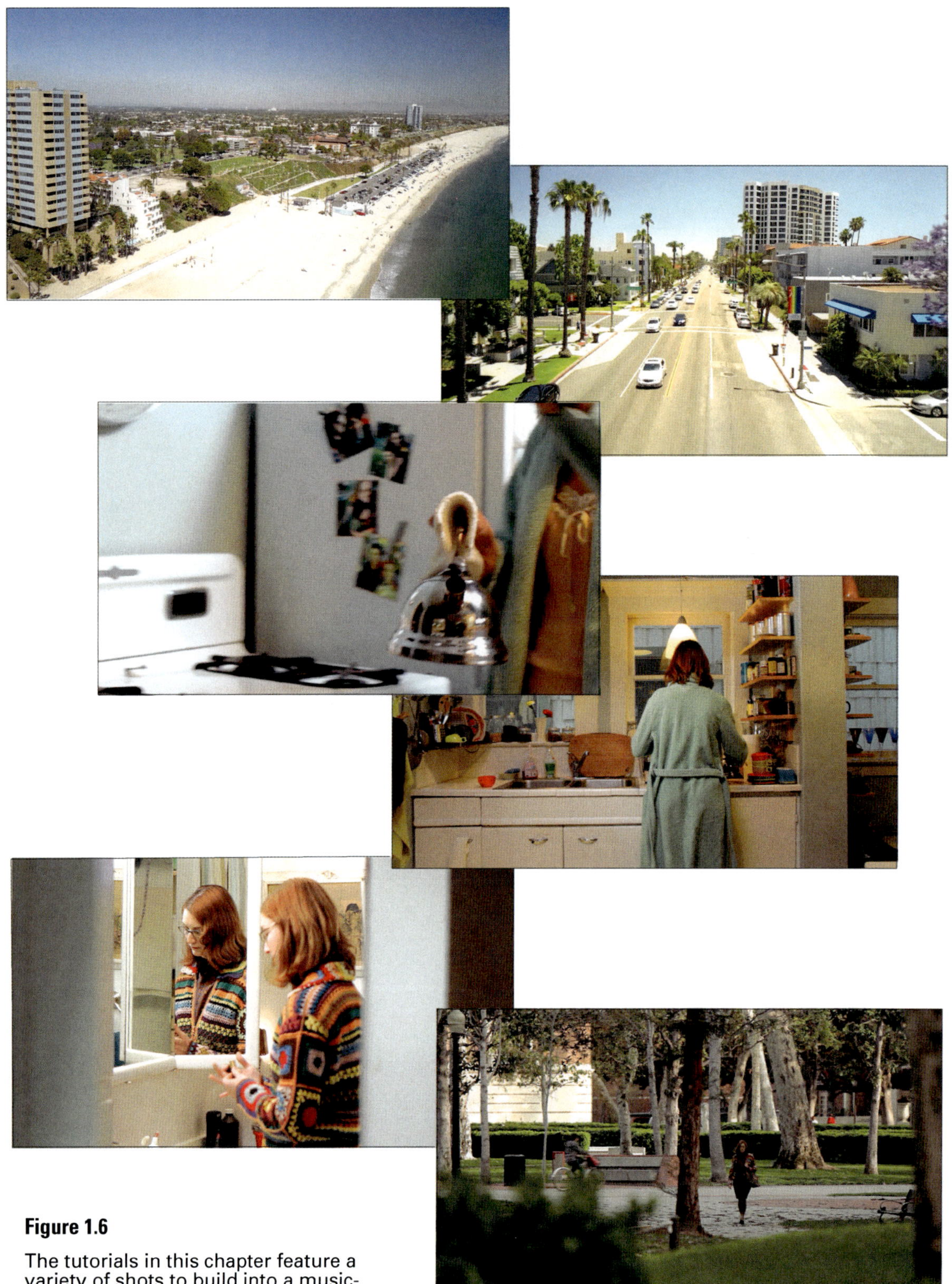

Figure 1.6

The tutorials in this chapter feature a variety of shots to build into a music-driven montage.

TUTORIAL: Set Up the Montage Project

The tutorials in this book are designed to walk you through the process of editing a movie in Premiere Pro so that you can take that knowledge and apply it to your next film or job.

This is the first of three tutorials in this chapter that will show you how to create a project, build a montage sequence, and refine it. In this first tutorial, you'll learn how to setup a project and get comfortable in the Premiere interface. You'll be working with footage from the feature film, *The Olivia Experiment* (Figure 1.6), which I directed. The footage in this chapter was shot MOS, which means it has no audio. In lieu of natural sounds, we're going to edit these shots to music.

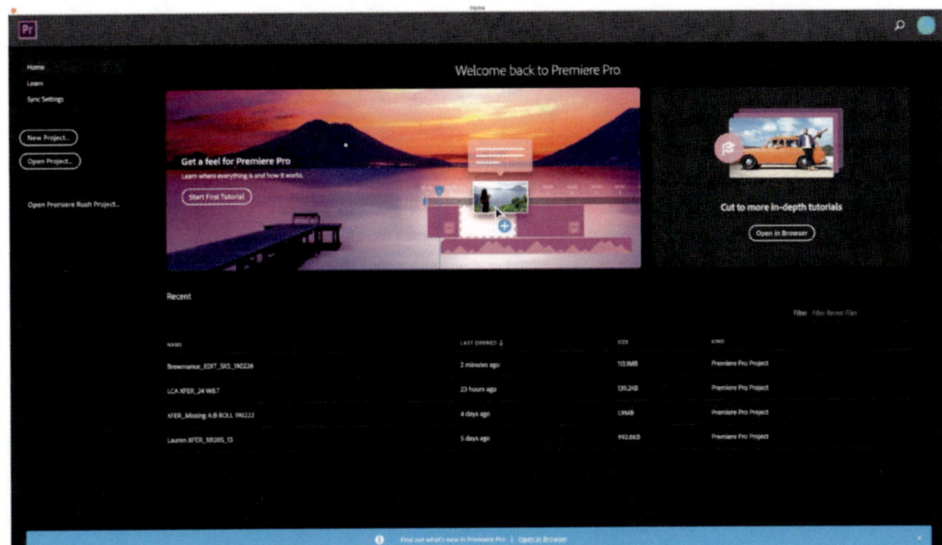

Figure 1.7

Launch Premiere and select New Project.

STEP 1: Make a New Project

Launch Premiere Pro and select New Project (Figure 1.7). The New Project window will appear, type in the name "Morning montage" for the name of the project. Now, browse to the location where you want to save the new project on your computer. Everything else can stay at the default settings so select Okay.

STEP 2: Switch to Assembly Mode

Every editor has their own way of building that first cut, but we're going to start with a special version of the Premiere interface that's designed just for that task. For the tutorials in this chapter, we'll be working in Assembly mode (Figure 1.1). Near the top of your computer screen, there is a horizontal menu featuring several different workspace options—choose Assembly from this menu (Figure 1.8). Assembly mode is a single monitor workspace that will be familiar to anyone who's used simpler editing software like Apple iMovie. The upper right quadrant contains the monitor, where you review your shots and your sequence. The lower right contains the Timeline panel, and the left side holds the Project panel, bins, and media.

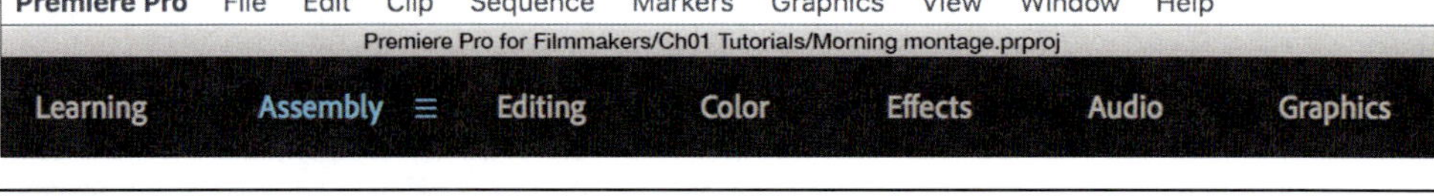

Figure 1.8

The Workspace presets menu is found at the top of the screen, just beneath the application menu bar.

The Assembly Workspace

Some people think the Assembly workspace in Premiere Pro is just for beginning editors. But lots of professional editors like to use the Assembly workspace when they're building rough cuts. It's also great for working on a laptop.

STEP 3: Import the Media

Your new project is empty. Since the tutorial footage is good to go, all you have to do is double-click on the background of the center of the Project panel, which is found on the left side of the screen, or go to File > Import, and navigate to the "Morning Montage media" folder that you downloaded from our website and import it. (Check out the downloading instructions in the Introduction of this book if you missed them.)

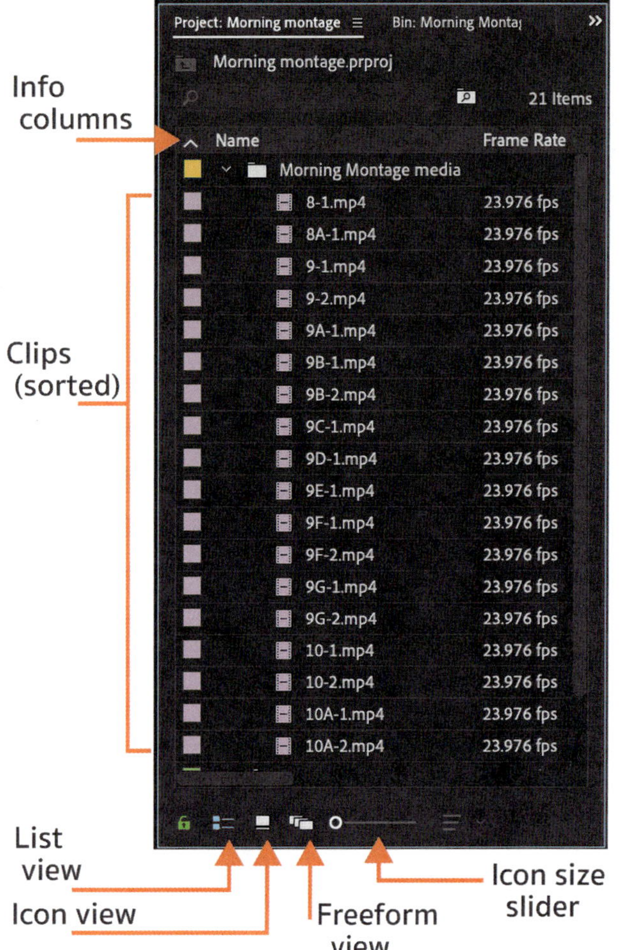

Figure 1.9

Import the footage and spin down the arrow to view the contents of the media bin.

STEP 4: Explore

Notice that the Project panel has a bright blue outline around it. This line indicates that this panel is currently active. If you click on the Timeline or the monitors panel, the blue outline will follow.

Spin down the arrow to the left of the Morning montage bin to see the contents of the bin in List view (Figure 1.9). As you can see, there are 18 shots, named according to filmmaking convention—scene number, camera angle, and take number. To the right of the clip names are various columns with info about each shot—frame rate, media start, duration, and more. You can sort the media by clicking on the header for each column. Try clicking on the Name column to reverse the order of the clips and clicking on it again to restore the original order.

Double-click on the Morning Montage media bin to open it in a new window. At the bottom of the bin, select the Icon view button (Figure 1.9). Use the slider next to the bin view buttons to make the clip icons larger or smaller. Play around with the width of your bin panel by dragging on the boundary to the right of the Bin panel—as you change the size of the Bin panel, the icons inside the bin will also resize. You can always choose Reset to Saved Layout from the pulldown menu next to Assembly in the workspace menu bar to return to the original view.

STEP 5: Make a New Sequence

Go back to the Project panel by clicking on its tab. We want to keep the Morning montage media bin dedicated to media only, so this will insure that the new sequence is saved in the main level of the project. Go to File > New > Sequence. When the New Sequence window opens up, name your sequence "Morning montage" in the field at the bottom of the window and select "Okay." (We cover advanced sequence options more thoroughly in Chapter 4.) The sequence will appear at the top of your Project panel and it will also open automatically in the Timeline. (It appears empty for now.)

That's it. Save your project (File > Save) and you're ready to work on the scene. We'll do exactly that in the next tutorial, but first you should know a bit more about viewing video clips and sequences in Premiere.

Navigating within a Shot or Sequence

One of the key functions required for editing is playing video. Not only do you need to be able to watch your raw footage and your cut, you also need to move backwards and forwards, sometimes quickly and also sometimes slowly. Many filmmakers compare moving within a shot to driving a car. It takes a little getting using to, but soon you'll be able to watch at normal speed, fast-forward to get to the good stuff, reverse a bit to hit your mark, pause, and step forward frame-by-frame—all without thinking about how you're doing it.

Here are some of the ways you can move around within the video itself:

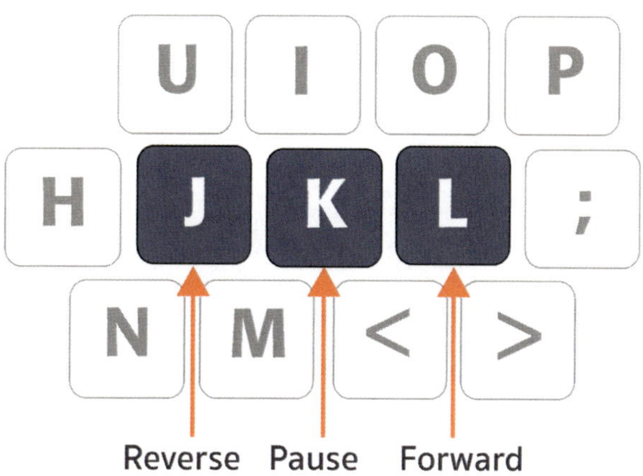

Figure 1.10

Use the J-K-L keys to play forward, backward, and pause within a shot or sequence. The more times you tap J and L, the faster it will go.

JKL keys These three keys are the easiest way to control the speed of your video while it is playing. L is play/fast-forward, J is reverse/fast-reverse, and K is pause. If you tap L multiple times, it will speed up with each tap until it maxes out. J starts out playing backwards at normal (1x) speed and speeds up with each tap as well. An important thing about J and L is that these keys continue to work while the video is in motion. So you can slow down, speed up, or reverse without having to pause playback (Figure 1.10).

Arrow keys The left and right arrow keys let you step through your media or sequence frame by frame in the Source, Program, and Timeline windows. Alternately, you can use the frame advance buttons on the Source and Program monitors (Figure 1.14). The up and down arrows will take you to the start and end of each clip in both the Source monitor and the sequence.

Dragging along the time rulers Every window that can play media also has a time ruler (Figures 1.4 and 1.14). You can position your cursor in the time ruler and drag forwards or backwards, a process known as *scrubbing*. As you drag through your shots or your cut, you can opt to *scrub audio*, which means you can hear it as you drag. This

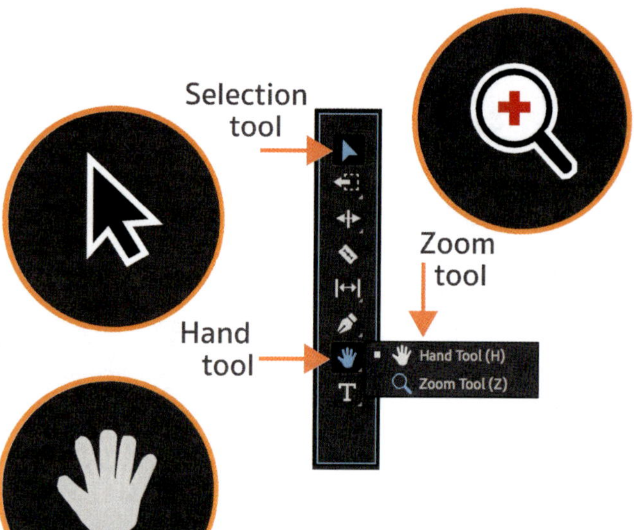

Figure 1.11

Found in the Tools panel, the Zoom, Hand, and Selection tools help you navigate in Premiere.

can be very useful if you're trying to find a specific sound. Audio scrubbing can be toggled on and off by typing Shift + S.

Zoom, Hand, and Selection tools These three tools, found in the Tools panel to the left of the Timeline (Window > Tools), help you navigate throughout Premiere (Figure 1.11). You already know the Selection tool well—it's the standard arrow cursor. But if you lose track of it, you can always find it at the top of the tools panel. Using the Hand tool, you can click and drag in the Timeline to change which part of your sequence you can see without accidentally making any changes to your cut. And the Zoom tool, found in the small menu under the Hand tool, zooms in the view on your sequence in the Timeline when you click and zooms out if you hold the Alt/Option key and click.

Spacebar = Play/Pause

The spacebar as play/pause button is probably the most important key command in Premiere. If you're not already used to using it thanks to other applications, it will soon become second nature.

TUTORIAL: Build the Montage

In the last tutorial, we set up a new project and got a tour of the Assembly workspace. In this tutorial, we'll continue working with the same project and use Premiere to build a first cut.

The most basic way to explain editing in Premiere is to say that it allows you to organize clips in a linear, chronological manner. The footage in this tutorial is in need of exactly that: it consists of a series of shots that show the morning routine of the main character of a feature film. As you work through the tutorial, you'll focus on putting the clips into an order that makes sense.

Taking your clips and building them into a sequence is the first step of editing any scene. As you create this first rough assembly, you'll be making lots of decisions about the story you hope to tell.

STEP 1: Review the Media

What's the first rule of good editing? Watch everything.

Start by skimming through the clips in the bin. You should already have the Morning Montage media bin open and set to Icon view. As you mouse over each clip, you'll scrub through the footage. Mousing from left to right will take you from the beginning towards the end. If you click and select a clip, the area around the clip will turn lighter grey (so that you know it's active) and a small, blue, time ruler with a grey square playhead will appear at the bottom of the clip

(Figure 1.12). You can click and drag the playhead to whatever position you want in the clip. Hit Play (spacebar) and watch the shot. Hit the spacebar again and it will pause. Try using the JKL keys to speed up, reverse, and pause playback. The arrow keys will jump from clip to clip.

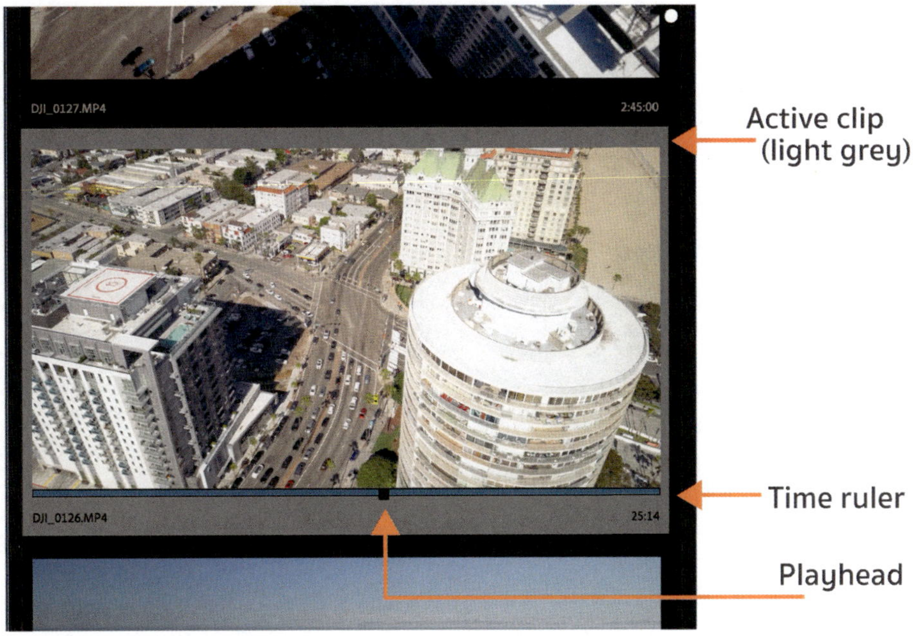

Viewing media in the bin is a good way to quickly get the lay of the land, but if you really want to watch a shot, it's much better to view it in the Source monitor. Just double-click on any clip in the bin and it will launch into the Source monitor window (Figure 1.14). Here you can also use the spacebar to play and pause as you watch, the JKL keys on your keyboard to go backwards and forwards at increasing speeds, and the up and down arrows to quickly jump to the start or end of a shot.

Figure 1.12

A time ruler in the highlighted clip in Icon View lets you navigate through the clip from inside the bin itself.

As you review the footage, the story will start to emerge. The first two shots (8-1 and 8-2) are aerial establishing shots designed to start the sequence. Next come the shots inside the house that show the main character making coffee and getting ready for work. The last four shots show multiple takes of her walking on campus. Now you have a rough story: A city near the ocean is established, a woman makes coffee early in the morning, she gets ready for work, and arrives on campus.

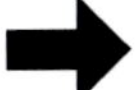

Why These Clip Names?

The clips in these tutorials are named using the traditional film naming convention of scene number, camera angle letter, and take number. If you need to know more about traditional film naming and organization, look at Chapters 10 and 13 of *The Digital Filmmaking Handbook*.

STEP 2: Make a Storyboard

Switch the "Morning Montage media" bin to Freeform view and rearrange the clips in an approximate order (Figure 1.13). What order is that? An obvious choice is chronological order but feel free to do whatever you like best or you can follow my choices in these instructions.

Start by arranging the shots in an approximate order. If you want to make some of the clip icons bigger or smaller in Freeform view, right-click on a clip and select Clip Size at the bottom of the menu. You can choose between small, medium, large, and extra-large.

Move the two aerial shots to the top of the bin—these are the establishing shots that are designed to start the sequence. Next, group the ten shots in the kitchen that show the main character making her morning coffee. Separate the two shots in the bathroom, where she's dressed for

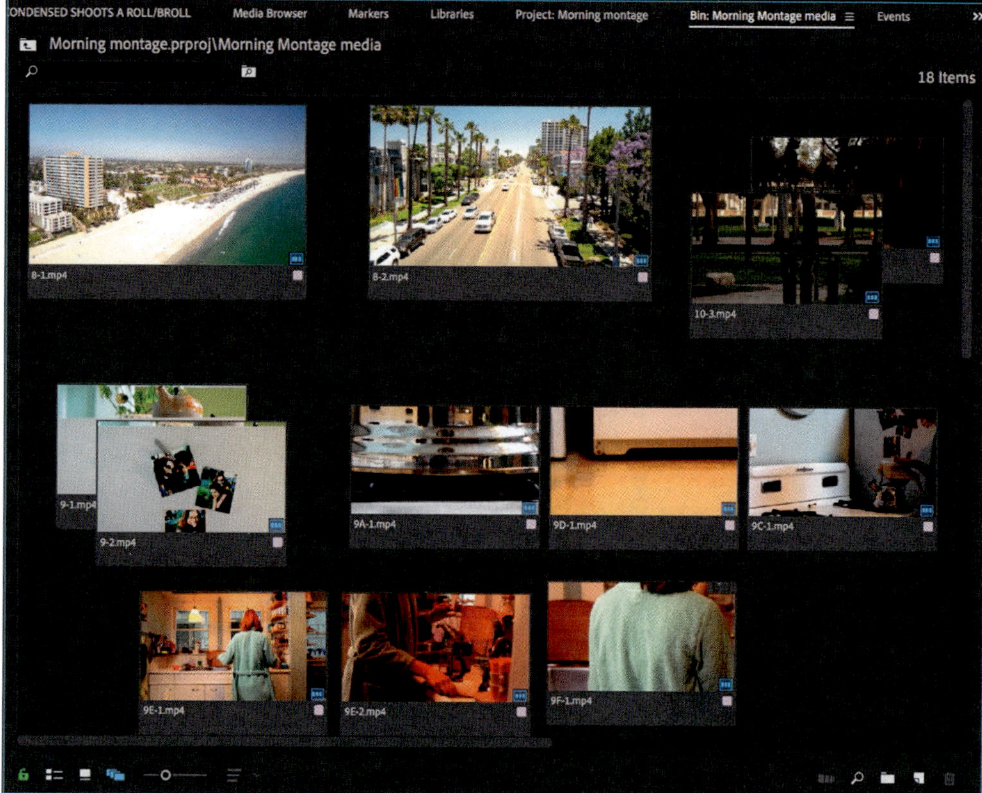

Figure 1.13

Shots arranged in Freeform View. You can arrange them without having to adhere to a grid, assign different sizes to different shots, and stack shots into groups, like a storyboard.

work and then move the four shots of the woman walking on campus to the end. Now you have a rough storyboard in the bin.

Don't worry about getting it perfect, this is just a first stab at figuring out the order for the shots in the montage.

STEP 3: Build Stacks from Similar Shots

Some of the footage in this bin are different takes of the same shot. Or they are slightly different shots that show the same thing. In other words, you will only use one of them. The Freeform bin view lets you move similar shots into stacks (Figure 1.13).

For example, shots 9-1 and 9-2 are two takes of the same thing—both pan down some photos on the fridge and land on the woman's hand as she turns on the gas burner. Drag them to a loosely overlapping stack. The same goes for shots 9G-1 and 9G-22. They have slightly different framing but otherwise show the same thing. Go through all the footage and stack anything that's more or less the same.

 Feature or Bug?

If you miss your mark with the mouse and accidentally double-click on the background of a panel, the Import window will appear. Just select Cancel—it's a bug or maybe a feature that seems like a bug. (Don't accidentally import the contents of your entire hard drive the way I did once.)

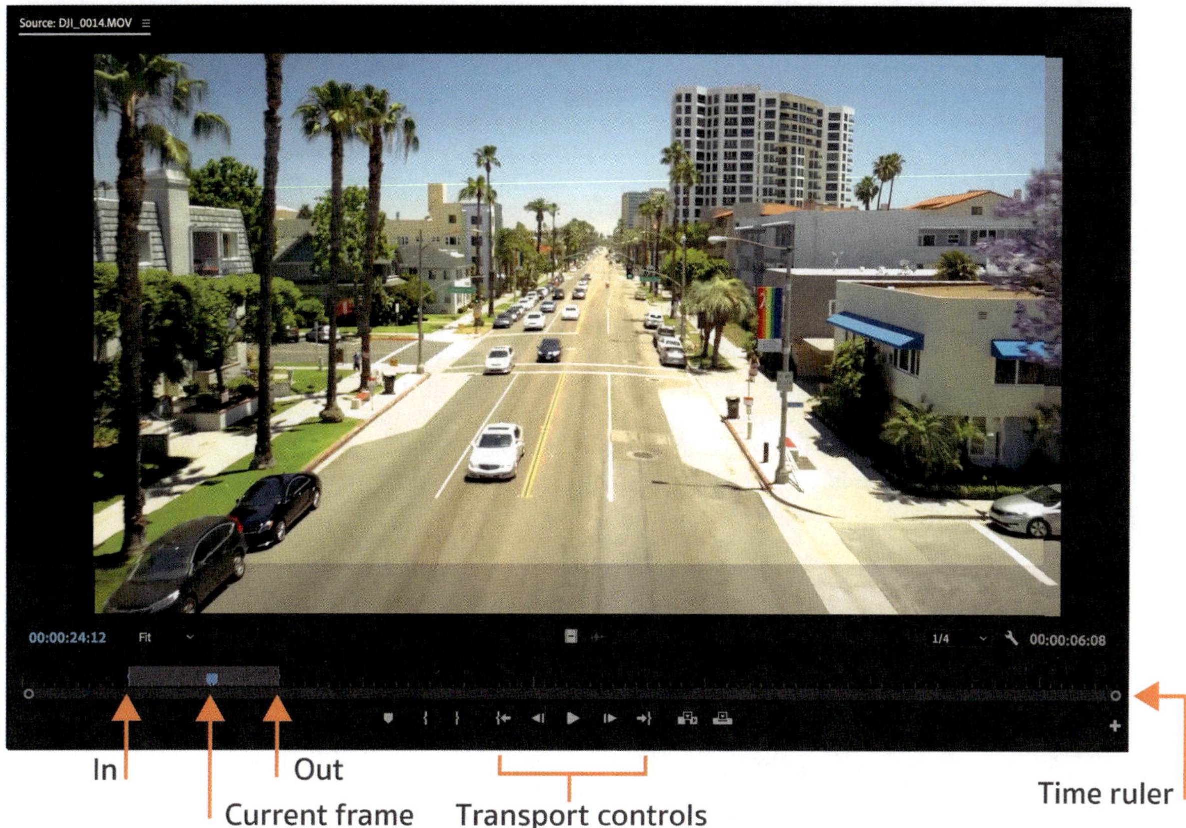

Figure 1.14

The Source monitor displays unedited clips, aka raw footage. A row of buttons below the video include transport controls (play/pause, frame advance, and reverse) and a time ruler that helps you navigate within each clip and shows highlighting when the start (In) and end (Out) points of a shot have been set.

STEP 4: Select the Best Takes

Now that you have stacked up all the similar shots, go through them and pick the one you like best. If you think you may want to return to this stacked arrangement later on, you can right-click on an empty area in the bin and choose Save As New Layout.

Once you've selected the best take from each stack, move the takes you don't want into a discard stack.

STEP 5: Trim Long Shots

You may have noticed that some of the shots are quite long, especially the two aerials and the shots on the university campus. There's no need to trim every single shot at this point, but we might as well slim down some of these extra-long shots so that they don't bog down our first assembly of the montage.

Double-click on the first aerial (8-1) to load it into the Source monitor. Now as you play the clip (Spacebar) you can use the I key (for "In") to choose the frame where you would like the clip to start. You're looking for a nice 4-5 second section where the camera movement is good, so use the JKL keys to navigate within the shot until you find the portion of it that you like.

Don't worry about being too precise here, it's just a first pass. I like the part of the shot that shows the tall buildings, so I set my In at about 3 seconds into the footage. Now set an Out (O) for the last frame of the shot, about 4 seconds later (Figure 1.14).

Notice that the Ins and Outs you set in the Source monitor also show up in the bin icons—the blue time ruler is smaller now, highlighting the part of the clip between the In and Out points. When you set the In and Out on a source clip they'll stay put until you change them.

Work your way through the other long shots and set Ins and Outs in the Source monitor. The Ins and Outs will remain active in your clips as long as you don't change them, so they will tell Premiere which portion of the shot to use when we add them to a sequence in the next step.

STEP 6: Add Your Shots to a Sequence

You can select multiple shots in the bin and drag them all at once by using the Shift key as you select them or by clicking in the bin and dragging a selection box around them. If you want to select multiple clips out of order, hold the Control (Win)/Command (Mac) key as you click on them. In Freeform view, the order that you select the shots matters because that's the order that they will get added to your sequence, so start at the beginning of your storyboard arrangement. If you have trouble seeing all of your clips on screen, use the zoom slider at the bottom of the bin to make them smaller.

When selected, each shot will have a bright blue outline around it. Grab one of the shots by clicking and holding the center of it and drag it into the video track portion of the Timeline. When you release, you'll see all of your selected shots appear in the sequence.

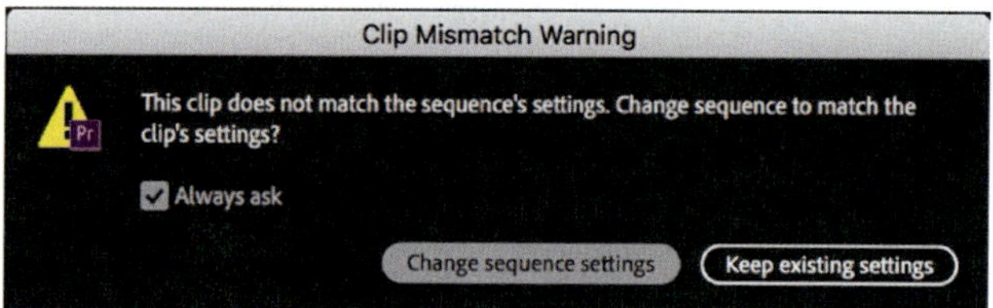

Figure 1.15

If you get this warning, select Change Sequence Settings so that your clip and sequence match.

You may get a Clip Mismatch Warning when you first drop the shots into the Timeline (Figure 1.15). If so, select Change Sequence Settings, which will ensure that your clip and sequence settings match.

You can also add shots to the Timeline one at a time. You'll notice that new shots will snap to the end of your first shot (Figure 1.17) and two little triangles will appear along the edit before you release the clip. This tells you that the shot has been added exactly at the end of the previous shot.

If you get to the point where your sequence is longer than the Timeline window, use the Zoom and Hand tools to navigate around your sequence. You can also resize the view by adjusting the zoom bar at the bottom of the Timeline.

When all of the clips are added to the sequence, your Timeline should look something like the one in Figure 1.16.

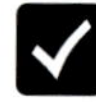 Zoom to Sequence

Here's a little trick: hit the backslash key (\) to make your sequence instantly fit into the Timeline window.

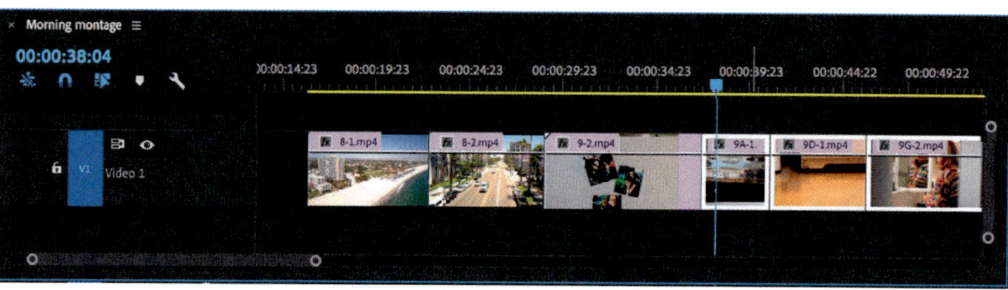

Figure 1.16

Drag your shots into the Timeline to build a sequence.

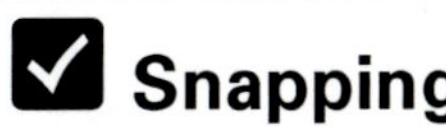

Snapping

Snapping causes the cursor in the Timeline to snap to each edit, which is super convenient. It's also super convenient to toggle snapping on and off as-needed. There's a button in the upper left corner of the Timeline that looks like a magnet and it toggles snapping (Figure 1.17). You can also toggle it by hitting the S key on your keyboard.

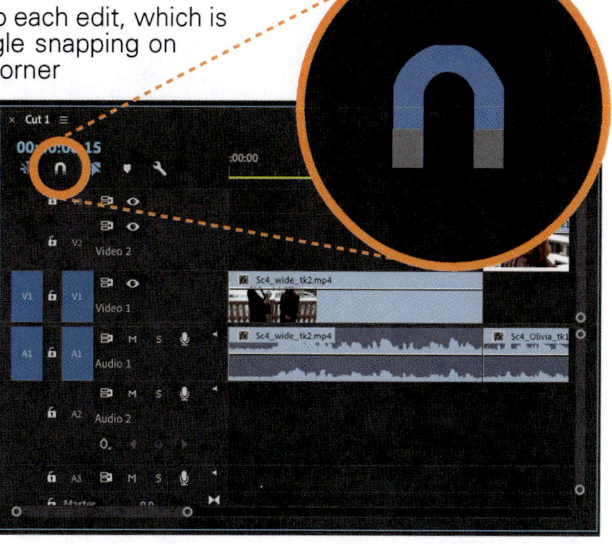

Figure 1.17

The Snapping button in the Timeline.

STEP 7: Watch Your First Cut

Position your cursor in the Timeline by clicking in the time ruler in the area above the tracks. The vertical blue bar of the playhead appears where you clicked. This blue line shows you where you "are" in the Timeline. Drag it all the way to the left to get to the start of your sequence. Alternately, you can repeatedly hit the up arrow key until you get to the start of the first shot.

Get ready to watch and hit Play (spacebar). If you want the full cinematic experience, for both Mac and Windows hit Control and the left apostrophe key (`) to go into full-screen mode. Hit it again or Esc to exit when you're done watching.

So what do you think? Was it good? Bad? Confusing? Do you need all the shots? Are they in the right order? Do you want to trim or extend some of them? And aren't you dying to add some music? We'll do all that in the next tutorial, but first let's dive a little deeper into the editing tools in Premiere.

Easy Ways to Edit

So far, we've been building a first assembly, but the truth is, editing is what happens from that point forward. If you're new to editing, it might seem intimidating, but the reality is that the simplest ways to edit involve skills you already use every day.

Drag and Drop

Drag and Drop editing is very intuitive because it's the same action we use all the time when moving things around on computers.

You may not have noticed it, but you already used drag and drop to build the sequence in the last tutorial. And there are many variations to it. You can drag and drop from bin to bin, from shots to sequences, and within sequences themselves. There are also ways to really dial-in exactly the how, what, and where of Drag and Drop, so we'll continue to build on this technique throughout the book.

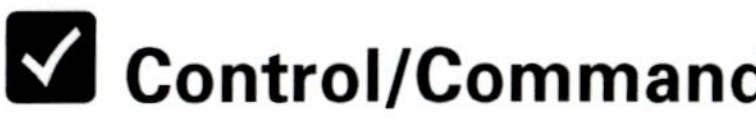

Control/Command

In this book, Control/Command is used as shorthand for Control (Win) or Command (Mac). Similarly Alt (Win) and Option (Mac) are referred to as Alt/Option.

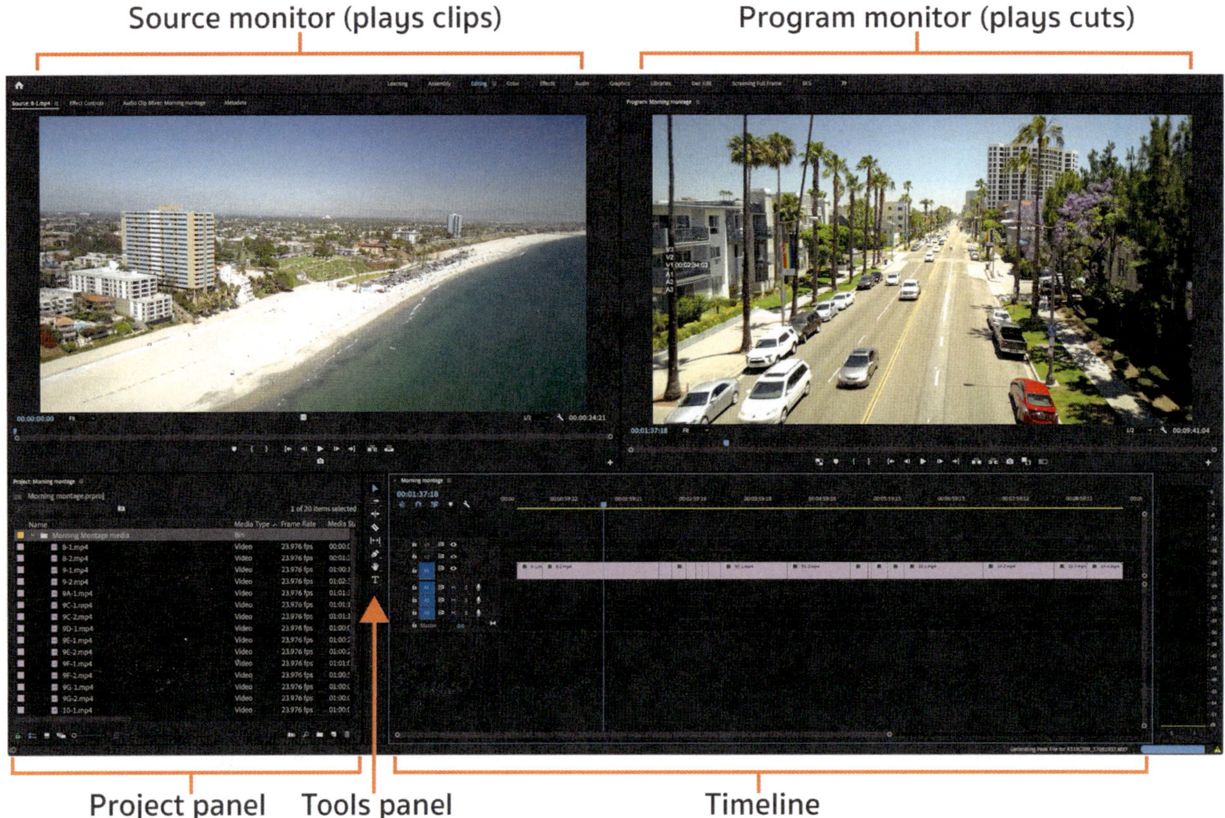

Figure 1.18

The editing workspace has a Source monitor on the left and a Program monitor on the right.

Cut, Copy, and Paste

Cut, Copy and Paste are also very intuitive ways to edit. They work just like they do in your operating system. You can click to select a clip, copy it (Edit > Copy), navigate to wherever you want to paste it (Edit > Paste) and you're done. You can also drag to select several clips and cut (Edit > Cut) to remove them from your sequence.

In bins, you can select clips, sequences, and other elements (audio, graphics, etc.) then copy and paste them into other bins. Inside the Timeline, you can select clips, or parts of clips, and copy and paste them into other places in the Timeline. And since Premiere allows you to have more than one sequence open in the Timeline, you can copy or cut media from one sequence and paste it into another.

If you prefer, you can use key commands instead of mousing to the Edit menu. The key commands are the same as the ones in your OS: Control + C (Win) or Command + C (Mac) to copy, Control + V (Win) or Command + V (Mac) to paste, and Control/Command + X to cut. You can also use the Delete/Backspace key to cut.

Top and Tail Trims

Top and Tail trimming lets you take an existing rough cut and trim away the beginnings and ends of shots as you play through your cut. It relies on two simple key commands, Q lops off the beginning of a shot and W lops off the end. The cool thing is that you can do this while your sequence is playing, so you can quickly slim down a rough assembly.

Switch to the Editing Workspace

Once you've assembled a first cut, you will spend most of your time using the Editing workspace (Figure 1.18). Consisting of a Source window, a Program window and a Timeline, the editing workspace will be familiar to anyone with previous editing experience. If you're still in Assembly mode from the last tutorial, use the text-based menu across the top of the screen to switch to Editing mode.

TUTORIAL: Finish the Montage

In the last tutorial you built a rough cut of your montage scene. Now you'll take it to the next level by fine-tuning your edit and adding music.

STEP 1: Use Drag and Drop to Rearrange Shots

Maybe some of the shots in your rough cut are not in the right order. You can easily use Drag and Drop to rearrange shots. To reorder a shot, first make sure Snapping is toggled on (S), and that you have the standard Selection tool (arrow cursor) activated. Click and hold the shot you want to move, then drag it up to the next video track (Figure 1.19). If you don't already have a second video track, Premiere will automatically create one for you. Drag it to the spot above where you approximately want it to go and release it.

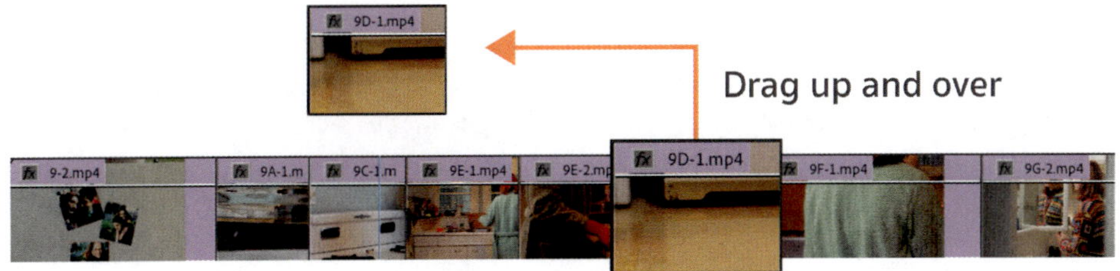

Figure 1.19

Drag the shot you want to move up to the next video track.

Now select the shots you want to move to make room for it. You can select multiple shots by clicking in the black area of the Timeline and dragging to select more than one or holding the Shift key and selecting each shot (Figure 1.20). Drag to reposition them in the Timeline to create a gap that's big enough for the shot you want to add. Continue rearranging your shots until you like the order. If there are shots you just don't need, select them and use the Delete key to get rid of them.

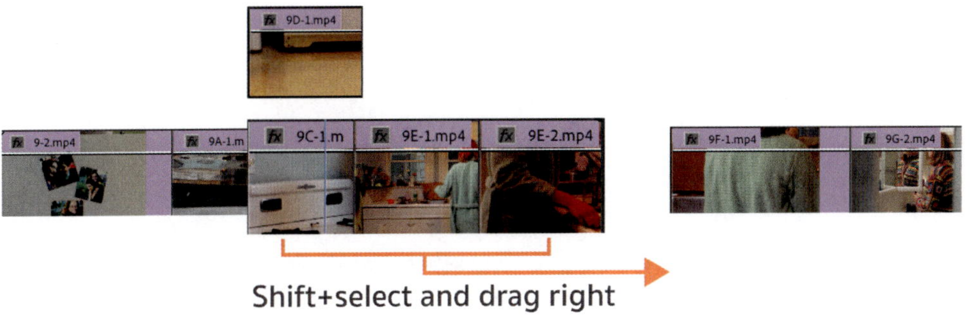

Figure 1.20

Drag-select or shift-select the shots you want to move to make room and drag them down the Timeline.

How Tracks Work

Video tracks play from the top down, meaning a shot on V2 will cover a shot on V1. Audio tracks play all at once.

STEP 2: Try Rearranging with Cut and Paste

You can also rearrange shots in the Timeline with Cut, Copy, and Paste commands. Click on any shot to select it (it will be highlighted) and then go to Edit > Cut to remove it from the sequence. Whenever you cut a shot, it remains in your computer's memory so that you can paste it anywhere you wish. To paste it without accidentally writing over your other shots, you'll need to navigate to the start of the shot where you want to add it (make sure Snapping is on) and then go to Edit > Paste Insert.

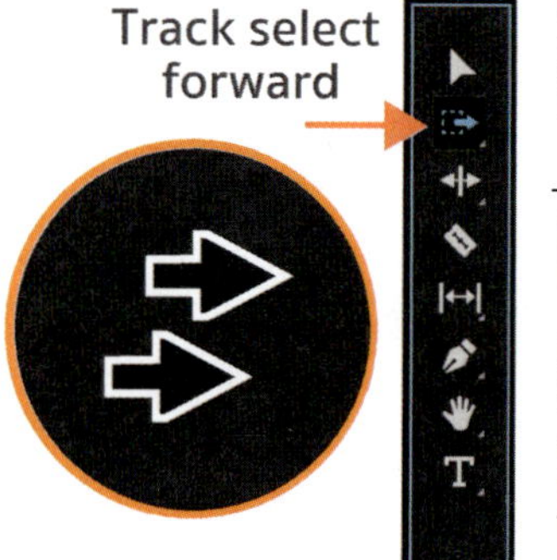

Figure 1.21

The Track Select Forward tool lets you quickly select large portions of a sequence.

Quickly Select Large Portions of Your Cut

Use the Track Select Forward tool to quickly select a large portion of a sequence. Found in the Tools panel (Figure 1.21), when active your cursor will change to a double-arrow and clicking anywhere in the Timeline will select every shot from that point forward. The menu under the Track Select Forward tool contains the Track Select Backward option—you can change the direction and select everything back from that point.

STEP 3: Trim Your Shots

Now that you've got everything in order, you can make a quick pass to trim the extra footage at the heads and tails of your shots. Top and tail trimming is the perfect way to do this. Go to the start of your sequence and start playing (spacebar). As you play, tap the Q key to lop off any media at the beginning of each shot that you don't need and the W key to remove media at the end. You'll find that you need to play sections of your cut multiple times as you decide where trim. The JKL keys will be very useful for this process, allowing you to play, pause, and play backwards. The up and down arrow keys are also great for jumping from shot to shot.

If you find using all those key commands while playing a bit too complicated, you can also drag in the time ruler until you find the spots where you want each shot to start and end, using Q and W while the video is paused.

Top and tail trimming is designed to make broad strokes, so don't sweat over each trim too much, just make a quick pass to get rid of the fat in your sequence and we'll show you how to make more careful trims in the next steps.

STEP 4: Drag to Shorten Shots

By now, your sequence should be looking good but there will be shots that you'll want to dial in more carefully. For example, there may be a lot of dead air at the beginning of the shot where the burner comes on. Turns out you can also select and drag the ends of each shot.

Shortening a shot is easy. With the Selection tool active, hover your mouse over the start of the shot of the burner. The cursor will change from an arrow to the Trim tool (Figure 1.22) when you are near the end of a shot. You may have to zoom in more for this to work easily. Notice

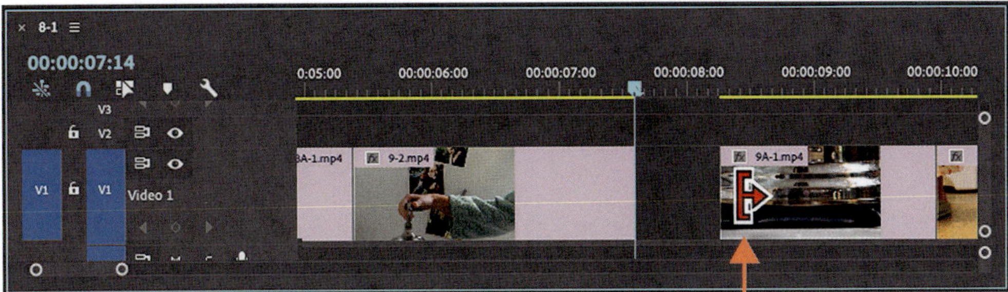

Figure 1.22

When you mouse over the end of a shot (aka an edit), the cursor will change to the red Trim tool and you can select that edit and drag it left or right to extend or shorten it. But if there's a shot right next to it, your range to adjust it may be limited.

that as you hover the mouse to the left and right of the start of the burner shot, the arrow in the Trim tool will switch direction.

We want to shorten the shot, which means we want to drag the start of it to the right, so hover the mouse just to the right of the start of the shot. When you see the red Trim tool cursor appear with the arrow pointing right, click on it to select it and hold. The start of the shot will appear highlighted in red. Still holding the mouse, drag to the right.

The start of the shot will move with the mouse as you drag and you can watch the Program monitor to see the contents of the shot changing as you move the mouse (Figure 1.23). Find the part of the shot where the burner ignites and release the mouse.

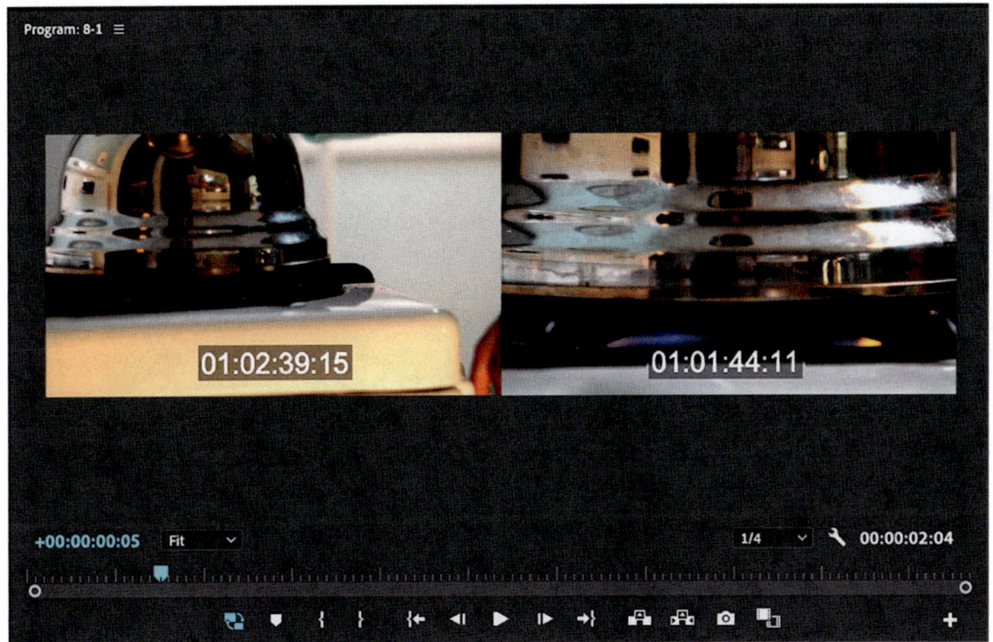

Figure 1.23

The program monitor changes to a two-shot view when you drag the end of a shot with the Trim tool. In this case, you'll see the last frame of the previous shot and the first frame of the burner shot, which changes as you drag to help you find the best spot to release the mouse.

☑ Zoom Level Matters

When you're working in the Timeline, the degree to which you are zoomed in effects what you can do. When you are zoomed way out, the cursor will move in large increments. To drag frame-by-frame, you'll have to zoom in more. Similarly, to get the Trim cursor to activate, you may need to be more zoomed in on an edit.

STEP 5: Delete the Gap

You'll see a black gap in the Timeline, which is where the material that you removed used to be, so let's fix that. It might be counter-intuitive, but you can select the gap by clicking on it. When selected, it will be highlighted in white. Just hit Delete and the gap will close.

STEP 6: Drag to Lengthen Shots

Now, let's extend the end of the first shot in your sequence. To lengthen a shot with the Trim tool, you'll need room to maneuver. Use the Track Select Forward tool to select all of the shots in your Timeline and drag them to the right.

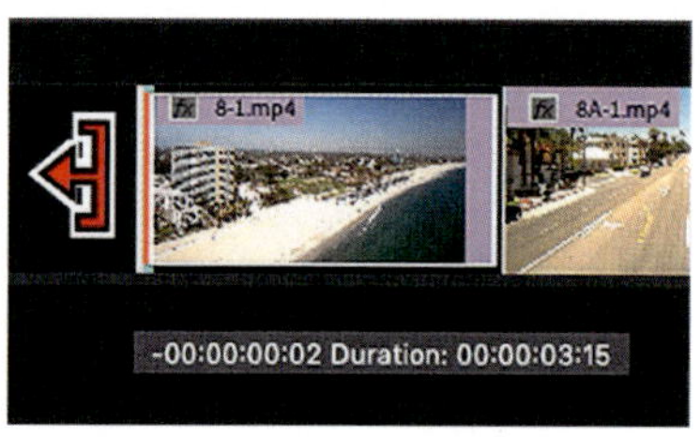

Figure 1.24

Make sure the Trim cursor points to the left as you drag to extend the shot.

Next, go to the start of the first shot that you want to lengthen. Make sure the red Trim cursor is activated and the arrow is pointing left. Click to the left of the shot and drag the edit to the right (Figure 1.24).

Notice that as you drag, a little window appears that tells you how many frames you are extending the shot and how the overall duration of the shot is changing. Drag until you add about one second to the shot and release.

Now take a look to see if you like your edit. Move the blue playhead to the start of your shot and hit Shift + K to Play Around. Premiere will back up a few seconds and play the area around your cursor. Keep working on shortening and lengthening the shot until you're happy with it.

Work your way through your cut shortening or lengthening any shots that aren't quite right and deleting any black gaps in the Timeline until you're happy with the montage.

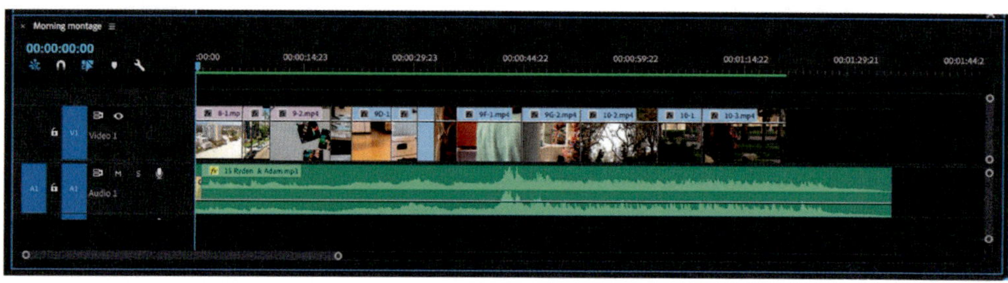

Figure 1.25

A music cue added to the montage sequence.

STEP 7: Add Some Music

We gave you a music cue to work with in the Morning Montage Music folder. If you haven't already imported it, please do so now. You'll see a clip indicated with a green waveform icon, which means it is an audio clip.

You can also use music from your personal library. Go to File > Import and navigate to your music library on your hard drive, find a song you think would work, and select okay. Feel free to add a few more. You might need to try out more than one cue to find the right choice.

Whatever your choice, select it best and drag it over to the Timeline. Aim for the lower area—the empty audio tracks—and drop it in (Figure 1.25). Hit Play (Spacebar) and listen.

Is it too loud? Music almost always comes in too loud.

Go to Window > Audio Clip Mixer and a new window with audio level sliders will open up. Hit play and you'll see levels moving in each track that has music (Figure 1.26). Drag the slider down to -8. Keep adjusting the slider up and down as the music plays, until you're happy with the volume. We'll cover sound in much greater depth later in this book, but the reality of editing is that you have to do some basic audio work from the very beginning. So welcome to your first temp mix.

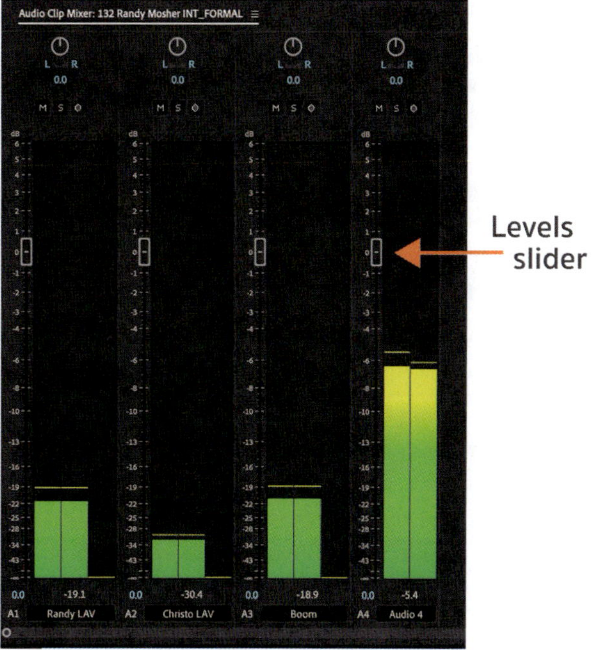

Figure 1.26

The Audio Clip Mixer window lets you adjust the volume of each audio track with a slider.

How'd It Go?

We just showed you a bunch of easy ways to edit the shots in your sequence. There's no right answer, so use the techniques we described as you please and work on your sequence until it feels good. Most filmmakers find that they need to make multiple passes on any given scene before they can consider it finished. Each pass consecutive pass often has a very specific goal—a pass on the getting the tempo of the cutting to match the music, a pass to make it visually dynamic, a pass to make it shorter, and so on.

If that was your first experience editing in Premiere, or maybe editing at all, I hope you liked it. In the next chapter, we'll dive deeper and explore sophisticated ways to edit with more complex material. If you want to take a look at our version of the scene from this chapter, it's called "Morning montage_music.mp4" in the "University scene cuts" folder.

Save Your Project

If you haven't already done so, name your project "Morning Montage" and save it (Control/Command S). We'll be using it again in Chapter 3.

Editorial Problems to Solve

There's so much more to editing (and filmmaking) than software tools. As you review your work on the disarmingly simple sequence in this chapter, consider these editorial challenges:

Matching action Editing the sequence where the actor makes coffee may require that her actions appear continuous from shot to shot. Play around with matching action as she walks to the counter in the wide shot and then proceeds to make coffee in the medium-wide side view. Do her arm movements work across the edit?

Clearing frame Having an actor walk out of frame gives you a way to shift locations. When the actor turns and yawns in one of the takes in the kitchen, she also exits frame. You can let her fully clear the frame then cut to a new scene, such as the one in the bathroom or the campus.

Shots that start in motion Traditionally, a shot with a camera move starts out with a static frame, then it moves and finally it lands on a new static frame. In this scene, some shots start out already moving: the aerial shots, the pan down the fridge to the kettle on the stove, and the slider shot of the feet. How do you cut these shots together? Notice that the speed of movement is relatively similar in all the shots—that means you should be able to cut from moving shot to moving shot without letting them settle until the last shot in the sequence comes to a stop on a static image.

Compressing time No one wants to watch someone make coffee (or do anything for that matter) in real-time in a movie. When she's at the stove, you can use the slider shot of the feet to compress time while the kettle boils. What can you do when she's at the counter making coffee to jump forward in time?

Cutting to music It's not a music video, but the fact is that when a scene has music, the music sets the pace for the scene. Does your cutting work with the music or against it? Can you make small changes to improve how the visuals work with the music? Remember one important thing: rhythm in editing has to do with the cuts from shot to shot, but it also has to do with the movement within each shot.

What to Watch: *The Godfather*

Probably one of the most famous visual scenes in the history of film, the baptism scene from *The Godfather* is famous for intercutting two wildly different scenes—a traditional Catholic baptism and a brutal gangster killing. Other famous montages include the Odessa steps scene from *The Battleship Potemkin* and the opening sequence of *Apocalypse Now.*

2

Editing Basics

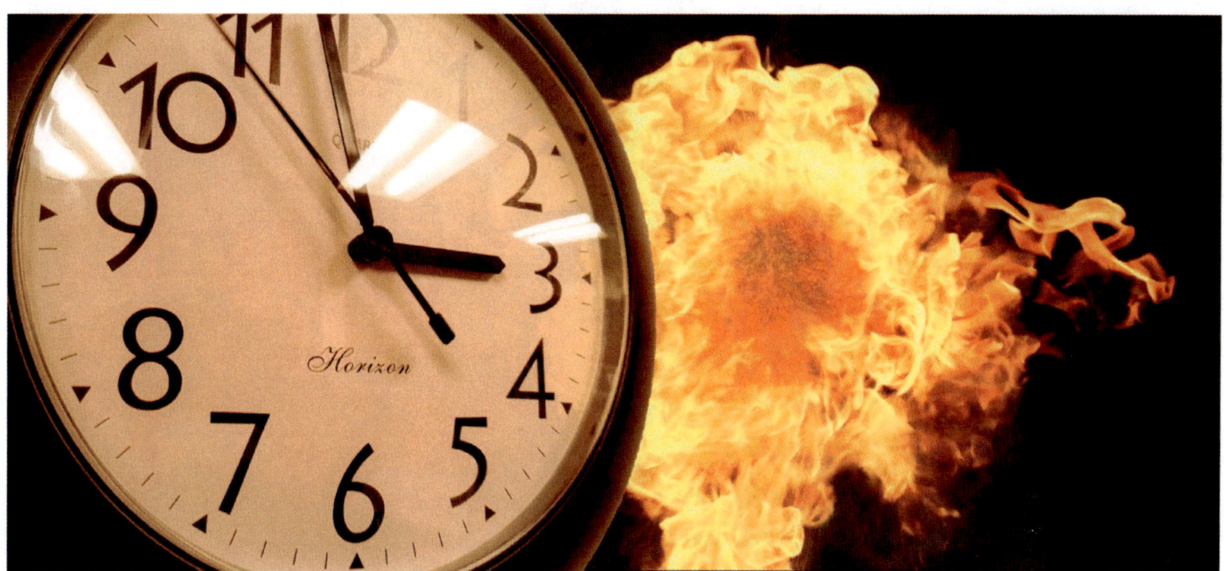

Figure 2.1

Getting your edits dialed-in down to the frame uses sophisticated editing techniques that have been honed by the masters of filmmaking over the past century.

Editing with Precision

THE EDITING METHODS WE'VE COVERED SO FAR are great for building an early cut, but sometimes you need to level-up. What's the difference between beginner editing techniques and advanced? Control.

Dragging and dropping is great, but it's very imprecise. That's why it's good for building rough cuts—you probably aren't ready to be precise at that point. But when you're working on an action movie and trying to cut from the countdown on an explosive device to the start of the explosion, you know exactly what you want to do and when: there's only going to be one frame when the clock strikes three and one frame when the explosion starts (Figure 2.1). It's frustrating to drag, aim, drop, and miss your target—even if it's only by a single frame.

This chapter gets to the heart of editing in Premiere. We'll go over the powerful tools that allow you to edit with precision and control, down to the frame. Prior to this, we've used editing techniques that are common outside of film editing applications. The techniques covered in this chapter are specific to filmmaking. They draw from the history of editing on actual film, were further developed during the era of editing with analog videotape editing, and have been refined in the current era of software-based editing. Today, they are not the only way to edit, but they form a crucial basis for filmmakers who wish to use Premiere to its fullest capacities.

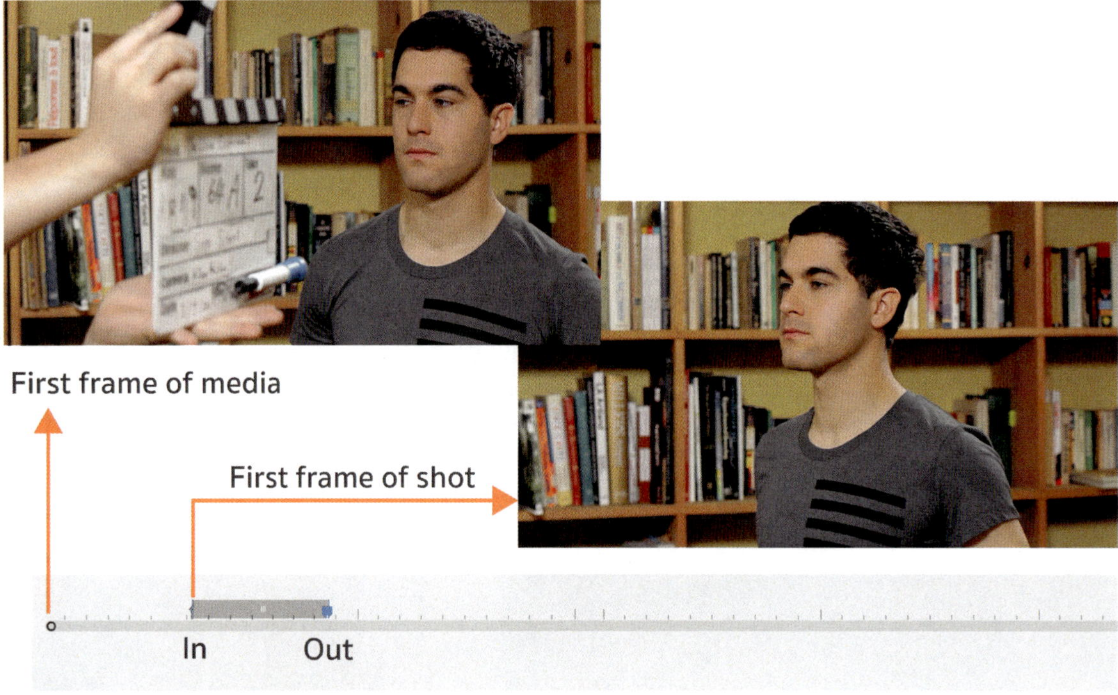

Figure 2.2

The first frame of media is almost never going to be the first frame of a shot that makes it into a film. Setting an In lets you tell Premiere where the shot really starts. And similarly, setting an Out lets you decide where it should end.

Ins and Outs

Since every shot has extra media at the start and end, editing applications allow you to set your own start and end points. In filmmaking, these are called *in-points* and *out-points*, or Ins and Outs for short.

(In this book, we use capital letters to clearly identify In and Out commands.)

Setting Ins and Outs allows you to determine when the good part of each shot starts and ends (Figure 2.2). Ins and Outs are so basic that it's hard to edit without them—in fact, you already used them in the Chapter 1 tutorials to trim the long aerial shots before you added them to your sequence, but there's much more that Ins and Outs can do.

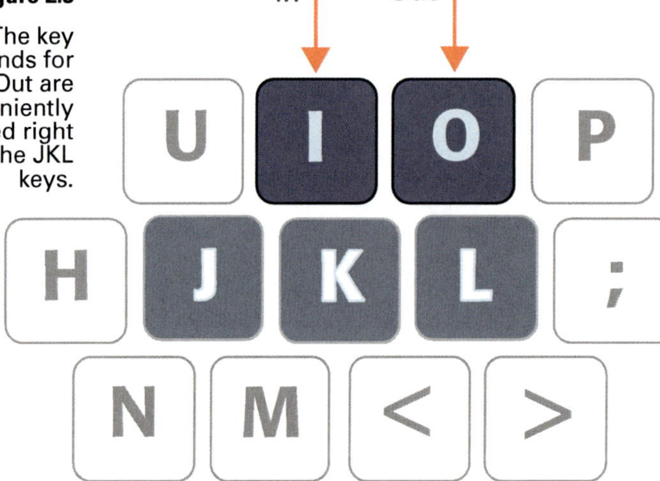

Figure 2.3

The key commands for In and Out are conveniently located right above the JKL keys.

Ins and Outs are not limited to source clips—you can also set them in a sequence. By doing so, you are telling Premiere which part of the sequence you want to be affected by any given action. This means that you can tell Premiere exactly where to add a new shot and also exactly which portion of the sequence you want to move or remove.

Ins and Outs are powerful tools that even the most experienced editors use all the time. That's why they have such a prominent place on the keyboard: I for In and O for Out (Figure 2.3). Premiere also has In and Out buttons at the bottom of both the Source and Program monitors. You use the buttons on the Source monitor to set Ins and Outs in your source clips and the buttons on the Program monitor (Figure 2.17) to set Ins and Outs in your sequence. You can use the Marker menu to find all of these commands, if you prefer using the mouse.

When Ins and Outs are set, you'll see corresponding marks in the time ruler(s)—they look like stylized brackets and the area between them will be highlighted (Figure 2.4).

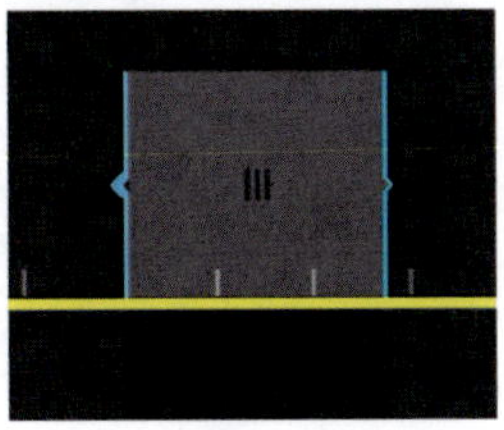

Figure 2.4

In and Out marks set in a clip or sequence appear as blue curly brackets in the time ruler, with highlighting between them to help you identify the part of the shot that is selected.

Ins and Outs affect how editing commands work—Drag and Drop; Cut, Copy, and Paste; and also the four new commands we're going to cover in this chapter: Lift, Extract, Insert, and Overwrite.

When editing commands are paired with Ins and Outs, filmmakers gain the ability to control how edits of shots and cuts behave over *time*, a crucial difference from editing, say, a word-based document or a still image. And this control of time, or duration, is perhaps the most basic task of editing a movie.

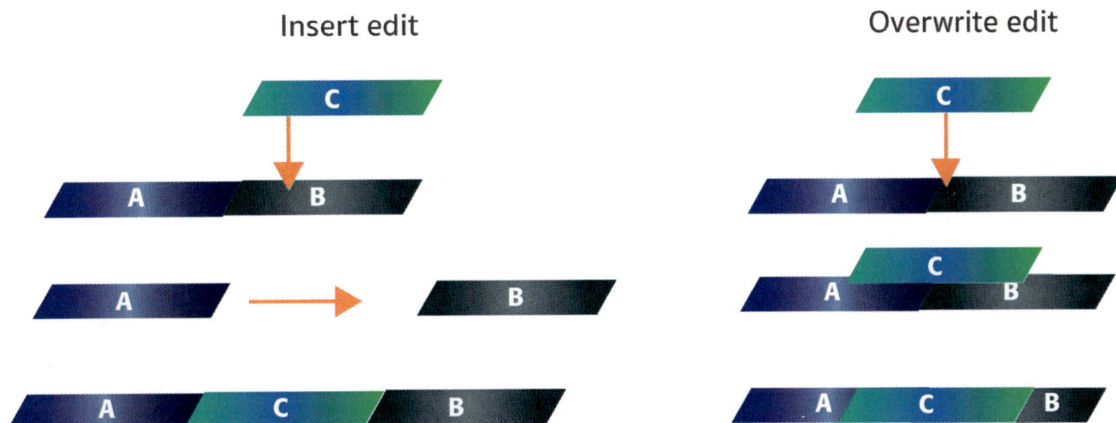

Figure 2.5

Insert (left) pushes other shots down to make room for the new shot. Overwrite (right) covers up anything that's in the way of the new shot.

Insert and Overwrite

The Insert and Overwrite commands tell Premiere how you want to add new material to your sequence (Figure 2.5).

Insert adds a new shot to the point of your choosing by pushing everything after that point later in time. That means you won't cover up any of the shots that are already in your cut. Overwrite will not move the shots that are already there. Rather, the added shot will cover any footage that fills the space it needs.

In Chapter 1, we showed you how to Paste-Insert clips into a sequence. It's often faster and more intuitive to use the Insert and Overwrite buttons at the bottom of the Source monitor (Figure 2.13) or the comma (Insert) and period (Overwrite) keys.

To perform Insert and Overwrite edits, you simply need to have a clip loaded in the Source monitor and a sequence open in the Timeline. If you use Insert or Overwrite without any Ins and Outs set, the whole shot from the Source monitor will get added to your cut at the point where your playhead sits. Adding Ins and Outs will define exactly where the shot starts and ends, before you add it to your cut.

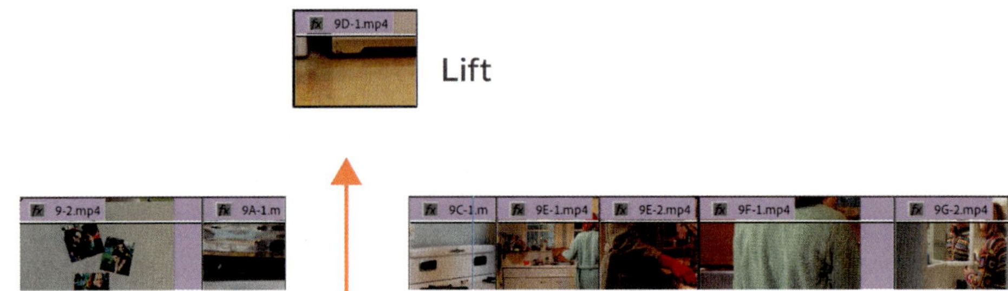

Figure 2.6

The Lift command removes a selection from your sequence and leaves a gap where it used to be.

Lift and Extract

You can also tell Premiere how to remove unwanted material from a sequence. For example, you might think a section of your first cut of the Morning Montage from Chapter 1 is too long. Setting In and Out points in the Timeline or Program monitor will designate which part of your cut is unnecessary.

You can then choose between *lifting* out the material between the In and Out, which will leave a gap in your sequence (Figure 2.6), or *extracting*, which will remove the material and close the gap (Figure 2.7). Lift and Extract are commands you will use all the time, so they are mapped to the keyboard at the semi-colon key (Lift) and the right apostrophe key (Extract). They are also found as buttons at the bottom of the Program monitor and in the Sequence menu.

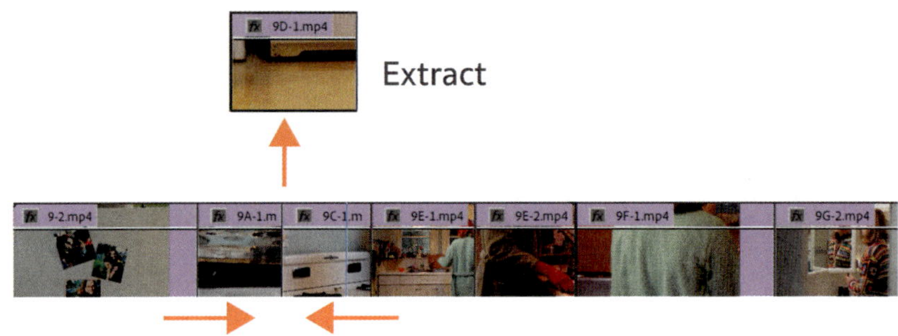

Figure 2.7

The Extract command goes a step further than Lift, removing the selection from your sequence and closing the gap where it used to be.

Three-Point Editing

When you make an edit by setting In and Out points for both the source clip and the edited sequence, it's known as *three-point editing.*

Obviously, two Ins and two Outs actually add up to four points (Figure 2.8), but you almost never set all four. Instead, you'll set an In and an Out on the source and an In on the sequence and Premiere will calculate the fourth point for you. In fact, you don't even need to set an In on the sequence. If there is no In point set, Premiere will instead use the blue playhead as the In. But Premiere always prioritizes any existing In point over the playhead.

Settings two Ins and one Out is by far the most common way to make a three-point edit, but you can also set two Outs and one In. The result will be a *back-timed* edit. This is useful if you have a source clip with a very specific duration—perhaps a shot of a hand picking up a weapon in a thriller. You're not going to linger on this shot, you just want the action, so you set Ins and Outs around it. Then in your sequence, you know that you want the shot of the gun to end right

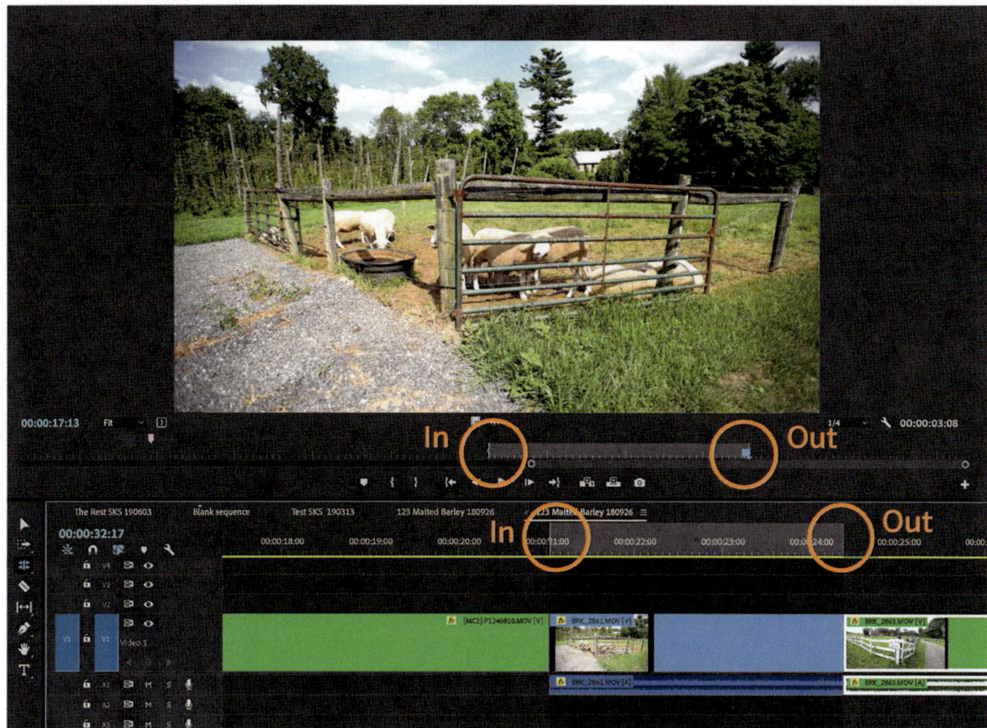

Figure 2.8

Here you can see a clip loaded in the Source monitor with In and Out points set and a sequence in the Timeline, also with Ins and Outs set. At least three of these four points are needed to make an Insert or Overwrite edit. But if you don't set Ins and Outs in the Timeline, Premiere will use the position of the playhead as an In.

as the victim's face reacts to the weapon in the close-up shot. You set an Out at that moment. Then you perform an Overwrite edit and Premiere calculates where the new shot should come in on the Timeline, covering any extra footage of the actor reacting to the gun before the crucial moment.

If you set Ins and Outs on both the source and the sequence, but the durations do not match, you'll get the Fit Clip window (Figure 2.9). Here, you can choose from a variety of options to make it work. Most users will prefer either Ignore Source Out Point or Ignore Sequence Out Point. The former means that the In and Out you chose in your sequence will dominate—there's no risk that you'll accidentally overwrite past the Out you set there. The latter means that the source clip settings will dominate—the part of the clip you selected will get added to the sequence in its entirety, regardless of how it changes the sequence. If you choose Fit to Fill, Premiere will change the speed of your shot, speeding it up or slowing it down so that it fits exactly. This is only rarely useful. Whatever your preference, you may wish to check the box next to Always Use This Choice, to avoid getting this message all the time.

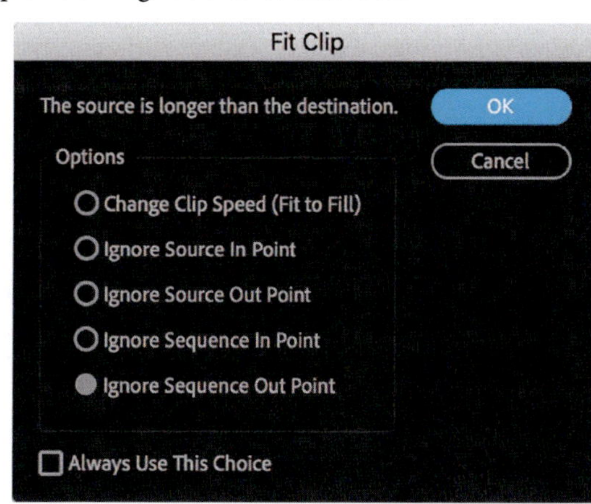

Figure 2.9

The Fit Clip window appears if you set Ins and Outs on both the source and the sequence, but the durations do not match. You can choose from a variety of options and you can also check the box at the bottom to keep this window from reappearing.

Undos and the History Panel

Undo might be my favorite thing about computers and Premiere Pro offers up to 100 levels of Undo (File > Undo or Command/Control + Z). As long as you keep your project open, you can hit Command + Z all the way back to the beginning of your session. But how do you know what you are undoing? After all, even a short amount of time spent editing can involve hundreds of actions.

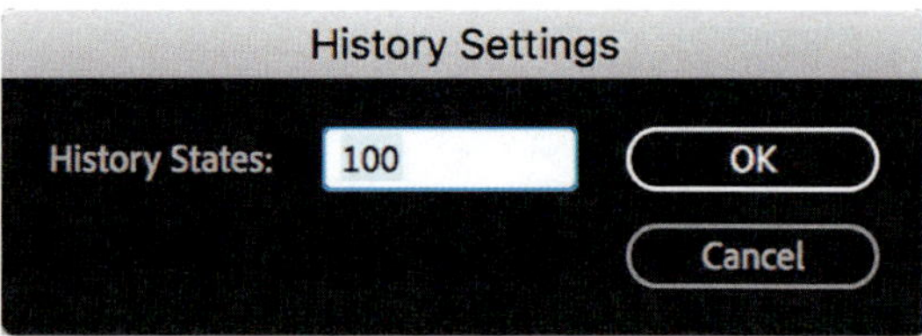

Figure 2.10

You can change the number of Undos to 100 in the History settings.

That's where the History panel comes in. Every action you make is listed in the History panel, up to a maximum of 100 actions. Instead of Command Z-ing a zillion times, you can just scroll up the list and click on the last action that you want to keep. Of course, undoing is linear so if you want to Undo an action ten steps back, you'll also Undo everything that came after it.

The default number of Undos is 32, so to get 100 you'll have to change the History settings (Figure 2.10), found under the History tab menu (Figure 2.11).

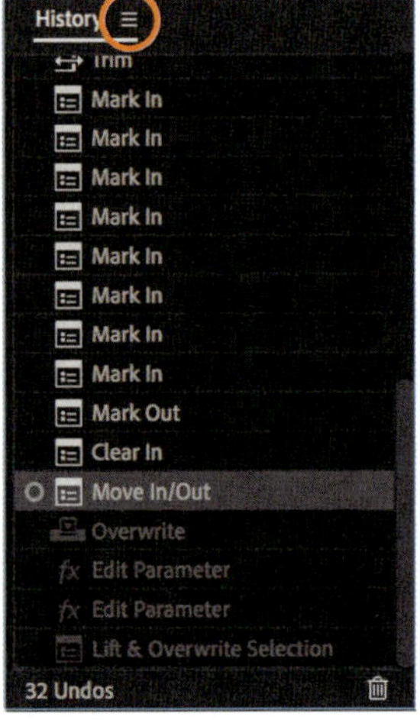

Figure 2.11

The History panel shows you every action you performed during your current editing session. By clicking on an action, you can undo everything that came after it. In this image, the greyed-out actions have been undone.

It can be hard to remember every little step you took as you were working, but the listing in the History panel does offer some clues. Each item has an icon that represents the tool or command that was used to create that action, along with a text-based description. Many of these icons match the buttons in the Source and Program monitors. While almost all editorial actions will be listed in the History panel, anything that is more about the program itself or the workspace will not be available to Undo: changes to the interface like sorting and resizing panels, and also any changes to Preferences. Some actions that occur in a sub-area of Premiere (such as titling or multicam editing) will only show up as a single action, that is, all your font and positioning adjustments will not be listed separately.

Also, be aware that if you Undo actions in the History panel, you can reverse that decision, but only until you perform a new action. That new action will erase the greyed-out thread of Undos and make them permanent.

TUTORIAL: Editing a Dialogue Scene

Explosions and action scenes need precise editorial control, but so do dialogue scenes. For this tutorial, create a new project and call it "University scene." Import the University Scene Media folder into it. We'll be working with this project in Chapter 3 as well. The scene in this tutorial is a traditional dialogue-driven scene that was filmed *master-shot style*. That means, there's a wide shot that covers the whole scene and three coverage shots—in this case, singles of each actor (Figure 2.12). This is a very simple scene and it's also very short but you can learn a lot from it.

There are four shots:

- Master Shot (2 takes)
- Single of Olivia, the main character (3 takes)
- Single of the female professor (2 takes)
- Single of the male professor (2 takes)

There's also a short script for reference (Table 2.1).

What is a Master Shot?

If you're unfamiliar with types of shots and other basic film terms, they are covered in Chapter 5 of *The Digital Filmmaking Handbook*, Planning Your Shoot.

Master shot

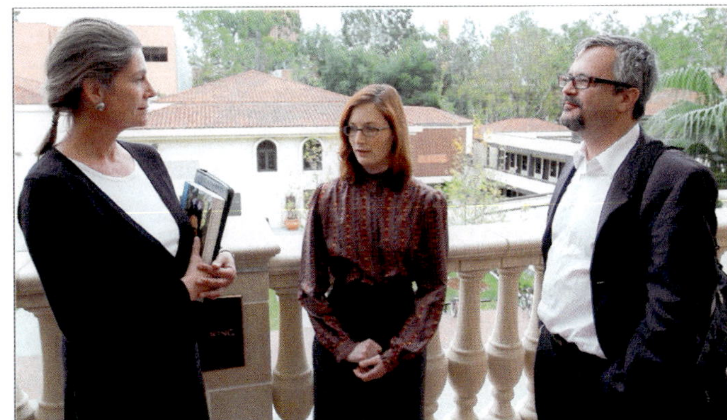

Single of professor

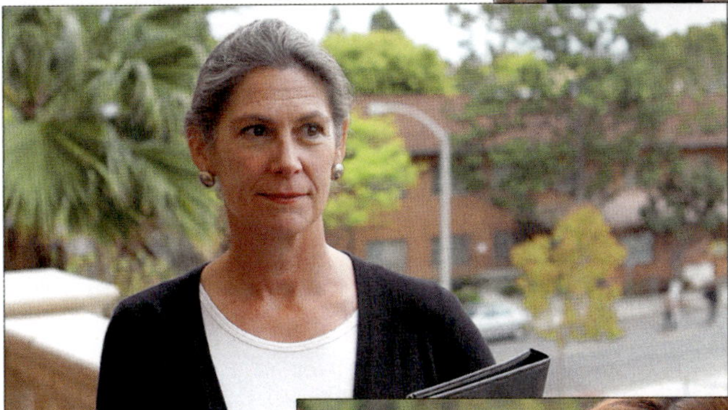

Single of Olivia

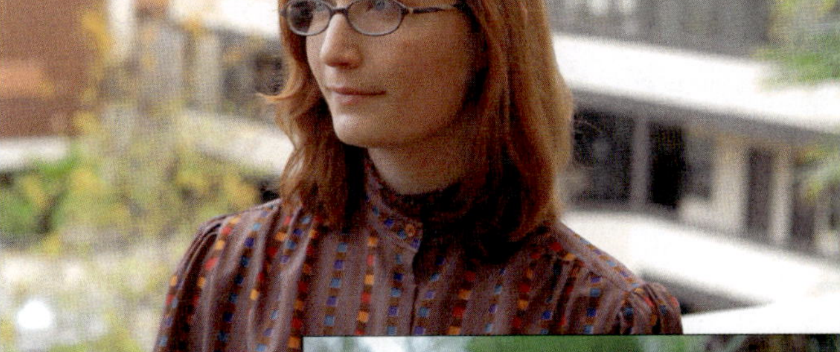

Single of male professor

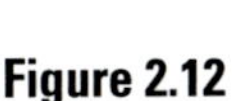

Figure 2.12

These four camera angles comprise the coverage for the scene in the tutorial. At the top is the master shot, which is wide enough to show everything that happens in the scene and below that are the singles of each character.

```
MAIN TITLE

EXT. MORNING SUNRISE

INT. OLIVIA'S KITCHEN

Olivia makes coffee. On her fridge are snapshots of
Olivia with an attractive young man we will learn
is JAMES.

EXT. U.C. BERKELEY CAMPUS – DAY

SHOTS of Olivia walking through campus.

EXT. FACULTY OFFICES – DAY

Olivia, now eloquent, discusses her thesis with
SENIOR PROFESSORS.

                    OLIVIA
      ...So in reality it wasn't the Simone
      de Beauvoirs but the Shulamith
      Firestones that paved the way for the
      Riot Grrrls....

                FEMALE COLLEAGUE
      That's a very positive step in defense
      of your thesis.

                 MALE COLLEAGUE
      Olivia! Congratulations on the
      Provosts' grant. I'm very happy for
      you.

He touches her arm. Olivia looks at him in a sudden
panic. The MALE COLLEAGUE gives her a puzzled look.

                    OLIVIA
      Thank you. Bye

Olivia hurries away.
```

Table 2.1

A script for the tutorial scene in this chapter.

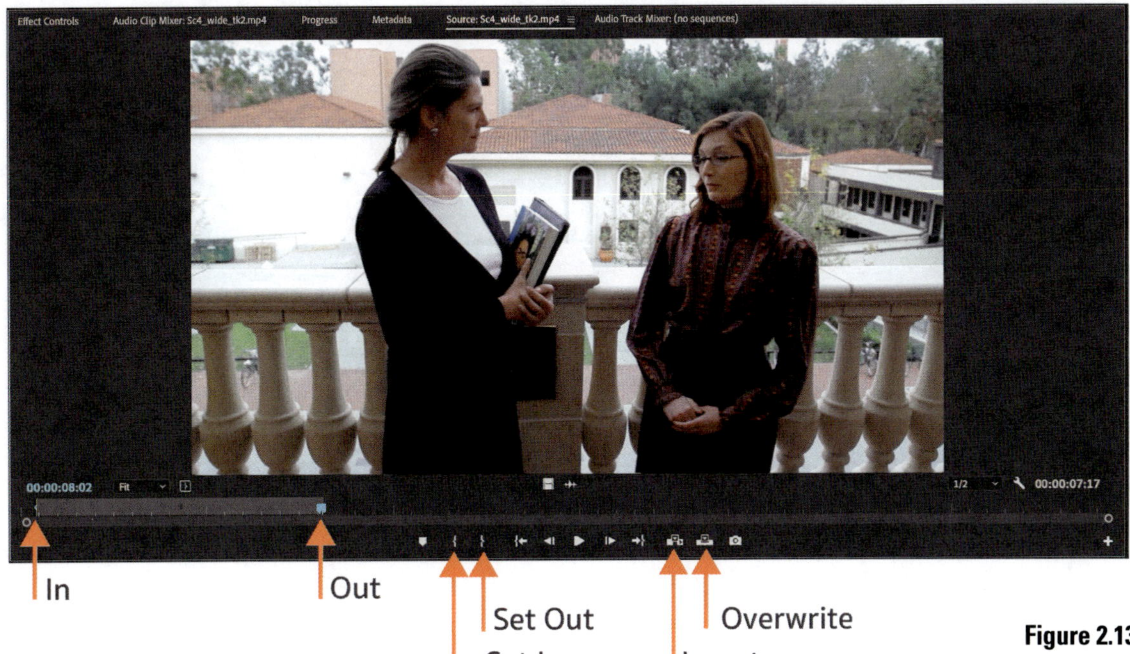

Figure 2.13

Use the Source monitor to set In and Out points in the master shot. You'll then see the In and Out marks in the time ruler with the area between them highlighted.

STEP 1: Use Overwrite to Build the Cut

We're going to start by editing the master shot into the Timeline. This will give us a solid base on which to build the scene.

There are many ways to add a shot to a sequence and you could use the methods you already know—Drag and Drop or Cut, Copy, and Paste—but in this tutorial we're going to focus on using the traditional editing commands: Insert, Overwrite, Lift, and Extract.

For that to work, we need to create a new sequence (File > Sequence > New). We'll use the default settings. Call your new sequence "University scene."

Now, let's build a simple version of the scene using take 1 of the master shot (Sc4_wide_tk1.mp4). Double-click on it in the bin to launch it into the Source monitor (Figure 2.13). For this first shot, we're simply going to edit the whole thing into the Timeline by clicking the Overwrite button (Figure 2.14). Make sure the playhead is at the very start of the empty sequence in the Timeline before you select Overwrite. (You can always use Undo if you want to try again.)

Use the backslash key (\) to Zoom to Sequence so that you can see it better and expand the tracks so that you can see thumbnails and waveforms. (Refer to the Basic Settings in Chapter 1.)

Figure 2.14

The Overwrite button is found at the bottom of the Source monitor.

? Describing Time

In filmmaking, time is written in hours, minutes, seconds, and frames. So instead of 1:07 for one hour and seven minutes, we use 01:07:00:00 in the format of hh:mm:ss:ff, also known as timecode. Premiere uses timecode notation to describe the duration of shots and sequences and also to indicate the position of the playhead. We'll use it going forward whenever we need to reference a specific time in a tutorial.

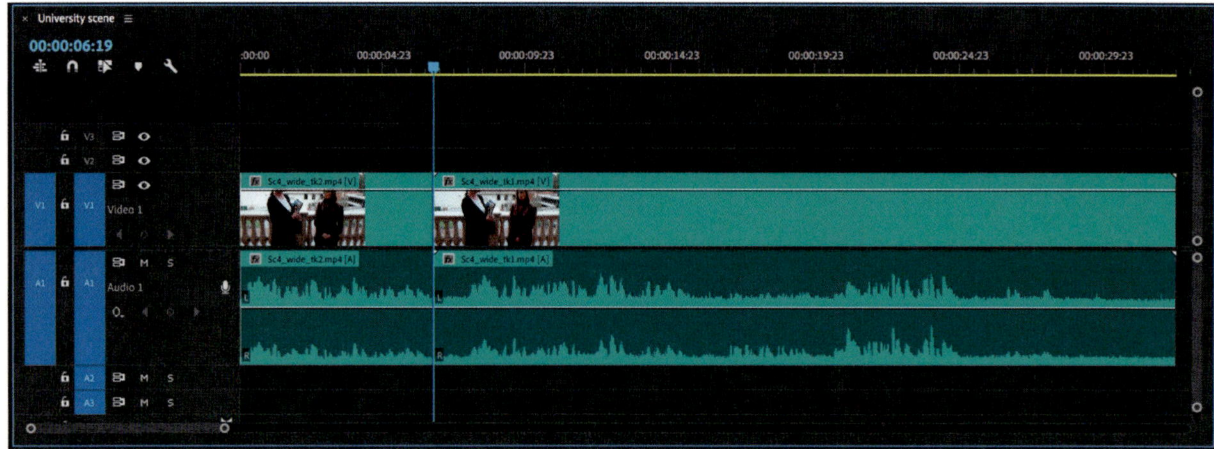

Figure 2.15

After inserting the line from the second master shot to the beginning of the cut, your Timeline should look like this.

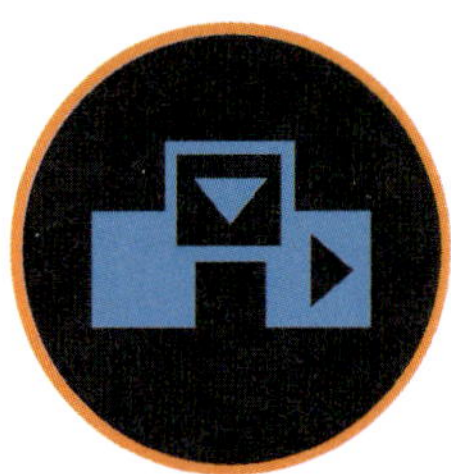

Figure 2.16

The Insert button is found at the bottom of the Source monitor.

STEP 2: Use Insert to Add a New Shot

Take 1 of the master shot is pretty good except for the first line—the actor had a bad cold that day and had trouble saying "Shulamith Firestone." But take 2 has a good version of the line. So we're going to use Insert to add that first line from take 2 of the master shot into the beginning sequence. (There's a script in Table 2.1 if you need to refer to it.)

Double-click to launch take 2 (Sc4_wide_tk2.mp4) into the Source monitor. We're going to set an In and an Out to mark Olivia's first line. Once again, the JKL and arrow keys are very useful for moving around in the clip as you navigate within the Source monitor. At about one second into the shot (00:00:01:00) set an In (I) and then set an Out (O) at the end of her first line, at about 8 seconds (00:00:08:00). Notice that the area between the In and the Out is now highlighted in the Source monitor time ruler (Figure 2.13).

Because we want to add this line to the start of the sequence, we're going to use the Insert command. Make sure that the Timeline playhead is positioned at the very beginning of the sequence and that you don't have any Ins or Outs set in the Timeline, then click the Insert button (Figure 2.16). You'll now see both takes in your sequence, with a partial take 2 ahead of take 1 (Figure 2.15).

Radio Cuts

When you build a cut based on the dialogue in a scene without worrying about the visuals, that's known as a radio cut—an old-fashioned term that means it would sound good on the radio or in a podcast. Radio cuts give you a good starting place. You build the structure of the scene based on dialogue so that you can focus on the visuals for the next pass. After Step 3, your cut in the tutorial could be called a radio cut.

What to Watch: *As Good as it Gets*

The most basic type of dialogue scene to edit is one with two characters—in fact the word *dialogue* actually means two people talking, as opposed to *monologue.* (I had to google and it turns out *trialogue* is actually a word.) Each added character increases the challenges in editing a scene. Two-person scenes are everywhere, but three-character scenes are much less common. *As Good as it Gets* has some great examples, like the scene in the car, "Good Times, Noodle Salad" with Jack Nicholson, Greg Kinnear, and Helen Hunt.

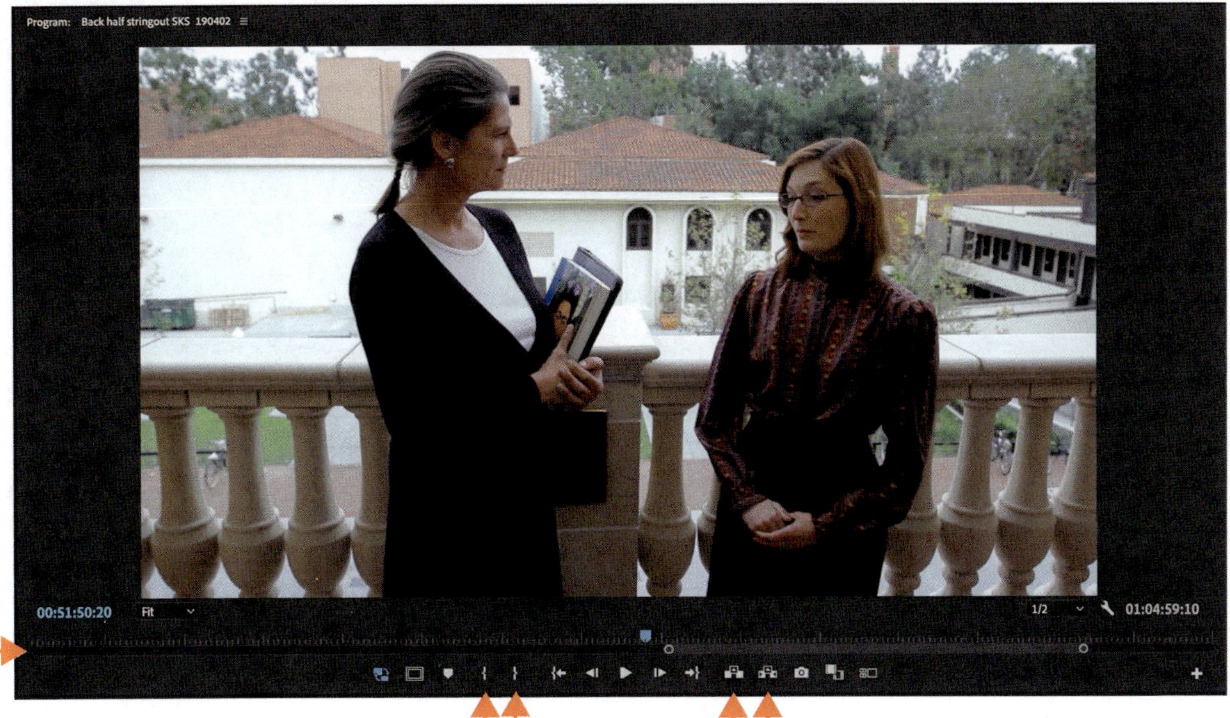

Figure 2.17

Use the buttons on the bottom of the Program monitor to set Ins and Outs, Lift, and Extract.

STEP 3: Use Lift to Remove the Extra Line

Now the first line of the scene is in there twice. We're going to get rid of it using Lift. This time, we'll add the In and Out points in the Program monitor (Figure 2.17). In the Timeline, use the arrow keys to move the playhead to the start of the second shot and set an In (I). Then play until you get to the end of the repeated line, at 00:00:16:00 and add an Out (O). This time, you'll see the area between the In and the Out highlighted in the Timeline (Figure 2.19) and also in the time ruler of the Program monitor. Use the Lift button at the bottom of the Program monitor (Figure 2.18) to remove the extra line. Select the gap between the two master shots and Delete.

You now have a full version of the scene based on the master shot. The dialogue is all in place, but we need to get rid of the jump cut.

Figure 2.18

The Lift button is found at the bottom of the Program monitor.

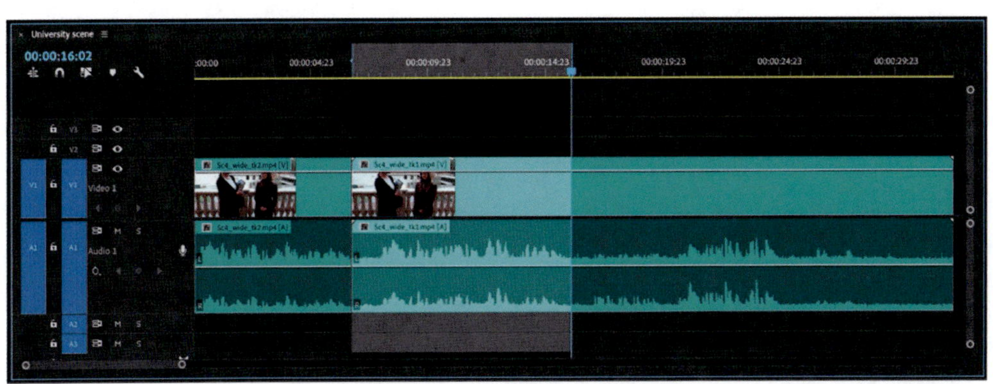

Figure 2.19

You can set Ins and Outs in either the Timeline or the Program monitor—they are the same and both display your edited sequence.

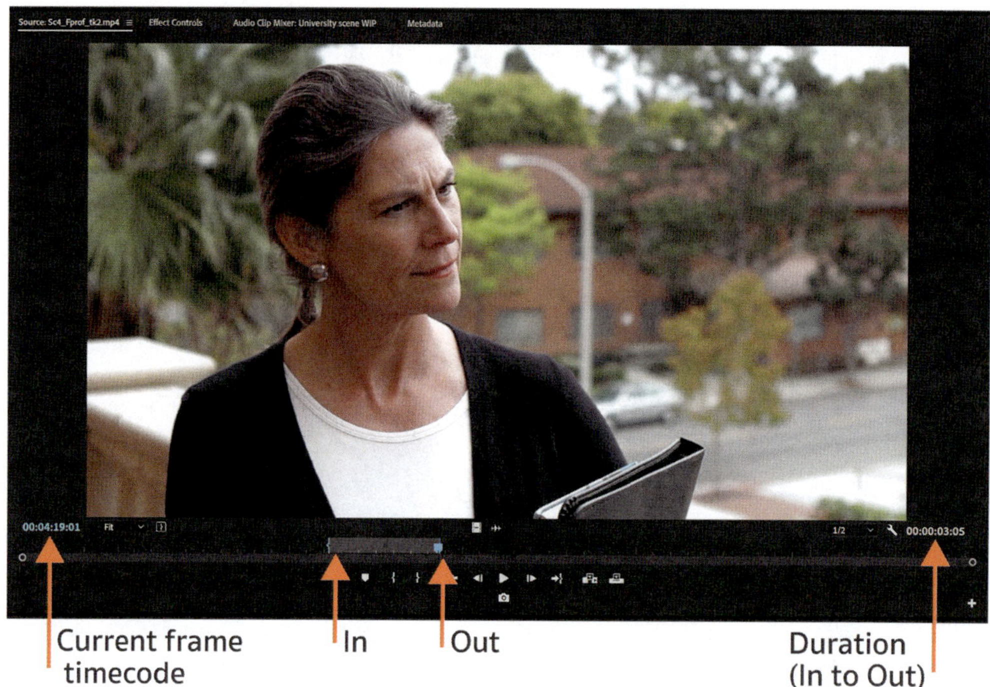

Figure 2.20

The single of the professor loaded in the Source monitor with In and Out points set. Note that the duration changes to reflect the length of the part of the clip selected by the In and Out marks.

STEP 4: Set Three Points to Insert a Single

Up until now, you've been making edits based on Ins, Outs, and the position of the playhead. Technically, that's a three-point edit because the playhead serves as an In when you don't have one set. Now we'll make a true three-point edit and use it to insert a single of the Female Professor that will hide the jump cut between the two takes of the master shot.

Let's use take 2 of her single, Sc4_Fprof_tk.mp4. Double-click on it to open it in the Source monitor and add an In at 00:00:09:07 right before her line "That's a very positive step in defense of your thesis," and an Out right after it at 00:00:12:02 (Figure 2.20). Now go to the Timeline and set an In (I) at the edit between the two master shots (00:00:07:01). You now have three edit points set: the source In, the source Out, and the sequence In.

In the Source monitor, click the Insert button (.) and you'll see the new shot in the Timeline (Figure 2.21) in between the two takes of the master shot.

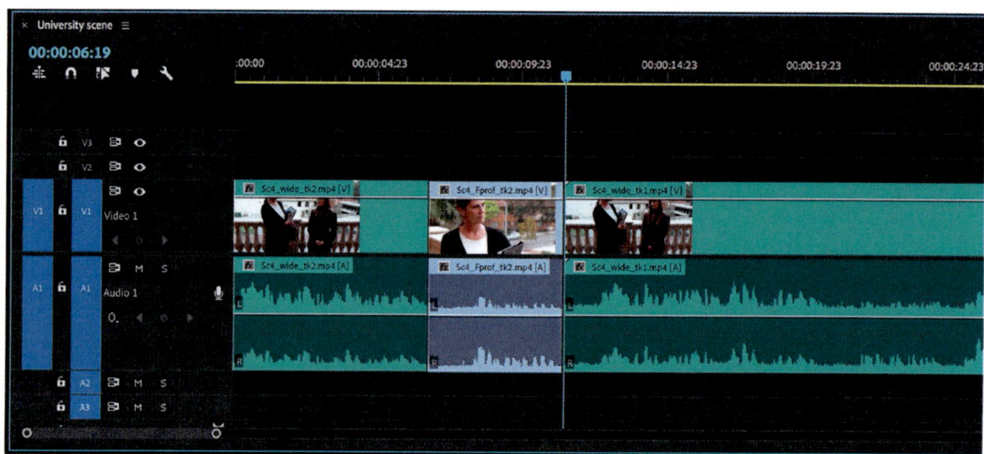

Figure 2.21

After you use three-point editing to add the professor's single to the sequence it will look something like this. (We labeled our shots with different colors to make it easier to see.)

Try Typing Timecodes

You can jump to any point in a shot or sequence by typing the time you want to go to into the Source monitor, Program monitor, or Timeline. The playhead will jump to that frame and you'll see the current frame timecode (Figure 2.20) updated to match. Try typing in the timecode references in this tutorial, but make sure you don't have any clips selected in the Timeline or you might move them accidentally.

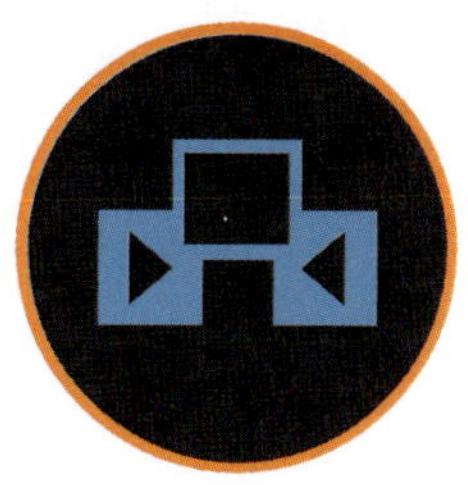

Figure 2.22

The Extract button is found at the bottom of the Program monitor.

STEP 5: Clean Up the Cut with Extract

To get rid of the extra line from the professor, set an In at the start of the second master shot (00:00:09:21) and an Out after it (00:00:14:08). This time, use Extract (') to remove that media and close the gap at the same time (Figure 2.22).

Now, let's get rid of the extra media at the end of the sequence.

Go to the end of the sequence, to about the point where Olivia exits frame, and play. There's not too much fat here, but you probably want to end the scene before the female professor closes her eyes.

Set an In at the point where you want the scene to end, then click the Extract button. (You don't need to set an Out because there's nothing else on the Timeline after this shot.)

You now have a cut based on the master shot that has all the lines you want, no jump cuts, and a clean ending. Go back to the start of the sequence and hit Play to watch the result. Your sequence should contain all of the dialogue in the script in Table 2.1

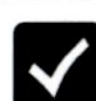

Removing Ins and Outs

When you set Ins and Outs in a source clip or in the Timeline, they stay there until you set new Ins and Outs. But since they affect everything you do, sometimes you just want to make sure no Ins and Outs are set. You can remove Ins and Outs by using the key command Option + I (Mac) or Control + Shift + I (Win) to remove an In or Option + O (Mac) or Control + Shift + O to remove an Out.

What Do You Think?

Watch your cut again. Is it smoother? More importantly, do you like how it turned out? Here's what I think: it's pretty good and it feels "seamless." But the professor isn't the main character and by showing a close-up of the professor, we're tossing the scene to her and not to Olivia. In other words, it's not doing a very good job of telling the story. And what is editing, if not storytelling?

If you want to look at what our cut looks like at this point, it's in the "University scene cuts" folder, called University scene V1.mp4."

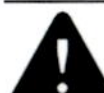

Save Your Project

If you haven't already done so, name your project "University scene" and save it (Control/Command S). We'll continue working on it in Chapter 3 by adding more close-ups and refining it with advanced editing techniques.

Narrative Problems to Solve

As with most feature films, it's not too hard to put a scene together if it's shot properly. What's harder is making more subtle storytelling choices.

> **Whose story is this?** In the cut we just made, all the lines are in and we covered an edit in the master shot with a cutaway. In other words, it's technically solid. But what about the story? The main character is Olivia, the woman in the center, not the female professor—would you know that if you saw this scene as is? How do you make the cut reflects the experience of the main character?
>
> **Is this scene funny or serious?** The film this scene comes from is a comedy, but like many comedies, not all of the scenes are funny. Instead, the comedy comes from how serious it is, at least for the main character. How do you deal with questions of tone as you edit? What editorial choices can you make that clarify the tone?
>
> **Are you telling the story you intended to tell?** This is a little harder to answer when you only have a snippet of a movie. But it's a question that every filmmaker has to ask themselves at some point. If you decide to drift away from the original script, you should make sure that's a conscious decision you can stand behind.

In the next chapter we're going to continue working on this scene and we'll address these and other narrative concerns.

3

Advanced Editing

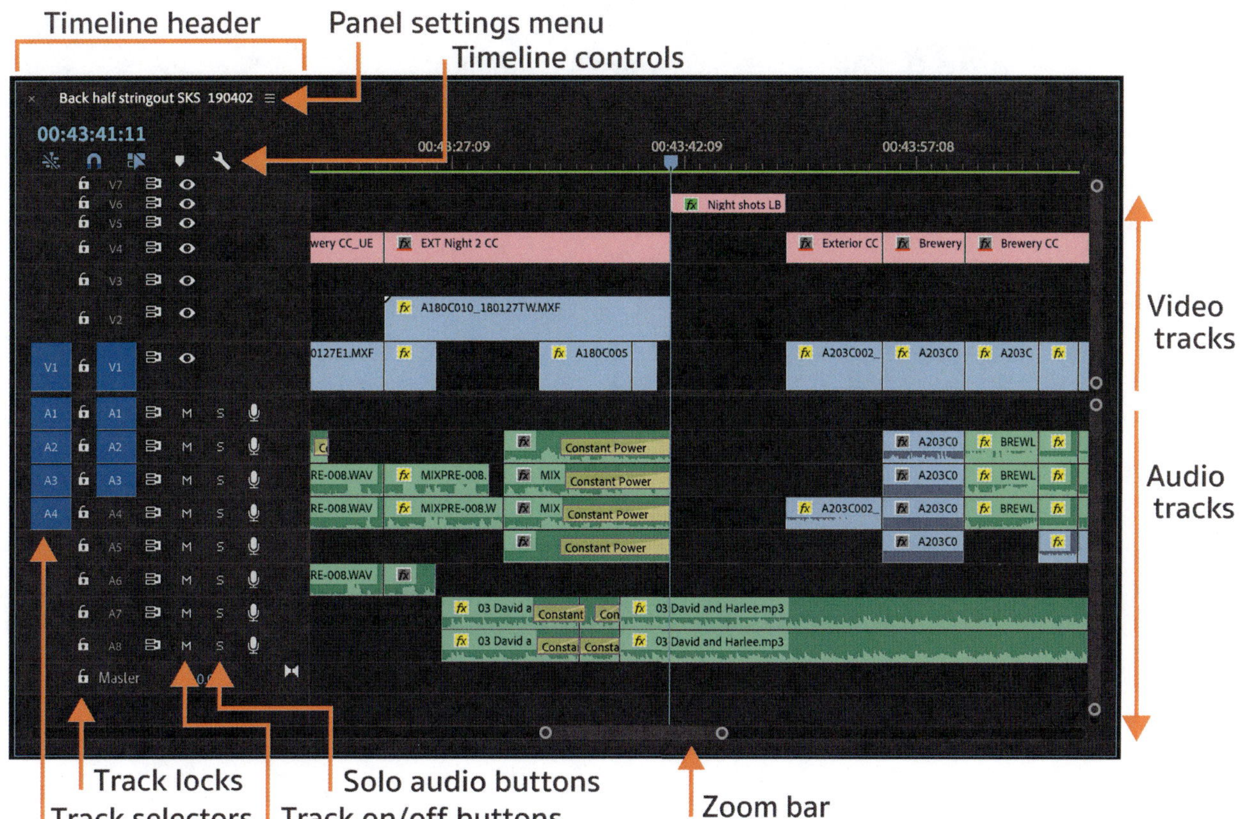

Figure 3.1

The Timeline is where you'll spend most of your time when you're editing in Premiere. It offers a flexible interface that can expand or contract according to the needs of your film.

Working in the Timeline

For many filmmakers editing is the fun part—you get to see all your hard work come together on a screen for the first time. But for others, it's the stressful part—the part where you see if the shots that you meticulously planned actually cut together, if the actors you chose and worked with so carefully suit the story, and if the script that took months or years to find or write holds up on the screen. In other words, it's where you, as a filmmaker, must confront your weaknesses and assess your strengths. But guess what? No matter where you fall on that spectrum, there's always one solution: editing.

In this chapter, we're going to explore the myriad ways of working in the Timeline, which is the place where most of the editing happens (Figure 3.1). If a simple sequence is loaded into it, the

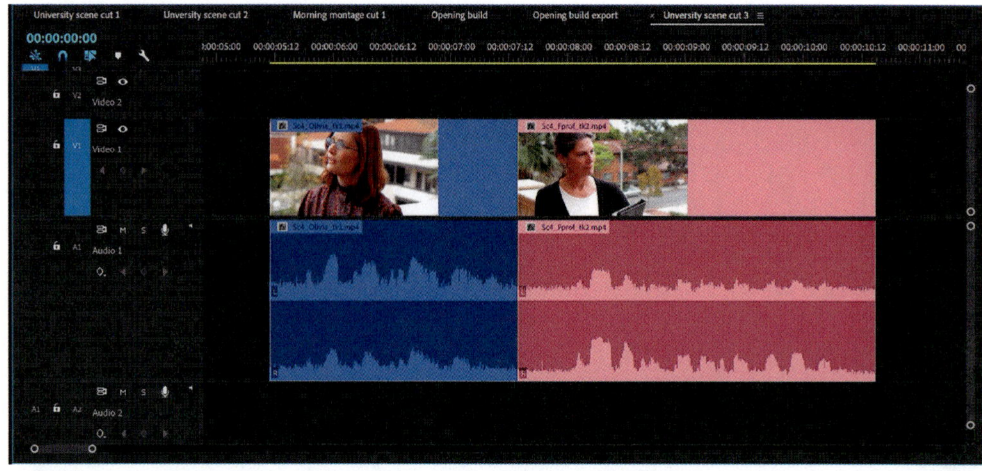

Figure 3.2

A straight cut is a simple edit across all the tracks in the shot(s).

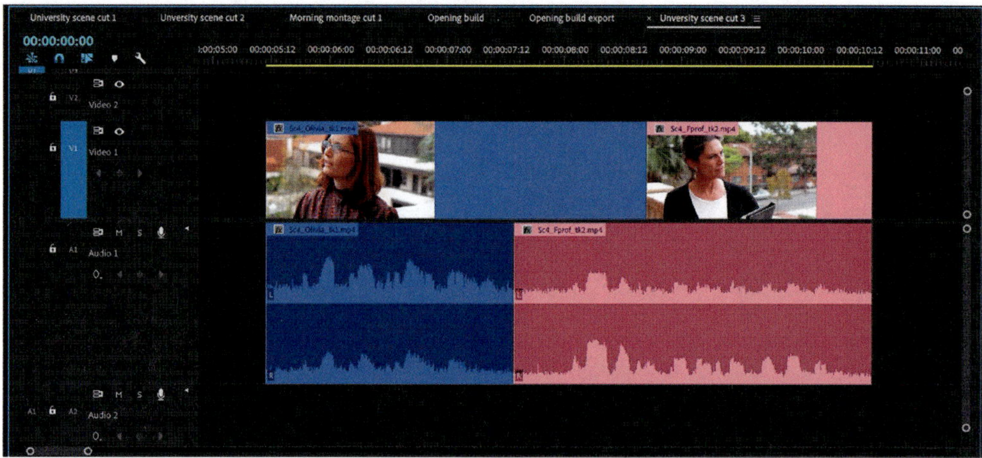

Figure 3.3

An overlapping edit is a cut where one element (video or audio) is extended separately from the other elements. In this example, the video of the first shot is extended beyond the audio. These kinds of edits are also called L-cuts because the result shape kind of resembles the letter L.

Timeline looks simple too. But the work you do there can get very complex—just look at the cover of this book, which shows a portion of the Timeline for a feature film. The Timeline expands and contracts to match your needs.

As we mentioned earlier, the Timeline is partner to the Program monitor. They work hand-in-hand, because they show two different views of the same thing. The Program monitor shows your film as an audience would see it and the Timeline shows it as a filmmaker sees it—many pieces that work together to (hopefully) add up to something greater. It's the difference between seeing the skeleton of a building and the glass-encased skyscraper it becomes. Or, to put it another way, the Program monitor is where you see your work-in-progress, the Timeline is where the work gets done.

We've already explored some basic Timeline editing techniques: Drag and Drop; Cut, Copy and Paste; Top and Tail trimming, and the classic editorial commands Insert, Overwrite, Lift, and Extract. But there's much more available to you when you're editing in the Timeline:

Multi-track editing So far in this book we've restricted editing to just one video track and two audio tracks but working across multiple tracks gives you much more room and freedom to work. Many who are new to editing find that editing across multiple tracks is very intuitive. In this chapter, you'll learn how to select and target different tracks, so that you can take full advantage of editing in the Timeline.

Nudging clips When you select a clip in the Timeline, you can use key commands to move it around the Timeline. Alt (Win)/Command (Mac) combined with the left and right arrow keys moves the selection frame by frame. Shift + Alt/Command moves it in increments of five frames. These tiny, controlled movements can really come in handy. You can also type in a specific number of frames in the numeric keypad, along with the plus or minus sign, to give Premiere a very specific nudge command.

Overlapping edits We've been working with edits that keep the audio and video tied together—that's also known as a straight cut (Figure 3.2). But when you edit the audio at the exact same time as the video, the edit is much more noticeable. In the real world, it's rare to make edits for both the audio and the video at exactly the same point. Instead, video or audio is overlapped, a type of edit that's also known as an L-cut (Figure 3.3). Overlapping edits seem more natural or more invisible.

Disabling clips When you don't want to see or hear a clip that's in the Timeline, but you're not quite ready to get rid of it entirely, you can toggle Clip > Enable to leave it in position but make it invisible and/or inaudible. Mac users have the keyboard shortcut Command + Shift + E, Windows users will have to program a key themselves.

Replacing clips You can drag and drop a clip into the Timeline and replace an existing clip by holding the Alt (Win) or Option (Mac) key as you drop it. The new clip will match the length of the clip it will replace. This is very useful if you are swapping takes or upgrading graphics and other temporary elements. For a bit more control, use right-click menu Replace with Clip command, which gives you some extra options.

Making Splices

Often, you'll find you need to make a cut in a piece of media in the Timeline to split it into two pieces. Edits like this are called *splices*. There are two ways to make a splice in Premiere:

Razor Tool If you click on the Razor tool in the Tools panel your cursor will switch from an arrow/pointer to a razor (Figure 3.4). Hover the Razor over any clip in the Timeline and a dotted line will appear on the clip that indicates where the Razor will cut the clip into two pieces. Now you can edit these pieces independently. You can also delete one if you don't need it using the Delete (or backspace) key.

Add Edit Very similar to the Razor tool is the Add Edit command, which creates a splice (Figure 3.5) in a selected clip using the keyboard: Control/Command + K. This can be more precise than the using the Razor tool because the edit will be made at the exact frame where the playhead is positioned. You can also Add Edits across all the tracks in a sequence by using Command/Control + Shift + K.

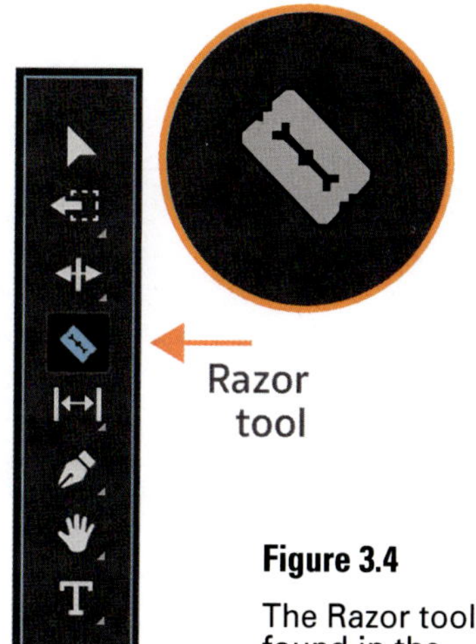

Figure 3.4

The Razor tool is found in the Tools panel.

You can identify splices in the Timeline by choosing Sequence > Show Through Edits. This will add a small icon that looks like a bowtie in across each splice in a piece of continuous media in the Timeline (Figure 3.5). Splices add great flexibility while you're editing, and when you're done with them you can simply select the splice itself and delete it to restore your clip.

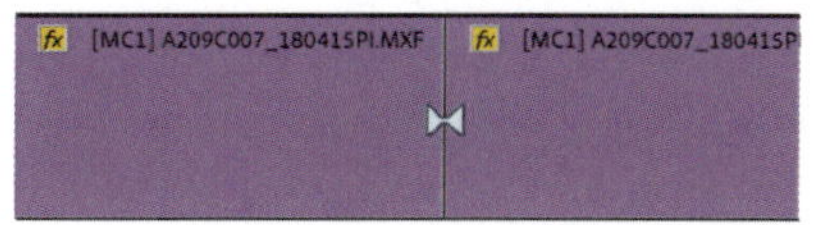

Figure 3.5

Splices in the Timeline can be identified by the bowtie icon.

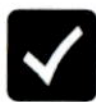 A Splice is a Splice is a Splice?

Premiere has some linguistic quirks when it comes to splices. Sometimes it calls them "edits," such as in the Add Edit keyboard command, and sometimes it calls them "through-edits." Either way, they are all the same thing.

Adding Dissolves

Sometimes you just want your cuts to be smoother. Video dissolves are less popular, but audio dissolves are something you'll use all the time. Both options are found in the Sequence menu—just select the edit, then choose Apply Video Transition, Apply Audio Transition, or Apply Default Transition to Selection to add dissolves across all tracks. You can adjust the length of each dissolve by double-clicking on it in the Timeline and changing the duration in the pop-up window. The default dissolve is about one second long.

☑ Modifier Keys

The modifier keys (Command/Control, Option/Alt, and Shift) affect how Premiere performs editing commands. For example, if you hold Control/Command while you drag and drop a clip within the sequence, Premiere will insert the clip, instead of overwriting it. Play around with the modifier keys (alone and in combination) as you try out the many ways to make edits in Premiere. Usually, you'll find that they offer a slightly different way of executing a command that's similar to the base command.

Timeline Safety Nets

Most media arrives straight out of the camera with one track of video and two or more tracks of audio linked together into a single clip. As a rule, Premiere Pro prioritizes keeping these clips in sync. For example, when you remove media from your cut with the Extract command, Premiere will remove the media from all of your tracks unless you tell it otherwise. If you trim the start of a shot on the video track, the audio will follow and vice versa. In other words, you have to make an effort to lose sync in Premiere.

But as your editing repertoire grows more sophisticated, you'll find that you need to edit audio and video separately with growing frequency. And that is when the risk of losing sync exponentiates. Luckily, Premiere has several features that help you stay in control of sync and the Timeline.

Sync Lock

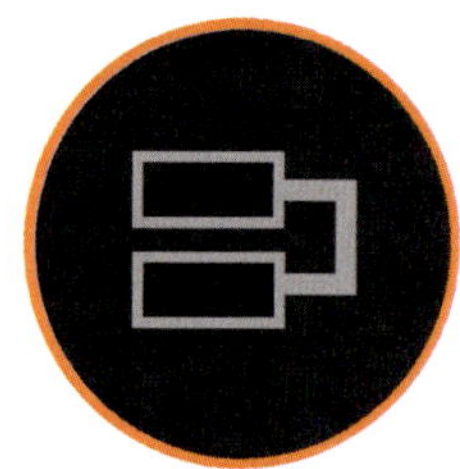

Figure 3.6

There is a Sync lock toggle for each track in the Timeline.

The main reason that clips generally stay in sync in Premiere is Sync Lock (Figure 3.6). It is the editing equivalent of auto-correct—it assumes you would rather keep your media in sync and compensates for anything you do while editing that would cause your media to lose sync. That means extending audio to match changes in video, adding gaps in the Timeline, and so on—whatever it takes. Some editors, including myself once upon a time, started out editing before features like Sync Lock were available. If that sounds like you and you'd like to keep it that way, you can just turn it off using the buttons found in the Timeline header for each track. But most of the rest of us will prefer to leave it on and not touch it.

Unlinking Clips

In order to edit the audio and video from a clip separately, you'll have to actually make a bit of an effort and either Unlink (Clip > Unlink) the audio and video files in a targeted clip or use the Linked Selection button (Figure 3.7) to toggle clip linkages on and off in the whole Timeline. Unlink is somewhat more permanent than Linked Selection—the media in your clip will remain Unlinked until you use Link to put them back together. Linked Selection is less permanent, in that it's tied to a toggle button that's conveniently positioned in the upper right corner of the Timeline—but it's reach is much wider since it affects everything in the Timeline. That said, you will find that you use the Linked Selection toggle all the time. These options will override Sync Lock, so be careful when you use them.

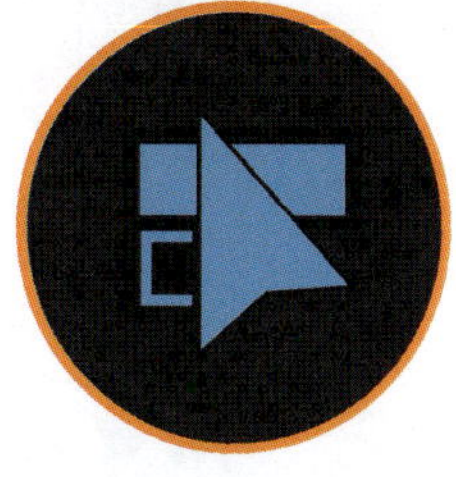

Figure 3.7

The Linked Selection toggle lets you turn clip links off in the Timeline so that you can edit with audio and video separately.

Out of Sync Indicators

Out of Sync Indicators are a warning in the Timeline that helps you identify a sync problem as soon as it occurs (Figure 3.8). If a clip has media (audio or video) that's out of sync, you'll see a small indicator outlined in red over the clip. There will be a number inside the indicator that tells you exactly how many frames you are out of sync and a plus or minus sign to tell you which direction to adjust the sync. Even if you've intentionally unlinked your media (Clip > Unlink), out of sync indicators are still useful. In this case, in order to see them you'll need to select Preferences > Timeline > Display out of sync indicators for unlinked clips.

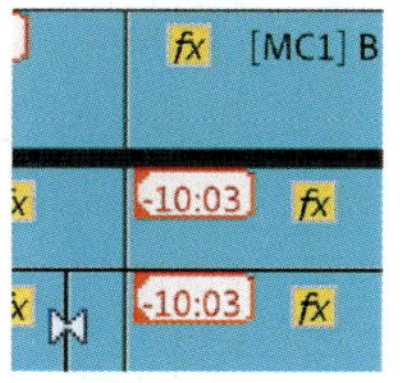

Figure 3.8

Out of sync indicators in the Timeline, show how far out of sync your media is.

Track Locks

You can lock the contents of each track, using the padlock buttons found in the track headers. When locked, you can't make any changes to that track. This can be useful when you've finished a cut and want to make sure there are no accidental changes to it. And sometimes it's useful to lock a track that you don't want to change while you're editing other elements.

Selecting Tracks

Once upon a time—that is, prior to digital editing, you only had one video track and two audio tracks. Today, the number of tracks available to you is virtually unlimited.

In and Out points give you control over how your edits stop and start. Track selection, also known as *patching*, gives you even greater control over how clips get edited into a sequence. By selecting and targeting tracks you can choose exactly where they end up in your cut in the Timeline.

Maybe your shot is a cutaway and you only need the video. Or you want to send video to the second video track, because the first video track is full. Or maybe you have a very specific plan for the contents of each track—music on some, dialogue on others, etc. Using track selection and patching, you can organize your tracks as you edit, saving yourself some time later on.

In the Timeline header, you'll see two columns with track names—V1 for video track one, A1 for audio track one, and so on (Figure 3.9). The left column contains the track selectors for the clip that's loaded in the Source monitor and the right column contains the track selectors for the tracks in the sequence that's loaded in the Timeline. When track selectors are active, they are blue.

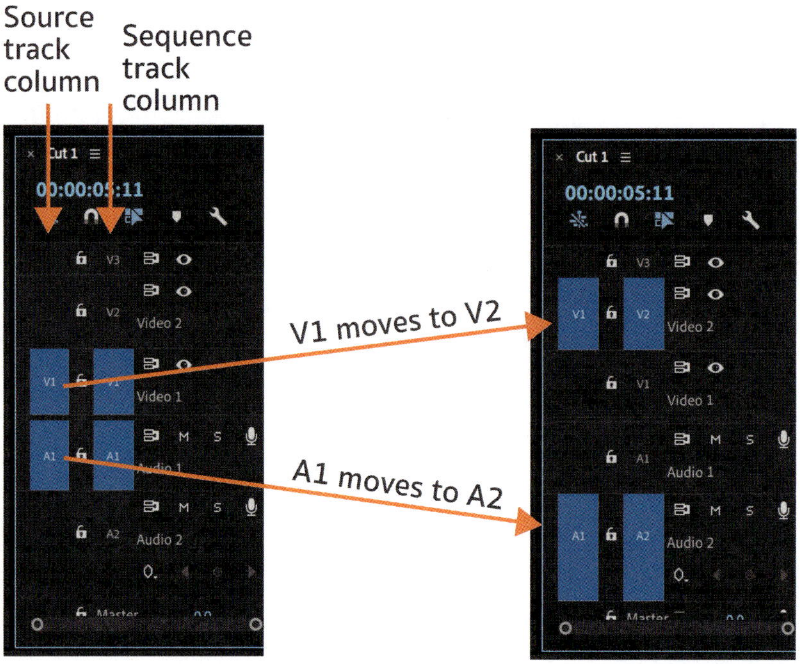

Figure 3.9

The left column of track selectors is for source clips and the right column is for sequences. Patching tracks lets you tell Premiere to make an edit and place the results on the tracks that you designate. Shown here, video on V1 and audio on A1 are sent to V2 and A2 in the Timeline.

You can choose the destination for each track from a source clip, a process known as patching and named for the old cable-based patch bays in post-production facilities. To patch your tracks, load a clip in the Source monitor. Only the tracks that are part of the clip will be available and they will be active (blue). By default, V1 on the source is aligned with V1 in the Timeline, A1 in the source is aligned with A1 in the Timeline, and so on.

To change the destination for one of your source tracks, drag the track selector in the source column up or down until the track selector lines up with the desired sequence track selector or simply click in the area next to the desired target track (Figure 3.9). If you don't want the media from a particular track to end up in your sequence, deselect that track selector so that it's no longer highlighted.

Restore Track Order

You're going to end up moving the source track selectors all over the place as you work and sometimes you just want to make it normal. Luckily, you can do that with the touch of a key, if you program it on your keyboard, or by right-clicking on any source track selector and choosing Default Source Assignment from the menu. I will admit, I use this one all the time.

TUTORIAL: Refining the Dialogue Scene

We just covered a whole bunch of tools and techniques that take editing in Premiere to the next level. In this tutorial, we'll put them to use as we do another pass on the University scene from Chapter 2. The first cut of the scene is a great starting place—now we can refine it by adding more shots to focus the story on the main character. Crafting the focus within a scene in terms of character is a very necessary part of editing scripted films.

Open the "University scene" project that you created in Chapter 2. This might be a good time to rewatch your cut and also to take another look at the script in Table 2.1 of the previous chapter. But before going any further, let's make a copy of your first cut so that you have a backup of it, in case you want to return to it. Select your sequence in the bin and go to Edit > Duplicate. Rename the new sequence "University scene backup." If it's not already in the Timeline, double-click on your main sequence, "University scene," to open it.

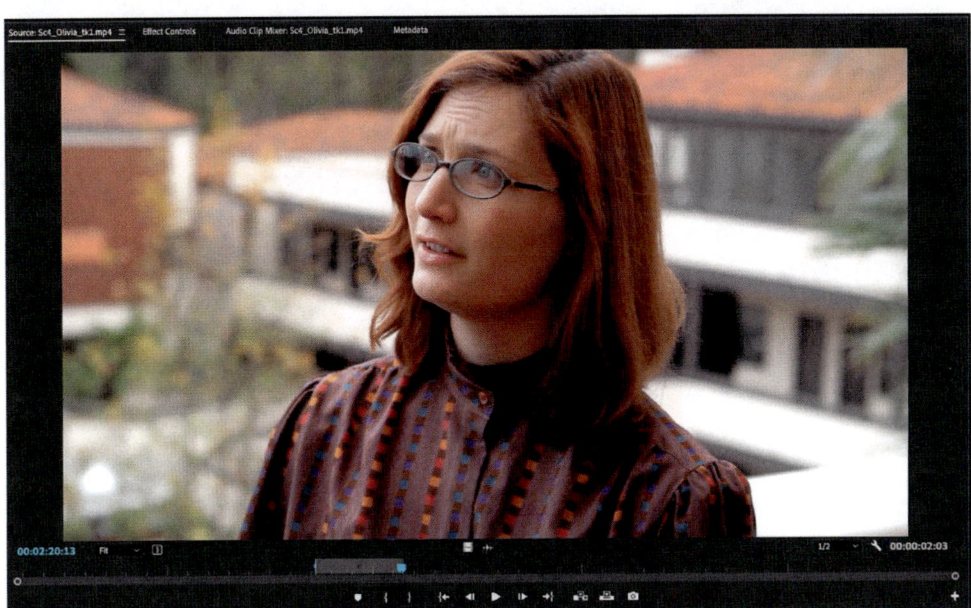

Figure 3.10

Add close-ups to focus the scene on the main character. Set an In and Out to select Olivia's line in the Source monitor.

STEP 1: Add a Single to V2

There's one easy way to bring the focus to a character and that's by using their close-up. In this case, we're going to add Olivia's close-up for the second half of her first line, prior to the single of the professor.

We'll continue to use three-point editing to add the close-up shot to the sequence, but this time we'll target video track two (V2) and audio track 2 (A2) in the Timeline to add the shot on different tracks.

Double-click to launch the take 1 (Sc4_Olivia_tk1.mp4) into the Source monitor and play around to find the start of the second half of her line, after the word "Firestones," around 00:00:07:08, and set an In. Set an Out at the end of her sentence, 00:00:09:14 (Figure 3.10). Now go to the Timeline and play your sequence until you get to the end of "Firestones" and set an In here as well. In the sequence, set an In at 00:00:04:16, also after "Shulamith Firestones."

Patch the V1 track selector on the source side to V2 by dragging or clicking. And since we don't want to overwrite the audio that's already in the cut, drag the A1 audio on the source side down to A2. Now on the Sequence side, deselect V1 and A1 and select V2 and A2. Your track selectors should like the ones in Figure 3.11.

Use Overwrite to add the new close-up into the Timeline and watch the results.

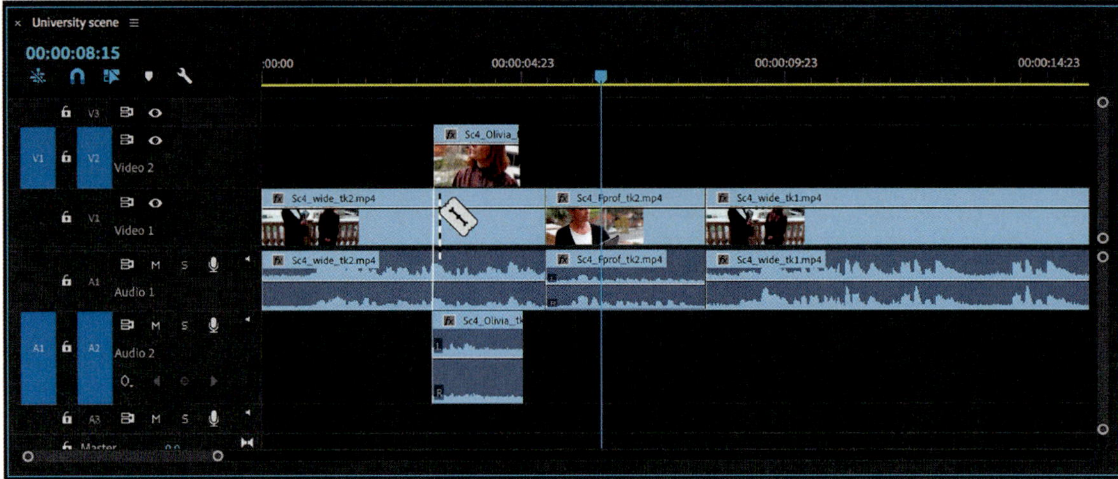

Figure 3.11

Patch the tracks so that V1 and A1 are sent to V2 and A2. Use the Razor tool to add a splice and delete the extra line on V1 and A1.

STEP 2: Add a Splice to Get Rid of the Extra Line

We now have Olivia's line on two tracks, but we only want to keep the audio that's from her close-up. We'll get rid of the extra line in the master shot by splicing it and deleting the part we don't need.

Select the Razor tool from the Tools panel and, with Snapping activated (S), drag the Razor to the start of the new close-up (Figure 3.11). Click within the master shot and a splice will appear across V1 and A1. You'll see the bowtie icon, which means that it's a splice across continuous media. Activate the standard Selection tool (V) and select the second half of the shot—the part with the extra line—and Delete.

There's a little bit of a gap between the Olivia close-up and the rest of the master shot, so let's pull the media on V1 and A1 back. Use the Track Select Forward tool (A) and click on the professor's closeup. That shot and all shots to the right will be highlighted. With Snapping active (S), drag backwards until they snap to the end of the closeup. Watch your cut—you should have a clean version of the scene so far, with no gaps and no extra dialogue.

Track Height Presets

If you have an arrangement of track heights that you prefer in the Timeline, you can save it as a preset. Save Preset is found under the Timeline Settings (wrench) menu and you can save that preset to a key of your choice using Edit > Keyboard Shortcuts (Win) or Premiere Pro > Keyboard Shortcuts (Mac). It's a little weird in that you can name your preset but then your preset is saved to a generic name for the keyboard shortcut, "Track Height preset 1," etc., which you then have to program to the keyboard. But it works.

Quickly Move a Shot to the Next Track

Use the Alt/Option key with the up and down arrows to move a selected clip in the Timeline to the next available track.

STEP 3: Make an L-cut in the Timeline

Sometimes, you can toss a scene to the main character by staying on them as they listen while others speak. Let's keep the focus on Olivia by extending her close-up a bit, over the start of the professor's line, using an L-cut.

Since Olivia isn't going to speak, we don't need her audio. Rather, we want to extend her picture but keep the professor's audio going under it.

Click on the Linked Selection button in the upper-left area of the Timeline header, next to the Snapping toggle, to deselect it. It should be grey/off. Now you can select audio and video from clips separately.

With the Selection tool (V) active, hover over the end of Olivia's close-up until you see the cursor change to the red Trim tool icon (Figure 3.12). Drag it to the right and release it about halfway through the professor's single. You just made an L-cut—it looks a little different than the ones we showed earlier in this chapter because it's split across multiple tracks.

Now watch this section. Is the professor's shot too short? Is the end of Olivia's shot at an awkward point like mid-blink? Drag the end of the shot back and forth until you like how it plays.

Figure 3.12

Drag out the end of the close-up of Olivia until it covers half of the professor's shot.

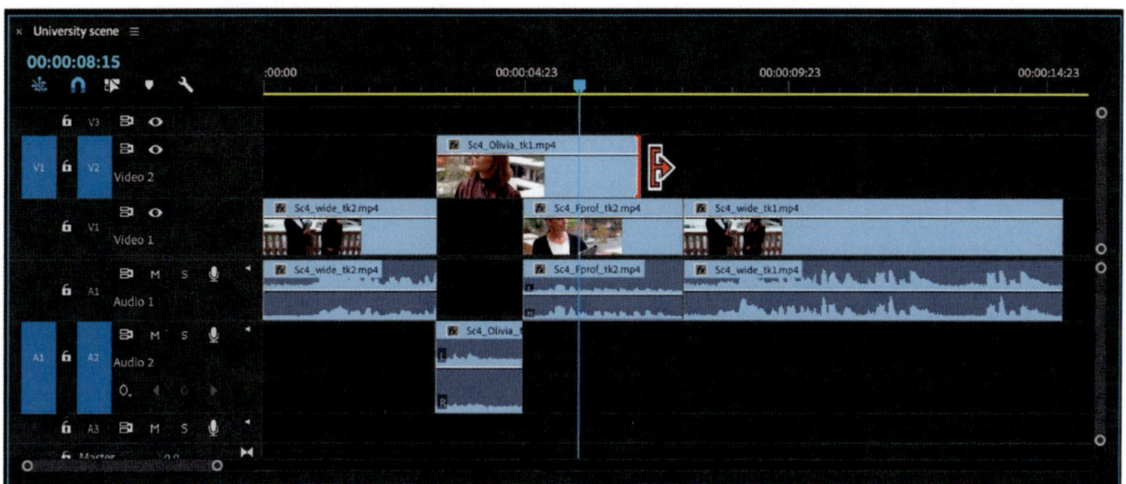

☑ More on Trimming

We introduced you to the standard Trim tool in Chapter 1. Simply hover near any edit in the Timeline and your cursor will switch to the red Trim tool and you'll be able to drag to shorten or lengthen the edit as long as there's space to accommodate it in your sequence. Premiere also offers a selection of advanced trim tools, Ripple, Roll, Slip, and Slide. We've devoted Chapter 7 to explaining how they work.

☑ Quickly Go to an In or Out

You can jump straight to any In or Out that you set in a shot or sequence by typing Shift + I or O. Alternately, you can use the Go to In and Go to Out buttons at the bottom of the Source and Program monitors or from the Markers menu.

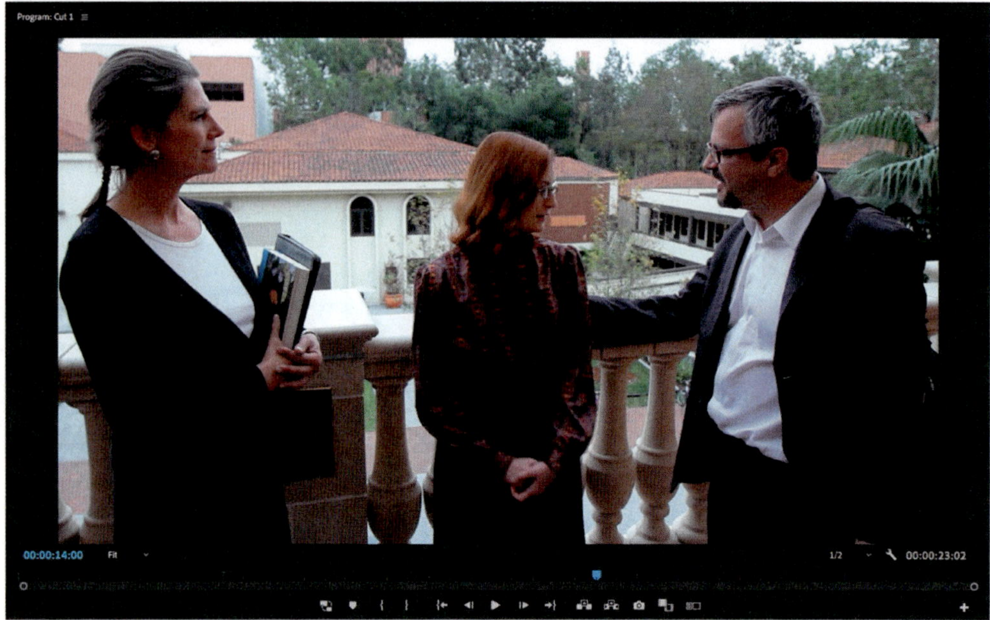

Figure 3.13

Find the moment where the second professor touches Olivia's arm and set an In.

STEP 4: Add Another Reaction on V2

We can further tilt the scene towards Olivia by adding more of her reaction shot. Let's add another shot of her after the male professor enters and touches her arm. Notice that she has a very strong reaction to this. It's helpful to put yourself in the place of the viewer when you're editing a scene like this one—where do you want to be and when? I think you want to see him reach out to her in the master shot, so that you understand what's happening, and then you want to see her face as she reacts in the close-up

Watch take 1 of her close-up, find the place where she reacts to his hand on her arm, around 00:00:16:17, and set an In (Figure 3.13). Then find an approximate point where the movement in the master shot matches the single, probably right after the male professor says "provost grant" at 00:00:12:13 and set an In in the sequence.

In the Source monitor, click Overwrite. (By the way, when you're editing into a track that's empty from your In-point forward, it doesn't matter whether you use Insert or Overwrite, the result will be the same.) Note that we didn't set any Outs, so everything in the single of Olivia after the In point was edited into the Timeline. That's because we really don't know where we want the shot to end.

 Toggle Source/Program Windows

Adding new material means you'll often go from the Source monitor, where you'll view clips and set Ins and Outs, to the Program monitor, where you'll view your cut. You can program the keyboard to Toggle Source/Program Monitor Focus with a key of your choice using Keyboard Shortcuts under the Premiere Pro menu (Mac) or Edit menu (Windows).

STEP 5: Use Extend Edit to Remove Extra Media

Once Olivia starts to exit in her close-up, the shot is over. It's much better to go back to the master shot to see the movement of her exit with all three actors and their reactions.

We want the audio to change along with the video, so turn Linked Selection back on (blue). You could use the standard Trim tool to shorten the shot, but instead, let's use Extend Edit (E). The Extend Edit command snaps the end of a shot to wherever the playhead is parked, assuming the shot is long enough to reach the playhead. (Ins and Outs do not affect the Extend Edit command.)

Play around and find a spot where she is on her way out of the shot and park the playhead there, around 00:00:17:17. Select the end of her close-up on either V2 or A2—you'll see the end of the shot highlighted in red on both tracks. Type E and the shot will get shortened to end at the playhead (Figure 3.14).

Let's use the same technique to get rid of the extra audio from the male professor in Olivia's single. Make sure Linked Selection is toggled off, find the end of his line (00:00:14:14), then select the start of the audio clip on A2 so that it's highlighted red and type E. You just made a second L-cut.

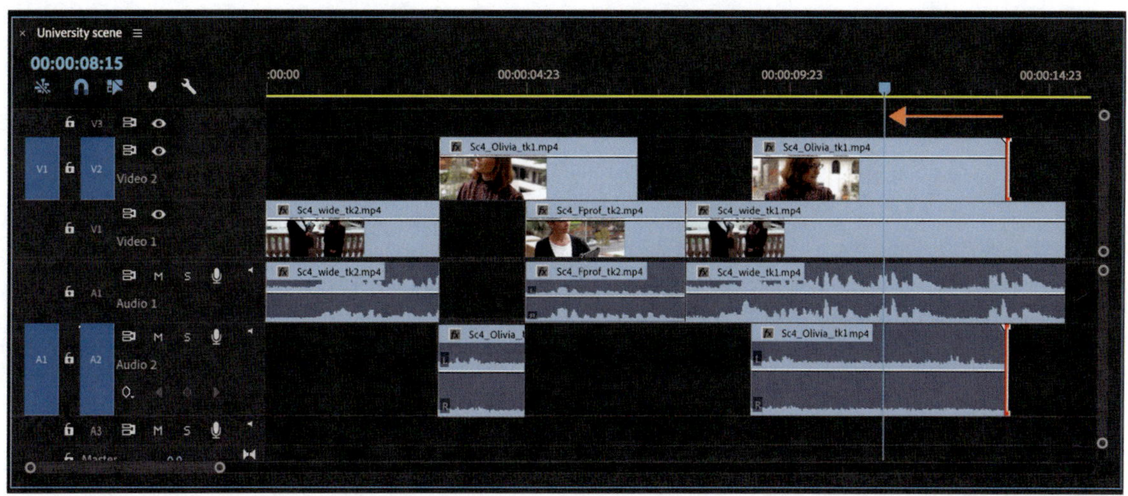

Figure 3.14

Position the blue playhead cursor at the point where you want the shot to end. Then select the end of the shot and type E to trim or extend the shot to the position of the cursor.

☑ X Marks the Clip

To quickly mark Ins and Outs around a shot, select it in the Timeline (make sure you have the right tracks isolated) and type X. You can also use Markers > Mark Clip.

STEP 6: Mark and Lift

We've got the second close-up of Olivia where we want it, and have cleaned up the extra audio from it, but there's still some extra lines in the master shot. We'll use a trick to get rid of it.

You can quickly set an In and Out around an entire shot by hitting the X key. But we don't want the whole shot, just the part that overlaps with the audio of the close-up. So we're gonna mark the audio track from the close-up, but then use those marks to lift exactly that portion of the master shot.

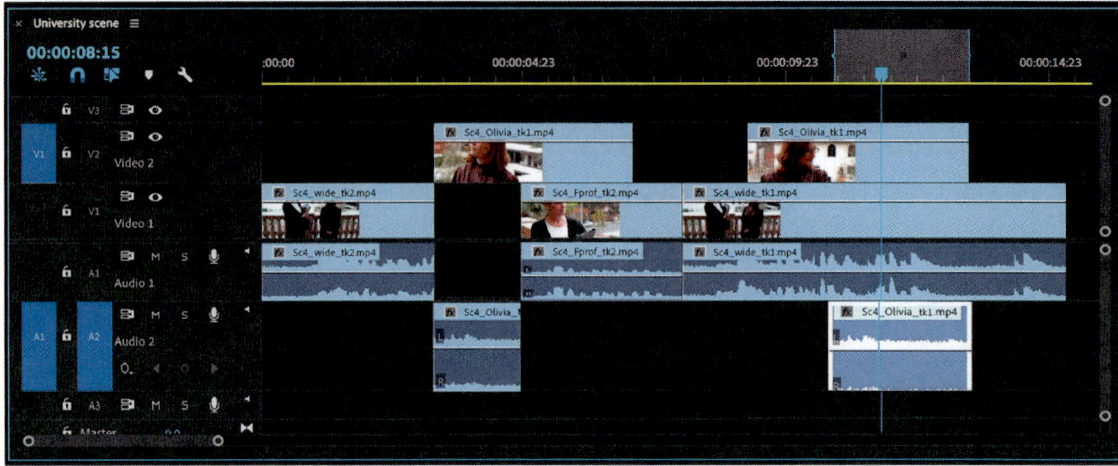

Figure 3.15 Deselect track V2, position the playhead in the close-up, and type X to mark it.

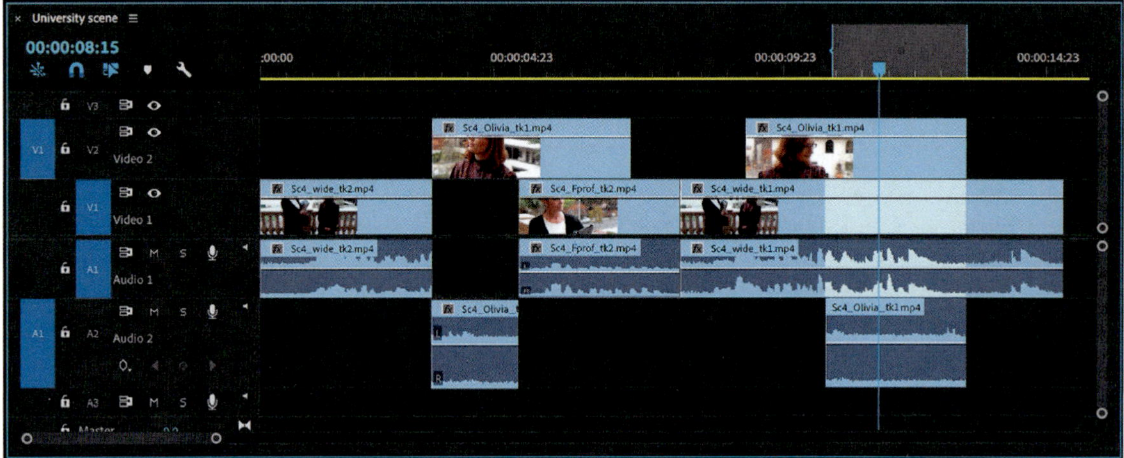

Figure 3.16 Deselect A2, then select V1 and A1, the marked area moves to the master shot.

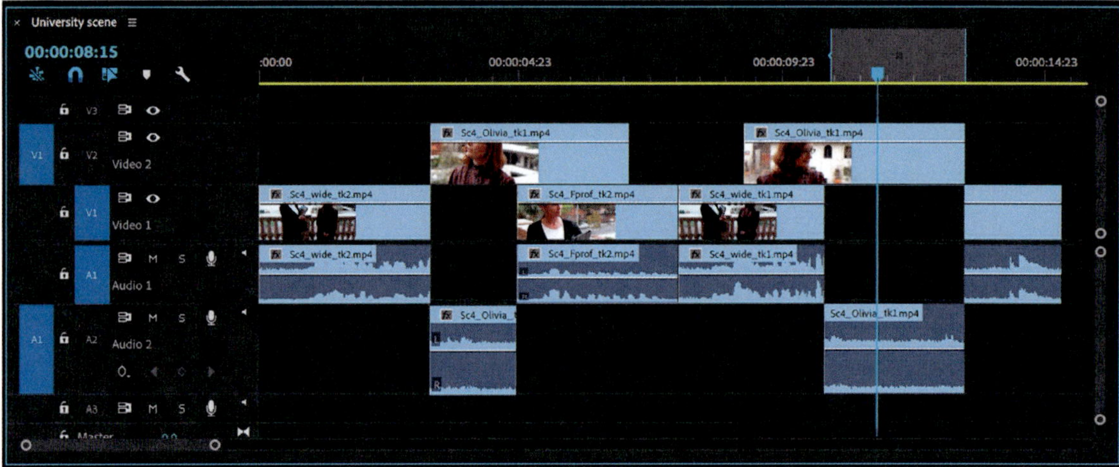

Figure 3.17 Use Lift to remove the marked portion of the master shot.

To select just the audio for Olivia's close-up, turn off V2 so that only the A2 track selector is on (Figure 3.15). Position the playhead inside the audio clip on A2 and type X. Note that In and Out marks appear in the Timeline exactly at the start and end of the audio clip and it's highlighted.

We're going to delete the media between those In and Out marks, but we only want to delete the media from the master shot on V1 and A1. So deselect A2 and select V1 and V2. You'll see the highlighting shift to V1 and A1 (Figure 3.16). We're going to get rid of the video as well as the audio because we don't need it.

Now use Lift (;) and the portion of the master shot between the In and Out on V1 and A1 will be removed (Figure 3.17). Take a listen—the audio should sound pretty good now.

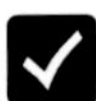

Isolating Tracks

Try using the mute or solo buttons in the track headers to listen with different tracks isolated. You can also turn off video tracks with the eye icon.

STEP 7: Adjust Shots with Nudge

Watch your cut again. Does the movement of Olivia as she exits frame flow well from the single to the wide? Sometimes you just need to move it a tiny bit to make it match better, something Adobe calls nudging.

We don't want to lose sync, so turn Linked Selection back on if it's off. Select the video and the audio of the last section of the master shot. Hold Command/Alt and use the left and right arrows to move the whole shot forwards or backwards frame by frame.

You can also nudge Olivia's close up. Matching action between a tight close up and a wide shot can be challenging. In this case, the easiest way to make it to work is to match the screen position—that is, matching the place where your eye is looking. That will make the movement feel continuous across the cut. Because we're all human, in the close-up, we're tracking her face so try to make the cut land at point where her face is, around the same place in the frame in both the single and the wide.

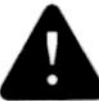

Be Careful When Nudging

Dragging to extend or move clips in the Timeline will automatically stop when you reach a new shot, offering protection against accidentally overwriting it. But nudging offers no such protections. You can easily overwrite material in your cut without any hesitation or warning, which can often be useful but not always. (The footage in our tutorial is on different tracks so there's less risk of this here.)

STEP 8: Use Layers to Review Multiple Takes

The professors are genuinely confused by Olivia's abrupt exit. The best way to highlight this is to add their close-ups to end the scene.

There are two takes of the male professor's reaction after she leaves. Sometimes it's hard to decide which take works best until you cut it into the scene. When that's the case, stacking the takes on multiple tracks is a great way to review them all in context, to help with the decision.

Load take 1 of the second professor's close up into the Source monitor and find his reaction after she crosses frame in his shot. Set an In, then set an Out after he turns back to the female professor.

In the Timeline, make sure that V1 on the source side is patched to V2 and all the audio tracks are deselected. (Since he doesn't speak, we don't need his audio.) Click Overwrite.

Let's drop in his other take and compare them. Set Ins and Outs at the same place in the second take. In the Timeline drag the V1 source selector to V3. If you don't have a V3, go to Sequence > Add Tracks and add one video track after Video 2. Use the Overwrite button to add it to the third video track.

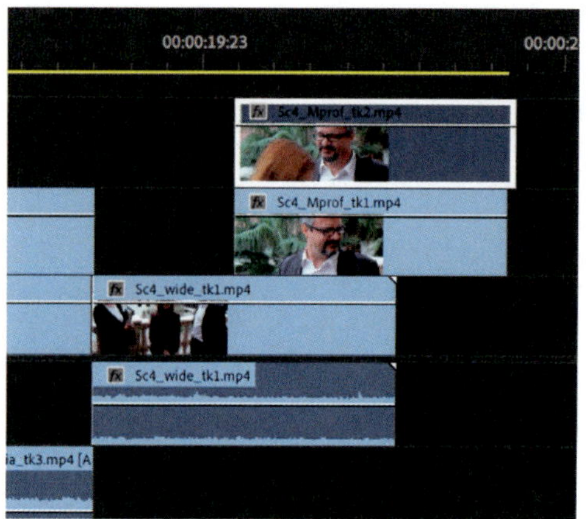

Figure 3.18 Stacking different takes of the same shot is a great way to help decide which take to use. The Disable/Enable command lets you watch each take without having to remove or rearrange the takes that are above it in the Timeline. Here, the upper shot is darkened because it has been disabled.

Now you have two takes of the same shot stacked on top of each other (Figure 3.18). You can view them separately by turn off each track with the eye icon, but there's a better way:

One cool thing in Premiere is that you can disable any clip (video or audio) in the Timeline. Select the clip on V3 and go to Clip > Enable (for Mac users, Command + Shift + E). The clip is now greyed out or darkened in the timeline. Play your cut and you won't see it, you'll see the shot that's on V2 instead. Play around by disabling and enabling the two takes. Drag the ends to shorten or lengthen the shot. Select the whole take and drag or nudge it to get it into the right place. When you have decided which take you prefer, you can delete the other one from the Timeline or simply leave it disabled. Follow the same steps to add the last shot of the female professor.

Match Frame

Sometimes you just want to go back to the original source clip when you're editing and Match Frame is designed just for that. Simply navigate to the frame you want to find in the Timeline, go to Sequence > Match Frame or type F, and the source clip that contains that frame will appear in the Source monitor, with the playhead parked on that frame. You'll find you use it all the time.

STEP 9: Evaluate Your Cut

So, how does it look? Are there any jump cuts or clipped lines of dialogue? Are there any long pauses that you can pull up? (If you want to look at our version, it's called "University scene V2.mp4" in the "University scene cuts" folder.)

If you think it's great, try another take on the scene. How about one where the point of view is that of the professors and not Olivia? Try adding the single of the male professor as he enters the scene. The techniques we covered in this tutorial give you the power to edit just about anything. With all these new tools, you might even want to take another whack at the Morning Montage from Chapter 1.

➡ More Beginner Editing Tutorials

There are more tutorials in this book and each one gets more advanced. But if you want to continue working on the basics, *The Digital Filmmaking Handbook* has a series of tutorials that cover editorial concepts, such as matching action and adding cutaways, in Chapter 14.

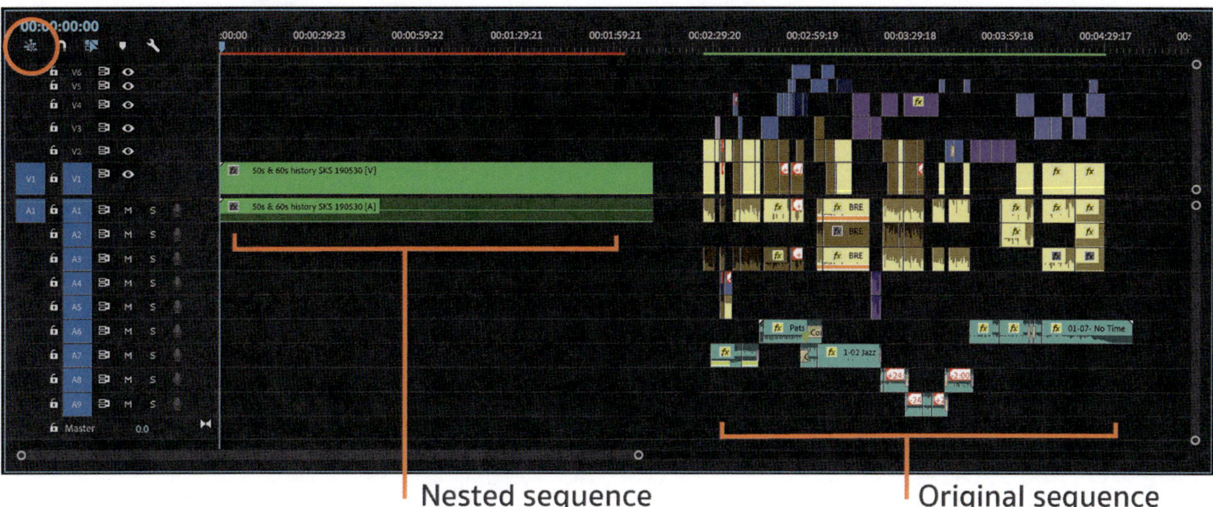

Figure 3.19

The Timeline shown here has the same sequence edited in twice: the first is nested and the second is not.

Putting Scenes Together

Eventually, as you work through the scenes in a film, you'll need to start putting scenes together. Most film editors start out with scene-based sequences and build them into longer sections—sometimes these are broken down by act, sometimes by reel, and sometimes by topic. The specifics vary according to what type of film it is and the personal preferences of the filmmakers. But one thing applies to all films: working out the transition or seam between scenes is a crucial step in finishing a film.

Scene Transitions

One hundred years ago (literally), the most common scene transition for silent films was a title card. Often it identified a new location, a jump in time, or both: "Meanwhile back at the ranch…" Using title cards and graphics for scene transitions is still common today. But most scripted films aim for seamless transitions—that is, transitions that feel organic, where you aren't taken out of the flow of the narrative. The most common type of scene transition today is a cut to an establishing shot of the new scene, accompanied with some sort of music or sound change that cues the viewer that one scene has ended and a new scene is starting. Sometimes a bigger transition is required—a sense of passage of time, or change. In that case a short sequence of shots, or montage, is used. But as with all things about editing movies, the devil is in the details. A wedding scene that ends with a kiss and dissolves to a shot of a baby sleeping in a nursery presents a very different story than if the kissing shot gets slammed with a hard cut to loud fast music and a car barreling down the freeway. Scene transitions have a huge effect on pacing and tone, adding drama, energy, humor, and many more subtle reactions.

Figure 3.20

This button in the upper left corner of the Timeline turns nesting on (blue) and off (white).

Nested Sequences

One way to put scenes together is by nesting them, so that you have a sequence within a sequence. Instead of seeing all your various clips and edits in the Timeline, instead you'll see a single clip that contains a link to the sequence you are nesting within the larger cut (Figure 3.19). This is kind of cool because it means your original scene is somewhat protected. You won't be able to change it much when it's nested, so there little or no risk of accidentally deleting a shot or shifting clips around. If you want to change a sequence that is nested, you'll have to open that original sequence in the Timeline and make your changes there. Those changes will be reflected in any cut that contains the nested sequence. The downside of nested sequences is that you have fairly limited options when it comes to adjusting the transition between scenes.

In the Timeline, there is a small icon in the upper left corner of the Timeline. Premiere calls it the "Insert and overwrite sequences as nests or as individual clips" button (Figure 3.20). Which manages to describe exactly what the button does, but in the most confusing way ever. Basically when it's on (blue), any sequence you drag into the Timeline will show up as nested. And when it's off (white), the sequence will show up as individual clips. Like most feature film editors, I use nested sequences rarely. But it's possible that on a series, nesting an opening credits sequence (that is always the same for every episode) would make a lot of sense. Nesting can also be good for parts of a film that are very delicate and complex, such as an opening sequence. It could help you avoid having to add many extra tracks of video and audio to your film that you won't need in the rest of the movie.

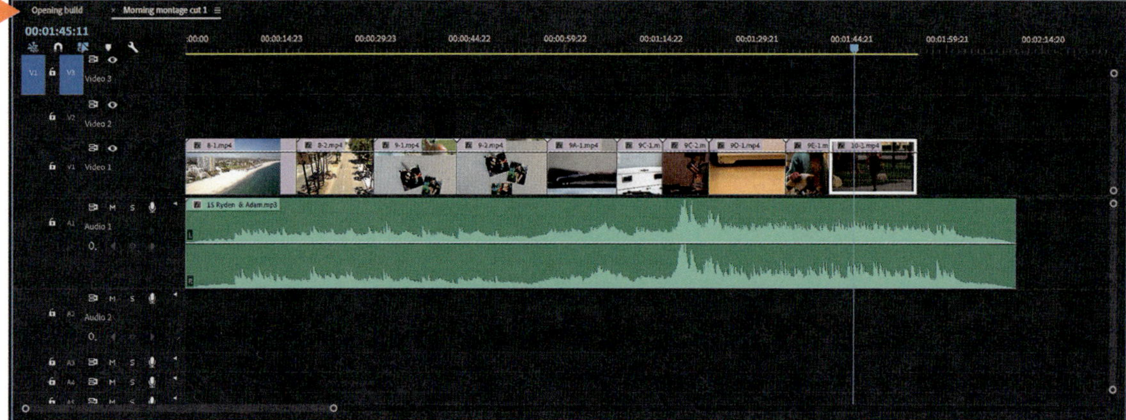

Figure 3.21

Each sequence in the Timeline has a tab. When you have more than one sequence open, you can use them to jump back and forth between cuts.

TUTORIAL: Build a Scene Transition

The scene you edited earlier in this chapter is meant to come right after the Morning montage scene that you created in Chapter 1. Putting scenes together is one of the most common tasks when you are editing a movie. In this tutorial we'll show you how to use Premiere to make a great scene-to-scene transition.

You're going to need the Morning montage project from Chapter 1 and the University scene project from earlier in this chapter.

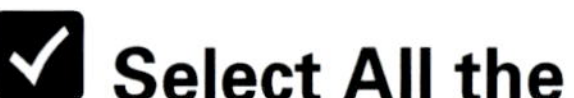

Select All the Tracks

You can quickly select or deselect all of the audio track selectors by holding the shift key as you click anywhere within the column of track selectors at the far-left side of the Timeline. This also works for the video tracks.

STEP 1: Cut the Scenes into a Sequence

Open both projects. When you have multiple projects open in Premiere, they'll show up as tabbed folders in the Project panel. Take your last cut of the University scene and duplicate it (Edit > Duplicate). Name the copy "Opening Build" and double-click to launch it into the Timeline and Program monitor.

Next, open your cut of the Morning montage from Chapter 1 and load it into the Timeline as well. You'll now see two tabs at the top of your Timeline (Figure 3.21).

Click on the "Morning montage" tab and select your whole cut in one of the following ways: drag and select the whole sequence in the Timeline or with the Timeline panel active, type Control/Command + A.

Copy your selection (Edit > Copy or Control/Command C).

Now select the Opening Build tab in the Timeline and position the blue playhead cursor at the very beginning of the sequence. Make sure that you have the V1 and A1 tracks selected.

Go to Edit > Paste Insert or Control/Command + Shift + V.

You may need to zoom out your Timeline view to see the both scenes.

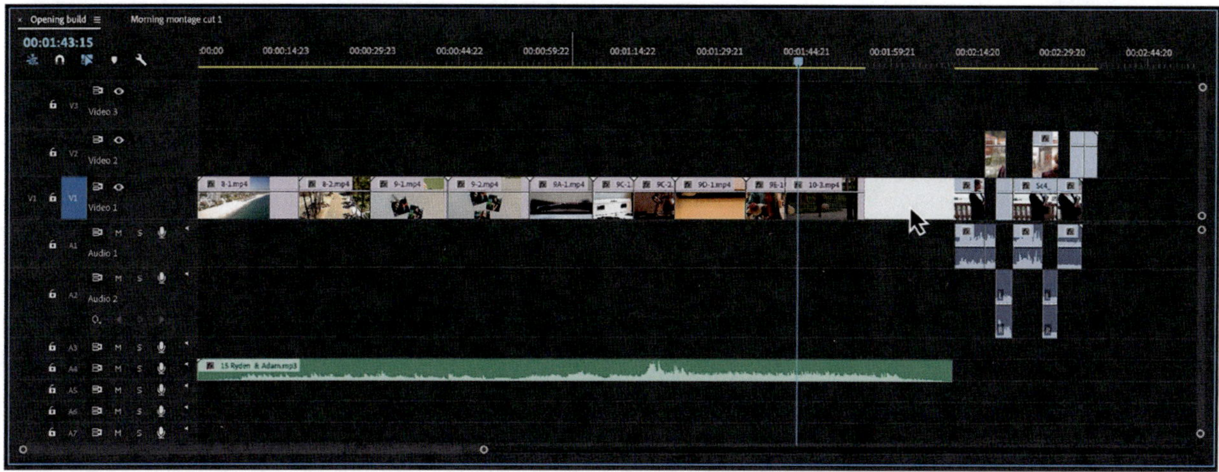

Figure 3.22

After you drag the music down to A4, use the arrow tool (V) to select the gap on V1, and Delete to close it.

STEP 2: Adjust the Seam

The transition from one scene to another is often called a seam. It's just another edit but it feels bigger. Depending on how you ended the music in your cut of the Morning montage, either the music stops abruptly or there's a black hole in the sequence or both.

Select the music in the Morning montage scene and drag it down to A4. Hold the Shift key as you drag to make sure it doesn't move horizontally (backward or forward in time). It's traditional to keep the music on separate tracks, completely isolated from the dialogue or other audio that's part of the scene itself.

Now you can select the gap between the two scenes on V1 and hit Delete to close it. Since there's nothing in the way on V1, the two scenes will now get butted together and the music on A4 will extend into the second scene (Figure 3.22).

Watch how your cuts fit together. It is working?

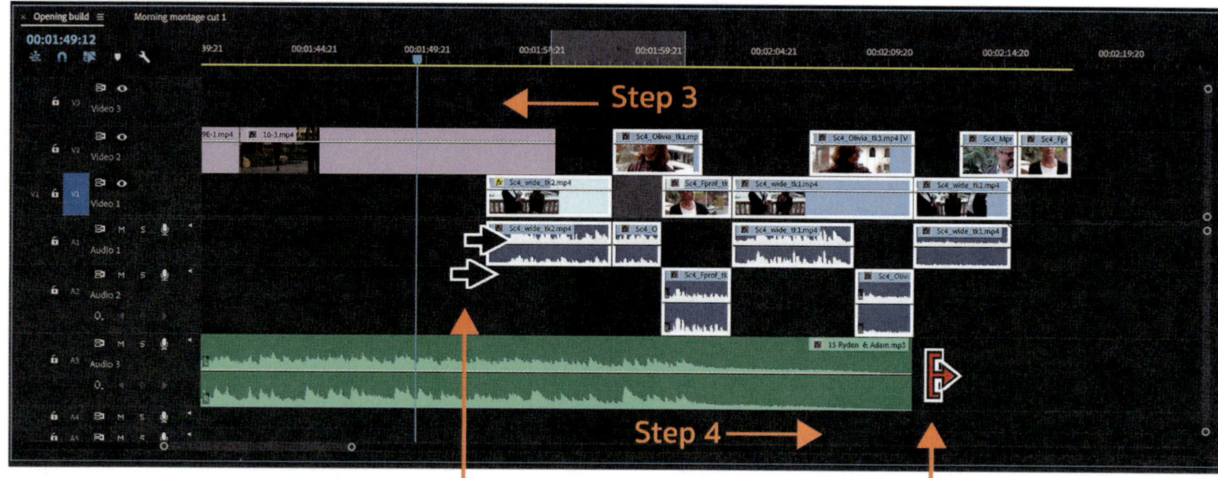

Figure 3.23 Use the Track Select Forward tool to select the entire University scene and drag it backward. Then, with the Selection (arrow) tool, select the end of the music. Your cursor will change to the red Trim tool. Use it to drag the end of the music forward in order overlap the music across the two scenes.

STEP 3: Try Overlapping the Audio

It can be easy to assume that every change you make needs to have a visual component. But often audio editing is a great way to make the visuals look better.

One way to make a scene to scene transition less abrupt is to have the audio of the second scene start before the video of the first scene finishes. We'll overlap the dialogue so that Olivia's first line in the University scene starts over the last shot of the Morning montage.

First, you'll need to zoom in on your sequence so that you can see all the elements you are working with. Sometimes zooming gets your sequence to the right size in the Timeline but the media you want to work with is not visible. In this case, the Hand (H) tool really comes in, um, handy.

Next, you need to make some room on the video track, so hold Shift and drag the last couple shots of the Morning montage up to V3.

Use the Track Select Forward tool (A) to select all of the media from the University scene and drag it back by a few seconds (Figure 3.23). Try aiming for somewhere in the middle of the words "Simone de Beauvoir." (It's easier to drag smoothly when Snapping is off.)

There's really not much room to play around here: you want to hit the sweet spot where there's enough of her line under the last shot of the montage and yet enough of the master shot visible so that it doesn't feel too short.

STEP 4: Adjust the Music Across the Seam

With the Selection tool (V), drag the end of the music to extend it over the start of the next scene (Figure 3.23). The effect we want is that we sort of land gently into the first dialogue scene of the movie. But if the song goes too far into the dialogue of the scene and become distracting, you'll need to trim the music and then add a dissolve to sneak it out:

With the arrow key selected (V), grab the end of the music clip and drag it somewhere around the end of the first master shot in the University scene. With the end of the music clip selected, go to Sequence > Apply Audio Transition or Shift + Control/Command + D (Figure 3.23).

By default, Premiere will add a one-second dissolve to the end of your music tracks. How does it sound? One second is pretty short for a music dissolve. So let's make it longer. Zoom in so that you can see the dissolve better.

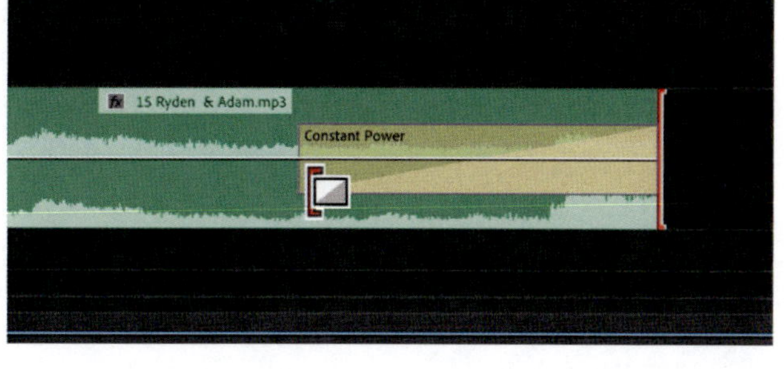

Figure 3.24

Adding audio dissolves and adjusting the length with the Trim Dissolve tool.

Make sure the edit at the end of the music clip is deselected, then hover your arrow cursor over the start of the dissolve (to the left side of it). Your cursor will change to a special Trim Dissolve cursor (Figure 3.24). Click and drag to the left (backwards in time) to start the dissolve earlier.

Keep trimming the end of the music itself and the start of the dissolve until you're happy with how it sounds. For me, it sounds best when I start the dissolve with Olivia's first line and have the music more or less out by the time we're in the next scene. But that really depends on your own taste and also the music that you are using.

If you want to take a look at our version, it's called "Opening Build v1.mp4" and it's in the "University scene cuts" folder.

Have you been wondering why the Morning montage is so long? You just put together the opening scenes of a movie. We're going to return to this sequence for a little sound design in Chapter 10 and to add titles in Chapter 11 because if you haven't already guessed, the Morning montage is actually the video that goes under the opening titles of the film. And we'll fix some technical issues using effects in Chapter 12.

☑ Close Extra Timeline Panels

As you're editing, you may find your Timeline cluttered with tabs, or panels. Use the pop-up menu in the upper left corner of the Timeline window to "Close Other Timeline Panels." (Make sure the sequence you are working on is active when you do this.)

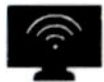

What to Watch: *Everything?*

The type of work we've covered in this chapter—editing dialogue and building scene to scene transitions—is something you see in every single film or series out there. These are some of the most basic components of filmic storytelling. The next time you watch something, pay special attention to how dialogue scenes are put together. Is there a strong point of view? Do we see more talking or more listening? And then, pay attention to how the director takes you from one scene to the next. Do they use music or establishing shots or other transitional devices? How do these moments affect the mood and pacing of the movie?

Big Picture Problems to Solve

As you put the scenes in your film together, you'll start to encounter one of the most challenging editorial tasks: building a story that holds up over time. Unfortunately, there's nothing in Premiere to help you with that. But we all have a huge database of films to draw from in our memories.

Is the structure of the story holding up? Taking the words of a script and transforming them into actual shots and scenes can result in huge changes to the story. So now that it's been shot, is the narrative flow still working? Or do you need to change the order of scenes and restructure the film to make it work?

Are there scenes that should be discarded or added? Everyone has heard of the infamous "cutting room floor" and there's a reason for that. Many lines or scenes—often brilliant on the page—simply aren't needed in the final film. And there's the opposite problem—sometimes you realize you need to add a scene for the movie to work. That's what *pick-ups* are for and mostly, it's during the editing process that they are identified.

How is the pacing and tone across multiple scenes? We mentioned pacing and tone within scenes, but there's also pacing and tone across sections or the whole film. As you build the film, you'll need to assess these elements on a bigger scale. If you're building to the climactic finish of the movie, you may not want to undercut drama with a scene that's light-hearted in tone. Similarly, if you have a fast-paced sequence of scenes, you may find that there are big sections of scenes that can be eliminated—often the beginning.

It usually takes multiple passes on a film to get these big picture elements to work right, so don't worry if you don't know the answers to these questions early on in the editing process.

➡ Three-Act Structure

Feature films are often built using three-act structure. If you're unfamiliar with this concept, *The Digital Filmmaking Handbook* explains how it works in Chapter 2, Writing, Scheduling, and Producing and also how it is applied in editing in Chapter 14, Editing.

What's Next?

The next three chapters provide the technical basis needed to understand how to set up your own film or series in Premiere. They can also be used as a technical reference, to answer questions and solve problems as they arise. If you prefer to continue on to the advanced editing chapters and tutorials, you can jump ahead to Chapter 7, Advanced Trimming.

4

Creating a Custom Project

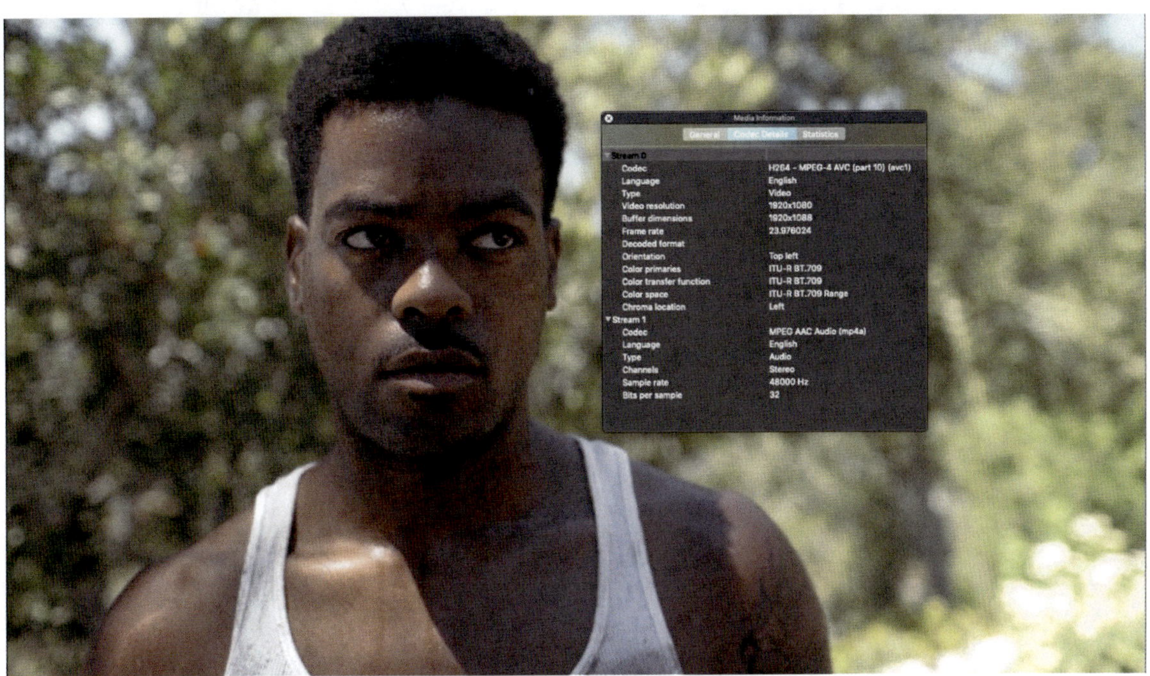

Figure 4.1

You can use the property inspector in any video player app (shown here, VLC) to get the media specs for your clips. This one is an h.264 file with 1920 HD video using the MPEG-4 AVC codec recorded at a frame rate of 23.976 with two channels of stereo 48 kHz AAC audio. There's also information about the color space and data rate.

What You Need to Know About Your Film

THIS CHAPTER AND THE TWO THAT FOLLOW contain some of the most important things you should know when editing with Premiere. It's the technical stuff. Some might say it's the boring stuff. Others might say it's the hard stuff. Either way, it's the necessary stuff (Figure 4.1).

We just spent three chapters going over editing in Premiere Pro with tutorial media. But what about your own movie? Films vary wildly and properly setting up a project can be one of the more challenging tasks.

Luckily, Premiere projects are very malleable. In fact, one of the reasons that setting up a project is so daunting is that there are so many options and a lot of them are things you've never heard of, even if you're an experienced filmmaker. (Mercury Playback Engine, anyone?) In this chapter, we'll explain what all those things mean so that you can assess whether or not they are important for your movie. We'll walk you through getting a film project—any film project—up and running in Premiere.

How to Use This Chapter

This chapter can be used as a reference to spot check various settings and preferences as you create a project. Alternately, it can be used as a giant tutorial. Armed with the media specs for the various tutorials in this book or perhaps from your own film footage, you can work your way through rest of the chapter—setting up a new project, setting up a new sequence, working through all of the preferences panels, and customizing the interface and keyboard shortcuts. At the end, you'll have a new project that's good to go and perfectly suited to your needs. I do this every time I start a new film or make a new project.

Where'd It Come From?

Before you can setup a Premiere project properly, it helps to know where your media came from. The more you know about how your film was shot or acquired, the easier it will be to set up the project.

Many directors are able to spew camera models, audio configurations, and video formats off the top of their head. Why? They spent a lot of time figuring out exactly how to shoot their film and they're not likely to forget such key decisions as which camera they used or how the sound was recorded. But if you're walking into the project later in the game, like many editors, you'll need talk to the director, the DP, and the sound recordist to get this information. Things that are really obvious if you were present on set are a lot less obvious if you start working on a film after the shoot has ended.

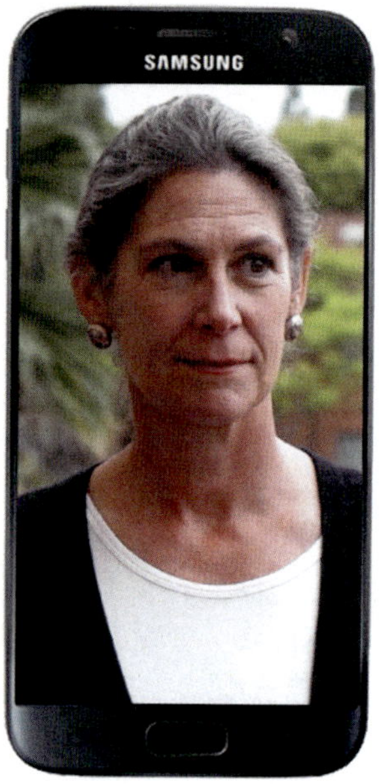

Figure 4.2 Web and mobile videos can opt for non-standard aspect ratios, like this tall mobile phone-oriented video.

You should also keep in mind any special considerations for your film. Every film is unique, but is your film unique in a way that affects the editing process? Was it a multicam shoot? Are there special elements for effects, such as green screen footage and backdrops? Were there any unique problems during the shoot? Unique solutions?

Information from the field is only half the equation—in order to decide how to best setup a project for editing, you need to also know...

Where's It Going?

If you shot a mini-movie on your phone and want to upload it to Instagram, that's wildly different from wanting to incorporate phone footage into a film destined for a theatrical release. Or maybe you shot 2K but want to make a tall-oriented video for cell phones or social media apps (Figures 4.2 and 4.3)? Typically, the choice is to work backward. In other words, figure out how you want to finish the film (4K projection, 2K, HD, YouTube) and make everything else conform to that. The more you are in charge of your own project (directing it, shooting it, editing it, deciding what your goals are) the easier this step of the process will be. But if you really don't know, we've provided some suggestions at the end of this chapter.

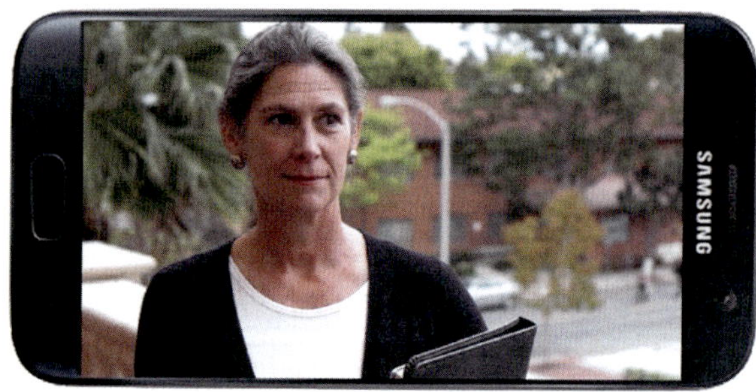

Figure 4.3 Orientation can make a huge difference for mobile video.

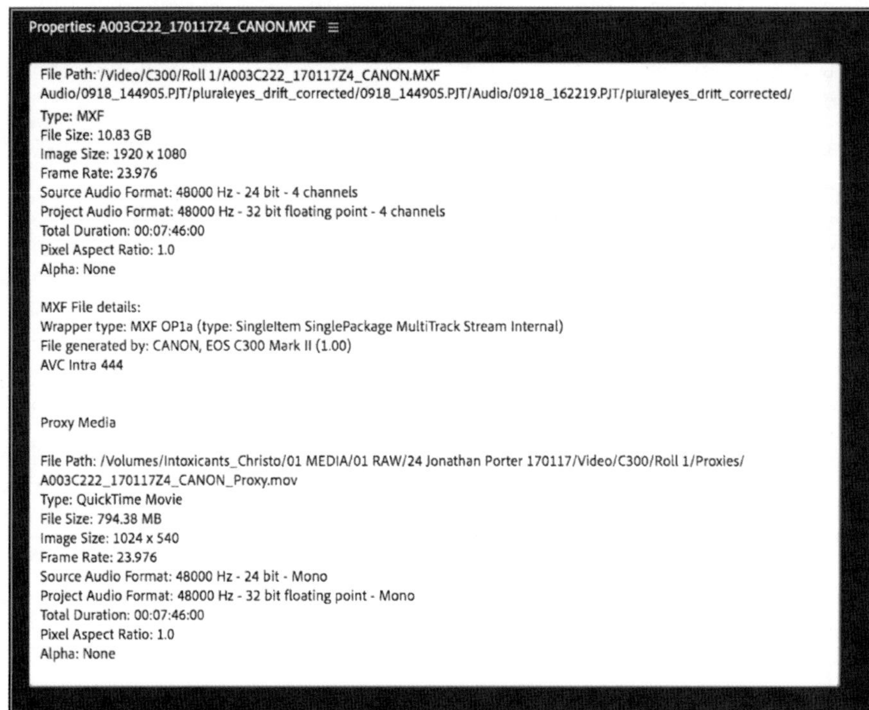

Figure 4.4

You'll find a very detailed list of information about any file in your project in the Properties panel (clip right-click menu). In this example you can see that the file has an MXF wrapper and is HD (1920 x 1080) with a frame rate of 23.976 and it was shot by a Canon C300 using AVC Intra compression with uncompressed 444 color. It also has proxy media attached which has a different set of media specs.

Media Specs

Every piece of media is defined by a set of specifications. You'll need this information to setup sequences in Premiere, create outputs of your cuts, and lots of other stuff in between. You can use applications like the QuickTime Player, VLC, or Windows Media Player to get the media specs for a clip (Figure 4.1). Unfortunately, the Premiere Info panel (Windows > Info) is a bit simplified and leaves out key details, such as codec, but the Properties window (clip right-click menu) offers much greater detail (Figure 4.4).

Even though Premiere accepts all types of media, having your sequence settings match your media specs will result in better performance and less rendering. It will help avoid unnecessary cropping or resizing and it will also determine the size and resolution of proxies and any graphics you might create for your film. Knowing this information about your media will help you understand how to use the information contained in this chapter and in the rest of the book going forward.

For example, the tutorial media that's associated with this book was exported from Premiere, using specifications that make it smaller, which is better for downloading (and uploading, if you're me). Because I'm using it all the time I have it in my head at the ready—h.264 1920 x 1080 MP4 AAC 48K two-channel mono (sources) or stereo (cuts)—that little list of gibberish is ingrained in my head and whenever I do an export of a sample cut for you, or create a new sequence, I can quickly check my settings to make sure it's right. There are so many variations available but, at least for the tutorials in this book, I only need to know this one set. But that's my project—here are the crucial video specs that you should know for yours:

Container file Every media file consists of a container file, also called a wrapper, that acts like a digital folder holding your video and audio in one place. The most common types of container files for films are QuickTime (MOV), Mpeg (MP4, MPV), Windows Media Video (WMV, also the older AVI), and Material Exchange Format (MXF). Usually you can identify the container file type by the extension at the end of the file name.

Video codec The video inside each container file is encoded using a special algorithm known as a codec. For projects that are not CGI, the video codec is usually determined by the camera. Most video codecs are proprietary, that is, created by the camera manufacturer, such as the R3D codec for RED cameras. But be aware that some cameras offer more than one video codec and if you're working with footage that was exported from another editing system, it's likely to either be from the Apple ProRes or Avid DNx family of video codecs.

Frame rate Almost everything shot in the US today has the frame rate of 23.976 (sometimes rounded up to 23.98). This is a variant of 24 fps (aka the frame rate of film) that works for US broadcast television. (Yes, over the airwaves.) The other frame rate you may encounter is 29.97 fps, which is what all projects destined for American television used to be until somewhat recently. Outside North America, media is either 24 fps or 25 fps.

Frame size Every frame of film or video is a rectangle, and that rectangle has two dimensions, width and height, and those dimensions are measured in pixels. Some video formats use these dimensions to identify the type of video: 1920 HD is 1920 pixels wide and 1080 pixels high, while 720 HD is 1280 pixels wide and 720 pixels high. Similarly, 2K video is 2048 x 1080 pixels, and 4K video is 4096 x 2160 pixels. That's where it gets a little more complicated. Not every 4K camera shoots exactly 4096 x 2160—some of them shoot 3840 x 2160, also known as UHD. But those formats are close enough that they are still referred to as 4K.

Aspect ratio Most newer video codecs are widescreen formats, so their aspect ratios are all in the same ballpark—either 1.78 (HD and UHD) or 1.85 (2K and 4K). The difference between 1.78 and 1.85 is very minor. So in general, mixing aspect ratios in the same project isn't a big deal. But some formats, such as anamorphic videos and pre-2006 American television format videos, have an aspect ratio that is quite different than widescreen and will require more significant resizing. We get into all this in Chapter 9, Mixing Media and Basic Effects.

Color handling Digital video color is defined by the color space (RGB or YUV/YCbCr), the amount of compression (4:4:4, 4:2:2, or 4:2:0), and the number of colors available or bit depth (anywhere from 8 to 24-bits). If your video is uncompressed, it's probably RGB 444 with 10-bit or higher color. If it's compressed, it's probably YUV/YCbCr 422 with 8-bit color. We cover digital color in all its glory in Chapter 13, Color.

You'll also want to know about the audio:

Audio codec Almost all professional audio is in the PCM format which usually takes the form of WAV or AIFF files. Other audio, especially audio downloaded from the web, is often MP3 or AAC. These codecs are considerably lower in quality than PCM audio. If you are working on a professional project, they are best avoided. But if it's a student project or destined for the web only, then they may be sufficient.

Audio mixing on the set Almost all production sound is recorded in mono. The exception would be a stereo recording of a music concert, for example. That's because almost all music is recorded in stereo. Clips from finished films and series are also usually stereo. The only media sources that might have 5.1 surround sound are clips from movies and you would only encounter that format if you had access to a source, such as a film production company, who gave you an unprotected version of the movie with the 5.1 mix. In other words, 5.1 is pretty rare as source audio.

Audio sample rate Today, it's very rare to come across audio that's not recorded at 48K (kilohertz) but if so, you should know what it is. The next most likely recording rate is 44.1K. Back in the olden days of the 1990's, this was considered "CD quality" which was the best they had at the time. Occasionally you'll encounter 96K audio, which is a very high-quality format. Many people consider it to be beyond the capabilities of the human ear to hear audio quality that's better than 48K.

In addition, you may find having this information helpful:

Camera model Some cameras have quirks that affect post-production, so it's always good to know which camera was used for the footage you are working with. Some cameras can switch from one media card to another mid-shot. The result shot is called a spanned clip and they can introduce issues if you don't import them correctly. Others, like RED and Panasonic P2 cameras, rely on the formatting of the media card to work properly in post. So make sure you check with your DP or camera manufacturer before you start to edit.

Audio recording configuration In addition to the production mix (mono, stereo, 5.1 surround), the sound recordist will also decide how the tracks are arranged and it can be very helpful to have their notes from the set. How many mics were there? What kind of mics? Did they do a mix track as well? (Sometimes sound recordists will mix down all the mics into a single track, in addition to recording each mic separately.)

Timecode Every digital camera assigns a number to each frame of video as it records and that number is called *timecode*. If you have to synchronize your media, timecode can be very useful. Generic timecode starts at zero for every shot. This is less useful in post. *Time-of-day* timecode matches the actual time the shots were recorded, so even multiple devices will share the same timecode without any special synchronization. And the most sophisticated timecode is synchronized across all devices, using a *timecode generator*. This ensures unique, matching timecodes for each shot from every device.

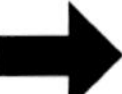

All About Media

Chapter 3, Digital Video Primer, in *The Digital Filmmaking Handbook* covers media specifications in depth, including all the technical details about how digital video and audio files work.

Setting Up a New Project

Creating a project is sort of easy and yet sort of hard. It's easy to click through the windows and ignore all the details. And that just might work. But it's better to set up a project that's truly dialed-in to your needs. When you launch Premiere Pro and select New Project from the Start screen, a New Project dialogue window will appear (Figure 4.5). There are three tabs in the New Project Settings window: General, Scratch Disks, and Ingest Settings.

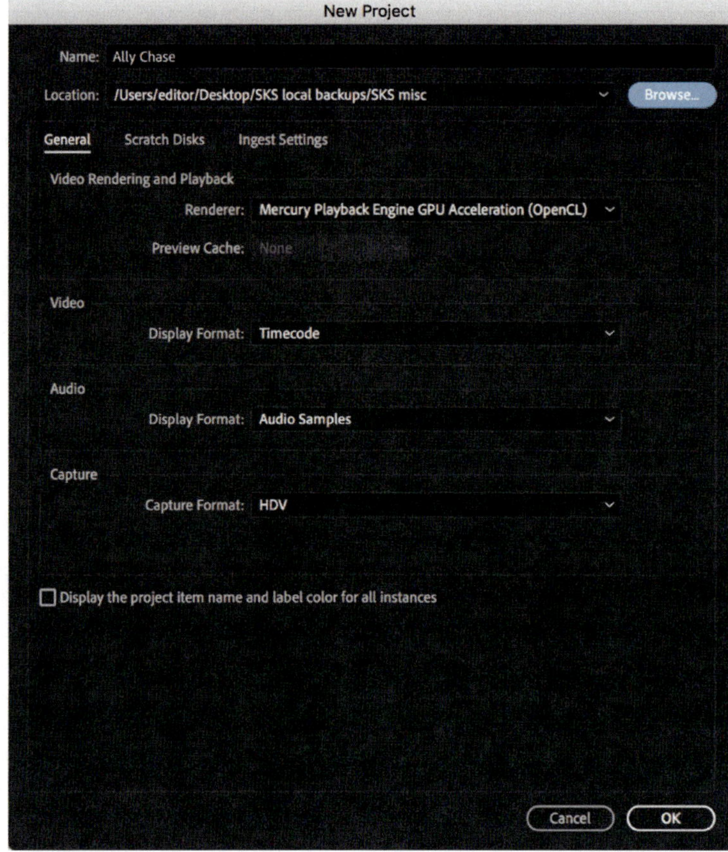

Figure 4.5

The New Project window lets you choose the location where you want to save your project file.

General Settings

Here, you'll be given a chance to name your new project and select a location for it. If you don't tell Premiere where to put your project file, it will default to a special Adobe Premiere documents folder on your primary hard drive.

You'll also choose a "renderer" which will determine how Premiere Pro interacts with your computer, affecting playback speed and quality. The Mercury Playback Engine is what Adobe calls the software underpinnings in Premiere Pro that enhance the real time playback and rendering of video. The Mercury Playback Engine can tap into your computer's GPU for added processing power, aka *GPU acceleration*. Depending on your computer, you can then choose from Open CL, Metal, or CUDA. If your computer doesn't have a GPU, you'll have to stick with software only, which is not as powerful.

Most of the options on the General tab beyond the defaults are inconsequential:

> **Video Display Format** sounds important, but that's a bit misleading because it doesn't affect how your video is displayed. Rather, it just affects how the various time counters in Premiere Pro work. Almost everyone will choose the default, "timecode," which separates time into hours, minutes, seconds, and frames. Premiere also allows for old school film footage counters, both 16mm and 35mm, and simple frame counters, which are primarily used for animation

Audio Display Format Similarly, you can choose between displaying audio samples or milliseconds. Sound editors can edit in much smaller increments than a frame of video, so instead of timecode, they use milliseconds or audio samples. Most filmmakers can just leave this at the default, milliseconds.

Capture Format This is for those who need to bring in video from a tape-based source. The two options are DV and HDV, both of which are obsolete. If you are using videotape in 2019, it's likely you will want the HDV setting, which is a widescreen format. (We have lots of information on capturing media from videotape archived on our website, *www.thedigitalfilmmakinghandbook.com.*)

☑ Finding Your Project

If you have a lot of windows open, it's easy to lose track of the project panel. To quickly find it, go to Window > Projects to bring it to the front of screen. Also, be aware that simply closing the project panel does not close the project, it just closes the window. If you want to close the project, you'll have to go to File > Close Project. If you're trying to find where your project is saved on your computer, it's useful to know that Premiere Pro projects end with the file extension PRPROJ. By default Premiere projects are saved on your main hard drive unless you specify a different location in your project settings (File > Project Settings > General).

Scratch Disks

Premiere needs a lot of accessory files and they are stored on *scratch disks*, which is a fancy word for designated media drives. (If you have them. If not, it's just your main hard drive.) If you use Photoshop a lot, you'll recognize the Scratch Disks tab, although the one in Premiere is bit more complex than the one in Photoshop. Just like Photoshop, Premiere Pro relies on hard drive space to improve performance while Premiere is running. That means that you always want to make sure that you have some extra space on your media drives for Premiere to use while you are editing.

The first four items—captured video, captured audio, video previews, and audio previews—are media. That means they should be stored on dedicated media drives if possible. Captures are media that you record on the fly and previews are render files. Because Premiere needs these files to function and the amount of disk space that they take up can vary, you should keep several gigabytes free on your media drives for them and also for application memory.

The next item—Auto Saves—is unique in this list because it's not media, it's just a place to save backups of your project when you have Auto Save enabled (and you should). As always, it's better to save backups on a separate drive. That way, if your main drive fails, you will (hopefully) still have access to your auto-saved versions. For that reason, using a dedicated, external media drive for them makes a lot of sense.

The following item, CC Libraries downloads, helps you share media and templates, such as font styles and graphic elements, across various Creative Cloud applications. For anyone who needs a shared database of media—like, perhaps an author who writes about Adobe applications—they are invaluable. Motion Graphics templates are files that let you share settings between Premiere Pro and After Effects. (We cover them in detail in Chapter 12.) Some Motion Graphics templates have media attached to them, not unlike CC Libraries, and here you can tell Premiere where to save these files. In short, both of these items can be treated as if they were media, which means they are best stored on dedicated media drives.

For films, I recommend avoiding the default Same as Project setting for any of the above, because it's safer to keep your media and your project on separate drives. For the tutorials however, I generally recommend saving your project on the same drive as your media. Why? It's easier: you won't have to work through all those scratch disk options and the tutorial projects only have a small amount of media, so your main drive should suffice. But if you have dedicated media drives, by all means use them.

Ingest Settings

The last tab in the New Project window shows the Ingest Settings. Premiere can create extra media during import—copies or proxies—and it can also save your media in a different format. For example, if your project is based on 4K video, you can use this window to tell Premiere Pro to automatically reformat it as 1920 x 1080 HD.

The default is that Ingest settings are not enabled, which is a fine way to start your project—you can always change that later. Ingest settings are discussed in detail in Chapter 5, Importing, Playing, and Proxy Media.

You Can Always Change Project Settings

If you decide to change any of these settings after you've created a new project, you can do so by going to File > Project Settings. You'll find three sub-menu items there that correspond to the three tabs in the New Project window.

Setting Up a New Sequence

Because Premiere Pro accepts so many media formats and lets you work with them in the same project, there aren't that many global project settings that are super important. It's the sequence settings that are most important. This is where you'll set the video and audio specs for your film that we discussed earlier in this chapter. For example, if you decided to work in 2K, this is where you let Premiere know that. The cool thing is that you can have as many sequences as you want in a project, and they can all have different sizes, frame rates, and so on.

When you make a new sequence (File > New Sequence), the New Sequence window opens (Figure 4.6). There are four tabs in the New Sequence window: Sequence Presets, Settings, Tracks, and VR Video.

Sequence Presets

This somewhat intimidating list of video formats is just a set of presets that were built to help you(!). The two windows on the right offer descriptions of each preset. The top window suggests uses for each preset and the bottom gives you all the specs in full detail (Figure 4.6).

If you have footage that exactly fits one of these choices, it can be a timesaver. If not, it can be a little confusing. In fact, if you know your media specs, it's often easier to create custom settings than to work your way through all these presets looking for one that matches your needs. In general, I prefer to create a custom preset for each new project and go through all the options at least once, just to kind of finalize all the technical specs in my own head. To do that, you have to skip these presets and go to the Settings tab.

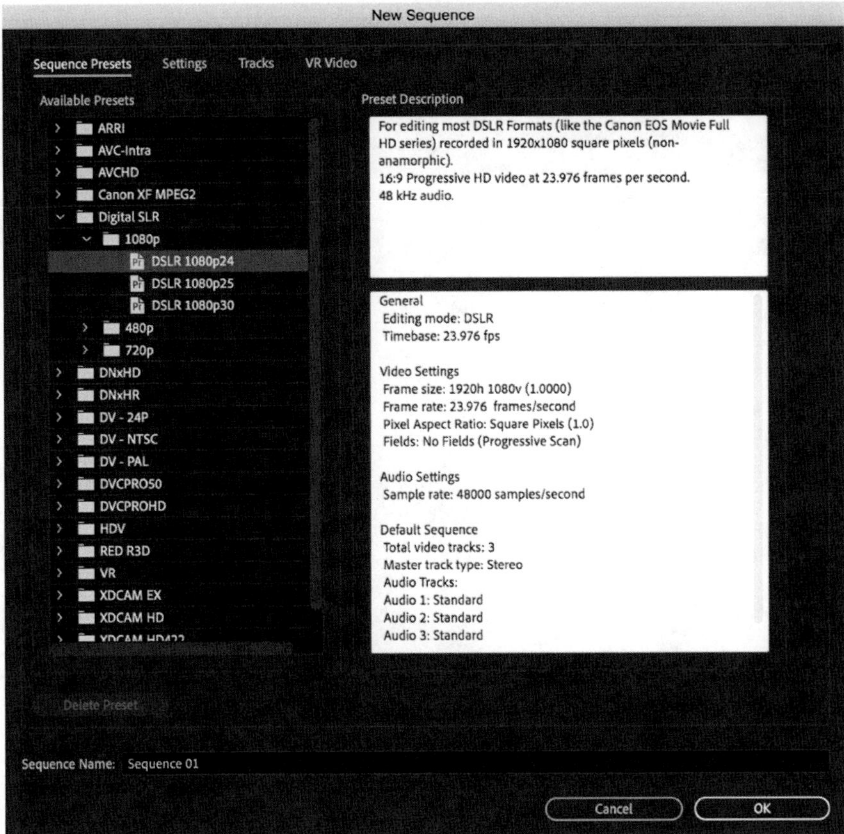

Figure 4.6

The New Sequence window has a bunch of presets available in the menu on the left and detailed info about each preset on the right.

? Where are the ProRes Presets?

Weirdly, there isn't a simple shortcut to creating an Apple ProRes sequence in the New Sequence window, even though it's arguably the most popular choice for film sequences. Instead, the sequence presets are organized by camera model and most cameras use proprietary codecs, not Apple ProRes which is an editing codec. But then again, some cameras do record ProRes and the Avid DNx codecs are there—so much for consistency. But no matter, you'll find the ProRes option on the Settings tab, buried in the Video Previews area near the bottom of the window. And you'll need to select Custom from the Editing Mode window to make sure it's available to you. Custom is a little hard to find the first time, because it's above the first option, Arri. And you'll need to select QuickTime as your preview file format. Like I said, ProRes is buried deep.

The Settings Tab

The New Sequence Settings tab is where the action is. It lets you customize your sequence settings to match the type of media you'll be working with (Figure 4.7). The first item, Editing Mode, is another list of presets—choose Custom if you want to make your own.

The rest of the items in this window allow you to select the video, audio, and preview (aka render) settings for your sequence:

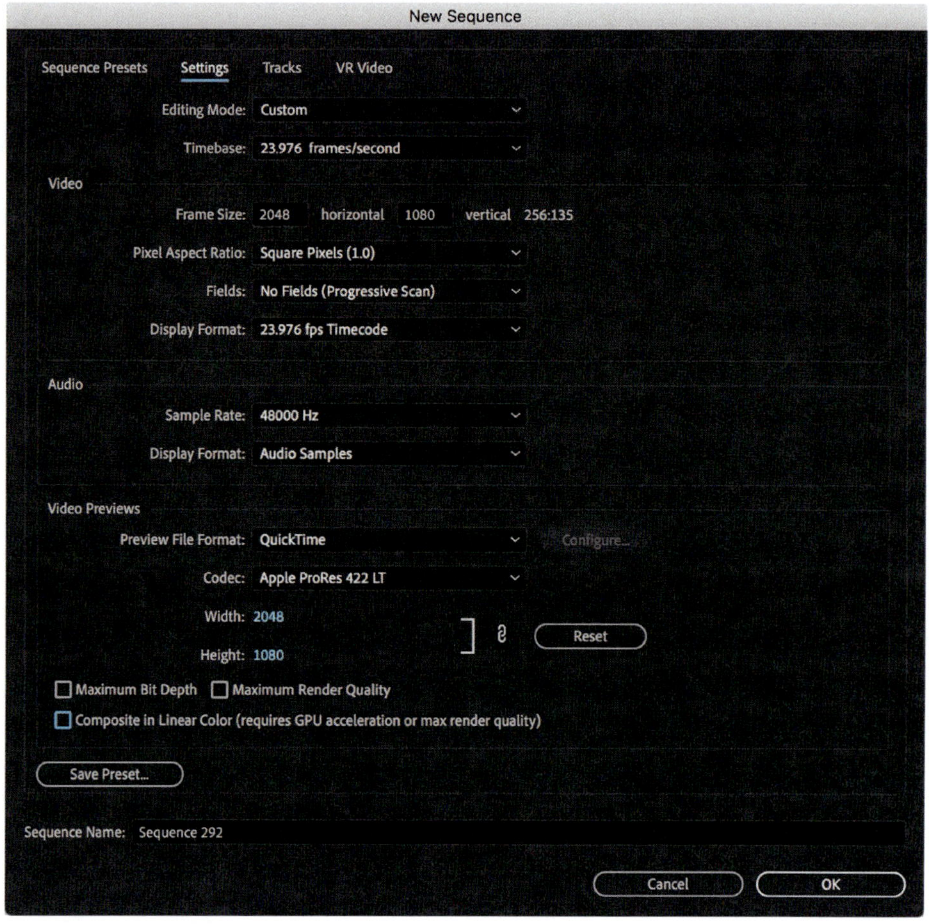

Figure 4.7

The New Sequence Settings tab lets you customize your sequence settings to match the type of media you'll be editing with.

Time base Most film projects in the U.S. have a time base (aka, frame rate) of 23.976. Broadcast television projects may have a frame rate of 29.97.

Video options consist of the image size (in pixels), the pixel aspect ratio (usually square), and fields (usually none). For 2K, the image size is 2048 x 1080; for most HD, it's 1920 x 1080; and for 4K, it's 4096 x 2160. Generally, your display format should match your time base, which is usually 23.976. If you want to make a special square or tall-oriented video for Instagram or mobile phones, this is where you set that up.

Audio Settings let you choose the sample rate (usually 48 kHz aka, 48000 Hz). The display format is the same as in the New Project window, a choice between two options for time counters.

Video Previews are render settings. I prefer to render at the same size as my sequence, usually either 2K or 1080 HD. You can select any codec you want for your renders. I usually choose an Apple ProRes codec, because even though Premiere considers almost every codec to be native, I think Premiere is optimized for Apple ProRes. I have no scientific backing for this assumption, but once upon a time, ProRes was the main codec for Premiere. Plus, much of film-oriented post-production is biased towards ProRes. To get to the ProRes codec, you'll need to choose QuickTime as your Preview File Format. Then, the ProRes family of codecs will be available under the Codec menu. Usually Apple ProRes 422 is sufficient, offering a decent-enough image quality for working (not finishing!) and small enough file size to not be too taxing on your system. There are also three innocuous little boxes at the bottom of this panel that affect how media in your sequence is rendered for playback. Maximum Bit Depth increases the bit-depth, which is useful for 10-bit or higher source video. Maximum Render Quality improves image quality for sequences with lots of resizing and other effects. Composite in Linear Color offers up a different algorithm for effects that blend images, such as dissolves. For now, I recommend leaving them unchecked because they can use a lot of processing power and slow your system down.

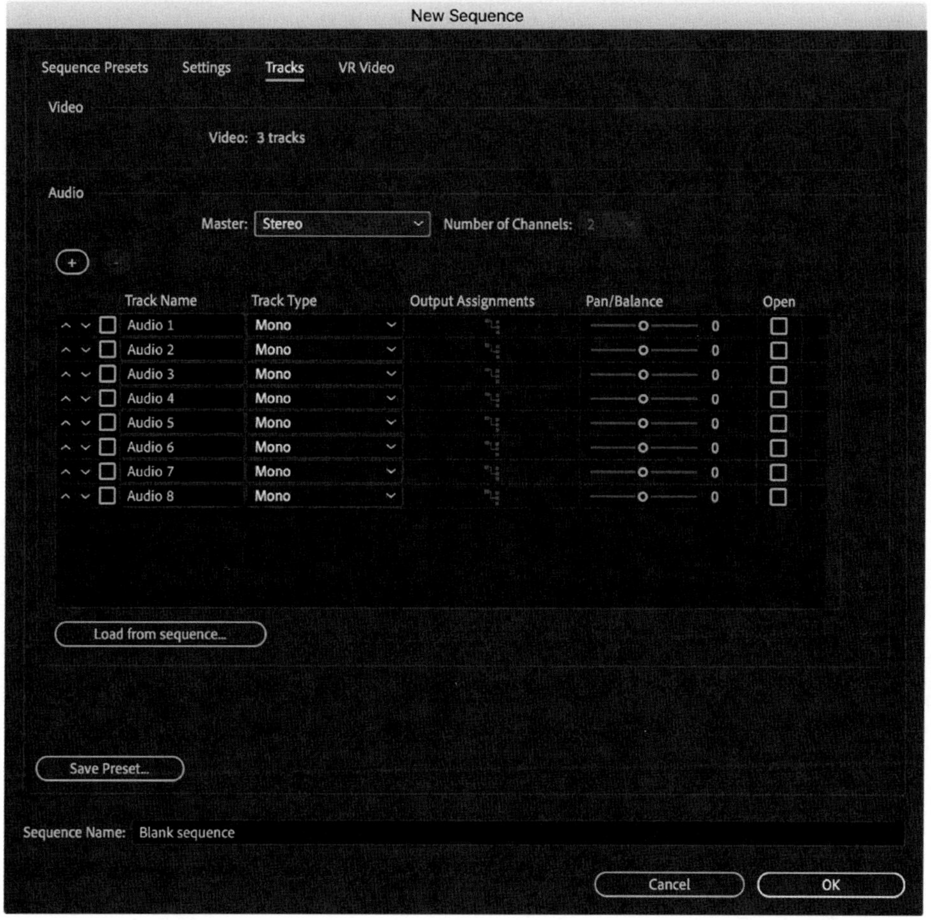

Figure 4.8

The New Sequence Tracks tab is where you tell Premiere how many video and audio tracks you want in your sequence as a default.

The Tracks Tab

The New Sequence Tracks tab is where you setup the number of tracks for a new sequence (Figure 4.8). The default is three tracks of video and four tracks of audio. That's plenty of video tracks to start with, but not enough audio tracks for most films. Click on the plus button to the left and keep clicking until you have eight to twelve tracks of audio. You can always add more of both to your sequence later on.

Audio Master Tracks

The audio master tracks configuration tells Premiere how your final audio will be output and it's one of the few settings you can't change later. You have the choice of stereo, 5.1, multichannel, and mono. Most film projects will choose stereo. Surround sound films will eventually end up as 5.1, but most filmmakers will work in stereo while they edit and save 5.1 sound for the final mix. Multichannel and mono are options generally used for special exports like sending audio to a sound editor. You'll find more information on this topic in Chapter 10, Audio Editing and audio export options are discussed Chapter 14, Finishing. For now, I recommend choosing stereo.

VR Video Settings

If you have a VR project, you'll need to configure the settings in this tab (Figure 4.9). Premiere only supports one type of 360-degree projection: equirectangular. You can then choose how you want it displayed: as a single image (monoscopic) or two different variants of stereoscopic images. Monoscopic 360-degree video is shot with a single lens, stereoscopic is shot with two lenses close to each other, which is more like natural human vision. Working with VR video is covered in Chapter 9, Mixing Media and Basic Effects.

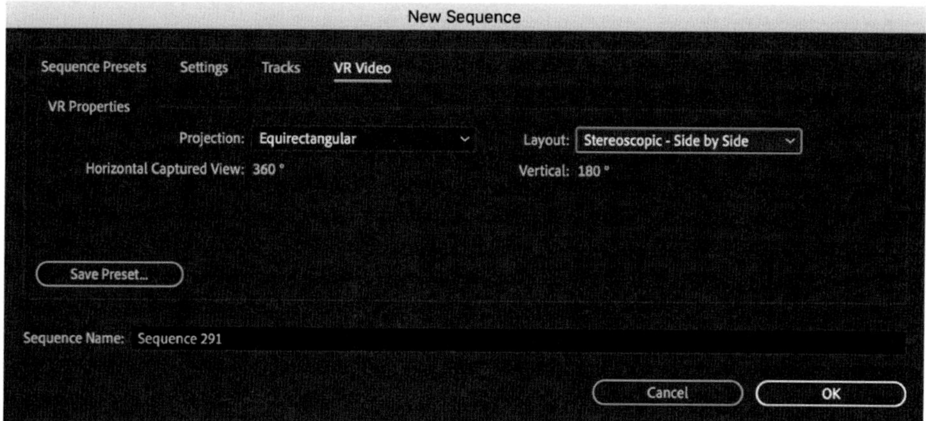

Figure 4.9
The VR settings tab.

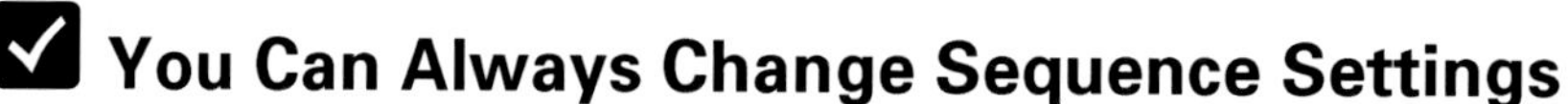

You Can Always Change Sequence Settings

If you decide to change any of these settings after you've created a new sequence, you can do so by going to Sequence > Sequence Settings. Here you'll find a window with all the options except for the master tracks configuration, which can't be changed after the fact. But there's an easy workaround—just make a new sequence with the master tracks audio configuration that you need and copy your cut into it.

Custom Sequence Templates

Making your own sequence template with custom settings is worth the few minutes it takes because you can use it over and over again as you create new sequences during the course of editing a movie. To do that, choose Custom, which is the first item on the Editing Mode menu list at the top of the Settings tab. Set up the settings as desired, then click on the Save Preset button in the lower left corner of the window. A new window will pop up that lets you add a name and description. Once you save your sequence settings template, you'll get kicked back to the main New Sequence window. Note that there is now a folder in the list of available presets called Custom and inside it is your new template. From now on, you can use your custom preset to create new sequences without having to go through all those settings again.

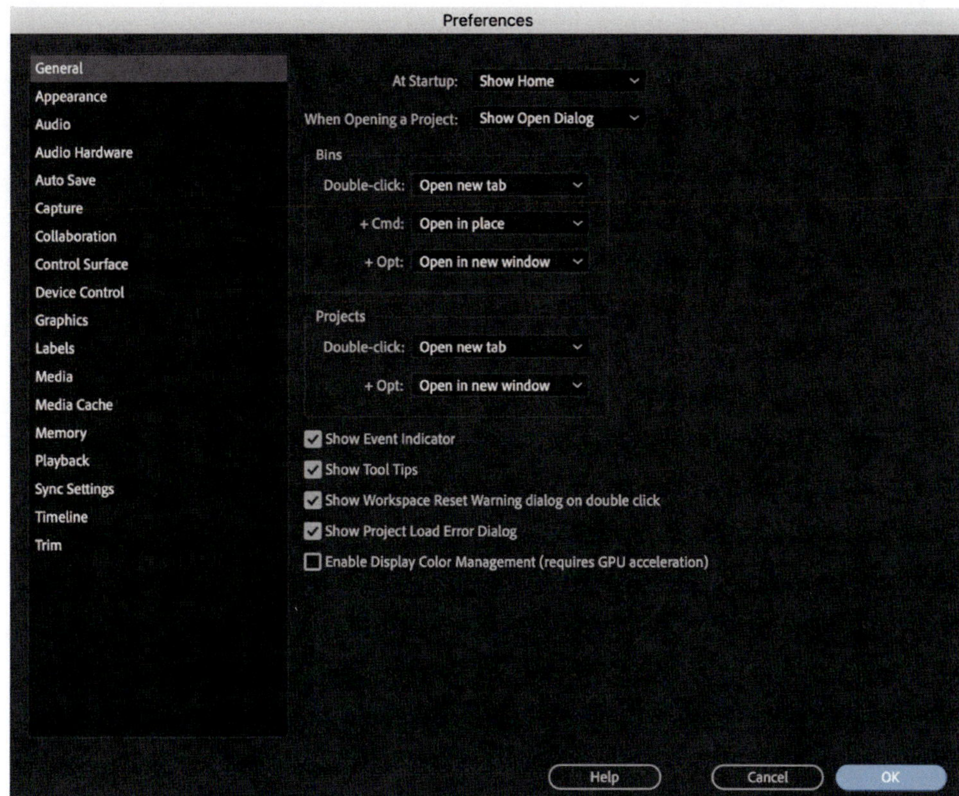

Figure 4.10

Premiere has eighteen Preferences panels.

Preferences

Premiere Pro offers a lot of customization and many of those choices are made in the Preferences window, which is found under either the Edit menu (Windows) or the Premiere Pro menu (Mac). It contains 18—yes, 18—sub-menus (Figure 4.10). In fact, there are so many that I'm skipping the ones that are self-explanatory like Appearance.

General

Most of these are pretty straightforward and really only concern your individual taste. How do you want your bins to open? Do you want Premiere to show tool tips? (If you're new to Premiere, yes!) The one item here that's of note is the Enable Display Color Management check box. This is a useful item to select if you're color grading or outputting to various delivery formats, so it's discussed more in Chapter 13, Color. But for normal editorial work, it's best to leave it deselected because it uses a fair amount of processing power and could result in slower playback and rendering.

Audio Hardware

If you have external speakers or a mixer, this is where you tell Premiere that you have them (Figure 4.11). You may also need to change some settings in your operating system at the Finder/Windows level.

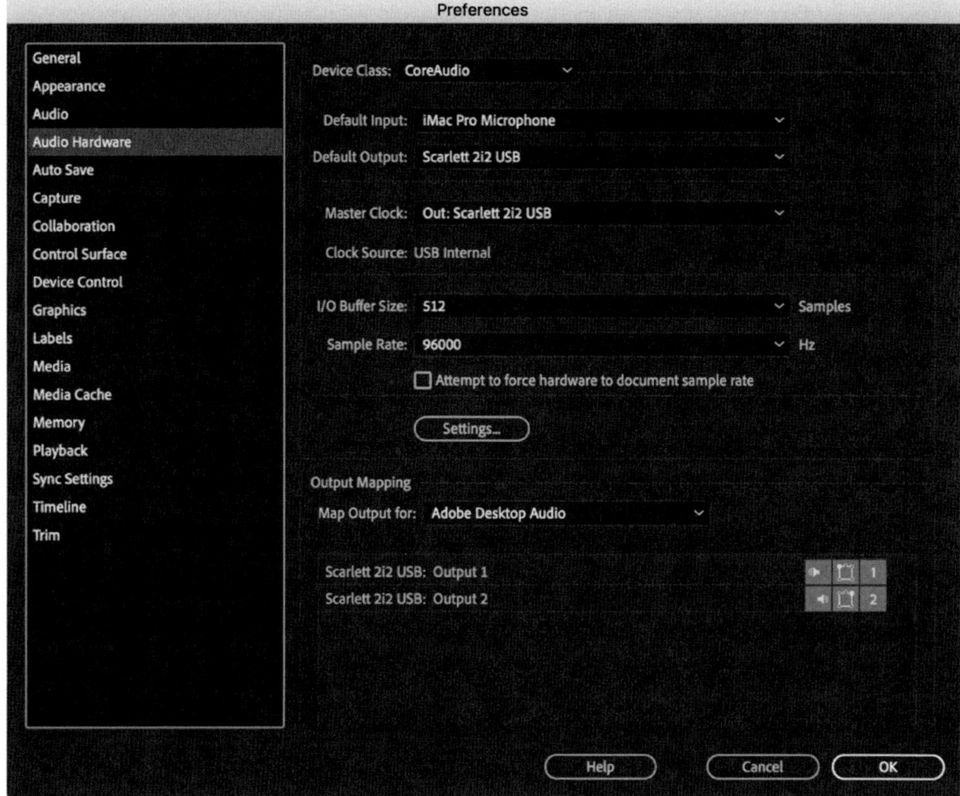

Figure 4.11

Audio hardware preferences should match your hardware configuration.

Auto Save

This one's pretty self-explanatory. You tell it how often to auto-save and how many backups to keep on hand. Generally, the defaults work fine here. By the way, the Auto Save location is set in the Scratch Disk tab of the Project Settings.

Be sure to deselect Save Backup Project to Creative Cloud if you have a dedicated project drive and want your backups to be local. You may be wondering why one would want to have project backups saved locally instead of the Creative Cloud. Your system might be networked locally, or already part of a remote backup system using another service such as Dropbox. There's no right or wrong answer here, just that this is where you get to tell Premiere that you don't want the backups on CC.

New in Premiere 2019 is "Auto Save also saves the current projects(s)." You definitely want to select this one. In previous versions of Premiere, auto-save copies of your project were saved to a special auto-save folder, but you had to manually save the main project yourself (File > Save). Now Premiere saves both, which is great. But only if you check the box.

Media

The Media preferences are important (Figure 4.12). If it's a professional project, it will have timecode, so you'll want to select Use Media Source. Default Media Scaling should usually be set to None. Any other choice here could cause Premiere to scale all your footage so that it automatically matches your sequence settings, which could have results that you don't like or slow down performance. (More on scaling media in Chapter 9, Mixing Media and Basic Effects.) Indeterminate Media Timebase sounds intimidatingly important but for most filmmakers it's not: this is where you tell Premiere what frame rate to assign to animation and sequential still image sequences. Choose 23.976 to match the rest of your project.

The next four checkboxes have to do with metadata, which for all intents and purposes is a fancy word for info. It's important to have "Write XMP ID to files on import" selected. The XMP ID is a unique identifier that Premiere uses to keep track of your files better. On the other hand "Write clip markers to XMP" isn't always necessary—if your markers consist of temporary notes as you edit, you won't need this. (More on markers in Chapter 6, Media Management and Troubleshooting.) "Enable clip and XMP metadata linking" should be selected. It means that any change to the clip metadata will be recorded in the XMP metadata and vice-versa. "Include captions on import" should be selected for any media that includes embedded closed-captioning. If you don't need this one, deselect it for faster importing.

Enable Proxies sounds really important but it's just another way to toggle the playback of proxies on or off (more on proxies in Chapter 5). Ignore it, you can deal with this elsewhere. "Allow duplicate media during project import" should be deselected. We haven't discussed duplicates in Premiere yet and it's not clear how much effect this preference has, but the fewer duplicates that Premiere creates, the better. (More on duplicates in Chapter 6, Media Management and Troubleshooting.)

The last checkbox, "Automatically refresh growing files," refers to media that is being edited as it's being shot, such as live sports or television. These files "grow" as the shoot progresses and as a result, they need to be refreshed regularly. New to Premiere 2020 is an option to automate playback of growing files in the Source monitor.

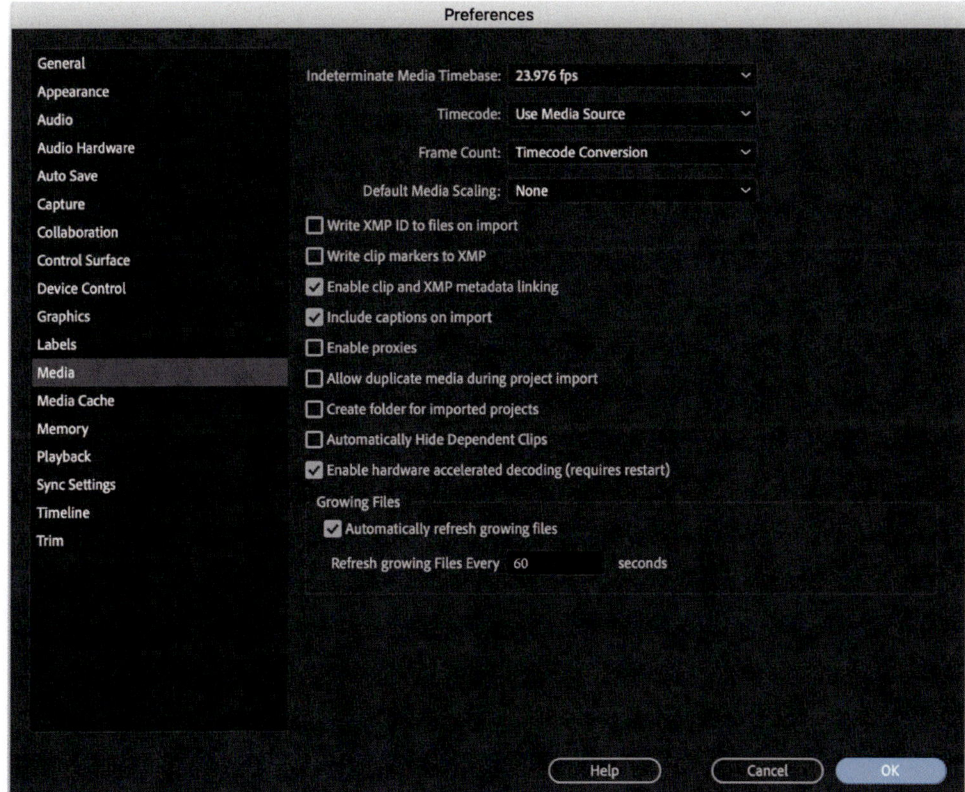

Figure 4.12

The Media preferences panel has options for how Premiere handles your media, including automated resizing and how metadata is saved.

Media Cache

Premiere Pro uses a folder called the Media Cache that contains a bunch of files that help with performance, such as video thumbnails and audio waveforms. Use the Browse button to select a location for this folder. Be aware that it can take up a fair amount of space so it's best to keep it on a dedicated media drive.

Another good reason to keep these Media Cache files separate from your other media files is that an element of standard system maintenance is to delete and rebuild the media cache and it's easier to do this if it's in a separate folder. The Media Cache files and the cache database can get corrupted during long term projects with lots of media so it's a good idea to rebuild them regularly.

The default for media cache management is set to "Do not delete cache files automatically." This is probably the best setting for most filmmakers. It allows you to decide when to delete and rebuild the media cache at your own convenience. Rebuilding the media cache database can take a while and performance in Premiere is pretty bad while it's happening. I delete and rebuild my cache every few weeks, on Friday night so that it has the weekend to rebuild.

Memory

This preferences panel lets you decide how to divvy up your RAM between the Adobe CC applications and your other applications. Adobe recommends a minimum of 8 GB but you should probably have at least 16 GB of RAM and plan to reserve 2-4 GB of it for other applications. That said, I work on a laptop with 8 GB (total) all the time and have no problems even with just about every Adobe CC app open at all times.

A small menu gives you the choice between optimized rendering for Memory or Performance. Most will prefer the results of Performance, but if you're doing final renders before exporting your finished film, you may wish to switch it to Memory, which may give you higher quality renders. (More on finishing in Chapter 14.)

Playback

We haven't talked about Trim mode or working with Adobe Media Encoder yet, but this is where you set some preferences for how Trim mode plays back your edits, more on that in Chapter 7, Advanced Trimming. As for Media Encoder, that's covered in the next chapter, but you should keep "Pause Media Encoder queue during playback" selected. Otherwise, your video won't play properly because Media Encoder is crunching data for you in the background. The rest of the options here affect hardware devices that are pretty much obsolete, like videotape players.

Timeline

The Timeline preferences cover a range of options. The first three options let you choose the default length for video and audio dissolves, and also a default length for images when you import a still into Premiere.

The next two items offer different options for how the Timeline behaves when playing back a sequence. These are a matter of personal taste.

After that is a fairly important one, Default Audio Tracks. (This used to be in the Audio preferences.) This lets you tell Premiere how to treat your source audio once it's placed in a sequence. For most editors, Use File, which doesn't change anything, is best. But you can use these preferences to convert audio from one format to another if you wish. Premiere does have one quirk—if you have a clip with two channels of mono audio, Premiere will assume it's stereo. You'll have to use the right-click clip menu to Modify > Audio and let Premiere know that it's not stereo. (Modifying audio is discussed in Chapter 8, Sync and Multicam.)

You should make sure "Display out of sync indicators for unlinked clips" is selected so that you can identify out of sync media at a glance in the Timeline (which we covered in Chapter 3). The rest of the checkboxes in this panel are various things you might like or dislike. The more you edit, the more they will mean to you but in general they are self-explanatory.

What Goes Where?

You may have noticed that there are lots of ancillary files associated with a Premiere project and the controls for where they are saved on your hard drives are spread across the Project Settings and Preferences.

So here's a little cheat sheet:

Project file location: Use Save As command to choose.

Render (aka preview) files: File > Project Settings > Scratch Disks

Auto save location: File > Project Settings > Scratch Disks

Proxies: File > Project Settings > Ingest Settings

Captured video and audio: File > Project Settings > Scratch Disks

Media cache and database: Preferences > Media Cache

Customizing the Premiere Interface

Some people like dark backgrounds, other like light, some like scrubbing audio, others prefer waveforms. Whatever your taste, Premiere lets you change just about everything about the way it looks, sounds, and plays back media.

There are a number of preferences and settings that you can use to customize the Premiere Pro interface:

General preferences (Preferences > General) Use to show tool tips and control how projects and windows open, also startup options.

Labels (Preferences > Labels) Lets you change the color of labels using a color wheel and set default colors for various types of media (Figure 4.13). To change clip labels, right-click on a clip or group of clips to bring up a menu that lets you set label colors.

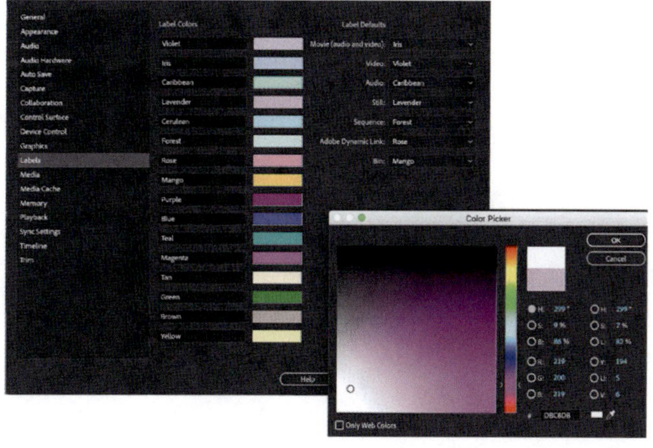

Figure 4.13

You can use Preferences to adjust the colors of labels in Premiere, which affect the entire interface.

Appearance (Preferences > Appearance) Change colors, brightness, etc. This might sound frivolous but it's not. Many editors prefer a darker and less colorful interface so that the film stands out.

Graphics preferences (Preferences > Graphics) Lets you choose between European/East Asian and South Asian/Middle Eastern text.

Drag and Drop Custom Panels You can literally drag and drop anything in Premiere, including panels. And when you try it, you'll see that panels have purple bevel-like drop zones that tell Premiere where to place the panel you are adding. They can go side-by-side, one above the other, and if you drag into the center, as tabbed windows (Figure 4.16). Personally, this took a bit of getting used to for me and I found myself accidentally creating strange layouts of the interface. Luckily you can choose Revert to Saved Layout from the Workspace menu to restore the interface to the default.

Source, Program, and Timeline Button Editors (Found under the "+" icon in the lower right corner of the Source and Program monitors and in the wrench menu of the Timeline, under Customize Video/Audio Header.) Button Editors let you add or remove buttons at the bottom of each monitor (Figure 4.14) and also the header for each track in the Timeline. Mousing over each button in the Button Editor will show the name of each button if you have the Show Tool Tips preference selected (Preferences > General). I like adding the Toggle Proxies button, the Safe Margins button, and the Toggle Multi-Cam View button. The Timeline buttons are different and most of them are already available to you by default. Exceptions include track-based audio level meters and controls, and keyframe options.

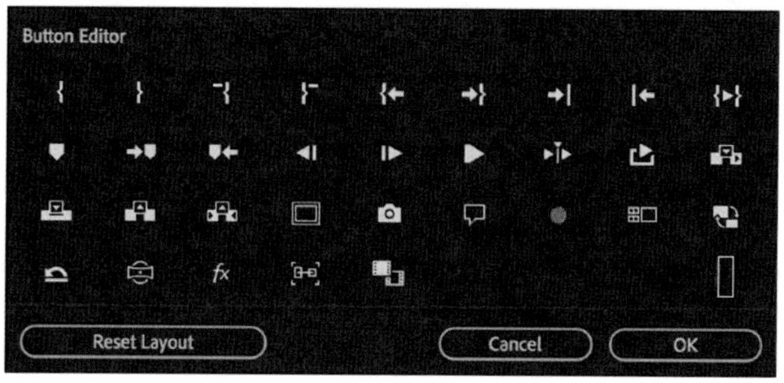

Figure 4.14

The Button Editor lets you customize the buttons at the bottom of the Source and Program monitors. There is also a button editor for Timeline track controls.

Bin View settings (A row of buttons at the bottom of each bin.) Here you can choose between List, Icon and Freeform view and adjust the size of the items in the bin. You can also select criteria for sorting.

Timeline Display settings (Found under the wrench icon near the upper left corner of the Timeline.) This menu gives you all sorts of choices for controlling the Timeline display. You can choose to show or hide video thumbnails, audio waveforms, dupe detection, clip names, and more. You can also set and save track height presets.

Source and Program Monitor settings Found under the wrench icon near the lower right corner of the Source and Program monitors, these menus let you choose between composite (i.e., normal) video and multicam. They also let you display timecode overlays on top of your video when playback is paused, which can be handy, especially on the Program side and gives you the option to change Overlay Settings, which can get quite complex. On the Source monitor it allows you choose to view the audio waveform of a clip, instead of the video. And the small menu next to it lets you select a playback resolution to improve performance on both Source and Program windows.

Panel settings menu (Found under the small menu icon next to the name of each panel in the upper right corner.) Panel settings let you choose between different bin views, whether to show thumbnails, and the font size for each panel. Here you can also choose the various Metadata columns to display in your bin (Figure 4.15).

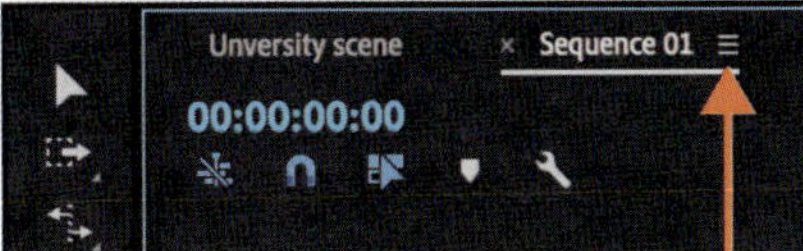

Figure 4.15

Every panel in Premiere has a panel settings menu, accessed on the panel tab, next to the name of the panel. Panel settings vary depending on the type of panel.

Workspace presets Don't forget that the most basic—and potentially most profound—way to customize Premiere is to arrange the panels in a way that truly suits you (and maybe only you). A two-Timeline workspace (Figure 4.16) is a favorite for a documentary filmmaker friend who finds it very useful for copying and pasting from a source sequence (top Timeline) to their actual cut (lower Timeline). When you find a unique workspace layout that works for you, save it using the panel settings menu in the Workspace menu bar along the top of the screen. I have a couple—a two monitor workspace, an enlarged Timeline view for when I'm dealing with a lot of tracks, and a custom single-monitor view.

Workspaces for two-monitor workstations Premiere workspace presets are all designed for single-monitor workstations but professional editing systems always have at least two monitors. You'll have to create your own saved workspace(s) to accommodate the second monitor.

Custom Keyboard settings (Edit/Premiere Pro > Keyboard Settings) Here you'll find keyboard presets based on Final Cut Pro 7 and Avid Media Composer (Figure 4.17). You'll also find that there are a zillion commands in Premiere that can be mapped to the keyboard.

➡ Custom Hardware?

If you want to go further and really build out a customized editing system with hardware like added monitors and specialized keyboards, Chapter 11 of *The Digital Filmmaking Handbook* covers all the elements of building an editing workstation.

Figure 4.16

Don't forget that the most basic, and potentially most profound, way to customize Premiere is to arrange the panels in a way that truly suits you and save them as a workspace preset. Shown here, a two Timeline workspace.

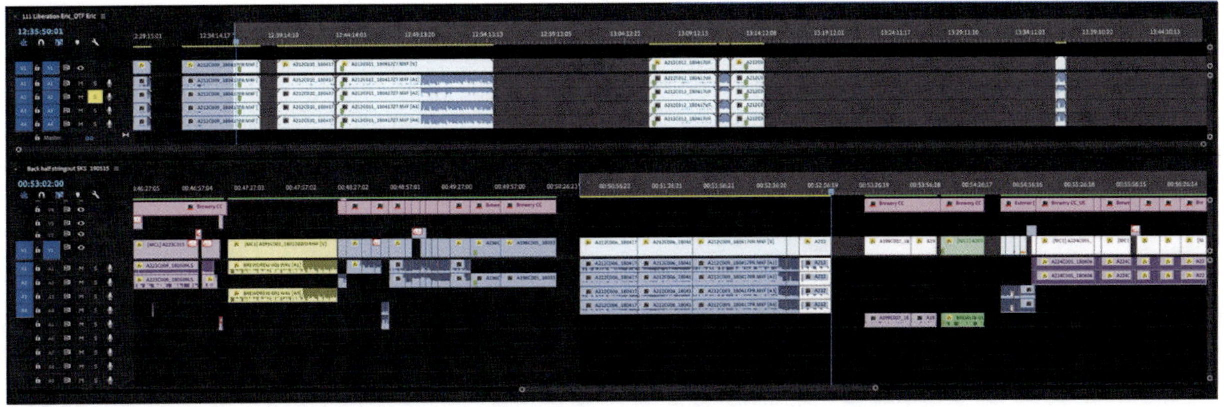

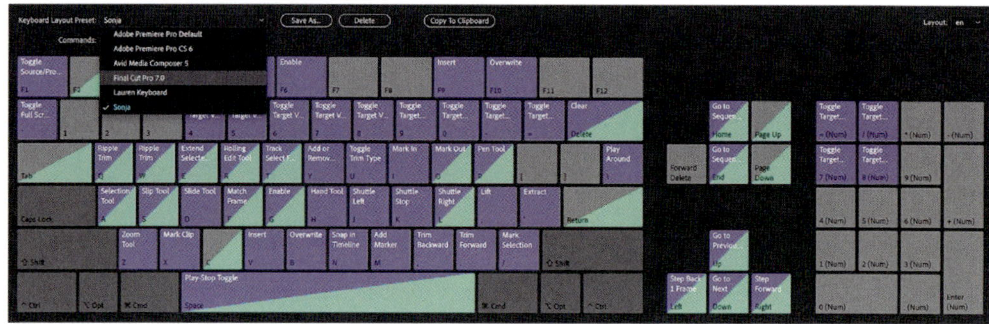

Figure 4.17

The Keyboard Shortcuts window. You can switch between some pre-built layouts for Final Cut Pro 7, Avid Media Composer 5 and Premiere Pro CS 6.

Get the Adobe Premiere Pro Reference PDF

The hardest thing about setting custom key commands in Premiere is knowing what they are called. But the Adobe Premiere Pro Reference PDF, available on their website, has a ten-page list of every single programmable key command. It's also searchable. Unfortunately, at the time of this writing it is a year out-of-date, but most of these key command references still work.

Project Planning Problems to Solve

Are you still wondering what video format you should work in as you edit? Here are some ideas:

If your footage was shot recently and you have no idea where it will end up, but you hope to finish it as a projected film, I suggest working in 1920 x 1080 HD. Most streaming services deliver in HD and UHD. Also almost everyone who will need to work with your film—your composer, graphics team, consultants, etc.—will find it easiest to use HD files. Working in HD doesn't require the extra hardware requirements (monitors, storage space, processing power) of UHD/4K and yet it still is a very high-quality image that will look good under most circumstances including theatrical projection. And since UHD and HD share the same aspect ratio, you won't have to worry about cropping and/or resizing when you up-res.

If you shot 4K or higher and it's a short-form project, you might consider sticking with 4K as you edit. You'll need a top-of-the-line workstation and all the help you can get from Premiere to playback 4K video in real-time. But these types of projects tend to be high-pressure and you may need to have a very high-quality cut available for screening or output at a moment's notice. In this case, it's worth sticking with high-resolution video and using proxies, rendering, and other settings to make sure Premiere can handle it. (Be sure to check out the section on Optimizing Premiere for Playback in Chapter 5.)

But what if you have multiple sources? Then it's even more likely that your decision will be based on your final goals for the film. And what if you have multiple goals for your finished film? That's actually the norm. In that case, you work at a resolution your computer can handle, finish at the highest quality level that you need, and then work your way down, quality-wise, to mobile streaming as you export your final versions.

5

Importing, Playing, and Proxy Media

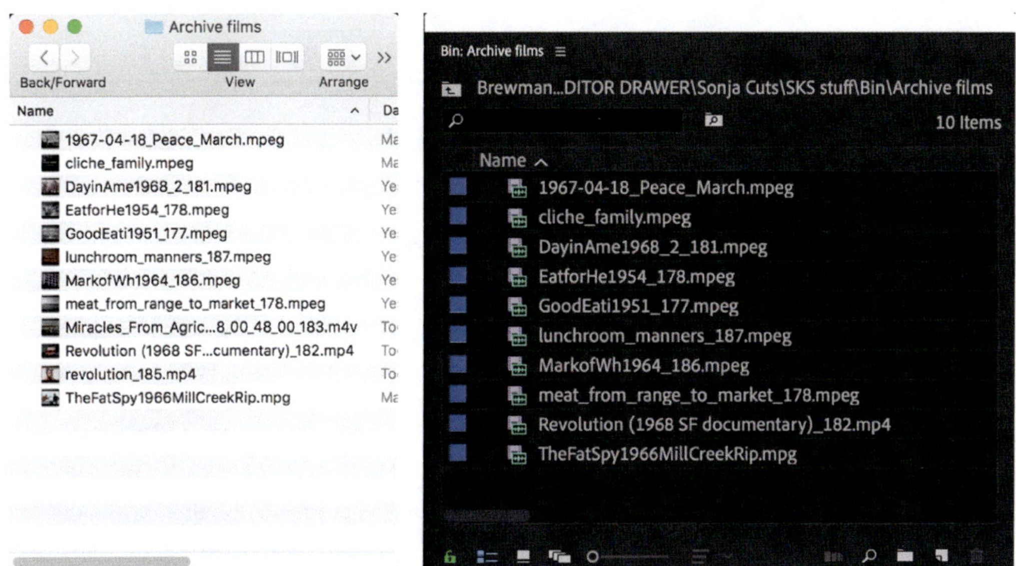

Figure 5.1

Your folders (left) will show up inside Premiere (right) using the same organizational structure that you created on your hard drive.

AT THE MOST BASIC LEVEL, Premiere is acting as an intermediary between the raw media stored on your hard drives and the final film that you plan to make.

That's a big job.

In order to do that, Premiere meticulously keeps track of your media, as does your operating system. How so? They each assign a number known as a *unique identifier* to every file and that number never changes. It's kind of like a social security number for digital media. If you move a file from one folder in Windows to another, Windows still knows it's the same file. If you rename a file in the Finder, the Mac OS still knows it's the same file. And the same thing is true inside Premiere.

What does that mean for you? It means that Premiere doesn't need extra organization to keep track of media, but you do. If you want to find a shot, it's much easier if you have it organized in a way that helps you recall where it is. There are a number of organizational strategies for films, but most filmmakers choose to organize by shoot date, by camera card, or by subject.

Whatever your choice, I heartily recommend organizing your media on your hard drive before you bring it into Premiere. That way, when you bring it into Premiere, your project will be a mirror-image of your hard drives (Figure 5.1).

Organizational Strategies

The Digital Filmmaking Handbook explains how to organize your media, such as dailies bins, both on the set in Chapter 10, Advanced Shooting and in post in Chapter 13, Preparing to Edit.

Don't Change the File Structure for Some Formats

RED, P2, and other formats rely on the directory structure created by the camera to decode the media. If your project was shot with one of these cameras, you should copy the entire card over and leave it intact. You can then organize these card-based folders into a system of folders organized by shoot date, or subject, or not at all.

Bringing Audio and Video into Premiere

Premiere offers two ways to get media into a project: Importing and the Media Browser, both of which can be affected by the Ingest settings:

Import

Importing media is the most basic way to bring media into Premiere. Why do I say it's basic? It's passive, meaning that Premiere does nothing to your footage. It doesn't change anything and simply creates a file inside Premiere that points to the media file on your hard drive. There are three ways to import: File > Import, drag-and-drop media files from your hard drive folder to a Premiere bin, and double-click on the empty background of a bin and use the Import window to navigate to your footage.

Import is a great choice when your footage is already good to go, such as the tutorial media for this book. You don't want to change your media in any way, and you don't have any special camera-related format issues such as spanned clips.

Spanned Clips

Some cameras have the capacity to keep shooting when a card runs out of space. They have two card slots and the camera can record the beginning of a shot on the first card and then, when that card is full, finish recording it on the second card. The result is called a *spanned clip*. Spanned clips require Premiere to take the last clip on one card, and the first card on the next card and put them together into one clip for you to edit with. If your camera can make spanned clips, then you want to use the Media Browser to bring in your footage, not the Import command.

The Media Browser

If the Project panel is the heart of your Premiere project, the Media Browser is the link to the outside world. It's a window into your operating system and it has some special powers, especially when it comes to importing media. It's similar to Import, but it's more like "Smart Import."

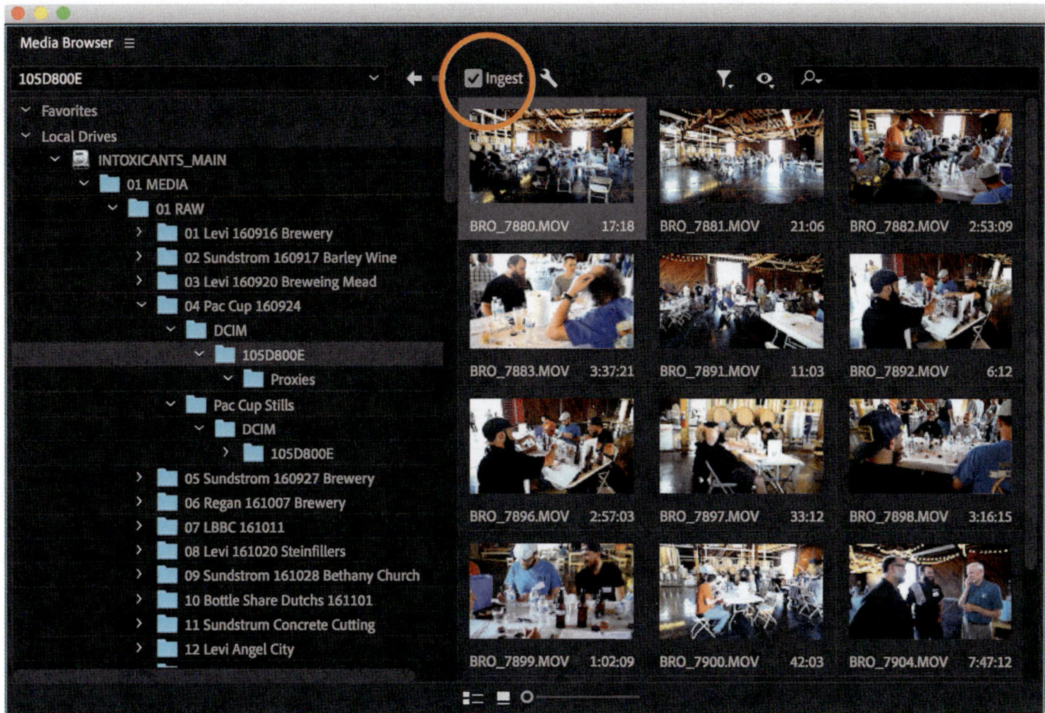

Figure 5.2

The Media Browser interface is the best way to bring media from your hard drives into Premiere.
By selecting the Ingest checkbox, you'll activate whatever Ingest Settings you have chosen.

At a casual glance, the Media Browser looks just like another window in Premiere (Figure 5.2). In fact, it looks like a simple replica of your hard drive(s). But it's more than just that. When you grab a clip through the Media Browser and drag it to a bin, Premiere interprets your file and brings it into your project in what it deems the best way possible. In most cases, it doesn't need to do anything, but if you have spanned clips, the Media Browser is smart enough to understand that they are really just a single shot. The Media Browser is also best for camera formats that rely on the directory structure of the camera card to interpret the footage correctly, such as Panasonic P2 and RED.

The Media Browser is designed to be similar to a web browser, so it has forward and back arrows at the top to help as you navigate. Also, unlike the Import command, it stays open so if you're bringing a lot of media into Premiere it may be easier to keep track of your work in progress.

One thing about the Media Browser that's slightly unintuitive is that there's no "Go" or "Okay" button. Instead, you drag items from the Media Browser directory into your Project directory or bin. You can also tell the Media Browser that you want it to bring in media using Ingest Settings by selecting the Ingest checkbox at the top of the Media Browser window (Figure 5.2). There's a small settings (wrench) menu next to it, which when clicked will bring up the Ingest Settings window.

☑ Give It a Rest

After you bring media into your project, Premiere will need to do some work, building thumbnails and waveforms, and creating proxies, copies, and transcoding media if you've selected these options in the Ingest settings. At the bottom right corner of the Timeline window, you'll see a blue progress bar that lets you know Premiere is still working on your files. Premiere can be slow or prone to crashing during this process so you might want to take a break while it works.

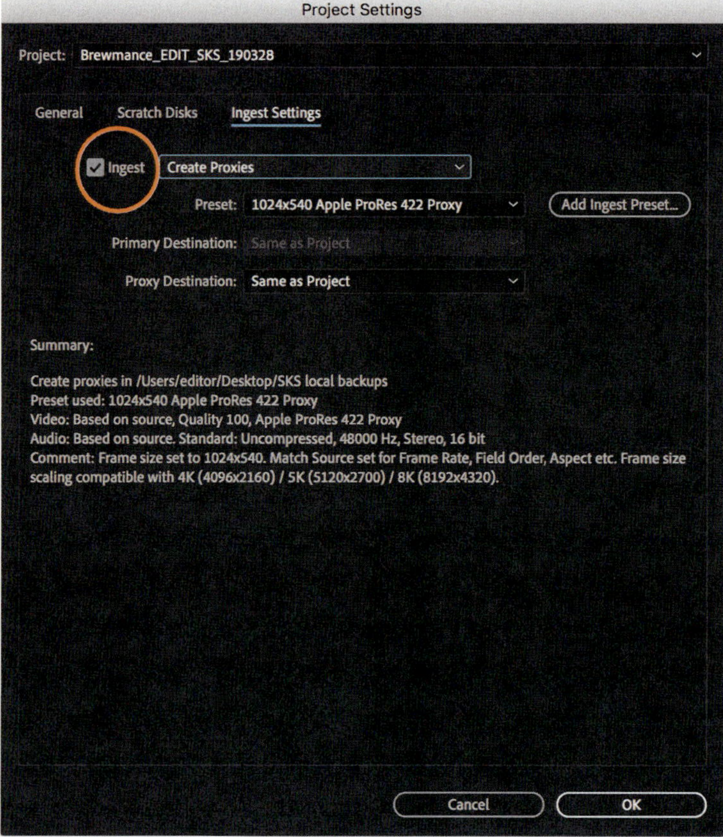

Figure 5.3

The Ingest Settings tab in the Project Settings window. Note the checkbox next to Ingest: this is basically an on/off switch for the Ingest settings and it's the same as the checkbox in the Media Browser, kinda like having two light switches for one light.

Ingest

Ingest is a weird word—there's a history behind it. Once upon a time, the process of bringing media into an editing application was called *capturing*. But as file-based formats began to takeover, people working in post-production needed a broader term, so they started using Ingest to cover all the various ways of bringing media into an editing system.

In Premiere, the Ingest settings (File > Project Settings > Ingest Settings) tell Premiere how to treat all media, automatically, whenever you add it to your project using both the Import command and the Media Browser. (Figure 5.3) There are three options in the Ingest Settings:

Copy is mostly used to take media from a camera card and copy it to a media folder on your hard drives during import. Most filmmakers will have already copied their media from their cards and onto their media drives before they launched Premiere. But if you haven't done that, choose this option—you definitely don't want to work directly from a card. This is also a good way to automatically create a backup set of your raw media as you bring it into Premiere. If you choose to copy, you'll get the additional option of MD5 verification, which is a safer way to copy (see next page).

Transcode will take your original media files and save them to whatever video or audio format (container file, codec, frame dimensions, sampling ratio, and frame rate) that you specify. Most projects no longer need transcoding at the outset, because Premiere can work with almost any type of media file in the same sequence. And if you decide to transcode some media later on, you'll probably use Media Encoder directly on a case-by-case basis. (More on transcoding with Media Encoder later in this chapter.)

Create Proxies does exactly what it says and builds a set of lower-resolution media files for every video clip that you import. These proxy media files are used to help Premiere work better if you are editing with large, high-resolution source video. While you're working, you can switch back and forth between the proxies and the original media as needed, which is a really great feature in Premiere. Proxies are covered in detail later in this chapter.

If you know exactly what you need, having Premiere automate these processes can be very convenient. And of course, you can always change the Ingest Settings later or just disable them. You can also transcode, copy, and create proxies on a case by case basis later as well.

Bringing media straight in via Import or the Media Browser is more or less instantaneous. But when you have activated the Ingest Settings, you are asking Premiere to make new files, which can take longer. Luckily, this can occur in the background because Premiere farms out this task to Media Encoder so that you can keep editing. Realistically, however, performance will not be great while Media Encoder is working.

Do You Need the Ingest Settings?

If you are winging it on a project because you're just learning and your project is small, you don't need to worry much about setting up ingesting to work exactly as needed from the outset. But if you're on a big show and you're responsible for bringing in hundreds of hours of footage, daily or weekly, you'll find it to be a big convenience. Ingest Settings are great for projects where you know you'll be doing the same thing every time you bring media into your project.

MD5 Verification

If you select Copy as an Ingest setting, you'll have the option to copy with MD5 verification. MD5 Verification is process that helps you confirm that your data was copied without any errors or corruption. A number known as a *checksum* is generated for both the original media files and the copied files and as long as that number is the same for both, the files themselves are guaranteed to be the same as well. In other words, MD5 Verification confirms that your copied files are identical to the originals. Checksums are used all the time when copying media in post, not just during ingest. You can perform a checksum when copying from one drive to another using built-in utilities in your operating system. (And you should.)

What If You Just Want to Change One Clip?

For example, you may have drone footage and the media format doesn't match the rest of your shoot. (Drone footage notoriously uses codecs that aren't great for editing with.) Or you bought a shot from a stock library that is a completely different format than the rest of your video. How do you change just that one shot to match the rest of your footage?

You could just change the Ingest settings and Import that one clip. But Ingest Settings are global—everything you import going forward will adhere to these settings. Sure you can change them back after you're done, but it's often better to keep your Ingest Settings aligned with your overall needs and treat special single-occurrence issues on a case by case basis.

Enter, Adobe Media Encoder.

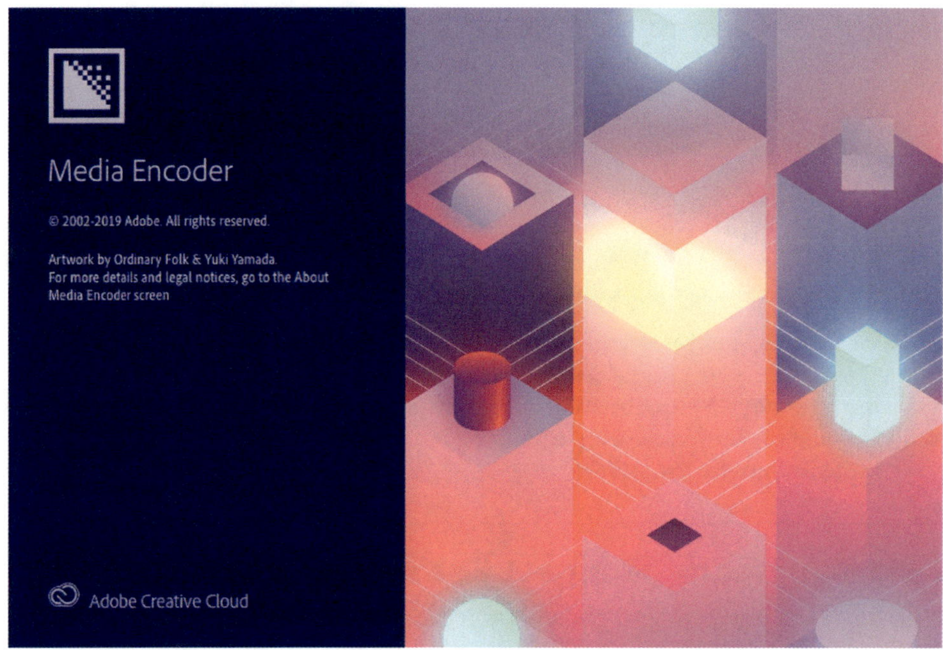

Figure 5.4

Adobe Media Encoder works hand-in-hand with Premiere Pro, often in the background.

Preparing Media with Adobe Media Encoder

Adobe Media Encoder is a companion application that works with Premiere Pro by processing both incoming and outgoing media (Figure 5.4). The integration between Premiere and Media Encoder is amazing—it often works invisibly, handling your need for proxies, copying, transcoding, and exporting in the background as you edit. And you don't have to actively tell Premiere to use Media Encoder, Premiere just does it.

Media Encoder also works as a standalone application. Whether it's a single shot, a whole camera card, or multiple days of shooting, if part of your project needs special treatment in terms of encoding, you'll find Media Encoder very useful.

The Media Encoder Interface

You'll see some familiar elements inside Media Encoder (Figure 5.5). The upper left window is the Media Browser, identical to the one in Premiere (Window > Media Browser). The upper right window is the encoding Queue, which is a list of files in line for processing. Below it is the Encoding preview window, when Media Encoder is working on your files you can watch its progress here. And the lower left window contains the Preset Browser.

The way it works is quite simple. You use the Media Browser in Media Encoder to navigate through your drives and find the media you wish to encode. Once you find it, you drag it into the encoding Queue. Now, you can choose between the standard (or System) presets or you can create your own. Media Encoder divides presets into two categories: encoding and ingest. Encoding presets are oriented towards the final step of filmmaking—exporting your finished movie to various formats. We cover encoding presets at length in Chapter 14, Finishing. For now, we'll stick to getting media prepared for editing—that is, ingesting.

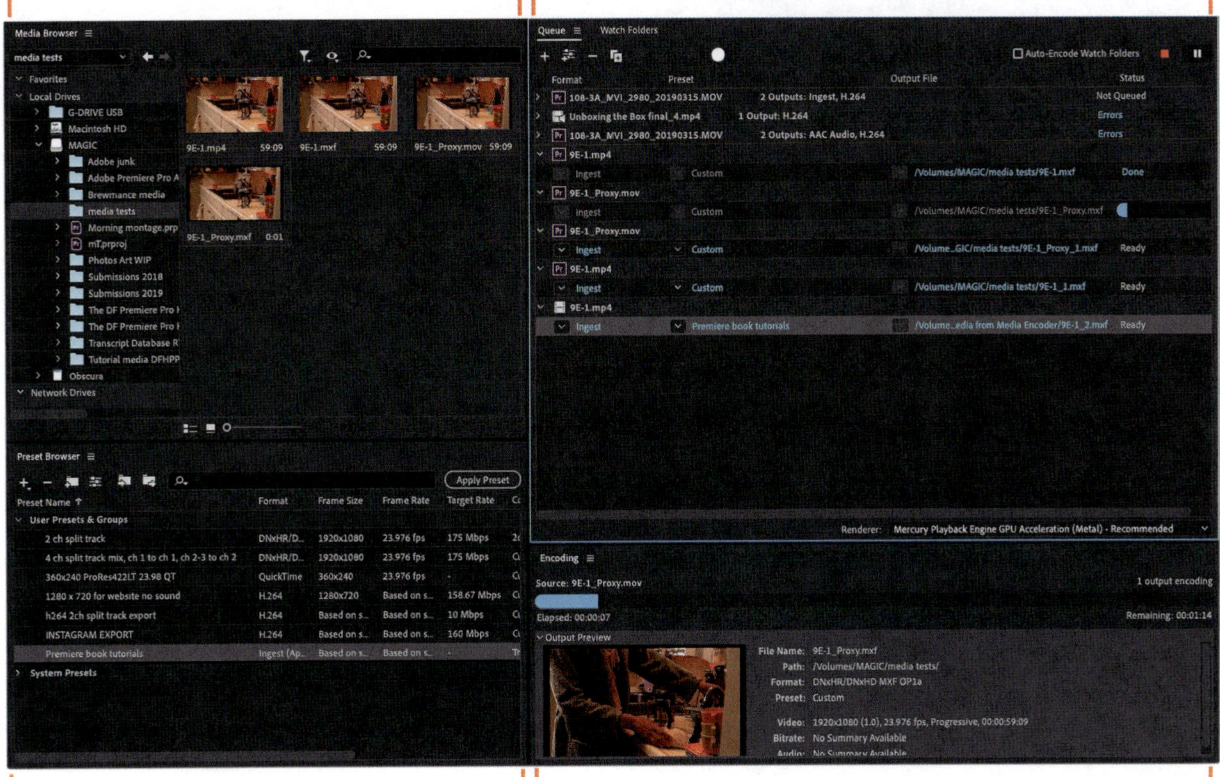

Figure 5.5

The Media Encoder interface includes the Media Browser, the Preset Browser, the encoding Queue, and the Encoding Preview window.

Ingest Presets

Ingest presets in Media Encoder look a lot like the options available to you in the Ingest Settings in Premiere that we discussed earlier. That's because Media Encoder and Premiere share these presets. The System Presets in the Preset Browser are geared towards exporting, with categories like Broadcast and Web Video, but odds are high that whatever you will need for ingesting is in there somewhere. However there's a distinct advantage to making your own custom presets. If you create a custom Ingest preset in Media Encoder, you can make it available in Premiere for future use. In fact, you can't create custom Ingest presets in Premiere, you have to create them in Media Encoder. (This is not true for export presets.)

Why should you make your own custom preset? Basically, you can get exactly what you want and even select a destination folder for those new files. For example, you may decide you want to change the codec for the tutorial media in this book. The tutorial media was encoded with the h.264 codec, which is great for exporting because it creates relatively small but high-quality HD video. It's not quite as great for editing because it doesn't have distinct frames, which means playback isn't always smooth. So you might decide you prefer an editing-oriented codec like Apple ProRes or Avid DNxHD. (You totally don't have to do this, btw, the h.264 codec is good enough for small editing projects.) And then, maybe you want to send those newly transcoded ProRes tutorial media files to a folder on a different drive.

To create your own custom ingest preset, go to Preset > Create Ingest Preset or click on the plus sign in the upper left corner of the Preset Browser. The Ingest Preset Settings window will open

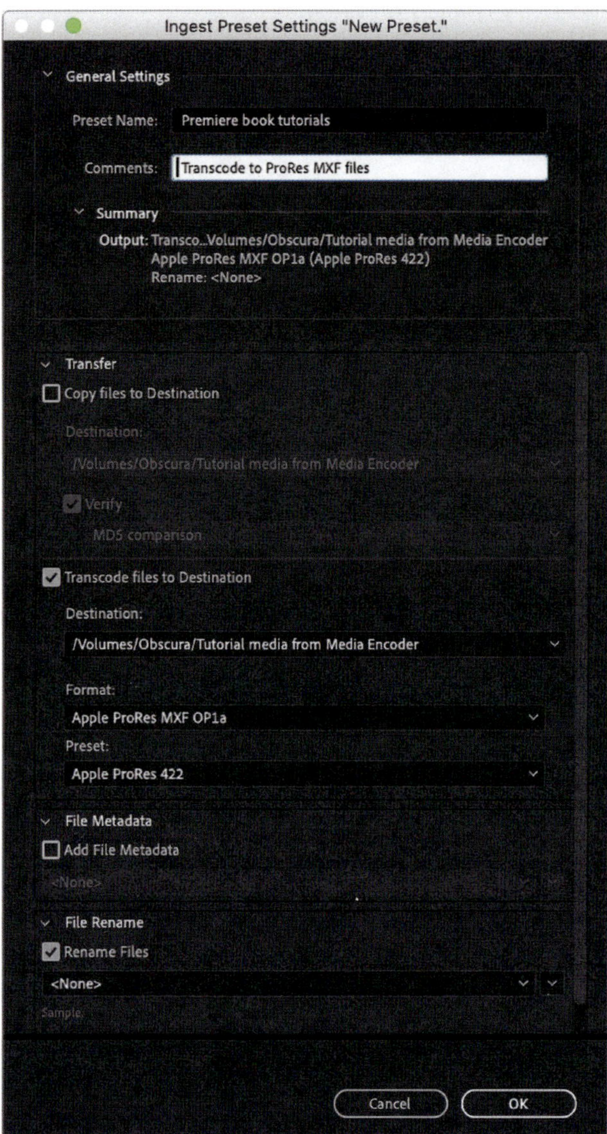

Figure 5.6

Custom Ingest presets that you create in Media Encoder can be used in Premiere.

up and here you can enter all the parameters that suit your needs (Figure 5.6). To change the codec, you'll need to select Transcode Files to Destination, then choose a destination folder, a format, and a codec. Under format, you'll get a list of various types of container files including options for audio-only files. The only formats that support Apple ProRes are Apple ProRes MXF OP1a and QuickTime, so choose whichever you prefer. Avid DNxHD is only available in the MXF format DNxHR/DNxHD MXF OP1a. And since these files are already HD, you might as well stick with an HD version of these codecs: DNx SQ 1080p 23.976 (Avid) or Apple ProRes 422. Don't forget to name your new preset before you hit Ok.

(If you glossed over the media specifications in Chapter 4, this might be a good time to review them.)

Your new preset will appear in the Preset Browser under the User Presets and Groups heading. And now if you go back to Premiere, and open the Ingest Settings, you can click on the Add Ingest Preset button to the right of the window, then navigate to your preset which is saved as a separate .EPR file on your hard drive. Adobe could really make this much easier, but even though it's a pain to set up, it's worth it if you have a lot of media to process.

Watch Folders

Sharing the Queue panel, under a separate tab, is the Watch Folders panel. Here you can designate folders for Media Encoder to monitor for new media that needs processing. Checking the box next to "Auto-Encode Watch Folders" will result in automatic processing of the contents of your watched folders. When you add a folder to the watch list, you can then select a preset to use when encoding the media.

Media Encoder Preferences

How Media Encoder functions is controlled by preferences, just like Premiere. You'll find them under the Edit (Win) or Media Encoder (Mac) menu and some of them will look very familiar. Most of the Media Encoder preferences have counterparts in Adobe Premiere, although they are spread around the seven Media Encoder preferences panels a little bit differently than in Premiere. You can refer back to the descriptions of Premiere preferences in Chapter 4 if you don't know what they do.

General preferences (Figure 5.7) control how Media Encoder works on a basic level. You can tell it to start encoding automatically, play a preview of each frame as it encodes, and notify you that it has finished encoding. The other options in this panel can vary depending on the type of media you are encoding and what type of computer hardware you are using. When you use

Media Encoder to encode a file, you have the option of adding metadata to the file and the metadata preferences are quite complex. Metadata is covered in Chapter 6, Media Management and Troubleshooting. Adding metadata to a clip is something you generally do when you are finishing a film, so that is discussed in Chapter 14.

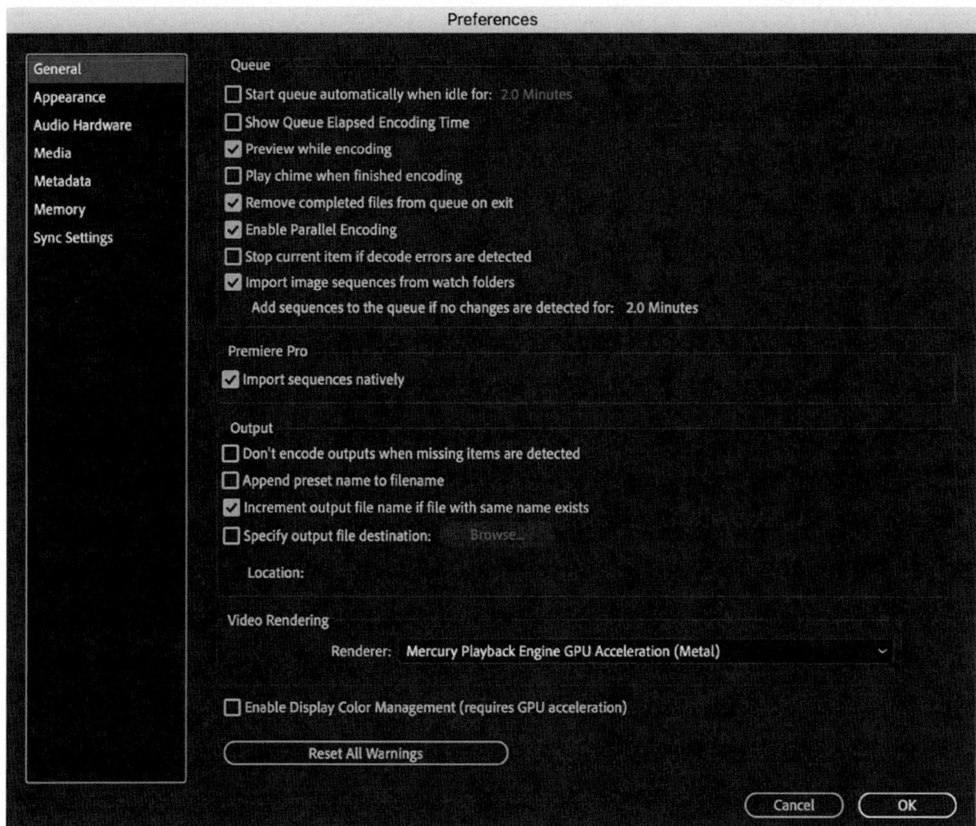

Figure 5.7

Media Encoder preferences look very similar to Premiere Pro preferences, but there are fewer of them and things are spread around a little differently.

4K or Larger Video Playback Settings

The bigger your media files, the more you'll need to rely on renders, proxies, and anything else that can enhance playback:

RAM settings (Preferences > Memory) Here is where you'll decide how much RAM to dedicate to Premiere Pro (most of it!) and how to optimize rendering (performance).

Video Previews (Sequence > Sequence settings) This portion of the Sequence settings window lets you choose the preview file format, aka the render format. Your choice depends on your hardware. If you have a top of the line system, you can select Maximum Bit Depth, Maximum Render Quality and Composite in Linear Color for better looking renders.

Render In to Out (Sequence > Render In to Out) Even if the render bar is yellow, meaning you don't need to render, let's be clear: you do when your video is 4K. If you really want optimized high-res playback, render first. Render In to Out will render your entire sequence or just the part selected by Ins and Outs if you have set them.

Turn off any background operations This isn't really a setting, per se, but you don't want to share processing power with any other application or background process, like Media Encoder.

Optimizing Premiere for Playback

A very smart assistant editor once said to me, "At the most basic level, my job is to make sure the cut plays back perfectly, every single day." She was right. There's much more to the job than that, but if that basic playback fails, so does everything else. The editor can't edit, the director can't direct, the people assembled can't watch the rough cut, and so on.

It might seem like getting video to play properly is so basic that it's not worth discussing, but an editorial project can force your computer to work at maximum processing power. And if your footage is very large—4K or more—even a top of the line computer may not be up to that challenge at times.

Premiere Pro accepts almost every kind of video you can imagine as native. There's nothing that it won't try to play. But will it succeed? Well, there are some things you can do to make that more likely.

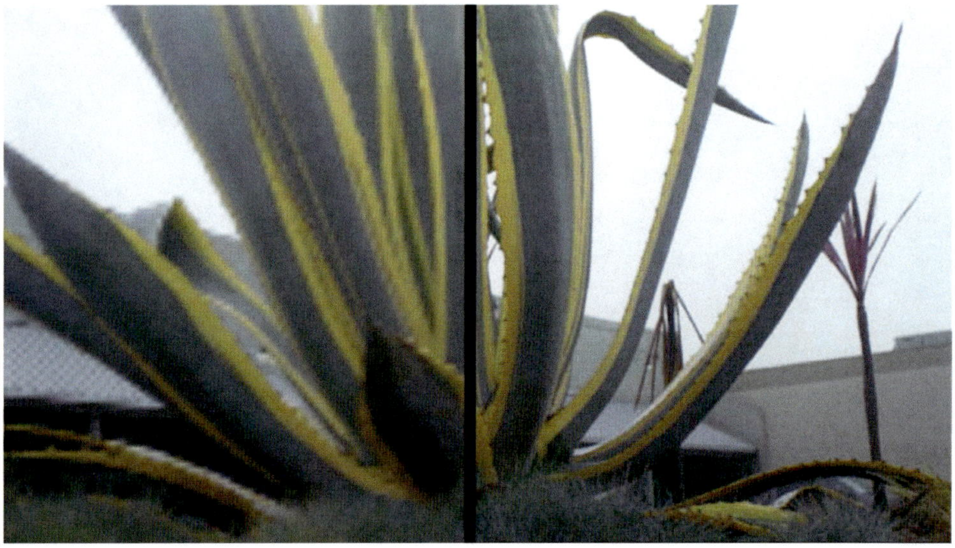

Figure 5.8

Full-resolution 4K video (right) and 1/8th resolution playback video (left). You can see the image quality is much lower in the sharpness of the plant and the lines on the roof to the left. And it looks much worse in moving video than it does in a still frame.

Playback Resolution

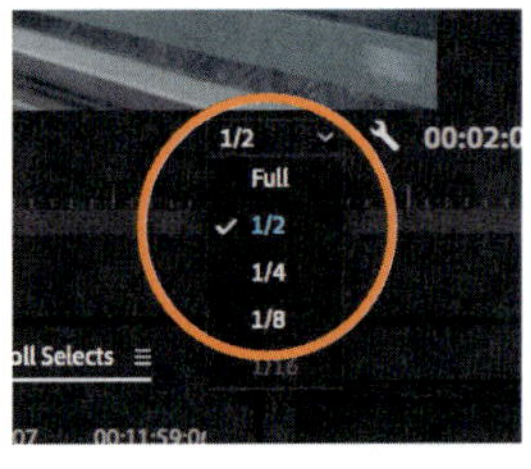

Figure 5.9

The playback resolution menu is in the lower right corner of the Source and Program monitors.

This is the easiest fix of all and it might be all you need (Figure 5.8). On the lower left side of the Program window (Figure 5.9), there is a little pop-up menu that lets you select the playback resolution. You can choose between full, half, quarter, eighth, and sixteenth. Even if your video is relatively small (1080 HD or 2K), that's still a lot of media for your processor to crunch through at the rate of 24 frames per second. Half or quarter resolution is a good choice here, depending on how powerful your computer is. Bear in mind that this resolution is for playback only. When you're parked on a frame, it will display a full-resolution image (unless you choose otherwise). Also, if you render your footage (we'll get to that in a minute), your footage will playback at the render quality you choose, which will override this setting.

Matching Sequence Settings to Media

If you only have one type of video in your film, another way to improve playback is to make sure that your sequence settings match the type of video that you're working with.

There's a super easy way to do this: just create a blank sequence and drop your footage into it. A dialogue box will open asking you if you want to change the settings or keep the existing settings. After you select Change Settings, your sequence and your media will match.

Unfortunately, if you have many types of video in your project, this won't work as well for you. Nevertheless, it can help to pick the most dominant type of footage that you have and set your sequence to match that one. (For more on mixing media in a sequence, check out Chapter 9.)

Thumbnails & Waveforms

Thumbnails and waveforms in the Timeline do not affect playback in theory, but they do affect overall speed and performance. Basically, anything that takes up extra processing power, such as redrawing thumbnails or waveforms as you play your sequence, can slow things down. I think audio waveforms can be really useful, video thumbnails not so much. After all, I can just look at the Program window to see what my shot looks like. Everyone has their own preference, but I recommend turning these off if you don't use them. They also take up hard drive space—not huge amounts but it can add up if you have a big project.

Flattening Your Sequence

If your project has lots of nested, multicam, or dynamic link sequences embedded in it, it may help to flatten them. Flattening means that each shot now resides in your current sequence and all references to nested or multicam source sequences are removed. Be aware that flattening is irreversible, so it's best to wait until you are closer to finishing your cut before you flatten anything. (Flattening nested and multicam sequences is covered in Chapter 14, Finishing.)

Rendering

Back in the 90s, rendering was a huge issue. You had to do it all the time just to be able to watch anything. Today, rendering is no longer required by any editing application. The fact is that Premiere works quite well without rendering but it works fantastically well if you do render. Render what? Anything with a colored indicator in the render bar of the Timeline (Figure 5.10).

When you have a sequence loaded in the Timeline in Premiere Pro, the render bar along the top of the Timeline tells you if your sequence is rendered or not. If your sequence settings perfectly match your footage and you haven't added any effects, it will be grey (matching the background) and that means there is nothing to render. Yellow means rendering is not required, red means rendering is required, and green means the media is rendered. But even the media that's marked yellow can still be rendered and playback will likely improve.

Another great thing about rendering in Premiere Pro: when you render a clip in one sequence, Premiere is smart enough to track it through your other sequences and reference the same render files, so you don't have to render the same shot multiple times and your hard drives won't get filled up with unnecessary extra render files.

Render Quality Settings

Premiere Pro renders your footage to match the settings of your sequence. If you have 4K footage in a 2K sequence, your renders will be 2K.

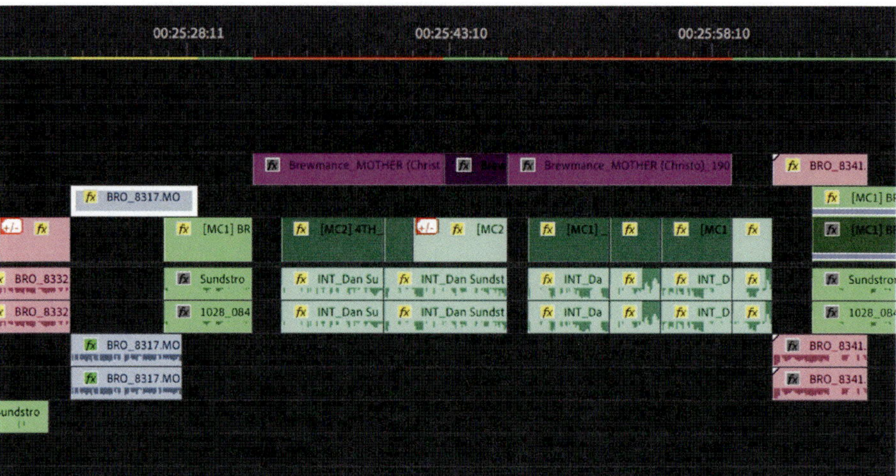

Figure 5.10

The Timeline render bar can be grey (nothing to render), green (rendered), yellow (not rendered and doesn't need to be), or red (render required).

Working with Proxies

You hear a lot about proxies these days, and with good reason. Premiere can work with so many types of footage, but the reality is that playing back all those formats in real-time can be a challenge for Premiere. In lieu of insisting that you transcode all your media to a single native format, which was how it worked in days of yore, Premiere allows you to bring in any format you like. And in order to improve performance, Premiere lets you create special low-resolution proxy files that are much less taxing for your computer to deal with. Proxies are more or less required for 4K (or larger) footage but even 2K and 1080 HD may benefit from them (Figure 5.11).

What is a Proxy?

Just as the name suggests, a proxy is a stand-in for high-quality video files. Everything is identical, except the resolution. Proxy files are much smaller and so these copies are easier for Premiere to play. They help Premiere perform better, especially if you have high-resolution originals.

Since proxies are just a copy, you can turn them off and play your original media at any time. A great thing about proxies in Premiere Pro is that once you decide to create them, they pretty much work invisibly. You won't see proxies in your Premiere bins, but they will exist as separate files on your hard drives.

Use Premiere and Media Encoder for Proxies

If you are going with a proxy-based workflow, stick with Premiere and Media Encoder to build your proxies (as opposed to something like DaVinci Resolve). It's not just easier, it actually adds functionality that you wouldn't get if you use another application. Specifically, you can turn proxies on and off with the click of a button inside Premiere.

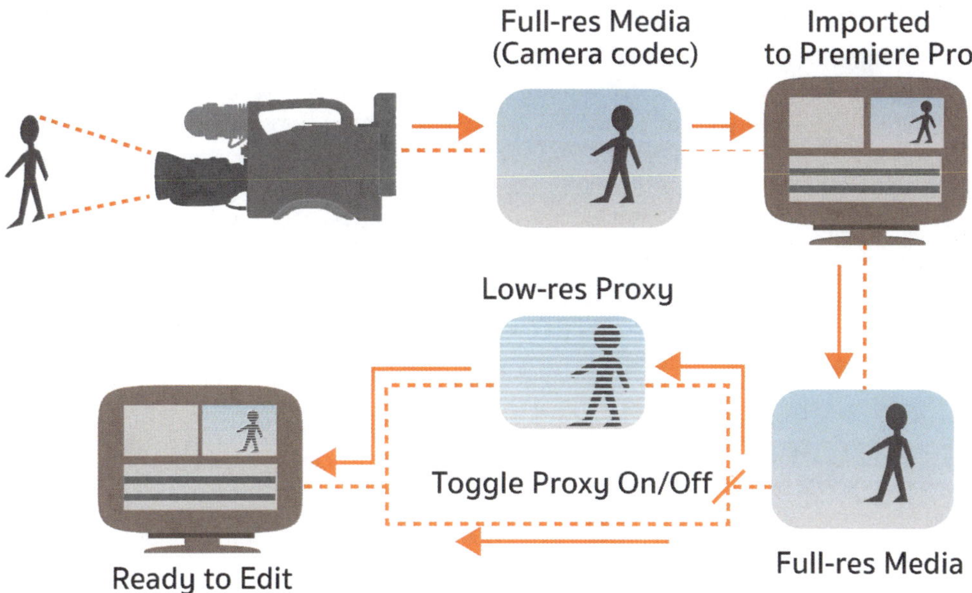

Figure 5.11

Full-resolution media and low-resolution proxies are interchangeable in Adobe Premiere.

How to Make Proxies

There are two ways to create proxies. You can create them automatically as you import footage, through the Ingest settings that we covered earlier, or you can create them later by right-clicking on a clip or group of clips and selecting Create Proxies from the menu. The Create Proxies window will open (Figure 5.12) and you'll have a choice of proxy presets to choose from. Here you can also add a custom ingest preset for your proxies that you created in Media Encoder, as explained earlier in this chapter. You'll have to select Add Ingest Preset and navigate to the preset file (.EPR) on your hard drive first.

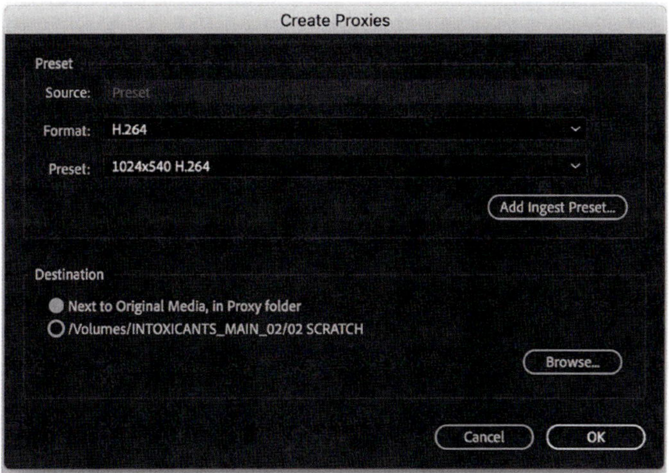

Figure 5.12

The Create Proxies dialogue window. You can use any preset you want but it's better if your proxy format has the same aspect ratio as your full-res media. The preset shown here has the same aspect ratio as 2K and 4K video.

What Type of Proxy Works Best?

Ultimately, the best proxy format is one that your computer can play without sputtering and the only way to know that is to make some test proxies and see how well they work. Keep in mind that while you can use any video format for your proxies, it will be better if the proxy format has the same aspect ratio as your original files. Otherwise, your image may get cropped, squeezed, or displayed with black areas along the edges of the frame. This may cause you to make false assessments about your film, like thinking a shot is framed poorly. In order to avoid that, follow these simple instructions:

- Proxies with the pixel dimensions of 1024 x 540 share the same aspect ratio as 2K (2048 x 1080), true 4K (4096 x 2160), 6K, and 8K.
- Proxies with the pixel dimension of 1280 x 720 share the same aspect ratio as HD (1920 x 1080) and UHD (3840 x 1080).

These are not the only aspect ratios out there, but they are the most common, especially for films.

So how bad (or good) do proxies look? If you have 4K footage and choose 1024 x 540 proxies, you're reducing it to 6% of the full resolution. That's a big reduction—you're likely to see posterization and other visual artifacts while playing. Then again, the Program monitor only takes up about 20% of the screen when you're editing. So unless you really need to watch your cut in full-frame mode all the time, the resulting proxy playback will generally seem much better than 6%.

When you want to watch full frame, for a screening or just because, use the Toggle Proxies button (Figure 5.13) to turn the proxies off so you can watch full frame and full res. Just beware that you may need to render it to get good playback, especially if it's 4K.

 **Film Math**

Remember when you were in high school math class and said, perhaps only to yourself, "I'm never gonna use this." Well, you were wrong. Filmmakers use math all the time. Aspect ratios are, you know, mathematic ratios. You can arrive at this ratio by dividing the width of a frame of film (say, 1920) by its height (1080). 1.78:1 can also be expressed as 16:9. Old school TV and films were 4:3 or 1.33 and 2K is 1.85.

Where to Store Proxies on Your Hard Drives

Like all things Premiere, you get to choose where your proxies are saved. There are two schools of thought on this. The first is to save your proxies next to your footage, i.e., in your dailies or camera card folders. The second is to put all your proxies into one folder, so that they can easily be moved around.

The first method works well for big, complicated projects. You'll always be able to find your proxies because they're right next to your raw footage. The second method works for smaller projects and is especially great for people who use laptops. You can copy all your proxies onto your laptop hard drive and take it on a plane with you. Either way, performance is always best on dedicated media drives, rather than your main hard drive.

Attaching and Removing Proxies

Sometimes proxies go missing, which is to say that Premiere Pro loses the link between the proxy and your master clips. As long as the proxies are still on your drive (likely), you can simply re-attach them to your media. Use the right-click menu to select Proxies > Attach Proxies.

If you are done with proxies, you can choose to remove them from your workflow. Select the clips you want to change, then right-click and select Proxies > Reconnect Full Resolution Media. This is a more permanent way to turn off the proxies. You'll no longer be able to use the Toggle Proxies button to bring them back. But unless you delete them, the proxy files will still be available on your media drives if you wish to reconnect them.

The Toggle Proxies Button

Premiere has a button called Toggle Proxies and it appears blue when you have proxies turned on and white when they are off. Probably you'll just leave them on all the time, but by moving this button to the area at the bottom of the Program monitor, you'll be able to confirm that fact at a glance. Go to the + (plus) icon at the bottom right of the Program window and click on it to open the Button Editor (Figure 5.13). Here you will find a bunch of buttons that you can add or remove from the row of buttons. Highlight the Toggle Proxies icon, drag it to a spot in the row of buttons, and select "Ok."

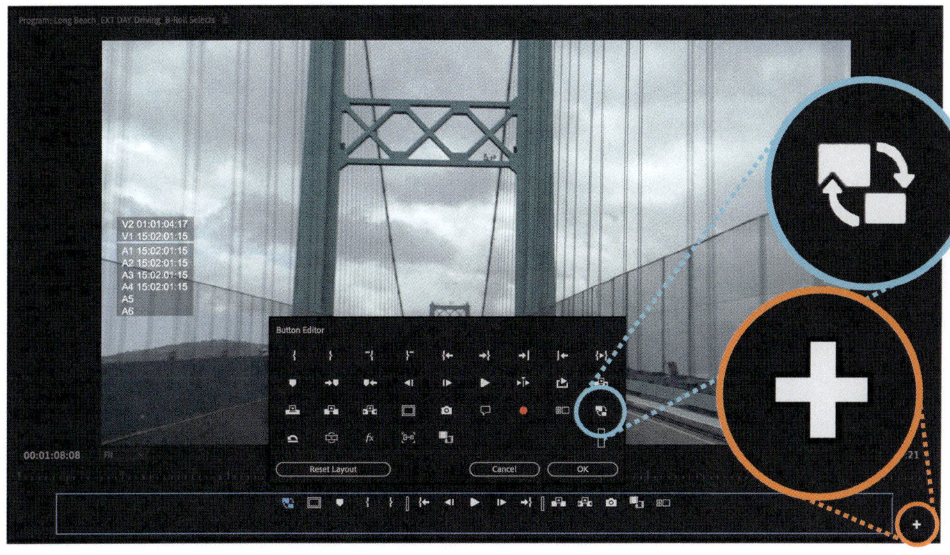

Figure 5.13

Click on the plus sign icon at the lower left corner of your Program monitor to bring up the Button Editor. Drag the Toggle Proxies button down to the row of buttons on the bottom of the Program monitor. When the button is blue, proxies are on.

Technical Problems to Solve

As you gather the media from your film and bring it into Premiere, here are some things to ask yourself:

> **What is the best way to organize your raw media so that you can always find what you need?** Dailies folders are best for feature films. Other types of projects may find that organizing content by subject matter works better—like if you have a documentary project with lots of archival media.

How will you handle small screenings? Even if you're the only person working on your film, you're going to want to screen it during the editing process. That screening might be a friend, a trusted advisor, or maybe you just take off your editor hat and put on your producer hat and sit in the back of the room. Whatever the case, you'll need to make some choices as to how you want to view the film. Full-screen is, of course, the recommended way to watch a film, so given that, what technical preparations will you make to ensure that it plays properly?

At what point(s) will you go back to high-res? If you're working with proxies, or using a lower-resolution playback setting, at what point will you stop working in low-resolution and switch to high? Some filmmakers may plan to wait until the very end, because their computers just can't handle large video. But even if that's the case, you can make a full-resolution export and play it on another system. It's important to remember that some problems with your media may not be as noticeable if you're working at low or proxy resolutions—very slightly out of focus shots, smudges on lenses, details within the shot itself such as the leg of a tripod in a shot or (famously) a Starbucks coffee cup in the background of shot in *Game of Thrones*. Viewing your film at full-resolution from time to time is an important part of the editing process.

6

Media Management and Troubleshooting

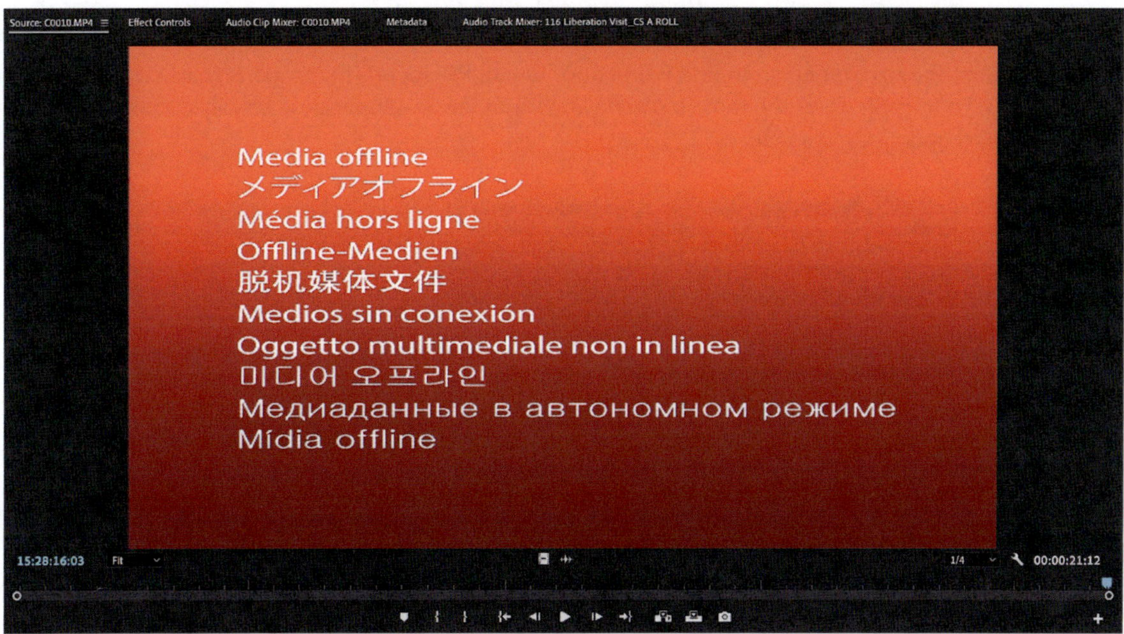

Figure 6.1

Missing, or offline, media is one of many issues you may encounter while editing in Premiere.

Media Management in Premiere

If you're creating small projects, like the ones for the tutorials in this book, you probably won't need to worry about media management. But the bigger your project, the more likely you'll need to perform complex operations along the way. Maybe you decided to add a second editor to take on some of the work, so you have to figure out how you're going to share the project and media. Or you have technical problems and some of your media goes offline and has to be restored from a backup (Figure 6.1).

Whatever the reason, it's good to know the nuts and bolts of how Premiere works and what to do if something goes wrong. The last chapter dealt with getting media into Premiere, this chapter provides a deeper understanding of how it works once it's inside Premiere.

Master clips

We started this book by explaining the key components of the Premiere interface, one of them being clips, or media. But there's a bit more to it. When you work in Premiere, you can duplicate clips into different bins, or save truncated versions of them (aka subclips), and you can edit them into as many sequences as you wish. So how does Premiere keep track of all that and how does it prioritize your actions as you edit? For example, if you change a clip, how does Premiere decide whether or not to change other iterations of the clip in your project?

The first time you bring a piece of media into a project, Premiere determines that piece of media to be a *master clip*. Master clips can be any type of media that you bring into Premiere—video from a camera, still images, audio, VR, or an animated sequence. These are the clips that act as pointers to your "real" media on your hard drives and Premiere uses a unique identifier to tie that master clip to the media on your hard drive. Once tied together, it's very hard to break this link. If you move your media from one hard drive to another, you might have to point Premiere in the right direction to find it, but once found, Premiere will recognize it and restore it across your project, in all those possible iterations of it—duplicates, subclips, clips edited into sequences, and so on.

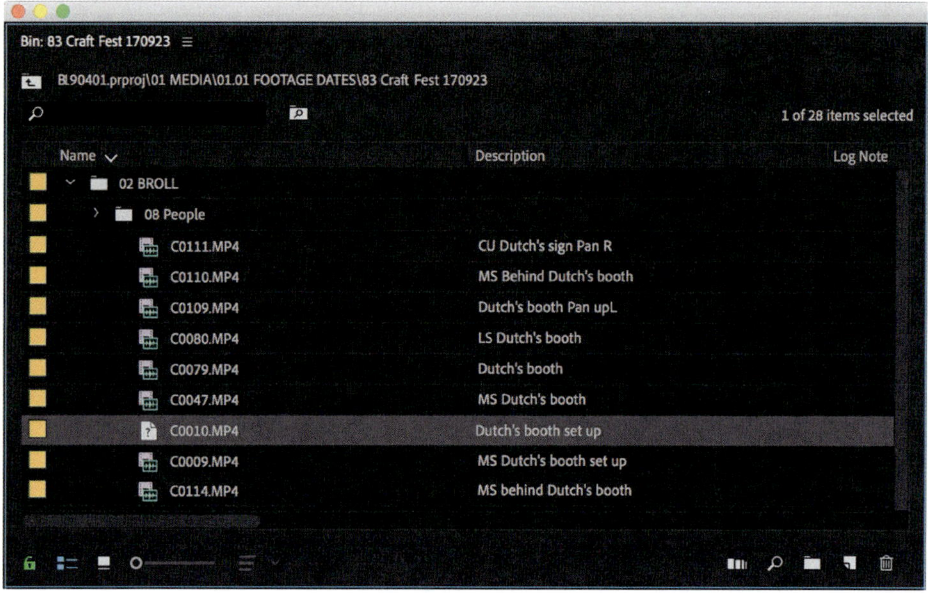

Figure 6.2

In bin List View, the clip icon is replaced with a question mark when media is offline.

So what does this mean for your workflow?

As a rule, any change done to a master clip in a bin ripples through all the other iterations of that clip in your project. So you will want to be careful to only make changes to master clips that you want to change globally. What kind of changes are we talking about? Anything you can do to a clip—adding markers, audio level changes, resizing, speed adjustments, color grading, and so on. (We haven't gotten into these topics yet but we're about to, going forward in the rest of the book.) So just to be very clear, we're talking about changes to the master clips in the bin, not clips that are edited into sequences. You can make all the changes you want to clips once you've edited them into a sequence without fear of accidentally changing something in another part of the project.

So why would you want to change a master clip then?

Global Changes

Sometimes, you do want to make changes that affect every iteration of a clip in your project. For example, if you shot with log color, you might want to add color effects to every single clip to make them look "normal" while you're working. Or if you're editing HD footage into an 2K sequence, you might want to globally adjust the size to avoid pillarboxing. As a rule, changing your master clips this way is a fairly advanced decision—the sort of thing a post-supervisor might dictate as part of the process of ingesting media on a big show. For most smaller projects, including feature films with one editor, this is something you'll decide to do as the need occurs. And when the changes you want to make are not global, or spanning large swaths of your media, then you really have no good reason to change the master clips. Instead, you'll just change the clips in your sequence.

Keep a Set of Clean Master Clips

The best workflow for most projects is to make a set of bins for master clips and set them aside as source bins that you won't change during the editing of your film. Feature film editors usually make a single bin for all the footage and fill it with sub-bins for each shoot day. The master clips will remain there for the duration of the project and although they'll get used constantly, they won't change them in any intrinsic way. If it's a scripted film, they'll also make a new set of bins organized by scene using duplicates of the master clips. Since the elements of a scene might be shot across different days, copies of all those shots can be pulled into a single bin for each scene. If it's not a scripted film, you might make secondary bins based on topic or some other organizing principle. This is the set of media that you'll use as you work.

The result is two major bins that act as directories for your media—dailies bins that are a resource for all the original footage as it was shot and work bins, which are organized by various needs during the course of editing the movie. Why all this caution? It's always good to have a clean version of your original clips, even if they're just "pointer" files. If your media goes offline, rather than hunting around you'll know exactly where it is.

Linking and Locating Media

Media goes offline. It just happens. Sometimes it's due to issues with a drive. Sometimes it's operator error. Sometimes Premiere just seems to lose the link—especially in the case of proxies. But whatever the reason, you'll need to get it back online.

If media goes offline unexpectedly, Premiere will let you know—you'll get a Locate Media window and as long as your media is still on your drives, you'll be able to easily guide Premiere in the right direction to search for it.

If you're looking through bins for offline media, it's easy to spot in List view: the master clip icon is replaced with a question mark icon when media is offline (Figure 6.2). But be aware that the question mark icon is also used when Premiere has not fully loaded the media for a project.

Make Offline vs Delete Media

Sometimes, you actually want your media to be offline. There are many reasons why you might want to remove media from your project. Perhaps it was temporary footage, such as rough animatics for a special effects sequence, and you no longer need it. Or it's something else that you no longer think is useful.

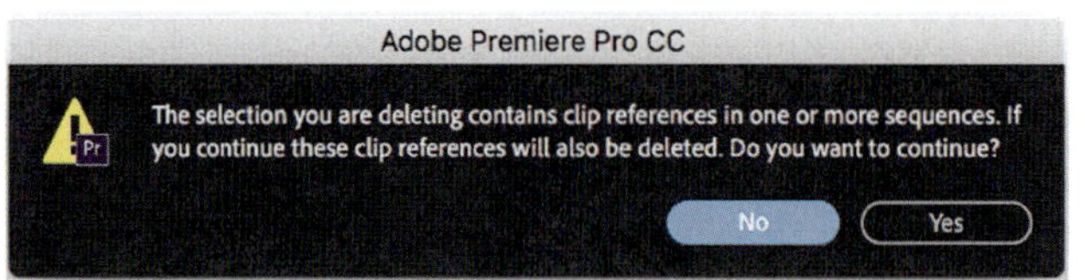

Figure 6.3

If you try to delete media that's been used in a sequence, you'll get this message asking you to confirm your decision.

It might seem natural to select a clip and hit Delete, but that's really not a great way to go about it. Yes, you'll successfully remove the clip from your project, but you'll also remove all traces of it. If it was used in a sequence, you'll see a black hole where it used to be. No data will remain and this will be irreversible. In fact, you'll see this warning message (Figure 6.3) from Adobe asking you if you really want to do this. The answer is no, you do not.

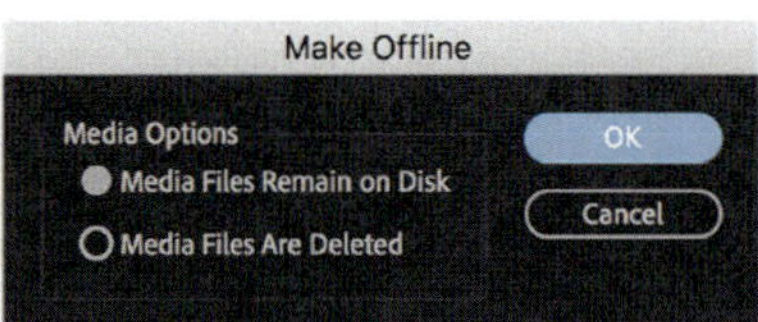

Figure 6.4

When you make media offline, you can choose between deleting the source files from your hard drive or leaving them intact.

By far, the best way to remove unwanted files from your project is the Make Offline command, found in the right-click clip menu. Make Offline removes the media from your project but keeps all the information about that media intact. When you choose Make Offline, you'll be given the choice between keeping the media on your hard drives or deleting it (Figure 6.4). Media Files Remain on Disk is the safe choice because it doesn't delete any of your actual media files, so you can always restore them. Then, if the media was used in a sequence, you'll see the offline media highlighted in red (Figure 6.5) and the source monitor will display the red "media offline" warning (Figure 6.1).

For me, the only time I would choose to actually delete the media from my hard drives is when I'm consolidating a project that's completely finished, for the purpose of archiving it. Even then, I would chose making media offline instead of deleting it, so that the project could be reconstructed at a later date if necessary. Also, if you just want to temporarily hide media in a sequence, I suggest disabling clips (Clip > Enable).

? Offline and Online Media

Offline is computer-speak for unavailable media. It could be unavailable because it doesn't exist on your hard drives, or because the link from the master clip in Premiere to the actual file on your hard drive was disrupted, whether by choice or by accident, or because you moved or renamed the media. *Online* means the media is available and linked to the master clips in Premiere.

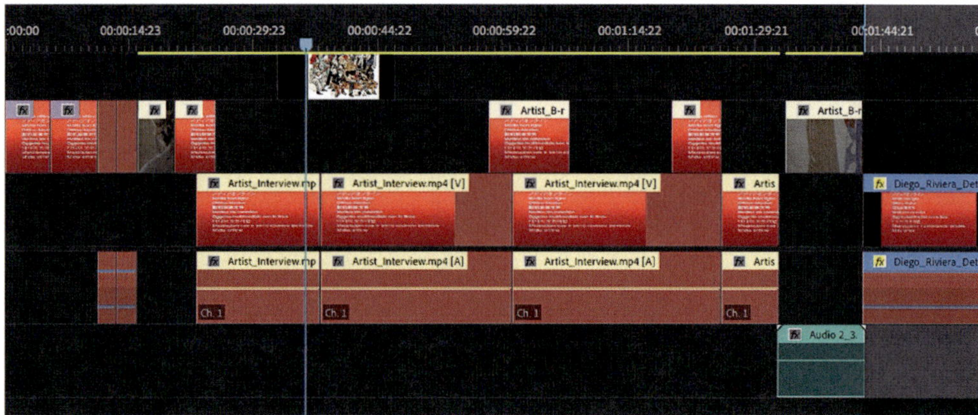

Figure 6.5

Offline media is displayed with red highlighting in the Timeline, so that you can see it at a glance.

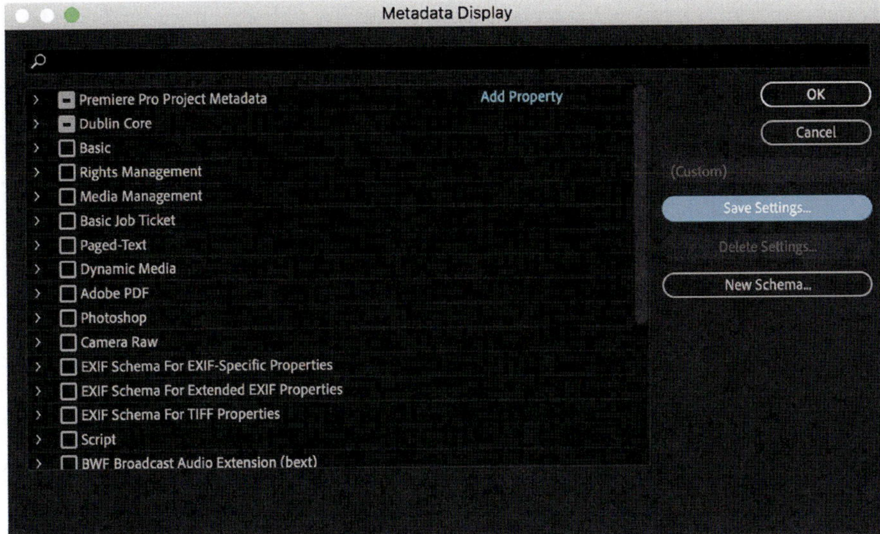

Figure 6.6

Metadata Display options including Premiere Pro Project Metadata and other popular metadata sets like Dublin Core and Dynamic Media.

Metadata

Everyone talks about metadata, but what is it? It actually sounds a lot more complicated than it is. Metadata is information about any digital file that is stored within the file itself. As far as video and audio files are concerned, the metadata usually includes all of the media specifications (container file type, codec, frame rate, etc.) that we discussed in Chapter 4. Because metadata can be just about anything, it can also include information such as copyright ownership, keywords, and much more. Metadata is grouped into different sets based on the type of information they contain and Premiere gives you access to many of these sets (Figure 6.6), but the ones most filmmakers find useful are the Premiere Pro Project Metadata, Dynamic Media, and Dublin Core (copyright and ownership info).

Premiere Pro Project Metadata

The Premiere Pro Project Metadata set is unique because it only works within Premiere and it translates directly to the bin column headings when you set your bin to List view. It includes many headings useful to filmmakers (Figure 6.7).

To add or remove columns in bin List view, open the panel settings menu for the bin and navigate to Metadata Display (Figure 6.6). Spin down the arrow next to Premiere Pro Project Metadata (first in the list) and you'll see all the possible column headings that you can add or

Name ^	Video Usag	Audio Usa	Media Start	Media End	Media Duratio	Video Duratio	Video Info	Audio Info	Tape Name	Log Not
A140C071_17091748.MXF	1	4	22:55:42:16	22:56:19:03	00:00:36:12	00:00:36:12	4096 x 2160 (	48000 Hz -	A145	audio c
A140C072_170917ZJ.MXF	1	8	22:56:33:00	23:01:30:23	00:04:58:00	00:04:58:00	4096 x 2160 (	48000 Hz -	A145	Boom c
A140C073_170917OZ.MXF	2	8	23:04:10:12	23:04:51:19	00:00:41:08	00:00:41:08	4096 x 2160 (	48000 Hz -	A145	
A140C076_170917EA.MXF	1	4	23:07:03:12	23:07:26:11	00:00:23:00	00:00:23:00	4096 x 2160 (	48000 Hz -	A145	
A140C077_1709172H.MXF	2	8	23:09:46:08	23:10:19:19	00:00:33:12	00:00:33:12	4096 x 2160 (	48000 Hz -	A145	
A140C078_170917II.MXF	2					00:00:33:04	4096 x 2160 (	48000 Hz -	A145	
A140C079_170917LZ.MXF	2					00:01:32:20	4096 x 2160 (	48000 Hz -	A145	
A140C080_170917G5.MXF	1	4	23:15:30:16	23:16:28:23	00:00:58:08	00:00:58:08	4096 x 2160 (	48000 Hz -	A145	
A140C081_1709172C.MXF	2	8	23:16:35:04	23:20:04:07	00:03:29:04	00:03:29:04	4096 x 2160 (	48000 Hz -	A145	
A142C009_1709168P.MXF	2	8	11:37:03:20	11:41:26:03	00:04:22:08	00:04:22:08	4096 x 2160 (	48000 Hz -	A142	
A142C010_170916JE.MXF	2	4	11:42:38:12	11:52:04:15	00:09:26:04	00:09:26:04	4096 x 2160 (	48000 Hz -	A142	
A142C011_170916LB.MXF	2	8	11:52:12:04	11:53:04:19	00:00:52:16	00:00:52:16	4096 x 2160 (	48000 Hz -	A142	
A142C012_170916YP.MXF	3	12	11:53:14:00	11:54:07:07	00:00:53:08	00:00:53:08	4096 x 2160 (	48000 Hz -	A142	
A142C013_1709169K.MXF	3	12	11:54:15:08	12:03:10:15	00:08:55:08	00:08:55:08	4096 x 2160 (	48000 Hz -	A142	
A142C014_17091690.MXF	3	12	12:03:38:20	12:04:07:19	00:00:29:00	00:00:29:00	4096 x 2160 (	48000 Hz -	A142	
A142C015_170916CU.MXF	2	8	12:04:20:16	12:11:01:03	00:06:40:12	00:06:40:12	4096 x 2160 (	48000 Hz -	A142	
A142C016_170916CY.MXF	2	8	12:11:10:00	12:14:59:11	00:03:49:12	00:03:49:12	4096 x 2160 (	48000 Hz -	A142	

A140C072_170917WT.MXF Multicam : A140C077_1709172H.MXF : 23:09:46:06
A140C072_170917WT.MXF79 Multicam : A140C077_1709172H.MXF : 00:13:13:06

Figure 6.7

Metadata columns shown in bin List View. Note that a popup menu in the Audio and Video Usage columns offers links to the sequences where each clip is used, which is very convenient.

remove from your bin. Once added, you can drag the column headings around to change the order to suit your preference.

Because the Premiere Pro Project Metadata set only really functions within Premiere, it's not that useful if you're hoping to share metadata across various apps. For that, you'll need to use the other metadata sets, and the most useful of these is the Dynamic Media set. Originally developed for audio editing, you'll now find that it covers the same type of info as the Premiere Pro Metadata set. But the difference is that this metadata is stored in your files on your hard drives, not in your Premiere project. So if you add log notes or keywords, these will translate to other apps as long as they can read metadata.

We're hoping that in the future, Premiere Pro Project Metadata will behave like "real" metadata. For now, Premiere Pro Project Metadata is just internal information—useful but misleading in its capabilities to interact with the world beyond the boundaries of Premiere Pro. As is, it's a fancy name for bin column headings.

Sorting Bins in List View

In addition to giving you an overview of the media specification for each clip in a bin, the metadata display columns (aka, bin headings) give you control over how each bin is sorted. Sorting by file name is an obvious choice, especially if your footage is named by scene and take numbers, but you can sort any column that you have active. The labels column (Figure 6.8) is a great choice. If you've organized your footage with colored labels (Edit > Label), clicking on this unnamed column to the left of the Name column will sort by label color. You might also find it helpful to sort by duration, especially with music bins, organizing cues from short too long. And of course you can create your own organizing methods using the Log Notes, Comments, and Description columns.

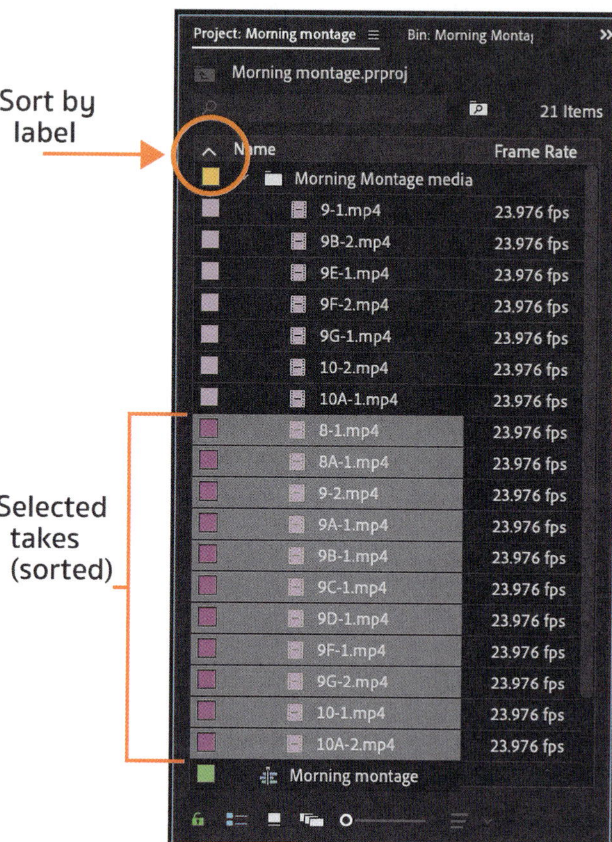

Figure 6.8

Select the label column, which is a blank space on the left side of the header (circled here), to sort clips by label in bin List View.

Media Encoder and Metadata

When you use Media Encoder to encode a file, you have the option of adding metadata to it. A very common reason would be to add copyright ownership information to each file. In Media Encoder Preferences open the Metadata panel—here you can choose to embed the metadata in the media file itself or store it in a special XMP sidecar file that is completely separate from the media file. There are many, many standardized metadata sets—some are for medical records, others are for the licensing of creative works, etc.—so the Preservation Rules menu lets you decide which metadata sets to include (Preserve All) or exclude. And the Output File Metadata menu lets you create a custom metadata template.

XMP Sidecar Files

In general, metadata is stored within each media file. But sometimes there's a need to store it separately. Some media file formats, like MXF, do not allow Premiere or Media Encoder to annotate the original file. Or maybe it's just better for your workflow to have it separate. Whatever the reason, if that's the case, the metadata is stored in a file called a sidecar that uses the Extensible Metadata Platform (XMP). This file rides along with the primary media file just like a sidecar on a motorcycle. If you delete the XMP sidecar file, your media will be fine but you'll lose the metadata.

Working with Timecode

Every frame of video has a unique number associated with it, known as timecode. You can navigate to any timecode in a shot by typing that number using your keyboard when you have the Source monitor activated. Every sequence also has timecode for each frame, so you can also type in the timecode with the Program or Timeline window activated. Navigating by timecode can be very useful if you have a script or transcript that includes timecode. It's also a great for taking notes.

If you rely on timecode a lot, you can choose to display timecode overlays in the Source and Program monitors. This option is found in the wrench tool menu at the lower right of each monitor panel. By default, timecode overlays are only visible when the video is paused (Figure 6.9). but they can be modified to continue to display during playback in the Overlay Settings (wrench icon).

You can also view timecode in a larger window (Window > Timecode) as your sequence plays, which is very helpful if you're taking notes.

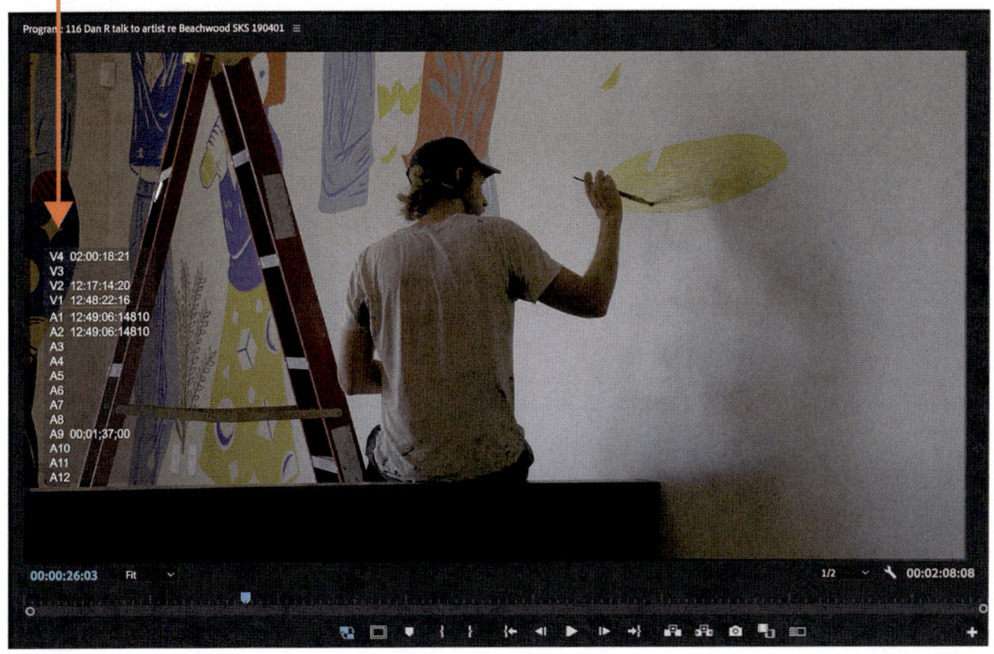

Figure 6.9

Timecode overlays in the Program monitor can be very useful. They are only visible when playback is paused.

Finding Media in Premiere

If you've only ever worked on short films and web videos, the idea that you might not be able to find a shot sounds ridiculous. But if you're making a feature doc or series with a shooting ratio of 100 to 1, it's a different story. That's a hundred hours of footage for every hour that ends up on screen. Or how about 1000 to 1? I've worked on more than one project like this. Even a traditional scripted feature, at 10 to 1 still means many, many shots and takes.

The bigger your project, the harder it can be to keep track of everything. Luckily, Premiere has several tools to help you find media.

Match Frame Bar none, this is one of the best tools in editing. At any point in your sequence, you can select Sequence > Match Frame and the shot that contains that frame will load in the Source monitor. It's also programmed to the F key.

Reverse Match Frame Although you won't use it as frequently as Match Frame, Reverse Match Frame can really come in handy. Basically, you park your cursor on any frame in the Source monitor and hit Reverse Match Frame (Sequence > Reverse Match Frame) and Premiere will take you to every instance that frame occurs in any of your sequences. Just hit Reverse Match Frame multiple times to skip through your various cuts. If you're trying to find where a shot was used, for example temporary elements that you want to replace, then Reverse Match Frame will help you find all occurrences of it.

Audio and Video Usage Columns are available in List view in any bin (Figure 6.7). Go to Window > Metadata, then select Metadata Display from the bin Panel Settings menu and open Premiere Pro Project Metadata from the Metadata Display window (Figure 6.6) to show the list of columns and add Audio Usage and Video Usage to your display. If a clip was used in any sequence, a number will appear in the column indicating the number of sequences it's been edited into. Click on the number and a menu opens with links to every sequence. The only downside is that if your media is synchronized into multicam sequences, these will show up here as well. But as long as you know that, you can ignore them.

Reveal in Project Sometimes you need to find the bin that contains a shot. You can right-click on any frame in your sequence or source clip and a menu will come up that offers Reveal in Project as an option. Selecting this will open the bin and highlight the clip in your project panel.

Reveal in Finder/Explorer You can select any master clip in your project, source monitor, or Timeline and use the right-click menu to get to the Reveal in Explorer or Finder command. Premiere will then open the folder on your hard drive containing the source media.

Searches You can search in the Project panel or in any bin. At the top of each panel is a magnifying glass and an entry field. You can enter any text and the bin will sort to show only items that match that text. There's also an icon that shows a folder with a magnifying glass on it—click on that and the Create Search Bin will open up (Figure 6.10). Here you can enter search criteria and save the results in a special bin. This bin will get updated if you add media to your project that fits your search criteria. You'll be able to set up search terms using any type of metadata used in your bin. Last but not least, you can use the Find command (Edit > Find) to search across your entire project.

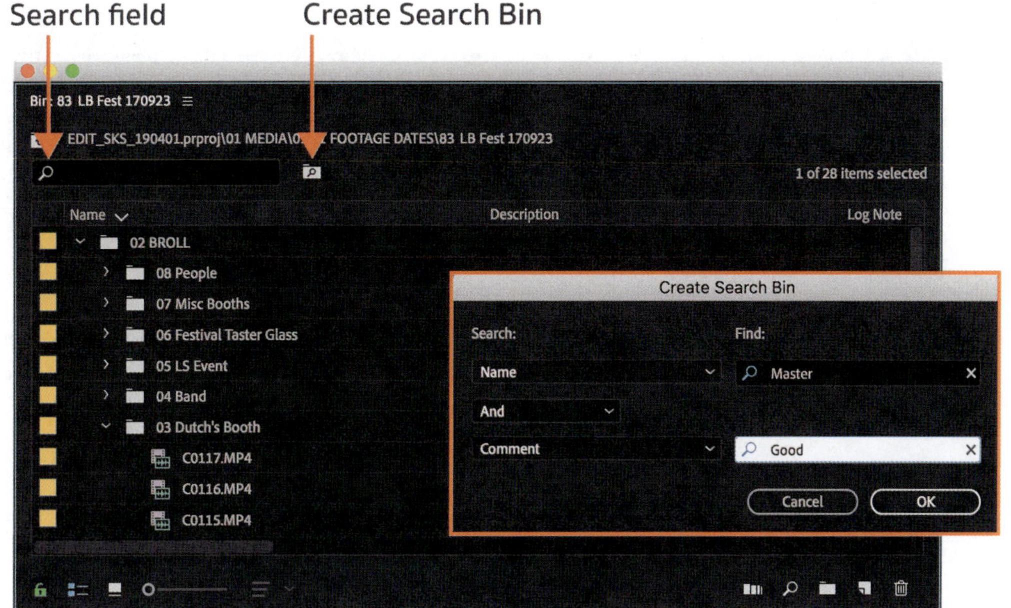

Figure 6.10

Search bins update automatically as new media is added to your project.

Backing Up

Every editor finds their own way of organizing and backing up their work because every editor has the experience of losing work. And relying on Auto-save is great, but sometimes it's easier to find stuff if you saved it yourself.

Here's how I do it:

I'm a big fan of manually backing up my project and renaming it every day. Basically in addition to the name of the film, I add the date in the format *yyyy/mm/dd*. Every day when I get to work, I use File > Save As and update the date.

What's the point of this? Well, basically it means I have a new project file every day, so if there's corruption in the project file I can work backwards through however many days until I get to one that works. Yes, you can just go through the auto-saves and achieve the same result, but there are many auto-saves per day (depending on your preferences settings), so it's a lot faster to have one main backup project per day. I rely on auto-saves more for immediate recovery from an unexpected crash.

In addition to backing up your project manually on a daily basis, it's also a good idea to back it up on cloud-based storage system such as Dropbox or the Adobe Creative Cloud. If your computer implodes and sets the office on fire, you're still gonna have a file that can be recreated with your cloud-based project backup and your off-site media backup drives—because of course you also have a backup set of your media drives stored at another location. Right?

Backing up within your project

I also back up whatever sequence I'm working on within the project on a daily basis. Sometimes it's just a scene, sometimes it's a rough cut of a whole movie. Just like I do with the Project file, I add the date to the end of the name of every sequence. Every day, I copy it into an "old cuts" bin and rename the one in my 'current cuts" bin to match today's date.

When I go back through these bins, I can follow a chronological trail of what I was working on. This works as a mnemonic device to help me find stuff. I'll see a week where I was building string-outs of the final scenes of the film and remember that it was around that time that I added or deleted this or that element of the film.

All this backing up might sound tedious, but eventually it will become a rote task, kinda like making coffee. You get to the office, open the project, Save As, find your sequence, dupe it (Command + D), rename it, done. Don't even think about it.

Troubleshooting

Unfortunately, problems occur with every editing system and Premiere Pro is no exception. Most crashes in Premiere have to do with an overtaxed system. But what part of your system is overtaxed?

Is it a crash or a hang? Premiere seems to get hung up a lot, and these hangs can last up to 10 minutes, but then it recovers. Restarting would ultimately take longer (as you wait for media to reload, etc.) so you may prefer to wait it out. You can check the Activity monitor (Mac) or Task Manager (Win) to see how dire things are. Mac users can also step out to the application switcher (Command + Tab) where, for certain tasks, you'll see a tiny progress bar at the bottom of the Premiere Pro icon (Figure 6.11). Identifying a true crash vs. a hang is difficult but I've found that most of the time, it's just a hang.

Figure 6.11

The Premiere Pro icon in the Mac OS application switcher displays a tiny, unintuitively-placed, progress bar that can help you determine whether or not Premiere is crashed or hard at work. Shown here a task is about 10% completed.

Is Premiere performing a background task such as exporting or generating Peak files (Figure 6.12). These tasks take up a lot of RAM and will definitely affect playback. It's best to wait until they are finished if you want good playback. There's a blue bar in the lower righthand corner of the screen that's active while media is loading, so keep an eye on that. When it disappears, you're good to go.

Is your media fully loaded? If you have a large project or slow drives, it might take Premiere a few minutes to get everything loaded when you launch the application. You'll see the gold Media Pending placeholder image in the Source or Program monitor, instead of your footage (Figure 6.13). It's best to wait until Premiere is done loading before you start trying to work, because this process requires a lot of RAM and Premiere is prone to crashing if you ask it to do too much at this time.

Figure 6.12

Premiere uses Peak files to help display audio waveform data. Generating them can take a lot of time when you first add media to a project. You will see this blue progress bar in the lower right corner of the Timeline when Peak files are being generated.

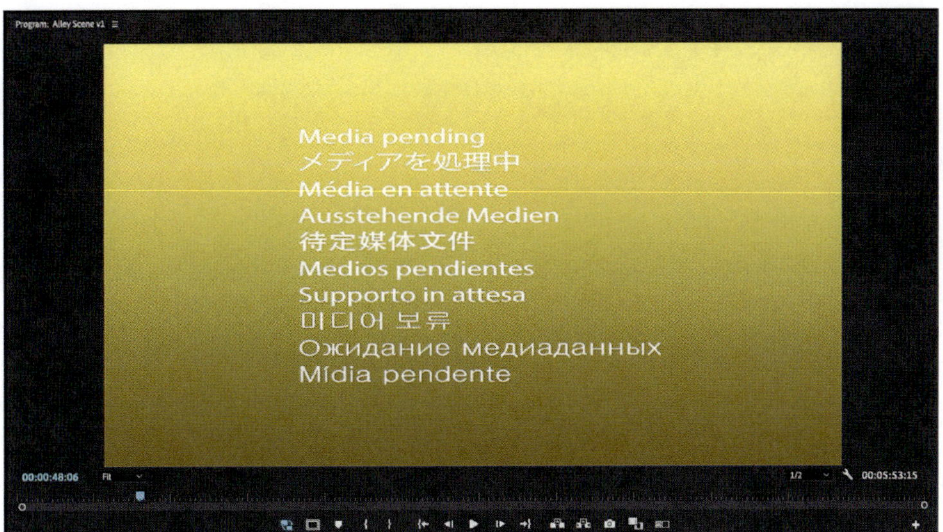

Figure 6.13

Adobe Premiere will display this placeholder image if it's not done loading your media. The best thing to do is wait. If you're bored, you can see if you can identify all the languages on this screen.

Is your hardware overloaded? Make sure that you have enough RAM, hard drive space on your main drive for application memory, and disk space on your media drives. At the very least, you should have 20% of your main hard drive free for application memory and your media drives should never be more than 90% full. The recommended minimum speed for media hard drives is 7200 rpm. Solid state drives (SSD) perform better than older types of drives. Fast drives won't help you if they are connected to your computer by slow cables, like standard USB.

Is it time for a software upgrade? Adobe upgrades Premiere Pro with alarming frequency. But their upgrades really do seem to fix common problems. It's recommended that you avoid upgrading mid-project, but on a long project that might be impossible. As always, back up your current project and save a copy of the older version of Premiere as well—make sure that you have a path back before you start the upgrade.

Is part of your media missing? Sometimes media gets changed after it's been edited into a sequence, for example you used Clip > Interpret Footage to change the frame rate and now the clip is shorter than it was when you edited it into your cut. If this is the case, Premiere will display a cross-hatched pattern on the clip, which indicates partially missing media (Figure 6.14). I've also seen this happen when the wrong proxies get attached to clips (due to duplicated file names which happens with certain cameras).

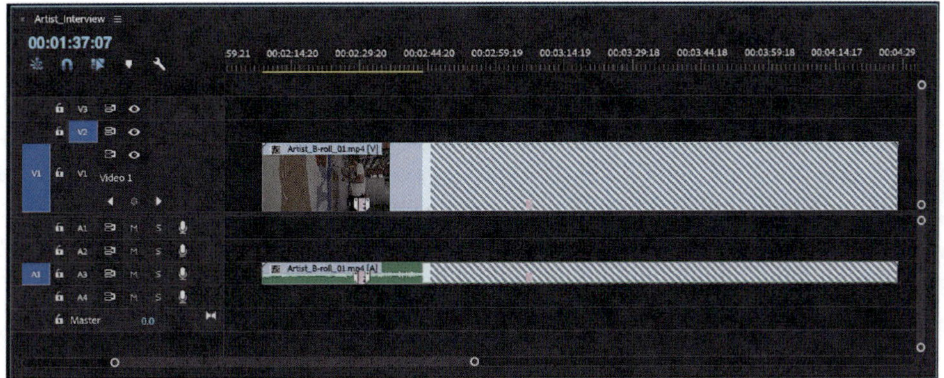

Figure 6.14

Partial media is indicated with crosshatching in the Timeline. When playing these clips, the part that's present will play normally and the crosshatched area will play as black.

⚠ Never Quit Premiere

Kidding, sort of. The truth is, quitting and restarting Premiere always seems to cause some trouble, even if it's just that you have to relocate a bunch of files you already located ten times or wait 20 minutes while the peak files rebuild. If you've got it up and running and it's working great, my advice is keep it on—I often go weeks between restarts.

Is your project file too big? Project files do not contain media, so they remain relatively small, often less than 100 MB. But the bigger your film and the longer you work on it, the bigger your project file can get. I've found that keeping them under 200 MB is best. What causes a project file to get bloated? Everything you create in Premiere Pro is a separate "object" for Premiere to keep track of and store as part of the project file—that includes every bin, clip, effect, music cue, adjustment clip, graphic, sequence, and so on. Other applications split some of these out into separate files, but Premiere keeps them all in a single project file. You might easily create 100 new items in a productive day of editing and over time this can add up. In addition, if you are sharing projects with editors on other systems that aren't sharing media on a networked server, Premiere will create lots of duplicate media (even if you ask it not to in the Preferences). More on duplicates and sharing later in this chapter.

Corrupt ancillary files Premiere Pro makes a lot of secondary files that get saved on your hard drive and they can get corrupted, especially over a long period of editing. Preferences, custom keyboard settings, custom workspaces, custom presets, renders and other preview files, and third-party effects, such as LUTs from camera manufacturers, are all stored as separate files. Preferences and settings are found on your main hard drive in Documents > Adobe > Premiere Pro (unless you've designated another location for them). As of Premiere 13 (the 2019 update), what used to be called renders are called Video and Audio Preview Files and they are stored in a folder of your choosing (File > Project Settings > Scratch Disks). By deleting these files, you'll force Premiere to rebuild them—but definitely back them up first.

Trash your preferences This kinda sucks because you'll have to reset them, but it has the effect of restoring Premiere to the default "factory settings" and is known to clear up a lot of strange issues. To easily delete the preferences as you're launching Premiere, hold down Alt/Option and release it once the splash screen appears.

Rebuild the Media Cache Trashing your Media Cache files forces Premiere to rebuild them, fixing any corruption in the cache. If you have a large project, this could take a while. You can find their location on your hard drives by looking at Preferences > Media Cache.

Rebuild the secret Media Cache (Mac only) Even if you specify an alternate folder for the Media Cache and scratch disks, Premiere still saves some files in the Mac OS Finder Library, which is normally invisible. Use the Go menu in the Finder to get there (Go > ~/Library/). The Library folder will open up, from there go to Application Support > Adobe > Common. Here you'll find a selection of Media Cache folders, depending on how you're been using Premiere and other Adobe applications. (Mine has Media Cache and Media Cache Files, probably from different versions of Premiere.) Trash the files inside these folders and Premiere will rebuild whatever is necessary next time you launch it. Just to be clear, these secret files could be taking up lots of space without you being aware—just today I found over 10 Gb in mine and I check it pretty regularly. On a laptop, 10 gigs matter.

Known bugs and other issues These change all the time, due to the fact that Adobe upgrades Premiere constantly. Just as an example, yesterday I realized that the version of Premiere I'm using has a bug that doesn't support the Dynamic Link feature (more on Dynamic Link later). So I upgraded and found a new bug—waveforms flashing on and off in the timeline. By the time you read this, those versions of Premiere will be old news, But each upgrade seems to fix some problems and introduce new ones. Luckily, Adobe has a web page to inform you about known bugs and other issues. It is found at *helpx.adobe.com/premiere-pro/kb/known-issues.html.*

Managing Group Projects

The more people who need access to a project, the more complicated it becomes. And the reality is that every group sharing scenario is unique. A daily television series, such as a talk show or the news, needs maximum access at maximum speed. That means a dedicated internal network that can deliver a single set of media to multiple workstations. For Premiere, these types of networks are usually available through proprietary, third-party vendors and often include in-house or on-call tech support.

If you don't need this kind of streamlined access, you might be able to setup your own server and local network. Another option is to simply create separate workstations with matching sets of media on external drives. This method can work for remote collaborators as well. I'll be honest and tell you that this doesn't work as well with Premiere as it does with Avid, primarily because Avid bins are separate from the project file. So you can just email an Avid bin to an editor across town, and they can open that bin in their own project and link it up with their set of matching media drives. With Premiere you have to send the whole project or build a smaller transfer project and send that. That can work great but there's one big caveat: duplicate media.

Sharing and Duplicate Media

Every time you copy a sequence from one project to another, Premiere creates a set of duplicate clips if they are not already in the second project. Premiere makes duplicates of any clip that it considers different or new. And prior to Premiere Pro 2020, the changes to a clip that make it different to Premiere included minutia such as added markers and labels. Luckily, in the latest version of Premiere, this has been improved—now only clips with added effects and audio changes get duplicated.

Duplicates are not actual media files, they are just pointer files. So they are very small. But if you are dealing with a feature film, every time you share the latest cut, hundreds or thousands of these duplicates are created. And over time, that can bog down your project and potentially cause you to lose the link to your original media bins, so any reduction in the number of duplicates that get created is a welcome improvement, although it could be improved further by not creating duplicates at all.

There is a setting available to control the creation of duplicates (Preferences > Media > Allow creation of duplicate media on project import), but it doesn't seem to do anything—duplicates still get made whether you have this selected or not. And there is another setting to simply hide them (Preferences > Media > Automatically Hide Dependent Clips). The fact is, there's very little you can do to avoid them if you're sharing projects in this way. Worse, once a duplicate is created it gets linked to the sequence, so now when you Match Frame, you'll be matching to the duplicate. Basically, it spreads like a virus.

With Premiere Pro 2019, another solution was added, the option to consolidate duplicates (Edit > Consolidate Duplicates). This command is pretty fussy—if you're renamed bins or clips, it may not work. It's also a global command, which is to say that it works on your entire project—all or nothing. And it is not restricted to source media, it will also remove duplicated sequences—something that might wreak havoc your backup system, for example.

All that sounds pretty dire. And it is, but it's a problem that's much worse for large projects, such as feature films; and projects with lots of footage, like documentaries; and projects that have a long post-production schedule. By the time six months of editing and sharing go by, it's likely that most of your cut will reference duplicates rather than your original media, which is a potential organizational nightmare.

If everything about your film is short, you can probably just ignore duplicates. If you're project isn't short, you may find that you have to spend some time doing serious housekeeping every month or so.

But there are two other ways to share projects within the Adobe framework that do not result in duplicated media: shared projects and team projects.

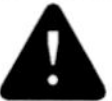

Turn on Project Locking

If you're using a Shared Project, be sure to turn on project locking (Figure 6.15), otherwise multiple users can have it open with no control over who can save or write over it.

Shared Projects

A slightly more sophisticated way to collaborate is to work in a Shared Project, rather than a standard project, and use media shared on a local server. This Shared Project will be available to anyone on your local network as a read-only project—you'll have to make sure you check the box next to "Enable project locking" in the Collaboration preferences panel (Figure 6.15) so that they can look at your project but can't change it. Locking the project means that whoever opens it first can make changes and the rest of the users can only review the contents at that time. It doesn't lock the project from other users on the network at all times, which you might infer. In other words, it's just a regular project with a little bit of added functionality (multiple people can have it open at the same time) and you'll have to build and maintain the local network that houses it yourself.

➡ Setting Up Networks

Building dedicated, local networks for post-production is covered in Chapter 11 of *The Digital Filmmaking Handbook.*

Team Projects

If you love working with Google Docs, then Team Projects will come naturally to you. Team Projects are internet-based, allow for multiple users to work on the same project, let you share work across multiple Adobe Creative Cloud applications, and use cloud-based media storage so that you don't have to build your own network. Team Projects require an additional subscription, Creative Cloud for Teams, and prices vary depending on how many users, how many applications, and how much cloud storage you need. At the base price, the Team Projects plan only comes with one application (Premiere Pro) and 100 Gb of cloud-based storage. You can add storage in 1 Tb increments per user for an extra fee, which can add up pretty quickly. But thanks to this new ability to add significant storage space, it is possible to edit a feature film with Team Projects and the cost might be comparable to multiple sets of physical drives.

Like all shared workspaces, there is an issue of conflicts among users and Adobe Premiere Team Projects are not as seamless as Google Docs in that regard. You'll find settings in Edit/Premiere Pro > Preferences > Collaboration (Figure 6.15). As with all things cloud-based, you are adding more elements to your media pipeline and that means there are more places where you may encounter problems. In a desktop-based workflow, you have drives, cables, and connectors. In a local network, you add more connectors and a local server. With cloud-based sharing, you have to deal with your internet service provider and Adobe's servers—which is to say, you may encounter issues that you can't control.

Team Projects are great for short-form content rather than feature films. And you can use Team Projects for smaller sections of your movie like the opening credits. If you're making a short film with a partner, it could be a great way to work, and the same goes for movie-related short form content such as trailers, teasers, and clips for the web.

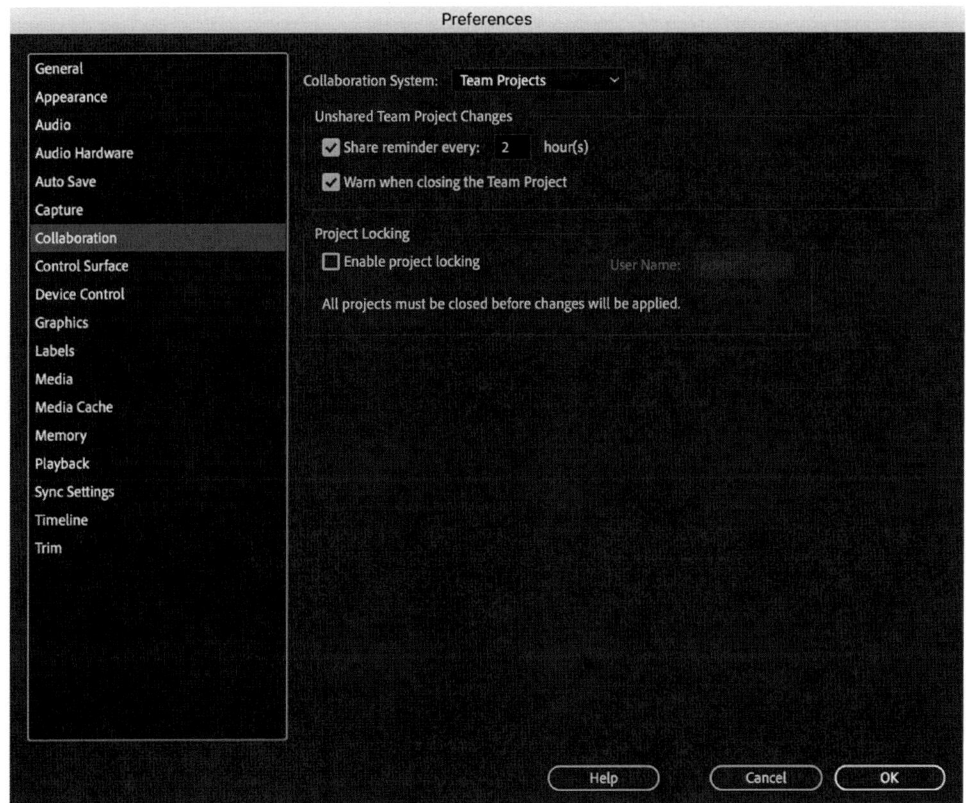

Figure 6.15

The Collaboration Preferences panel.

Organizational Problems to Solve

Keeping your project and workflow organized requires that you know what you need. But when it comes to editing films, the plan you started out with will often need to change along the way.

Here are some of the questions to ask yourself at several stages during the course of editing your movie:

> **How many people will be involved in the editing of your film?** Are you a one-person show? Or a traditional film with one editor and one assistant editor? Or many people, wearing many hats? The more people you have, the more workstations you need, and therefore, the more complicated it gets to share projects, sequences, and media.
>
> **How long do you plan to be working on this film?** The longer it takes to edit your movie, the higher the likelihood of drive failures. Sad to say but hard drives fail all the time because editing involves intensive use of media drives. Make sure you're prepared with a regular backup schedule and a set of off-site backups of your media.
>
> **Is a collaborative workflow right for your project**? Do you need fast turnaround of notes and other feedback? If so, Premiere Pro Shared Projects or Team Projects might work for you.

Just remember that it's totally fine to change your workflow mid-stream but proceed cautiously if that's the path you need to take.

7

Advanced Trimming

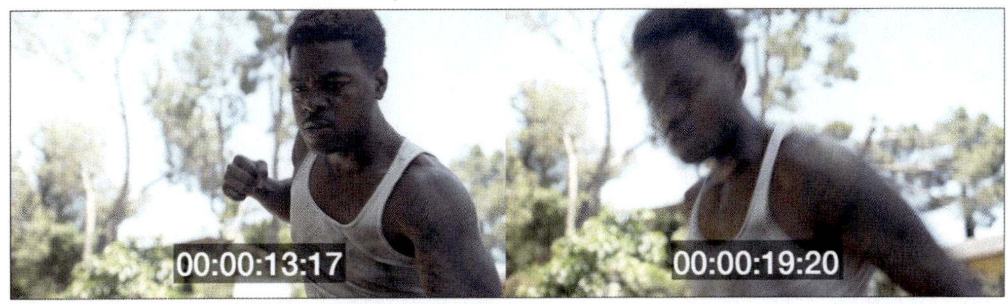

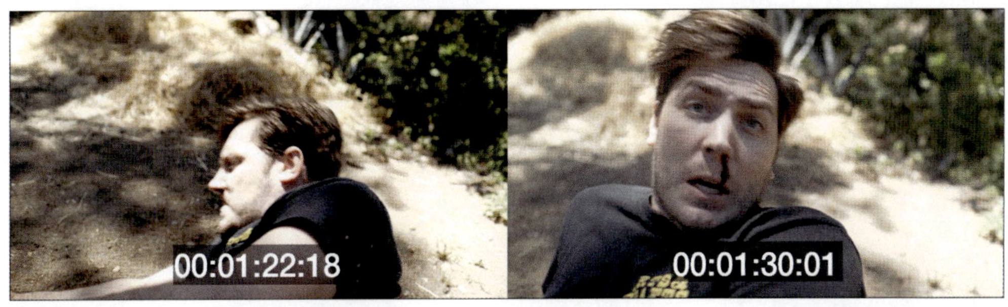

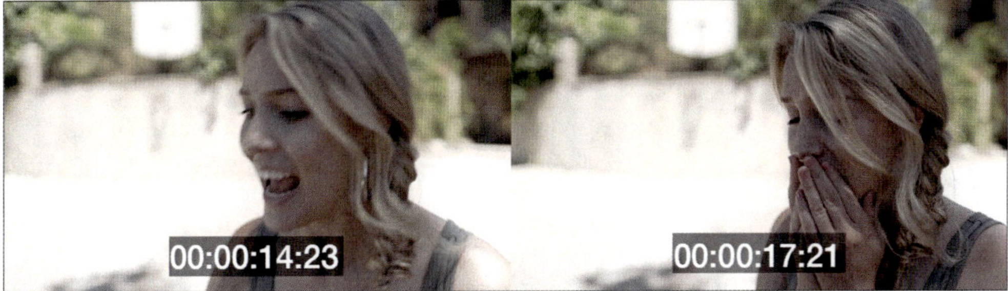

Figure 7.1

Scenes with lots of movement and camera angles are fun but challenging to edit. The trimming tools in Premiere are especially useful for scenes like this.

Fine-tuning a Scene

YOU BUILT A ROUGH CUT, ADDED CUTAWAYS, AND MAYBE EVEN WORKED IT OVER A FEW TIMES. But your film is still not perfect. Maybe the action from one shot to another doesn't quite match, maybe you want to adjust how an edit falls within a line of dialogue, or maybe you want to work through your film cut-by-cut to make sure it's the best it can be (Figure 7.1).

We introduced you to editing in Premiere in Chapters 1-3, but that was just the start. In this chapter, we'll cover the most sophisticated—and at times the most challenging—ways to edit in Premiere: Ripple, Roll, Slip, Slide, and Trim mode.

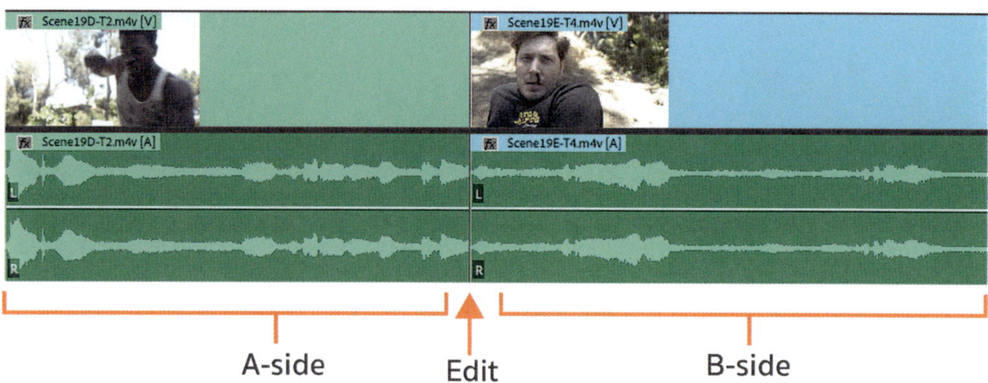

Figure 7.2

Anatomy of an edit: the A-side, the B-side, and the edit itself. These terms are helpful when talking about edits and how they work.

Anatomy of an Edit

An edit is the cut point between two shots. In an edited sequence, the shot that ends at the edit is called the *A-side* of the cut and the shot that begins after the edit is called the *B-side* (Figure 7.2). Using these terms can help you discuss the details of a cut and how it works: "The A-side needs to be shortened" or "The B-side comes in too late." The A-side is also referred to as the outgoing shot and the B-side as the incoming shot.

If you're new to editing, thinking about edits this way can help you see them better—as something with two parts. When you see an edit that isn't working right, it helps to try to assess which side of the edit is causing the problem. Of course, it can be both sides but often it's not. And even if it is both, it often works better to pick one side of the edit and work on that, then move on to the other side.

Two more useful film terms: the start of a shot is referred to as the *head* and the end is the *tail.* Heads and tails can also be used to refer to the start and end of scenes or even a whole film.

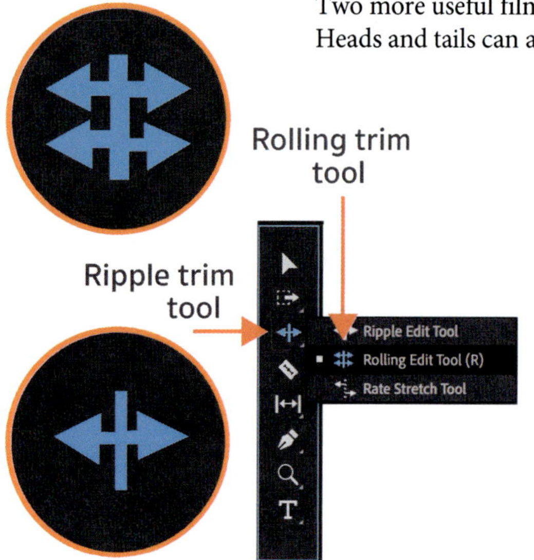

Figure 7.3

The Ripple tool in the Tools panel and the Roll tool, found in the menu under the Ripple tool.

Ripple and Roll

Earlier in this book, we showed you how to extend or trim the end of a shot by dragging on the end of a clip with the standard Trim tool. And you probably noticed that you were limited to working within empty areas of the Timeline—if your clip butted up to another shot, you couldn't drag it any further.

The Ripple and Roll tools remove this limitation. They let you adjust the ends of clips by dragging them in the Timeline, even when there is another shot right next to them. You'll find Ripple and Roll tools in the Tools panel (Figure 7.3) and when selected, your cursor will change to special Ripple and Roll icons as you hover near edits in the Timeline.

Ripple lets you shorten or lengthen a shot in the Timeline and the shot that's on the other side of the edit will follow it backward or forward in time accordingly. Unlike standard Trim (Figure 7.4), when you use Ripple to shorten a shot, no gap will be left in the Timeline (Figure 7.5). Ripple only works on one side of an edit at a time.

Roll lets you drag the edit itself, so that both shots change (Figure 7.6). If you drag to the left, the end of A-side gets shorter and the beginning of the B-side gets longer. If you drag to the right, the A-side gets longer and B-side gets shorter. Of all the trim tools, Roll works in the most intuitive way—it does what you probably expected from standard Trim and moves the edit itself, leaving no gap.

It can help to think of them this way: Ripple adds or removes media and these changes "ripple" through the rest of your sequence, shortening it or lengthening it accordingly. Roll just pushes or "rolls" the edit itself back and forth and nothing else changes.

When you Roll an edit all the way to the next edit, you'll effectively delete the shot from your sequence. When you use Ripple to shorten a shot all the way to the next shot, you'll delete it as well. In both cases, if you run out of media in your source clips, you won't be able to trim any further. The figures below show you how the same 20 frame trim changes when you use standard Trim, Ripple, and Roll.

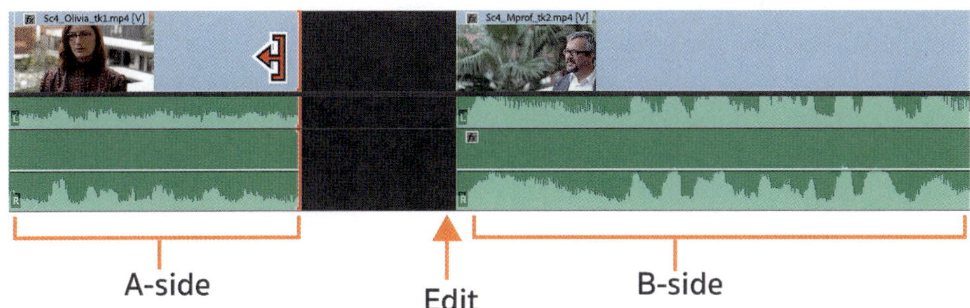

Figure 7.4

A standard trim shortening the A-side by 20 frames. The B-side of the edit is untouched, leaving a gap in the Timeline.

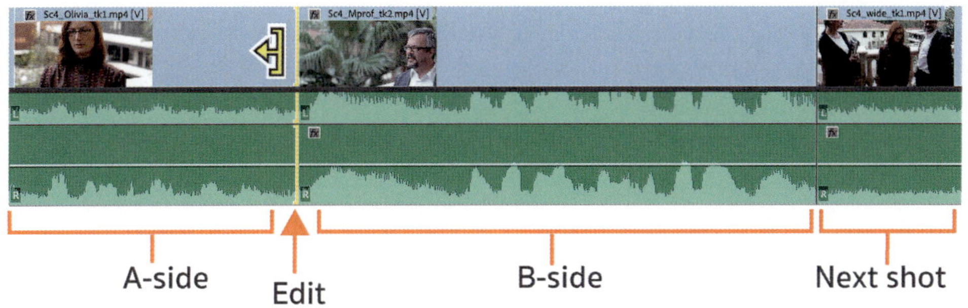

Figure 7.5

Here, the same 20-frame edit is executed using the Ripple tool. Instead of leaving a gap in the Timeline, the whole rest of the sequence is dragged forward. The content of the B-side shot is the same as in the original edit but it has been pulled up, along with the shot after it.

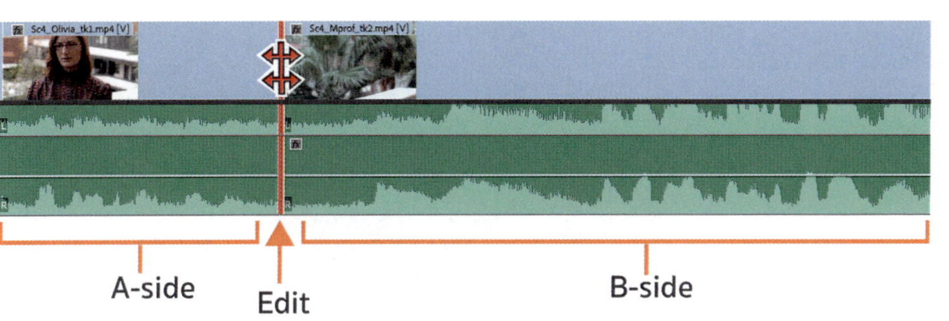

Figure 7.6

The same 20-frame edit using the Roll tool. This time the head of the B-side is extended to fill the gap. Notice that the thumbnail of the B-side has changed from Figure 7.5, because the first frame of the shot is different now.

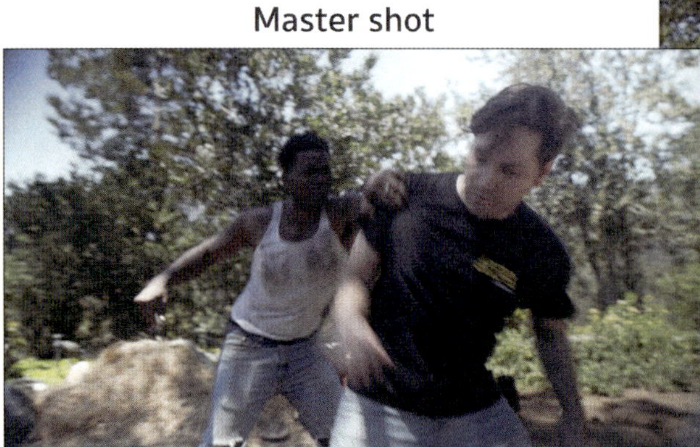

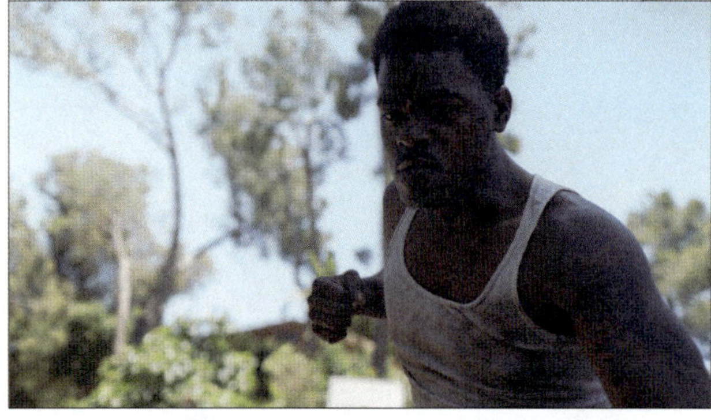

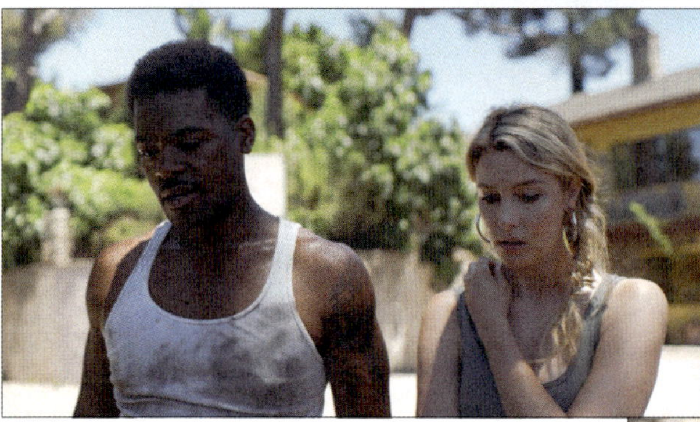

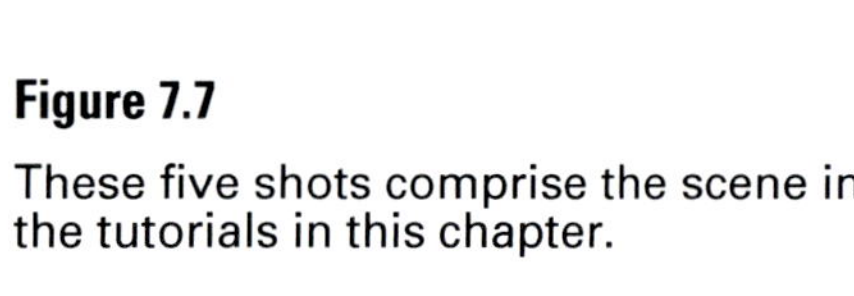

Figure 7.7

These five shots comprise the scene in the tutorials in this chapter.

```
EXT. JACKSON'S HOUSE - DAY

                    JACKSON
      Get off my property. (To his wife)
      Let's go!

He gives her a shove towards the house. Lance
reacts, grabbing his shoulder. Jackson pushes Lance
toward the hillside, but Lance gets the best of him
with a straight punch that knocks him to the ground.

                    LANCE
      You touch her again, I'll kill you.
      (To Jackson's wife) You okay?

                 JACKSON'S WIFE
      Uh-huh.

                    LANCE
      I'm leaving now. But you remember what
      I said. Now she's your wife, Jackson,
      and I respect that, but don't you hurt
      her anymore.

                    JACKSON
      You come near her again, I'll kill
      you. That's a promise.
```

Table 7.1

The script for the *Jackson's Hole* fight scene.

Editing an Action Scene

Action scenes are really fun to edit. They usually have several camera angles, so there are lots of editorial choices to make. But every camera angle you add to a scene makes it that much more of an editing challenge. And matching action from one shot to the next means that even a single frame can make a huge difference in how it plays.

For the tutorials in this chapter, you'll edit a scene from the dark comedy *Jackson's Hole*, directed by Juri Koll. The scene has three characters: Jackson, Jackson's wife, and Jackson's brother Lance. In this scene, old rivalries between Jackson and Lance explode into a fight (Table 7.1). To start, we're going to focus on just the action part of the scene, which has five camera angles: a wide master shot, a reverse wide shot, and singles of the three actors (Figure 7.7). When this scene is fully edited, it will only be about 45 seconds long.

We'll use four short tutorials to explore each of the advanced trimming methods—Ripple, Roll, Slide, Slip, and Trim mode—and use them to build this scene into a polished cut.

Customize Your Timeline View

You will need to see video thumbnails and audio waveforms in the Timeline as you work your way through this chapter. Use the Timeline Display Settings menu under the wrench icon in the Timeline and select "Show Video Thumbnails" and "Show Audio Waveforms." The video track needs to be fairly large in order to see the thumbnail images, so adjust the track height by dragging the lines between the track selectors on the left side of the Timeline. And remember that you may need to zoom in to get the trim tools to work properly.

TUTORIAL: Ripple

In this first tutorial you'll use the Ripple trim tool (Figure 7.8) to shorten shots and get rid of extra material. Make a new project called "Jackson's Hole," and import the folder called "Jacksons Hole fight" into it. Take a minute to review the footage.

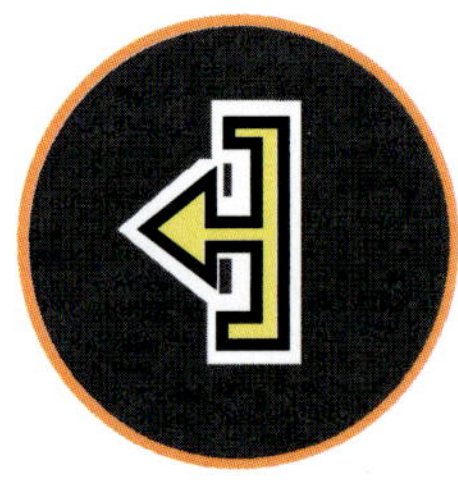

Figure 7.8

When the Ripple tool is active, you'll see this yellow cursor appear when you hover near an edit in the Timeline.

STEP 1: Build the Scene

Arrange your workspace as you wish (I'm using the Editing workspace preset) and make a new sequence (File > New > Sequence), call it "Jacksons Hole fight" and select "Ok" to accept the default settings. The new sequence will automatically open in the Timeline. (Just a quick note—I've colored each shot with a different label to make it easier to see the edits in the images in this book. You don't have to do that but if you want to make yours look the same, the label colors are listed with each shot below.)

Drag the shots into the Timeline in the following order:

Scene 19B-T1, Wide master shot (mango)

Scene 19C-T1, Reverse wide shot (rose)

Scene 19F-T1, Single, Jackson's wife (teal)

Scene 19D-T2, Single, Lance to two-shot with Jackson's wife (blue)

Scene 19E-T4, Single, Jackson (cerulean)

In the Timeline, you'll see small triangles at the heads and tails of each shot. This tells you that the entire clip is in your sequence (Figure 7.9).

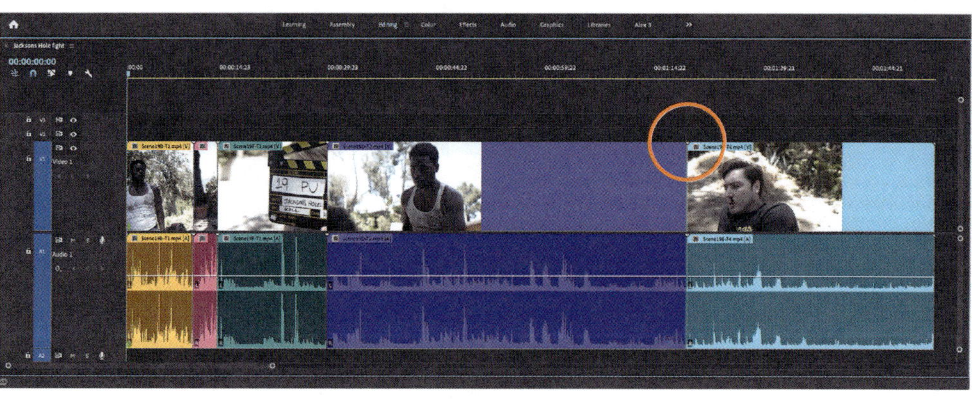

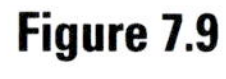

Figure 7.9

Note the small triangles (circled) at the edits that indicate that the end of the source media is in the sequence.

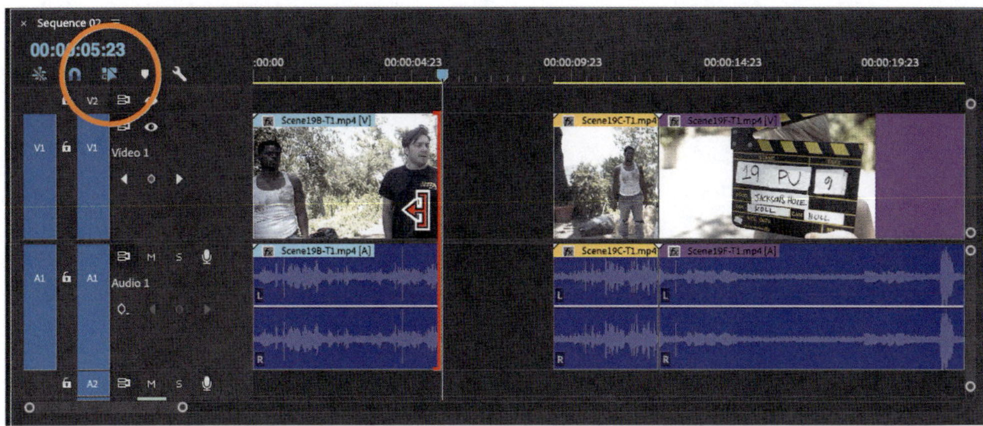

Figure 7.10

Shortening the over-the-shoulder shot with standard Trim results in a gap in the Timeline.

☑ Linked Selection

We covered the Linked Selection Timeline toggle in Chapter 3, but you'll be using it all the time as you do the trimming tutorials in this chapter. It's found in the row of buttons near the upper left corner of the Timeline and we've circled it in Figure 7.10 for you.

STEP 2: Try a Standard Trim First

Watch the cut as it is. This rough first assembly has a lot of fat in it. Let's start by getting rid of the extra material at the heads and tails of each shot. The first shot starts okay but we want to get out before we see that Jackson's wife doesn't fall, at 00:00:06:13 into the sequence.

Make sure Linked Selection is on and the Selection (arrow) tool is active. Move your mouse to the end of the first shot (Scene19B-T1). You will find it helpful to toggle Snapping in the Timeline on and off as you work (S)—Snapping is great to get from one edit to the next, but it makes dragging smoothly almost impossible.

You may have to move the mouse around to find the sweet spot where it turns into the red Trim cursor (Figure 7.10). Click on the A-side of the edit and drag the end of the shot to around 00:00:06:13, then release.

You may also need to zoom in further (+) to get the level of control needed to perform this action. As you zoom in, the increments that things move gets smaller—so keep zooming in until you can move in single-frame increments.

When you release the mouse, you'll see that you have made the trim but there's a black hole in the Timeline. You could easily select the black gap in the Timeline and delete it, but there's a better way…

STEP 3: Try Again With Ripple Trim

Hit Undo (Command/Control Z) until the sequence gets back to the original state. This time grab the Ripple tool from the Tools panel (Figure 7.3).

Now when you hover the mouse around the end of the shot, you'll see the yellow Ripple icon in the Timeline (Figure 7.11). Just like standard Trim, Ripple is directional—you'll see the tool cursor change directions accordingly as you move your mouse around the edit. When you select an edit with the Ripple trim tool, it will get highlighted with a yellow bracket that points towards the side that will be affected.

With the yellow Ripple cursor active, click on the A-side of the edit and drag it to 00:00:06:13, just like you did in Step 1. Release the mouse—this time there's no gap in the sequence. Notice that the rest of the sequence has been pulled along with the shortened A-side, so the whole sequence is shorter.

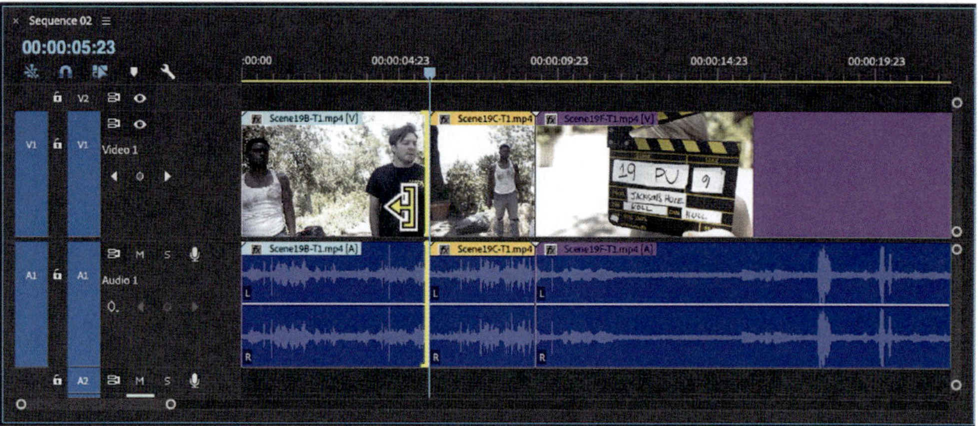

Figure 7.11

In the Timeline, an edit selected with Ripple trim is highlighted with a yellow bracket. Ripple trim only affects one side of the edit and both the cursor and the bracket point to whichever side of the edit you selected—in this case they point to the A-side.

⚠ Make Sure the Trim Cursor is Yellow

If you're trying to make a Ripple trim and the cursor is red, that means you are only making a standard Trim, not a Ripple trim. Go to the Tools panel and make sure the Ripple tool (Figure 7.3) is highlighted in blue. The Ripple trim cursor is always yellow.

STEP 4: Make More Ripple Trims

Now let's use Ripple trim to shorten the B-side of that same edit—click to the right of the edit and drag right to shorten it.

As you drag, take a look at the Program monitor (Figure 7.12). When you drag an edit with the Ripple tool, the Program monitor changes to a two-frame display. On the left is the last frame of the A-side and on the right is the first frame of the B-side. Watch the B-side in the Program monitor as you drag and try to find a frame where the position of Jackson's wife matches her position in the A-side, when the timecode in the B-side of the program monitor reaches 00:00:01:05. Release the mouse and watch your cut—Play Around (Shift + K) is great for this.

How does it look? Does the action match across the edit? If not, you can adjust the B-side some more by dragging to the right or make it longer/start earlier by dragging left. You can also go back to the A-side and adjust it. But don't worry about getting it perfect. We'll do that later. For now just try to get it in the ballpark and if it looks great, even better.

Next, shorten the end of the second shot by Ripple trimming the A-side so that it ends around 00:02:17:00—right in the middle of the action. The reaction of Jackson's wife takes forever to start. Use Ripple to trim the head of the shot to right before she says "Hey!" Let's get out of her shot quickly, right as her hands move to her head around 00:00:16:20, and before she says her second, ad libbed line.

Work your way through the rest of the shots, using Ripple trim to clean up slates and other sloppy starts and ends, by working first on the A-side and then on the B-side of each edit. You can move from edit to edit in the Timeline using up and down arrow keys (you'll need to make sure the track selector for V1 is highlighted in blue for this to work).

When you're done trimming each shot in the sequence, it should contain all the dialogue in the script for the scene (Table 7.1) and not much else.

 Save Your Project

We'll be using it for the rest of the tutorials in this chapter.

 Check Out Our Versions

The folder called JH Tutorial Cuts contains the four versions of this scene, one for each tutorial in this chapter, so that you can check your work against ours.

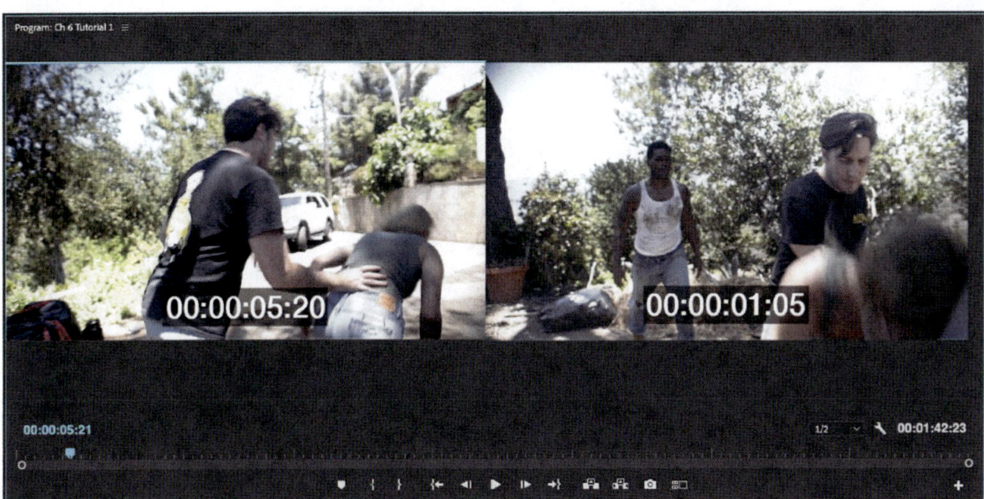

Figure 7.12

As you drag the edit with the Ripple tool, the Program monitor changes to a two-frame view. This can be helpful if you are trying to match action or make any other type of edit that is based on finding the right visual point in a shot. If your Ripple trim is based on audio, you'll see waveforms instead.

Choosing Coverage

When a scene has many things going on at once, there are more choices to make when you edit it. It helps to think about what you would want to see at each point in the scene. Usually, you want to see the action start, whether it's someone throwing a punch or a strong line of dialogue. But then what? Which character's reaction is the most important? How do you balance the through-line of the action itself against the story of the characters in the film? If a bomb explodes in a wide shot and then you cut to five close-ups of characters reacting, it might feel like you missed the moment. But if you don't show any reactions, the moment might be underwhelming.

The answer is always "story." Is your film about the bomb squad? If so, it may be best to cut from the explosion to the interior of the bomb squad truck as it races to the scene, intercutting from then on until they are all at the same place. Or is it about the immediate effects of the bombing? If so, you need to show the aftermath and reactions of the people at the scene. Often, you'll want all the above. Whatever you choose, you'll need to find a balance between the larger story, the scene at hand, the actual coverage that is available to you, and a visual style.

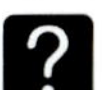 Ad Lib Dialogue

During the course of shooting, it's likely that the actors will add some ad lib lines, especially in a scene with lots of action. In the scene from *Jackson's Hole*, the actor playing Jackson's wife has a couple ad lib lines during her close-up. They aren't in the script but they help the scene feel more natural and realistic.

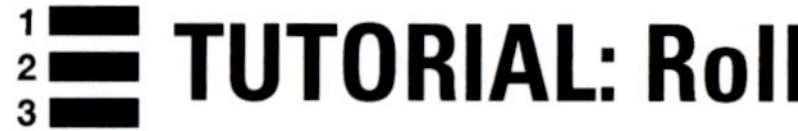

TUTORIAL: Roll

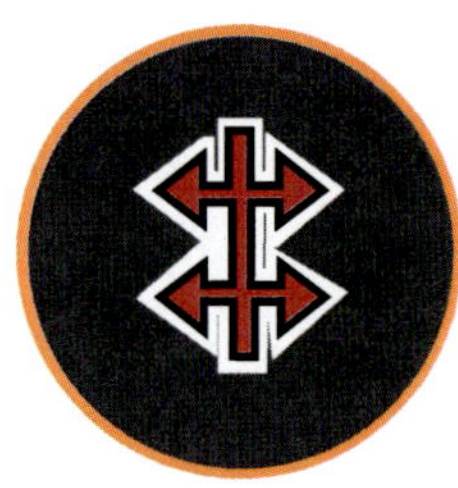

Figure 7.13

When the Roll tool is active, your cursor changes to this double-sided red arrow when you hover near an edit in the Timeline.

In the last tutorial, we built an assembly of the fight scene from *Jackson's Hole* and trimmed each shot using the Ripple tool. All the lines are in and the order of shots seems okay, but it needs some cutaways. We want to see Jackson's reaction after getting punched and we want to see the reaction of Lance and Jackson's wife after Jackson threatens to kill Lance.

In this tutorial, we'll add these cutaways and adjust them using the Roll tool in the Timeline (Figure 7.13).

STEP 1: Place the Cutaway

First let's find the cutaway of Jackson to place after the punch. Double-click on his shot (Scene19E-T4) in the bin to launch it into the Source monitor. Set an In right before he spits (00:01:21:00) and an Out before he starts to gear up for his line of dialogue (00:01:24:05). Patch the source audio from A1 to A2 in the sequence and drag or use overwrite to add it to the sequence during Lance's shot. This way we'll have the audio from both shots in the cut.

In this area, the coverage is limited. The actions of Lance do not match the actions of Jackson but you can still find a way to get the cutaway in. When Lance stands up, the single turns into a two-shot with Jackson's wife, but the camera wobbles as Lance changes position. You can hide the camera wobble with the cutaway. Find a place after Lance starts to stand, around 00:00:19:00, leave the playhead there and use Overwrite to add the cutaway to the sequence. You should have a new shot on V1 with audio on A2 (Figure 7.14).

Watch it—it's not going to be perfect, but we'll be working on that.

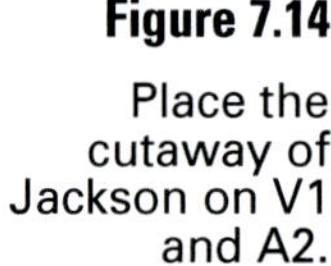

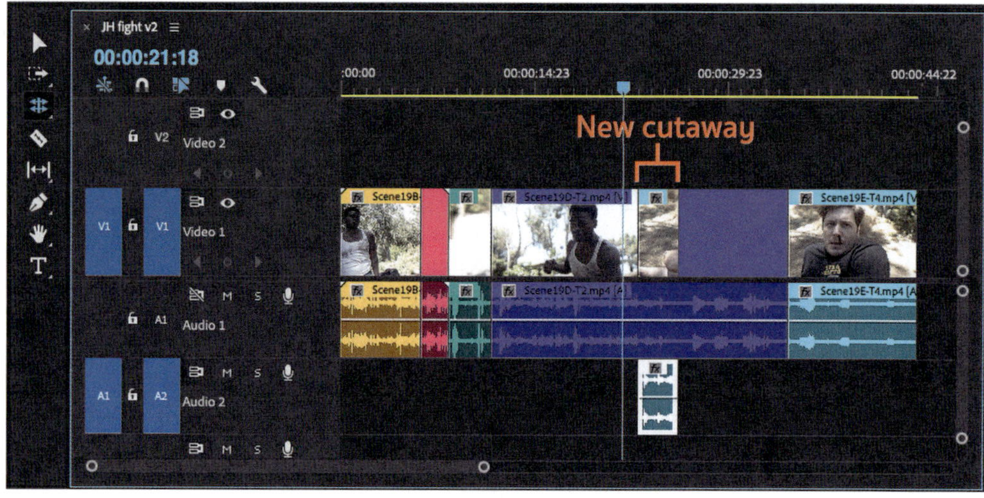

Figure 7.14

Place the cutaway of Jackson on V1 and A2.

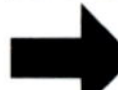

The Language of Film

Learning the vocabulary to discuss films as works-in-progress is covered in Chapter 14, Editing of *The Digital Filmmaking Handbook.*

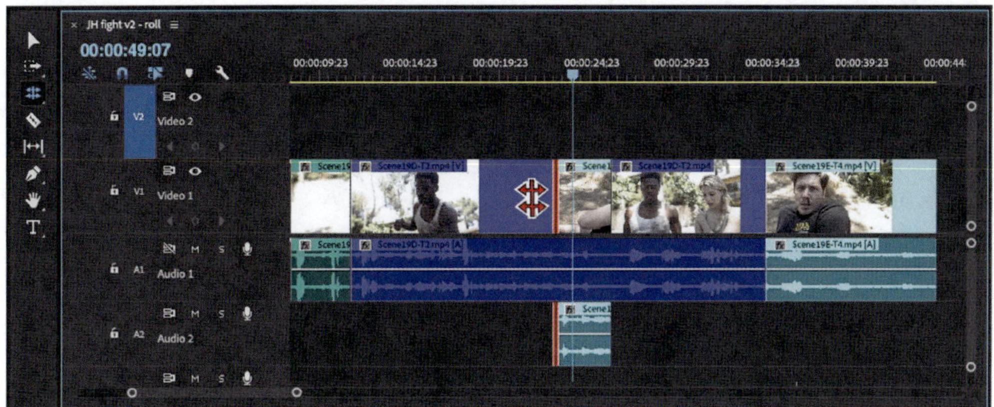

Figure 7.15

Use Roll to adjust the edits at the head and tail of the new cutaway.

STEP 2: Roll the Cutaway

Next, we're going to adjust the cutaway using the Roll tool. The reason that rolling works well here is that we want to keep the timing of the dialogue intact—we don't want to make it longer or shorter. So by rolling the shot, we can change how it starts and ends without changing the dialogue or the timing of the rest of the scene.

The Roll tool is found in the menu under the Ripple tool in the Tools panel or you can use the key command N. Activate it and select the edit at the start of the cutaway. The cursor turns into the red, double-arrow Roll cursor (Figure 7.15). Select the edit and drag it in either direction until you're happy with it. Make sure that you always drag the audio along with the video (keep Linked Selection on). Play Around (Shift + K) to review the changes as you work.

Now do the same for the end of the cutaway. I found that Jackson's extra roll before the spit looks natural, so I extended the head of the cutaway to include that. And I extended the tail as long as possible before he starts to talk.

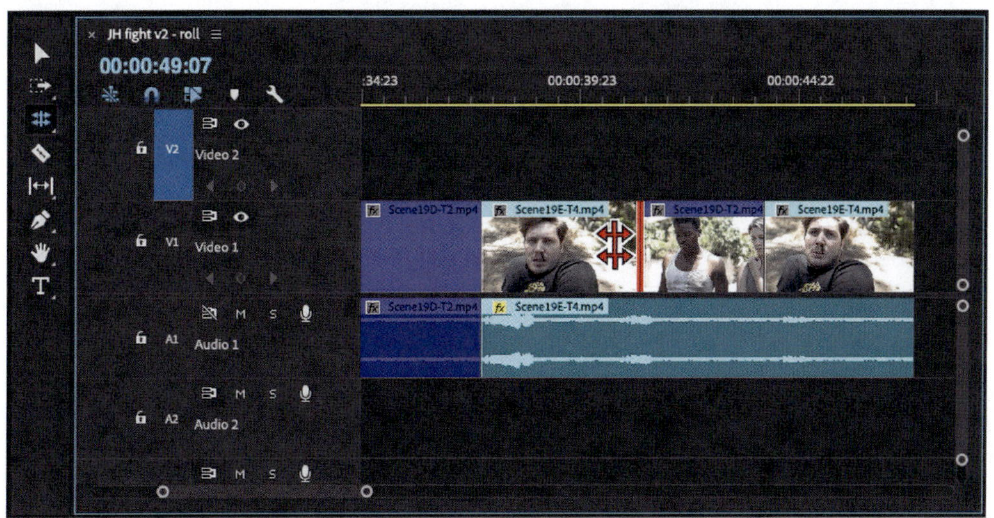

Figure 7.16

Add a reaction shot to the sequence. If there's no dialogue, reaction shots are often added as video only.

STEP 3: Roll the Reaction Shot

Let's insert a reaction shot of Lance and Jackson's wife after Jackson threatens to kill Lance but before his last line, "That's a promise."

Go to the end of the shot of Lance and Jacksons wife in the cut and use the F key to Match Frame the last frame of the shot into the Source monitor. (You'll need to have the V1 track selector highlighted.) We don't want to use the same part of the shot, so play forward and find a good part of the reaction as Jackson speaks, like when Lance clenches his jaw around 00:00:43:16. Set an In and about two seconds later, set an Out.

Go to the Timeline and set an In after Jackson says, "You come near her again, I'll kill you." Make sure you have V1 patched to V1 but deselect the audio tracks—we don't want to add a double line here. Use Overwrite to add the reaction into the shot of Jackson (Figure 7.16).

Now use Roll on both the head and tail of the reaction shot to adjust it. See how far you can push it, after all, Lance is the main character—but beware that if you Roll all the way to either end, you'll replace the video of Jackson's shot. At some point, the director calls cut and the camera starts to move, so you'll want to get out of the two-shot before that happens.

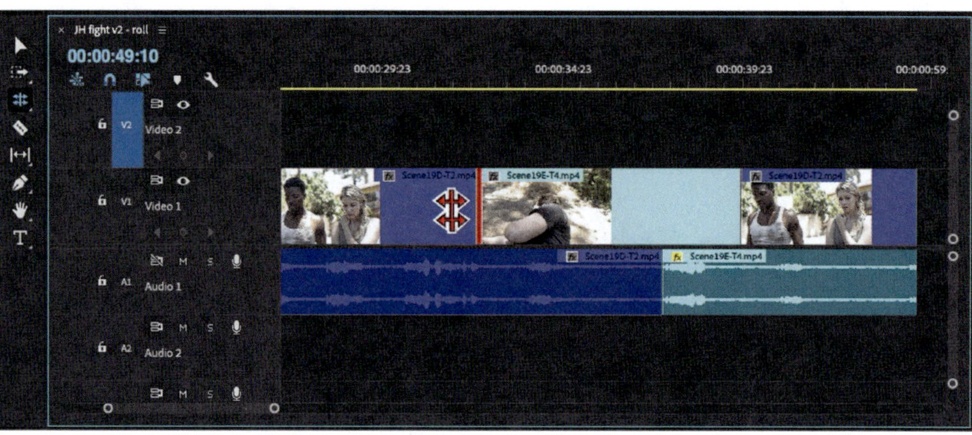

Figure 7.17 Toggle off Linked Selection so that you can select only the video edit, then use Roll to make an L-cut.

STEP 4: Use Roll to Make an L-cut

Roll is the perfect tool for making L-cuts.

Go to the edit after the two-shot where Lance says, "But don't you hurt her anymore." The next shot should be a single of Jackson saying, "You come near her again, I'll kill you." We're going to use Roll to overlap Lance's line with Jackson's shot.

First, you'll need to toggle off Linked Selection. Activate the Roll tool (N) and select the edit. Now you can drag it left to extend Jackson's single over Lance's dialogue (Figure 7.17).

You can also drag it to the right if you prefer to make the L-cut going the other way and you can choose to L-cut the audio edit instead—although in this case it won't do much good, you'll just end up with lip flapping.

That's it! The more you use Ripple and Roll, the easier they get—you'll eventually find that you use them all the time.

Slide and Slip

Slide and Slip are a level up from Ripple and Roll. Instead of adjusting where a single edit falls, you are adjusting both ends of a shot (Figure 7.18). These aren't going to be tools you use all the time—think of them as precision tools you use to attack special problems.

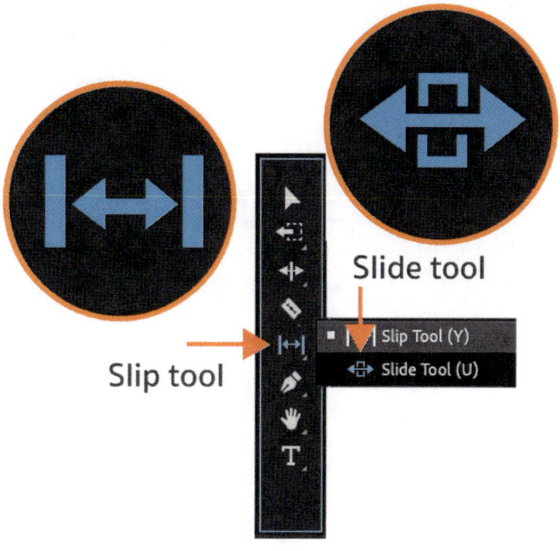

Figure 7.18

Slide and slip in the Tools panel.

Slide lets you move a shot backward or forward in a sequence without changing the overall length of the sequence (Figure 7.19). As you drag, the shots that surround the selected clip will shorten or lengthen as needed to make up for the shift in position of the selected shot. It's like making a rolling edit on both ends of a shot at the same time. Three shots are affected when you slide a shot: the clip you selected, the clip before it, and the clip after it. With Slide you are limited by the length of the source media in those shots that bracket the clip you are moving. You are also limited by the duration of all three shots combined. Since the overall duration of the sequence won't change, you can't drag past the beginning of the preceding shot or the end of the following shot.

Slip allows you to select a clip in the middle of any sequence in the Timeline and drag to adjust its contents so that it starts later or earlier without affecting any of the shots around it (Figure 7.19). In other words, it stays the exact same length and it also stays in the same position within the sequence—what changes is the content of the shot

Original three-shot sequence

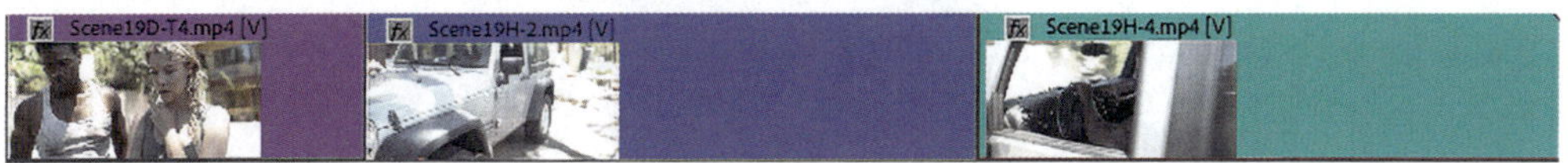

Center shot Slides across sequence

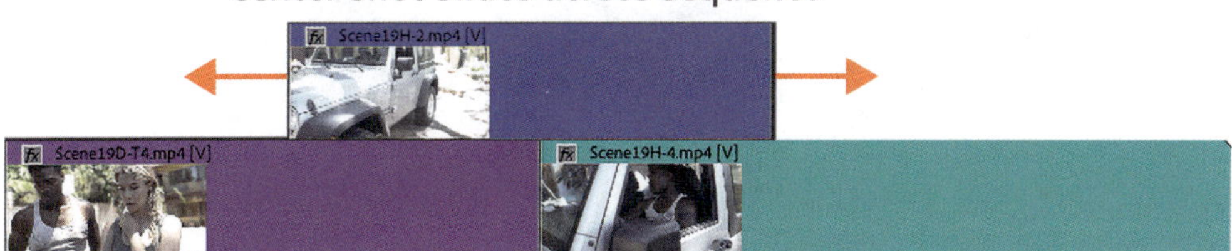

Contents of center shot Slip to shift visible portion of shot

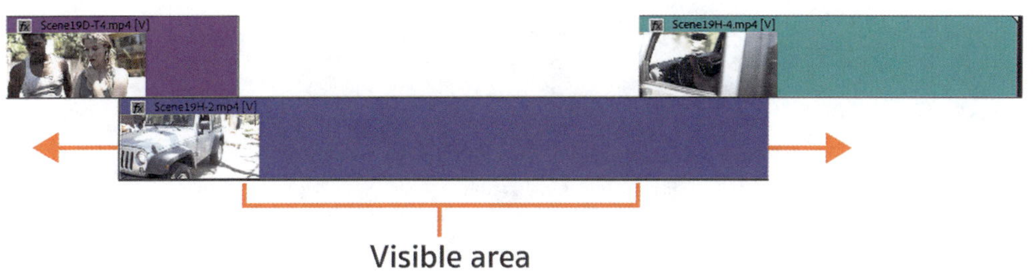

Visible area

Figure 7.19

Slide and slip change the center shot in a three-shot sequence. It's easier to visualize how they work by seeing them as two layers of video, even though they actually work on a single track.

itself. It's as if you matched frame to your source footage, changed the In, and used Replace to change the clip in the Timeline. Except you don't have to go through all those steps to get there. And better yet, you can drag back and forth until you get the contents of the shot exactly right.

Figure 7.20

The Slide tool changes to this cursor when you hover over shots in the Timeline.

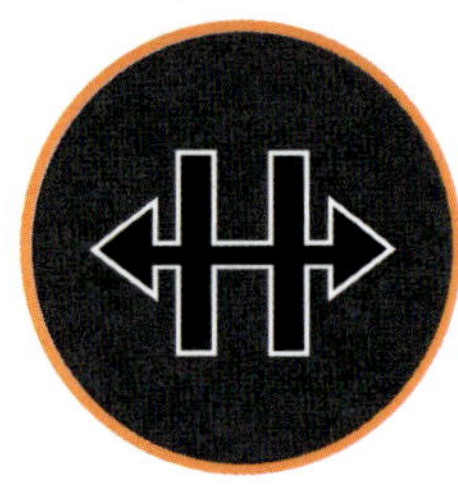

Watch Your Sync

It's easy to lose sync when you use Slip and Slide. And sometimes you won't care about sync, like with certain reaction shots and cutaways. But either way, you'll want to know when you've lost sync. Go to Preferences > Timeline and select Display Out of Sync Indicators for Unlinked Clips.

TUTORIAL: Slide and Slip

Both Slip and Slide are mostly used to fine-tune a cut. Slip is particularly useful for adjusting shots with very specific timing needs—actions, lines of dialogue, etc. Slide is great for shifting cutaways and other insert shots. Slip and Slide may sound complicated but they work on an intuitive level once you get used to them. The more you use Slip and Slide, the easier it is to use them.

So in this tutorial we'll walk you through working with them. We're going to start with Slide (Figure 7.20) because it's easier. Slide is the perfect tool for adjusting cutaways. Remember that cutaway we added earlier, of Jackson on the ground after Lance punches him? We placed it to

Figure 7.21

The Program monitor in four-frame mode while sliding a shot.

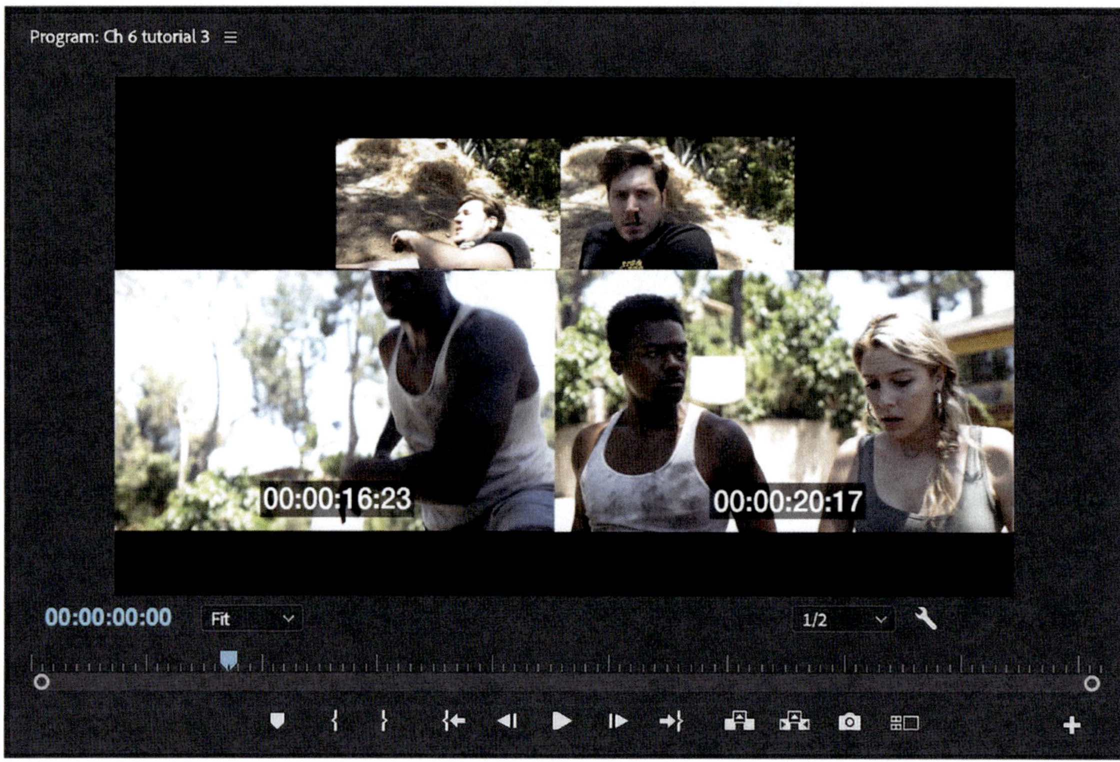

cover the wobbly camera move when Jackson stands up. But if you don't sees Jackson stand, the geography is confusing. So we're going to use Slide to find a better spot for it.

STEP 1: Slide the Cutaway

Activate the Slide tool, found in the menu under the Slip tool, fourth down in the Tools panel (Figure 7.18) or you can type U. Make sure Linked Selection is toggled on—we want the audio and video to move together. Select the cutaway of Lance and drag it to the right. As you drag, check out the Program monitor—it's changed to a four-frame view (Figure 7.21). This might look complicated but it's not. Remember that Slide affects two edits, the edit at the head of the shot you are sliding and the edit at the tail. In this case. The small frames on top show the first and last frames of the shot you are moving—the cutaway of Jackson. Notice that as you drag, these frames stay the same. That's because you're not changing the content of Jackson's cutaway, you're just changing its placement in the sequence.

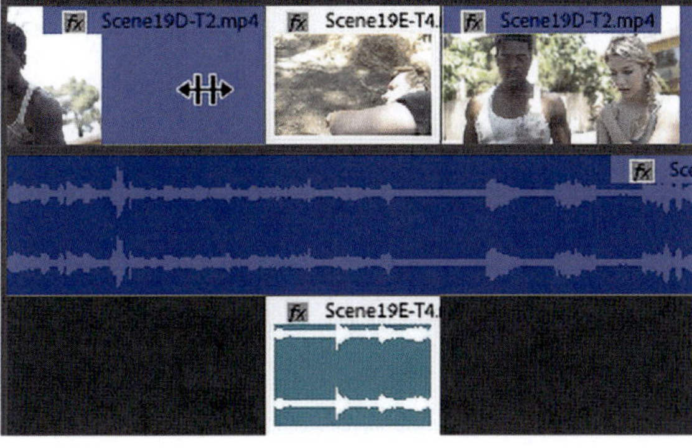

Figure 7.22

Sliding a shot in the Timeline. Note the special Slide cursor.

The larger two frames at the bottom of the Program monitor in four-frame view are the shots that are changing. That is, the two halves of the two-shot As you drag, the contents of these frames will change, showing you exactly how sliding Jackson's cutaway will change the shots around it. You've got a lot of room to slide—I ended up placing it quite a bit later, after Lance says, "Are you okay?" (Figure 7.22).

Figure 7.23

The Program monitor in four-frame view when slipping a shot.

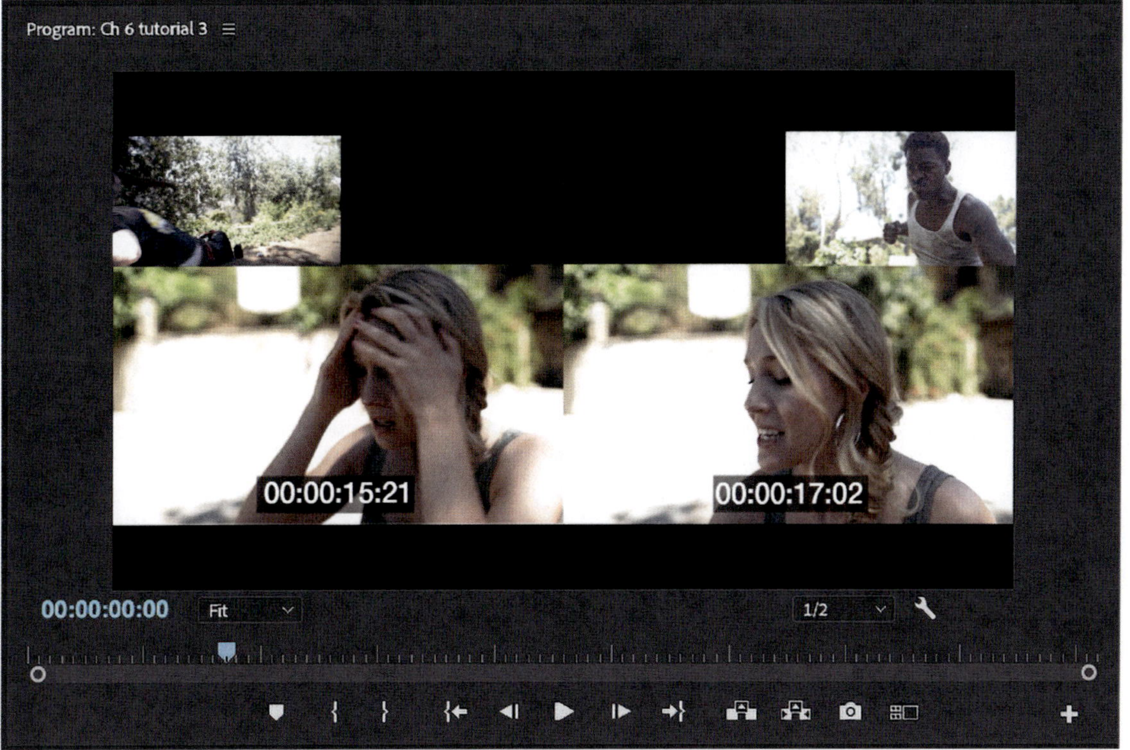

STEP 2: Use Slip to Change the Contents a Shot

To practice Slip, let's work on a part of the cut we haven't dealt with much: the single of Jackson's wife as she reacts to the fight, which is the third shot in the sequence.

In the first tutorial, we trimmed it so that it just contains her first line, "Hey" and her hands going to her face. But she has another line, "Stop, get..." which could be used as an alternative initial reaction to the fight. We're going to use Slip to shift the contents of the shot so that it includes that line instead.

Activate the Slip tool (Y), select the shot and drag to the left (Figure 7.24). As you drag, you can look at the waveform in the audio track to see when her next line occurs (you'll have to release the shot to see the waveform).

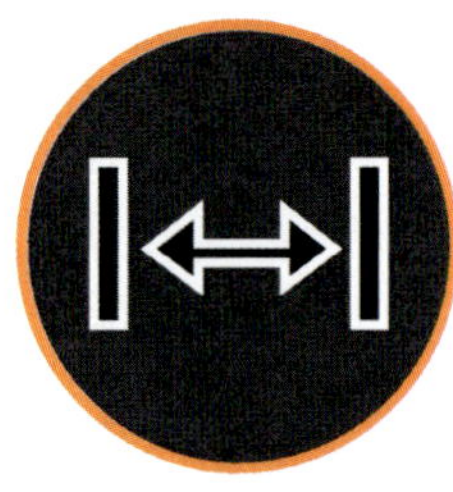

Figure 7.24

The Slip tool shows up as this cursor when you hover over shots in the Timeline.

This time, as you drag the four-frame view will appear in the Program monitor again (Figure 7.23). Slipping affects three shots: the outgoing reverse wide shot of the fight, the shot of Jackson's wife, and the incoming single of Lance. This time the lower portion of the four-frame view shows the first and last frames of the Jackson's wife single because that is the shot you are changing. The smaller upper frames don't change because you're not changing the placement of the center shot, rather you are changing the content.

After you drag the center shot left about 2 seconds, you'll get the second line in position (Figure 7.25).

For extra points, let's make an L-cut with the audio so that we have both her lines. With Linked Selection off, drag her audio to A2, being careful to keep it in sync with Snapping on. Select the audio on A2 and use Roll to drag the start of her audio to the left, until her first line, "Hey!" appears in the waveform. Now she reacts off-camera to the start of the fight, then has a second reaction on-camera a bit later. You can start to see how these four types of trimming work together as you're editing a scene.

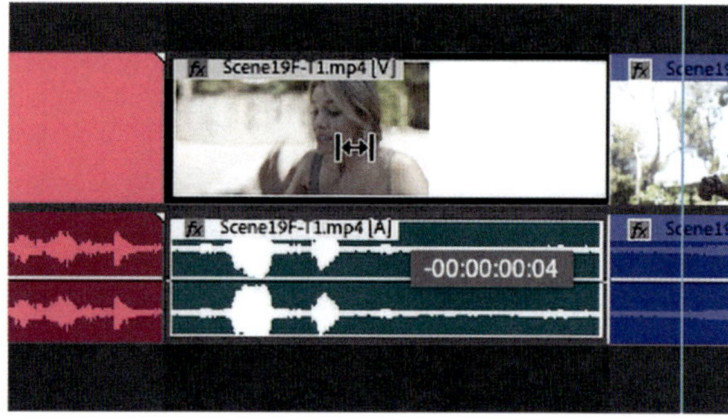

Figure 7.25

Slipping a shot in the Timeline. Note the special Slip cursor.

Trim Mode

Premiere has a special editing interface within the main interface called Trim mode (Figure 7.26). You get into Trim mode by double-clicking on any edit in your sequence. Once in Trim mode, hitting Play (spacebar) will play a loop of the area around the edit you clicked on. This allows you to quickly and repeatedly watch the edit as you adjust it. It will start playing a few seconds before the edit, or *pre-roll*, and continue a few seconds after the edit, or *post-roll*, looping until you hit Pause.

The Trim mode interface is designed for small adjustments—a few frames in either direction. A row of buttons at the bottom of the Trim mode interface let you move the A-side, the B-side, or both in increments of one and five frames. As you move your edit backward or forward in time, counters on each side of the edit tell you how many frames you've moved that side of the cut. The arrow keys make it easy to jump to the next edit—use the down arrow to move back and the up arrow to move ahead, just like in the Timeline.

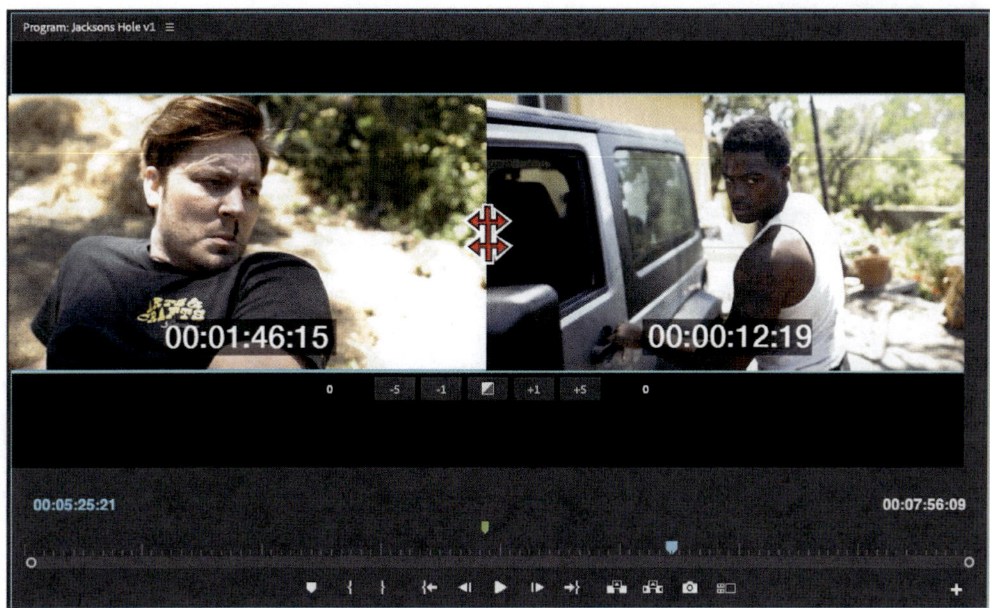

Figure 7.26

The Trim mode interface.

Ripple and Roll in Trim Mode

Trim mode allows you to make three types of trims: standard, Ripple, and Roll. (It does not allow for Slip and Slide.) The tool you use when you double-click on an edit to launch Trim mode matters—the Selection tool (arrow) will give you Trim mode with standard Trims and the Ripple tool will give you Trim mode with Ripple trims. These types of edits are the same in Trim mode as they are in the Timeline (described earlier in this chapter). Most filmmakers will prefer Ripple trims, because adding gaps to a sequence as you edit is only rarely desirable.

Trim mode has a two-frame interface, on the left is the last frame of the A-side of the edit and on the right is the first frame of the B-side. Premiere will automatically switch from the Trim or Ripple cursor (depending on which tool you used to launch Trim mode) to the Roll cursor depending on the position of your mouse within the Trim mode monitor. So you can easily make a variety of very detailed adjustments to the cut.

As complicated as all this sounds, Trim mode is easy to use once you start working with it. You get a lot of instant feedback as to what you are doing and the effect it's having on the cut. Also, you can work incrementally, using Ripple and Roll interchangeably. So what starts as you deciding to shift a cut by a couple frames, ends with you moving it forward (Roll), then just the A-side backwards (Ripple), then the B-side forward a bit more (Ripple), and so on.

 Try Adjusting Pre-roll and Post-roll

Depending on the type of film you are making and your personal preferences, you may need longer or shorter pre-roll and post-roll when working in Trim mode. You can change them in Preferences > Playback. Be aware that these changes will also affect the pre-roll and post-roll of the Play Around command (Shift + K).

Make it Bigger

The Trim mode window is pretty small, but you can go full-frame with it (Window > Maximize Frame). Better yet, you can drag the left border of the Trim mode window to the left, giving it most of the width of the screen, since you don't need to see the Source monitor. This way, you can still see the Timeline as you trim.

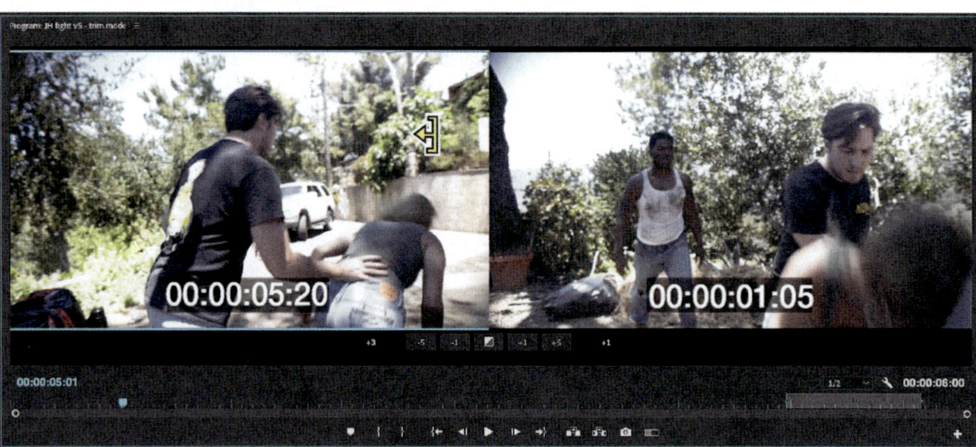

Figure 7.27 Small adjustments on each side of the edit in Trim mode will help you find the perfect place to match the action on both sides of the cut.

TUTORIAL: Polishing in Trim Mode

By now, your cut of the fight scene from *Jackson's Hole* should be looking pretty good. But you can still make it better. Let's start by polishing the first edit in Trim mode.

STEP 1: Match Action in the First Edit

The first cut in the scene is one of the most dynamic and it's also one of the most delicate. Since all the fighting in this scene is fake, you have to carefully avoid showing any of the cheated movements by the actors. And as is commonly the case, the action on the A-side doesn't quite match the B-side. On the B-side, Jackson's wife falls much farther, all the way out of frame. On the A-side, she only stumbles part way and Jackson doesn't follow through with the move either.

But that's okay, it's still possible to match the action. Before going into Trim mode, make sure that Linked Selection is on.

To enter Trim mode, select the Ripple tool and double click on the edit between the first and second shot. Trim mode (Figure 7.27) will open in the Program window. Note that the normal buttons at the bottom of the Program monitor are still there, but there's also a second, new set of buttons right below the frames in the window. Hit Play to start looping playback. This is a good way to look at the edit and try to figure out what's wrong with it.

Try adjusting the A-side so that it ends as Jackson pushes his wife. To trim the A-side only, mouse over it in the Trim mode window. When you see the yellow Ripple cursor pointing left, click on the A-side frame (Figure 7.27). A blue highlight will appear on the A-side, letting you know that this side is active.

Now all your actions will only affect the A-side. Use the Trim buttons to add or remove frames, then hit Play to see how it looks. When you think it looks good, switch to the B-side (hover and click when the Ripple trim cursor appears pointing right). Then add or remove frames until you have the A-side and the B-side frames look like they might match. Hit Play to see how they look in motion. Continue working back and forth from the A-side to the B-side until you're happy with the cut.

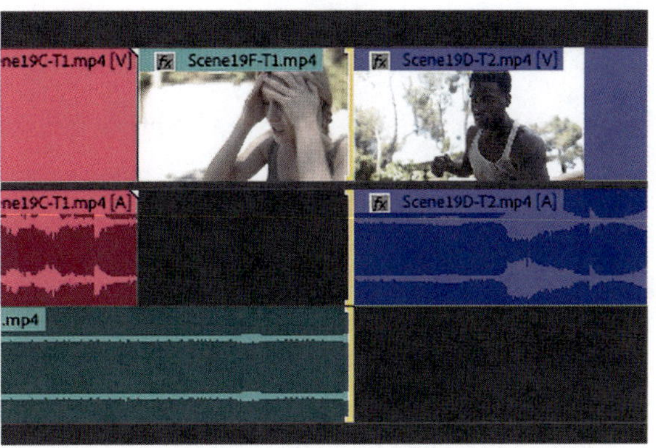

Figure 7.28

You can shift-select to add tracks while you're in Trim mode. Note the yellow Ripple trim brackets highlighting the selected edits in the Timeline as you work.

STEP 2: Try Dynamic Trimming

How about that fake punch at the start of Lance's single? As far as fake punches go, it's a pretty good one. Let's see if we can make it look better. One of the coolest things you can do in Trim mode is adjust your edit while playback is looping. You might prefer a shorter pre-roll and post-roll as you attempt this (Preferences > Playback). I set it to 1 second before and after.

Go to the edit between the reaction shot of Jackson's wife and the single of Lance as he punches Jackson (Figure 7.28). This one's easier, because we only need to adjust the B-side of the cut (the punch). But it's a little trickier because the audio is split onto two tracks. As sequences get closer to a fine-cut, it's very common to have audio and video split across multiple tracks.

Make sure Linked Selection is on and with the Ripple tool active, double-click on the B-side of the edit, on the single of Lance. In Trim mode, you'll see the blue outline on the B-side of the shot. Hit Play and start adding and removing frames with the trim buttons, watching the edit as it plays. I like seeing a little bit of the punch before impact but not too much. Remember that sound design is going to make all this seem much better.

Once you get the B-side the way you want, switch to the A-side to trim the shot of Jackson's wife. But first, take a look at the Timeline when you click on the A-side with the Ripple tool. The audio on A2 for the A-side is not selected. If you trim now, you'll change the video of Jackson's wife but not her audio. Luckily, you can choose which tracks are changed in Trim mode without leaving Trim mode. Just shift-select the A-side of the audio for Jackson's wife on A2 in the Timeline (Figure 7.28). Now her audio will get trimmed, along with the video.

Figure 7.29

You can use Trim mode to make very complex L-cuts but beware that it's easy to lose sync.

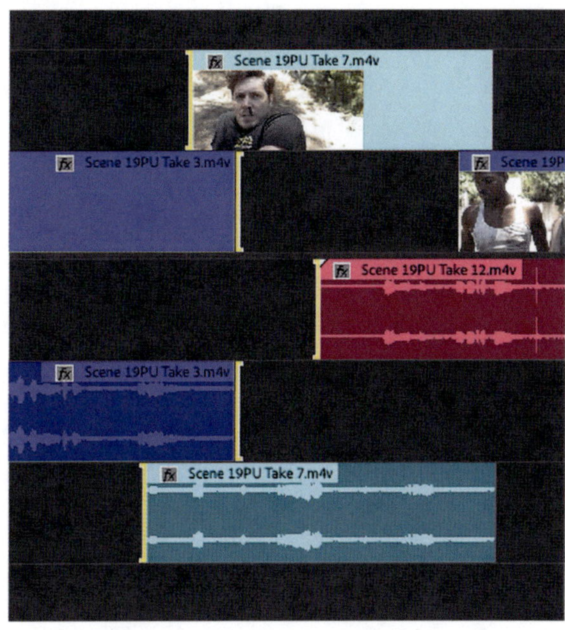

☑ Complex Trims

You may have noticed in the last step that when you shift-select to add or remove tracks in the Timeline, you can also select in different directions. That is, you can Ripple trim to adjust the video in the opposite direction from the audio (Figure 7.29). This is basically just another way to make an L-cut but it can get very complicated if you have a lot of tracks in your sequence selected in different directions.

Next-level Polish Problems to Solve

Now that you've done some serious editing, think about how you can make your film better:

Watch your geography If a scene relies too heavily on close-ups, you can lose track of the relationships between the actors and their movements. Dialogue-driven scenes can get away with staying on close-ups but for action-oriented scenes, maintaining a sense of the geography is crucial. Whenever someone enters or exits the scene or when the elements of the scene are moved around significantly, it helps to cut back to a wide shot so that the audience re-orient themselves. Try imagining a scene like the University scene from Chapters 2 & 3 without the master shot—would you even understand what prompts Olivia to leave abruptly?

Polish edit by edit Start at the beginning and work your way through the cut shot by shot in Trim mode, using the up and down arrow keys. As you look at each edit, try to see if anything bumps as you watch it. Often you'll find there's just an extra frame that causes the edit to be less than perfect.

Editing with style Pacing, rhythm, and the shaping of scenes are all qualities that emerge in the editing process. Will you build to a rapid-fire, staccato rhythm of shots getting shorter and more active in content until the drama explodes? Or will you stay wide and give the viewer a sense of perspective as the story unfolds. There are many, many questions to consider when it comes to editorial style and only you know the answers.

How will sound design help your cut? The editing process might feel like you're working in a void, but there's so much that enhances a film after the editing is finished. It's never too early to start thinking about sound design. In the *Jackson's Hole* scene, the sound of the fight will greatly enhance the drama. What else would you add?

Practice some more There's a folder called "Jacksons Hole ending" with some extra shots. You can add them to the end of the scene you edited in the tutorials and use the trimming techniques you learned in this chapter to work them in.

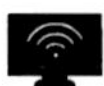 What to Watch: *Fleabag*

Want to see more sucker punches and bloody noses? Watch season 2, episode 1 of acclaimed comedy series *Fleabag*. There are several great examples of how to edit a surprise punch in the face.

8

Sync and Multicam

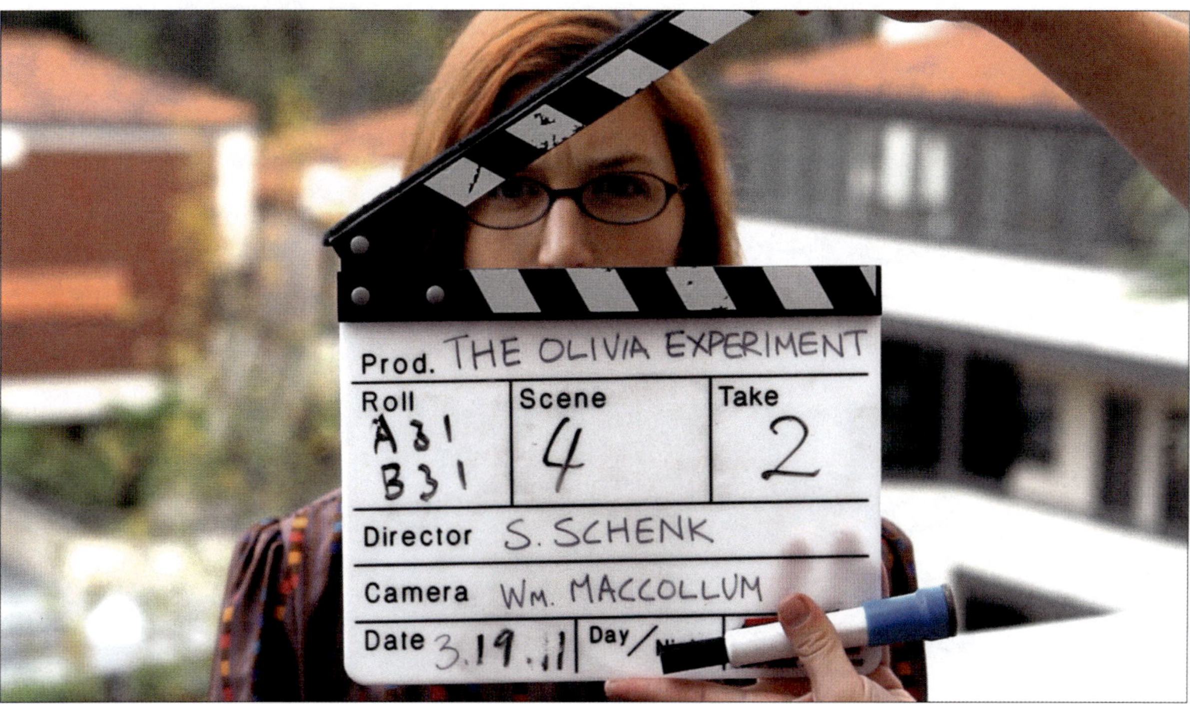

Figure 8.1

A traditional slate clap creates the sync point for multiple devices.

MULTICAM MEDIA IS EVERYWHERE. Sports, concerts, talk shows, reality television, game shows, sit-coms, the list goes on. It can also be found in some unexpected places. Comedic feature films often use two (or more) cameras to insure they capture both sides of conversation, especially if improvisation is expected. Action sequences are usually shot with multiple cameras even if the rest of the film is shot single-camera. And documentaries often shoot interviews with two (or more) cameras to allow for editing without the need for cutaways.

In this chapter, we'll show you all the ways that you can combine multiple sources into easily editable groups, starting with the most fundamental task: synchronizing media (Figure 8.1).

A word to the wise—of all the chapters in this book, this one covers topics that are either not covered in the documentation, not covered well, or are just plain wrong—okay let's be kind—out of date. We learned this stuff the hard way, working on a massive project for over a year that spanned multiple editors, assistant editors, and cameras from the Sony AS7 to a Nikon DSLR to a 4K cinema camera. This project put Premiere (and those of us working with it) through the wringer. And we learned a lot along the way. As with all things post, there's no right or wrong, there's just right for you and wrong for you. But I do hope we clarify some of the mysteries around Premiere, many of which have to do with multicam media, sync, and related audio issues.

Basic Sync

Sync is so basic, it can seem invisible. A standard video clip recorded by a camera consists of one track of video and two tracks of audio. They are synchronized, because they were recorded at the same time with the same device.

When media is recorded by different devices, synchronization is a process that happens later, in post-production. The editor or assistant editor takes all the footage from the various devices and builds them into synchronized clips (Figure 8.2).

These clips can be very simple—one track of video and several tracks of audio—or very complex—several tracks of video and many tracks audio. The more devices that you record with, the more complicated the synchronizing process becomes.

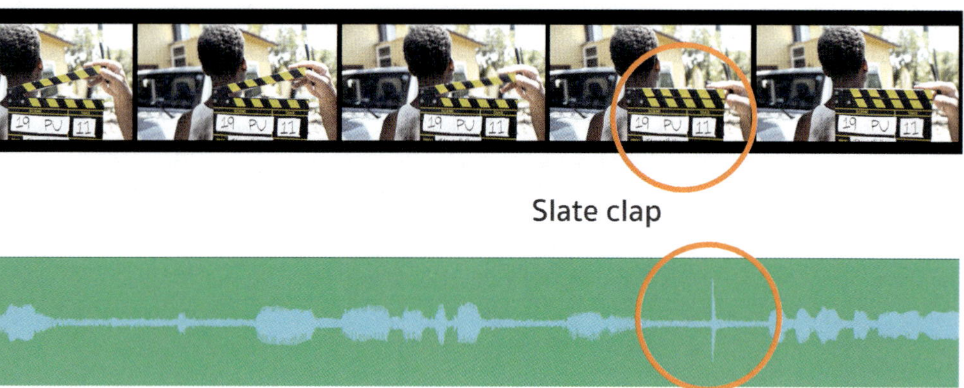

Figure 8.2

Media gets synchronized by lining up the video and the audio waveform at the exact frame where the slate is clapped.

Automated Sync

Professional shoots have more gear and some of that gear is used to generate matching timecode across all devices. That way, when you get into post, your audio recording will have the same timecode as your camera recording. If you're lucky enough to have matching timecode footage, you can tell Premiere to sync automatically based on timecode.

If you don't have matching timecode, Premiere can still sync your footage automatically, using a process where it will analyze the audio from your camera mic (attached to the video clip) and try to match it to the audio in your sound clip(s). (There was a piece of software called PluralEyes that invented this process, but now it's incorporated into most editing applications, including Premiere.)

For this to work, you need to have recorded audio on your camera and you also need that audio to match your production sound because Premiere compares the waveforms against each other to sync the two sources. For example, if your camera was a block away, shooting down the street at the actors, the audio picked up by the camera won't include their voices. When Premiere tries to analyze the camera audio against the production audio, it won't find anything to match it up against. But if the camera is closer, it might still pick up enough of the dialogue over the roar of traffic to sync automatically.

When they work, these automated sync methods are almost like magic. It just takes a few seconds and it's done. But these methods can fail for a variety of reasons and if so, you'll have to set the sync points yourself.

Setting Sync Points

Generally, sync points are set by marking an In on each piece of media you want to synchronize. You can also set markers as sync points. This is where the classic film slate comes in. A short, hard sound with a visual component—like that of the slate closing—creates a sync point. There's only going to be one frame where the slate clap is heard and one frame where you can see the top of the slate hitting the bottom (Figure 8.2). By settings Ins at all the slate claps across multiple sources, you tell Premiere exactly how to sync your media.

But what if you don't have a slate? Any short, hard sound with a visual referent on camera will work: hand claps, door slams, car doors, even glasses clinking in a toast (Figure 8.3). And what if you can't find a distinct, hard sound to use as a sync point? You can still sync by matching sounds and visuals, it just will be less precise and probably take longer. For example, in the English language sounds from letters like B, K, and so on, are hard sounds so it can be easier to find lip sync with words that contain them.

Hopefully you won't have to deal with that, but if you do encounter this problem, be aware that as long as the audio and the camera were recording, a solution exists.

Why Sync Gets Complicated

The more cameras and audio devices that you need to group together, the harder it can be to sync your media. Here are a few common but challenging scenarios:

Distant cameras In a multicam shoot that's relying on slates for sync, slating can get difficult when the various cameras are not near each other. In that case, each camera may get slated separately, which can make it a little harder to sync them in post.

Poorly organized media If your footage isn't labeled clearly on the set, it can be hard to figure out which pieces of media go together.

Missing camera mics If audio was not recorded with each camera, you won't be able to automatically sync based on audio. To do this, Premiere needs your camera audio to match the waveform against your sound recording, so camera audio is very important.

Long and short clips combined When you have a long continuous piece of audio and many short pieces of video or a camera that's continuously rolling while another camera is grabbing short insert shots, you'll have to deal with multiple sync points. If synching automatically doesn't work, this could take a while. This scenario is common with documentary, reality, and "series" takes in feature film shoots, where cameras roll for multiple short takes without cutting between them.

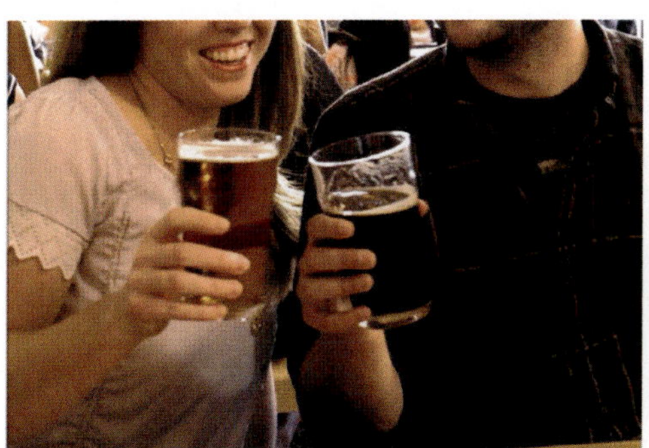

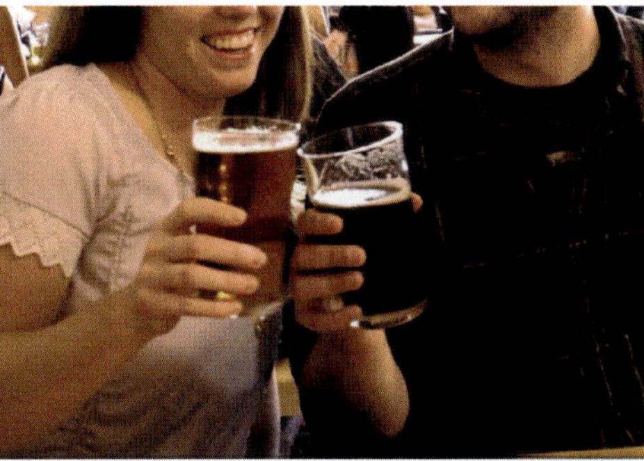

Figure 8.3

Any short, distinct sound, such as two glasses clinking, can serve as a sync point.

➡ Double-System Sound

The traditional feature filmmaking processes of recording double-system sound and synchronizing dailies are covered in Chapter 10, Advanced Shooting and Chapter 13, Preparing to Edit of *The Digital Filmmaking Handbook.*

Merged Clips

So here's a bit of Premiere history. Long ago, Premiere did not yet support multicam editing, but of course it needed to allow for the synchronization of dailies. And that was done through a feature called Merge Clips. Since that time, Adobe added multicam functionality to Premiere but they also left Merge Clips intact. So you have a choice. Sort of.

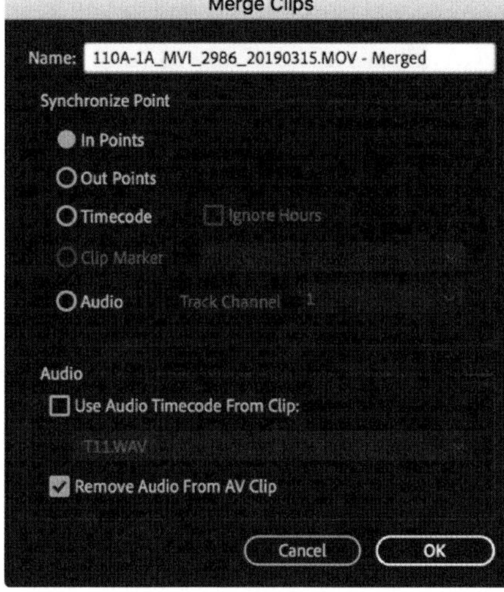

Figure 8.4

The Merge Clips window lets you choose how to sync your media.

Merged clips can work great for synching sound to video but there are serious limitations that make them less useful for many filmmakers. First of all, you can only merge a single stream of video. So that right there eliminates its usefulness for many. If you have a true multicam shoot with more than one video camera, Merge Clips is not for you.

Secondly, merging clips more or less breaks the link from the original clip. That means, you can't match frame back to the original source clips. For many filmmakers, this is a deal breaker. Getting back to your original media is crucial for many post-production processes, from sound editing to color correction to consolidating a finished film and archiving it. With Merge Clips the filenames stay intact (so long as you don't change them), so the link isn't 100% lost, however the possibility of automated processes is diminished. In addition, much of the metadata attached to the original source media fails to make the transition to a merged clip. Given the importance of metadata in modern filmmaking, that is also often a deal breaker.

So with all those caveats in mind, Merge Clips can be a great choice for simple projects that have a need to synchronize audio with a single video source but have no plan to backtrack to the raw media and upgrade it when the film is completed. (I know, we haven't talked about any of this yet—it's all in Chapter 14, Finishing.) It might work well for student assignments, casual YouTube posts, and other projects with a quick turnaround—films that aren't going to go through the rigorous, traditional film finishing process.

If that sounds like your film, merging clips is really easy. Just select the clips you want to merge, right click on one of them and select Merge Clips from the pop-up menu. The Merge Clips window will appear (Figure 8.4). Most people will choose to sync automatically using Audio, but you can also set In points, Out points (for tail slates), or automatically sync with timecode. The result will be a new clip with the word "Merged" added to the name of the original video clip. (Your original clips will be left intact.) This new merged clip behaves exactly like all your other clips: if you double-click on it, it will launch into the Source monitor. From there you can edit it into the Timeline and work with it just like any other clip.

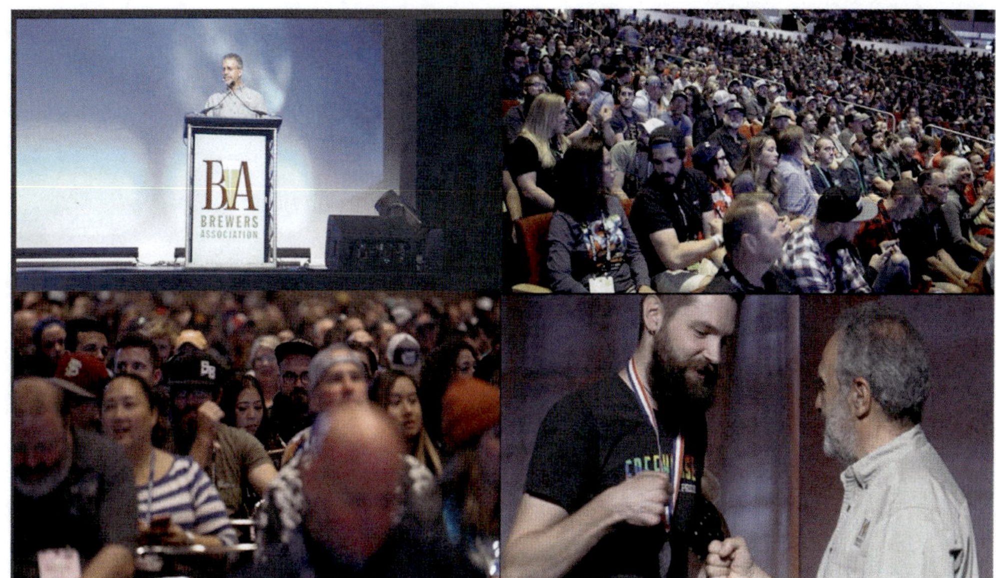

Figure 8.5

Multi-camera view in the Source and Program monitors displays all the cameras in a grid.

Multicam Sequences

For most films, the ideal way to synchronize media in Premiere is to build multicam sequences. Even if your footage only has one camera.

As the name suggests, a multicam sequence isn't a clip, it's a sequence. Or more accurately, it's a sequence that acts like a clip. If you double-click on it, it opens in the Source monitor just like a clip does. However, if you have more than one camera, you'll see a split screen view that shows multiple tracks of video (Figure 8.5). And since it's neither a clip nor a standard sequence, it has its own icon in List view (Figure 8.6). But because it's actually a special type of sequence, you can also open it in the Timeline. Just right-click on a multicam sequence in a bin and select "Open in Timeline" from the menu. Here you'll see all your various video and audio sources (Figure 8.7). If you need to make changes or adjust sync, you can easily do it here.

With multicam sequences, you can use Match Frame to navigate back to your source clips, from either the Source monitor or the Timeline. So unlike merged clips, the link between your original media and multicam sequence stays intact, which is preferable for most filmmakers.

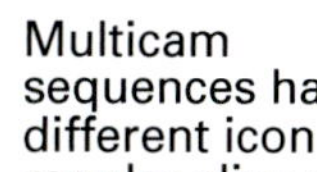

Figure 8.6

Multicam sequences have a different icon than regular clips or sequences in a bin.

Multicam sequences behave a lot like nested sequences. If you mute a track in a multicam clip, that track will be muted wherever you've used it. This can cause lots of problems if you're not careful. The same goes for adding or removing effects and so on. For this reason, I recommend treating your original synched multicam clips like gold: once you make them, lock them in a vault and don't touch them. Yes, you can edit with them. Yes, you can change the audio levels or add effects after they are edited into your film sequence. But don't make changes to the original multicam sequence itself unless you want those changes to ripple through every instance where the multicam footage is used in your project.

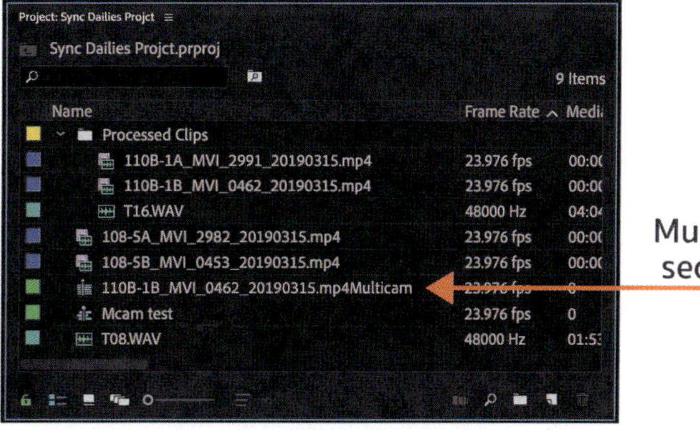

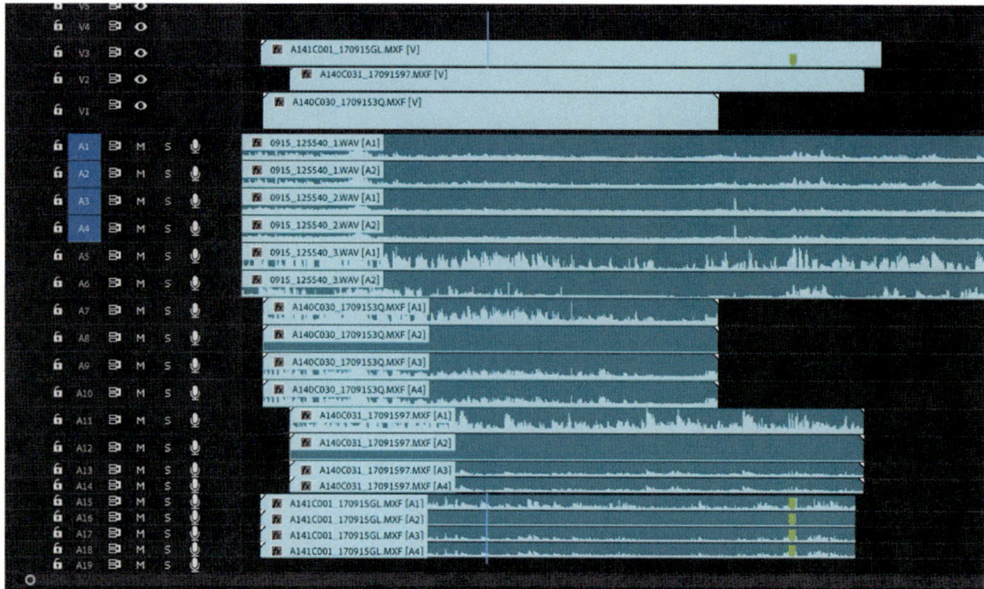

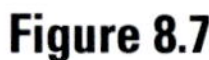

Figure 8.7

Use the right-click menu on a multicam sequence in a bin to open it in the Timeline and you'll see how it all fits together. Note that this is just a three-camera sequence, so it's easy to imagine how complicated a multicam sequence with many cameras can get.

Preparing Multicam Footage

Organizing your footage is the key to building multicam sequences. If your shoot is complicated—and multicam shoots often are—it may take a while to figure out which audio clips go with which video clips. Most big multicam shoots have higher budgets, so the odds are good that your footage will have timecode. On smaller projects like indie films, hopefully the crew has used some sort of naming convention on the set. In a worst-case scenario, you'll simply have to review the footage and figure it out yourself, a process that can be very time consuming. Luckily Auto Sync can speed up that process. You can just select all the shots in a bin and tell Premiere to sync them and hope for the best. Happily, it often works great.

It's very helpful to know which camera is the main camera. Traditionally, the main camera is always labeled as "Camera A," the second camera is B and so on. The A camera generally rolls the whole time, so typically you'll use that camera as the basis of your multicam sequence.

Next, you should make a plan for how you want to build the multicam sequences. Do you want one big sequence that contains the whole shoot or do you want several shorter sequences? This generally depends on the content of your project. For something like a recording of a live event, it makes sense to put it all into one sequence. But really long clips and sequences can be cumbersome when editing. If there are natural breaks such as costume changes in a live concert, intermission during plays, or downtime in sporting events, it's generally a good idea to break it into shorter multicam sequences that follow these natural breaks. For scripted feature films, you'll build multicam sequences for each take. Sometimes there's a series, which is a group of multiple takes where the director does not call cut between takes. In that case, you would build the whole series into a single multicam sequence.

➡ More on Multicam

If you want to know more about shooting multicam footage and best practices on the set, it's covered in Ch 10, Advanced Shooting of *The Digital Filmmaking Handbook*.

Making a Multicam Sequence

To synchronize multicam footage, select the clips that you know go together using Control/Command to select them in order. The order in which you select the source clips for a multicam sequence is important because whichever video file you select first will be designated as the primary source. It will get sent to V1 and that means it will have the first position in the camera bank. If you are grouping takes from a traditional film shoot, you'll probably want the master shot to be the primary source. For most other types of shoots, you'll want the main camera—usually Camera A—to be the primary source.

With your sources selected, go to Clip > Make Multicam Sequence or select it from the right-click menu. The Create Multicam Source Sequence window will open up and that's where you'll find all the settings to customize your multicam sequence (Figure 8.8):

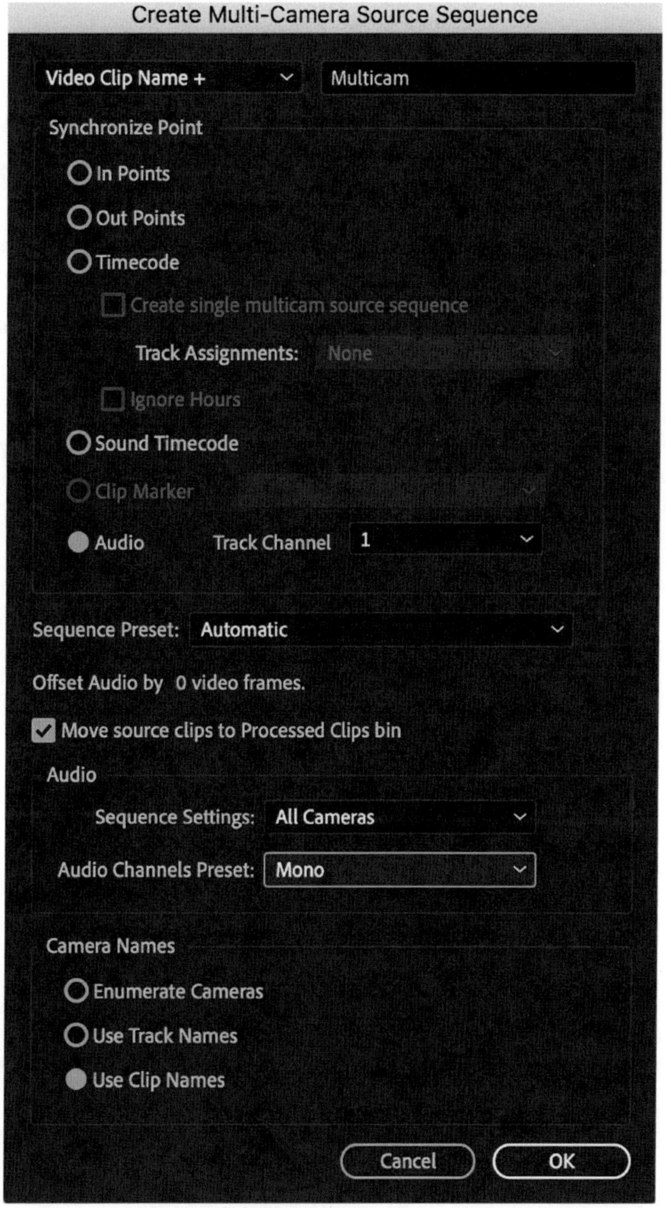

Figure 8.8

The Create Multicam Sequence window.

Video Clip Name + This is how Premiere will name your multicam sequence. The default is that it will take the name of the first video clip that you selected, aka the primary source, and add the word "multicam" to it.

Synchronize Point We covered sync points earlier in this chapter and the issues are the same, whether you have ten cameras or one. If you're synching automatically with audio, you can tell Premiere which track to use as a guide from your camera clips. The default is track 1 and since most camera mics record two identical channels, that should work. If you have an on-board shotgun mic or other audio source patched to channel 2, choose track 2, and if you aren't sure you can try Mix Down which will combine all your tracks and use that as a guide.

Sequence Preset The automatic setting seems to get it right, but you can setup a custom sequence preset for multicam sequences and select it here. Be aware that the sequence preset that works best for multicam may not be the same as the sequence preset that works best for editing your film. For that reason, it's often better to stick with "Automatic."

Move source clips to Processed Clips bin After making a new multicam sequence, the clips that were used to build it will be moved to a new bin called Processed Clips. This bit of housekeeping is usually helpful.

Audio > Sequence Settings This is probably the most important setting and we'll cover it in detail in the next section.

Audio Channels Preset: Again, the automatic setting generally gets it right, but I prefer to tell Premiere exactly what I want. For feature films, that means mono. For live concerts, if your audio was recorded in stereo choose that. And for special events in 3D or 360° video, you may have 5.1 production audio. But for most filmmakers, mono is the way to go.

Camera names Here you have a choice as to how each camera is named, which is useful if you have a lot of cameras. These are the names that will show up in the camera banks when you're editing, so naming them in a way that makes sense for your project can be very helpful. When clip names are long, it's better to use the track names or enumerate (aka, use numbers to identify) the cameras. After you build a multicam sequence, you can rename the tracks, so I prefer to use track names and change the camera names as needed after the fact.

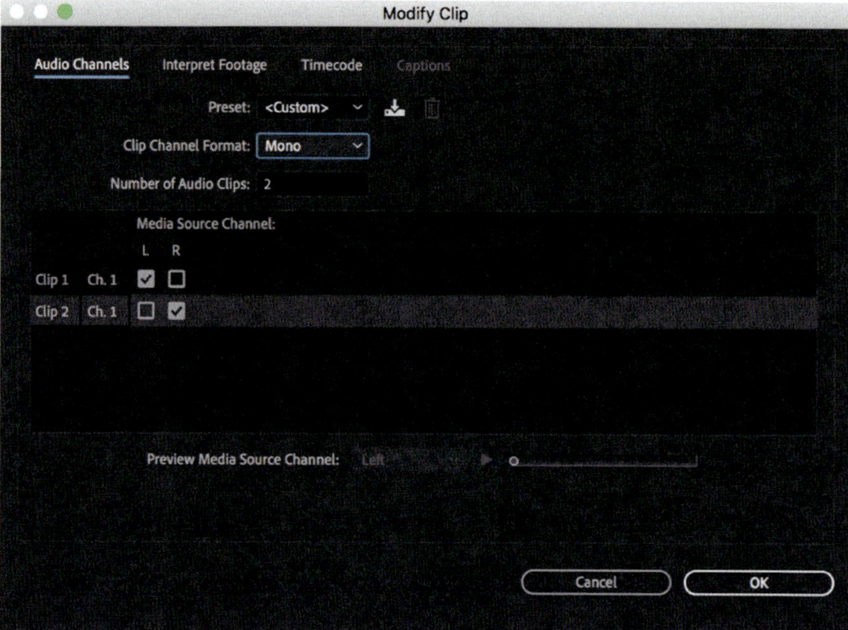

Figure 8.9

The Modify Clip window with settings to convert a stereo clip to two channels of mono sound.

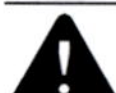 Make Sure Mono Audio is Set to Mono

If the Default Audio Tracks are set to Use File (Preferences > Audio Preferences), when you import any clip with two channels of audio into Premiere it will get interpreted as stereo. (Stereo audio always has two channels.) This is great for music, but if your production audio is actually mono, you'll have to rectify this by right-clicking on a clip in a bin and selecting Modify > Audio Channels from the menu. Make sure that the Clip Channel Format is set to mono, the number of audio clips should be two, and Left is selected for Clip 1, Channel 1 and Right is selected for Clip 2, Channel 1 (Figure 8.9). Be sure to do this before you build multicam sequences.

Switching

Back in the olden days when television was live, a typical shoot had three cameras but only a single live feed. Someone would have to operate a switcher, a device that allowed them to edit from camera to camera on the fly. Digital multicam editing still reflects this history—the way that you setup a multicam sequence affects how switching between cameras works later when you're editing.

Get the Audio Settings Right

There are two types of multicam sequence you can make in Premiere—multicam where only the video switches as you edit and multicam where audio follows video as you switch. Audio settings are what make this determination. There are three audio scenarios (Figure 8.10) that Premiere is equipped to handle for multicam: Camera 1, All Cameras, and Switch Audio. Camera 1 and All Cameras will give you multicam sequences where only the video switches and Switch Audio will give you a multicam sequence where audio follows video as you switch.

As always, the key to getting what you want is choosing the right settings.

Camera 1 is the best setting for shoots that have a single source of good audio. That audio was either fed to the main camera or recorded as a separate audio-only file. Don't be daunted by the fact that this setting is named Camera 1—if you have a separate audio-only file, Premiere will automatically designate it as the main audio source instead of the camera audio. All the audio that's not from the primary source will still be present in the multicam sequence but those tracks will be muted. This is a bit of automated housekeeping that is very convenient if you know for a fact that you don't need the rest of the audio. Be aware that whatever camera you chose first when you selected the clips to build your sequence will be the basis on which Premiere builds this sequence. When you edit this type of multicam footage, only the video will change as you switch cameras.

All Cameras is just like the Camera 1 without the housekeeping—none of the audio tracks will be muted in the resulting multicam sequence. If you think you need all of your audio or just don't know what you need yet, this might be a better choice than the Camera 1 setting because it will avoid some complications that may arise due to how the audio is bussed when you choose Camera 1 (more on that in a bit).

Switch Audio means that each camera has also recorded the sound that needs to go with it. This is common in reality TV shoots: every camera is paired with a sound recordist, so the audio on that camera goes with what you see in the shots it recorded. When you edit this type of multicam footage, you'll be able to use the Audio Follow Video setting when you edit, so that whenever you switch cameras, the audio will switch as well.

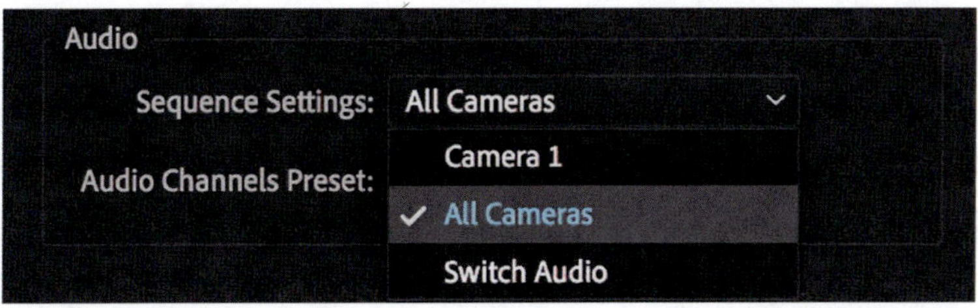

Figure 8.10

The Audio Sequence Settings menu in the Create Multicam Source Sequence window gives you options that affect how multicam editing works later on.

Troubleshooting Multicam Sequences

It's hard to get a complicated multicam sequence exactly right on the first go. So the best practice is to check each multicam sequence after you create it by opening it in the Timeline (Figure 8.11). Just use the right-click menu in the bin and select Open in Timeline. Your multicam clip will open as a sequence in the Timeline and you can now edit it just like any other sequence. You'll want to check sync, clean up any strangeness (like shots from the same camera spread over multiple tracks), remove extraneous tracks, and rename tracks if you chose that option (Figure 8.12).

Audio in Premiere can get especially complicated when it comes to multicam sequences. You have maximum control over how it gets assigned to each camera and also how it gets sent—or *bussed*—to different tracks as you edit. You may need to adjust the audio configuration by bussing and panning tracks and also making sure you have the correct number of tracks in your multicam sequence. With the multicam sequence open in the Timeline go to the Audio Track Mixer, found in one of the tabs in the same window as the Source monitor or at Window > Audio Track Mixer. Here, there's a small menu to the right that lets you tell Premiere how many tracks you want in this sequence. Then there's a small audio track assignment icon for each track (Figure 8.13) that brings up the Track Output Channel Assignments window which gives you options for how this track gets bussed when you edit the multicam clip into your film. Typically, you'll want a one to one relationship for the tracks in your multicam sequence. That is, the total number of tracks in the Audio Track Mixer should match the number of tracks in the multicam sequence and track 1 should be bussed to track 1-2 and panned to the left (-100), track 2 to 1-2 and panned to the right, (100), and so on. If tracks are accidentally bussed to the same output channel, you may hear them mixed together when you're editing. (You can always check the Properties of any multicam sequence to quickly see how audio has been mapped.) That's a lot to check on. But on a positive note, whatever works for one multicam sequence in your project is likely to work for the rest. So once you figure out the quirks, you'll be able to quickly apply them to the rest of your media.

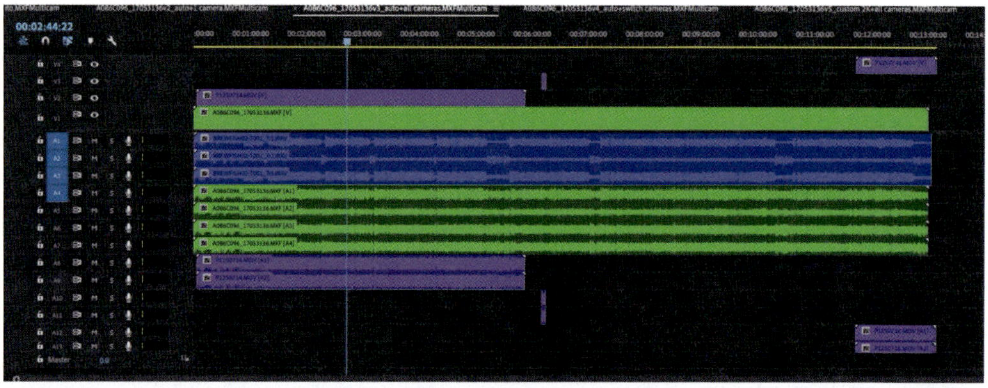

Figure 8.11

In this multicam sequence, the B camera (purple) got split onto successive tracks, which makes for cumbersome editing and one of the B camera clips is really short, probably due to In and Out points set in the source clip, (aka operator error).

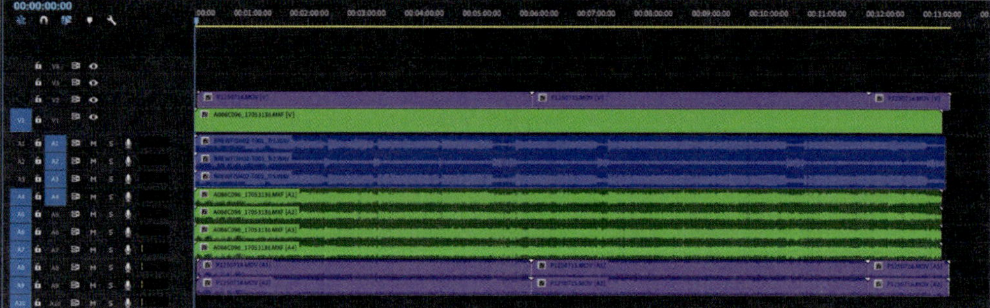

Figure 8.12

It's easy to extend the short B-camera shot on V3, then collapse all the B-camera shots onto a single track in the Timeline. This sort of minor clean-up is very common with multicam sequences and makes a huge difference when editing with it.

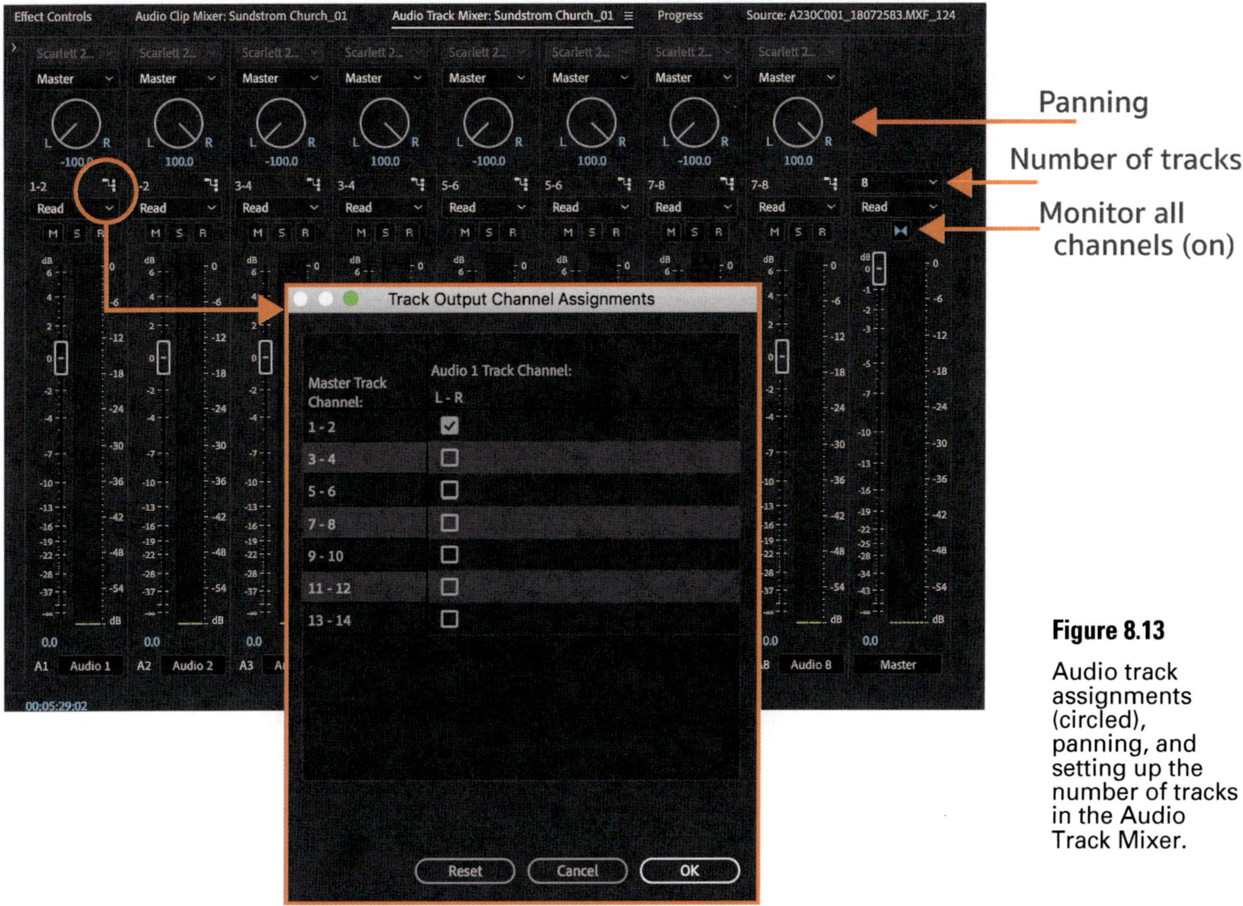

Figure 8.13

Audio track assignments (circled), panning, and setting up the number of tracks in the Audio Track Mixer.

Don't Use the Audio Track Mixer to Set Levels

The changes you make in the Audio Track Mixer affect the whole sequence, so don't use it to adjust audio levels—instead, use the Audio Clip Mixer for that. The Audio Track Mixer is mostly used when you create final exports and we cover that in Chapter 14, Finishing.

TUTORIAL: How to Sync Multicam Dailies

Traditionally, synchronizing dailies is not necessarily a multicam task, but it's more and more common to have more than one camera on the set. And since Merge Clips does not work for many, the solution is to build multicam sequences even if there's only one video source. The skills involved in synchronizing separate video and audio clips lie at the heart of multicam editing. In this tutorial, you'll learn to get comfortable with the concepts and methods needed to sync dailies and build multicam sequences.

When you have a complicated array of camera angles, audio recordings, and separate slates for each camera, you may not be able to simply set sync points in all your shots and use automated processes to make a multicam sequence. In this case, your best bet is to synchronize the footage yourself in the Timeline.

We'll start with using the automated processes in Premiere and then move on to building a custom multicam sequence in the Timeline.

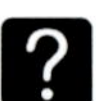 **Dailies**

Depending on the type of camera you used, or the limitations of the shoot itself, you may have decided to record your audio on a separate device, a process known as double-system recording. If so, your sound and picture will need to be synchronized before you can edit with them. Once upon a time this process, known as synching dailies, took hours to complete, but with digital editing applications like Premiere, it's generally fast and easy.

STEP 1: Try a Blind Auto-Sync First

In general, it's worth giving automatic sync a shot before you sync anything yourself—it's possible that Premiere will figure it all out for you. Create a new project with the default settings (File > New > Project) and import the media folder called Two-cam Sync Tutorial. You'll see a selection of video and audio clips. Select all (Command/Control + A), right-click, and choose "Make Multicamera Sequence." The Create Multicam Sequence window will open (Figure 8.8).

We're going to use the easiest method first—automatic sync via audio. Select Audio from the Synchronize Point options, make sure "Move source clips to Processed Clips bin" is selected, choose "All Cameras" from the Sequence Settings menu and "Mono" for the Audio Channels Preset. "Camera Names" is a matter of personal preference. Hit "Ok" and wait for the results.

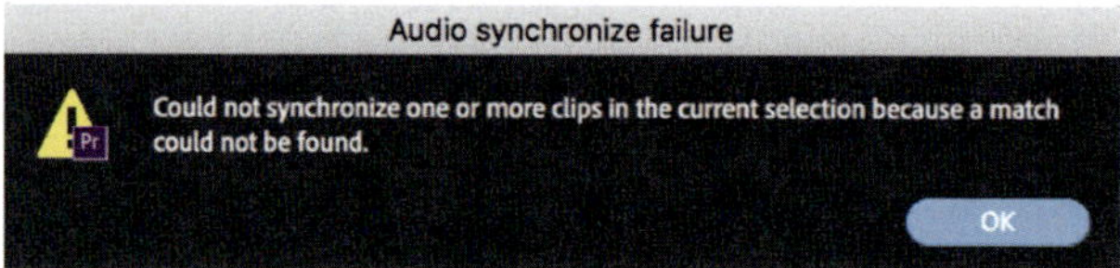

Figure 8.14

When Premiere fails to auto-sync multicam sequences, you'll get this message.

STEP 2: Inspect the Results

Despite the dire warning (Figure 8.14), Premiere did sync one set of clips into a multicam sequence. Take a look at your bin. You should see a new sub-bin called "Processed Clips" and a new multicam sequence in the main bin called 110B-1A.mp4Multicam. That means you'll have to sync the second group yourself. But first, take a look at the multicam sequence that Premiere

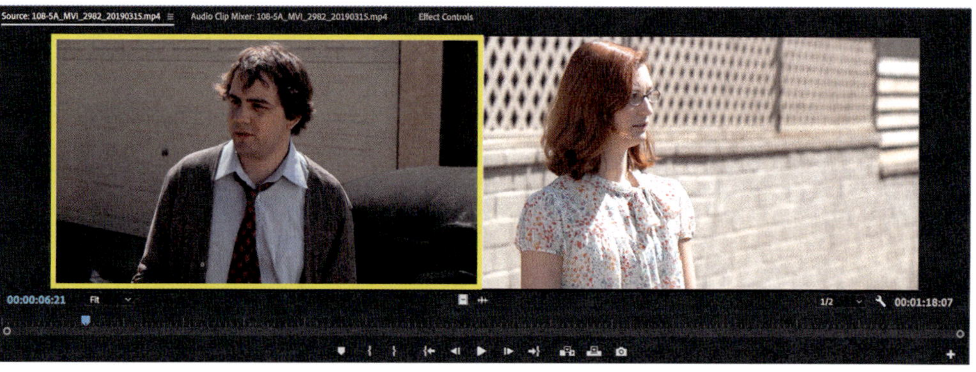

Figure 8.15

This camera arrangement is awkward because the eyelines don't match, so swap the shots in the camera banks.

created by opening it in the Source monitor. To see a multi-camera view, you'll have to select it from the Display Settings (wrench) menu. How does it look? Sometimes the order of the cameras is awkward—in this case the A camera is second and it would probably be easier to edit if they were swapped (Figure 8.15) so that the eyelines match.

STEP 3: Rearrange the Cameras and Audio

Switching the camera positions is easy—we'll just rearrange the tracks in the multicam sequence in the Timeline. Right-click on the multicam sequence in the bin and select Open in Timeline. This is how you can see the underpinnings of any multicam sequence—it's also where you can edit it as needed (Figure 8.16). With multicam sequences, V1 is always the first camera in the multicam bank, V2 is second and so on. In this case, simply going use drag-and-drop to swap the footage on V1 and V2. Keep Snapping on and take care to only move it horizontally (i.e., keep sync).

While we're at it, we might as well clean up the audio. Olivia's audio is on A2, but she's the main character so swap her audio with the audio on A1, the male actor's audio. There's nothing on A3 so we can delete it. A4 has the boom and A5 and A6 are camera mic. We can move them up and disable or mute the camera mics.

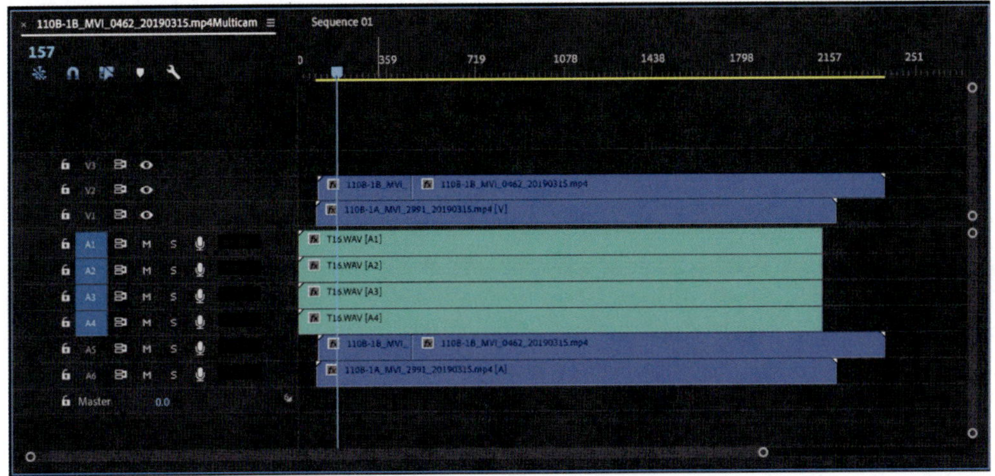

Figure 8.16

Viewing a multicam sequence in the Timeline. The media on V1 will get displayed as the first camera in multicam view. Audio recorded separately will get prioritized and placed in the sequence starting with A1. Simply drag the contents of each track to rearrange them.

Bug Watch: No Sound!

Sometimes when you open a sequence and hit play, you'll hear no sound for some of your clips, even though you see levels moving in the audio monitor. This appears to be a bug and the fix is to mute and unmute any of the audio tracks that has content in it. It should start playing properly after that. Completely unconfirmable evidence suggests that this might be a bug that's related to multicam sequences. If that doesn't work, open the Audio Track Mixer and turn the Monitor All Channels button on (Figure 8.13). It looks like a little bowtie and when it's on, it's blue. (Its normal job is to temporarily override audio settings such as muted or soloed tracks.) But it's more serious purpose, at least for now, is to make this bug evaporate. Toggle the bowtie button on and off and your silent audio problem should disappear. If this doesn't work, it may not be a bug, it may be the way the audio is configured in the multicam sequence.

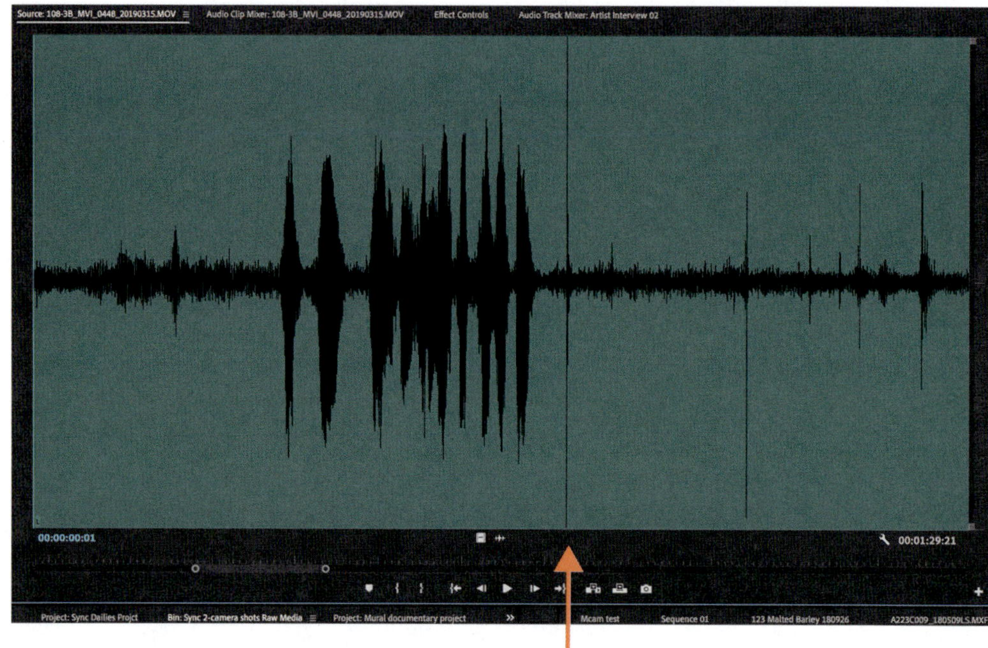

Figure 8.17

A slate clap has a distinctive sharp line in the audio waveform.

STEP 4: Sync the Other Clips Manually

To build a multicam sequence yourself in the Timeline, you'll need a blank multicam sequence to start with. Take the multicam sequence you made in Steps 1-3 and duplicate it. Rename it, 108-5 Multicam, open it in the Timeline, and delete the media. You now have an empty multicam sequence that you can use to sync the rest of the media.

The file called 108-5.WAV contains the audio you'll use as a basis for this new multicam sequence, so we'll add those tracks first. Load the audio clip in the Source monitor and find the slate clap. Slate claps are fairly easy to identify visually—they look like a sharp spike in the waveform (Figure 8.17). Set an In point on the frame that contains the slate clap (01:54:32:04) and edit it into your sequence starting on track A1. You should see four tracks of audio in the Timeline.

Next load the video clip that starts with 108-5A—that's the scene number, take number and camera letter. Launch it into the source monitor, find the slate and set an In (00:00:07:04). Send the video to on V1 and patch the audio to A5, then Overwrite. Follow the same steps for 108-5B, patching video to V2 and audio to A6. All the slates on all the tracks should be aligned at the first frame of the sequence. Watch the sequence and be sure to make sure that the audio matches the video in both cameras. Since there's only one good mic for this second multicam sequence—the boom on A4—you can Open in Timeline and disable, mute, or delete the other tracks.

That's it. Double-click on the new multicam sequence in the bin and load it into the Source monitor. You can now work with it like any other source clip. You won't need to go back to viewing it in the Timeline unless you have a problem to correct.

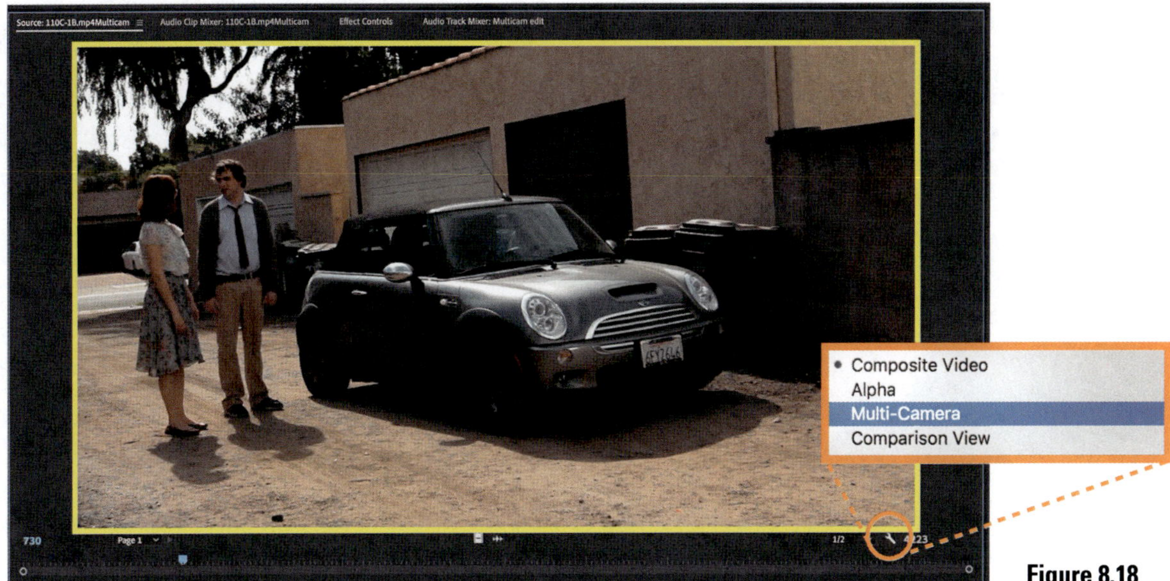

Figure 8.18

The Source monitor shows a yellow outline when the clip displayed is multicam even if the monitor is not set to multicam view. To see all the cameras, select Multi-Camera from the wrench menu.

Editing Multicam

Okay, so finally we are going to talk about actually editing with multicam media. Clearly, building multicam sequences is the hard part. But once you start editing with them, you'll forget that immediately. Multicam sequences make dealing with lots of cameras incredibly easy—and fun.

Multicam in the Source Monitor

When you launch a multicam clip into the Source monitor, you'll only see one of the cameras (Figure 8.18). In other words, it will look like any ordinary shot. But there will be a yellow outline around the image that identifies the source as multicam. In order to see all the cameras, you need to go to the Source monitor Display Settings menu (wrench icon) and choose Multi-camera from the list. (Normal single-camera view is called Composite Video.) Your monitor view will now display a split-screen view of all the camera angles in the multicam sequence

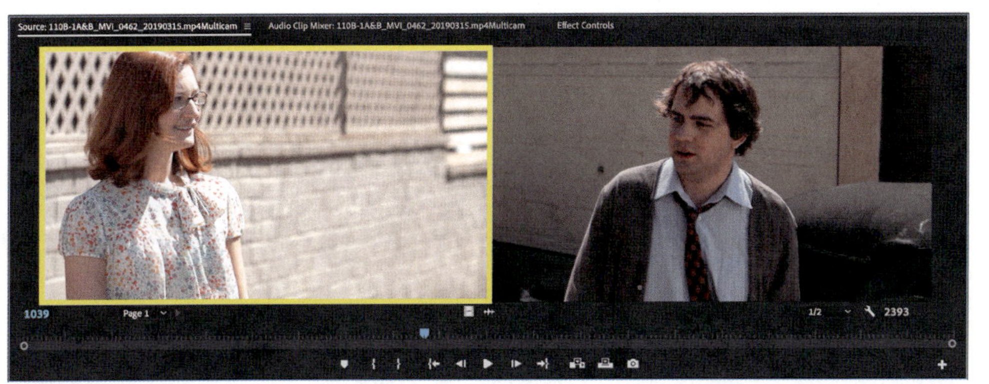

Figure 8.19

When you switch the Source monitor to Multi-camera View, you'll see all the cameras available to you at the frame you're parked on. The simplest way to edit multicam is to select a camera (yellow outline) and then edit as if it were ordinary source media.

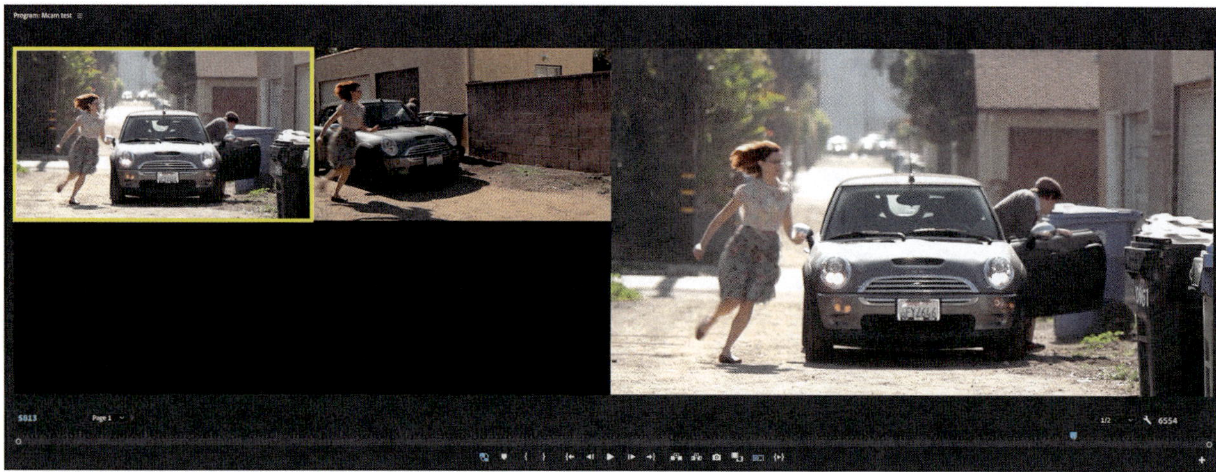

Figure 8.20

Multi-camera view in the Program monitor looks a little different. It's actually a small editing interface with all the source streams on the left and the active stream in the large window on the right. Shown here, the Program monitor is in standard switching mode, which is indicated by the yellow outline around the active camera angle.

(Figure 8.19). The most basic way of editing multicam footage is to select the camera in the Source monitor by clicking on it—the yellow outline will move to that camera angle to show that it's active—and then edit it into a sequence as you normally would, using Ins and Outs, patching tracks, and choosing between Insert and Overwrite.

Multicams are Nested Sequences

Multicam sequences are a special type of nested sequence, so you'll need to have nesting toggled on in the Timeline. (We covered nested sequences in Chapter 3.) Also, any changes you make to the multicam sequence when you use "Open in Timeline" will trickle through anywhere that you used that multicam sequence as a source. It's natural to match frame back to your multicam sequence, open it in the timeline to figure out what's what, and solo a track to listen to it, but be sure to unsolo it after you're done.

Multicam in a Sequence

Once you have multicam footage edited into a sequence, you can view it in the Program monitor (wrench menu > Multi-Camera). You may need to enable multicam mode (Clip > Multi-Camera > Enable). Here you'll see a special multicam editing interface (Figure 8.20) with all the source cameras on the left and a larger view of the active camera (yellow outline) on the right.

Multi-Camera View in the Program monitor is special because it's "live" in a sense. When you click on any of the video streams to switch cameras, the camera will switch in your sequence in the Timeline as well. In other words, if you click on a camera, you'll actually change the contents of the shot in the sequence.

There are two multicam editing modes available to you in Program monitor: *standard switching* and *live switching*. Whenever sequence playback is paused, you are automatically in standard switching mode. Standard switching is identified by the yellow outline around the active camera (as opposed to a red outline). When you click on a source camera in the Program monitor, the whole shot will change in the Timeline.

Live switching is identified by a red outline around the active camera and is more like what you might be familiar with from other editing applications (Figure 8.21). Live switching only works when the sequence is playing—every time you select a camera as it plays, a splice is added to the

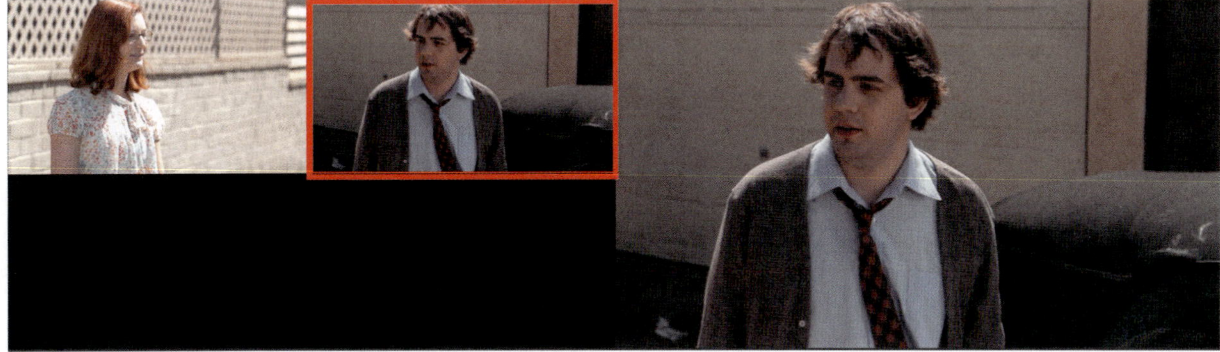

shot in the sequence and the shot changes to the camera you selected. To activate live-switching, you have to hit Play first. The outline for that camera will turn red and you'll now be in live switching mode until you pause playback.

Figure 8.21

The camera with the red outline is the one that's currently active in live switching mode.

For most feature films, you'll treat multicam footage the same way you treat single-camera footage—you'll launch it in the Source monitor, mark the good parts with Ins and Outs, then edit it into your sequence. But sometimes a whole scene is contained in a single multicam sequence. If that's the case, you can simply set In and Out marks to get rid of the slop at the beginning and end, then edit the whole shot into a sequence, whether is a sequence for the scene or the whole film. Even though it's called a multicam "sequence," it's still just another piece of source media. You never edit in the multicam sequence itself, rather you add it to a new sequence and edit there.

One last thing—Multi-camera view means you're playing multiple video streams at once. This is very taxing on your computer and requires a lot of RAM and GPU processing power to work properly. In the case of full-resolution 4K (or higher) video, you may not be able to play more than one stream at a time, so you'll have to lower the playback resolution and/or use proxies.

☑ Toggle Multi-camera View

Found under the "+" icon in the lower right corner of the Source and Program monitors, the Button Editor lets you add the Toggle Multi-camera View button to the bottom row of buttons on the Source and Program monitors. Clicking this button will switch back and forth from single cam to multi-cam view (Figure 8.22)

Use the Keyboard

The numbers 1-9 are programmed to Select Cameras 1-9, so using them lets you switch cameras very quickly, which can be important in live switching mode. You can also customize the keyboard and move them to the keys of your choosing.

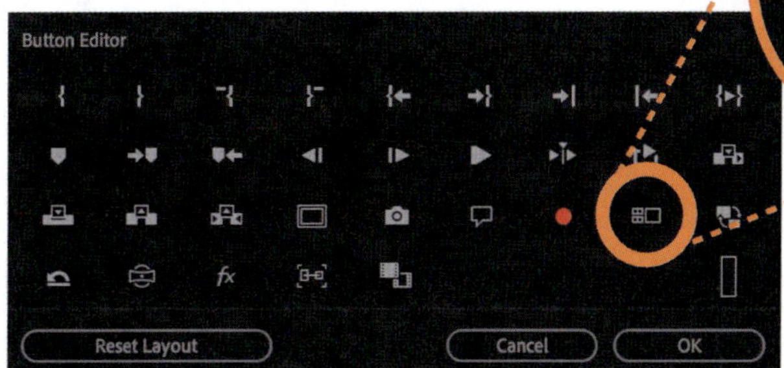

Figure 8.22

Add this button to your Program monitor to quickly get into multicam mode.

Match Frame and Multicam

The first time you hit Match Frame on a multicam clip in your sequence, the multicam sequence will get pulled up in the Source monitors. To get to the original source video clip, you'll have to tap Match Frame again, this time on the Source monitor. If you want to bring up the multicam clip in the Timeline, choose Reveal in Project from the right-click menu in the Source monitor. That opens the bin containing the multicam sequence. Then right-click on it and select Open in Timeline from the menu. Your multicam sequence will now be displayed in the Timeline and you can Match Frame on any track to bring that media up in the Source monitor.

Undoing Multicam Edits

Be aware that all the edits as you live-switch cameras are treated as a single action in the History panel. So you can't just undo the last edit, you'll undo the entire pass.

Stylistic Problems to Solve

Multicam editing introduces a whole new set of conveniences and problems when you're editing. Here are a few things to consider:

Single-cam vs multicam comedies Shooting single camera results in such a distinctive look that it is one way to define genres. Hour-long single camera comedies (such as *Girls* and *The Office*) feel very different than half-hour multicam comedies (sitcoms like *Big Bang Theory).* What is that difference exactly? It's the feeling of watching something "live." Sitcoms are often shot with a live studio audio on a stage. Sports and talk shows are also commonly shot multicam and are likewise known for being "live."

Where would you place the cameras? Try to imagine shooting a concert, a football game, or a live political debate. Where would you place the cameras so that they cut together? What about a traditional three-camera sitcom?

Edit the extras We gave you some additional clips to work with in the Sync Tutorial. Not only can you use them to practice building multicam sequences, it's also another scene to edit. You can edit it multicam style, single-cam style, or both.

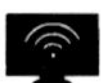

What to Watch: *A Beautiful Day in the Neighborhood*

This scripted film goes behind the scenes of the classic children's show, *Mister Rogers' Neighborhood.* It was filmed on the actual stage where the original TV series was recorded at WQED in Pittsburgh and gives a fascinating glimpse of multicam history.

9

Mixing Media and Basic Effects

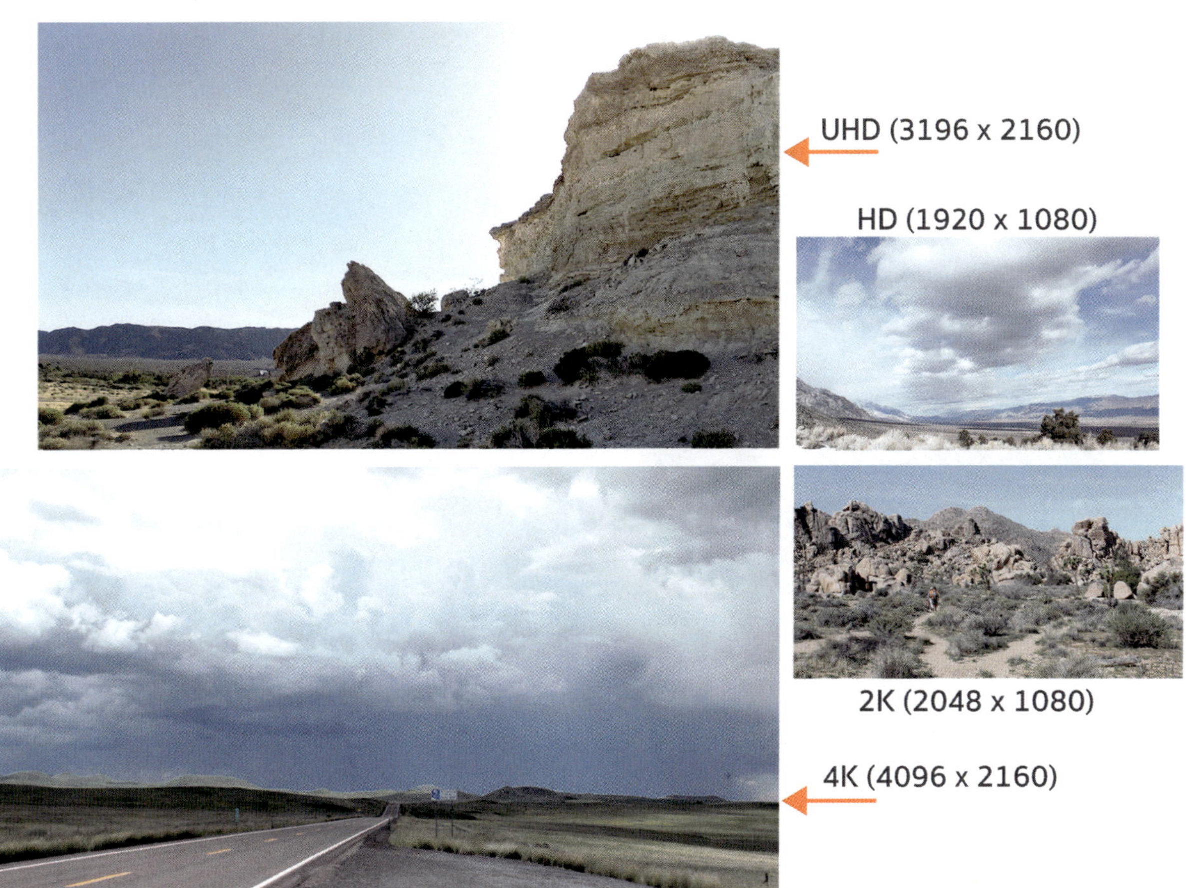

Figure 9.1

A comparison of UHD, HD, 2K, and 4K video frame sizes. As you can see, 1080 HD and UHD share the same aspect ratio, which is not quite as wide as that of 2K and 4K.

Working with Different Types of Video

Premiere is very adept at handling different types of media. It seems like there's nothing it can't work with: multi-layered stills, 360-degree media, and video of all shapes and sizes (Figure 9.1). But as a filmmaker, your goal isn't just to make a video that works inside Premiere, you need it to work on screens in the real world.

That means that if you have footage from different cameras or sources, you will probably end up needing to resize some or all of your video. If you have slow-motion footage, you'll need to make sure it plays at the right speed. And if you are adding stills to your film, you'll need to crop, reposition, and add movement to them.

All of these changes are considered effects, but they're not special. Instead, they are part of the basic palette of editorial tools that filmmakers use all the time. This chapter will introduce you to some of the ways to manipulate media using the basic visual effects available in Premiere, plus a little help from some other Creative Cloud applications.

Watch Your Aim

The text and icons in Premiere can be pretty small. As you click on Position or Motion in the Effect Controls panel, be sure not to click on the small "FX" or stopwatch icons. These will disable your effects or toggle keyframes on and off, respectively.

Resizing Options

Premiere will resize media for you, using a combination of the media scaling preferences, the size of your sequence, and scaling options that you set on a shot by shot basis.

By setting preferences, you can tell Premiere how you want all of your media scaled on import (Preferences > Media > Default Media Scaling). Here you'll find three resizing options: Set to frame size, Scale to frame size, and None (Figure 9.2).

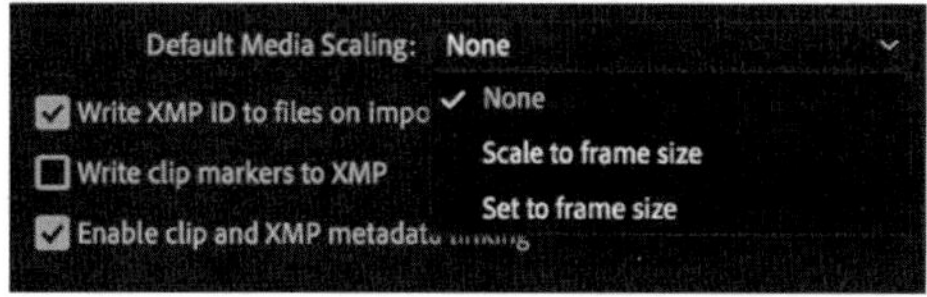

Figure 9.2 The Default Media Scaling menu in the Media Preferences panel tells Premiere how you want to handle resizing media that does not match the size of your sequence.

Set to frame size does exactly what you expect—it non-destructively resizes any piece of media that doesn't match your sequence settings to fit those sequence settings, without changing the resolution or aspect ratio of the master clip. That means if you drop an HD shot into a 2K sequence, it will not fit the frame exactly because the aspect ratio of HD and 2K are not the same. In other words, it might not work perfectly but if you don't like the way it resized your footage, you can always change it later. If you want your clips to more or less match and prefer not to spend time resizing yourself, I recommend choosing this option.

Scale to frame size After several tests, it's hard to say that "Scale to frame size" does anything at all when set as a preference. In the past, it used to actually resample your media to match the default Project settings. But now, there are no default Project settings for media size—instead, you set the media size for each sequence. My guess is that this is a leftover from previous versions of Premiere and is probably best avoided.

None The third choice is to not let Premiere resize your media at all. (Preferences > Media > Default Media Scaling > None). Premiere will do nothing and it's all on you. If you edit a 4K clip into a 2K sequence, it will playback as is—4x too big for the frame and therefore, extremely cropped. You'll have to resize it yourself. In doing so, you'll give up convenience but gain control. This is the option I prefer.

All of these scaling options are mutable—you'll be able to change them as you wish later on. Once media is already in an edited sequence, you can choose between these three options from the Clip menu (Video Options > Set/Scale to frame size).

But if you choose "None" or have parts of your movie that require custom scaling, there's a better way to resize media...

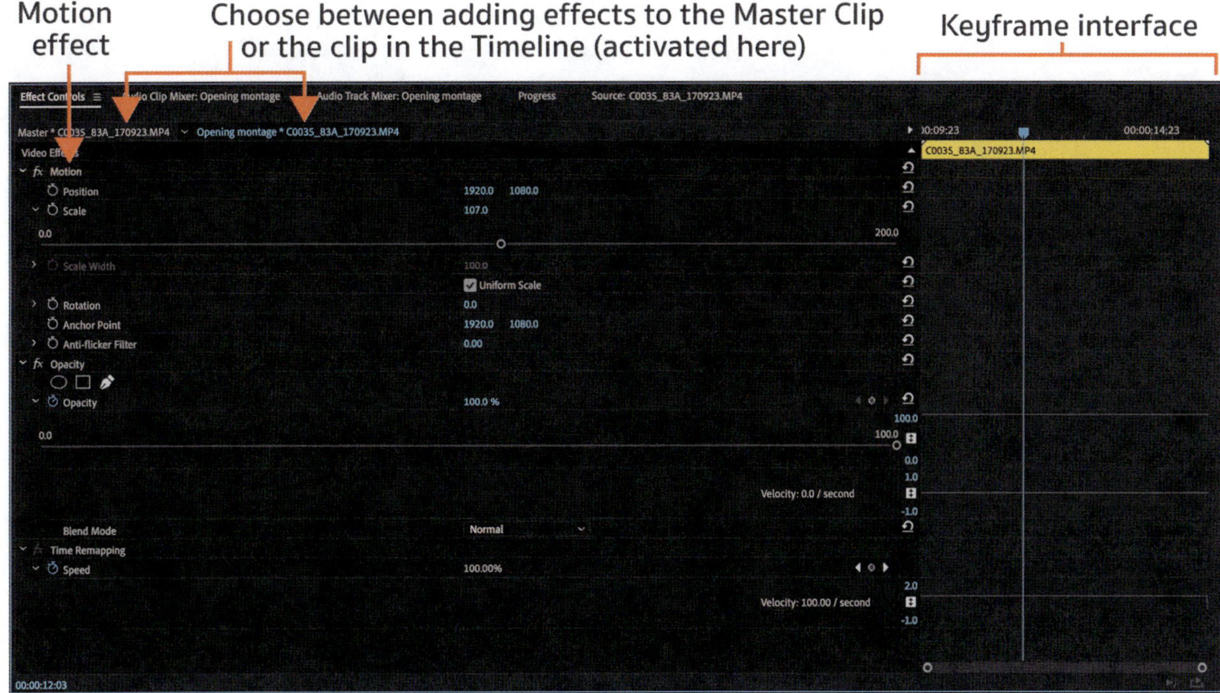

Figure 9.3

The Effect Controls panel acts as a command center where you can add, remove, review, and edit the effects applied to clips in the Timeline. All video clips have three basic effects pre-applied to them: motion, opacity, and time remapping. To the right is an area dedicated to the visual mapping and control of keyframes.

The Effect Controls Panel

To resize and reframe media in Premiere in a more customized way, you'll use the Effect Controls panel (Figure 9.3). Like many panels in Premiere, the Effect Controls panel is more than just a window, it's an interface where you can add, remove, and adjust effects applied to clips in the Timeline. It's found under a tab next to the Source monitor (Window > Effect Controls Panel) and when you select any clip in the Timeline, you'll see a list of effects (both video and audio) that have been applied to that clip. The Effect Controls panel also lets you adjust each effect by setting parameters and keyframes, which control how each effect is applied over time.

All video clips come equipped with three basic effects already applied to them: Motion, Opacity, and Time remapping. These are called *fixed effects* by Adobe and they are set to neutral, so they have no effect on your media until you adjust them. But the fact that they are applied to every clip by default is super convenient because it means that you can adjust the size of any clip in a matter of seconds.

Scale and Position

In order to resize media, you'll use two options within the Motion effect: Scale and Position. To adjust the Scale of any clip, first make sure you have it selected in the Timeline, then open Motion effect and open Scale within it. Use the slider to drag and make your clip larger or smaller. The slider is limited to 200%, so if you want to go larger, you'll have to type in a number.

These changes to Scale will keep your shot centered in the frame, but that's not always going to be the right choice. If not, you'll then use Position to reframe the media. Position isn't quite as intuitive at a glance. You can type in coordinates but most of us wouldn't choose to use this method. Instead, click on the word Motion or Position, then you can click and drag in the

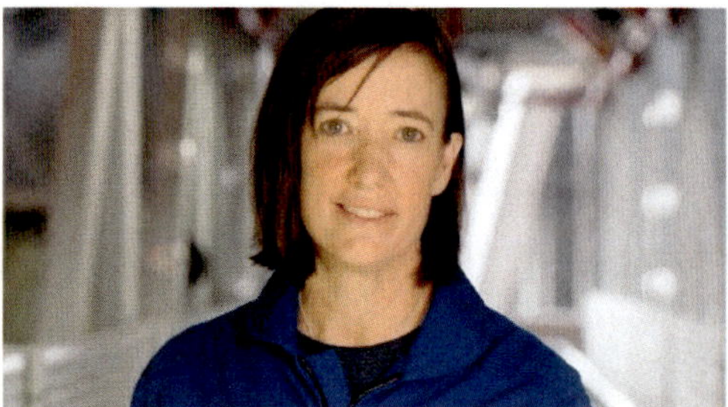
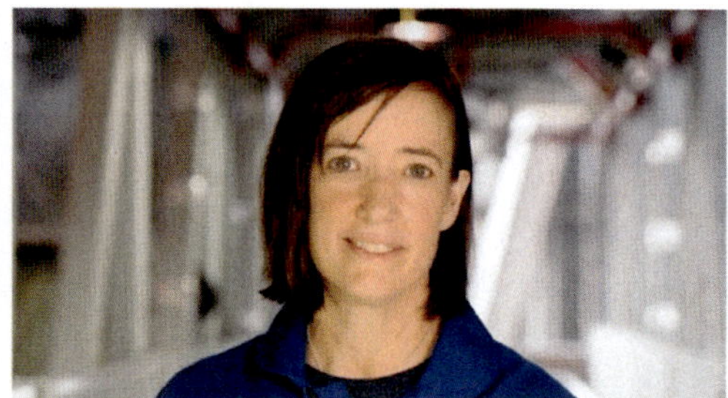

Figure 9.4

With a tightly framed shot like this interview with a NASA astronaut, even a small amount of repositioning can make a big difference.

Program monitor to reframe the shot. (For versions of Premiere prior to 2020, you have to click on a tiny box icon to the left of the Motion effect.) Even a small amount of cropping, such as going from 1920 HD to 2K, can mess up a perfectly good composition and if so, repositioning is crucial (Figure 9.4). There's a lot more to the Effect Controls panel, including the ability to add keyframes and change how a clip is scaled and positioned over time. We'll get into that later in this chapter. For now, the focus is on simply getting different types of media to work together in a sequence.

Presets

If you have to resize a lot of footage in the same way, you should save a preset of your Motion effect settings. Just right-click on the Motion effect—actually click on the word Motion—and a small menu will open with the option to save presets. Give it a name and it will be saved to the presets section of the Effects panel (Window > Effects). Now that you have a preset, you can select multiple clips in the Timeline and drag the preset onto them to change them all at once.

☑ Auto-Reframe Effect

New to Premiere 2020 is the Auto-Reframe Effect (Window > Effects > Video Effects > Transform). Drop it on a clip in your sequence that isn't the right size and click Analyze in the Effect Controls panel. I found it had similar results as Set to Frame Size (Preferences > Media > Default Media Scaling), which we discussed earlier.

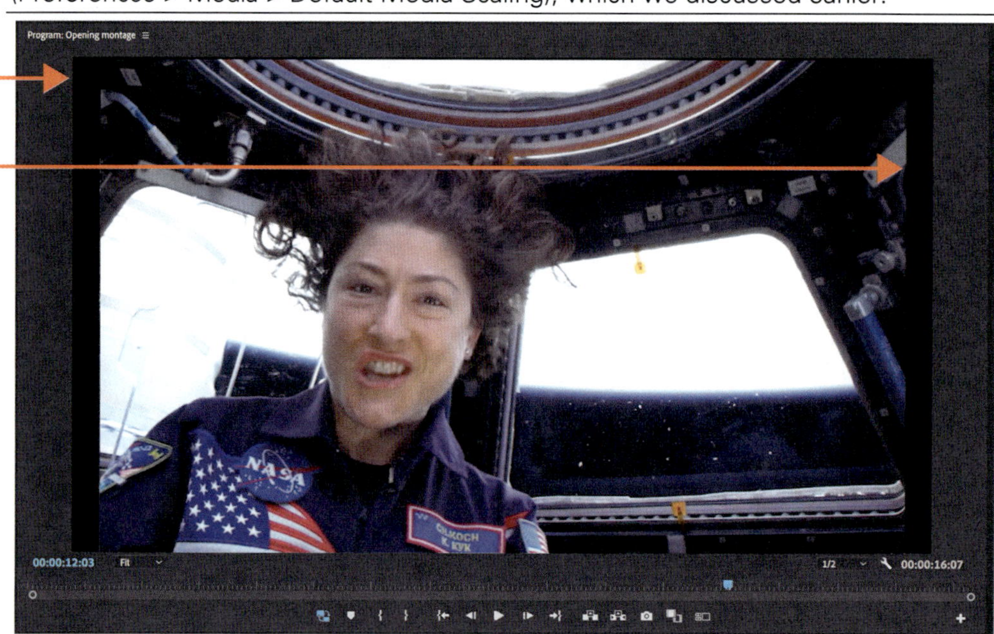

Figure 9.5

When the dimensions of your shot are smaller than that of your sequence, you'll see black bars on the sides or the top and bottom of the frame, like this HD footage in a 2K sequence. When your shot is larger, you won't see any black, but the image will be cropped.

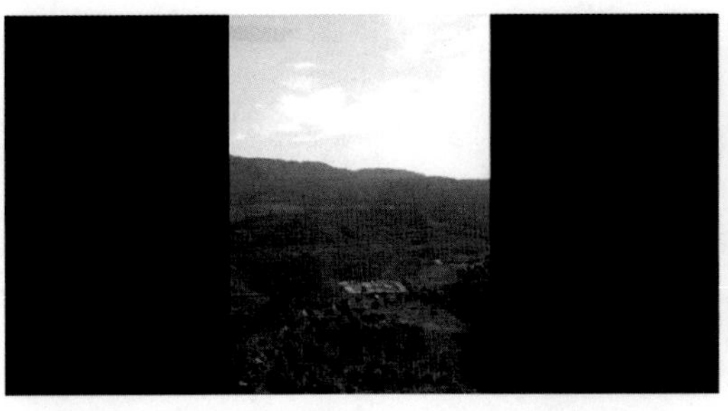
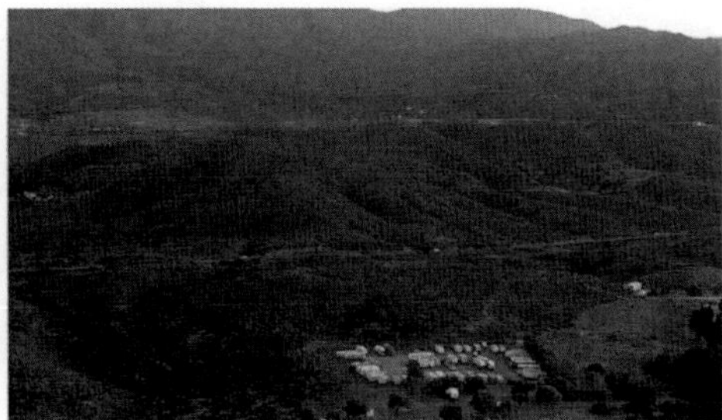

Figure 9.6

Web and mobile videos can opt for non-standard aspect ratios, but if you're trying to incorporate "tall" mobile phone video into a widescreen film project, you'll face some challenges. Either you'll have more than half the screen empty or you'll have to blow up the image so much that you'll lose more than half of it.

Common Resizing Scenarios

Resizing to match popular video formats is a common task, here are some scenarios you may encounter:

Matching 2K and HD If you have both 2K and HD video in your film, you're going to have to choose which one you want to finish in and adjust the other to fit that aspect ratio. Luckily 2K and 1920 x 1080 HD are almost the same size (Figure 9.1), so the amount of resizing that you'll have to do will not affect image quality. To increase HD to 2K, set the scale in the Effect Controls panel to 107%. The aspect ratios are not identical (Figure 9.5), so you'll get a little cropping at the sides. To decrease 2K video to 1920 x 1080 HD, set the scale to 94%.

Mixing 2K or HD with 4K You'll have to choose whether you want to enlarge the 2K/HD video 200% or reduce the 4K video to 50% (Figure 9.1). Reducing means no risk of image quality loss, but your whole film will be lower in quality (2K instead of 4K). Bumping 2K and HD up to 4K is a huge increase and it will not look great, so it's not recommended. But if you have an isolated sequence—say, archive footage in a doc—it might be acceptable to have certain scenes that look different than the rest of the film and worth it to have your whole project finish at 4K. Similarly, HD that is 1280 x 720 (aka 720p) is quite a large jump in size if you're scaling it at 2K.

Dealing with different 4K video sizes There are many different 4K cameras, but they don't always shoot the exact same frame size. So you'll have to make small adjustments to make these various sizes work together.

Creatively cropping 4K video If you shot 4K but plan to finish in 2K or HD, you have a lot of leeway when it comes to cropping your image to fit the smaller frame size. A frame of 4K is four times the size of 2K, so you have all that extra space to work with and you won't have to worry about image quality. By simply placing a 4K image into a smaller sequence, you'll end up with the image centered in your sequence. By adjusting Position and Scale, you can create a shot that's very different from the original. You might even be able to make several shots out of a single 4K clip.

Dealing with "tall" videos Traditional video has a landscape orientation—the width is greater than the height. But if you end up with mobile phone footage in your project, odds are high that it will be recorded in portrait orientation (Figure 9.6). If you're integrating this video into a film, you'll have to choose between enlarging and cropping or having a video that fills about a third of the screen. But if your project is going onto the web, you might be able to just stick with the original aspect ratio.

What about 6K and 8K? Mixing 4K with 8K will have the same issues as mixing 2K with 4K. You'll use the solutions described above when mixing these types of video with anything smaller. But on a positive note, as video for films moves away from HD, the math gets easier.

Old Video and Film Specs

Older video is usually either SD (640 x 480) or widescreen (720 x 480). It has a frame rate of 29.97 if it's from North America and 25 fps if it's from most other parts of the world. 16mm and 35mm film has a frame rate of 24 fps and very old silent film has a frame rate of 18 fps.

Mixing Frame Rates

Video has a third component related to size: time, specifically the number of frames in a second of media. The higher the frame rate, the more information contained in a shot. That's why slow-motion video starts at around 60 fps—in order to play smoothly and slowly, more frames are needed.

Premiere allows you to easily mix frame rates in a sequence. You can simply edit a clip with any frame rate into a cut and Premiere will adjust it to play at the frame rate of the sequence. You might notice some stuttering with motion on shots that have movement, especially fast action within the frame and pans, but in general it will look pretty good. As you might suspect, the smaller the shift in frame rate, the better it will look. Going from 24 fps to 25 fps (PAL) is going to look a lot better than going from 24 fps to 29.97 fps (NTSC). That said, there's not a lot you can do when you are stuck with mismatched frame rates. But there are a couple options in Premiere that you might want to try if the automatic frame rate conversion is problematic.

Interpret Footage With the clip selected in the bin, go to Clip > Modify > Interpret Footage. At the top of this large dialogue window (Figure 9.7), you can check the dot next to Assume Frame Rate and then enter a different frame rate for any clip. This change will affect the clip from this point going forward, but it won't change any instances of it that you previously edited into sequences. You may need to use this command to get 60 fps slowmo to play correctly in a 24 fps sequence, although many cameras that record 60 fps or higher slowmo will include metadata that tells Premiere how to correctly play the footage.

Transcode in Media Encoder or elsewhere You can always convert footage before you start editing with it, using any transcoding app. Since each transcoding application uses a different algorithm, it may be worthwhile to experiment and compare the results.

Clip menu > Speed/Duration This option is usually used as an effect, to create slow-mo for example. But sometimes a shot is recorded at the wrong frame rate and you might be able to correct it here. Perhaps the camera operator was shootings slow-motion footage at 60 fps and on the next shoot, they forgot to switch it back to 23.976. In the Clip Speed/Duration window, adjust the speed using a percentage or by setting a specific length for the shot. You can also choose reverse motion here.

Time interpolation options

When you adjust the frame rate of a clip, Premiere has a few different algorithms that make the new frame rate work. With the clip selected in the Timeline, go to Clip > Video Options > Time Interpolation. You can choose between three options in the Time Interpolation menu: Frame sampling, Frame Blending, and Optical Flow. (These options are also available in Clip > Speed/Duration if you select it from the Timeline.) Frame Sampling is the most basic option and the default—you don't need to go to Time Interpolation to get it. In Frame Sampling, frames are either doubled or removed to get to the right frame rate. Frame Blending also doubles frames but it blends them together to get smoother motion. Optical Flow creates new frames using special calculations and is processor-intensive, so it requires rendering. It is optimized for movement that doesn't have motion blur. As you might guess, experimenting with Frame Blending and Optical Flow is the only way to know if one of them works best for you.

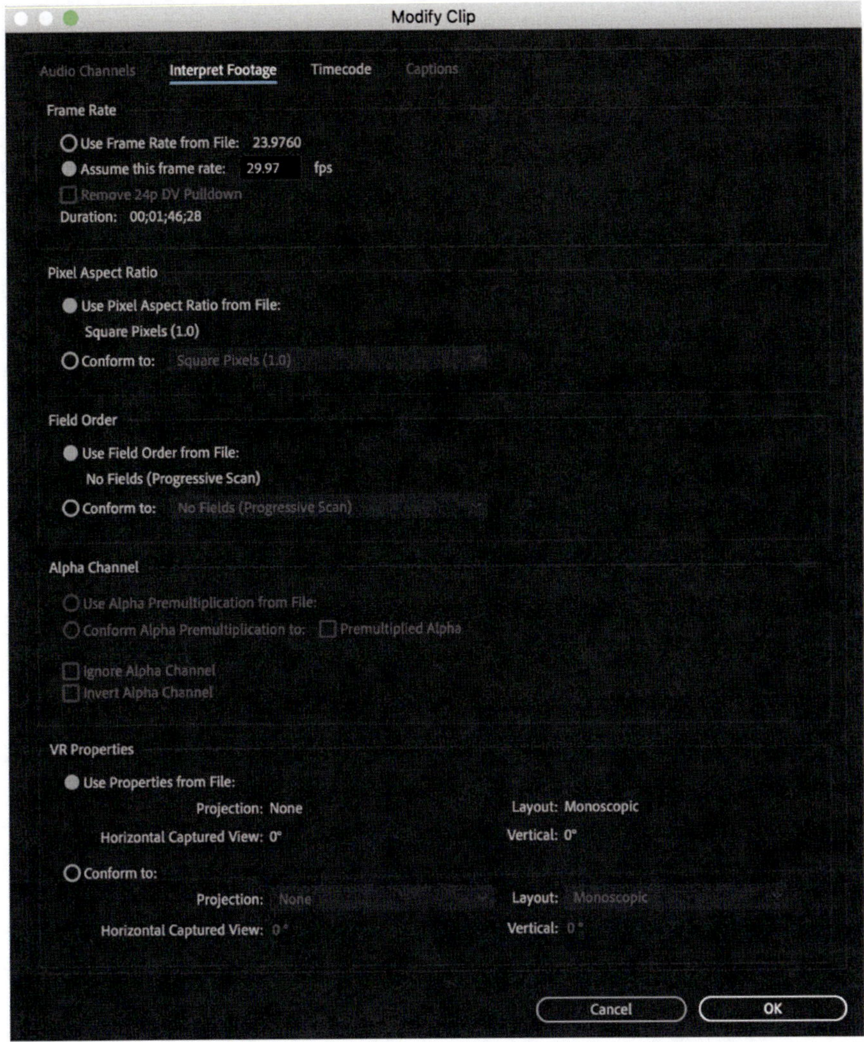

Figure 9.7

The Modify Clip panel gives you lots of options for changing your media. Everything from changing frame rates to controls for alpha channels to adjusting VR properties.

360º Video

Working with 360-degree video can be surprisingly simple. That's because it's just a frame of standard video that's recorded in a special way. First, you'll need to check that the VR Properties (Figure 9.7) for your 360-degree clip are set right (Clip > Modify > VR Properties). You'll most likely want to choose equirectangular projection and stereoscopic side by side layout.

When you open a 360-degree clip in the Source monitor, you'll see the full 360-degree image (Figure 9.8). To change it to something more like normal perspective, select VR Video > Enable from the Settings (wrench) menu (Figure 9.9). The presents a new viewer that includes controls on the bottom and right that let you navigate around the full 360-degree frame. If your final

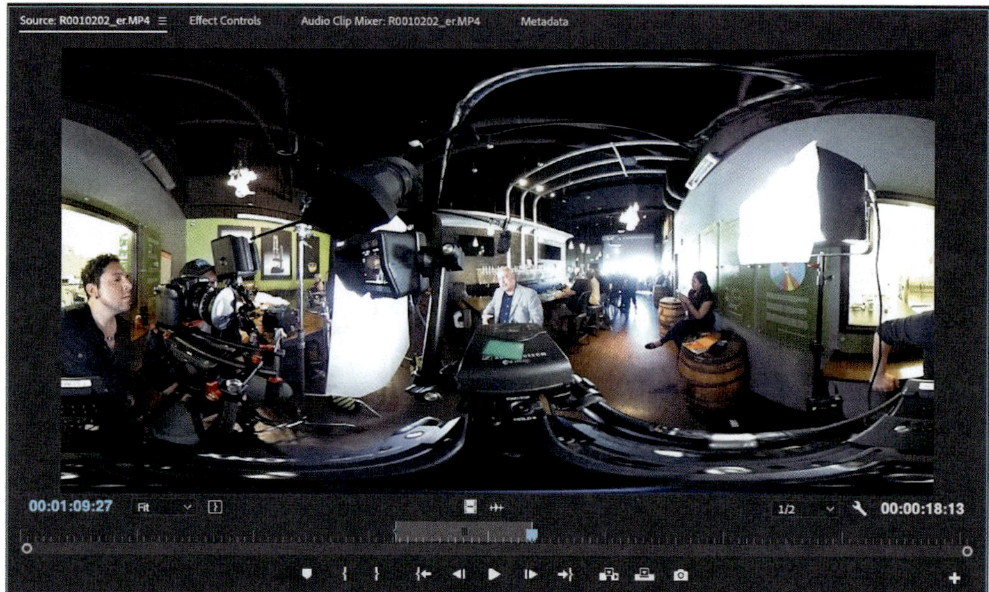

Figure 9.8

Raw 360° video in the Source monitor.

video is 360-degrees, you'll also need to make sure your sequence is set up for 360-degree video (Sequence > Sequence Settings).

One cool thing about 360-degree video is that you can pull a bunch of shots from any one clip. In the clip shown here, I could pull a shot of the guy talking in the interview setup, a shot of the woman on the right, a shot of the people at the bar, and a shot of the camera person.

To reframe the 360-video in a standard video sequence, edit it into your sequence. VR Video should be disabled. Add the VR Projection effect to the 360-degree clip (Window > Effects > Video Effects > Immersive Video > VR Projection). This effect allows you to adjust the shape of the 360-degree video. Using a combination of VR Projection, Scale, and Position, you can find standard video shots within the 360-degree image.

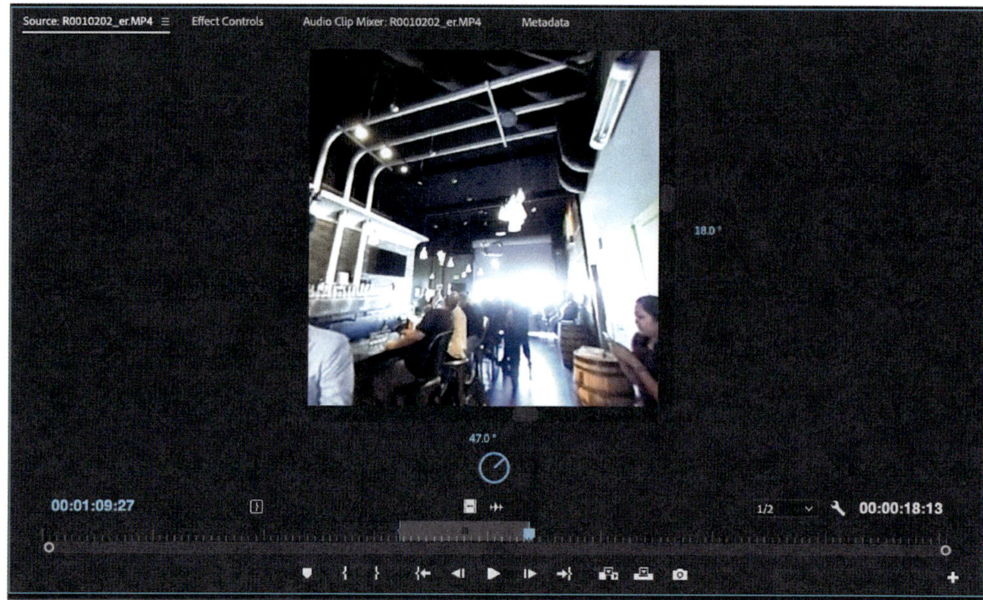

Figure 9.9

Enabling VR video gives you a new view of the same clip, with controls to adjust the point of view.

The only issue is that the resolution of the video frame is spread across the whole image, so each clip you pull will be lower in resolution. The shots I just described are a tiny percentage of the frame, so even if it's 4K video, the resolution of these shots will most likely be lower than 2K.

➡ Working with VR

Coverage of all aspects of working with 360-degree footage—from cameras and shooting to editing, sound, and post-production are spread throughout *The Digital Filmmaking Handbook*. You can find a list of these resources in the index at the back of the book.

Editing Unscripted

Documentary projects will stretch the boundaries of any editing application. Other types of unscripted projects, such as reality shows and improvised comedies, face similar issues. After all, a documentary might get shot over several years, or reach deep into the past. A big reality show can have more than ten cameras and twenty cast members. And a scene in an improvised comedy can have a great many takes that do not match in any way. In short, they all deal with unpredictable situations and rather than designing a scene shot by shot, they aim for *coverage*. Generally, the result is copious amounts of media, from many sources. That presents a host of creative and technical challenges.

In this section, we'll look at the tools in Premiere that help when editing these types of films and show you how to deal with mixing different types of media in the same sequence—both stills and video. While unscripted projects are more likely to need these tools and techniques, they are potentially relevant to films of any kind.

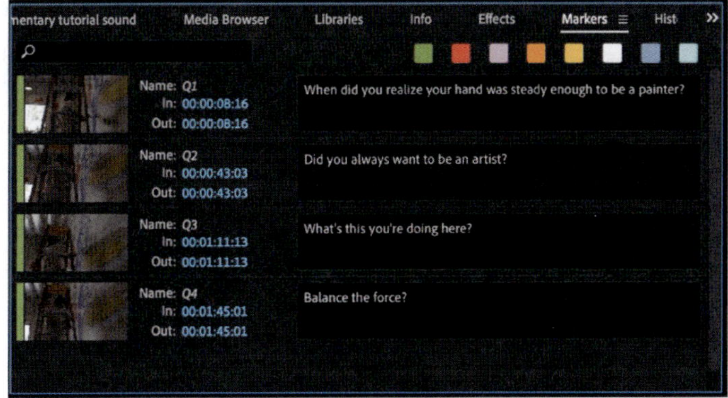

Figure 9.10

The Markers panel gives you a storyboard-like layout with room to log your shots and easy access to labels.

What to Watch: *The Family* docuseries

The Family is a fascinating documentary series that spans several decades, so you'll see a wide variety of archival media mixed with footage shot by the filmmakers and still images. In addition, it's a great example for other unscripted filmmaking techniques such as shooting interviews with two-cameras so that you can cut from one to the other, and beautifully constructed recreations with actors. And it shows how graphics can be both visually compelling and informative, helping the viewer understand the linkages between a huge amount of complex and often disparate archival materials.

Logs, Labels, and Markers

When you have a lot of footage to wade through, it can be helpful to take notes. logging is available in several of the Bin List view columns, labels help you organize by adding color to different types of media, and markers let you add comments to any frame in a shot or sequence (Figure 9.10). They're all effective ways to help you navigate your media so that you can find stuff as you edit.

Logging in Bin Columns

Back when most video was tape-based, logging each shot was required. Now, it's something you do on an as-needed basis. But the bigger your project, the more useful it can be. There are several information columns available to you in Bin List view that can be used for logging—the Description, Log Note, and Comment columns all allow for any sort of text entry. The Good column is a simple checkbox, which can be useful for sorting shots.

If you don't see these columns in Bin List view, go to the Panel Settings menu on the tab for the panel containing your bin and select Metadata Display. Open the first sub-menu, Premiere Pro Project Metadata, and you'll see a large list of all the various bin columns that are available to you. Once you've added the logging columns to your bin display, you can log each shot in the bin or in the Clip portion of the Metadata panel (Figure 9.11). Alternately, you can use the Metalogging workspace preset (Window > Workspaces > Metalogging) if you have a lot of clips to log—it's a custom designed panel layout just for logging bin columns and metadata.

If you think you want these columns to appear in every single bin in your project, go to your main Project window and select the Metadata Display columns there. Each bin will inherit these columns.

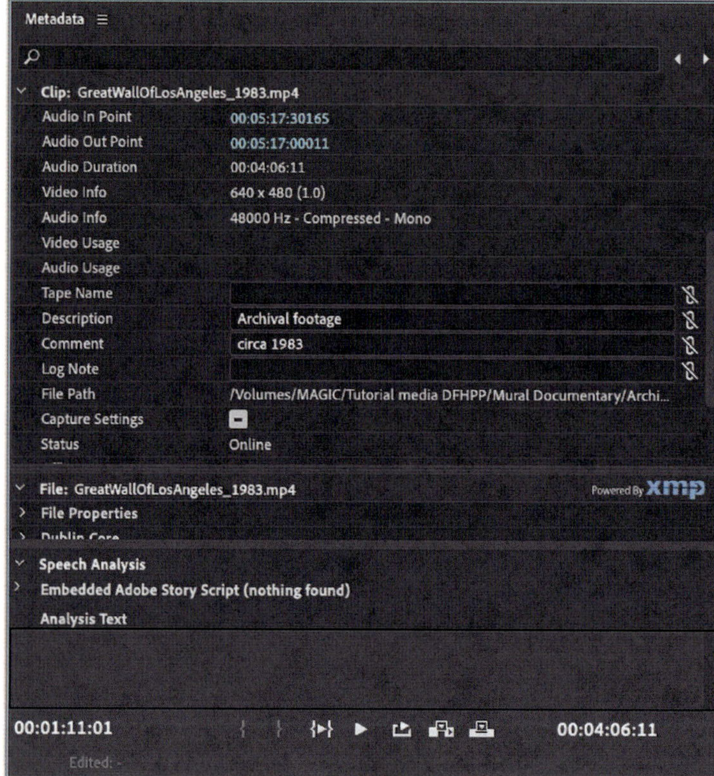

Figure 9.11

The Metadata panel.

Key Preferences for Metadata

If you want to make sure that they translate to apps beyond Premiere Pro or across multiple systems, be sure to check the first three boxes in the Preferences > Media panel: "Write XMP ID to files on import," "Write clip markers to XMP," and "Enable clip and XMP metadata linking."

Logging in Metadata

If you want your log notes to get added to your media files on your hard drive, you'll need to use another metadata set because the Premiere Pro Project Metadata set only works within a Premiere Pro project. There are several other metadata sets listed when you open Metadata Display but the best file-based metadata set for filmmakers is Dynamic Media. It contains a list of properties that are very similar to those in the Premiere Pro Project Metadata, including Comments, Log Comments, and Good. Information added to this metadata set gets saved in your source media in the XMP format (Extensible Metadata Platform). File-based metadata is either written to your media container file or when that's not allowed, a special sidecar XMP file is created to go along with each media file (see also the metadata section in Chapter 6). Unlike the Premiere Pro Project Metadata, you can't add Dynamic Media log notes in Bin List view. Instead, you'll have to go to Dynamic Media in the Metadata panel (Window > Metadata > File > Dynamic Media) and enter your log notes there.

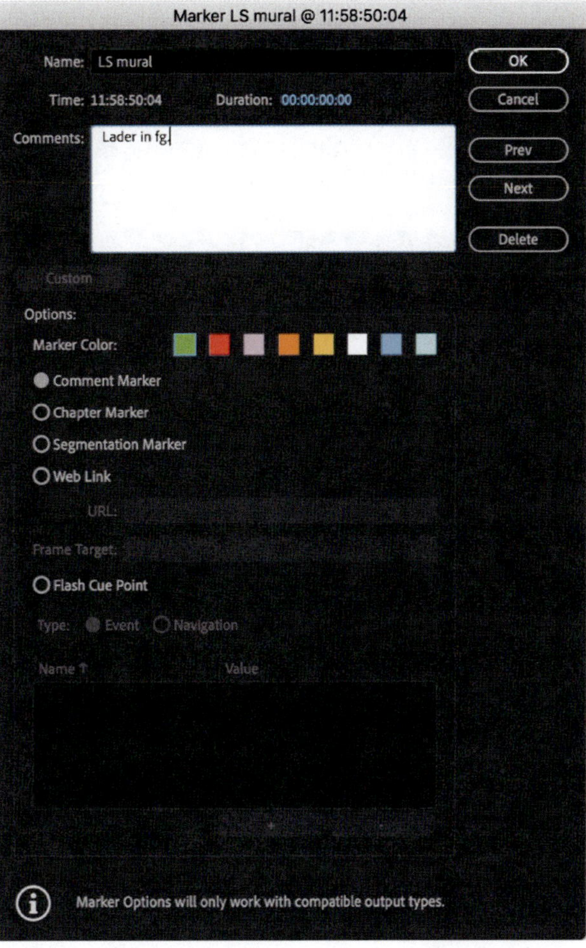

Figure 9.12

The Marker interface lets you log Comments, change Marker Colors, and navigate from marker to marker.

Using Labels to Organize Media

Colored labels are a deceptively simple way to organize your media. The default in Premiere is that different types of media are assigned different colors. You can change these colors in Preferences > Labels panel. You can also come up with your own labelling color scheme. On a documentary, you might choose one color for all interviews, another color for archival media, and another for verité footage. Or you could use different colors to indicate different locations, topics, scenes, or shoot days. The options are pretty much unlimited.

Using Markers in Premiere

When you need to make notes within a shot or edited sequence, you'll use markers. You can add markers to clips in the Source window and also when selected in the Timeline. You can also add markers to sequences in the Program window or the Timeline. Clip markers appear in the video and audio tracks of the clip itself and sequence markers appear in the time ruler in the Timeline (Figure 9.13).

To add a marker to a clip or sequence, just type the letter M. You can do this as you're playing which is very convenient. Then you can go back and double-click on any marker to bring up the Marker interface (Figure 9.12). Here you can give the marker a name, add comments or log notes, and choose a color for the marker. You can also choose between different types of markers. The most common type is a Comment Marker, which is simply a place to add text-based notes. The other types of markers are Chapter Markers (for DVDs and Blu-ray discs), Segmentation Markers (for specialized video servers), and Web Link Markers (where you can add a URL, useful for embedded video in websites and other HTML environments).

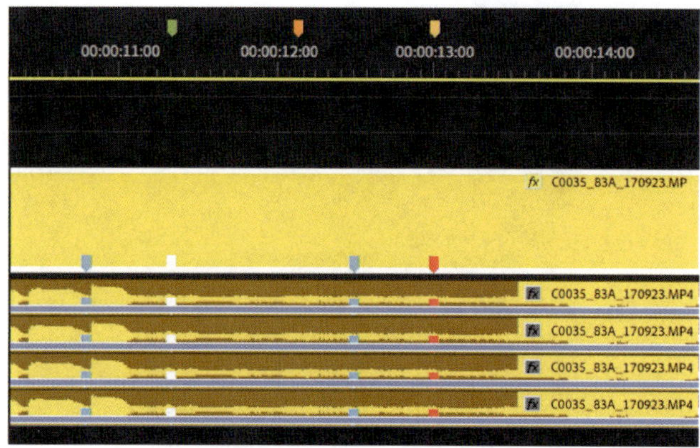

Figure 9.13 Clip and sequence markers in the Timeline.

By default, markers are added to the XMP metadata in your source media files. If you don't need this, you can disable it in Preferences > Media Preferences > Write clip markers to XMP.

Once you've added markers, you can view, edit, and search them in the Markers panel (Window > Markers). One drawback is that the name column in this panel is not adjustable, so keep your marker names short.

Markers have their own menu at the top of the Premiere Pro interface. Here you have some options for navigating markers and you can also choose Ripple Markers, which means that the markers in your sequence will move when you insert or delete media in a sequence. (It's a little confusing that editing marks—In, Out, etc.—are included in the Markers menu since they are a very different type of marking and they aren't affected by the Markers interface or panel. Just be aware that only the lower half of this menu is relevant to the type of Markers we are discussing here.)

Exporting Markers

You may want to export your markers as a list to email or print it. You can do so by choosing File > Export > Markers. You'll have the option to export them as Comma Separated Values (.csv) for spread sheets, text files (.txt) or as a web page (.html). The web page option is by far the most useful for sending or printing notes, because it includes thumbnails of the frame for each marker, comments, and timecode information in an easily readable format.

1 2 3 TUTORIAL: Editing a Documentary Scene

For many projects, dealing with media is very easy because it's from a single source. But documentaries can have a huge variety of source media and figuring out how to make it all work together can be a challenge. This tutorial walks you through the process of adding and resizing several types of video and in doing so, you'll get to edit a short documentary scene as well.

The documentary scene in this tutorial is about mural art. There's archival footage from the 1930s and the 1980s, both of which are SD video and we also have some recent 2K and HD shots courtesy of Shutterstock (Figure 9.14).

That's three types of video that need to work together in a way that's visually interesting. The goal for this documentary is to finish in 2K, so you're going to have to conform all the media to 2K. And this tutorial will help you do exactly that.

STEP 1: Setup a 2K Sequence

Create a new project and call it "Mural Documentary." Create a new sequence (File > New > Sequence > Settings tab) and set it up according to these specs:

Editing Mode: Custom
Timebase: 23.976 fps
Video Frame Size: 2048 x 1080
Pixel Aspect Ratio: Square
Fields: No Fields
Display Format: 23.976
Audio Sample Rate: 48000 Hz
Video Previews: QuickTime
Codec: Apple ProRes 422
Width and Height: 2048 x 1080

Also, check your preferences and make sure that Default Media Scaling is set to None (Preferences > Media). This tutorial will show you how to resize them yourself.

Import the contents of the Mural Documentary tutorial media folder. You'll see several folders where the media has been organized by content—Archival videos, Shutterstock clips, and Stills.

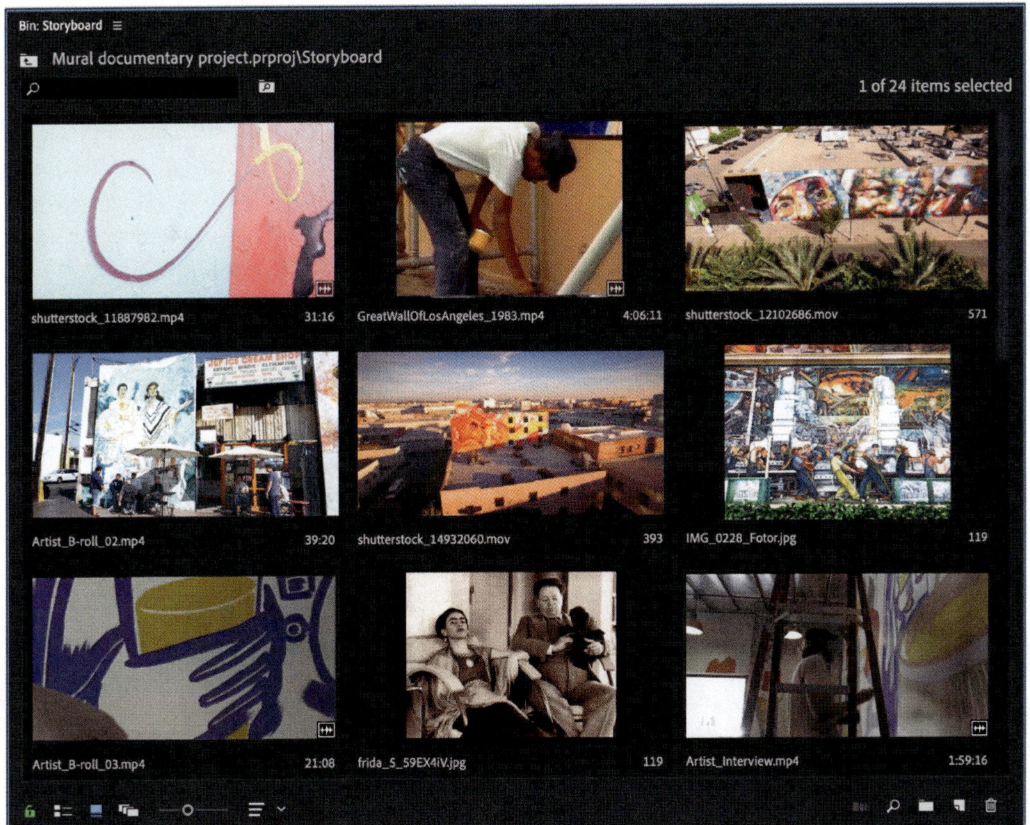

Figure 9.14

Documentaries and other unscripted projects face additional challenges due to lots of media and a variety of sources. In this scene, there's footage from the present day, the 1980s, the 1930s, a variety of still images, and footage from the Shutterstock library.

Table 9.1

A voice-over narration script for the documentary scene.

Mural documentary narrator:
The tradition of mural painting in southern California has deep ties to Mexican art in the 20th century. One can draw a direct line from today to artists like Diego Riviera, known for his massive murals installed across the U.S. during the Works Progress Administration era of the 1930's.

STEP 2: Use Markers to Log the Narration

The voice-over narration (Table 9.1), read by Ben Long, is the heart of this documentary. It's called Documentary VOs.WAV and found at the main level of the tutorial media folder. Typically with voice-over recordings, you'll get a string of takes in a single clip. As a result, it can be very helpful to log the voice-over takes using markers. Take a minute to note the icon for an audio-only clip in the bin—a small green waveform.

Launch the voice-over audio in the Source monitor by double-clicking on it. A larger green waveform of the clip will appear in the source monitor. Drag the zoom bar at the bottom of the Source monitor out so that you can see the whole clip. It's pretty short, so it's easy to distinguish the three takes in the waveform. Familiarize yourself with the material by listening to the clip.

Now let's find the start of the first take and set a marker by typing M. A marker will appear in the Source monitor time ruler with a pea green tab, the default color for markers in Premiere. Double-click on the green tab to open the Marker interface (Figure 9.12). Here you can name the marker, change the label color, and add a description. It's best to stick with short names, so name it Take 1 and select Okay, then do the same for takes 2 and 3.

Now open the Markers panel (Window > Markers)—you'll now have a log of the takes with timecodes. To the right is the Comments field, so you can review the takes and type notes here (Figure 9.15). You can use Shift + M to step forward through the markers in the Markers panel, and also the Source monitor and Timeline, and Shift + Control/Command + M to go back. Pick the take that you like and double-click on it to relaunch the Marker interface and change the Marker Color to red. I suggest take 2 because it's slower which gives a little more room for the imagery. Now you can easily jump to your favorite take whenever you need it. Whatever your choice, add it to A1 of the new sequence.

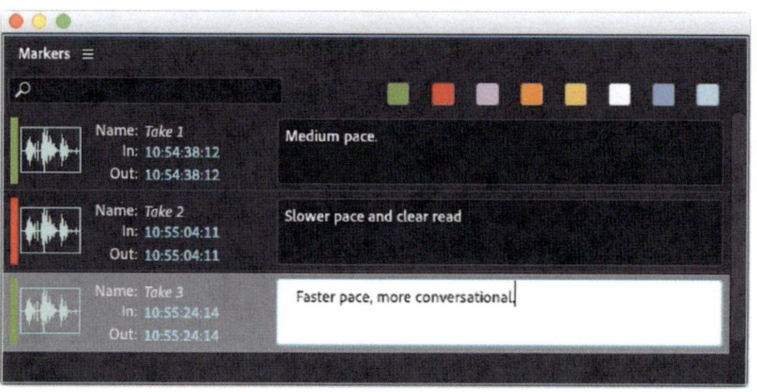

Figure 9.15

Use Markers to log takes of voice-over narration and add comments and colors.

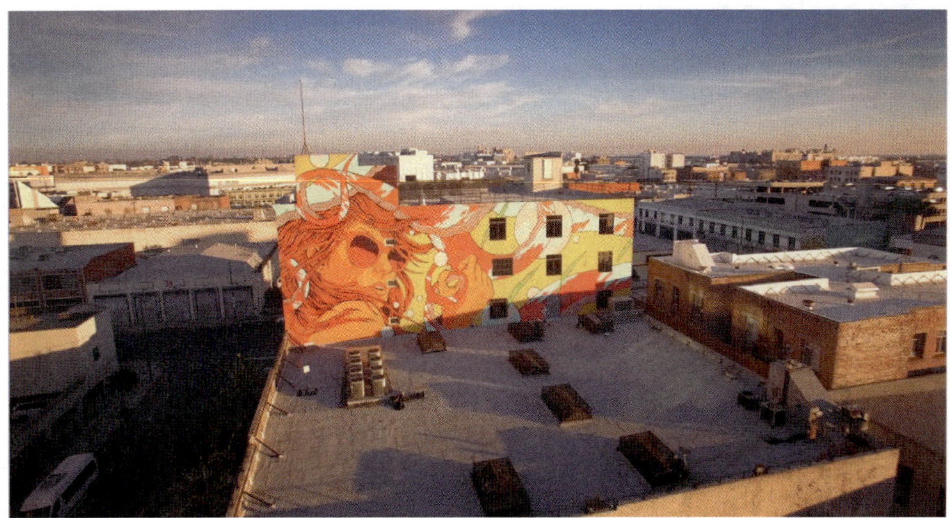

Figure 9.16

Footage libraries can be a great resource for documentaries. This drone shot of a mural in Los Angeles was provided for this tutorial by Shutterstock.

STEP 3: Add the B-roll

Next, we'll use the b-roll to cover the voice over. For this scene, we have modern day b-roll of murals in Los Angeles, archival video of Diego Rivera in the 1930s, and archival video of Judith Baca's mural project in Los Angeles in the 1980's. (You might find it helpful to add markers to these shots as well, or to add descriptions in the Log Note column in Bin List view.)

Let's start with the contemporary footage in the Shutterstock clips folder—there are three 2K shots showing murals in Los Angeles (Figure 9.16), and two HD shots of guys spray painting a mural. The clip names aren't indicative of their content, so it's easier to look at them in bin Icon view. Use these five shots to cover the first line or so of the voice-over. Some of the clips have sound but we don't need it.

How does it look? The 2K shots look great, but the two shots of guys spray painting are HD so there's some pillarboxing (Figure 9.17).

To get rid of it, select one of the pillarboxed shots in the Timeline and go to the Effect Controls panel (Window > Effect Controls) and spin open the Motion effect submenu. In the Scale area, type in 107—that's the percentage that you need in order to increase 1920 x 1080 HD to fill a 2K frame. Now, take another look. Is the composition awkward? With the word Motion highlighted in the Effects panel, click and drag the shot in the Program monitor to adjust the framing. Hold the Shift key as you drag up and down to keep it from moving side to side. Do the same for the other shot (Figure 9.17).

Figure 9.17

Correct the pillarboxing and reposition the shots (before and after) using the Motion effect in the Effect Controls panel.

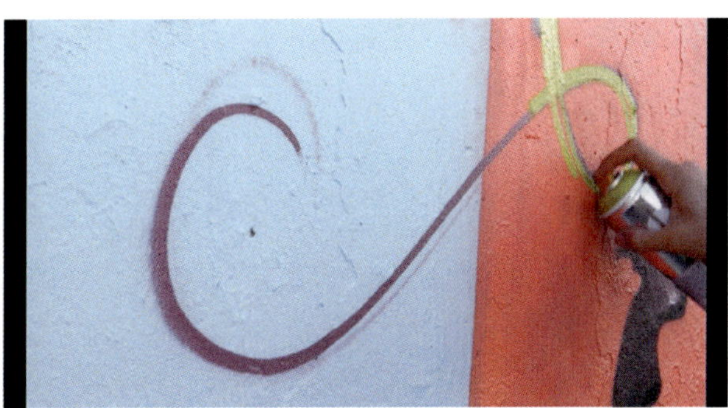

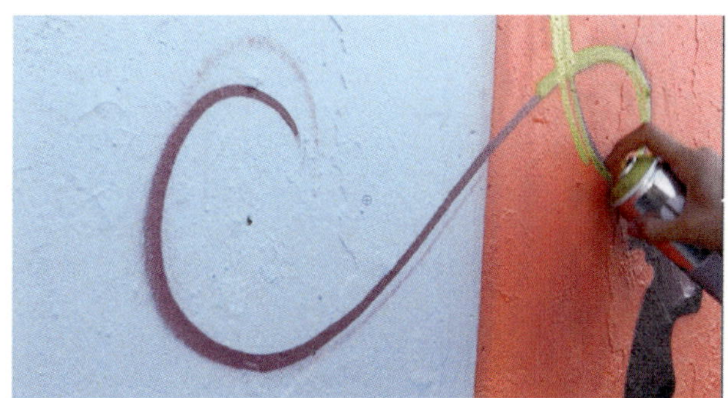

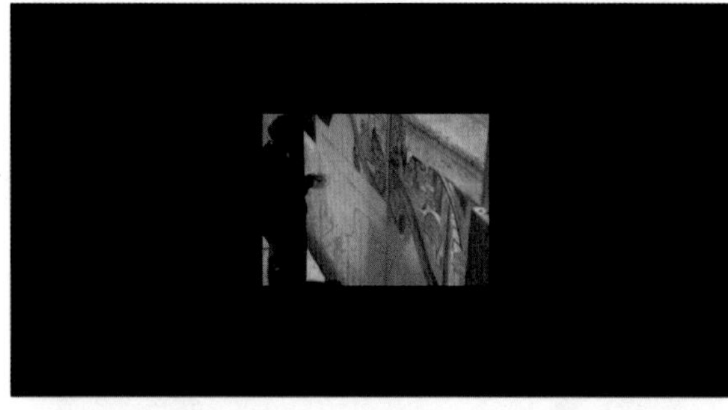

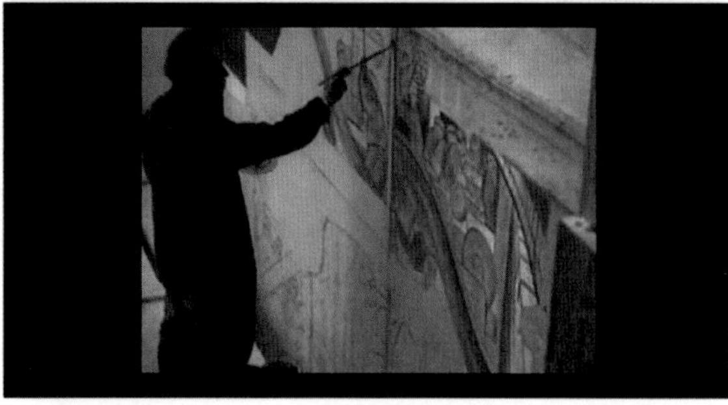

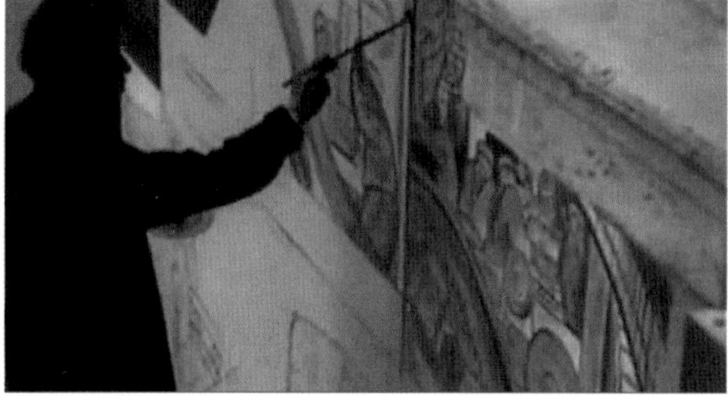

Figure 9.18

The original SD video clip is very small compared to a frame of HD video (top). Resizing it to fit the frame better involves` some creative choices.

STEP 4: Resize the Archive Video

The next line segues to historical topics and we have some cool archival footage to help illustrate this history in the Archival videos folder.

The black-and-white archival clip shows Diego Rivera in the process of painting a huge mural in Detroit in 1932. The color archival footage of Los Angeles artist Judy Baca was shot in 1983 and shows the making of her massive mural, The Great Wall of Los Angeles. Both shots are SD (Standard Definition) video, which is 640 x 480 pixels.

Add a shot or two from each into the Timeline, to cover the rest of the narration and take a look. Compared to the 2K footage, they are tiny and, well, square. This footage predates the preference for widescreen media.

When you are making this big of an adjustment between two formats, you will have to make some creative choices (Figure 9.18). Perhaps you'll enlarge the archival footage a bit, but not make it full frame. This leaves the effect of the original footage intact. Or maybe you will like the effect of a degraded image once you make it full frame.

Select one of the new shots in the Timeline, then navigate to the Effect Controls panel. Spin down the triangle to open the Scale portion of the Motion effect. The slider on the Scale effect only goes to 200 so you'll have to type in a larger number. Try 340 to get it to fill the frame. Select the Motion position box and drag the image around to reframe it. Use the Effect Controls panel to adjust the Scale and Position of each of the archive clips until you're happy with them.

Render to Improve Playback

All these different types of video in a single sequence can make it hard for Premiere to play it back in real time. So take a minute to render your sequence (Sequence > Render In to Out).

STEP 5: Adjust the Speed of the 1930's Film Clip

This is something you'll only rarely encounter, but the footage of Diego Rivera was shot at 18 fps because it originated on film. You can tell because it is slightly sped up—it's common for 18 fps film footage to get transferred to video at the standard film rate of 24 fps, which results in faster motion. This clip was then transferred to multiple formats, so now you have a clip that's 60 fps. When you edit it into your sequence, Premiere will adjust the frame rate so that it plays at the frame rate of your sequence, 23.976 fps, automatically. But it will still appear slightly sped up. Luckily, we can easily improve the motion in this clip by slowing it down to 75% because 18 fps is 75% of 24 fps. (More film math!)

Select a shot from this clip in your Timeline and go to Clip > Speed/Duration and enter 75% as the speed (Figure 9.19). If you select Ripple Edit, the clip will get longer and any shots after it will get pushed down the Timeline. If you don't select Ripple Edit, the speed will change to 75% but the duration of the shot in the Timeline will stay the same, so the shots after it will retain their position in the Timeline. Now take a look at the clip in your sequence—does the movement look more realistic?

The documentary scene might look a little unfinished this point. That's okay. We're going to add some still photographs in the second tutorial, so save your project, we'll be using it again.

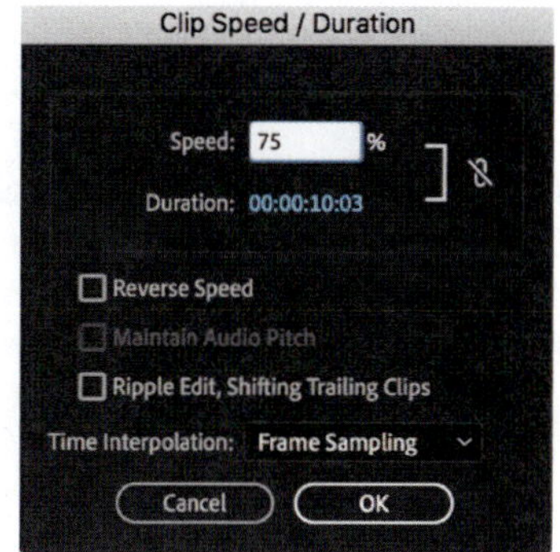

Figure 9.19

Set the speed of the 1930's film clip to 75% in the Clip Speed/Duration window.

☑ Check Out Our Versions of the Mural Documentary

The folder called Mural Doc Cuts contains the two versions of this scene, one for each tutorial in this chapter, so that you can check your work against ours.

Importing Stills into Premiere

One of the great advantages of Adobe Premiere Pro is the integration it has with other Adobe Creative Cloud applications. And that relationship is very noticeable when you are dealing with other types of media, especially still photographs.

Because photographs are not necessarily made to be part of a film, preparing them can involve some extra steps that you don't have to worry about with video and audio. Here are some of the things you should keep in mind if you plan to add photos to your movie:

Aspect ratio Just as video frames have an aspect ratio, so do still images. But video frames tend to stick to certain standardized ratios (4:3, 16:9, etc.). Photos tend to be much more varied. When you decide to bring photos into Premiere, you'll have to choose whether to maintain the original aspect ratio or to resize and conform it to your video aspect ratio in Premiere.

Orientation Photos not only have different aspect ratios, they can also have different orientations. Photos shot with a wide rectangular frame have *landscape* orientation and photos with a tall rectangle have *portrait* orientation.

High-resolution photos Photographs often have a resolution, or pixel depth, of 300 ppi (pixels per inch), which is about 4x the pixel depth of a frame of video (72 ppi). If you plan on zooming or cropping in Premiere, that extra size can be very useful. If not, you might consider resizing your photos before you import them using an image editor like Photoshop.

Low-resolution photos Images that you find on the web tend to have the same resolution as video, 72 ppi. But they often have smaller width and height, so the result is that they won't fill an entire frame of video. You'll have to choose between enlarging them to fit your video, which means degraded image quality, or keeping them as they are and having them not fill the frame.

Figure 9.20

If your still image has layers, there are several import options.

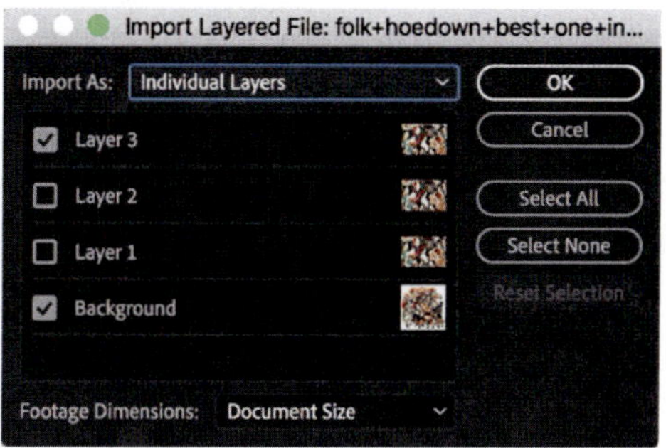

Layers Images from image editing apps like Photoshop can consist of multiple layers, including a special transparency layer or *alpha channel*. When you bring a layered image into Premiere, the Import Layered File window will appear (Figure 9.20) and you'll have to tell Premiere how you want it to handle these layers. Premiere can flatten them into a single image (Merge All Layers), flatten selected layers into a single image (Merged Layers), bring each layer in as a separate clip (Individual Layers), or build a sequence with the contents of each layer on a separate track of video (Sequence).

Color space. There are two types of color space commonly found in photographs: RGB and CMYK. RGB is used for digital video, computer screens and photographs displayed on computers. CMYK is used when photographs and other images are destined for print. Most photos that you encounter will be RGB, but if you do have CMYK images, it's best to convert them before you bring them into Premiere using an image editor like Photoshop.

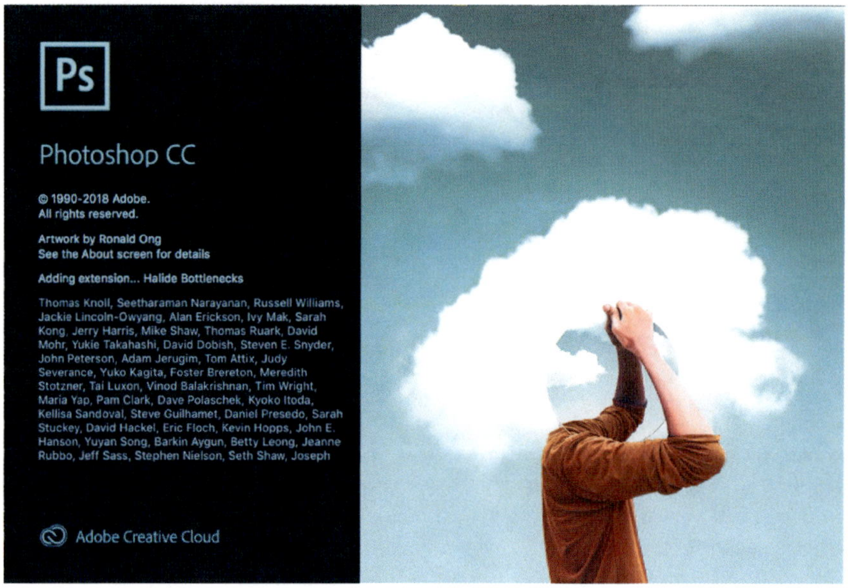

Figure 9.21

Adobe Photoshop was designed to edit still images and, thanks to Creative Cloud integration, works hand in hand with Premiere.

Prepping Still Images in Photoshop

It can make a lot of sense to process your photos in Photoshop before you bring them into a Premiere Pro project (Figure 9.21). In particular, you may want to do a little standard image tweaking, such as adjusting black and white levels, contrast, brightness, white balance, and saturation. Some images might have sloppy edges, such as scanned photos or images taken from negatives. In Photoshop you can quickly crop out any junk. And sometimes you may want to straighten them out as well, especially if they are scans.

Lastly, if your photos are massive, you may wish to scale them down a bit (Figure 9.22). Remember that the resolution of a frame of video is 72 ppi while many still images have a resolution of 300 ppi. Your still image is likely to be four times as big as your video frame, maybe even larger. That's not necessarily a bad thing—it gives you room to add zooms or cropping. But if you know your stills are way too big, you can correct for that early in the process.

One thing to know when you're resizing images in Photoshop: the Image Size window is kind of like a calculator. Change one value and the others will change accordingly. When resampling is off, you'll resize without changing the overall pixel dimensions of your file—make any one element bigger and the others will get smaller. But if resampling is turned on, you'll resize any element that you change and the others won't adjust to compensate for that change. That means the overall pixel dimensions will change. So when you do want to enlarge or reduce the image, you'll need to turn resampling on.

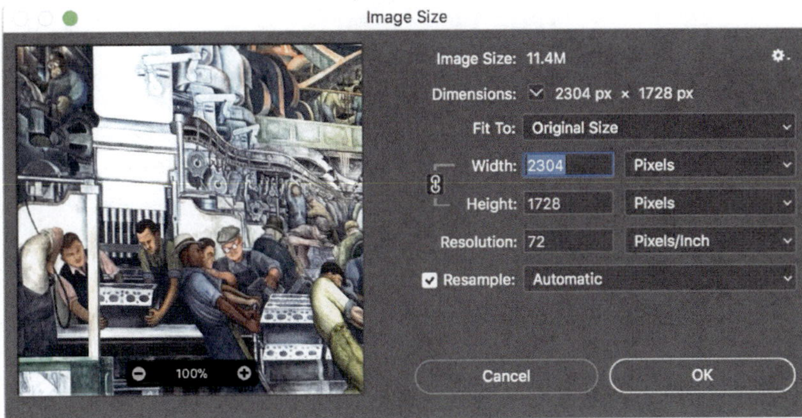

Figure 9.22

The Image Size interface in Photoshop.

Edit in Photoshop

Once you have still images imported into Premiere, you can always go back to Photoshop to edit them some more. Just select the clip in either the sequence or a bin, then go to Edit > Edit in Adobe Photoshop. Your photo will open in Photoshop and you'll be able to work on it there, save it, and return to Premiere to find it updated. This seamless integration with other Adobe applications is one of the true highlights of Premiere Pro.

There's much more to still images than just editing photographs. Graphics, titling, and working with sequential stills for animation are covered in Chapter 11, Titles and Graphics.

➡ Learn More About Digital Photography

Ben Long, co-author of *The Digital Filmmaking Handbook*, is also the author of an excellent photography book, *Complete Digital Photography*. If you want a deeper understanding of how to edit digital images, this book is an ideal choice.

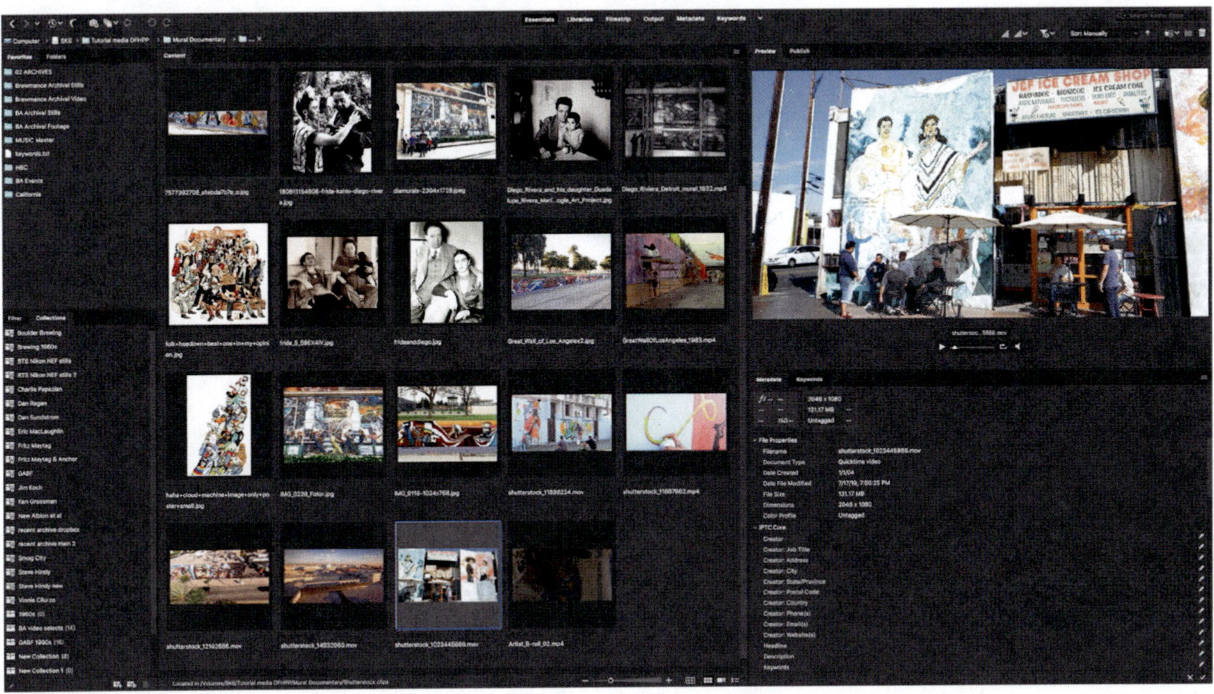

Figure 9.23

Adobe Bridge is a media cataloguing application that can be very useful if your project has a lot of still images.

Adobe Bridge

Organizing lots of still images for a film or animation project can be challenging. But luckily, an Adobe Creative Cloud subscription also includes a media cataloguing application, Adobe Bridge (Figure 9.23). Bridge can work with all kinds of media, but it's best suited to photography and still graphics. There are many things you can do with Bridge and there are a handful of them that are of particular benefit to filmmakers.

Reviewing Stills at a Glance

Bridge lets you peruse your media in three different ways. You can browse folders on your hard drive directly in Bridge. One advantage that Bridge has over your OS is that you can select View > Show Items from Subfolders and see everything inside a folder, without having to click through each subfolder separately. You can also organize your still images in virtual folders that Bridge calls "Collections." When you rearrange images in these virtual folders, the media on your hard drives remains untouched. So you can make one set of folders organized by content and another set organized by location, just to cite an example. And since they are pointer files, they won't take up any more space on your hard drives. Bridge will build "Smart Collections" based on criteria you set, such as keywords or dates (Figure 9.24). If you add media that matches these criteria to your hard drives, Bridge will update the smart folder. Last but not least, you can view images in full-frame mode (spacebar), using the arrow keys to navigate.

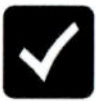

Export Still Frames From Premiere

You can use Export Frame (Shift + E) to save any frame of video in Premiere as a still image—options include TIFF, JPG, and PNG.

Add Metadata and Keywords

Bridge isn't just a passive photo viewer, it also can annotate files by adding metadata and keywords. Cameras include information about how a file was shot (codec, frame rate, aspect ratio, etc.) and sometimes footage from the set even comes with information such as the shot and take number. Adobe Bridge can amend existing files with new or changed metadata.

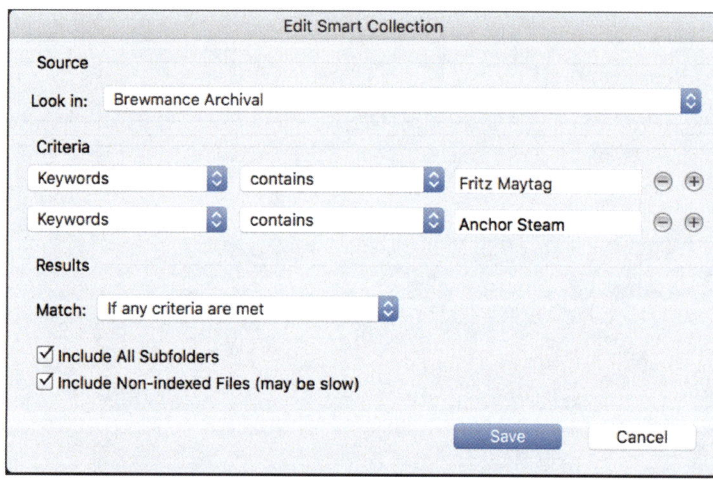

Figure 9.24

Smart Collections in Adobe Bridge will sort through your stills and create a special folder for you based on criteria you set.

Some things you may want to add include copyright information, contact information in case someone wants to license the materials, and names of people in the shot. Keywords are a very useful type of metadata because you can design a list of keywords tailored specifically to your project, such as topics in a documentary.

Bridge and External Drives

Unfortunately, Bridge has some blind spots when it comes to external drives. If you remove an external drive while Bridge is running, Bridge will lose track of all your files and folders related to that drive. That can really be a problem for laptop users who tend to not always have their external drives online. But as long as you quit Bridge before you unmount the drives and remount the drives before you launch Bridge, you will not have this problem.

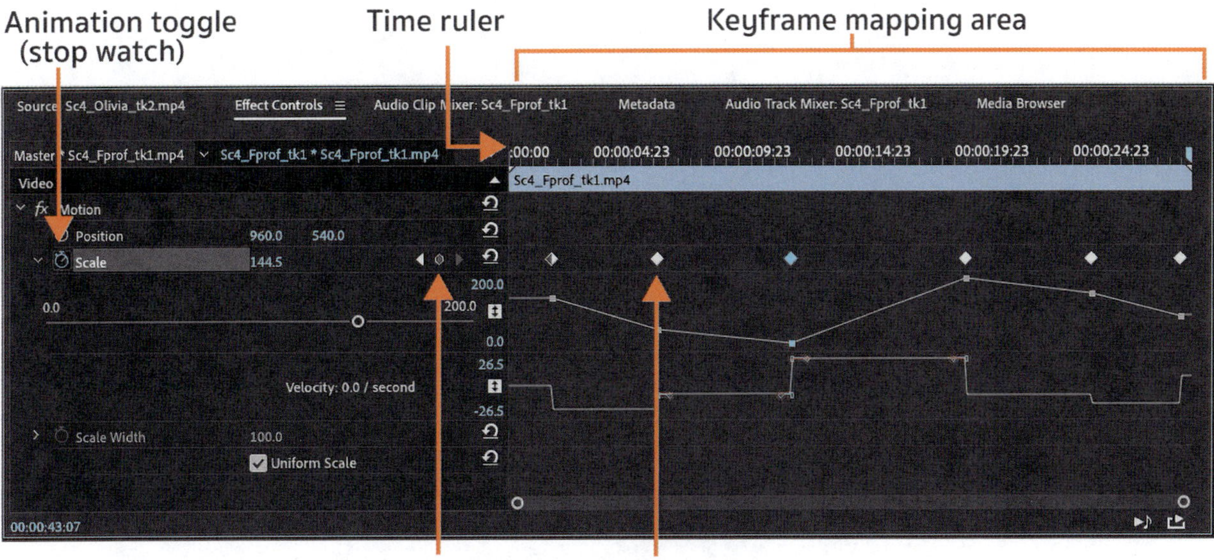

Figure 9.25

Shown here, keyframes in the Effect Controls panel are set to create zooming movements. Note that the keyframe mapping area also has a time ruler that corresponds with the one in the Timeline and the Program monitor.

Adding Movement with Keyframes

Still images are, well, still. And often that doesn't work in a motion picture. Adding movement to still images can serve to focus the viewer's eye and also help with still images that don't fit properly in a traditional widescreen video frame. Keyframes designate exactly how the Scale and Position of a still image change over time (Figure 9.25). And of course adding movement with keyframes isn't limited to still images. You can use the same techniques for video clips and they work especially well for video that is larger than your working resolution. In fact, adding movement can help you take full advantage of 4K footage in a 2K or smaller project.

What Are Keyframes?

The word *keyframe* originates with the animation process of selecting key frames—a frame that is very well-rendered—within a sequence and interpolating the frames between them to save time and effort when hand drawing frame-by-frame animation. Keyframes work that way in video as well, but all the interpolation, or *inbetweening*, is handled invisibly by Premiere. For example, you can crop a shot tightly with Scale and Position by setting a keyframe on the first frame of the shot in the Timeline. You can then add another keyframe at the end of the shot and change the Scale and Position to make it as wide as possible. Premiere will figure out the movement from the cropped frame to the wide frame, effectively creating a zoom out. You can apply keyframes to any effect on any piece of media—video, sound, stills, etc.—but in this chapter we focus on using keyframes to create movement in stills. We'll continue to cover how they work with audio, color, titles and graphics, and visual effects later in this book.

To add keyframes in Premiere, you'll use the Effect Controls panel, which includes a visual map that shows keyframes on the right side of the interface (Figure 9.25).

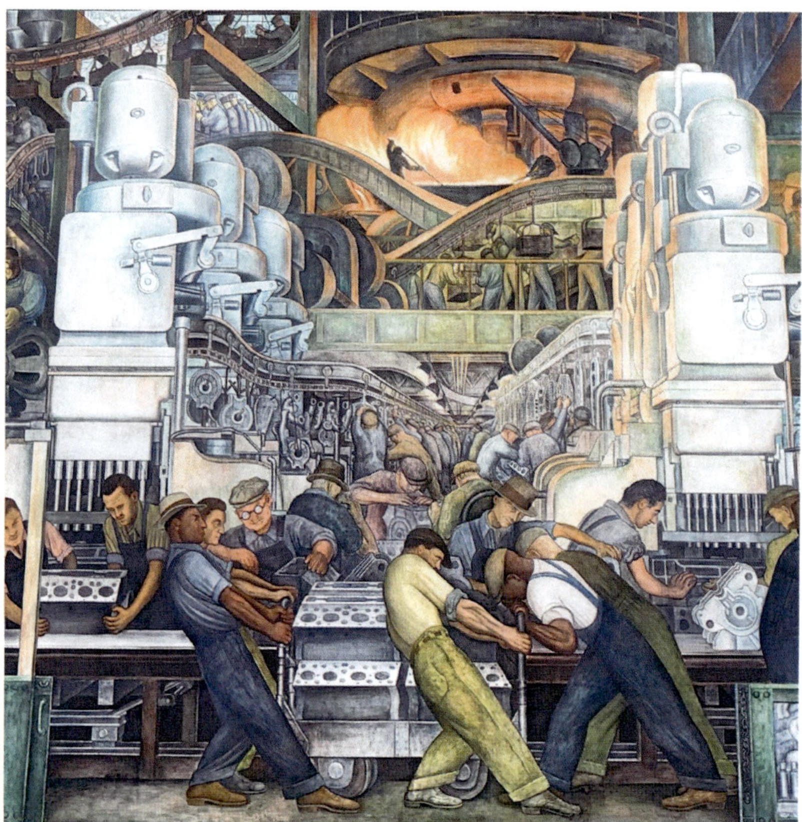

Figure 9.26

This image of the WPA mural by Diego Riviera is beautiful, but the fact that it's square makes it hard to fill a frame of video with it.

TUTORIAL: Add Stills to the Doc Scene

Even though it may seem like there are lots of different sizes in video, the reality is that there are just a handful. But the variety of sizes and shapes in still images is almost infinite. And while archive media is often smaller than digital video, still images—even old ones—can be much larger. This is great, because it gives you lots of room to work with, but the other issue is that still images rarely fit the aspect ratio of video (Figure 9.26). In this tutorial, we'll add some photographs and an illustration to the documentary scene that you started in the previous tutorial, and we'll deal with the issue of conforming the shape and size of still images to that of digital video by resizing and adding movement with keyframes.

STEP 1: Add the Still to Your Sequence

Check out the Stills folder in the Mural Documentary project. There are images from the two artists from the archival videos, Judy Baca, and Diego Rivera. We're going to start with the image of the mural by Diego Riviera (Figure 9.26). This image is beautiful but it's square. And standard widescreen video is not. Let's add it to the sequence on video track 2. Because it's so much bigger than a frame of 2K video, you'll only see a tiny portion of it in the Program monitor.

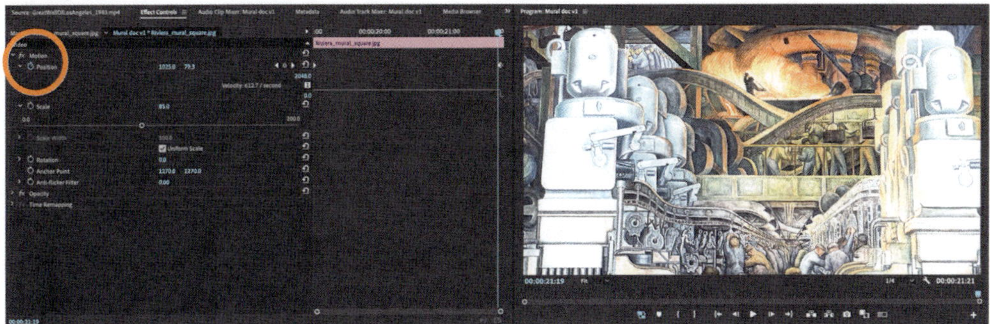

Figure 9.27

Reframe the image so that we see the upper portion. Turn on the animation toggle (circled) to activate keyframing.

STEP 2: Set Keyframes

In the Effect Controls panel, change the scale to 85%, so that it fills the width of the video frame. We're going to create a tilt down movement, so activate Position and drag the image so that you see the upper portion of the frame (Figure 9.27). Go to the first frame of the mural still. In the Effect Controls panel, click on the animation toggle (stopwatch icon) next to Position in the Motion effect (Figure 9.28). This activates keyframes in the selected clip and a keyframe will automatically get set on the frame where the playhead is parked.

Figure 9.28

This stopwatch icon is the Animation Toggle, use it to activate keyframing (blue is on).

Now navigate to the last frame of the shot and click on the Add/Remove Keyframe button (Figure 9.25). Select the new keyframe (it will be highlighted in blue) and adjust the position while holding the Shift key so that it drags in a straight line. Reframe the still so that you see the bottom portion of the image. Play the clip, you should see a nice, straight tilt from top to bottom of the image.

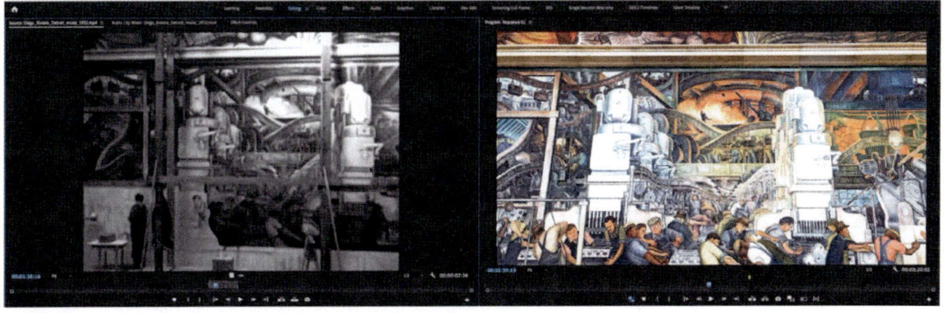

Figure 9.29

Use Scale and Position to resize the still image and the archival video clip in order to draw a comparison between them.

STEP 3: Finish the Doc Scene

There's a lot more material to work with here. Add more stills from the tutorial media bin and use keyframes to make them move. Try making a zoom by using keyframing Scale from small to large. Use Scale and Position to resize both the still image and the archival video clip to draw a comparison between the two (Figure 9.29). Pay attention to the voice-over as you make add stills and movement, the goal is to illustrate what the narrator is saying. You might find it useful to splice the voice-over between phrases and add some space so that the imagery can play out longer and more naturally. Last but not least, try adding some music from your personal library. Music can dictate pacing and you may find that your cut is too fast or too slow once you've added music.

Removing Resizes

In general removing effects in Premiere is easy—you just select them in the Effect Controls panel and hit Delete. But resize effects are fixed effects and that means they are part of every clip in Premiere, so you can't just hit Delete. Instead you'll have to use Remove Attributes, found in the right-click menu.

Unscripted Problems to Solve

Hey, the name alone ("unscripted") implies that these types of projects are unique. Consider the following to enhance your unscripted project:

Research and write In Chapter 10, we're going to record some new additional voice-over for the documentary. We're going to give you a script but you can also write your own. Do some research online about the topics in the documentary and try to come up with additional material to record.

Document is a verb If your unscripted project is a documentary, you'll have to decide just what level of "documentation" you are providing. Is this a carefully researched project, with qualified experts and verifiable backup documentation? Or is it something more experimental and less realistic? As you work on your documentary, be sure to make a decision about this and remain consistent throughout your film.

How will you structure your story? Chronology? Emotional arcs? Peeling back layers of investigation? Building to a big event or revelation? All of these structural strategies can work for documentaries and sometimes you might need more than one.

10

Audio Editing

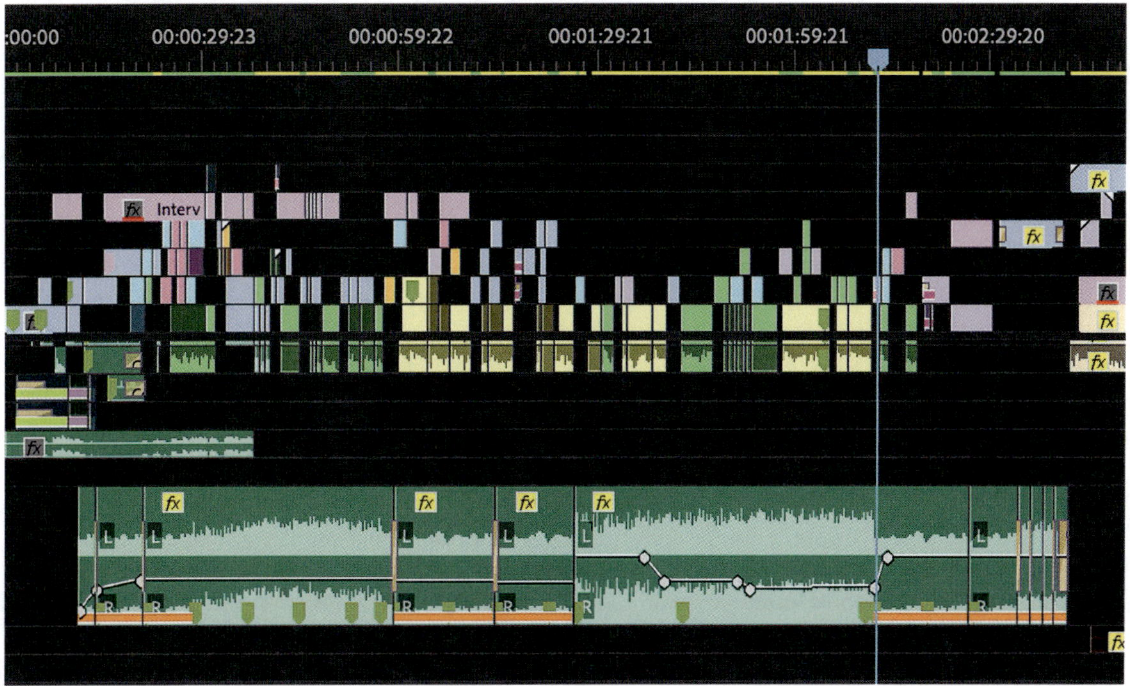

Figure 10.1

Editing audio clips in the Premiere Pro Timeline.

Sound is Story

EVERYTHING YOU DO WHEN YOU EDIT AUDIO for your film has the goal of serving to tell a story. Remembering that fact can make it easier to navigate the myriad choices available to you as you begin to edit the sound for your movie.

For most films, the sound editing process can be magical—it's where the make-believe world you created on the set truly comes to life. Scenes shot on stages or otherwise "fake" locations suddenly seem real. Performances that seemed strange are now nuanced as they reflect the sounds of the world beyond the frame (horn honks, applause, crickets, a blaring television). Transitions from scene to scene become small films in their own right.

When you edit the sound for a movie, you'll find there are two primary tasks: creating and improving. Creating—or sound design—involves building a world that tells the story you want to tell. Improving—or sweetening—is all about fixing problems by adjusting levels, equalization, and adding special filters.

In this chapter, you'll learn all about designing and improving sound in Premiere. But there are many moving parts when it comes to editing audio (Figure 10.1). And while many sound editors are also filmmakers, not as many filmmakers are sound editors. We'll try to keep a balance between what filmmakers need to know and the highly detailed set of tools that sound editors use daily.

Four Types of Sound for Movies

There might be an infinite number of sounds to add to your movie, but they can be broken down into these basic categories:

Dialogue There's a saying in post-production, "Dialogue is king." For the most part they're talking about how to mix, but unless you are working on a silent film, an experimental film, or a music video, dialogue is going to be central to the story. The best dialogue is always recorded on the set. That allows it to acquire qualities that match the performances and the location. But there are types of dialogue that are recorded separately: wild lines (usually off-screen dialogue), dubbed dialogue (aka ADR or looping), and voice-over narration.

Sound effects When you think of audio editing, sound effects (aka SFX) are likely to be the first thing that comes to mind. Rocket ship engines whooshing by, punches and body falls, the clicking of something innocuous like knitting needles in a horror movie—sound effects are the cat's meow. (Sorry, couldn't resist.) But sound effects are also mundane—doors opening and closing, cars starting, fingers on a computer keyboard. Either way, this will be one of the most creative and fun parts of building the sound design for your film.

Ambience I'm just gonna say it: I love ambience. You find some fairly generic ambience track—suburban light traffic with a distant playground, lapping ocean and clanking boat gear as the tide rises, bird that go silent—and suddenly your film is transported. In feature film sound design, the ambience is often consistent within a scene—the roar of the factory doesn't change just because the camera angle changes. For docs and unscripted projects, it can feel more "real" if the ambience shifts with the camera angles in your edit. As you can see, there are many creative choices to make with ambience. Special types of ambience for films include room tone and walla. Room tone is a sound recording of a room or location without dialogue and walla is the sound of people talking in the background, like at a party or restaurant.

Music This is the most self-explanatory category of movie sound. Everyone has a favorite film score. Most films get edited with music that will eventually get replaced, known as temp score. In addition to score, there's also *incidental* music, which is music that's tied to the location and the ambience. For example, a scene shot in a night club or a scene shot in a car with the radio on. In scripted films, this music is added in post—all those people dancing to the band are faking it and dancing to silence. Or maybe a very low volume version of the song so that all the beats are right. Whatever the case may be, it will be easier for post if you add the music after the fact.

What to Watch: A Scene without Video

Find a film you haven't seen before and after the main credits, turn off the video (or just turn away from it). Listen to all the sounds in addition to dialogue. See how much of the setting, story, and characters you can identify without seeing the visuals.

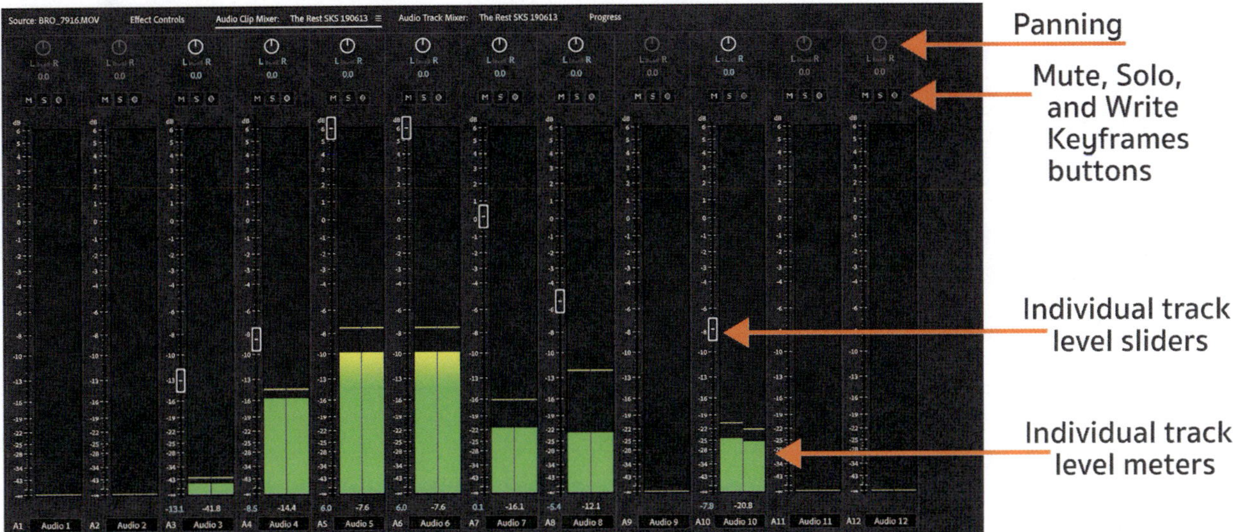

Figure 10.2

The Audio Clip Mixer is where you set levels for each piece of audio in a sequence.

The Premiere Audio Interface

The audio editing components in Premiere are similar to most other editing applications: you edit sound in the Timeline, just like you edit every other type of media. You can use every editorial process we've discussed so far on audio alone. But there are additional tools that you'll need as you start to edit the sound of your movie…

The Audio Clip Mixer

Don't let the name fool you—the Audio Clip Mixer is primarily used to adjust audio in sequences, although it can be used for individual source clips as well. This is where you set levels for each piece of audio in a sequence as you edit in the Timeline (Figure 10.2). It's found in one of the default tabs in the Source monitor panel or you can bring it up from the Window menu. Each track in your sequence or source clip will show up here and you'll be able to adjust the levels, the panning (left, right, center), and you can also mute or solo tracks. The mute and solo buttons here correspond to the mute and solo buttons on the tracks in the Timeline. When you mute a track here, you'll see the mute button activated in the Timeline as well, and vice versa.

Every change you make to the levels or panning in the Audio Clip Mixer works on a clip by clip basis: every time the sequence moves on to a new clip, you'll have to make a new adjustment. If you have a group of clips that need the same audio treatment, you can shift-select or lasso them and adjust them all at once. One thing I love about Premiere is that you can play a sequence and adjust levels for each clip dynamically as your sequence plays, which is a big timesaver compared to stopping, changing a level, and starting again.

? Tracks, Channels, Streams, and Layers

These terms are used interchangeably to describe multiple elements within a clip or sequence.

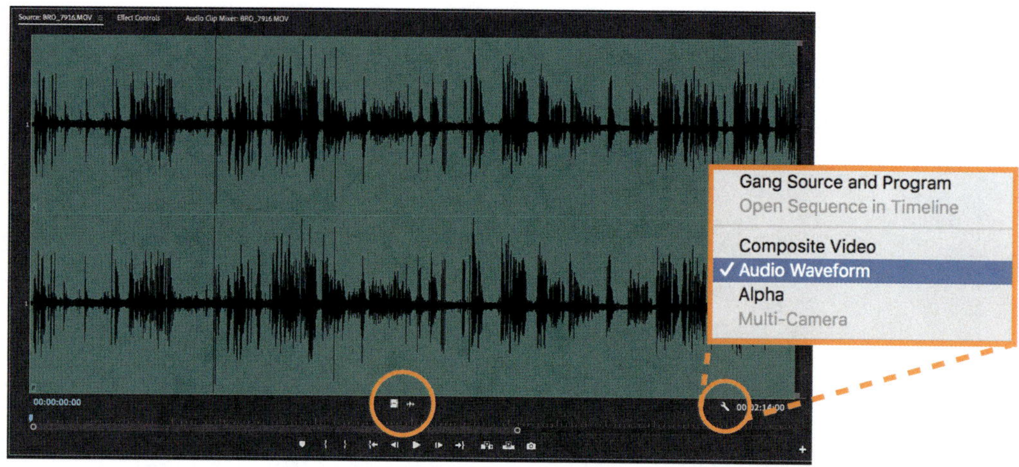

Figure 10.3

Audio waveforms can be displayed in the Source monitor by clicking on the waveform button in the bottom center of the monitor or by selecting Audio Waveform from the Display Settings menu.

Viewing Waveforms

A crucial component of editing sound is the ability to see it. That sounds wrong, but that's exactly what waveforms do—they show you distinct sound waves that correspond to the audio in a clip.

To view waveforms, first of all you have to make sure Premiere generates them by selecting Preferences > Audio > Automatic Audio Waveform Generation. And of course, you need to be looking at a clip that has audio attached to it. Clips such as drone footage or MOS b-roll might not have audio tracks. You'll see a tiny waveform badge in each clip that includes audio in bin Icon view.

There are two ways to view clip waveforms:

Source Monitor The main viewer in the Source monitor displays video, but you can switch to audio waveforms with the click of a button (Figure 10.3). At the bottom of the image, just above the time ruler, there are two icons: a small filmstrip and a waveform. Clicking on these buttons switches the view from video to audio. (If your media is audio-only, it will display the waveform view automatically.) You can also use the Display Settings menu (wrench icon) and select Audio Waveform to change the display. As you can see in Figure 10.3, if a clip has two channels of audio, there will be two waveforms stacked in the display.

Timeline You can view waveforms for each clip in the Timeline. From the Timeline Display Settings menu (wrench icon), select Show Audio Waveforms. You can also

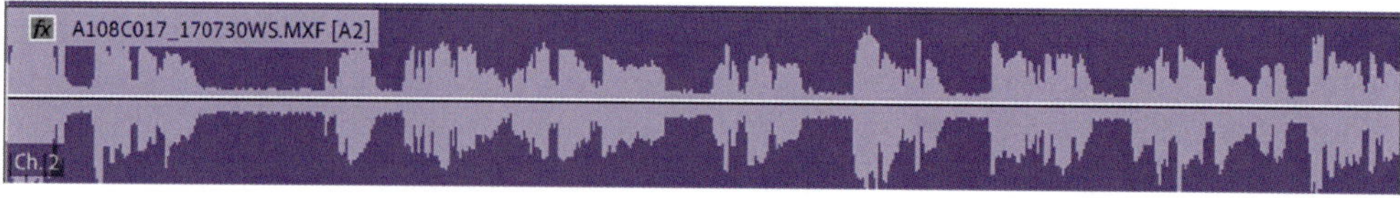

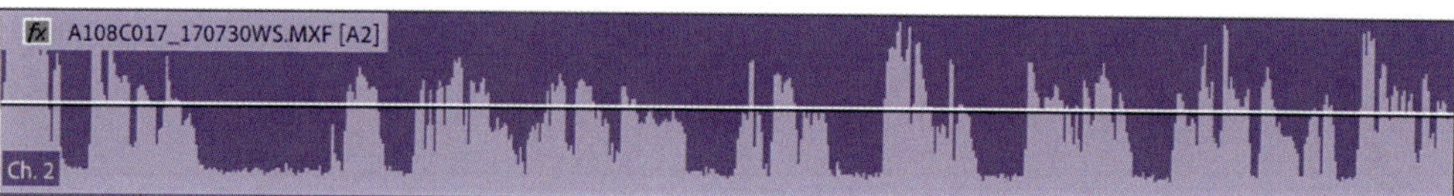

Figure 10.4

In the Timeline panel menu you can choose between standard audio waveforms (top) and rectified audio waveforms (bottom).

choose between two different types of Timeline waveforms, standard and rectified. Standard waveforms look exactly like the ones in the Source monitor. Rectified waveforms are slightly different and are designed to make waveforms for audio recorded with low levels that are easier to see (Figure 10.4). Since a lot of audio is recorded low, you'll like using rectified audio waveforms. They're found in the panel settings menu for each sequence.

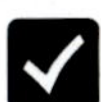

Missing Waveforms?

If you see a flat line instead of a waveform, and yet you hear sounds when you play, it may be that Premiere has not generated a waveform for the clip you are monitoring. If that's the case, you can have Premiere make a new one: Clip > Generate Audio Waveform. And if you're in the Timeline make sure that you have Show Audio Waveforms selected in the Timeline Display Settings (wrench) menu. Last but not least, there seems to be a bug that causes the waveforms for some clips to not be visible. As of the time of this writing, it hasn't been fixed. But luckily it only affects some clips in a project, not all of them. That said, it's a problem.

Level Meters

In addition to seeing the content of your audio, you also need to know how loud it is. Level meters show you the range of volume, or loudness, in your audio clips and tracks as you play them. A typical peak meter (Figure 10.5) displays volume in a range from 0 dB (loudest) to -60 dB (quietest). While your audio is playing, the meters show colors that range from red (too loud), to yellow (loud but acceptable), to shades of green. Since every piece of sound—especially dialogue—covers a range that can span from low to loud, the goal is to have your meters staying mostly in the green area, averaging at around -12 dB and avoiding the red area entirely. When audio does get into the red area, above 0 dB, the result is that the audio will get clipped. Clipping is the audio equivalent of overexposure—part of the sound went over the peak limit will get cut off, resulting in sound that is strange or distorted. If any sound goes over the peak limit, the peak indicators, at the top of the level meters will turn red and stay that way until you stop playing.

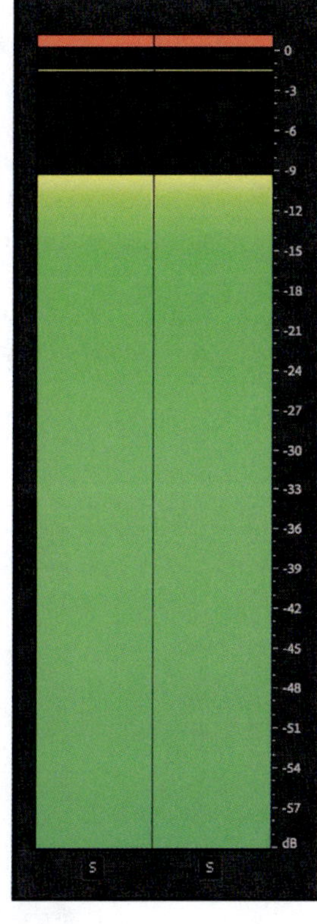

Figure 10.5

The Audio Meters window is found next to the Timeline and this one shows output levels for a stereo sequence, so there are two level meters. Along the right side is a loudness scale, measured in dB. The peak indicators at the top are red, which means that some of the sound that played recently was over the safe limit.

There are several ways to view level meters in Premiere:

The Audio Meters window (Window > Audio Meters) is found to the right of the Timeline in the Editing and Audio workspaces (Figure 10.5). It changes according to the number of tracks your sequence master is set to—if you are working in a stereo sequence, it will show two tracks. Even though it's next to the Timeline, the Audio Meters window displays levels for whatever sound is playing at the moment—both source clips and sequences.

The Audio Clip Mixer has a bank of level meters for each track in your sequence, but you'll only be able to see the levels for clips and adjust them as they pass under the playhead (Figure 10.2). The level you set here will only extend to the head and tail of each clips. If you're fast, you can set levels for multiple tracks as they play.

The Audio Track Mixer has a bank of level meters for each track in your sequence but it's very different from the Audio Level Mixer because it only changes the levels in sequences (not source clips) and adjustments you make here will affect every single clip in that track. So if you decide your overall mix for the music is too loud, you can go to your music tracks here and quickly lower the volume across the board. The Audio Track Mixer is not used much when you're editing sound. You'll only use it when you need to set up special track configurations for sequences and exports of your movie. In general, it's best avoided until you are ready to output a cut or tweak your final mix. We discussed it a bit already, in Chapter 8, Multicam Editing and we'll discuss it further in Chapter 14, Finishing.

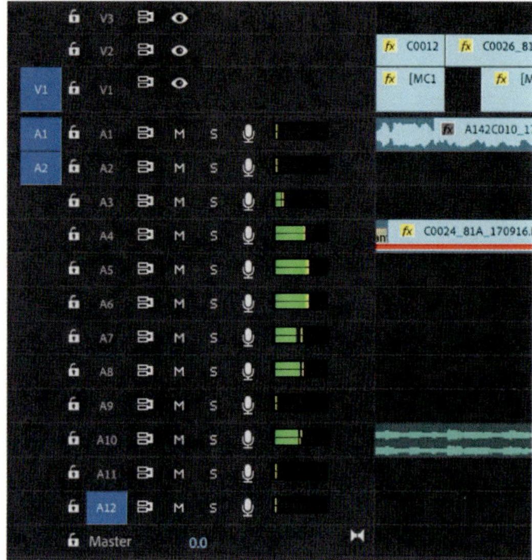

Figure 10.6

Timeline Track Meters.

Timeline Track Meters can be added to the header of each audio track (Figure 10.6). If you have lots of audio tracks, this can be very useful because they allow you to monitor each track separately and you don't need to dedicate screen space to the Audio Clip Mixer. For example, if you have 24 audio tracks the Audio Clip Mixer window would get pretty wide to accommodate them all. You can add them from the Timeline Display Settings (wrench) menu. Select Customize Audio Header, then drag the Track Meters button down to the empty area in the track header of your first audio track. Track-based level meters will be added to all of your tracks.

Level Meter Options

Right-click on the Audio Meters window to bring up a menu that offers different types of level metering.

Rubber Bands and Keyframes

Each audio clip in the Timeline has a *rubber band* that represents the audio level (Figure 10.7). If your audio volume hasn't been adjusted, the rubber band will be in the center of the track. (You may need to increase the size of your tracks to see better. To temporarily increase the size of any track, double-click in the empty area on the right end of the track header and the track will get bigger. Double-click again to bring it back to normal size.) To grab the rubber band, make sure you have the Selection tool (arrow) activated, then hover your mouse over the rubber band in the center of the clip. The cursor will display a double up and down arrow that means you can now click and drag the rubber band. If you drag it up, the whole rubber band will move up, making the volume increase across the whole clip. If you drag it down, the volume decreases.

Rubber bands become very versatile when paired with *keyframes*. We discussed keyframes in terms of adding movement to stills and video in Chapter 9. Audio keyframes work in a similar manner—they are special anchors that indicate a point of adjustment or change to an effect that

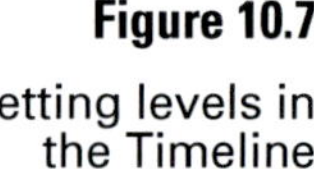

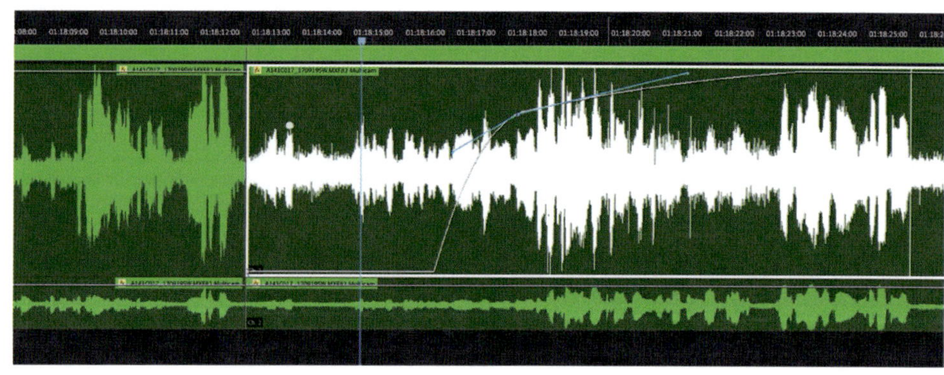

Figure 10.7

Setting levels in the Timeline offers lots of control, thanks to rubber bands, keyframes, and customized interpolation ramps.

has been applied to a sound clip. Volume control is considered a fixed effect in Premiere and that means you can adjust it with keyframes.

Any keyframe you add to the rubber band in the Timeline gives you an anchor point that you can drag up to increase volume or down to decrease it. Premiere will then compare each keyframe with the one that follows it and interpolate the changes, creating a ramp.

There are several ways to add keyframes:

- In the Timeline track header, there's a small menu that looks kind of like an empty oval shape, click on it to bring up the menu and select Track Keyframes > Volume (Figure 10.8). Now the oval shape is filled with a plus sign and the keyframe controls to the right of it are activated. The small circle to the right of the oval is the Add/Remove Keyframe button. Position the playhead anywhere within an audio clip in the Timeline and click on the Add-Remove Keyframe button to add a keyframe. Note that you'll have to add at least two keyframes in order to create a ramp.
- You can map Add-Remove Audio Keyframe to a custom key on your keyboard.
- You can add them in the Effect Controls panel. (More on that later in this chapter.)
- You can use the Write Keyframes button in the Audio Clip Mixer (Figure 10.2) to automatically add keyframes as you drag the level sliders up and down while your sequence plays. This is a fast way to add lots of keyframes.

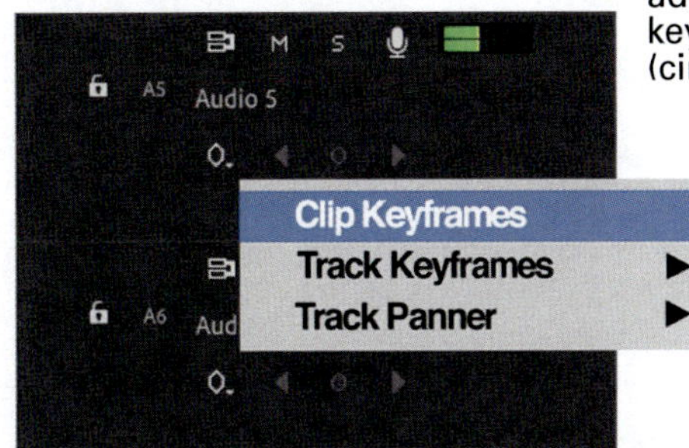

Figure 10.8

The Show Keyframes menu is in the Timeline header for each track. Don't confuse this menu (oval) with the add/remove keyframe button (circle).

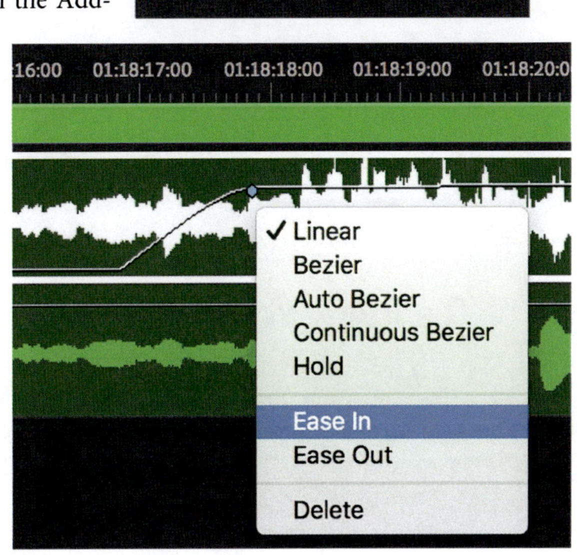

Figure 10.9

The Bezier controls menu for keyframes lets you adjust the curve of the ramp between keyframes.

You can control how Premiere performs the interpolation between keyframes by right-clicking on the keyframe to bring up a small menu that offers a set of options (Figure 10.9). Here you'll find different ways to shape the ramp. If all that sounds complicated, it's not. When you work with rubber bands and keyframes, you'll see a visual map of how your audio levels are adjusted within each clip. Clicking and dragging keyframes to change the rubber bands is one of the easiest and most intuitive way to adjust audio levels for many people.

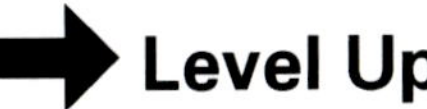

Level Up

If you don't know the basics of how audio works—setting levels, technical terms like dB, etc.—they are covered in-depth in Chapters 8 and 15 of *The Digital Filmmaking Handbook*. Audio is an area of filmmaking that crosses into scientific territory, and yet it isn't that hard to understand. I highly recommend learning more if you're serious about sound for your films.

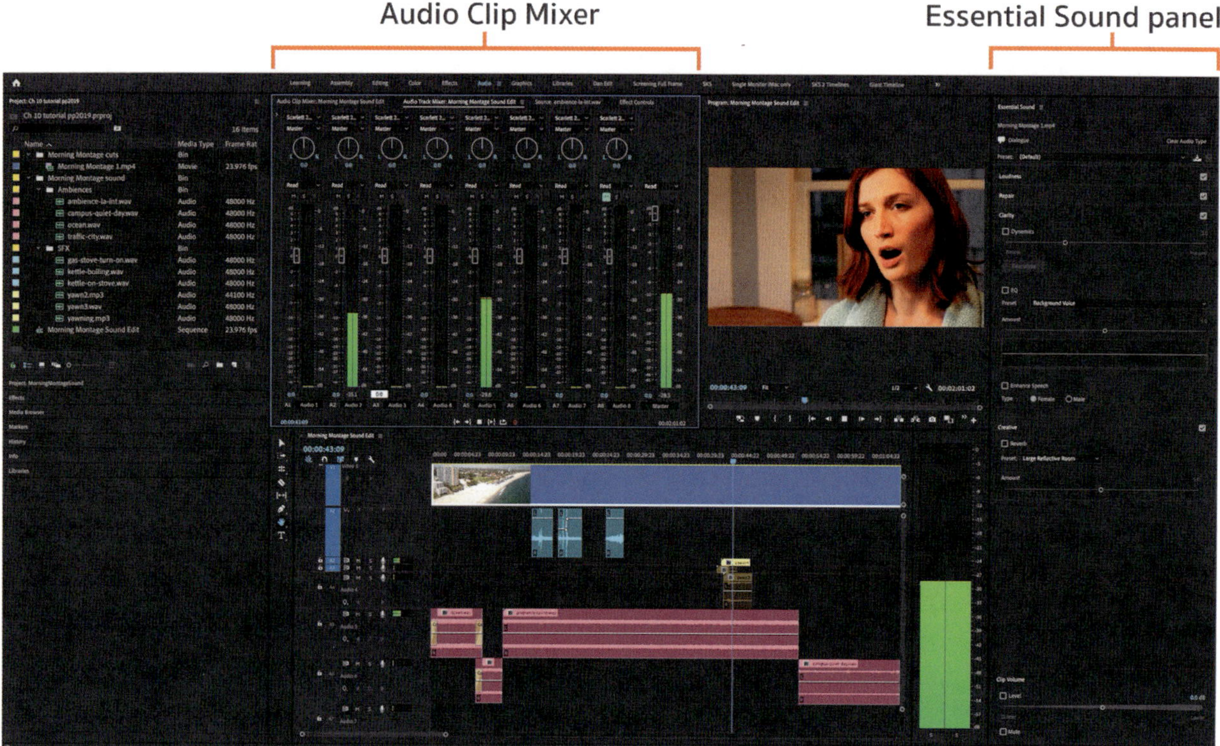

Figure 10.10

The Audio Workspace preset arranges panels in a way that brings audio interface elements to the foreground.

The Audio Workspace

If you haven't noticed by now, Premiere loves presets, so of course there is a special audio editing interface preset available to you, the Audio workspace (Figure 10.10). It's still a traditional two-monitor workspace but instead of the Source monitor, the Audio Clip Mixer is on the left, the Program monitor is smaller but still on the right, and the Timeline is below. All of these panels are squeezed to the center to make room for the Essential Sound panel on the right and a large Project panel on the left. This workspace is a decent place to start, but like most Premiere presets, you'll probably discover your own custom workspace for sound editing that you like better. For me, the editing area of this workspace is too small, especially the Timeline. Lots of sound editors use a giant Timeline—if they have a two computer monitors, often one of them will be entirely dedicated to the Timeline. That's because serious sound editing requires a lot of audio tracks and it's hard to see them unless you are able to dedicate a large portion of the screen real estate to the Timeline alone.

Master Tracks

Source audio can come in one of the three traditional configurations: mono, stereo, or surround sound. Most production audio is mono (think "one mic = one stream.") In a typical film, all music is stereo and also some sound effects. Surround sound is rare as a source.

Any sequence you create in Premiere can handle all of these types of source audio, and in fact it can handle them all in the same sequence. But when it comes to playing that audio from your sequence, all of your various sound clips are going to get sent to the speakers using the Master Tracks configuration you chose in the settings for your sequence when you created it.

If you have been working with the default settings, you are working on a stereo sequence. All the audio in your cut is getting split across two streams and one stream is going to the left speaker and the other is going to the right. Ninety percent of all films are edited on computer workstations equipped with a pair of stereo speakers and then get exported to a digital file that also gets played on devices (television monitors, computers) that also use pairs of stereo speakers. And even many VR projects end up relying on headphones, which are also stereo. For that reason, most filmmakers work with a stereo temp mix (aka Master Track configuration) during the editing process (Figure 10.11).

Your Master Track configuration will be reflected in the number of meters you'll see in the Audio Meters panel. It will also result in differences in the display of the Audio Track Mixer. And you'll see differences in the Master Tracks themselves, which appear at the bottom of the stack of audio tracks in the Timeline—you know, those tracks you've been ignoring and in fact, can probably continue to ignore.

You might be wondering, what about a film that needs a surround sound mix for theaters or home systems? If your film is headed for the full, theatrical, higher-budget route, usually you'll work in stereo during the rough cut, then your sound mixer will create the surround sound mix along with various other mixes that will likely be required for your film after you finish editing it. Final mixes are discussed in detail in Chapter 14, Finishing.

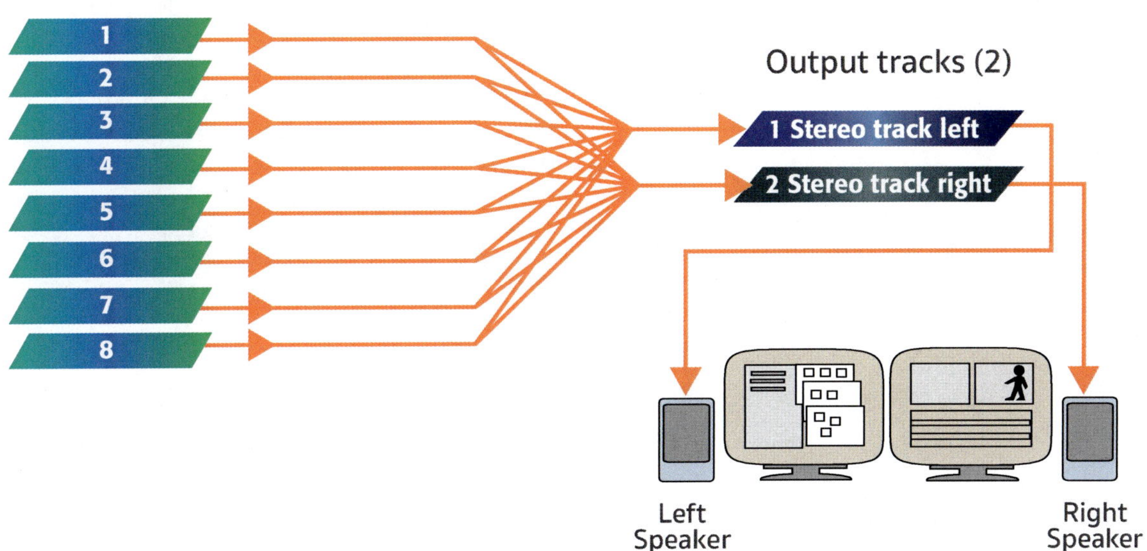

Figure 10.11

Input tracks are the ones you edit with, in a sequence. Output tracks, aka master tracks, are what gets sent to your speakers. Shown here are 8 mono input tracks in a stereo output sequence. Stereo mixes always have only two tracks.

Types of Audio Tracks in Premiere

The Master Track configuration you choose limits the number of *output* tracks. But sequences in Premiere can have an unlimited number of *input*, or source, audio tracks. When you create a new sequence, you tell Premiere exactly what you want these tracks to be. In addition to the types of audio we mentioned earlier—stereo, mono, and surround sound—there are also two other types available to you that are somewhat unique to Premiere—standard and adaptive. Mostly, they're sort of the same. It used to be that stereo sources, like music, took up two tracks and mono sources, like production sound, took one track. So you had to designate separate stereo and mono source tracks in a sequence. Now you can mix mono and stereo sources in any of the following track types: mono, standard, and adaptive. Adobe has done away with the stereo source tracks option, probably because it isn't necessary now. In other words they all will work unless you're working in 5.1 surround sound, in which case you'll have to choose that. And if you're confused, it's not you—this area of Premiere is needlessly complicated.

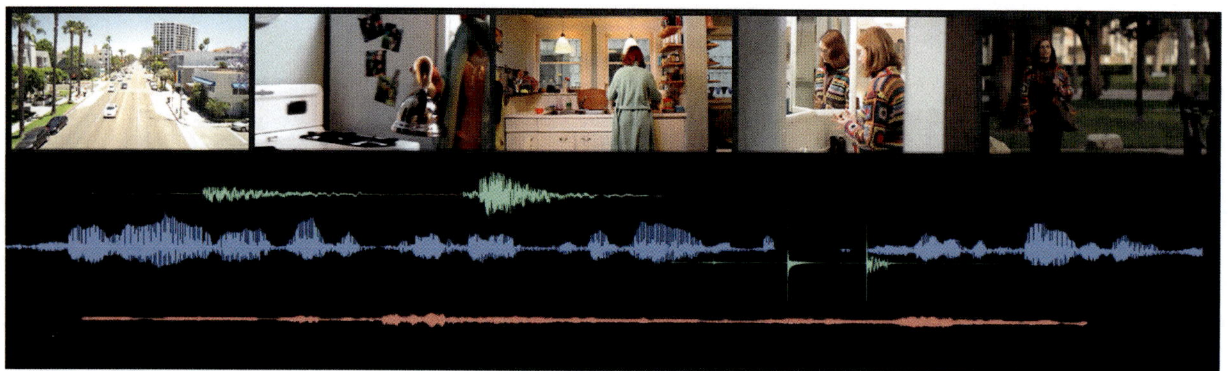

Figure 10.12

For this tutorial, you'll build an audio environment from scratch for the montage scene from Chapters 1 and 3.

TUTORIAL: Building a World with Sound

Earlier in this book, you edited two scenes from a feature film into a sequence called Opening Build. The footage for the first part of it, "Morning montage," has no sound except for the music that you added. In this tutorial we're going to use sound design to bring it to life (Figure 10.12). We'll show you how to add sound effects and ambience to create a sense of environment and we'll also cover basic techniques for mixing your audio. You'll need to import the media in the "Opening Build Sound" folder into a project—you can use the "University scene" project and "Opening Build" sequence that you created in Chapter 3 or you can create a new project and use the file called "Opening build v1.mp4" which is included in the "Opening Build Cuts" folder. This file contains an edit of the two scenes.

STEP 1: Hold a Spotting Session

Hey, this isn't specific to Premiere but why leave out the fun stuff?

If you're using Opening build v1.mp4, create a new sequence and drop it onto V1 and A1. If you're using your own cut from Chapter 1 or 3, make a copy of it and open it in the Timeline. Either way, name your new sequence "Opening Build 2." Give yourself some room to work by adding tracks (Sequence > Add Tracks) so that you have eight audio tracks. Drag any music down to A8 and mute it—you want to be able to watch the visuals and imagine potential sounds without any distractions. If you're using Opening Build 1.mp4, drag the audio down to A7.

Now watch the scene and make a list of all the sounds you might want to add to bring it to life. You can use markers to make notes on the cut itself if you prefer. Here's a hint: we're giving you some sounds to work with for this tutorial, but you can always find (or record!) your own. Think in broad strokes—actions that seem strange without sounds attached to them, ambiences that are missing. Remember, it's easy to go crazy adding every little sound—especially when a scene has no natural sound at all like this one. But in this case, we're going limit ourselves to just the stuff that seems weird without sound, knowing that the music will obliterate anything that's too subtle.

STEP 2: Add sound effects

The first scene is a stylized montage that will eventually become the main title sequence of the film. Because the music is the key audio element, you only need to add a few sound effects to make it come to life. The SFX bin has several sound effects that you can use for this scene.

Let's start with the gas burner (Figure 10.13). Double click on gas-stove-turn-on.aiff to open it in the Source viewer. The sound effects in this tutorial are stereo, so you'll see a double waveform for it in the Source monitor. Listen to it and mark an In right before the sound of the gas igniting is heard, at about 00:00:01:04. The gas ignition is a hard sound and it needs to be synchronized to the exact frame where the burner flame appears in the video. Find that frame in the Timeline and set an In there as well. Use Overwrite to add the sound to A1 and watch your edit.

Drag the head of the audio effect back so that the full clip is in the Timeline and listen again. It sounds a bit loud. Open the Audio Clip Mixer (Window > Audio Clip Mixer) and adjust the level slider for A1 down to about -8 dB.

Next, add the kettle whistling sound effect (kettle-boiling.wav). You can add it on the same track, since they don't overlap. The kettle is a soft sound—it doesn't have to sync to a specific frame. I added it near the end of the shot of the feet to motivate the cut to Olivia grabbing the kettle and let it run to the end of that shot. Don't worry about how it cuts out abruptly, we'll deal with that in a bit.

Go back earlier in the scene and add a clank of the kettle as it gets set on the stove (kettle-on-stove.wav). The sync moment here is harder to find. The first hit in the sound effect clip is best because it's a double hit, which kind helps kind of helps you cheat the sync here.

The last sound effect you need is the yawn. Here, you have three choices (yawning.mp3, yawn2.mp3, and yawn3.wav). It's common to pull in several options of a sound effect while you're working because they can sound very different when aligned with picture. Find an

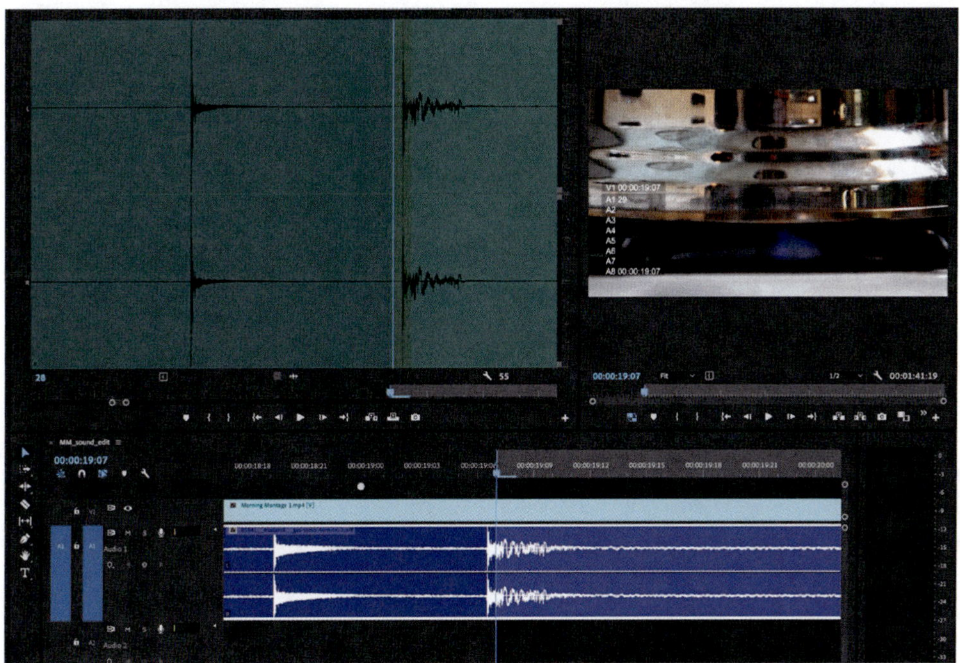

Figure 10.13

Add the gas burner ignition sound effect.

approximate place for the first yawn to start in the sequence and drag it onto A2. Add the other yawns to A3 and A4, respectively. Now you can use the Mute or Solo buttons to audition the three options. Which one fits the movement of the actor best? Which one sounds more like her voice (which you hear in "University scene" that follows the montage)? When you pick a yawn, you can leave the others available in the sequence by disabling them (Clip > Enable) or just remove them.

Now listen to your cut. How does it sound? Maybe a little sparse?

Scrubbing Sounds

You can turn audio on and off while scrubbing by typing Shift + S. Normally when you speed up sound, the pitch increases, and it decreases when you slow it down. Selecting Preferences > Audio > Maintain Pitch While Shuttling makes it easier to understand dialogue at any speed.

STEP 3: Add Ambience

Ambience can make a world of difference and this scene covers a lot of locations—there's a city by the ocean, traffic on streets, Olivia's apartment, and a university campus. Adding ambience is generally easy, because you usually don't have to sync it with anything.

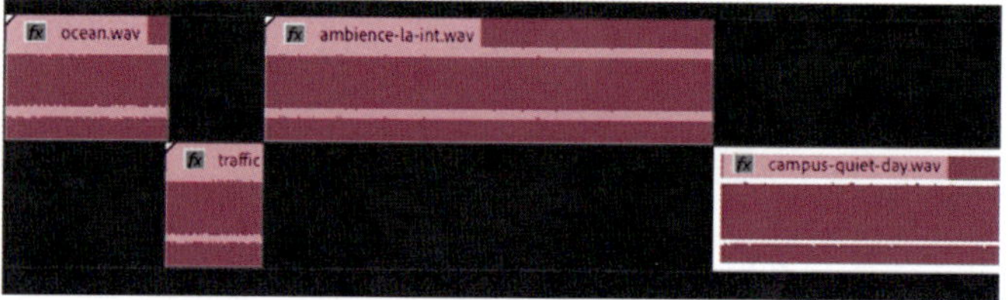

Figure 10.14

Checkerboard the ambience onto tracks A5 and A6.

In the Ambiences bin, you have ambience tracks for each location. Take a minute to review them.

Since the sound effects are on A1-4, start by adding ocean ambience (ocean.wav) to A5, under the drone shot of the city and the ocean. Next add the city traffic (traffic-city.wav) under the drone shot of the street on A6, then the apartment ambience (ambience-la-int.wav) on A5 through all the shots in Olivia's apartment. This is a technique called *checkerboarding*—you split the ambience tracks between two tracks, which gives you room to overlap them later on, when you're mixing (Figure 10.14). Add the campus (campus-quiet-day.wav) to A6 and take a listen. If they sound way too loud, go ahead and lower the levels in the Audio Track Mixer until they sound more natural.

STEP 4: Adjust the Mix

You already adjusted some of the levels as you were working, which is normal. But now let's fine tune them and add some crossfades.

The first step of mixing usually involves organizing the audio tracks so that each class of audio (dialogue, SFX, ambience, and music) has its own set of tracks. Luckily, your sequence should already be like that. You have SFX on A1-4, ambiences on A5-6, and music on A8. So you can easily isolate each class of sound. By the way, although the yawn is a sound effect, you would normally put that onto the dialogue tracks because it's meant to be the sound of the lead actor's voice. But it's already on its own track (A4) and there isn't any other dialogue in the scene, so it can stay where it is.

The next step is to work your way through each class of sound, setting the levels as needed. If this scene had real dialogue, you would start with that, since that is usually the audio that's most important for the story. In this case, the sound effects need the most work. Listen to all four sound effects and make sure the levels sound right. You don't need anything to be super-loud but you do want it to stand out a little bit from the ambience. I put the kettle clank and the gas burner ignition around -15 dB, the whistle at -6 dB and the yawn at -3 dB which is a bit loud on purpose.

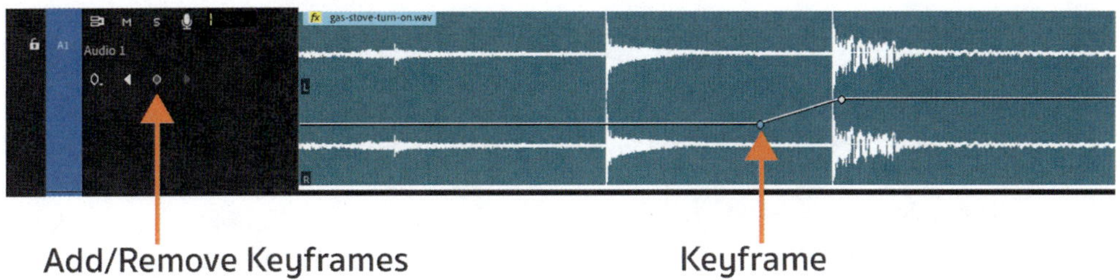

Figure 10.15

Use rubber bands and keyframes to add ramps between level shifts in the stove ignition sound effect.

STEP 5: Rubber Bands and Keyframes

Next, I want to make some fine adjustments.

I like the sound of the burner ignition but the clicking that comes before it is too loud. I'm going to use the rubber bands in the timeline to lower them. Go to the Timeline Settings menu (wrench icon) and select Show Audio Keyframes. Now select the clip in the Timeline so that it's highlighted, place the playhead after the first click and add a keyframe by clicking on the small Add Keyframe button in the header of A1 in the Timeline (Figure 10.15). Add another keyframe right after the second click. Now drag the first keyframe down to lower the sound of the clicks. Notice that a short ramp is created between the second click and the sound of the gas igniting (Figure 10.15). This audio clip isn't long enough to extend throughout the shot, so let's fade it out. Add another keyframe a couple seconds after the burner ignites and one on the last frame of the shot. Drag the last keyframe all the way down to the bottom. Now listen to the clip with A1 isolated using the Solo button in the Timeline or the Audio Clip Mixer.

The kettle whistling also needs a fade at the end. Add a keyframe in the middle of the clip and at the end. Drag the one at the end all the way down to the bottom. How does it sound? You can drag keyframes from left to right if you don't like their position. I think a short fade on the kettle sounds better than a long one, so I'm going to drag the first keyframe to the right, closer to the end of the shot. And then I want the whole thing to end a bit earlier, as she's clearing frame. So drag the keyframe at the end to the left.

Finally I like the yawn, but I think the second half of it is too loud. So I'll use two keyframes in the middle to build a little ramp to lower the second half of the clip. And I'll add a keyframe at the end to keep the level down after the ramp.

 Find More Sounds

We've given you a selection of sounds to work with for this tutorial but more sound effects are easy to find online. So be sure to do a little googling and seek out some interesting sounds that might work for you. If you're a student, your school might have a sound library and if you work for a production company or studio, they're likely to have one as well.

STEP 6: Adding a Fade Across Two Tracks

As for the ambience clips, sometimes it sounds great to have a hard cut from one ambience track to another, other times, you'll want the shift to be less noticeable. In this case, each change in the ambience works with the shifts in location. Even though cutting from the wide shot of the city with the ocean to the closer shot of traffic on a street isn't technically a location change, there is a shift in perspective and it also feels like we're farther away from the water. So extending the city with ocean ambience here would sound weird. Adding a crossfade at this edit is a matter of personal taste.

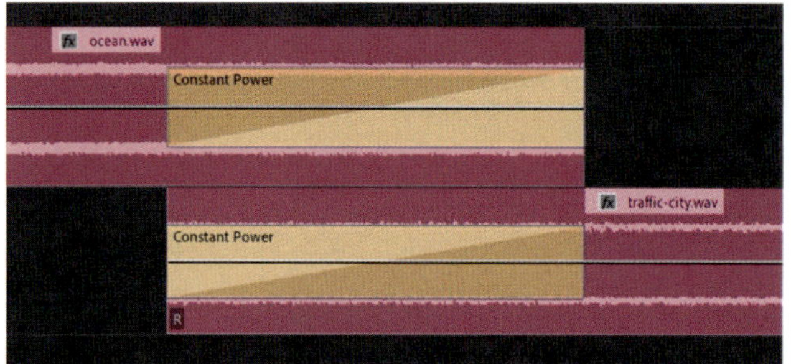

Figure 10.16

A crossfade on two separate tracks of audio.

To crossfade between clips on separate tracks, you'll have to extend the media on the A-side, the B-side or both (Figure 10.16). Drag the ends of the clips to extend them by a couple seconds. If you run out of media, use Slip to give yourself some room—after all, it's ambience so you don't have to worry about it synching up with anything.

Select the end of the A-side and go to Sequence > Apply Audio Transition or Shift + Command/Control + D. The default length for dissolves is one second, so drag the end of the effect to shorten or lengthen it. Now do the same thing for the audio on the B-side. The idea is to align these two effects over each other, centered on the cut in picture and the cool thing about doing dissolves like this is that you can make them different lengths For example, you might want a slower fade in on the city traffic but a shorter fade out on the ocean sounds. Listen to this ambience transition with the tracks isolated. Now it's a much softer, less noticeable shift to the traffic. Go ahead and add more crossfades in the ambience tracks if you like softer transitions.

STEP 7: Mix Some More

Now that you've got it all cleaned up, unmute the music and listen to the overall relationships of the sound in the scene. Do the effects stand out enough against the music? What about the ambiences? I ended up increasing the levels of the exterior ambiences so that they could be heard better but they might be a little too loud. We kept the campus ambience running throughout the university scene that comes after the montage because it helps smooth out the ambience shifts from shot to shot a little bit. If you want to watch our version, it's called "Opening Build sound.mp4" in the "Opening Build cuts" folder.

That's it, you're done with the temp mix. This might seem like a lot of work, but that's because this scene started with nothing, in terms of sound. Try watching the first music-only version of this scene and then this new version. It seems a lot more like a film now. Save your project and name it "Opening Build" (File > Save As), we'll return to it in the next chapter to add the opening titles.

? Sound Effects vs Audio Effects

It might be a little confusing, but sound effects (aka, SFX) are sounds that you add to your film: door slams, dog barks, car-bys, etc. Audio effects are digital treatments that you can apply to the sounds in your film: reverb, pitch shifting, equalization, noise reduction, and so on.

Audio Effects in Premiere

Everything we've talked about so far has been about creating a sound environment for your movie, but there's another hugely important topic in sound editing: improving or fixing the audio in your film. And that's where audio effects come in.

Audio effects work best when you know what you want. Is there some sort of high-pitched noise in your audio that you can remove with a notch filter? Or perhaps you want to add reverb to mimic the echoes of a cavernous concert hall?

There are many audio effects available to you in Premiere and they break down into several categories:

Filter-based effects, such as equalization, target specific frequencies in your audio clips and boost, limit, or remove those frequencies. Equalization is often the go-to effect for filmmakers to improve the quality of sound and also to remove problematic sounds such as hums. We'll get into EQ more later in this chapter.

Dynamic effects (compressors, gates, limiters, expanders) affect the dynamic range of the sound by limiting it, compressing it, or expanding it. In movies, these are used to remove problematic sounds, such as noise.

Time-based effects alter the timing of the audio signal to change the quality of the sound, resulting in echo, reverb, flanging, and more. Often these are used to create or enhance the feeling of the space in which a scene occurs.

Modulation effects add motion and depth to sound, such as increasing vibrato or tremolo.

Pitch-shifters raise or lower the pitch of a sound. In films this is used to counter any naturally-occurring changes in pitch when you manipulate the speed of a sound.

Transitions are dissolves or fades. In Premiere there are three types of pre-programmed crossfades and they leave a little to be desired. But you can also build your own fade by using rubber bands and keyframes in the Timeline and you can create a crossfade transition by overlapping the sound on two tracks in the timeline and fading it in or out using the rubber bands.

Working with audio effects in Premiere involves four panels: the Effects panel, the Effect Controls panel, the Clip FX Editor, and the Essential Sound panel. You'll notice that first two panels also include video effects and transitions. That's because Premiere handles audio and video effects in the same way—you find the effect you want in the Effects panel and then you adjust it in the Effect Controls panel. But to really tap into the full potential of each audio effect, you'll use the Clip FX Editor panel which brings up a special interface unique to each effect.

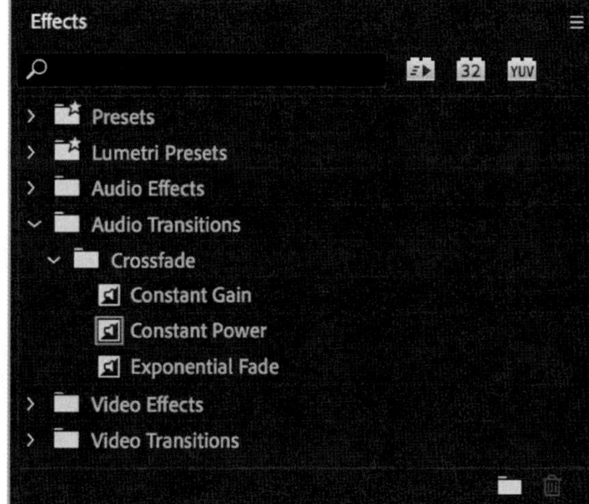

Figure 10.17

Audio Effects are found in the Effects panel.

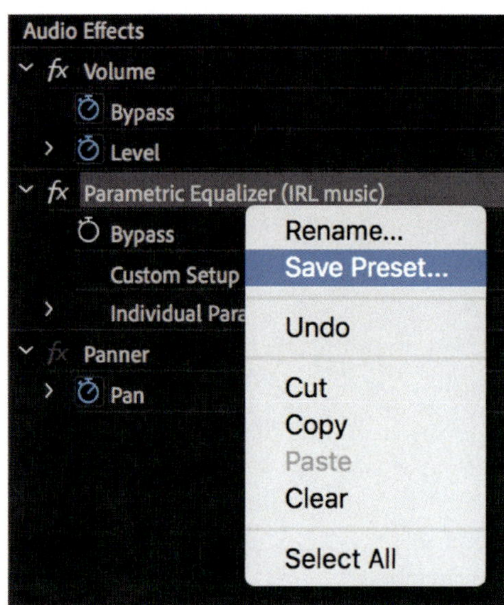

Figure 10.18

Right-clicking on the name of an effect in the Effect Controls panel brings up a menu that lets you save or rename a custom preset.

Master Clip Effects

If you put an effect on a master clip that effect will affect all instances of that clip in any of your cuts. If you put an effect on a clip in a sequence, it will only affect that one instance of the clip. This includes effects that are outside the Effects panel, such as Gain. Generally I prefer to add effects to clips in sequences and avoid master clip effects.

The Effects Panel

The Effects panel (Window > Effects) contains a set of sub-folders, three of which are relevant to editing sound: Audio Effects, Audio Transitions, and Presets (Figure 10.17).

Audio Effects The Audio Effects folder offers a large selection of effects that can improve the quality of your sound. Many of them have very specific purposes—you'll only need them to target unique problems in your audio clips.

Audio Transitions Just like video transitions, audio transitions offer ways to change how audio sounds across an edit. But there is only one way to transition audio across a cut—the dissolve. Adobe calls it a Crossfade and there are three types of crossfade available to you.

Presets If you use a customized audio effect often, it may help to save it as a preset. You do this in the Effect Controls panel by right-clicking on the name of the effect to bring up a menu with the option Save Preset (Figure 10.18). Once saved, the new preset will be found inside the Presets folder (along with any other presets you saved, including video presets).

Sounding Familiar?

Unlike other editing applications, sound editing in Premiere often shares the same windows, folders, and interfaces with video editing—keyframes, fixed effects, presets, the Effect Controls panel, the Effects panel—but of course you'll use them differently. It's nice to not have to learn two separate tool sets for audio and video.

The Effect Controls Panel

The Effect Controls panel (Window > Effect Controls) displays all of the effects that have been applied to the clip you have highlighted in the Timeline. If your clip is linked to video or multiple audio clips, you'll see the effects for them listed here as well. (You can use Linked Selection to isolate just the audio for a clip so that you don't have such a long list of items in the Effect Controls panel.) In the Editing or Audio workspace, the Effect Controls panel is found on one of the tabs in the same window as the Source monitor (Figure 10.19) and you can also find it under the Window menu. The Effect Controls panel lets you make changes and adjust each effect by setting parameters and keyframes.

Unique to Premiere is the fact that there are fixed effects for audio, just like there are fixed effects for video, and you'll find them attached to each audio clip in the Effect Controls panel. These

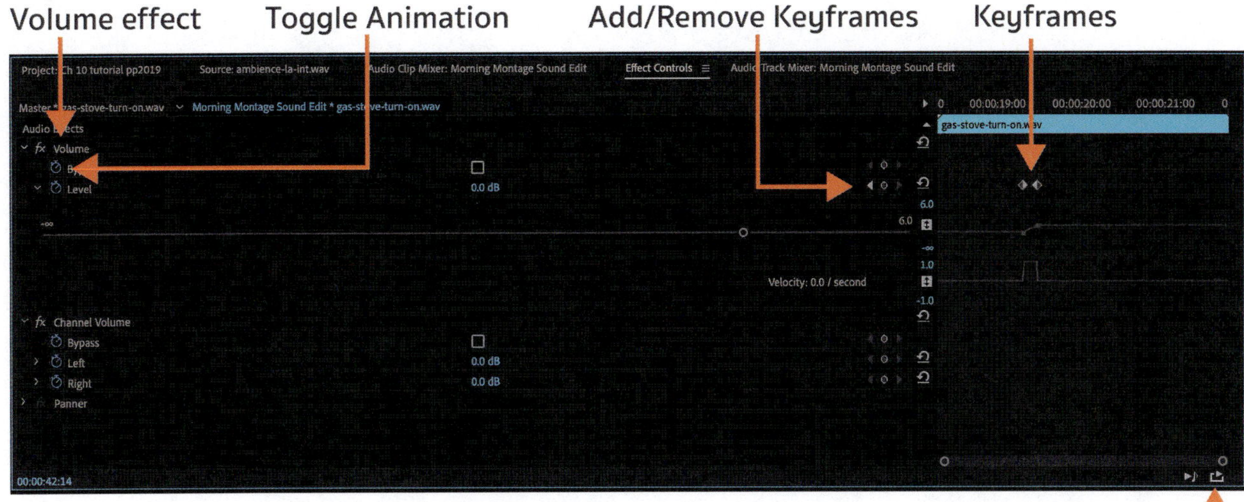

Figure 10.19

The Effect Controls panel is used for audio effects as well as video.

fixed audio effects are Volume, Channel Volume, and Panner. Volume is for adjusting levels, Channel Volume lets you adjust the levels for each track in a stereo clip independently, and Panner lets you pan tracks to the left and right. Most filmmakers prefer to use the Audio Clip Mixer instead. Fixed effects are always present on any audio clip but they are set to neutral, so they have no effect unless you adjust them. And like video fixed effects (motion, opacity, and time remapping), you'll have to use Remove Attributes to clear them.

You add effects from the Effects panel by dragging them on to your clips in the Timeline or straight into the Effect Controls panel (make sure you have the audio clip selected in the Timeline). As you add effects, they'll show up in this list.

The Clip FX Editor

Most of the audio effects in Premiere are editable. Spin down the triangle next to an effect in the Effect Controls panel and you'll be able to see the Edit button (if it is indeed editable). This will bring up a new Clip FX Editor window with a special interface that lets you customize the effect. It's kind of like having a mini app for each effect within Premiere (Figure 10.20). There are a large number of audio effects in Premiere and most filmmakers learn to use them on an as-needed basis. The most important categories of audio effects for filmmakers are removal of unwanted sounds (hums, noise, etc.) and changing the quality of sounds (equalization, pitch shifting, adding reverb, etc.). It's definitely worth playing around with effects in the Clip FX Editor panel to see how they work. After all, you can easily remove them by selecting the effect in the Effect Controls panel and hitting Delete.

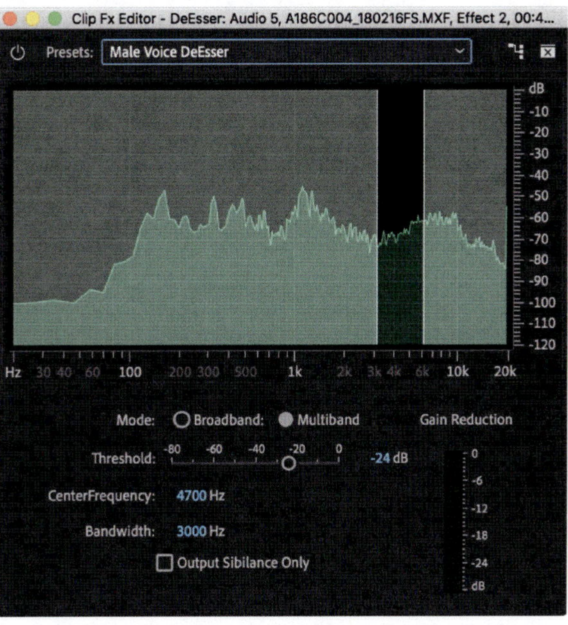

Figure 10.20

The Clip FX Editor showing the DeEsser effect interface.

Audio Effects Plugins

There are many specialized audio effects packages that can be added to Premiere as plugins.

The Essential Sound Interface

The Essential Sound panel (Window > Essential Sound) is a special window that has a selection of controls to help make it easier for you to improve the sounds in your film (Figure 10.10). Premiere calls it a panel but it helps to think of it more as an interface or an app, because it works actively to add multiple, pre-programmed effects to your audio. A menu near the top lets you assign a type of audio to your clip (Dialogue, Music, SFX, or Ambience). Once you do that, the window changes to offer a series of effects to improve your audio.

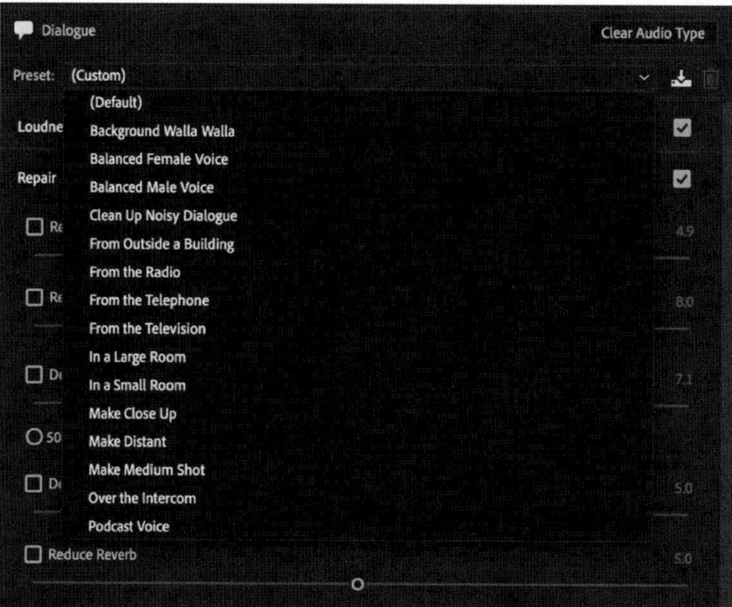

Figure 10.21 The Essential Sounds panel has a large menu of dialogue presets. Walla Walla is a town in Washington state, the correct audio term is walla. Either way it's silly.

After using the Essential Sound interface, if you look at your audio clip in the Effect Controls panel, you'll see that Essential Sound has added multiple effects to your clip. All of these effects are available to you in the Effects panel, but the beauty of Essential Sound is that it figures out the group of effects that you need and has also figured out how to apply those effects. It can be a big timesaver and I find that the results are often better than if I were to do the same process step-by-step on my own.

The Essential Sound panel is great for filmmakers who may know a lot about sound don't have the same level of expertise with all the specialized audio tools that a sound editor has. The presets for dialogue (Figure 10.21) are especially useful.

Gain, Speed, and Duration

Three very common audio effects are not found in any of the audio effects panels—instead they are found in the right-click menu when you select a clip with audio in the Timeline or bin: gain, speed, and duration.

Gain

Gain is the first thing you should adjust if your audio was recorded low. Boosting the gain lifts up the overall loudness of the entire audio clip. To bring up the Audio Gain window (Figure

10.22) right-click on a clip in the Timeline or a bin and select Adjust Gain By and enter a number. If the gain has already been adjusted, you'll see exactly how many dB it was boosted or diminished next to the "Set Gain to" option. If you're more comfortable with video than sound, it can help to think of gain as the audio equivalent of boosting the black levels. Or, you know, adjusting the video gain on a camera.

At the bottom of the Gain window, you'll find the *peak amplitude*, also measured in dB. This reveals the maximum audio level within the clip at this gain setting. If you're using the 0-60 dB scale, you want this number to stay under 0 dB. In the example in Figure 10.22, the peak amplitude is -5.5 dB, so you wouldn't want to raise the gain much more than 3-4 dB. You can also use the Audio Gain window to *normalize* the sound in a clip, which is a way to automate gain adjustments based on a dB setting of your choice.

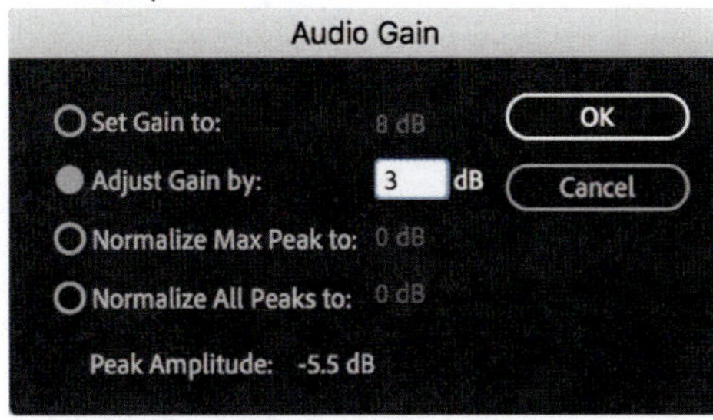

Figure 10.22

Audio Gain adjustment window.

Speed and Duration

These time-based effects are very simple to use in Premiere. Simply right-click on a clip and select Speed/Duration from the menu. The Clip Speed/Duration window will appear (Figure 10.23) and you can either adjust the speed by percentage or the overall duration. The chain icon means that these two adjustments will work together. You can select Maintain Audio Pitch to avoid having the pitch get higher as you increase speed and lower as you decrease it. And you have the option to reverse the speed as well, which also uses the percentage or duration inputs. Be aware that if the clip you selected has video attached, the video will also change. To adjust audio without affecting the video, you'll have to make this adjustment in the Timeline and make sure Linked Selection is off. If you select Ripple Edit, the clip will get longer and any shots after it will get pushed down the Timeline. If you don't select Ripple Edit, the speed will change but the duration of the shot in the Timeline will stay the same, so the shots after it will retain their position in the Timeline.

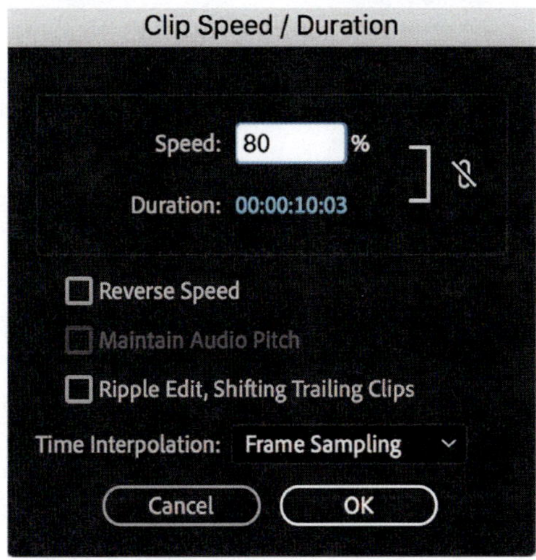

Figure 10.23

The Clip Speed/ Duration window. Note that this works for both audio and video.

EQ in Premiere

There are many, many audio effects and filters—most of them serve very specific needs. But there's one type of audio effect that you'll use on every single project: EQ.

EQ—aka, equalization—is a special type of audio adjustment that lets you boost or diminish sounds at different frequencies. EQ is kind of like the audio version of color grading—you can use it to stylize or improve the original media and you can also use it to fix problems. If you shot in a room with the low hum of an HVAC system, it may be possible to diminish it by lowering the sounds in that range of frequencies. If one of your mics was low-quality, you might improve the sound it recorded by boosting the bass and the low middle end of the audio frequencies.

Because there are so many things you can do with EQ, there are also many different EQ-based filters and effects. The classic old-school telephone filter is just an EQ adjustment that boosts the high frequencies and diminishes the lows.

Premiere offers many different EQ effects and if by chance you have any audio plugin packages installed, you can rest assured that there will be several more.

So which one do you use? As with everything else in post, the simpler EQ effects are easier to use, the more complex ones are more likely to succeed. Start with Graphic Equalizer (10 Bands) or Parametric Equalizer—these have fewer frequencies to manipulate. And of course, it all depends on what you are trying to do. If you've never worked with EQ before, it might help to think of it as a very dialed-in version of bass and treble boosting on a speaker. Except instead of just bass and treble, you have a range of ten to thirty intervals to work with.

If you just want to do some standard vocal boosting, I recommend using the Essential Sound Dialogue presets. But if you have a real problem to fix—a mic that wasn't working right or some sort of noise in the audio track, then you should definitely try one of the EQ effects listed above. The Parametric Equalizer was created to replace the now-obsolete EQ effect. I'd say that's a good basic equalizer to start out with, as is the 10-Band Graphic Equalizer (Figure 10.24).

Figure 10.24

The Graphic Equalizer (10 bands) effect is a good starting place for adjusting EQ. It has a convenient selection of presets available in the menu at the top.

The only way to get to know how to use an equalizer is to start playing around. Use the Loop Playback button (Figure 10.19) to continuously play the audio as you adjust the various frequencies. You'll be able to immediately hear how any change affects your sound.

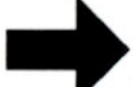

More About EQ

To learn the basics of equalization, read "EQ Is Your Friend" in Chapter 15 of *The Digital Filmmaking Handbook.*

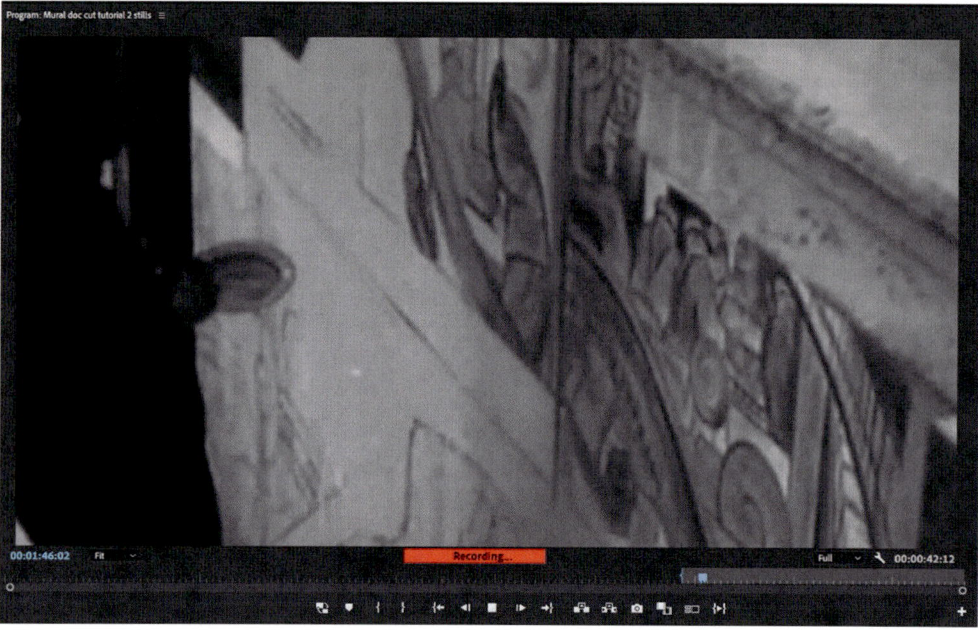

Figure 10.25

The Program window displays a red warning when recording is in progress in the Timeline.

Recording Audio in Premiere

Not all sounds come from outside sources—you can actually record audio directly into Premiere if you have a microphone (Figure 10.25). This is very convenient for projects that need narration, dubbing, or wild lines.

The high-end way to record dialogue is to rent a specially equipped sound stage and use special equipment. But you can certainly try to do it yourself in the editing room with a good microphone and a clean sound environment. It might be easier on the actor and you'll be able to do as many takes as you like without worrying about the clock. You'll also be able to drop it in on the spot and see if it works.

The most difficult issue with replacing dialogue is matching both performance and audio quality. If it's just a word, you might be able to sneak it in but if it's a whole line, it may sound better to replace the dialogue for that actor in the whole scene.

Excerpt: Diego Rivera, *My Art, My Life* "As I rode back to Detroit, a vision of Henry Ford's industrial empire kept passing before my eyes. In my ears, I heard the wonderful symphony which came from his factories where metals were shaped into tools for men's service. It was a new music, waiting for the composer with genius enough to give it communicable form. [...] I felt that in the society of the future as already, to some extent, that of the present, man-and-machine would be as important as air, water, and the light of the sun."

Table 10.1

The voice-over script for the documentary scene.

TUTORIAL: Record Voice-Over for the Doc

Remember how we added all that footage to the end of the documentary scene from Chapter 8? We're going to record some voice-over to lay under those shots. We've prepared a short script for you to record (Table 10.1).

STEP 1: Prepare

Premiere lets you record voice-over as your sequence plays, straight into a track in the timeline. That's awesome but you may not want to hear the sound of your cut and have it bleed into your voice recording. Turn down the volume on your speakers before you start.

Next, make sure your audio hardware is setup right: (Preferences > Audio Hardware). You'll need to setup your external microphone input here. If you don't have an external mic, you can stick with the default, "Built-in Microphone."

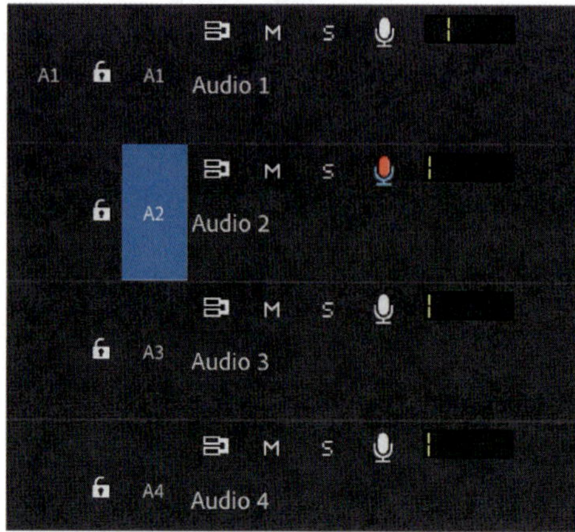

Figure 10.26

Use the small microphone button in the header for any track in the Timeline to record audio straight into your sequence.

STEP 2: Record

In the Timeline, the microphone icon to the right of the track selectors, mute, and solo buttons is the voice-over record button (Figure 10.26). Clicking this button will let you record voice-over straight into the Timeline, onto any track you choose. When you select record, you'll get a three-second countdown and then you'll see the red "recording" warning in the Program monitor (Figure 10.25). When you're done, click the microphone icon again to halt recording.

STEP 3: Mix

Adjust the levels of the new voice recording in the Audio Clip Mixer until it sounds good. Do you want the voice-over to sit on top of the rest of the audio in the film (louder) or fit in more naturally (softer)?

STEP 4: Try Normalization and Auto-Ducking

Normalize and Auto-Duck are two ways to automatically get voice-over narration to conform to the existing cut. Normalize is set in the Gain window (right-click > Audio Gain). You can tell Premiere Normalize to a maximum level or Normalize all peaks to a certain level that you specify. The effect of normalizing is that you tell it to stay below a certain level and Premiere figures out the details for you.

Auto-ducking works in the opposite way. Instead of changing the main sound—the narration—you diminish the music to highlight the dialogue. Auto-duck is found in the Essential Sound panel—after you designate your music cue as "Music," you'll see a section called "Ducking." Check the box and you'll have some control parameters available to you.

Extra points: Now that you have this line in the doc scene, take another pass on editing the scene. Pay special attention to the video and stills that cover this new VO.

Adobe Audition and Dynamic Link

So you played around with some audio effects in the Clip FX Editor and you have no idea what you were doing. Naturally, you might infer that therefore Audition, Adobe's dedicated sound editing application, is not for you (Figure 10.27). That's a reasonable conclusion. But here's the deal, the effects editors in Audition are not that much more difficult to learn than the ones in Premiere and yet they often give much better results. In my opinion, if you're gonna spend some time learning how to apply, say, a notch filter, then you might as well farm it out to Audition and do it there. Especially given that Audition is seamlessly integrated into Premiere.

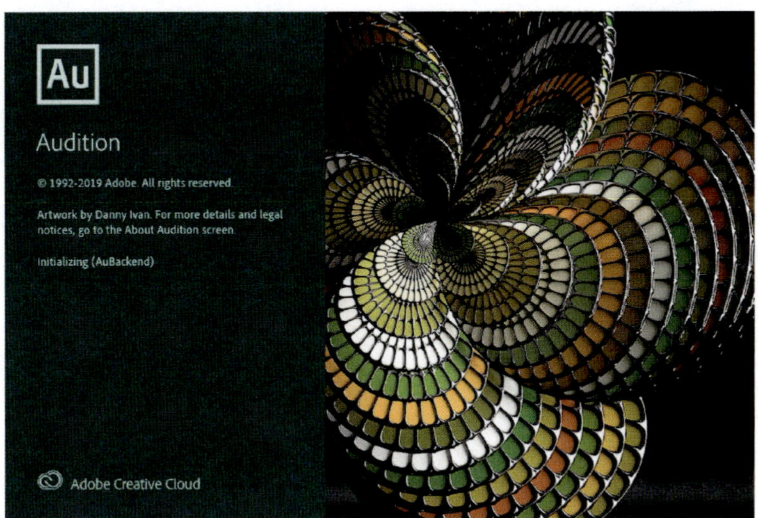

Figure 10.27

The Adobe Audition splash screen.

The reality for most filmmakers is that you're not going to mess around with audio effects much unless you have a true need for them. Like maybe you have a scene you shot that is absolute perfection but one of your wireless lav kept crackling throughout the day. You've already tried all the options in Premiere but the scene is so great, wouldn't it be worth spending a few hours or days to try to fix it in Audition?

There's no way to offer a detailed description of Audition in this book—it deserves its own book—but we can tell you how to use Audition and Premiere together.

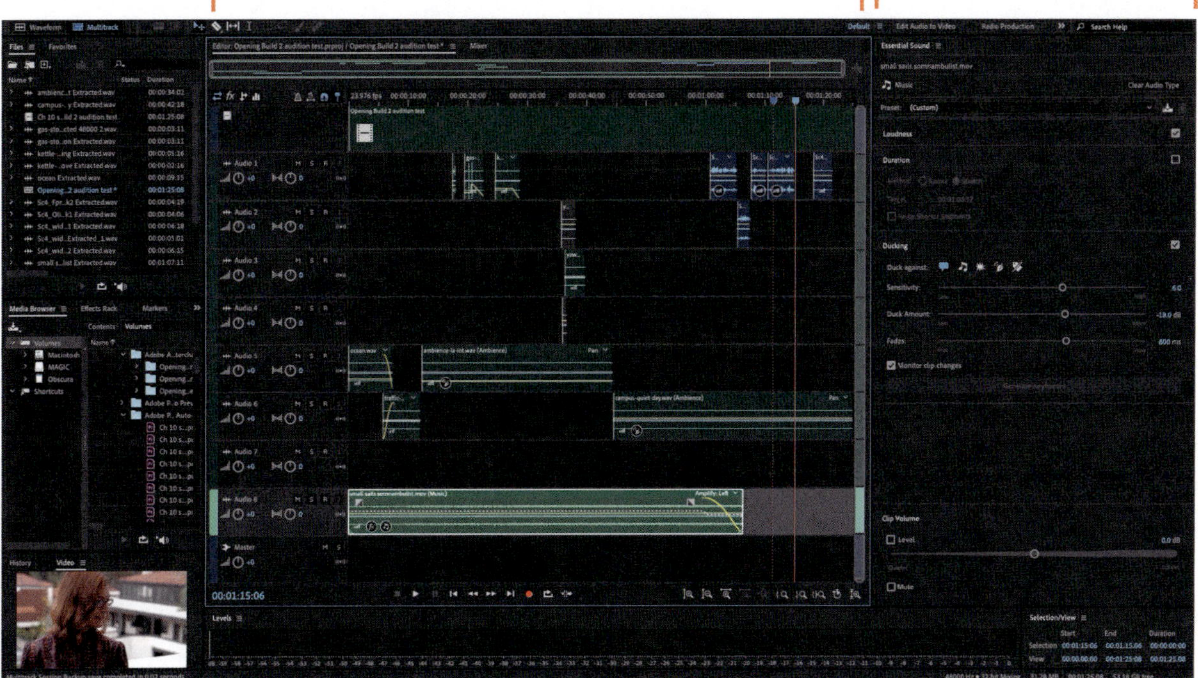

Figure 10.28

A Premiere Pro sequence in the Adobe Audition interface. You'll notice some familiar windows: Essential Sound, Media Browser, and an audio-centric version of the Timeline.

Sending Audio to Audition

Thanks to Adobe Dynamic Link, working with Audition and Premiere Pro together is seamless. Simply highlight audio in the Premiere Timeline and go to Edit > Edit in Adobe Audition and select Clip or Sequence, depending on your needs. When you send a single clip to Audition, it will automatically open with the Editor panel in Waveform view. You'll recognize the Essential Sound panel to the right. You'll be able to make live edits to the clip in Audition and see them reflected in your cut in Premiere, which is a beautiful thing. Audio clips that are being edited in Audition get the words "Audio Extracted" added to the clip name in the Timeline.

If you chose Sequence, you'll get a dialogue box with some parameters to set, such as handles and whether or not to keep existing effects attached. Be sure to check "Open in Audition" at the bottom. Audition will launch and an Adobe Audition Interchange version of your sequence (Figure 10.28) in a new Audition Session project (.SESX). Once open, you'll recognize your sequence in the Editor window which has two views: Multitrack, which shows the whole sequence much like the Timeline in Premiere, and Waveform, which is a detailed waveform display of individual clips. Working on a whole sequence in Audition is more likely to be something you'll save for the final sound design pass on a locked film.

Sound Design Problems to Solve

There's so much you can do with sound. Here's a few things to try out:

Perspective How does the sound design change as your main character moves through a scene? Are we (the audience) hearing what they hear? Or what we would hear if we were present? If a scene has more than one character, whose point of view would be best to foreground?

Try adding sound effects for the *Jackson's Hole* scene The fight in the *Jackson's Hole* scene you edited in Chapter 7 mostly occurs off-camera. Adding sound effects will make it sound more like a real fight occurred. The types of SFX used for fights are known as "hits" and "body falls." Try adding them and also some ambience to your cut of this scene.

Do a dialogue editing pass on the University scene Probably the least sexy and most necessary type of sound editing is dialogue editing. It's one of those things that is invisible when it works and completely distracting to the viewer when it doesn't. So what is it? When you edit a movie, you pull many different shots together. Some of them come together smoothly, others have noticeable differences and many of those differences are part of the dialogue. Sometime the energy of a performance is different, other times the lines vary from take to take, and most commonly, the edit that works for picture doesn't work for sound, resulting in a line that's slightly clipped or otherwise less than ideal. Try pulling up pauses, ums, and stumbles, replacing a word or partial word with the same line from another take, and filling gaps between words or lines with room tone or fill.

Do a sound design pass on the documentary scene Follow the steps in the first tutorial in this chapter but apply them to the doc scene instead. Add ambiences for the shots from Shutterstock and add hard effects like the sound of spray painting. Just because it's a doc doesn't mean you can't build an environment with sound. And now that you added that new voice-over, there's a whole set of sounds suggested by the text.

11

Titles and Graphics

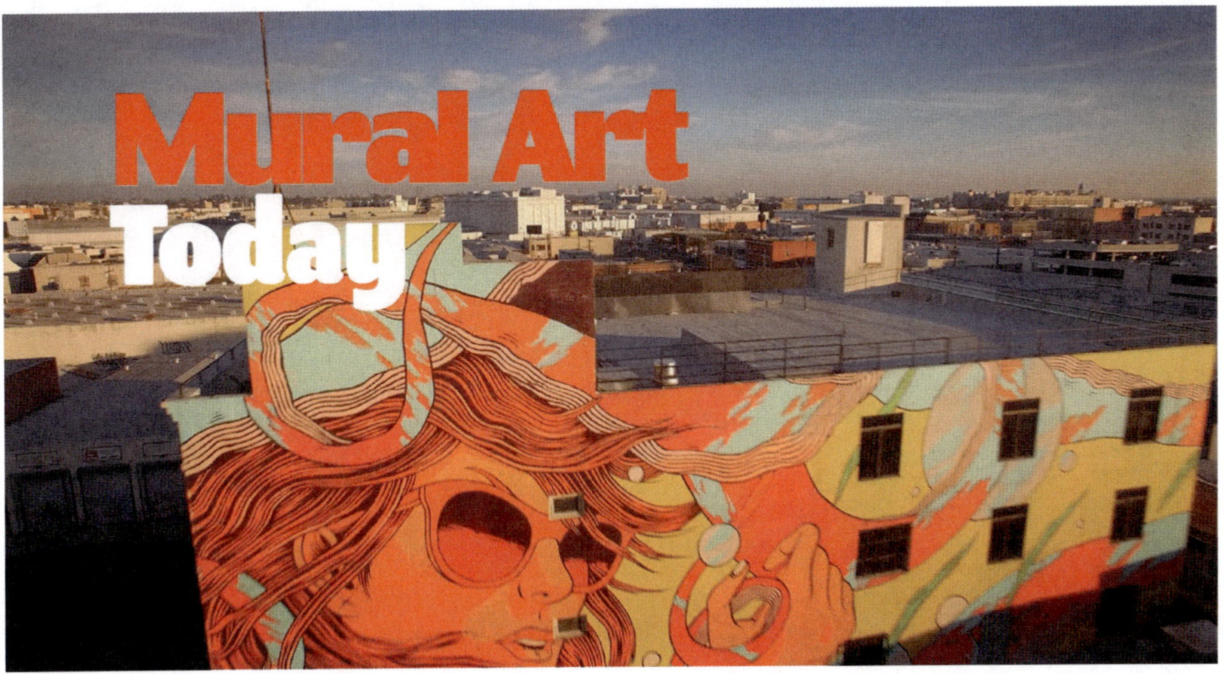

Figure 11.1

Most film titles are simply text over video or text over black.

ALL FILM TITLES ARE INFORMATIONAL—main titles, opening credits, lower thirds, subtitles, location cards, time and date stamps, end credits—every single one of these is there to tell the audience about the film. What varies, greatly, is the style.

Television, internet-based projects, and documentaries tend to use more graphics, animation, and effects than scripted movies. They also use more titles throughout the project (Figure 11.1). You might see location cards, time and date stamps, lower thirds, and other elements that provide sign posts for the viewer. Feature films, on the other hand, rarely have titles outside of the opening and the end credits, although it's possible to see full-frame titles to introduce a new scene or location—a tradition that goes all the way back to the era of silent cinema. And of course, every now and then you see a feature film that uses a fully-animated opening sequence to start the movie and even some interstitial animation along the way.

In other words, there are no rules and yet the type of titles used, how they look, and when they appear serve to tell the viewer what kind of film they are watching. And more importantly, they set the tone and provide an initial introduction to the story you are about to tell. In this chapter, we'll cover the titling and graphics tools available to you in Premiere Pro, and we'll spent a little time in Photoshop as well. We'll also show you how to bring animation into a Premiere Pro project.

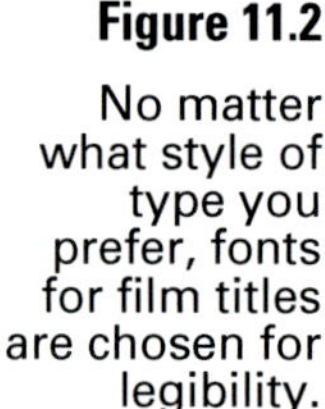

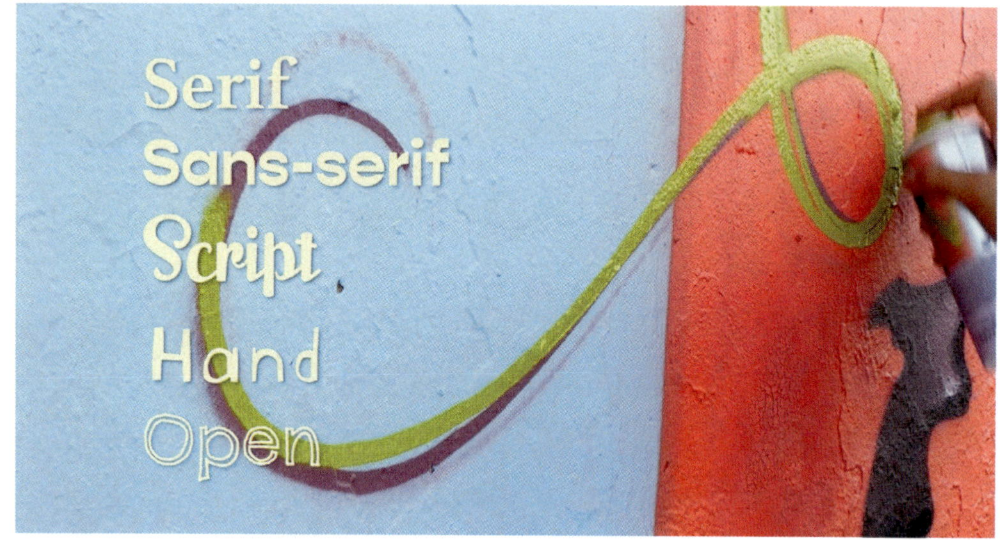

Figure 11.2

No matter what style of type you prefer, fonts for film titles are chosen for legibility.

Choosing a Font

Choosing type for film titles is very different than for web sites or books. First of all, it's easy for standard fonts to be perceived as illegible when they are displayed over moving video. Even when text is placed over black or another simple, colored background, it's going to be low resolution compared to print. Video is 72 ppi and print images are usually 300 ppi. So you're going to be looking for fonts that stand out, especially if they are created in a style that is more subtle than heavy block print (Figure 11.2).

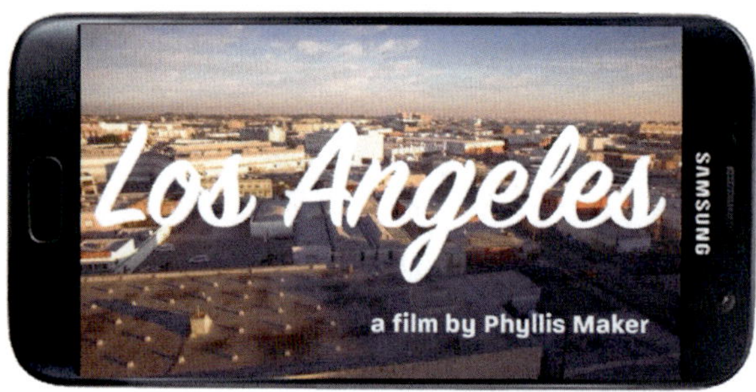

Figure 11.3

Text that works on a phone may not work the same in a theater.

Phones vs Theaters

This might be the greatest conflict in cinema today and it's fully apparent when deciding on which font to use for your titles. Typically, it's considered a bit inelegant to blast the audience with a giant full-frame title in a theater. In fact, huge titles at that size are actually less readable than smaller ones. On the other hand, so many viewers (myself included) watch most of the media they take in on their phones (Figure 11.3), in which case you need to make sure it reads when very small. There's no easy answer here. although it's certainly possible that you might create different theatrical and streaming versions of your film and change the titles accordingly.

Readability

When it comes to film titles, legibility is a key issue—especially if the title plays over video. Many fonts are designed for paragraphs of printed text, like the one you're looking at right now. Almost none of these fonts will be of use to you for your film. Similarly, delicate fonts with very thin lines and highly condensed fonts look great until you put them into a film. And don't forget that the viewer has a limited amount of time to read a film title, unlike a book reader who can take as long as they want. So making sure film titles can be taken in at a glance is important.

Here are a few things to keep in mind when it comes to readability:

Standard upper and lowercase type is easier to read than all caps.

Medium-weight or bold fonts are usually the easiest to read on a screen. Very fine lines disappear when placed over video and heavy-weight type can be hard to read as well.

Condensed type is harder to read than standard type. Type that's widely-spaced can also be problematic.

Script and handwritten font styles can be more difficult to read.

Less is more Literally, the shorter your words the easier they are to read and the result will potentially be more visually interesting as well.

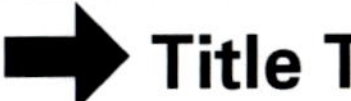

Title Titles

To learn more about the types of titles used in films, read Chapter 17 in *The Digital Filmmaking Handbook.*

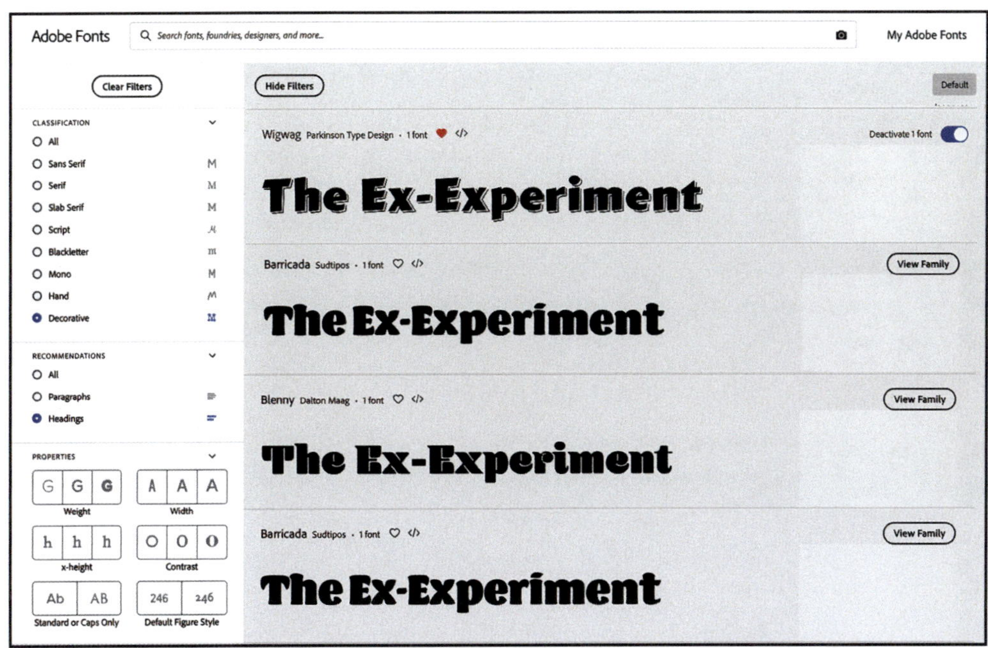

Figure 11.4

The Adobe Fonts web site has a great interface for auditioning fonts for film titles. If you select Headings from the filter list, you'll tend to get fonts that stand out.

Installing Adobe TypeKit Fonts

If you have an Adobe Creative Cloud subscription it includes access to the Adobe TypeKit library of fonts. Go to the Graphics menu in Premiere and select Add Fonts from Adobe Fonts. This will take you to the Adobe website, which has a great interface for picking fonts for film titles (Figure 11.4). Just type the name of your film into the Sample Text box and you'll see it displayed in every font. Use the filters on the left to narrow down the choices. If you don't know much about fonts, this interface is a great learning tool.

When you like a font, just activate it and you're done—it will immediately be available in Premiere after downloading. You might notice the text below the activate slider: "Licensed for Personal & Commercial Use. Learn More." The licensing is included in the price of your Creative Cloud subscription. This is important because you have to license fonts for film titles, just like you have to license music and other creative works that you use in your movie. At the time of this writing, the Adobe licensing agreement does say that you can use the fonts to produce film or video content for commercial exhibition, broadcast use, or distributed online through services like Vimeo and YouTube. It's almost a little too good to be true since font licenses can cost hundreds of dollars. Definitely one of the things that makes the price of a Creative Cloud subscription worth it.

Tracking
T r a c k i n g
Keming
Ker ning
Leading
Leading
Leading

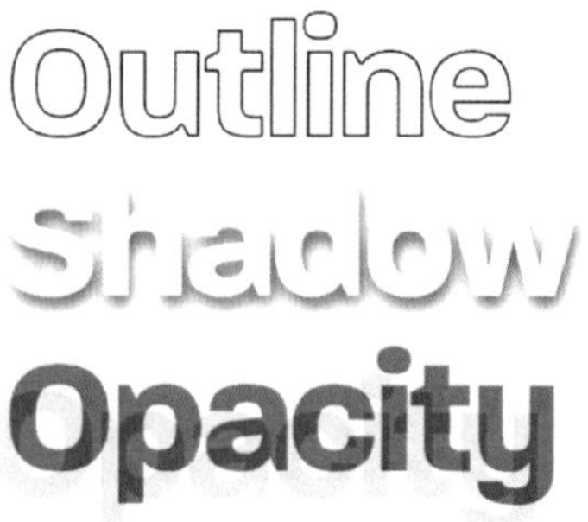

Figure 11.5 Standard text formatting options include tracking, kerning, leading, and strategies to separate text from the background.

Formatting Text for Film Titles

No matter what application you use to build titles—Premiere, Photoshop, Illustrator, or After Effects—you'll find a similar set of options (Figure 11.5) available for editing the appearance of fonts:

Alignment You can choose between left, center, right, and justified, which spreads out words to create text blocks with sharper edges on both the left and right margins. The paragraphs in this book are justified but it's rarely used for film titles.

Tracking evenly adjusts the spacing between letters.

Kerning adjusts the space between any pair of letters. Sometimes certain pairs of letters have awkward spacing, appearing connected or too far apart—the letters V and A are notorious for that—kerning allows you to fix that issue.

Leading adjusts the vertical distance between two lines of text.

Fill is the color of the main body of each letter.

Outlining (aka Stroke) is used to separate titles from the background and can be a different color than the fill.

Shadows also separate titles from the background, especially when the background is video. You can see how much the white text on a white page pops thanks to a shadow.

Position and scale seem so basic they're not worth mentioning, and yet when they change over time, they can yield dramatic effects.

Opacity can be changed to make titles semi-transparent. A small reduction in opacity (80-90%) can make titles feel more integrated into the background image without actually making them appear transparent.

Keyframing lets you adjust any of the above parameters over time. You might choose to have your titles fly-in, which involves keyframing their position and scale, or fade by keyframing the opacity. We explained how keyframing works in Chapters 9 and 10, but we'll go into how it works for titles, including some advanced keyframing techniques, later in this chapter.

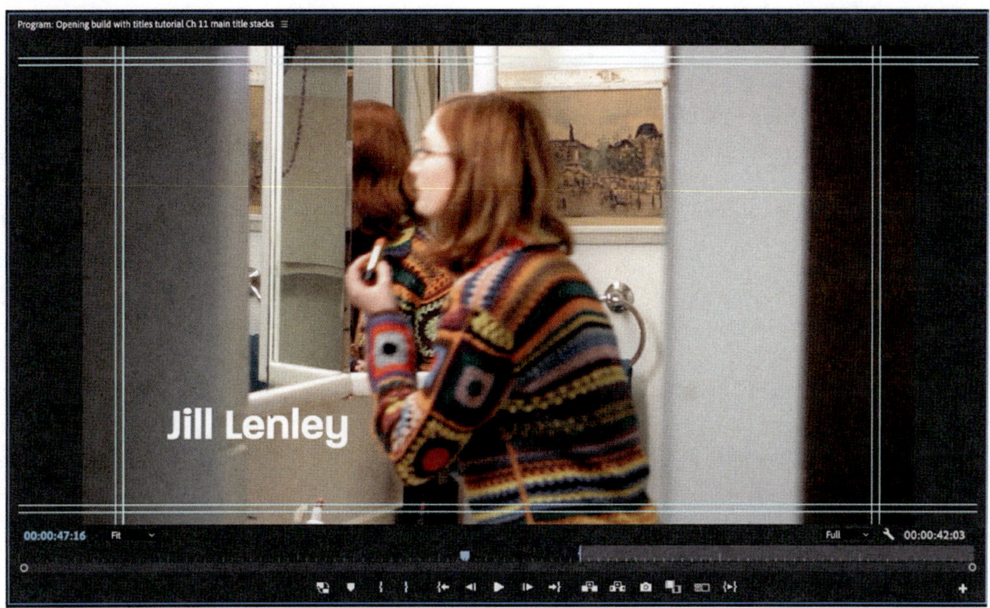

Figure 11.6

Safe margin guides help avoid accidental text cropping.

Guides and Safe Margins

The edges of the screen are considered off-limits for titles in film and television projects (Figure 11.6). That's because every monitor is different and anything too close to the edges may get cropped. A general rule of thumb is to avoid the outer 10% of the screen. All still and video editing applications offer on-screen guides to help you keep your titles from going off the edge. Sometimes, if you are working for a specific network or distributor, they'll have custom guides to identify which parts of the screen are off-limits—they may need an unexpected area for their logo and other on-screen graphics. Of course breaking the rules can look very cool, and if you film is destined for the web, you might be able to get away with it. But keep in mind that what looks good embedded in the framework of a web page could still get cropped when viewers elect to play it back in full-screen mode.

Making Titles in Premiere Pro

You might think that you need a dedicated graphics app to build your titles, but you can make them in Premiere although the tools are somewhat limited. Titles created in Premiere start with fonts, which are scalable, vector-based graphic objects. If you have any experience with web design, you already know that you never have to worry about resolution with vector-based objects. You can make them as big or small as you want and they will remain crisp and clear. (But they are still ultimately limited by your final film resolution, of course). Font-based titles also remain editable—that is, you can change any of the attributes discussed earlier at any time during the editing process.

There are two ways to make font-based titles in Premiere Pro, from scratch using the Type tool (Figure 11.7) or with presets in the Essential Graphics panel (Figure11.8).

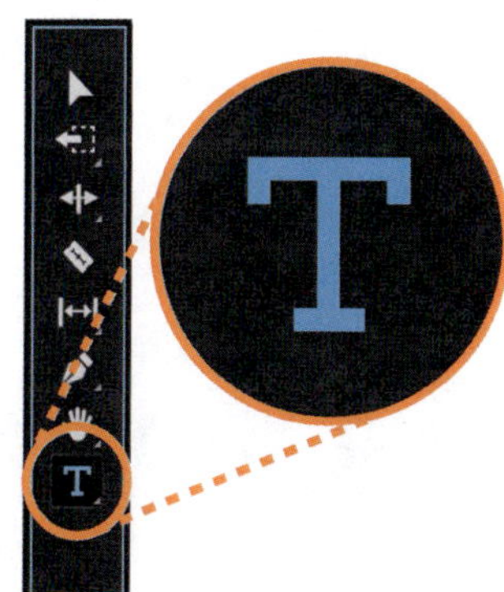

Figure 11.7

The Type tool is found in the Tools panel.

The Type Tool

The easiest way to make titles is to use the Type tool, found at the bottom of the Tools panel (Figure 11.7). Simply select the Type tool, then click in the area of the Program monitor where you want the text to appear and start typing. A box outlined in red will appear around your cursor in the Program monitor to let you know that the Type tool is active. Once you've created some text, you'll see a new clip appear in your Timeline on the next available video track in your sequence.

One thing that's unusual about titles in Premiere is that when you make a new title with the Type tool, you won't see a new graphics clip in your Project panel or bin. In Premiere, titles are actually effects—the Text effect. But you can still highlight, copy, and paste any title into other sequences if you wish. If you do prefer to have a title clip to refer to in your project, you can convert the title to a Master Graphic by highlighting it in the Timeline and going to Graphics > Upgrade to Master Graphic. A new clip will appear in your Project panel and you can rename it and organize it as desired. If you double-click on a Master Graphic, it will launch into the Source monitor like any other piece of media. This can be very useful if you need to use the same title over and over again. Of course, if you delete it, it will also behave like any other piece of media in Premiere and disappear without a trace, leaving black holes in your Timeline.

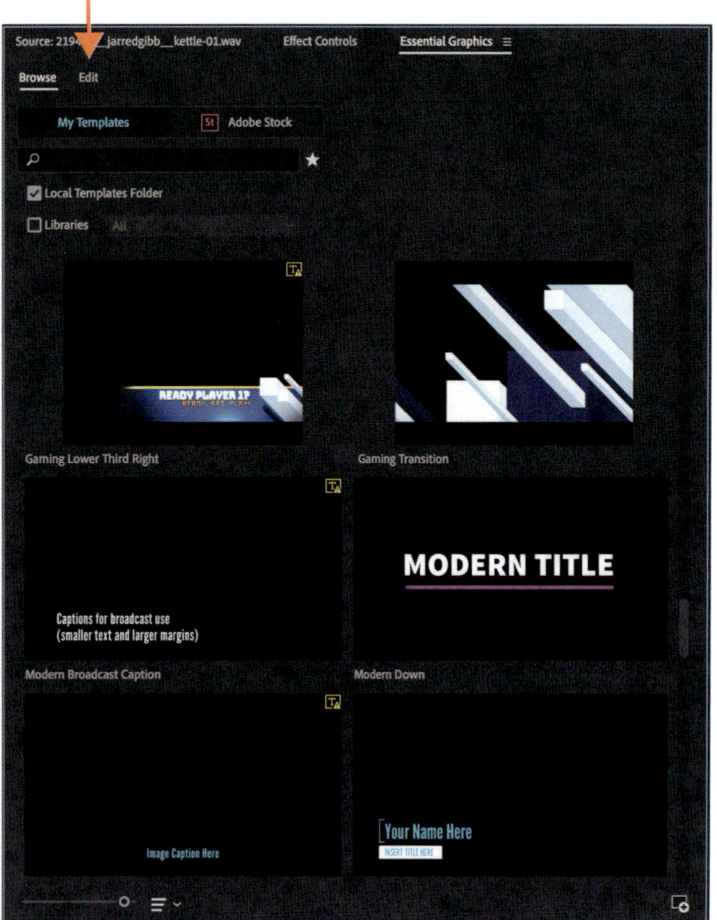

Figure 11.8

Instead of creating titles from scratch, you can use the presets in the Essential Graphics panel and customize them as needed.

Essential Graphics Presets

If you want something a bit more complicated, you can start with the presets found in the Essential Graphics panel (Window > Essential Graphics). Here you'll find a selection of title presets on the Browse tab—everything from news and sports graphics to spinning lower thirds and elaborate end credits (Figure 11.8).

To use one of these presets, simply click and drag it into your Timeline, preferably onto an empty video track. If Adobe needs to load fonts from the Creative Cloud, it will do so automatically.

Most projects that use elaborate graphics like the ones available here will eventually want to create custom graphics. The presets available in the Essential Graphics panel are saved in the Motion Graphics Template format, which has the file extension MOGRT and is also compatible with After Effects. In fact, After Effects also has an Essential Graphics panel and motion graphics templates created in After Effects can be imported into Premiere Pro (Figure 11.8), where key elements such as type attributes are editable. In other words, if you have some skills in After Effects, you can repopulate the Essential Graphics panel with your own highly-customized presets. (We get into After Effects in greater detail in Chapter 12.) But if that's a little too advanced, these existing presets are a good starting place and you can always customize them within Premiere by changing the font, colors, and other text attributes.

You can also save your own Motion Graphics Templates in Premiere—just highlight a title in the Timeline, then go to Graphics > Export Motion Graphics Template and select Local Templates the destination in the pop-up window. Then go to the Essential Graphics browse window and you'll now see your own template under the My Templates button. You may have to check the box next to Local Templates Folder at the top of the Essential Graphics browser.

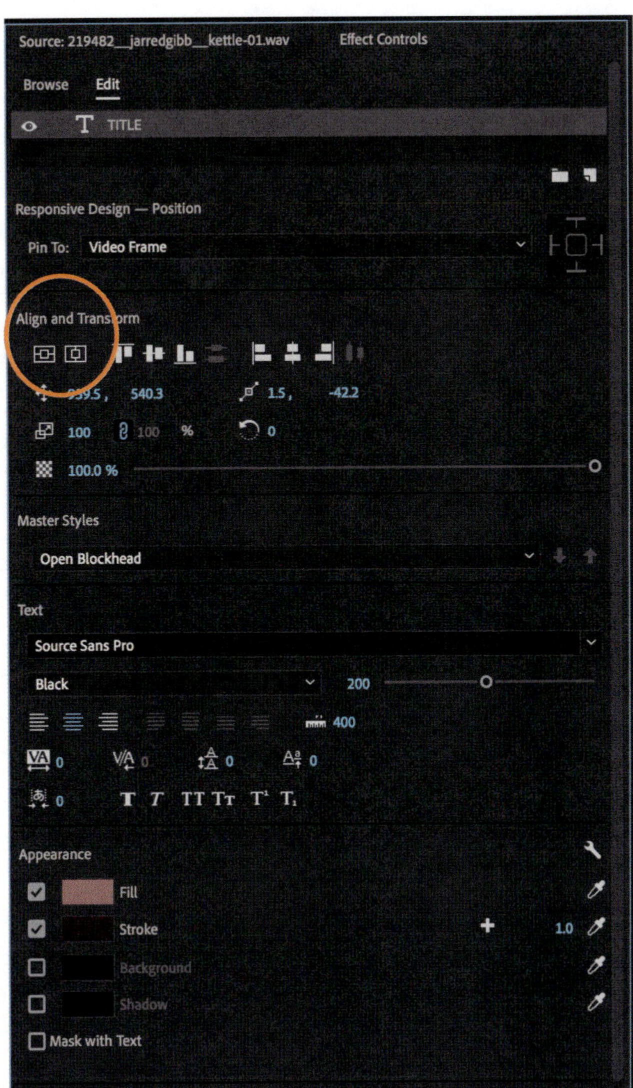

Figure 11.9

The Essential Graphics editing interface adds two alignment buttons that are not available in the Effects Control panel. They're great for centering text on screen.

Editing Type in Premiere

You can edit type in the Essential Graphics editor (Figure 11.9), found under the Edit tab in the Essential Graphics panel, or the Effect Controls panel (Figure 11.10). In both panels, you can change the font, size, alignment, and color. You can make fine adjustments to the tracking, kerning, and leading. You can also add outlines or drop shadows to make text easier to read when placed over a frame of moving video.

The Essential Graphics editor has some convenient formatting options if you want titles centered in the screen. This sounds pretty basic but it's a welcome addition that's been missing for many years in most editing applications. In the Align and Transform area, click on the vertical and horizontal alignment buttons (Figure 11.9) and your text is perfectly centered, no more guessing. (For this to work with older versions of Premiere, you must center-align your type first.)

The Essential Graphics editor is also a good place to start when you want to customize one of the Essential Graphics presets. These presets are often built out of multiple effects—glows, 3D effects, and transformation over time are common elements in addition to standard text attributes. When you customize a preset in the Essential Graphics editor, Premiere will gather and adjust that group of effects together for you. You can also create and save your own special text-oriented formatting presets called Master Text Styles. What's the difference between Master Text Styles and the Motion Graphics Templates we mentioned earlier? Motion Graphics Templates are groups of effects that show up in the Essential Graphics browser. Master Text Styles only include attributes of the Text effect (not the other effects like glows, etc.) and they show up in the Master Styles menu in the Essential Graphics editor.

☑ The Graphics Workspace

The graphics workspace is similar to the editing workspace, with the addition of the Essential Graphics panel. You can also access the Essential Graphics panel and add it to any other workspace as well (Window > Essential Graphics).

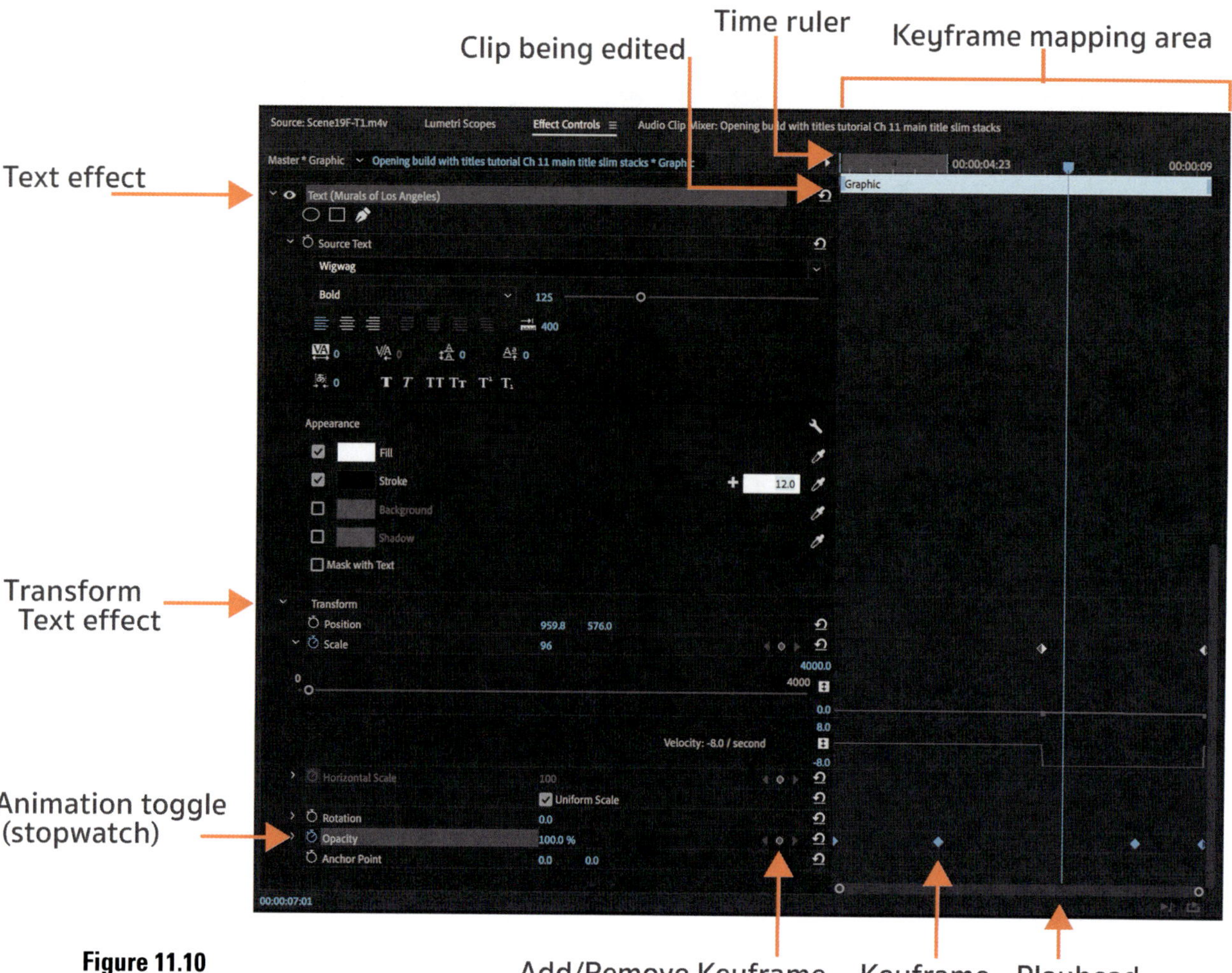

Figure 11.10

You've already been using the Effect Controls panel for audio and motion effects, but it's also used to edit titles. Found under the Text effect, the Transform area is where you add keyframes to change titles over time.

Which One Should You Use?

There are a lot of different types of titling presets (standard Text effect presets, Essential Graphics presets/Motion Graphics Templates, Master Graphics, Master Text Styles, not to mention Creative Cloud text styles which we discuss later in this chapter) and two different interfaces in which to manipulate them (Effect Controls panel and Essential Graphics editor). The presets choice is really a matter of personal preference and workflow. As for the two text editors, you'll probably end up needing to use both of them. The Text effect in the Effect Controls panel doesn't offer alignment presets, Master Text Styles, or custom Motion Graphics Templates, but the Essential Graphics editor doesn't have a keyframing interface.

If you're wondering why you might need that, read on.

Animating Titles in Premiere

There's a reason that titles for film are often called motion graphics—movement over time is intrinsic to the medium of film and even the simplest movie titles tend to be animated in some way. Titles that fly-in, spin, grow, shrink, and disappear slowly can all be created with keyframed animation in Premiere—that is, changing the attributes of scale, position, rotation, and opacity over time.

Advanced Keyframing

Animation in Premiere is based on keyframes, which are anchor points within a clip in the Timeline that dictate the size, position, and transparency of s piece of media at a given point in time. For titles, you can add keyframes to any of the items under the Transform section of the Text Effect in the Effect Controls panel (Figure 11.10).

For example, a very simple use of keyframes in a title would be to set a keyframe on the first frame of the title and set the position off-screen to the left, then set a second keyframe on the last frame of the title and set the position off-screen to the right. When you play the title, you'll get text that crawls across the screen left to right (Figure 11.11). The speed of the crawl is controlled by the length of the title clip in the Timeline—the longer the shot, the slower the crawl.

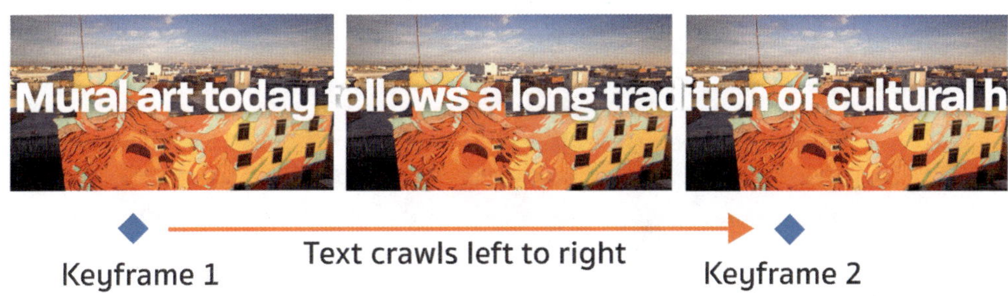

Figure 11.11

Keyframes let you adjust simple parameters to transform text over time. Shown here, two keyframes that change Position.

Now if you added two more keyframes, one a couple seconds into the shot and another a couple seconds toward the end and used them both to enlarge (or Scale) the type, the text would crawl in from the left as it grows larger, then start to shrink back down as it crawls off screen on the right (Figure 11.12). If you were to keep adding keyframes for rotation and opacity, you can see how things can get pretty complex. Figuring out how to place keyframes to get the animation you want is a little bit of a logic puzzle.

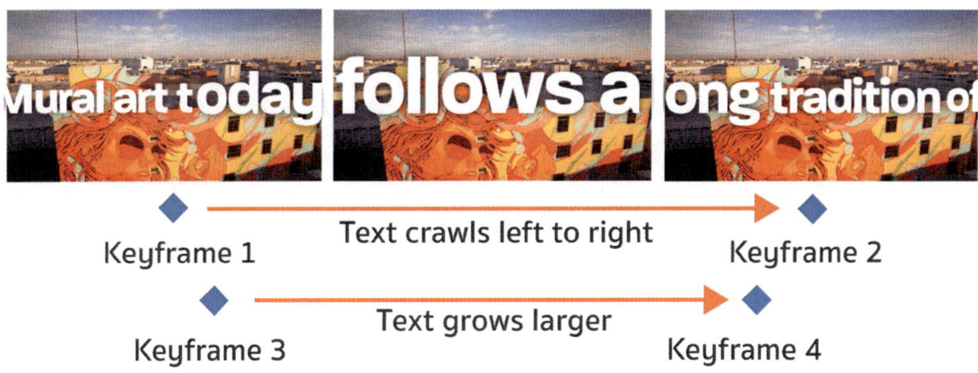

Figure 11.12

The more keyframes and more parameters you add, the more complex the animation. Here, we've added two keyframes that change Scale.

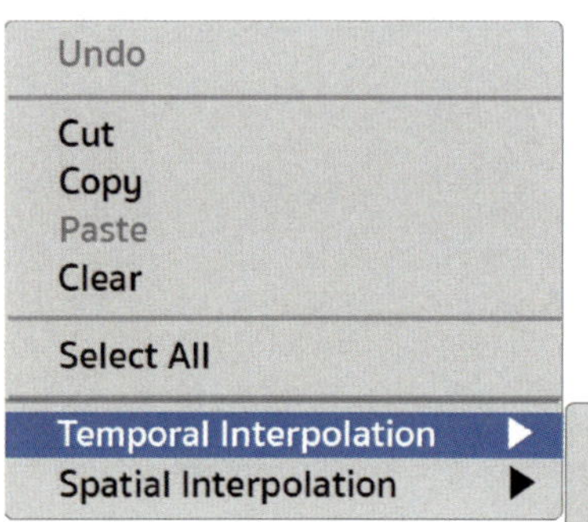

Figure 11.13

Right-clicking on keyframes brings up a menu that lets you choose from a selection of curved ramps to get different interpolations between keyframes.

To set keyframes in Premiere, first take notice of the keyframe mapping area on the right side of the Effect Controls panel (Figures 11.10 and 11.14). Along the top is a time ruler with a playhead cursor that matches your position in the sequence in the Timeline. Just like other time rulers in Premiere, you can drag the playhead and change your position in a sequence. You'll see this change reflected in the Timeline and the Program monitor. For titles, the keyframe mapping area only shows the clip you have selected in the timeline. The visible area will shift to fit any Text effect clip you have selected in the Timeline (by clicking on it, not with Ins and Outs) and a visual of that clip will show just beneath the time ruler. Each keyframable parameter in the Transform section of the Text effect has a Toggle Animation button that looks like a small stopwatch. When you select it, it will turn blue (on) and a keyframe will automatically be set wherever your playhead is parked. For that reason, it generally makes sense to park the playhead on the first frame of the title media before you start to add keyframes. To add additional keyframes, move the playhead and click on the Add/Remove keyframes button to the right (Figure 11.10). Beware: don't click the animation toggle again or you'll remove your existing keyframes.

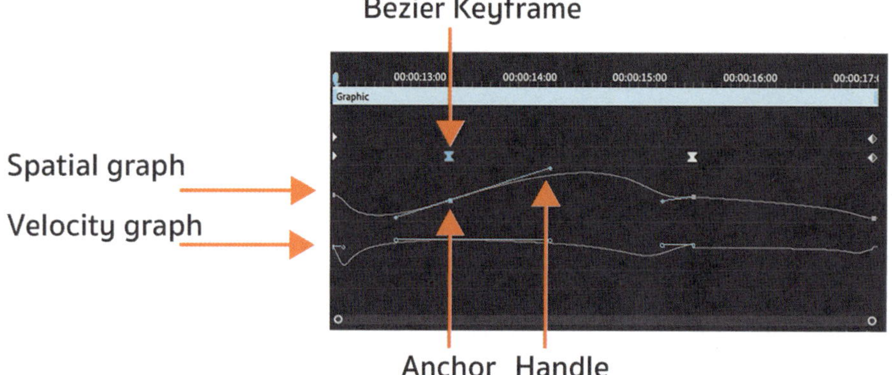

Figure 11.14

The two graphs in the keyframe mapping area, spatial and velocity, have editable Bezier curves, to let you dial in the shape of each ramp.

Changing Interpolation

When you set keyframes, Premiere interpolates the changes from one keyframe to the next in a linear manner. But you can also tell Premiere how to interpolate that shift between keyframes, so that the change starts out fast, then slows down, or vice-versa. To change the interpolation, just right-click on any keyframe. You'll get a small menu that lets you choose between different types of Bezier curves (Figure 11.13). Each of these curves results in a different shift, or ramp, between keyframes. Try the Ease In or Ease Out options to give your keyframe interpolations a gentle ramp.

To see a visual representation of these interpolations, look at the keyframe mapping area of the Effect Controls panel, just below the keyframes themselves. Spin down the triangle next to the parameters under Transform in the Text Effect—you'll see two maps, spatial and velocity, if applicable (Figure 11.14). The velocity graph is named a bit confusingly—it doesn't change the speed between keyframes, to do that you would just move the keyframes themselves. (They can be selected and dragged in the keyframe mapping area of the Effect Controls panel.) Rather, it changes the speed within the duration that is specified by the keyframes. When you click on a keyframe, you'll see the handles and anchor point of a Bezier curve appear and the keyframe icon will switch from a diamond (linear) to an hour glass (Bezier). Bezier curves aren't just a visual representation—you can also manipulate them directly by clicking and dragging the handles to control the shape of the curve and this will affect how your transformation plays out. Sometimes a standard, linear ramp doesn't work and this is how you fix that problem in Premiere. Bezier curves aren't that hard to work with once you get used to them, but they definitely are a bit outside the average filmmaker's toolset.

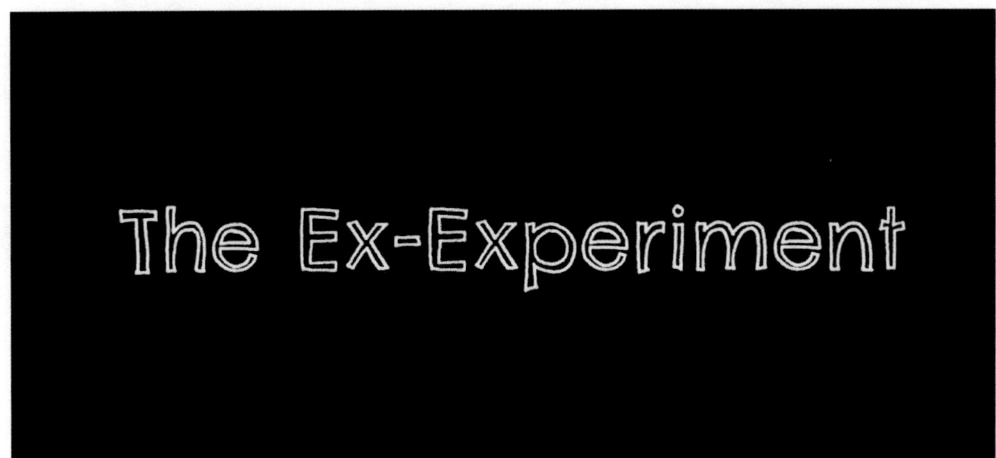

Figure 11.15

Open fonts look great over plain black or white backgrounds, but not always over video.

TUTORIAL: Making a Main Title

We worked on the scenes in the Opening Build sequence in four tutorials so far and built it out with music and sound design. Now we're going to create a main title for it in Premiere. Open your latest version of the Opening Build project or alternately you can use "Opening Build sound.mp4" from the "Opening Build cuts" folder and import it into a project. The music montage, which you built in Chapter 1, was designed as a visual bed for the opening titles. There's a lot of time for the opening credits—about one minute and fifteen seconds before the dialogue from the first scene starts. We're going use the titling tools in Premiere to build a simple, animated, text-over-video main title.

STEP 1: Find a Font

If your titles are simple, fonts choice is everything. So go to the Creative Cloud app, select Fonts from the bottom of the menu on the left, and then use the font picker on the Adobe Fonts site to activate at least five fonts to audition for the main title. I chose the following: Asphalt, Wigwag, Blockhead OT, Cuisine, Paralucent, Chelsea Market Open, Suave Script Pro, Milk Script, Bello Script Pro, Bello Caps Pro, Gopher, and Peachy Keen. There's a pattern here: I chose some big, blocky fonts because those always read well over video, I chose some script fonts because they're pretty and it's a female-driven rom com, and I chose some open fonts because I like how they look (Figure 11.15).

Large Font Families

Big typefaces, like Helvetica, are really more like large families of fonts. You'll have many options including condensed fonts, italics, and different weights, from thin to heavy. Some font families, like Gill Sans, even include special decorative fonts. The advantage to working with a large typeface is that you can use that font family for all your titling needs, and you'll be unlikely to face the issue of fonts that don't look good together.

STEP 2: Place the Main Title in Premiere

Back in your Premiere project, make a copy of the last sequence and call it 'Opening Build Titles" or if you're using Opening Build sound.mp4, make a new sequence and drag it onto V1 and A1. Select the Type tool from the Tools panel, click in the middle of your Program monitor, a red text box will appear on the screen, and type in the name of the movie, "The Ex-Experiment." It will default to something not suited to film titles, such as Minion Pro. Notice that a new title clip will appear in your Timeline on V2 (Figure 11.16). Use the align buttons in the Essential Graphics panel (Window > Essential Graphics) to center the text on the screen (Figure 11.9).

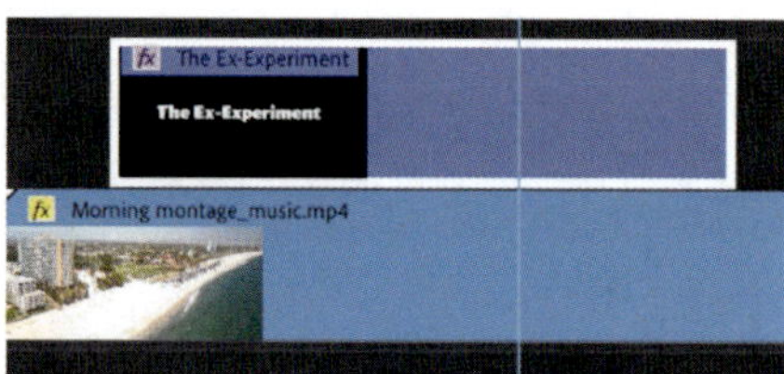

Figure 11.16

When you create a new title with the Type tool, a new clip will appear in the Timeline.

Now, we need to decide where the main title will fall. Usually main titles are placed near the beginning or at the end of the opening sequence. Let's try putting it first, over the aerial of the city, starting at about 00:00:01:12 and extending it all the way to the end of the second aerial shot of the city, about 00:00:12:10.

STEP 3: Auditioning Fonts

Now we're going to audition fonts by making a stack of copies of the main title card on successive video tracks. Select the title clip on V2 and hold the Alt/Option key as you drag it to V3—Premiere will add a V3 track if there isn't already one there. Make sure you have snapping selected (S) so that the clip stays in the same position on the new track. You'll now have an exact copy on V3. Continue Alt/Option-dragging until you fill your video tracks with enough title cards for the fonts that you want to audition.

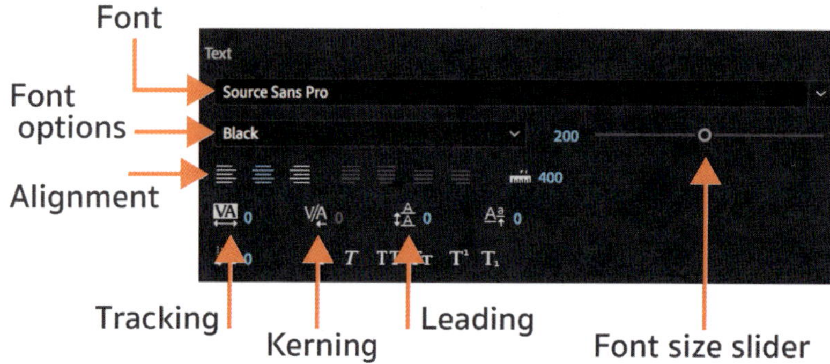

Figure 11.17

Text formatting options in the Essential Graphics editor.

Next change the font on each track starting with V2: Activate the Selection tool (V) and select the text in the Program monitor. In the Essential Graphics panel make sure you're on the Edit tab. In the Text area (Figure 11.17), you can now change the font in the pulldown menu. Just below it is another pulldown menu, where you can select different variations of that font, if available. Many fonts have more than one version but they'll often default to the most common choice, "Regular" or "Medium." But odds are high that you'll want the bold, black, or maybe a special decorative option. Next, use the font size slider to adjust the size. You might be used to using point sizes for fonts, but that measuring system is irrelevant for text in films. The slider just represents a percentage, in Figure 11.17 it's set to 200%. You'll also see here controls for basic alignment (right, center, left, and justified) and text controls (tracking, kerning, and leading). These choices are a matter of personal taste, but for the animation to work right in this tutorial, you need centered alignment.

Watch the various versions of the main title by disabling (Clip > Enable) or turning off tracks (eye button) and pick a font to move forward with. I chose Wigwam—easy to read, a little funny.

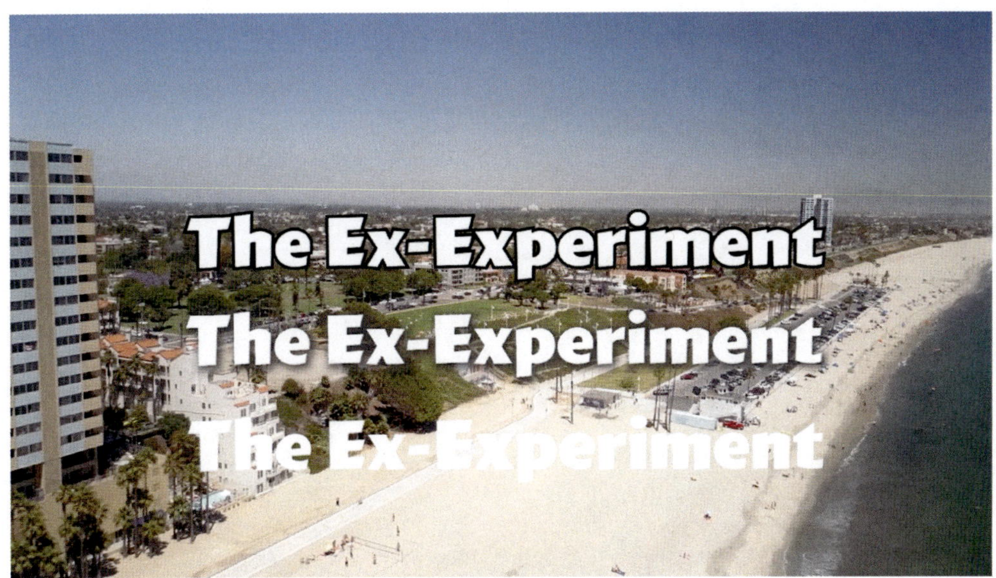

Figure 11.18

Outlined text (top), drop shadow (middle), and plain text (bottom). With a busy background like this, titles need some help to stand out.

STEP 4: Separating Text from the Background

Because this title is going to play over video, it's going to need a little help to make it stand out from the background. But we don't want to really call attention to this bit of help, so that means we will choose between a very fine outline and a drop shadow (Figure 11.18).

To try out a fine outline, select Stroke in Appearance section of the Essential Graphics editor. Click in the center of the rectangle to the left of the word "stroke" to choose a color for the outline. Black is a good choice, but a grey might work just as well and be less noticeable. How does it look?

The downside of outlines is that they can look a little cartoon-y. Next try a drop shadow instead. Deselect stroke and select Shadow. Here you can control the Opacity,
Angle, Distance from the text, Size, and amount of Blur (Figure 11.19). To make a subtle drop shadow, you want it to be fairly close to the original text, with a fair amount of blur, and also a fair amount of transparency (Figure 11.20).

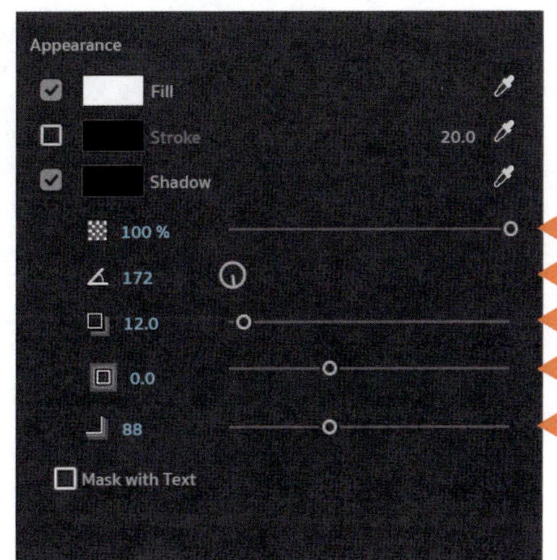

Figure 11.19

Select Shadow and use the controls below it to adjust Opacity, Angle, and Blur.

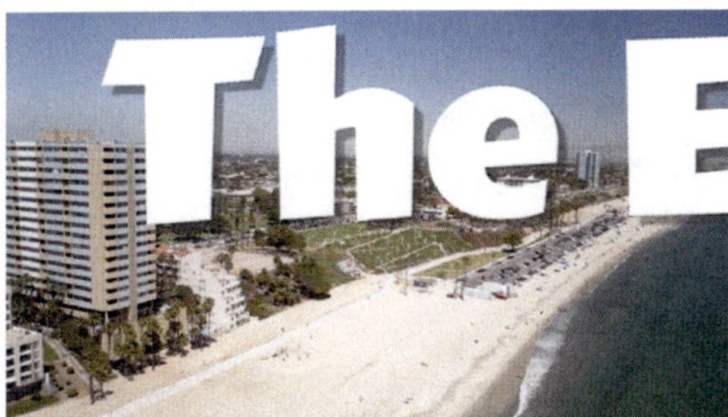

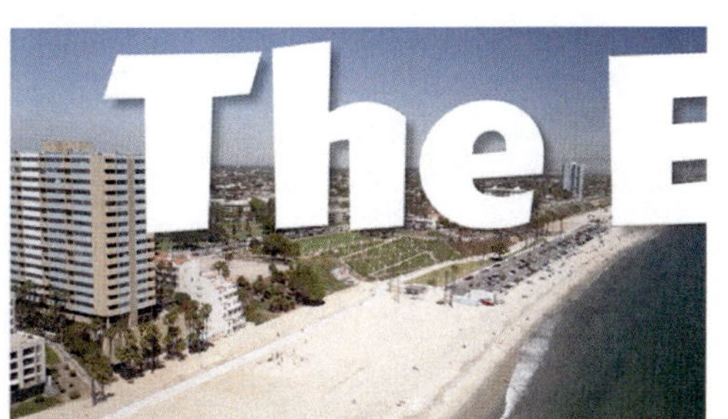

Figure 11.20

What could be less realistic than a shadow on the sky (left)? But a little blur goes a long way (right).

STEP 5: Add Movement to the Main Title

Now, let's animate the title. First we'll have it fade on slowly over the wide aerial. Open the Effect Controls panel and then select the title clip in the Timeline (Figure 11.21). You'll see an effect called Text near the top of the Effect Controls panel. Scroll down so you can see the Transform area of the Text effect. Position the playhead on the first frame of the title and select the toggle animation button for Opacity. Set the opacity on the first frame to 0. Then about 5 seconds later, add a keyframe and set the opacity to 100%. Play your title. It should now have a slow fade in.

Next, let's have the main title recede with the movement along the street in the second shot. Position the playhead on the first frame of the second aerial shot, then toggle on animation for Scale—a keyframe will be set on that frame automatically. Now go to the end of the second aerial shot and set another keyframe and change the scale to 70%. Watch what you've done so far: the title now moves with the camera in the second shot. Let's have it fade out at the end. Add another keyframe for opacity (100%) a few seconds before the end of the title and another opacity keyframe set to 0% on the last frame. You can drag each keyframe to make adjustments. Be sure you only have one keyframe highlighted blue when you drag though, or you'll end up changing everything. Play around with the Bezier curves as well, especially for the Opacity interpolation. Too see them, you'll have to spin down the triangle next to Opacity, then double click on the anchor below each keyframe (Figure 11.21).

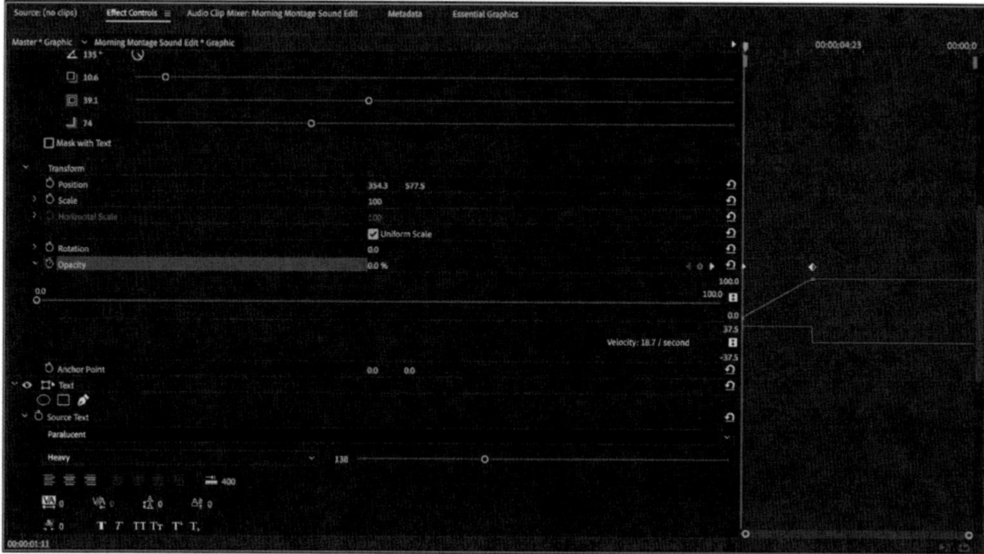

Figure 11.21

Transforming Opacity on a Text effect is the same as a fade, but with keyframes, you can control it at every step.

STEP 6: Add the Rest of the Opening Credits

Hey, there's a whole minute or more left for you to fill with opening credits. Make up some names for the cast and crew and add them to the sequence, up until the dialogue for the next scene starts. Try using some of the presets from the Essential Graphics panel and customizing them to go with your main title. Check out our cut: Opening Build Titles.mp4

 Titling in After Effects

After Effects is a great app for creating titles. All of the topics discussed in this chapter are relevant and the specifics of working in After Effects are covered in Chapter 12.

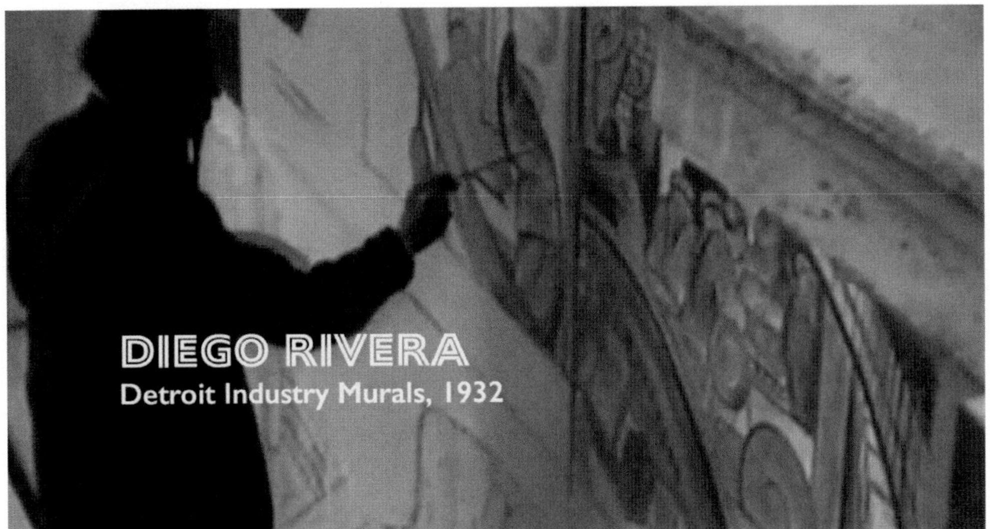

Figure 11.22

Photoshop is a great choice for building a batch of static lower thirds.

Designing Titles in Photoshop

If you have a lot of titles and you want them all to match—for example, a batch of lower thirds—it can be easier to make a template in Photoshop and build your titles there (Figure 11.22). One strategy is to make a layered document where each layer has a separate title on it. Then you can import the entire layered document into Premiere as Individual Layers so that each layer becomes a separate clip in Premiere.

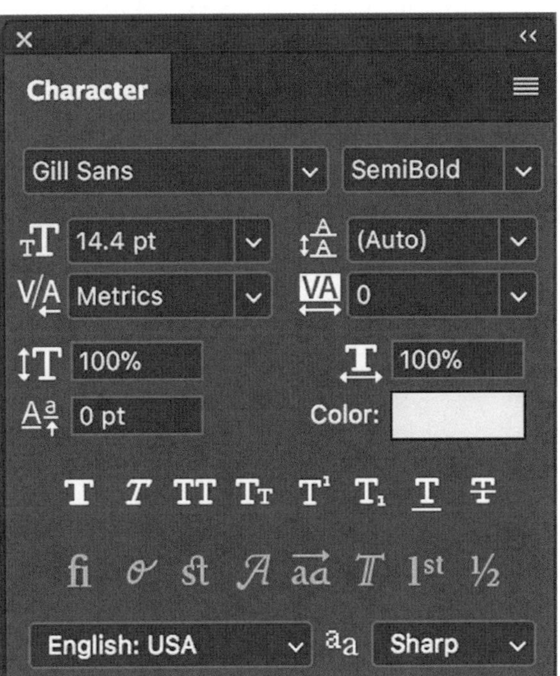

Figure 11.23

The Character window in Photoshop contains all the standard type formatting tools.

Because Photoshop is well-integrated with Premiere, you can create a new photoshop file from inside Premiere (File > New > Photoshop File) which will prompt you create a document the same size as your sequence and launches Photoshop. (You can also use the Edit in Photoshop command in the File menu to quickly make changes as needed after you import your graphics back into Premiere.)

Photoshop is a big program, just like Premiere. Luckily, you don't need to know all of it to make titles. You'll immediately recognize the Type tool in the Photoshop Tools panel and it works just like the one in Premiere. Once you have some text to work with, you'll find the Character panel (Window > Character) has all of the standard text editing controls (Figure 11.22) and if you need to adjust alignment, that's found in Window > Paragraph. Type layers in Photoshop have special properties. Right-clicking on a Type layer (Figure 11.23) brings up a menu with Blending Options, which is where you set drop shadows and other text effects.

Here are some things to consider if you decide to make titles in Photoshop:

Image size Make your document the same size as your video and remember that all video is 72 ppi. There's no reason to go any bigger unless you plan to add movement that enlarges your titles in Premiere. If you create a new Photoshop file from inside

Premiere (File > New > Photoshop File), Premiere will automatically assign it the same size as your sequence.

Title safe guides You can get film and video title safe guides by creating a new document in Photoshop, selecting the Film & Video tab at the top right of the New Document window, and choosing the preset that fits your video size. You will have to click the View All Presets button to get to a 2K or 4K preset. Your image will open with title safe guides visible. You can toggle them on and off by typing Command/Control + ; (semi-colon).

Export a guide frame from Premiere If you plan to place your titles over video, you can quickly export a still frame from your sequence in Premiere using the Export Frame button or Shift + E. I prefer the lossless TIFF format for stills, but you can also use PNG or JPEG.

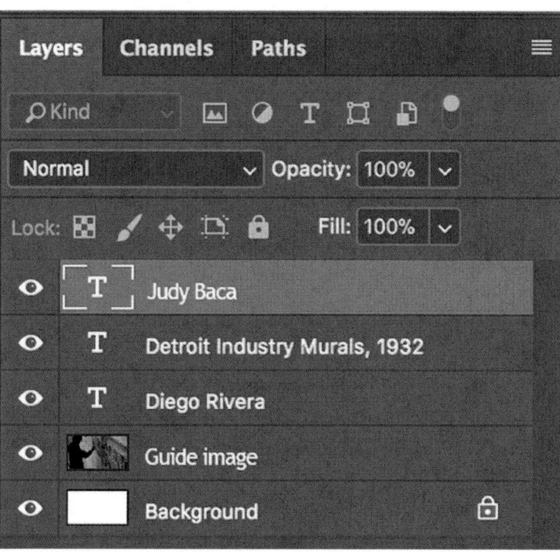

Figure 11.24

Type layers in Photoshop have special properties. Right-clicking on a type layer brings up a menu with Blending Options, which is where you set drop shadows.

Work in layers Premiere doesn't let you create titles with layers but it does let you work with layered stills created in Photoshop, so use the Photoshop layer functions to build a single document that contains all your titles on separate layers (Figure 11.24). Be sure to save it in the PSD format, which supports both layers and transparency. And when you bring it into Premiere, choose Individual Layers or Sequence to keep those layers separate and editable in Premiere.

Stay in the RGB color space Still graphics in Photoshop may default to the CMYK color space, which is used for print, so make sure you're working in RGB, which is used in video and computer graphics (Image > Mode > RGB Color).

Rasterization When you save a Photoshop file as PNG or bring a layered PSD file into Premiere, the fonts in your document get *rasterized*, that is, they get changed from editable vector-based fonts to bitmapped images. You won't be able to use the Type tool, the Text effect, or the Essential Graphics editor to change them. However, if you saved them as PSD files, you will be able to use Edit in Photoshop (found in the right-click menu) to go back to your source file in Photoshop, where the text will remain editable. Changes you make in Photoshop will be reflected in Premiere after you save.

Dedicated Graphics Tracks

It makes a lot of sense to keep your titles and graphics on a special, dedicated track in the Timeline. That way, if you want to watch without them or export a textless version of your film, you can simply turn those tracks off.

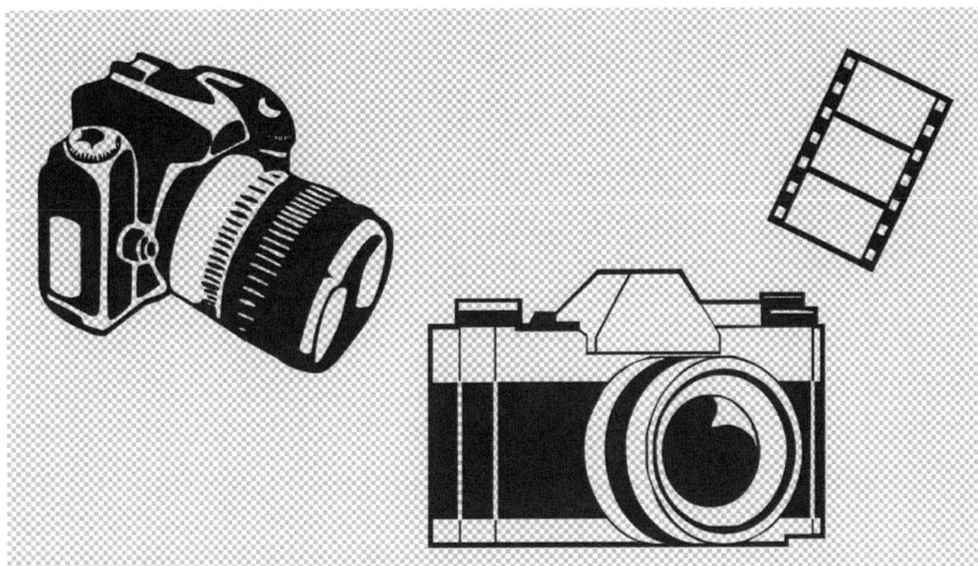

Figure 11.25

Alpha channels allow for a transparent background in both still images and video clips. Adobe apps use a checkerboard pattern called a transparency grid to let you know the image is transparent. In Premiere, you'll have to select Transparency Grid from the wrench menu in the Source monitor to see it.

Importing Other Graphic Elements

Many film projects need to incorporate other types of graphics besides titles, like logos and animated sequences. These are almost always created outside of Premiere, in a dedicated graphics application

Media with Alpha Channels

Logos and other identifying graphics are usually created with a transparent background, also known as an alpha channel (Figure 11.25). To get your text layers to be transparent in Premiere, you'll want to save your photoshop file in the PSD format. For single-layer transparent images you can also use PNG. You may need to tell Premiere how to interpret a file, whether it's a still or video, that contains an alpha channel. The Modify Clip window (Clip > Modify > Interpret Footage) has several options (Figure 11.26). Generally the default setting should work but if not, try the others. And if the wrong part of your image is transparent, the logo rather than the background, select Invert Alpha Channel to swap them. When you load a source clip with transparency in the Source monitor, the transparent area will appear black unless you select Transparency Grid from the wrench menu (Figure 11.25).

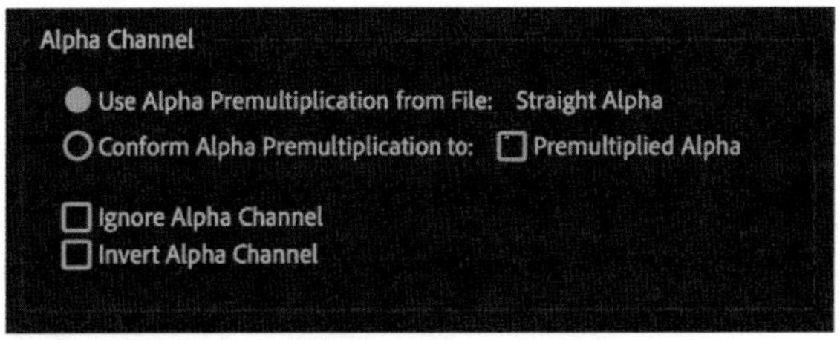

Figure 11.26

Use the Interpret Footage window to get to the options for Alpha Channels in Premiere.

Creative Cloud Libraries

Creative Cloud subscribers can build Libraries that contain graphics, color palettes, text styles, and other visual elements that are then shared across various Adobe applications including Premiere, After Effects, Photoshop and Illustrator (Figure 11.27). (If you're not a Creative Cloud subscriber, you can still build a library but it will only work within Premiere.) For filmmakers, that means you can design your titles in Illustrator or Photoshop, save the text formatting attributes to your Library as a style preset, and use it as-needed in Premiere or After Effects. If you have still graphics, you can drop them in there as well—for example, guide image exports from Premiere for making titles in Photoshop or company logos. If you have multiple

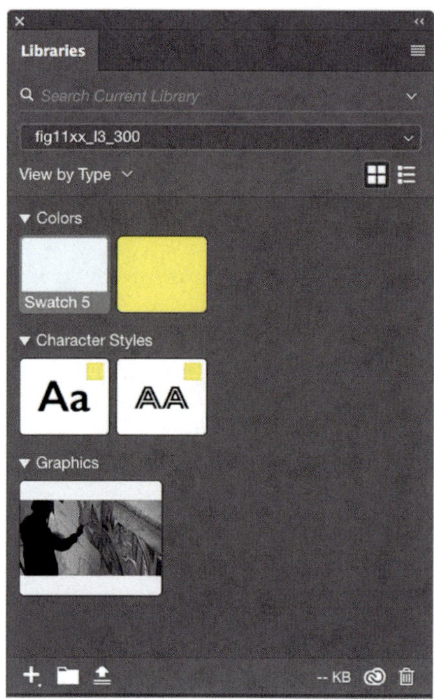

Figure 11.27

Creative Cloud libraries are incredibly useful if you're working with media across several Creative Cloud apps.

users or need to access the same items over and over again, it's very convenient and worth the small amount of time it takes to build a custom library.

Importing Full-frame Animation

Full-frame animations created outside of Premiere are often saved as folders of sequential still images, as opposed to a single video clip. Usually they will be named sequentially as well (animation001.png, animation002.png, etc.) and if you import correctly, Premiere will detect that this a set of sequential stills and build them into a video clip for you. First, you'll need to do a little prep work, make sure that your image files do not have layers and make sure the file names are sequential. Then, before you Import the image sequence you need to tell Premiere what frame rate to use for it. You'll find this in Preferences > Media > Indeterminate Media Timebase. Normally, you'll choose the same frame rate as your sequence which is probably 23.976 fps. Now, go to File > Import and navigate to the first sequential image file. Select it, then select Options from the bottom left corner of the navigation window. You'll see a check box next to the words Image Sequence at the bottom of the window, make sure it's checked, then select Import. It's slightly counter-intuitive to only select the first image in the sequence and not all of them, but the Image Sequence option will be greyed out if you select more than one image.

☑ Credit Rolls

Thanks to the presets in the Essential Graphics panel, creating credit rolls is a breeze. Just select Roll in Edit tab of the Essential Graphics panel. Make sure the title clip is selected in the Timeline. (If you select the text itself in the Program monitor you won't see the Roll option.) When you view rolling titles in the Program monitor, you'll see a blue scroll bar that lets you navigate through the credit roll. Simply lengthen or shorten your title media in the Timeline to slow down or speed up the roll. The hardest part is collecting the information and spell-checking it before you add it to your film.

Informational Problems to Solve

Here are a few things to think about regarding titles and graphics for your film:

Does your film need more information beyond the main title and credits? Are there things you can clarify with an added layer of information?

How will you incorporate that information stylistically? Does it need to match the main titles or does it need a completely different style?

How can you use fonts and graphics to codify your film? As a horror movie, a serious documentary, a funny film, etc.? Look at the trailers and posters for popular films to see what they did.

Try adding lower thirds to the documentary scene from Chapter 9. Try building them in a layered Photoshop file and importing them into Premiere.

12

Visual Effects

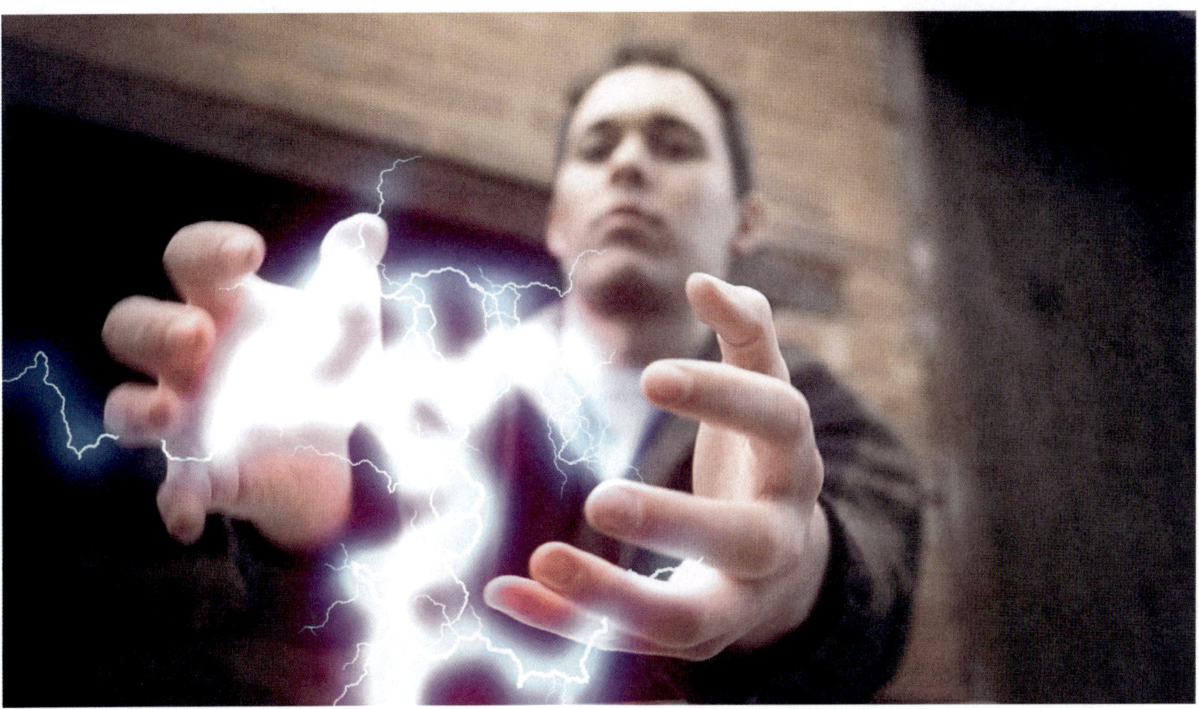

Figure 12.1

Effects generators add lens flares, lightning, and other visual elements to existing footage. Shown here, the Boris FX Sapphire zap effect.

VISUAL EFFECTS ADD A LAYER OF THE IMPOSSIBLE TO YOUR MOVIE—wings on angels, flying objects, non-existent locations, chain lightning from your fingers (Figure 12.1). But even if your film does not need effects that are quite so special, you're still likely to use effects in your film. For example, almost all shots of screens in movies—laptops, television sets, mobile phones—have their contents added in post-production because it's just about impossible to shoot a screen in real life so that it's readable to an audience. And changing backgrounds or simply enhancing a night sky so that you can see the moon and stars are also common uses of effects. The other main use for visual effects is to fix problems—kind of like practical magic. Visual effects allow you to remove wires and harnesses from stunt actors, correct camera problems such as shaky shots and lens artifacts, and get rid of cables, lights, drone shadows, and anything else that accidentally makes it into a shot.

In this chapter, we're going to focus on the effects found in the Premiere Pro Effects panel to correct image problems and create content. We'll show you how compositing works and offer some quick fixes for problems that you may encounter with your movie. And we'll give a broad overview of Adobe After Effects and show you how to use it, both in tandem with Premiere and on its own.

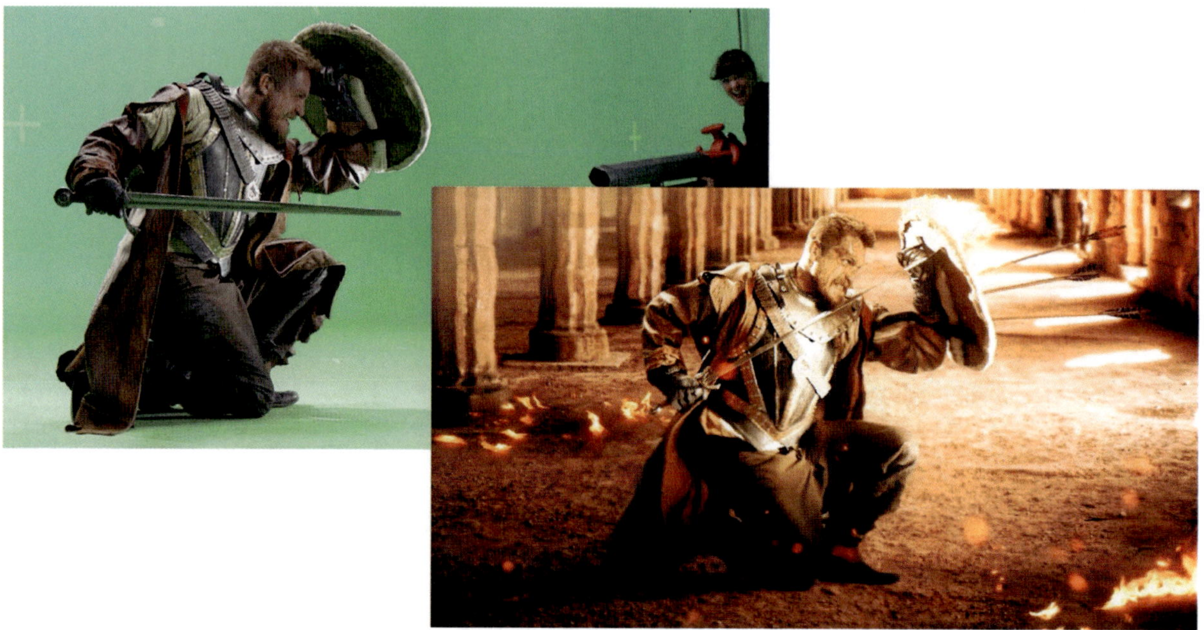

Figure 12.2

Visual effects can completely change a scene or shot. A whole bunch of effects from Red Giant were used to build this composite from the green screen source footage.

Types of Visual Effects

There are a lot of visual effects available to you in Premiere—in fact, one of the hardest things about working with effects in Premiere is knowing which effect you need. Running through the gamut of these effects one by one isn't very efficient because there are so many of them and they have very specific intended uses. On top of that is the fact that you can add even more effects to Premiere in the form of plugins, such as those made by Red Giant, Boris, and Mettle, to name a few. So it's helpful to talk about what you can do with visual effects in Premiere and that breaks down into five broad categories...

Additions to the original image, either by introducing new elements with *effect generators* or compiling layers via *compositing*, are the most exciting types of effects for filmmakers. Effects generators (Figure 12.1) are used to create elements such as lens flares, lightning, film grain, and also practical things like on-screen timecode. Compositing lets you merge layers of video and other media by designating which parts of a layer are transparent, for example a green screen backdrop (Figure 12.2).

Distortion effects take part of your original digital video image and change it. Blurs, warps, film grain, noise reduction, image stabilization, sharpening, cropping, removal of lens distortion, and flipping vertically or horizontally are some common distortion effects.

Time manipulations include slow-motion, fast-motion, freeze frames, and speed ramps.

Transitions affect the shift from one shot to another and are applied to splices in the timeline, rather than to the clips themselves. The most basic video transition is the dissolve but there are many other options: wipes, page turns, etc.

Color effects are used to fix problematic color, adjust overall color, and constrain color to fit restrictions for certain types of distribution channels. We'll go over color effects in detail in Chapter 13.

Working with Effects in Premiere

If you've been reading this book straight through, we've already introduced you to the effects interface in Premiere Pro. Visual effects work the same as titles and audio effects: you'll find specific effects in the Effects panel, drag them onto clips in the Timeline, and adjust their parameters in the Effect Controls panel. You'll then use keyframes in either the Effect Controls panel or the Timeline to customize how they appear over the course of each shot. We covered keyframing, resizing, motion, titling, and audio effects in Chapters 9, 10, and 11. Everything discussed in those chapters also applies here. If you are unfamiliar with any of these processes, you should read "The Effects Controls Panel" (page 149), "Adding Movement with Keyframes" (page 167), "Rubber Bands and Keyframes" (page 176), and "Advanced Keyframing," (page 203).

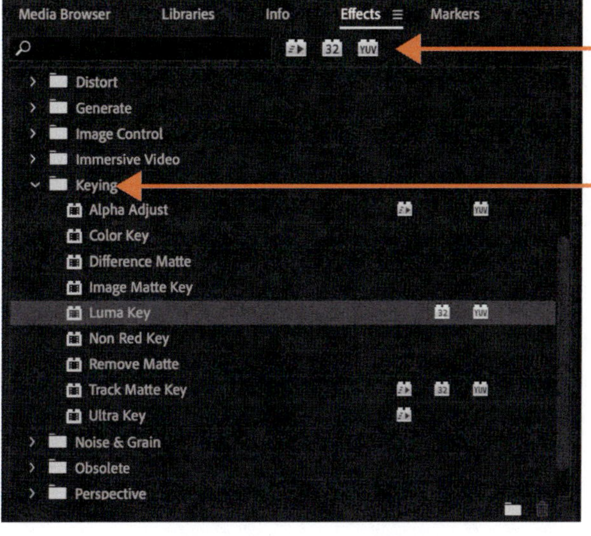

Figure 12.3

The Effects panel in Premiere has a large selection of video effects. Luckily, the Effect filtering buttons and search field at the top mean you don't have to open every single folder to find an effect.

The Effects Panel

The Effects panel holds a set of folders that each contain different types of effects (Figure 12.3). For visual effects, there are three key folders: Video Effects, Video Transitions, and Presets. When you open the Video Effects folder, you'll see that there is yet another layer of sub-folders, each containing a different family of visual effects. If you know what you're looking for, you can enter it into the search field at the top of the Effects panel.

The Effects panel has some properties that you should know about before you start adding video effects to your film. Premiere has three classes of effects—accelerated, 32-bit, and YUV. At the top of the Effects panel, you'll find filtering buttons for each of these types of effects (Figure 12.3). By selecting or deselecting them, you'll change the list of effects that you see.

So what do they mean?

Accelerated effects use your computer's GPU to enhance playback, which means they do not require rendering if your computer supports Adobe's Mercury Playback Engine. Despite the fancy name, these are standard effects in Premiere—there are only a handful of effects that are not accelerated in the current version of the software. (An important one is the Luma key effect, which we'll explore in a tutorial later in this chapter). Accelerated effects can be enabled or disabled in the Project Settings (File > Project Settings > General), where you need to select one of the Mercury Playback Engine options as the renderer for your project if you want accelerated effects. (Renderer options for setting up a new project are covered in Chapter 4.)

32-bit color effects Bit-depth accounts for the level of color detail in a video image, but it affects more than just color—higher bit-depth can improve the results of many different types of effects. Standard bit-depth video has 8 bits per channel and high bit-depth video has 32 bits per channel. The result is that 8-bit video has millions of colors and 32-bit video has trillions. When it comes to visual effects, more information means better results, especially with effects that need precise color information to work well, like chroma keying or alpha channels. So if you have high quality source media (10-bit or 12-bit footage, 16-bit graphics, etc.) you should use 32-bit effects whenever possible. One important thing to remember is that if you are using multiple effects on a shot, the bit-depth of your final image will be determined by the effect with the lowest bit-depth that has been applied to it. So if you mix 8-bit and 32-bit effects in the same shot, the resulting image will be 8-bit.

YUV effects operate in the YCbCr color space of digital video and these are all effects that are related to color processes. YCbCr is abbreviated (somewhat confusingly) as YUV and is the native color space of a lot of digital video codecs, as opposed to RGB (digital screens and uncompressed video) and CMYK (print). We'll go over color space for digital video in Chapter 13, Color.

Fixed effects are already applied to your clips and are only found in the Effect Controls panel (not the Effects panel). For video, the fixed effects are Motion (including Scale and Position), Opacity, and Time Remapping. These effects are set to "neutral" until you change their parameters.

Effects Panel Presets

Premiere has a bevy of pre-built effects available for you in the Presets folder. And you can also add your own custom-made presets as well. The selection of visible presets also changes based on whether you have chosen accelerated, 32-bit, or YUV effects filtering in the Effects panel.

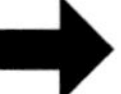

Digital Video Primer

If you need a refresher, Chapter 3, "Digital Video Primer," in *The Digital Filmmaking Handbook* covers the basic components of digital video. We also cover color and compression in Chapter 13 of this book.

Editing Effects

Once you've added an effect to a clip in the Timeline, you'll be able to edit it in the Effect Controls panel. Unfortunately video effects do not have the same cool app-like interface that audio effects have but you can toggle them off and on, add keyframes, and adjust parameters here. You can also edit keyframes in the Timeline. (We covered advanced keyframing in Chapter 11.) In the Timeline, each video clip in a sequence has a small FX badge that changes colors, depending on the type of effects that are applied to that clip. It's grey when the fixed effects are set to neutral/default, yellow when fixed effects are applied, purple when any other type of effect is applied, and green when both fixed and other effects are applied together. But it's not just a badge, it's a menu. Right-click on it and a list of the effects that have been applied to that particular clip will open up (Figure 12.4). (This might tie with the wrench menus for the least-intuitive placement of a significant menu in Premiere.)

Use this Clip Effects menu to select the effect you want to edit and a rubber band will appear in the clip in the Timeline. Command/Control click on it to add keyframes and drag them up or down to adjust the intensity of the effect you have chosen to edit. You can also drag keyframes left and right to adjust their timing within the clip. Depending on the effect you have chosen, you may be able to adjust the curve of the rubber band in the Timeline using anchors and handles, or you may have to adjust it in the Effect Controls panel.

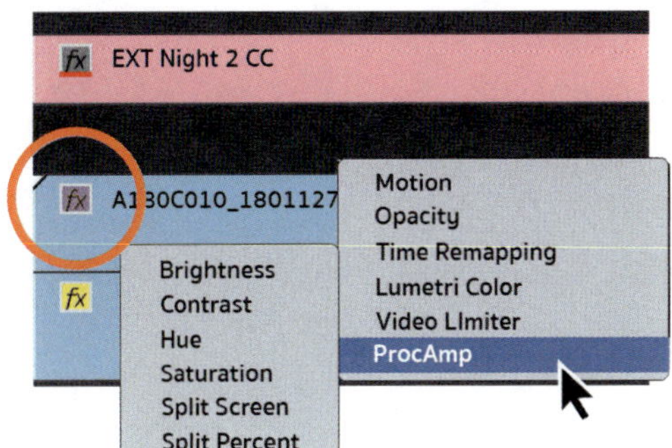

Figure 12.4

Each Clip Effects badge (circled) actually contains a right-click menu that lets you choose which effect you want to edit using keyframes in the Timeline.

☑ Seeing Keyframes in the Timeline

As you work with effects, you'll need to make sure you tell Premiere to Show Video Keyframes in the Timeline Display Settings menu (wrench icon).

Adjustment Layers

When you add effects to clips in Premiere, the most common choice is to drag them straight onto the clip itself in the Timeline. While there's nothing wrong with this method, you can also create an *adjustment layer* to put the effect on a separate layer above the clip. You might be wondering, why bother? There are two primary reasons why adjustment layers are incredibly useful. First of all, if you put all your effects on a dedicated effects track using adjustment layers, you can then turn them on and off with a click of the eye icon on in the Timeline controls. Second, adjustment layers affect anything that's visible on the tracks beneath them. So if you have a composited image on V2 and a background on V1, placing an adjustment layer effect on V3 or higher, will affect both the background and the foreground. To create an adjustment layer, select your sequence in the bin, then go to File > New > Adjustment Layer. The adjustment layer will show up as a piece of media in the bin. You can now place it in any track in your sequence and apply effects by dragging them onto it.

Time Remapping & Speed Ramps

Premiere does have a folder of Time effects in the Effects panel, but these are generally kind of silly. The time-based effects that are most useful to filmmakers are found elsewhere: slow-mo, fast-mo, and speed ramps. If you just want a simple speed change, you can use Clip > Speed/Duration, which we covered in Chapter 9. But if you want something more complex, the best choice is to use Time Remapping, a fixed effect that is already applied to every clip and edit keyframes in the Timeline to create a ramp (Figure 12.5).

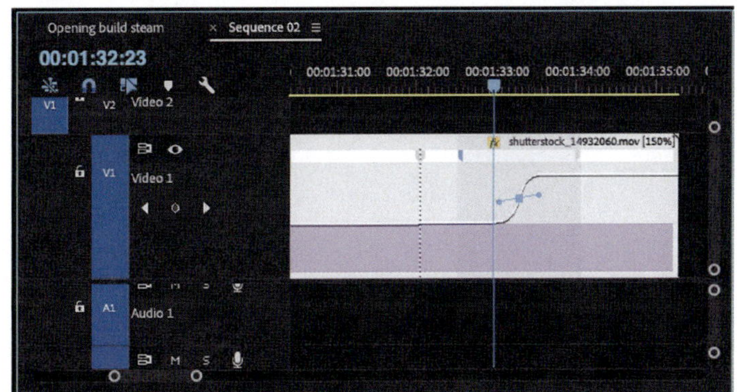

Figure 12.5

Making a speed ramp with keyframes and Time Remapping in the Timeline.

☑ Freeze Frames

In Premiere, freeze frames are called Frame Holds. Select a clip in the Timeline and park the playhead on the frame you want to freeze, then go to Clip > Video Options > Frame Hold. There are quite a few ways to make a Frame Hold and these can be found under Clip > Video Options > Frame Hold Options.

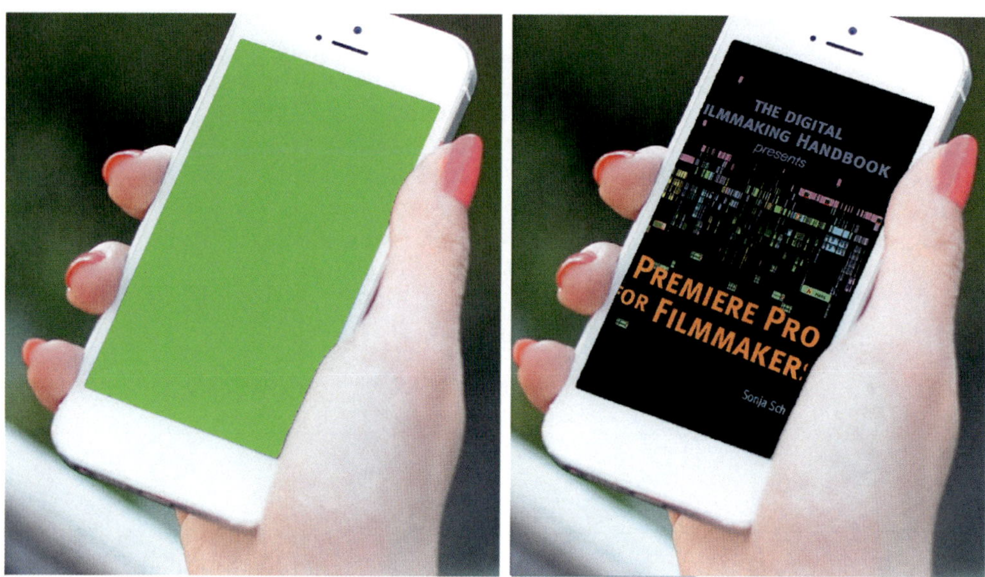

Figure 12.6

The contents of screens like computers, phones, and televisions are usually composited after the shoot.

Compositing

One of the most powerful visual effects tools for filmmakers is compositing, which simply means blending multiple layers of video into a single image. The simplest form of compositing is knowing as a picture-in-picture effect (PiP), where a smaller layer of video is positioned on top of a full-frame image (Figure 12.6). More complex compositing effects are called *keys*. Key effects use transparent areas to add a layer that only contains part of the whole image. A very common choice is to use a key to put a person into a different background, like the image in Figure 12.2. *Green screen* footage is composited using a *chroma key* effect, where all of the green pixels are rendered transparent. Footage with a high-contrast ratio can rely on a *luma key*, which renders a particular luminance value as transparent (usually black or white). And of course *alpha channels* are a form of compositing. (We covered them in Chapter 11.) Alpha channels are a type of digital stencil, called a *matte*, that separate a portion of the image from the rest. Because each pixel can have transparency that ranges from invisible to full opacity, digital mattes can be very sophisticated. They also allow you to track that portion of the image over time, known as a *traveling matte*.

In Premiere, you'll find a selection of keys and mattes in the Keying subfolder in the Effects panel (Window > Effects > Video Effects > Keying). You'll find a huge number of picture-in-picture presets as well (Window > Effects > Presets > PiPs), but you can easily create your own by dropping the smaller shot on V2 and adjusting Scale and Position in the Motion effect. You may also wish to crop the edges (Window > Effects > Video Effects > Transform > Crop). One of the realities of compositing chroma and luma keys is that they are very easy to use, unless they don't work well (due to how the footage was shot, etc.) and then it can be very difficult to get them to work.

 **Visual Effects and Proxies**

As a rule, you will want to use high-resolution footage when you are working with visual effects, so turn proxies off or reattach high-resolution media to the shots you are working on.

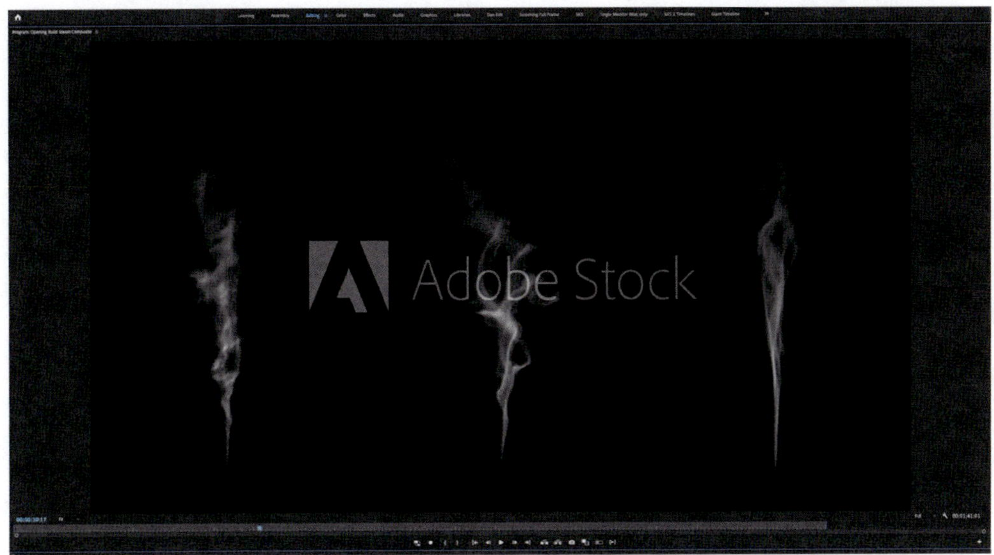

Figure 12.7

This shot from Adobe Stock footage has three different steam jets against a black background that's perfect for luma key compositing.

TUTORIAL: Compositing Steam to a Kettle

Did you think we didn't notice the fact that when the kettle whistles in the Opening Build sequence from the Chapter 11, it has no steam? We're going to fix that right now with a basic compositing tutorial.

STEP 1: Adobe Stock Steam

First you need some steam. Luckily, Adobe Stock has a large library of shots of steam over black. You want black or green because it's easier for compositing. And since the University scene is HD, an HD clip will suffice. Adobe lets you download a free, watermarked preview shot. This is good enough for the tutorial. I chose a shot with three jets of steam (Figure 12.7)—ID# 170863829— in case you want to use the same shot. Import it into the University scene project. If you don't have an existing project, create a new one and import the file called Opening Build Titles.mp4. This is the most recent version of the scene.

STEP 2: Rate Stretch Tool

Add the steam shot to the Timeline around the point where the actor takes the kettle off the stove, approximately 27 seconds into the scene. This is the same spot where you can hear the kettle whistling. It definitely seems fake without the steam. Place the stock steam shot on an empty track above the main video track. You'll notice that it's quite a bit longer than the shot that needs the steam, which is only about three seconds long. We're gonna use the Rate Stretch tool to shorten it, and in the process make the steam move faster.

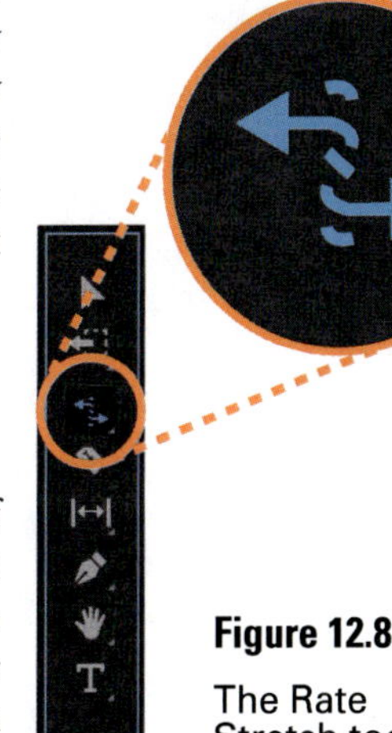

Figure 12.8

The Rate Stretch tool is found in the Tools panel, in the sub-menu under the Ripple tool.

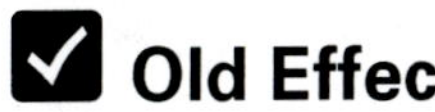

Old Effects

There's a folder of Obsolete effects from previous versions of both Premiere and After Effects—don't use them unless you need to work with an older project.

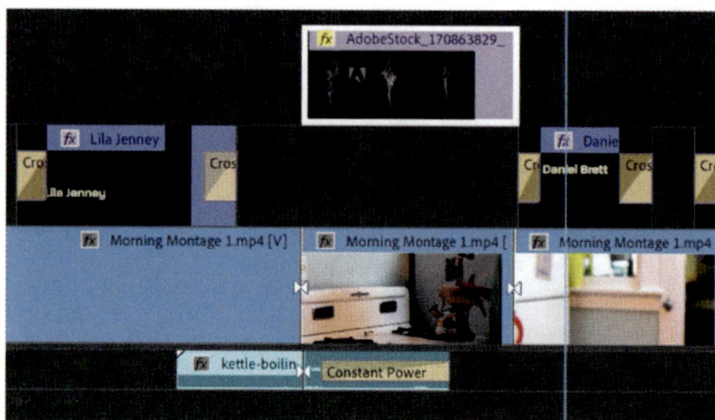

Figure 12.9

Add the steam shot to the next available track in the Timeline. Use both the Rate Stretch tool and trimming to get it in position.

The Rate Stretch tool is found in the Tools panel, in the sub-menu under the Ripple tool (Figure 12.8). To be honest, this is the Premiere tool I use the least—usually there are better ways to adjust the speed of a shot. But in this case, it's perfect because the shot is both too long and too slow, and also we don't need to worry about sync sound.

Grab the end of the shot and drag it back toward the end of the kettle shot. (If you have trouble selecting it, make sure to aim your mouse within the shot itself, not the black empty part of the Timeline.) Now watch it. Mine was too fast on the first try, so I lengthened it a bit with the Rate Stretch tool, then used Add Edit (Control/Command + K) to cut it so that it exactly fits the shot where she picks up the kettle (Figure 12.9).

STEP 3: Crop Effect

In a lot of editing applications, cropping is part of the Position or Scale attribute. In Premiere, it's a separate effect. You'll find it in the Effects panel (Window > Effects), under the Video Effects sub-folder called Transform. (Make sure you have the effect filtering buttons turned off so that you can see everything.) Grab the Crop effect and drag it onto the steam shot in the Timeline. Now open the Effect Controls panel (Window > Effect Controls) and scroll down to the Crop effect.

Spin down the triangle icon to see the Crop options. Of the three jets of steam, I like the one on the left side of the Adobe Stock shot. To remove the other two jets of steam, we're going to crop the right side of the shot. Spin down the triangle next to the Right cropping option and drag the slider from the left to the right (somewhat counterintuitive) until you have cropped out the extra jets of steam (Figure 12.10). Whoops, looks like the watermark is gone too.

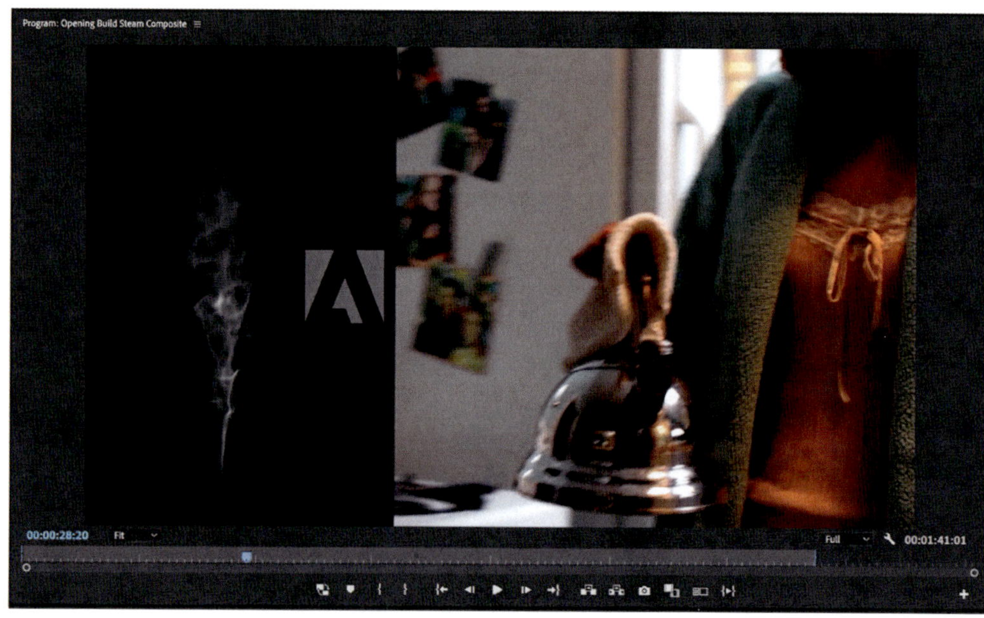

Figure 12.10

Use the Crop effect to trim the steam shot from the right until you only have one jet of steam visible.

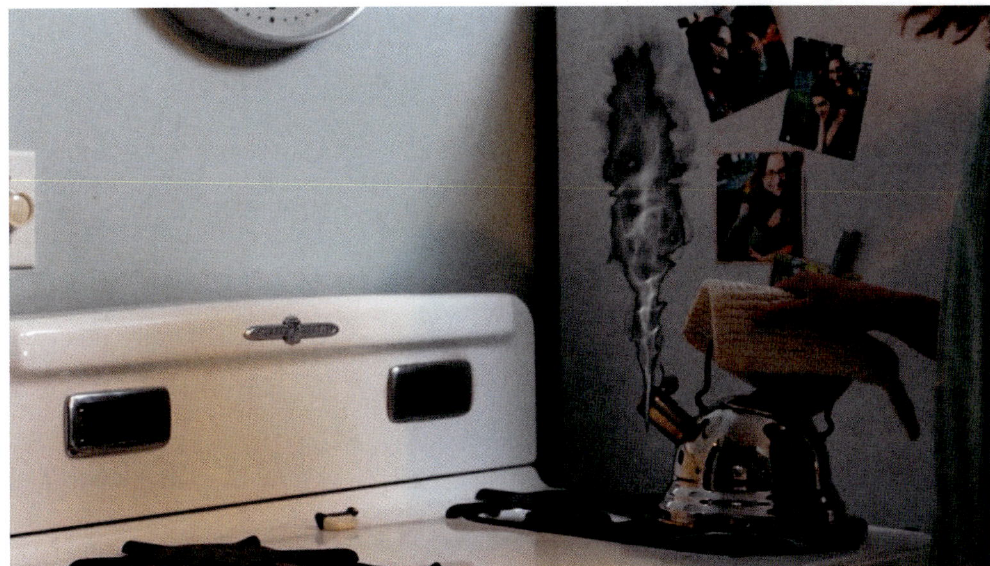

Figure 12.11

Play around with the Luma key sliders, Threshold and Cutoff, until you're happy with the amount of the steam video that remains visible. Remember to check the results in motion, things that look great as still images can look terrible as a moving image.

STEP 4: Luma Key Effect

Now we're going to use a luma key to remove the black background so that only the steam is visible. Go to the Effects panel and grab the Luma Key effect from the Keying sub-menu and drag it onto the steam clip in the Timeline. You'll see the Luma Key effect added to the list in the Effect Controls window as well. In the Timeline, you'll notice that the render bar at the top has turned red—this effect needs to be rendered to play properly. But it plays fairly well as-is, so we'll save rendering for the end. Take a look—guess what, mine looks pretty good—the black background is gone. If yours doesn't look so great, adjust the Threshold slider until it does. This is the easiest part of the whole tutorial and really it never gets old (Figure 12.11).

STEP 5: Repo and Track with Keyframes

Now we need to reposition the steam so that it appears to be coming out of the kettle. If the last step was the easiest, this is the hardest. Luckily the steam is already the right size, so we don't have to resize or crop it further. We're just going to adjust the Position and use keyframes to track it as it moves with the actor.

Select the steam shot in the Timeline with the arrow tool, so that it's highlighted. Then position the playhead on the first frame of the shot. Go to the Motion effect in the Effect Controls panel and toggle on the Position animation by clicking the stopwatch icon next to Position. A keyframe will appear on the first frame of the shot. Next, select the word Motion so that a blue box with handles appears outlining the steam shot in the Program monitor. Now you can reposition the steam shot by dragging it with your mouse.

If you play the sequence now, the steam will start as if it's coming out of the kettle but then the kettle will move and the steam will stay put. So we need to add more keyframes. It helps to start with the broad movements, then dial it in with more keyframes as needed. Add another Position keyframe when she taps the kettle with her sleeve, about 14 frames into the shot. Spin down the triangle next to Position and click the Add/Remove Keyframe button which is a small circle to the right (not the stop watch icon), then tap Motion again and drag the steam shot to follow the position of the kettle. Add another keyframe when the kettle comes all the way forward, about

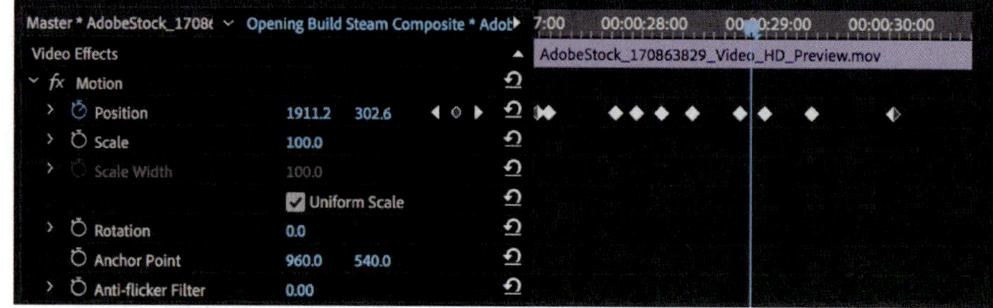

Figure 12.12

It takes about ten keyframes to track the movement of the kettle.

48 frames into the shot and repo again. And one more on the last shot before the mouth of the kettle clears frame, about 55 seconds into the shot, and one last one at the end of the shot to continue the movement even though the kettle is no longer visible (Figure 12.12).

At this point, you might want to watch your work in full-frame mode. Do another pass adding keyframes and repositioning as needed. I ended up with ten keyframes. I would say it could be a lot more perfect and you could add a matte to get rid of the steam crossing her arm in an unrealistic way, but the steam is pretty subtle and it's a lot more realistic than a whistling kettle with no steam at all. Last but not least, select and render the steam shot (Sequence > Render Selection). After I rendered mine, I decided to add some Opacity keyframes to minimize the steam when her arm crosses in front of it. By the way, this steam shot is low res and it's also 29.97 fps, so if you had a full-res version at the right frame rate, the movement of the steam would look a lot better. If you want to check out our version, it's called Opening Build Steam Composite.mp4 in the Opening Build cuts folder. And if you want to practice some more, try compositing some steam coming out of her lipstick in the shot in the bathroom.

Quick Fixes

One of the primary uses for visual effects in films is to fix problems. Here are some common solutions…

Image Stabilization

If you have shaky footage, it might be worth trying to stabilize your footage, especially if it's going to play on a big screen. The bigger the image, the more distracting (and nauseating) shaky footage can be. Image stabilization works by zooming in on your shot so that there's room to shift the shot and correct for extraneous movement (Figure 12.13). The higher-resolution your footage, the more room you have to work with. For example, if your camera acquired 8K video but you're delivering at 4K, you'll have plenty of room to stabilize shots. But even if you have this kind of luxury, image stabilization can only do so much. It's very good at correcting for smaller movements, such as gently swaying handheld shots. It's less good at fixing wild, fast swings.

Visual Effects Plugins

You can vastly extend the capabilities of both Premiere Pro and After Effects by adding plugin packages, such as those offered by Boris FX, Red Giant, and Mettle. You'll get customized tools for very specific tasks and although they're not free, you can often find free trial downloads for a limited time or with limited features.

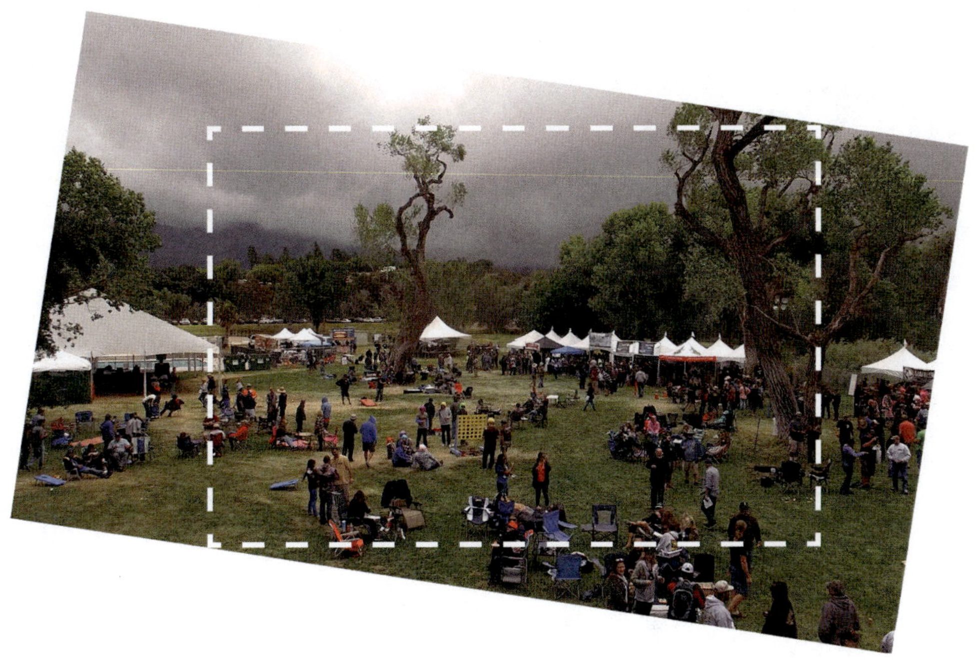

Figure 12.13

Image stabilization works by enlarging the problematic video so that there's room to reposition it, and then cropping it to fit the frame size of your sequence. This shot is 4K and the final film will be 2K, so there's plenty of room to maneuver without worrying about reducing the resolution too much.

In Premiere, the Warp Stabilizer VFX (Window > Effects > Video Effects > Distort > Warp Stabilizer VFX) is the only automated image stabilization option. The Warp Stabilizer requires that the shot you want to stabilize is in a sequence that matches the shot's exact dimensions. So if your source footage has different dimensions than your primary sequence, you'll want to create a new sequence for your stabilized shot that matches it. Then, after it's stabilized, you'll nest that sequence into your cut. (We went over how to nest sequences in Chapter 3.)

When you first apply the Warp Stabilizer, you'll get a message letting you know that Premiere is analyzing your shot. This can take a while but luckily it works as a background operation and you can track its progress in the Effect Controls panel. Once finished, you can view it and then use Smoothness, Method, and scaling options to dial it in. For example, if you're stabilizing handheld footage, you might not want it to fully remove the motion. Rather, you just want to smooth it out a bit. Reducing the standard Smoothness of 50% to 25% might have more natural-looking results. We used the Warp Stabilizer to smooth out some handheld footage for the After Effects tutorial later in this chapter—it's an impressive and powerful tool.

☑ Copying, Pasting, and Removing Effects

To copy effects from any clip in the Timeline and paste them onto another clip, select the clip in the Timeline, and go to Edit > Copy. This will copy the video along with any effects or attributes that have been applied. Select the destination clip then use the Paste Attributes command (Edit > Paste Attributes). Be careful not to use regular Paste or you'll replace the whole video clip. You'll be able to choose which class of effects to copy by checking the boxes in the Paste Attributes window (Figure 12.14) before you select OK.

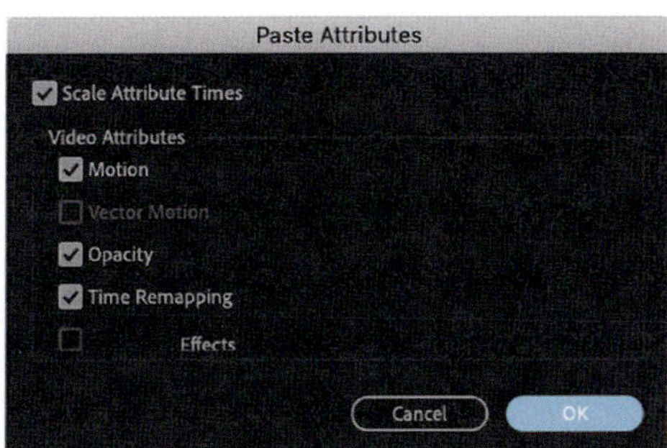

Figure 12.14

Use the Paste Attributes command to copy effects from one shot to another, including fixed effects and audio effects.

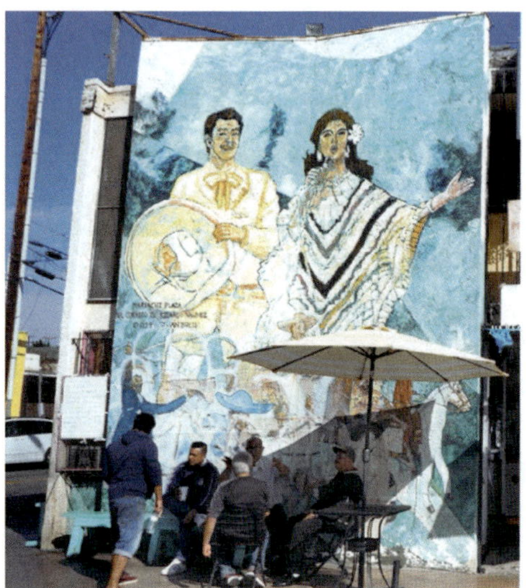

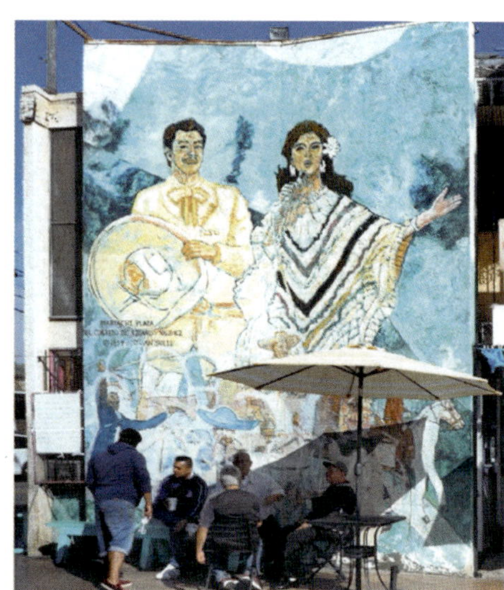

Figure 12.15

Extreme wide angle lenses result in a distorted image (left). But a simple Corner Pin effect can easily straighten it out (right). Beware that if you have too much distortion, the resulting cropping can lower the resolution of your image.

Getting Rid of Lens Distortion

Wide angle lenses notoriously add distortion to the video image—you'll see exaggerated and curved lines at the edges of the frame. And drones use very wide-angle lenses, so lens distortion is very common with drone footage. Luckily, Premiere Pro offers a large selection of lens distortion removal presets, with several options for each popular drone model. If the lens distortion isn't too crazy, you might have better luck with Corner Pin (Window > Effects > Video Effects > Distort > Corner Pin), which lets you shift the position of each of the four corners in the frame. By pinning the upper corners of the Shutterstock footage in Figure 12.15, I was able to easily straighten out the vertical lines.

Wire Removal

Wire removal effects were developed to remove wires when objects or actors are suspended in flying shots. But they're incredibly useful for removing more prosaic items. Cables from mics, cables on the floor, ends of C-stands, and outdoor power lines can all be removed this way. Premiere Pro doesn't have built-in wire removal effects, but if you have a Creative Cloud subscription, you can use the CC Simple Wire Removal effect in After Effects instead. In fact, we've got a whole tutorial on the topic, later in this chapter.

Blurs and Sharpening

Blurs are used to creatively add a rack focus, to create an appearance of bokeh in a composited background shot, and to censor objectionable content. Sharpening can help make the overall image look better. In the next tutorial, we'll fix a rack focus by adding more blur.

Nesting Compound Effects

When you're creating very elaborate effects that span multiple clips and video tracks, you should consider building them in a separate sequence and then nesting that sequence into the main cut of your film. That way, you won't have to dedicate more than one video track to it and there's less risk of accidentally changing it.

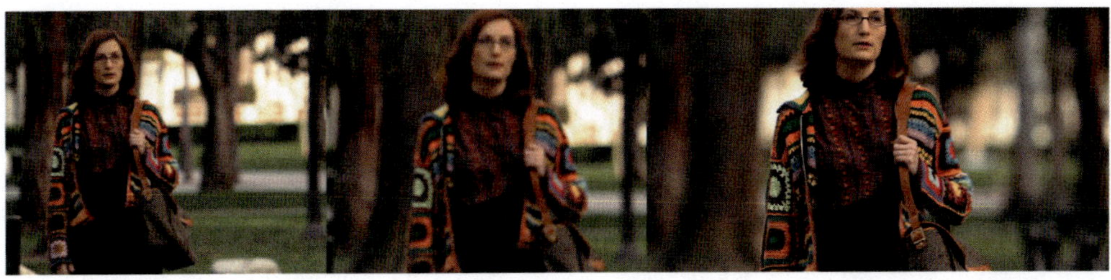

Figure 12.16

This rack focus shot isn't long enough for our title sequence.

TUTORIAL: Adding a Rack Focus

Your film has a shot that drifts in and out of focus. What's the solution? Blur more!

The final shot of the main title sequence for the Opening Build starts to go out of focus, which seems intentional, but then it comes back into focus for a few seconds before blurring again. In this tutorial, we'll show you how to make a clean shift from sharp focus to soft without the extra back-and-forth. This technique can cover a flawed shot like the one in this tutorial and it can also be used on a shot that is fully in focus, to add a rack focus after the fact (Figure 12.16).

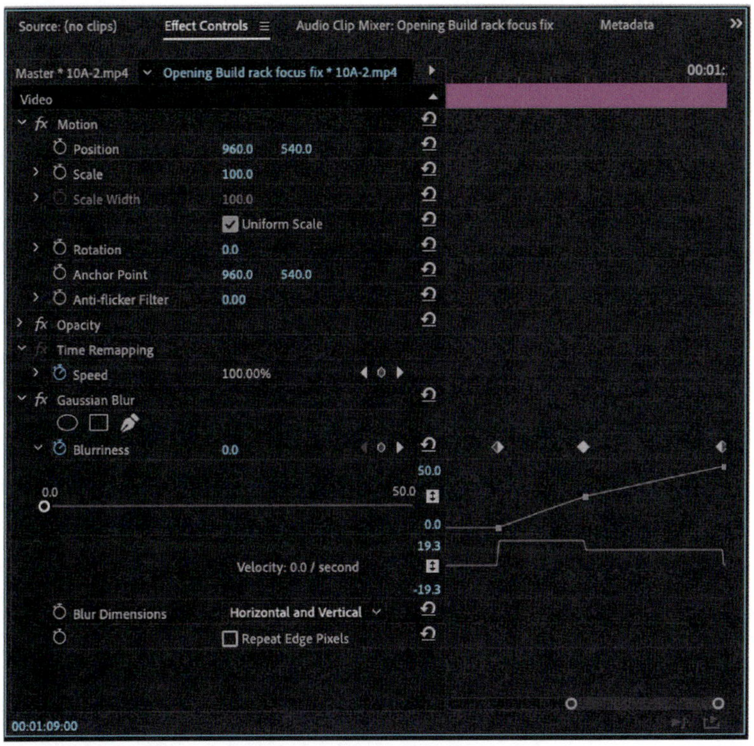

Figure 12.17

Gaussian Blur controls in the Effect Controls panel.

STEP 1: Add the Gaussian Blur Effect

For this tutorial, you'll need either your project from the last tutorial with the steam shot composited, or "Opening Build Steam Composite.mp4" from the Opening Build cuts folder in the Tutorial media. You'll also need the shot called "10A-2.mp4" from the Morning Montage media folder. Add it to the end of the montage, before the dialogue scene starts—you'll need a clean version of this shot without titles composited onto it.

Add the Gaussian Blur effect to shot 10A-2.mp4 in the Timeline (Video Effects > Blur and Sharpen > Gaussian Blur), then open the effect up in the Effect Controls panel (Figure 12.17).

STEP 2: Set Keyframes

The shot already has a rack focus up to about 1 minute and 15 seconds into the sequence, then it suddenly goes back into focus. Add a Blurriness keyframe before that return to focus and a second keyframe when focus is sharp, about one second later. Set the Blurriness to 25 on the second keyframe. Now let's make the rack continue by adding a keyframe at the end and setting the Blurriness to 50.

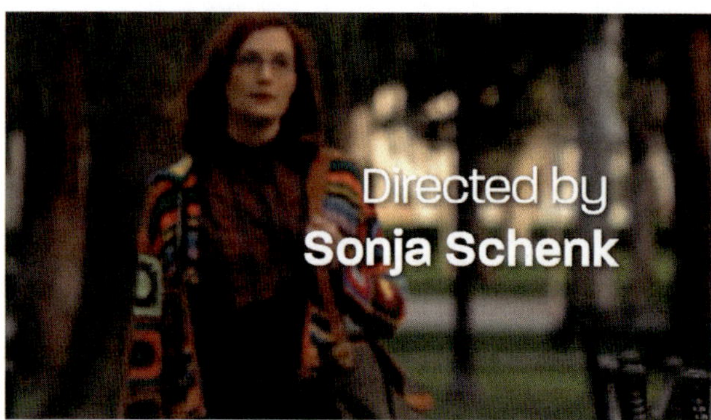

Figure 12.18

Blurry backgrounds, aka bokeh, are perfect for highlighting foreground elements like titles.

STEP 3: Add a Point of Focus

The rack focus is long and it's kind of annoying to stare at an out of focus shot for that long, but that's okay—it's a perfect background for another title card (Figure 12.18). And since it's the last shot in the sequence, that's a spot that's usually reserved for something important, like—ahem—the director's credit. Check out our cut: Opening Build Rack Focus Fix.mp4.That's it. It's amazing what such a simple effect can do to improve a shot.

Immersive Effects

VR effects are a special set of effects that are used on 360-degree video. They are found in the Immersive Video sub-folder (Window > Effects > Video Effects > Immersive video).

After Effects

The most popular motion graphics application for many years, After Effects is part of the Creative Cloud suite and thoroughly integrated into the Premiere Pro workflow (Figure 12.19). It's shockingly easy to farm out a problematic clip to After Effects, adjust it, and quickly view the results in Premiere, thanks to Adobe Dynamic Link. It's also helpful that when you're working in After Effects, you'll recognize many elements from Premiere, including lots of the same or similar panels, commands, and buttons.

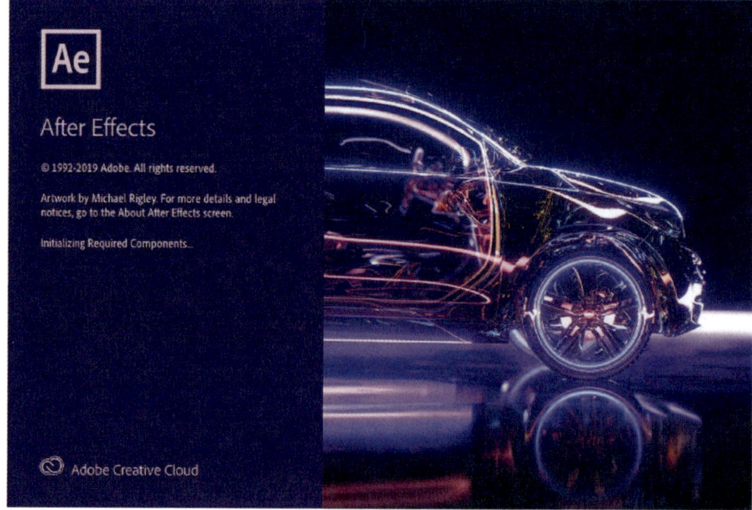

Figure 12.19

Adobe After Effects is one of the most popular visual effects and motion graphics editing applications in the film industry.

The extension of Premiere into After Effects (and also Audition and Photoshop) via Dynamic Link is easily my favorite thing about editing in Premiere. It's truly a feature that no other editing application can compete with.

Sending Clips to After Effects

To send a clip or section of your sequence to After Effects, just select a clip or series of clips using the mouse in the Timeline (not with Ins and Outs) and use the right-click menu or the Edit menu to choose Replace with After Effects Composition. After Effects will launch with a new project (.AEP) and your clip(s) will be available as a composition, which is the After Effects equivalent of a sequence. Back in Premiere, the clips you sent to After Effects will be labeled with the color Rose. (You can change this color in Preferences > Labels > Label Defaults > Adobe Dynamic Link.) The render bar above it will be red, meaning that rendering is required, and your clip names will have the words Linked Comp and the name of your After Effects composition and project added to them. In other words, they will stand out in your Timeline (Figure 12.20). Everything you do to those clips in After Effects will be reflected "live" in Premiere, so you can work in both applications at the same time with no need for importing and exporting media.

It can be a good idea to make a copy of your original clip or sequence on a different track in your Timeline as a reference/backup. You can keep it disabled unless you need it.

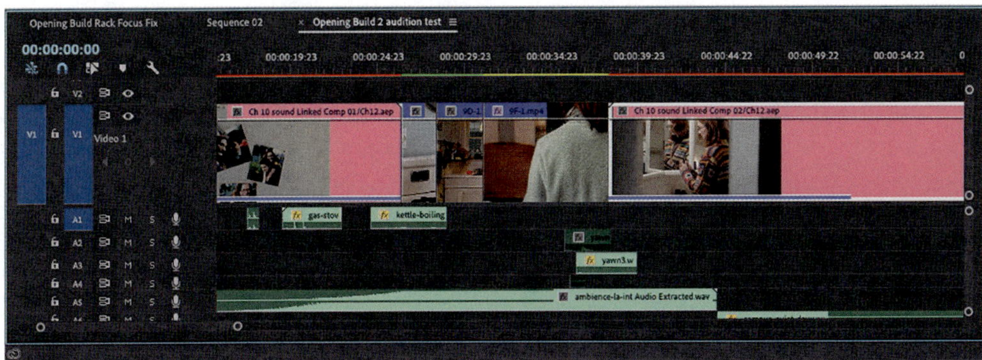

Figure 12.20
Clips in the Premiere Pro Timeline that are Dynamically Linked to an After Effects composition are labeled bright pink and require rendering for playback.

 You May Need to Upgrade

If you're having trouble getting Dynamic Link to work, it may be because you don't have compatible versions of Premiere and After Effects installed.

The After Effects Interface

The main workspace in After Effects consists of three windows: the Project panel, the Composition panel, and the Timeline (Figure 12.21). The Project panel is exactly what you'd expect—a directory of media (or "assets," so corporate!) and compositions that can be organized into folders. Just like Premiere, assets can be any type of media—stills, audio, and video.

The Timeline is where the editing happens but it is quite different than a standard video editing Timeline. Instead of tracks, each piece of media in After Effects gets a dedicated layer, which

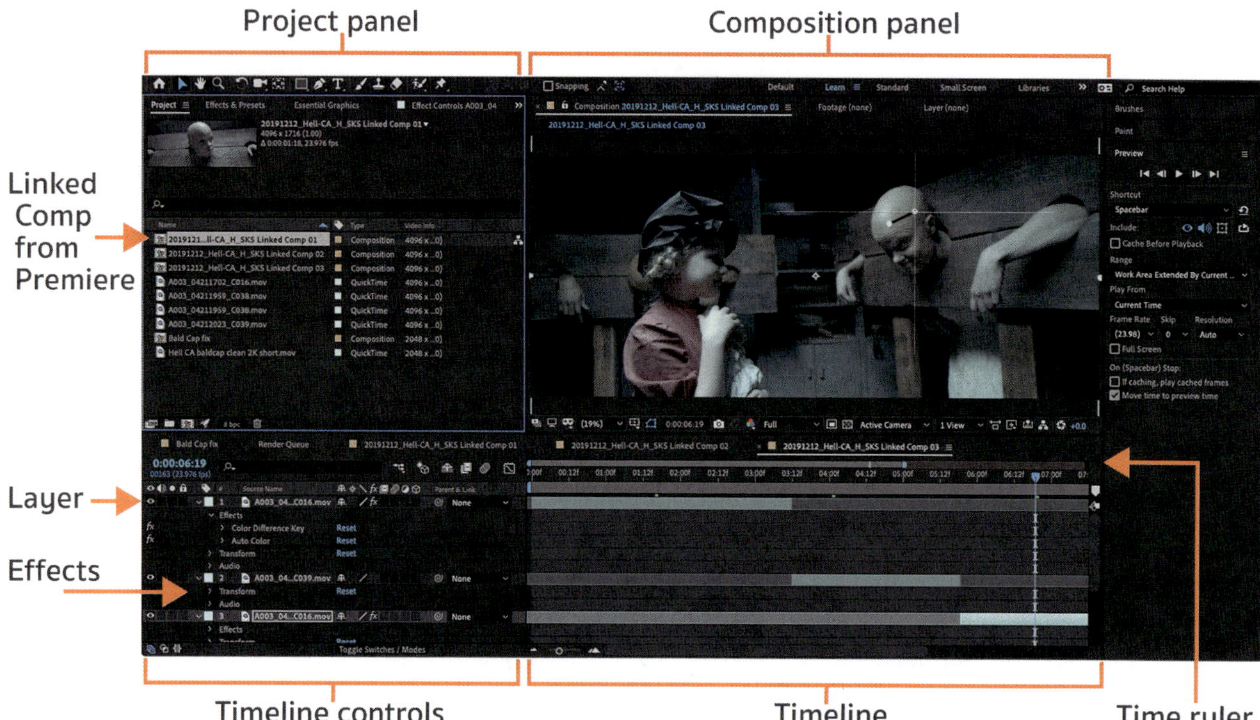

Figure 12.21

The After Effects interface consists of a Project panel, a Timeline, and the Composition panel which serves as a playback monitor and also a workspace. In the After Effects Timeline, each clip gets a separate layer.

comes with a set of fixed transformation effects already applied. On the left are the Timeline controls for each layer. Just spin down the triangle next to the name of the layer and then spin down the triangle next to Transform to see the controls for Anchor Point, Position, Scale, Rotation, and Opacity with the familiar stopwatch icon to turn on keyframing. As you add effects to your layers, you'll see the controls for each effect added here as well. The right side of the Timeline shows your clips in a chronological view with a zoom bar, a time ruler at the top, and a playhead to indicate your position.

The Composition window is a monitor that plays back your edits from the Timeline and it's also a workspace where you can edit visual effects. The default view sets your image size at 12.5% which is tiny, but in After Effects you can see and manipulate shots that go beyond the edge of the frame. 12.5% gives you lots of working space which is very helpful when adjusting Position and Scale. You can change the default image size using the Magnification Ratio Popup menu found at the bottom left of the Composition panel. If you have no need for extra working space, you can always change it to "Fit." By default, After Effects plays every single frame in your composition, so if your computer is not powerful, it will not play in real time. You can lower the resolution to improve playback in the Resolution/Down Sample Factor popup menu found at the bottom center of the Composition panel.

After Effects Preferences and Settings

After Effects has a boatload of Preferences and Settings, but if you're using it with Premiere via Dynamic Link, they will be automatically set to match your Premiere sequence settings (frame rate, width and height, and pixel shape). You should, however, adjust the Media & Disk Cache, Memory, and Audio Hardware Preferences to suit your system (After Effects (Mac) or Edit (Win) > Preferences).

Editing Effects in After Effects

After Effects has a bevy of built-in effects, found in the Effects & Presets panel (Windows > Effects & Presets) and they work similarly to the way effects work in Premiere. Each effect has a bit-depth icon next to its name, with a number telling you the bit-depth of that effect, ranging from 8-bit to 32-bit. As with Premiere, higher bit-depth means better-looking results, but also more rendering time. And happily, there's a search field at the top of the panel so that you don't have to dig through every folder to find an effect.

Add effects to clips in the Timeline by dragging them onto the clip itself, either on the right side of the Timeline or in the Effects area under each layer name in the Timeline header to the left. (You'll only see the Effects area after you have effects applied to a layer.) The Effect Controls window will open automatically when you add an effect to a clip. It's a lot like the Effect Controls panel in Premiere.

Motion Graphics Templates

The Essential Graphics panel in After Effects is very different from the one in Premiere Pro, which we covered extensively in Chapter 11. In Premiere it serves as a library of motion graphics templates and an effects editor. In After Effects, it only has one function—to build motion graphics templates for use in Premiere. After you create an effects-based treatment for a composition that you think would be a great template for other clips in Premiere, open the Essential Graphics window (Window > Essential Graphics) and you'll see your current composition listed under Master. Drag the effects you want added to the template from the Timeline to the Essential Graphics panel. You may encounter some limitations because not everything can be saved as a template—the effects here need to be compatible with Premiere. Add a name for your template and save it. Motion graphics templates from After Effects are saved in the unpoetically named MOGRT format. Once saved, you can open the Essential Graphics panel in Premiere, import your new MOGRTs, and apply them to your media. (We explained how to import MOGRTs into Premiere in Chapter 11.)

Rendering/Exporting

If you're working in After Effects, you will eventually need to render your compositions. Render, in the After Effects parlance, is more like Export for Premiere and other video editing applications—it results in a new media file that is saved on your hard drive. You have the choice between rendering/exporting in After Effects or outsourcing your render/export to Media Encoder. What's the difference? Not much. Both work in the background and both are likely to slow your system down but not so much that you can't keep working. With Dynamic Link media there's another option, Render and Replace in Premiere, found under the Clip menu. We'll get into Render and Replace in Premiere in the next section. (Suddenly I see why Adobe recently chose to change the name of "render" files in Premiere to video and audio "previews"—it is indeed confusing.)

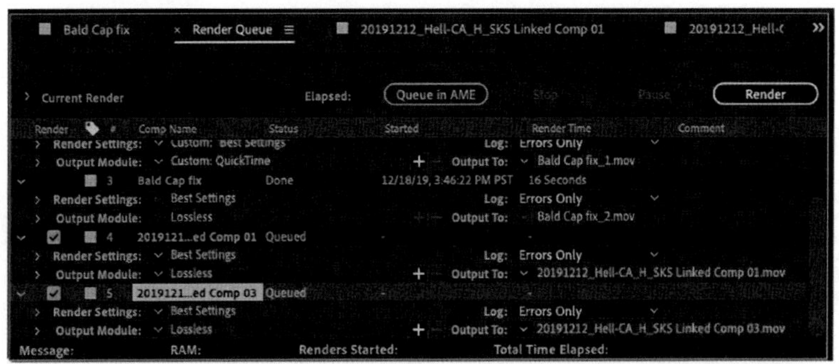

Figure 12.22

The Render Queue in After Effects.

The Render Queue

The interface for rendering/exporting in After Effects is called the Render Queue (Figure 12.22) and it lives in a tab in the Timeline panel (Window > Render Queue). To render a composition you'll have to choose Composition > Send to Render Queue. The Render Queue is much simpler than the Media Export window in Premiere. In fact, it only offers four options, each of which is highlighted in blue and clicking on them brings up options:

Render Settings are where you can elect to use proxies for your render or not—generally you will not want that. Otherwise, most of your important Composition Settings are already set up if you're using Dynamic Link (Figure 12.24).

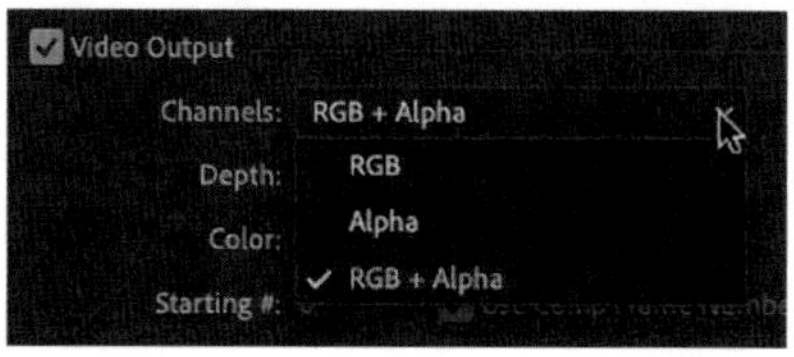

Figure 12.23

Choose RGB + Alpha in the Output Module if you need transparency in your export.

Output Module sounds very sci-fi. By default, rendering in After Effects is lossless and uses an uncompressed codec which should work for most filmmakers. The other important thing here is that if you are rendering a clip with a transparent background, or alpha channel, you'll need to choose RGB + Alpha, as opposed to the default, plain RGB (Figure 12.23).

Log is a menu that tell After effects what sort of feedback you want on your export, i.e., did it drop any frames? The default is "errors only," which will only bother you if there's a problem.

Output to lets you choose a location and file name for your rendered media file.

Render and Replace in Premiere

When you edit a clip from a Premiere sequence in After Affects via Dynamic Link, Premiere will offer a special Render and Replace command (Clip > Render and Replace) that allows you to export that clip and save it as a new file stored on your hard drive. In other words, this isn't just a preview, it's a completely new clip that is intended to replace your original media file. This new media file loses the link to After Effects, so it's no longer editable there, but you can reverse this decision by choosing Clip > Restore Unrendered.

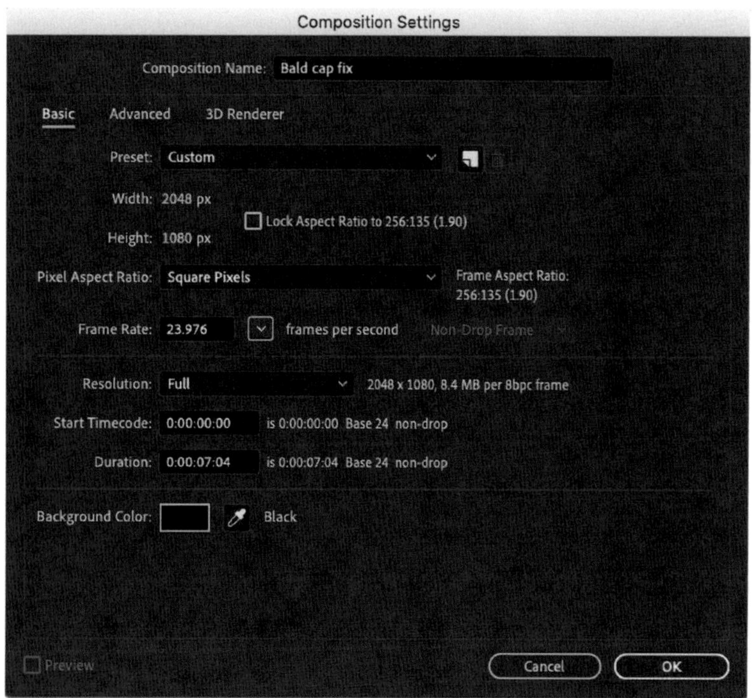

Figure 12.24

The After Effects Composition Settings will automatically match your Premiere sequence settings if you used Dynamic link. But when you create your own composition, you'll have to adjust the settings to match your media.

When you opt to Render and Replace, you'll get a dialogue window giving you some options. They are somewhat unclear, giving you choices like Source, Format, and Preset. Source means the media specs for the resulting file will be based on the specs for the source you choose from this menu and the options are Sequence (based on your sequence settings), Individual Clips (based on the media specs of your source clips), and Preset (based on settings from a preset). Format is a list of limited container file options based on your choice of Source.

And Preset is a list based whatever you selected for Source and Format combined with the presets available from Media Encoder, including ones that you create yourself. (We cover creating ingest presets in Media Encoder in Chapter 5 and encoding presets in Chapter 14.)

If you just want to make your cut play properly in Premiere, you might find something here that works for you. It you want an uncompressed, high-resolution export, stick to rendering in After Effects or create a custom encoding preset in Media Encoder. And if you really just want quick and dirty playback in Premiere, use the Render In to Out command from the Sequence menu.

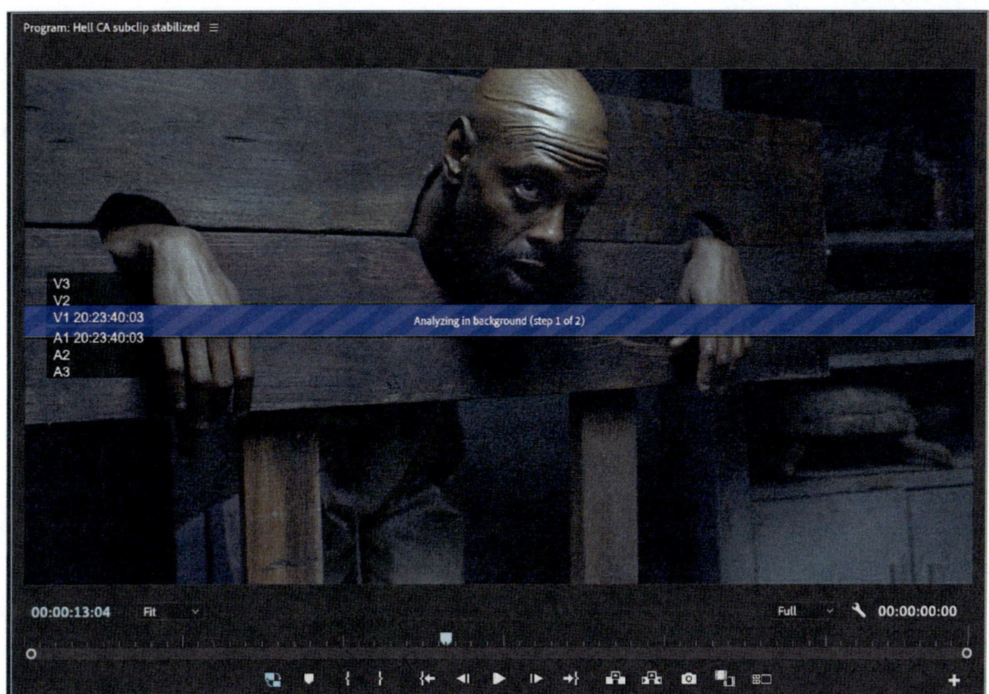

Figure 12.25

We used the Warp Stabilizer effect in Premiere before sending this clip to After Effects to fix the wrinkles on the actor's bald cap.

TUTORIAL: Bald Cap Fix in After Effects

Hell CA is a slyly funny horror film directed by Bonné Barton about three veterans who get stuck in a creepy town on their way to Coachella. The shoot involved a lot of makeup effects and that often means clean up in post. In this case, one actor's bald cap is less than ideal with an obvious seam and lots of wrinkles.

We're going to use After Effects—independently of Dynamic Link since you don't have the rest of the movie—to diminish the problem. We did a little prep for you in Premiere to get the clip ready for this tutorial. First of all, it's a handheld shot and the more movement in a shot, the harder it is to make effects work well if they require tracking. So we subclipped the part of the shot we needed in Premiere and applied the Warp Stabilizer to reduce motion (Figure 12.25), then we rendered it out as a new clip.

The original footage is 4K, but unfortunately that is too big for the tutorial media, so the clip we'll be working with in this After Effects tutorial is 2K and saved with the h.264 codec. But in a perfect world, you would be using the original 4K media in order to get the best results.

STEP 1: Make an After Effects Composition

Launch After Effects and create a new project. Use File > Save As and call it Hell_CA_fixes. Open the Media Browser (Window > Media Browser) and navigate to the "Hell CA media" tutorial media folder. It contains two clips but you only need the one called "Hell_CA_baldcap.mp4". (The other clip is for Chapter 13.) Drag it into the Project panel, then go to Composition > New Composition. The Composition Settings window will open up. Make sure it's set to match the footage, which is 2048 x 1080 square pixels at 23.976 fps and that Resolution is set to Full (Figure 12.24). You may need to select Custom from the Preset menu and manually enter this information. Call the new composition "Bald Cap fix" and hit Okay. Double-click to open it in the Timeline, then drag "Hell_CA_baldcap.mp4" into it the left side of the Timeline, you'll see it appear in the first frame of the first layer of the composition. By the way, After Effects has a set of Workspace presets just like Premiere—I'm using Essential Graphics (Window > Workspace > Essential Graphics).

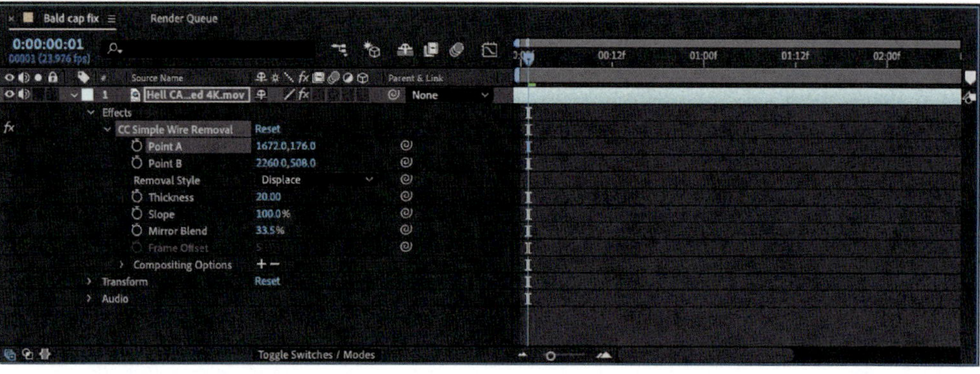

Figure 12.26

Drag the CC Simple Wire Removal effect onto your clip in the Timeline. You'll see it in the Timeline header after you spin down the triangles in the Timeline controls.

STEP 2: Add the CC Simple Wire Removal Effect

Let's take a second to assess the problem: the bald cap has lots of wrinkles, plus you can see the seam where it's attached to the actor's forehead. They're not wires but they do have a line-like shape, so the wire removal effect should work well here.

Open the Effects & Presets panel (Window > Effects & Presets). Type "wire" in the search field to bring up the CC Simple Wire Removal effect, located in the Keying folder. Drag it onto your clip in the Timeline. To view the effect, spin down the triangle to the left of the clip name, then spin down the triangle next to Effects. You'll see CC Simple Wire Removal listed—now spin down the triangle next to that to see the controls (Figure 12.26).

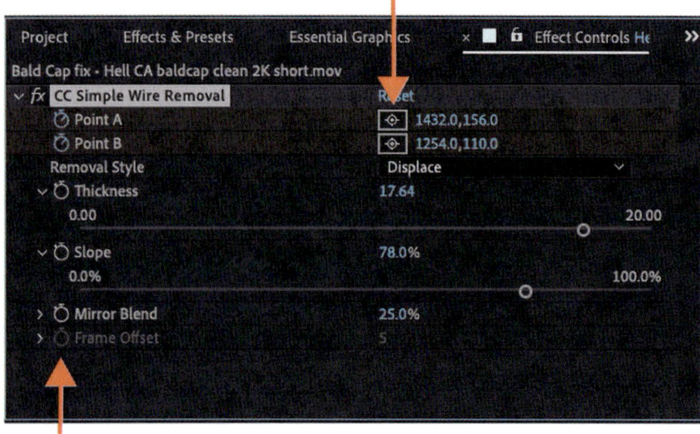

Figure 12.27

The CC Simple Wire Removal effects in the After Effects Effect Controls panel. Note the crosshair buttons which are used to select the start and end of the "wire" you want to remove.

STEP 3: Define the Line You Want to Remove

Double-click on the wire removal effect to open it up in the Effect Controls panel, which will appear in a tab in the same panel as your project (Figure 12.27). The way this effect works is that you set two points (A and B) to define a line that you want to remove. We're going to start with the line where the bald cap is attached to his forehead. It's not a straight line, so we're going to have to use more than one wire removal effect to clean it up. But first, let's work on the main seam, right across his forehead.

Make sure your playhead is on the first frame of the shot in the Timeline, then click on the Animation toggle (stopwatch icon) for Point A and Point B in the wire removal effect. Two keyframes will appear in the Timeline. In the Effect Controls panel, click on the small box contain a set of crosshairs to the right of Point A. Crosshairs will appear in the Composition panel and you can drag them to wherever you want the line to start. Select the crosshairs for Point B and drag them to where you want the line to end. The default Removal Style is Displace, which is best but if you just want to clearly see the line as you draw, change it to Fade. Once it's in position, restore it to Displace (Figure 12.28).

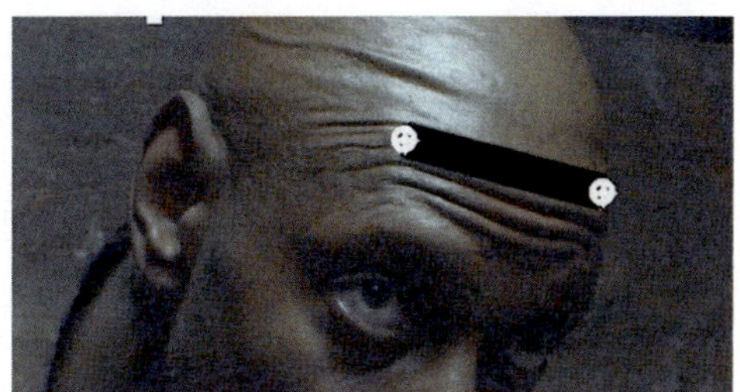

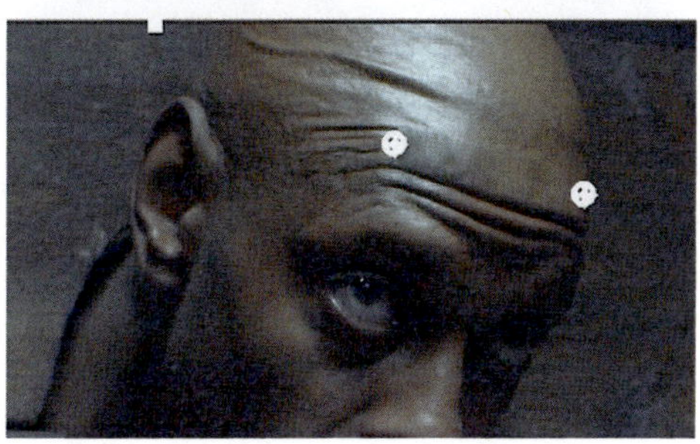

Figure 12.28

Choose Fade from the Removal Style menu (top) to see your line and Displace to make it disappear (bottom).

Next, you'll want to make the line fairly wide so drag the Thickness slider until the seam disappears—I set it at 17.64. The Slope slider changes how sharp the edges of the line are. For me, a slope of 78% worked well. The Mirror Blend slider changes how the surrounding pixels are blended into the removal line. Play around with it—for this first line, it grabbed too much of the actor's real brow lines to be of use.

STEP 4: Track Motion with Keyframes

Now we're going to track the motion of this line across the shot by adding keyframes and adjusting the positioning of Point A and Point B. (This is where the image stabilization we did to prep the clip for this tutorial really helps. We'll need far fewer keyframes as a result.)

Back in the Timeline, drag the playhead to the last frame of the shot and click on the Add/Remove Keyframe button for both Point A and Point B. In the Effect Controls panel, click on the crosshairs and move both Point A and Point B to match the position of the bald cap seam in this frame.

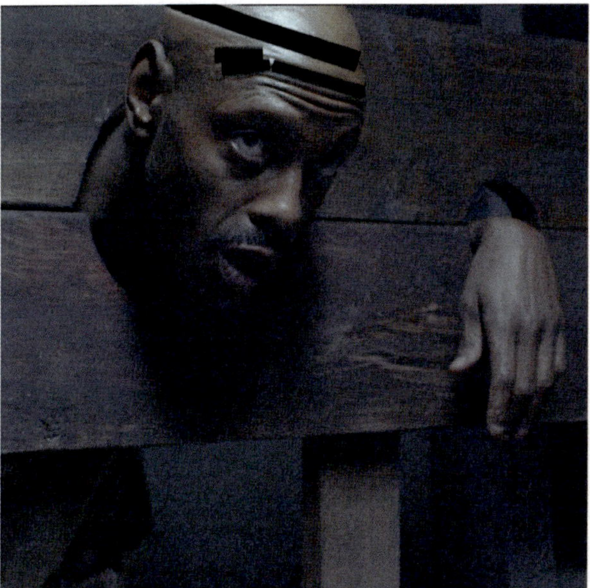

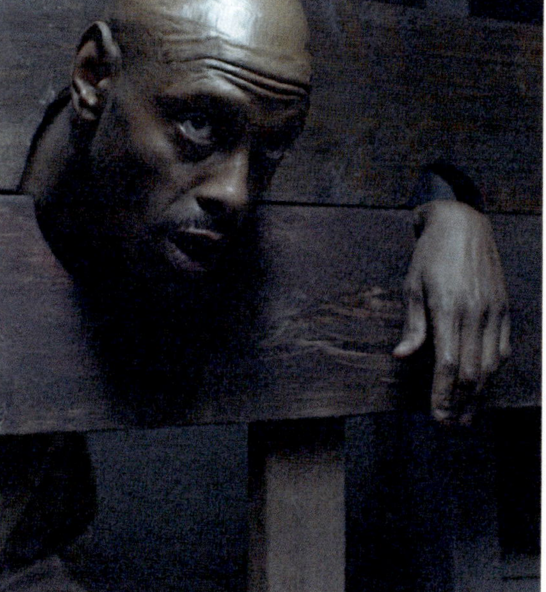

Figure 12.29

We ended up using four "wires" to remove the worst offenders from the actor's bald cap.

Watch the shot. Looks like we need some more keyframes. Work your way through the shot, setting and adjusting Point A and Point B until the line tracks the motion in the shot. If you notice weird migrating dark areas in your "line" when you watch the shot, be aware that the wire removal is pulling pixels from the area around your line to cover it. So you have to make sure that your line isn't too close to the real wrinkle on his forehead, or it will pull the shadow from that wrinkle into your line and it will start to look very strange. I'll be honest, this is not an easy fix to make. Just remember that your goal with this fix is to not draw the eye to it. A viewer will naturally be looking at the actor's eyes so as long as there aren't any strange movements in your fix, it will be an improvement.

STEP 5: Remove More "Wires"

Go back to the Effects panel and grab the CC Simple Wire Removal effect again and drag it onto your clip in the Timeline. You'll see it listed as CC Simple Wire Removal 2. Use it to remove another line—perhaps the left side of the same seam that angles down toward his temple. Note that you can also keyframe the thickness, slope, and mirror blend parameters if you really want to dial them in. You may find that the keyframes you added in the first wire removal effect are points that you'll need keyframes for the new wires you add. Add as many wire removal effects as you wish until you've cleaned it all up (Figure 12.29).

That's it! You can see our version in the Hell CA cuts folder: Hell_CA_baldcap_fix.mp4. This is a pretty tough fix and it worked surprisingly well.

Visual Effects Problems to Solve

Sometimes it feels like the sky is the limit, when it comes to visual effects. But just like all the other techniques covered in this book, they exist to help you tell your story. So given that, here's a few things to ask yourself:

Are there any shots with the crew or gear visible? Nothing takes you out of the fantasy world that a film creates faster than a visible microphone, light stand, or crew in a reflective surface.

Are there any screens you need to replace with higher-resolution composites? As we mentioned earlier, it's almost impossible to shoot screens with proper exposure and resolution so that viewers can read them. Do you have any cell phone or computer screen shots that require compositing?

Are you trying to do too much with one effect? Rather than trying to do it all in one go, try breaking down your effects work into smaller pieces.

What is the best order to apply effects? In the last tutorial, we stabilized first, then we worked on fixing the wrinkles in the bald cap. As you assess the shots in your film that need fixing with visual effects, which effect should you start with? This might require some trial and error but eventually you'll develop a spidey sense for it.

Can you make it better by making it worse? Sometimes you can see too much—too much detail, too much focus, too much background. The natural instinct is to add effects to your film but do you have any shots that will be served by diminishing the original footage by cropping, resizing, or blurring?

13

Color

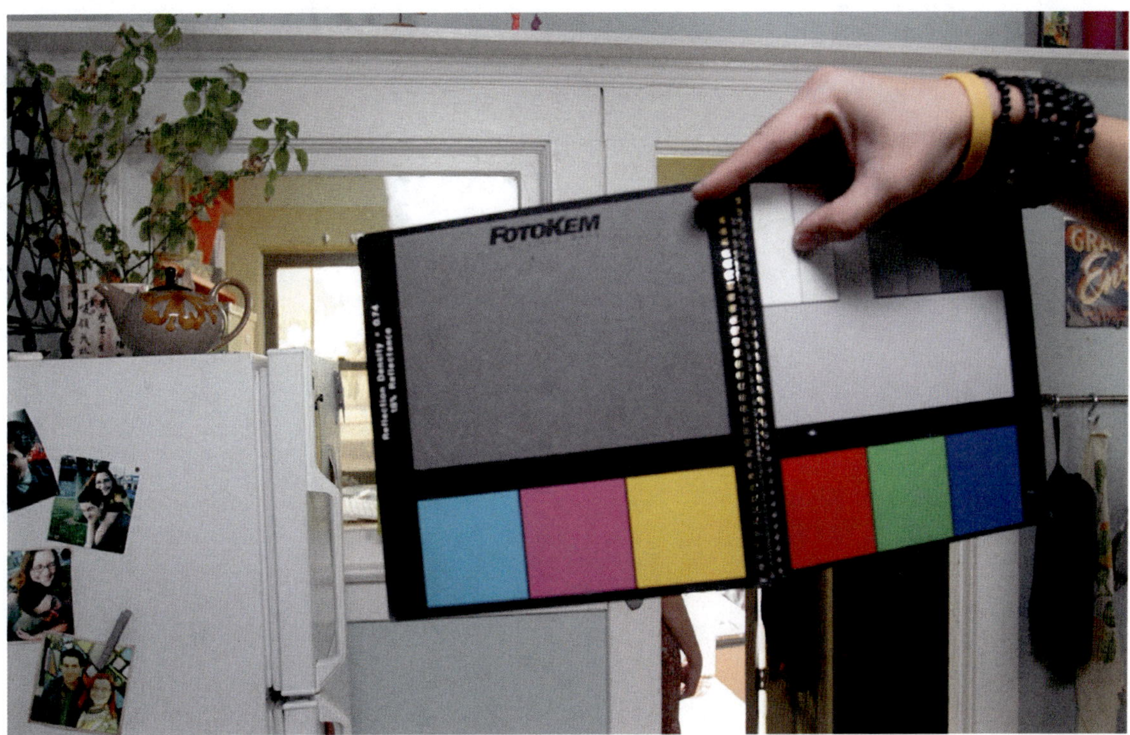

Figure 13.1

Color charts recorded on the set are helpful for adjusting color in post and making sure color settings conform to industry-standard specifications.

CAST, HUE, SHADE, TINT, TONE—WHATEVER YOU CALL IT, COLOR IS MAGICAL. For filmmakers, it adds a crucial element, which is beauty. But color is more than what you see—it's also a set of data that behaves according to laws of physics. And, not to intimidate you, but there are rules (Figure 13.1). Color for broadcast and streaming services must follow very concrete specifications laid down by distributors, international consortiums, and even the federal government. Filmmakers will find that their color needs break down into three categories: enhancing aesthetics, fixing problems, and work-in-progress adjustments. In this chapter, we'll cover all the above, focusing specifically on how to use the tools available in Adobe Premiere Pro to accomplish these tasks. Or should we say, tool? The Lumetri Color effect is not the only color effect available in Premiere Pro but it's pretty much one-stop shopping.

☑ The Color Workspace

Premiere Pro has a Workspace preset just for color and it's identical to the Editing workspace with the addition of two key panels—the Lumetri Color panel (Figure 13.2) and the Lumetri Scopes panel (Figure 13.13).

Lumetri Color in Premiere

A couple years ago, when Adobe introduced the Lumetri Color effect for Premiere and After Effects, it caused a stir—you could now grade the color in your film without leaving Premiere. And Lumetri Color is pretty cool. So what is it, exactly? Lumetri Color is an effect, just like any other video effect available in Premiere but it has a set of expanded tools that makes it feel almost like an app, all of which are found in the Lumetri Color panel (Figure 13.2).

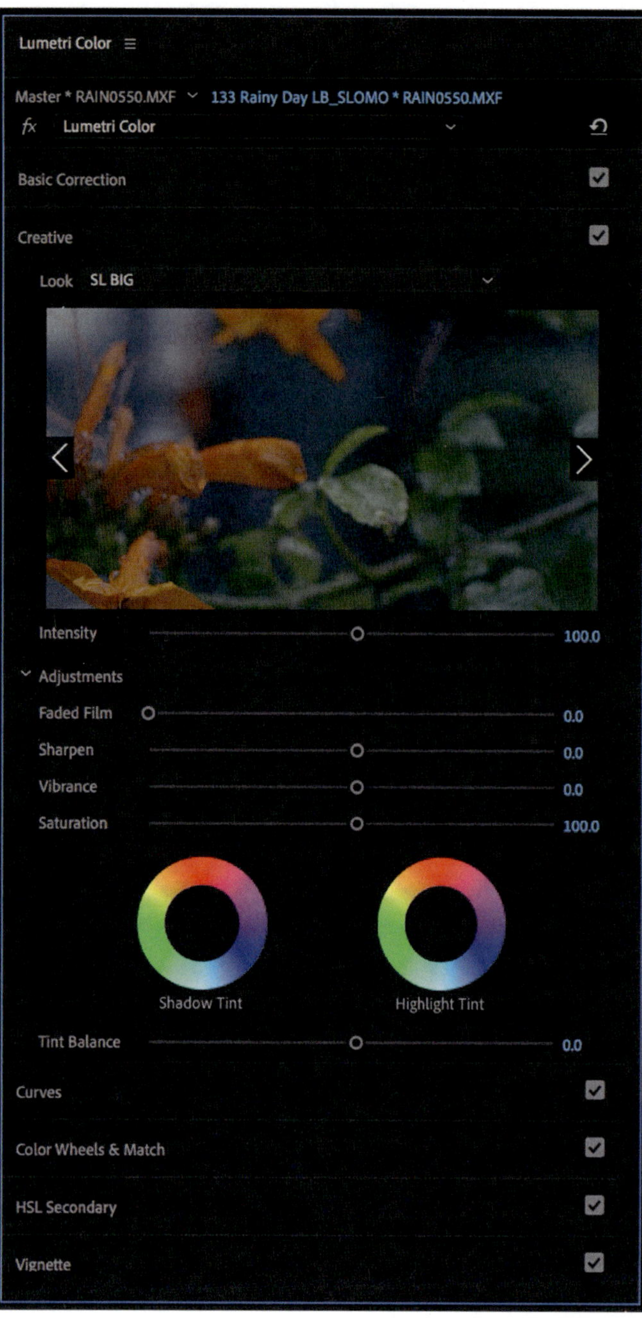

Figure 13.2 The Lumetri Color panel is one-stop shopping for color effects in Premiere Pro, with LUTs, Looks, color wheels, curves, color masking, and more.

The Lumetri Color panel (Window > Lumetri Color) gives you an active interface for making adjustments to the Lumetri Color effect and is divided into six areas. Basic Correction contains all the usual tools to correct color: white balance, exposure, black and white levels, saturation, and more, all controlled by sliders. Happily there is a Reset button at the bottom if you go too far. At the top, there's also a menu for applying LUTs to your media. Creative lets you choose from a huge selection of preset Looks and gives you some slider options to take your color grade a bit farther than Basic Correction. (We're going to dig deeper into LUTs and Looks in the next section.) The next three areas—Curves, Color Wheels & Match, and HSL Secondary—offer alternative ways to control the color of your media. And the last section lets you add a vignette to your image.

To add Lumetri Color to your media, simply click on the Lumetri Color menu at the top of the Lumetri Color panel and select Add Lumetri Color Effect. Alternately, you can navigate to it in the Effects panel and drag it onto your clip in the Timeline or into the Effect Controls panel, which has the same set of controls as the Lumetri Color panel albeit much smaller. It's easier to do your work in the Lumetri Color panel and you'll instantly see the changes to your media in the Program monitor. You may also want to use the Lumetri Scopes as you work. They're found in a tab in next to the Source monitor if you're in the Color workspace or you can go to Window > Lumetri Scopes. The Lumetri Scopes are a set of special software-based monitors that include waveforms, vectorscopes, parade views, and histograms—you can pretty much view the color and luminance of your media in every way possible. You need the Lumetri Scopes to make sure that you aren't overprocessing your color—they're the video equivalent of audio level meters. In the rest of this chapter, we're going to show you how to use all the above to make your film look its best. We'll start with the basics—how to make your media look good while you're editing a rough cut—and move on to the artistic—creative color grading—and the pragmatic—using scopes to make sure your color conforms to the rules of international distribution standards.

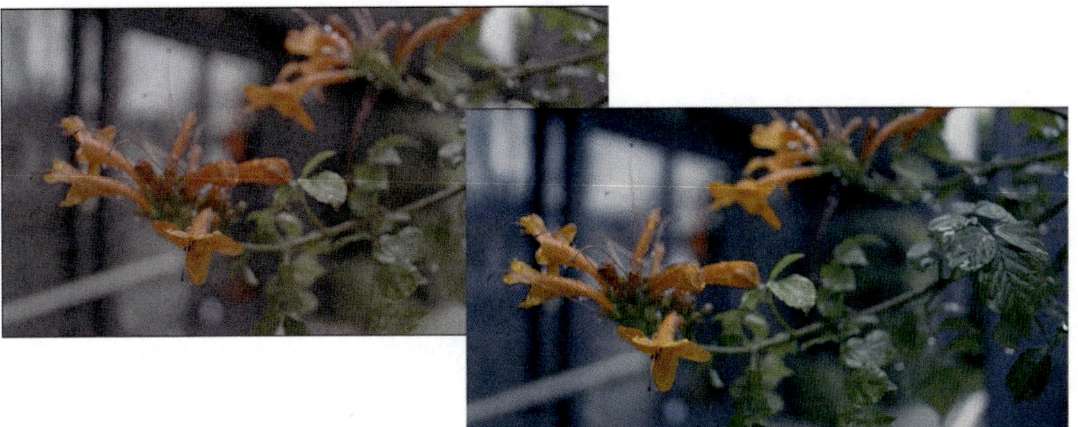

Figure 13.3

Original log color media on the left and with a Lumetri Color Look applied on the right.

Work-in-Progress Color

Sometimes you just need the color in your film to look decent while you're editing. More and more cameras shoot with some variation of a logarithmic, or log, color profile which looks grey and dull until you color grade it (Figure 13.3). And it may be that you need something more creative to make your rough cut watchable. Luckily there are some quick fixes available in Premiere.

LUTs

The proprietary log color profiles used by many cameras are designed to get the most information from the camera's sensor but they need to be unpacked, or translated, to look good to the human eye. Look Up Tables, or LUTs, are the key to unpacking log color. Similarly, raw video also requires a LUT to look right. In post-production, when a Look Up Table is applied to log media, you'll see the footage as it was intended to be seen. In other words, LUTs are a "make it normal" effect. Depending on how your media was acquired, you may find that a LUT has already been applied to your clip when you Ingest it—some cameras can assign LUTs via metadata and Premiere will read this info from the file and add the LUT automatically.

Figure 13.4

Choose from a selection of LUTs found in the Input LUT menu in the Basic Correction area of the Lumetri Color panel.

If you do need to add a LUT, the easiest way in Premiere is through the Lumetri Color effect. At the top of the Basic Correction section of the Lumetri Color panel, you'll see the Input LUT menu (Figure 13.4). Here, you'll find a selection of LUTs that are available in Premiere. Each LUT is named according to the camera model and settings that it is designed to work with: ALEXA_Default_LogCRec709 is a LUT designed for the Arri Alexa camera using the default settings for media recorded in the proprietary Arri Log C color space and constrained to meet the requirements for Rec. 709. If that's a match for your footage, you're all set—just select a clip or group of clips in the Timeline, select that LUT from the Input LUT menu in the Lumetri Color panel—it will be applied to your clip(s) and you'll see the it added to the list in the Effect Controls panel. If you don't see your camera model in the list, you can add LUTs to the list or create your own. LUTs are often available from the various camera manufacturers' websites.

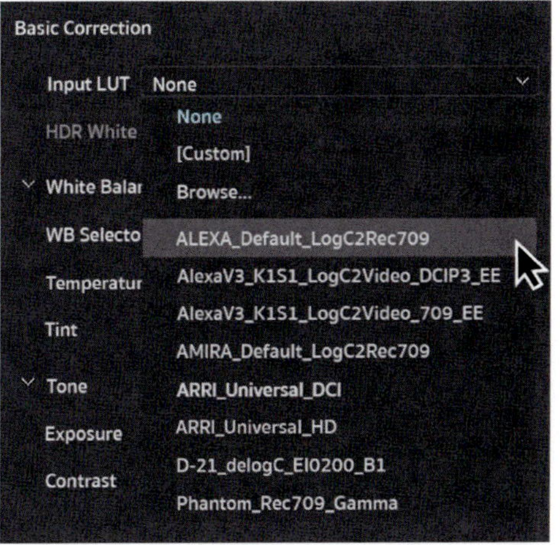

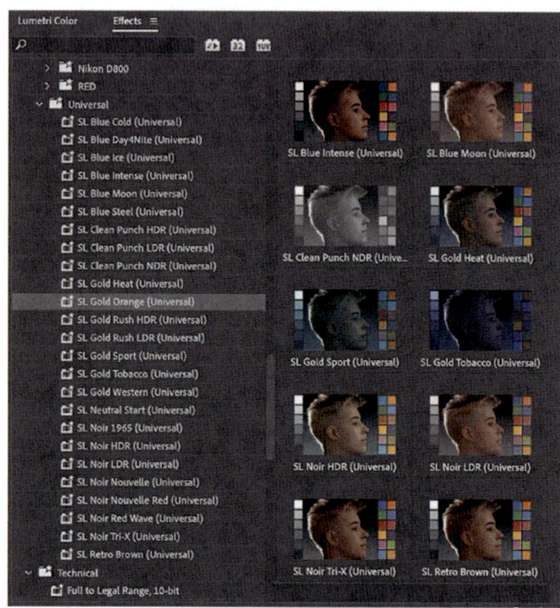

Figure 13.5

The Lumetri Presets folder in the Effects panel has a huge selection of preset looks designed to work with specific cameras or mimic classic film stocks.

☑ Color and Proxies

By all means, go ahead and color grade your proxies during the rough cut phase if it helps when screening your film. But when you start the true color grading process, you'll need to work on the high-resolution original media, not the proxies.

Looks and Presets

If you want something more intense than the functional color upgrade of an applied LUT, you can try a Lumetri Color preset or Look. Looks are found in the Creative portion of the Lumetri Color panel (Figure 13.2) and there are many available. Here you'll see a preview window with a frame of your video—you can use the arrows to the left and right in the Preview window to flip through the various Looks and see how they affect your footage. Most of the Looks are either designed for specific camera models or designed to mimic classic 35mm film stocks.

Another option is the Lumetri Presets folder, found in the Effects panel (Window > Effects). There are a ton of options here and you can see the results of any preset on an image of a model with a color chart (Figure 13.5).

Make It Easy to Get Rid of Temporary Color

If using LUTs or Looks is the right choice for your film while you edit it, remember that you may want to remove them later on, when you hand your film off to a colorist. With that in mind, there are some things to consider before you add temp color effects to your film.

Avoid Master Clip effects if you can It may sound like a good idea to add LUTs to every single master clip after ingest, but Master Clip effects can be problematic later on, mainly because you have to remove them one by one. If your LUT gets corrupted or doesn't work right after a software update, you may have to go through every single shot in the project to get rid of it. And the same goes if you need to prep an untreated version of the film to give to your color person.

Use adjustment layers The easiest way to add effects to large swaths of your film and remove or disable them with a single click is by using adjustment layers (File > New > Adjustment Layer). Dedicate a video track in your sequence to them and you'll be able to turn it on and off as needed. Or you can quickly select all the contents of that track and delete them. Be aware that if you change the settings on a LUT in an adjustment layer, those changes will affect all instances of that adjustment layer in your project. (We covered how to create and use adjustment layers in Chapter 12.)

Keep it simple It may be tempting to dial-in custom color for every scene, but unless you have a lot of time to spend on temporary color, it's better to have just a handful of color effects to make your movie watchable. Say, one for night exteriors, one for day interiors, one for the scene with fluorescent ceiling lights, and so on.

Disabling and Removing Color Effects

When you remove any effect in Premiere, you can choose between disabling or removing them completely. Disable any effect by clicking on the FX toggle to the left of the name of each effect in the Effect Controls panel. You can also disable all Master Clip Effects by right-clicking on any effect in a bin that has a Master Clip effect applied to it and selecting Disable Masterclip Effects from the menu. In either case, you'll see a backslash through the FX toggle in the Effect Controls panel that indicates that effects are disabled. To bring them back, simply click the FX toggle again. To Remove effects entirely, you can either select them in the Effect Controls panel and Delete or you can right-click on clips in a sequence and select Remove Attributes from the menu, which gives you some control over what gets removed. Note that Remove Attributes will only work on Clip effects and not Master Clip effects.

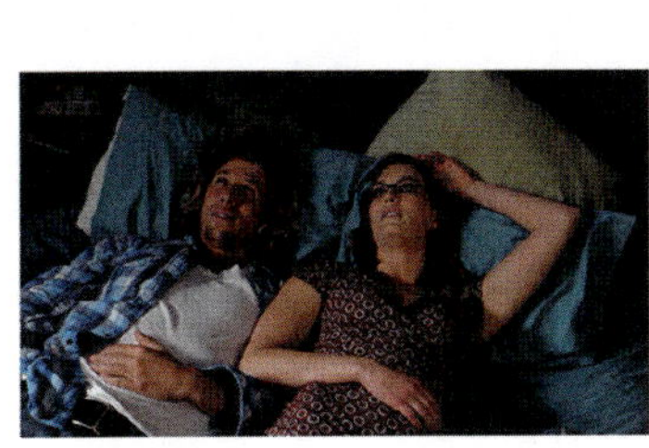

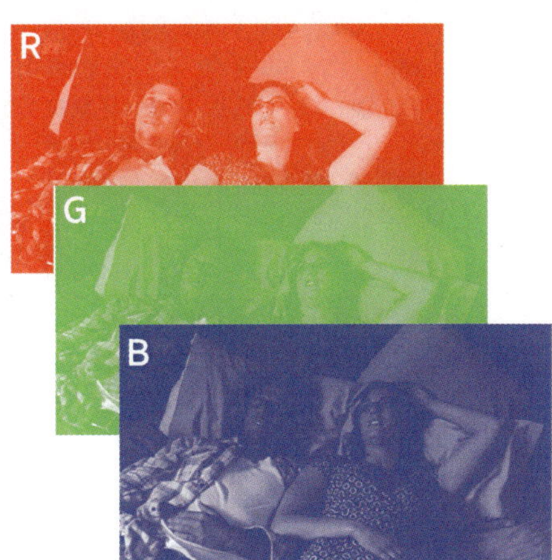

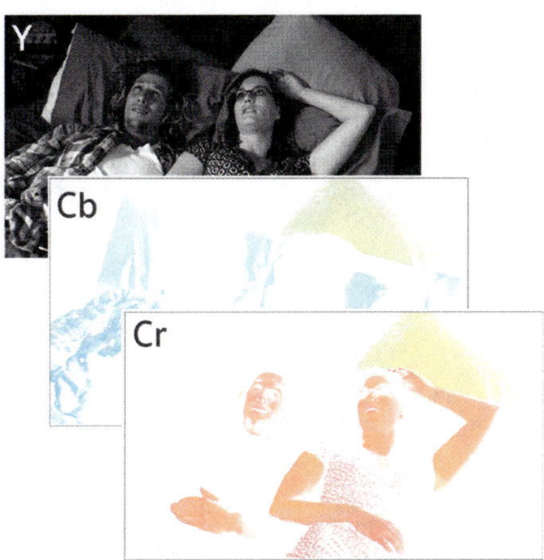

Figure 13.6

The full spectrum of analog color is converted to three channels in a digital video color space. RGB color consists of Red, Green, and Blue channels, and YCbCr color has one channel of light and dark information, or luminance, and two channels of color.

Digital Color Basics

So far, we've been talking about some easy fixes for work-in-progress color, but if you're serious about color, you need to understand how it works. Color in digital video is broken down into three elements—color space, color sampling or compression, and bit depth—and every video codec is defined by how it handles each of these color components (in addition to other video specifications like image size, frame rate, etc.). And as you might suspect, each of these elements can affect the quality of your final film.

Color Space

When it comes to color for films, we want it to look the same in many different situations—the color in a film projected in a theater needs to look the same when broadcast on regular television and also when streamed to a computer or mobile phone. And each of these scenarios involves a potentially different color space (Figure 13.6). What exactly, is a color space? It's the way that color is organized for various devices. The human eye can see millions of colors and there's no need to organize them but for devices such as cameras, monitors, and printers, programmers and engineers restrict the way the device interprets color by using one of several different digital color systems:

RGB For filmmakers, RGB is the primary color space. It's what your computer monitor is using as you edit your film. If your film is headed for streaming on the web, your final digital master file will also use the RGB color space, as will projects destined for theatrical distribution. The RGB color space consists of three channels—Red, Green, and Blue—which are the primary colors in an additive, light-based, color system.

YUV and/or YCbCr Also of importance to filmmakers is the YUV color space. YUV was invented to help describe color video in a way that worked during the transition from black and white to color television. YUV also has three channels—the Y stands for luminance which is light intensity of an image and the U and V are two color difference channels that add up to a full color image. Without getting too technical, U is all the colors minus red and V is all the colors minus blue. Just to make it more confusing, in digital video, YUV is actually an abbreviation for YCbCr—it's just easier to say and remember. (True YUV is actually an analog color space.) If your final film is going to be aired on traditional broadcast television—something that's less and less common—your final digital master file will need to use the YUV/YCbCr color space.

CMYK (Cyan, Magenta, Yellow, and Black) is primarily used for printing.

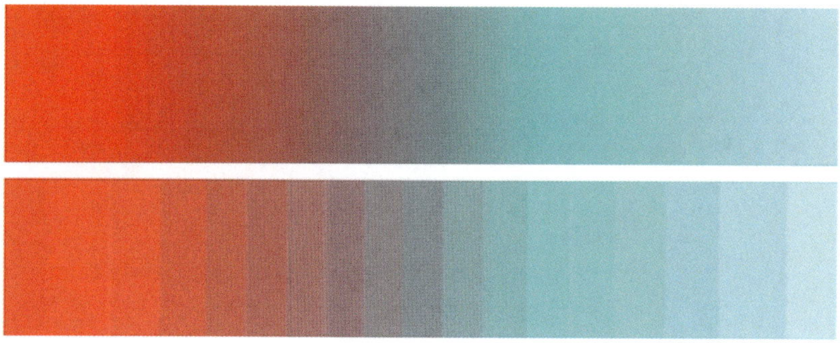

Figure 13.7

More bit depth means more colors, and more colors mean better gradients. Shown here, a high bit-depth gradient (top) yields a smooth transition from red to cyan, while a low bit-depth gradient (bottom) results in banding or posterization.

Color Sampling and Compression

In order to have the highest quality color in an image, your digital video needs to be uncompressed. Compression starts in the camera, so you'll need to shoot with a camera that records with an uncompressed codec. But the reality is that many cameras shoot with compressed codecs and they achieve smaller file sizes is by reducing the color information, yet this compressed footage is still very high in quality. That's because the human eye is better at seeing values of lightness and darkness than it is at seeing color. So compressed camera codecs discard some color information but keep the full range of luminance and the resulting video looks pretty good to most people. Uncompressed video has four samples for each channel, which is written as 4:4:4 or sometimes just 444. Digital files that use the RGB color space always have a color sampling ratio of 4:4:4, while digital files that use the YCbCr color space can have a color sampling ratio of 4:4:4 (uncompressed), 4:2:2, or 4:2:0. These last two have an uncompressed luminance channel and two compressed color channels. Codecs often have these numbers in their names, like Apple ProRes 422 HQ, so that you can immediately understand the type of compression used in the codec.

Bit Depth

In addition to color space and color sampling, the other element that affects the quality of color in a digital video file is bit depth, which is the amount of color information stored in each pixel in a frame of video. Most digital video uses 8-bit color which means each pixel contains a total of 256 colors. Since there are 3 color channels in every digital video pixel, that adds up to over 16 million colors can be assigned to any given pixel. That's a lot, but 8-bit color is not the highest quality, although it's considered to be very good. 10-bit might not sound that much bigger than 8-bit, but these numbers are exponential so video with a bit depth of 10 has over a billion colors and 12-bit color has even more. Why would you need so many colors? The more colors you have, the more subtle the gradations between colors (Figure 13.7). This means that you have a finer degree of control over changes and improvements to color when you are grading your film. By the way, the terms for bit depth do get confusing because you can talk about the bit-depth of a channel (8 bits), a pixel which contains three channels (24 bits), or a pixel with three channels plus an alpha channel (32 bits). So 8-bit color can be referred to as 24-bit color or 32-bit color. In Premiere, the color bit depth numbers refer to bits per pixel.

Logarithmic and Linear Color Profiles

It gets a little more complicated. Color can be scaled in a linear manner or logarithmically. Linear color means there is a straight light from black to white and each color on that spectrum has equal weight. But the reality is that we don't see the full spectrum equally—our vision is biased towards the midtones. Logarithmic color accounts for these biases in human sight and uses a curve instead of a straight line, giving more weight to the center and less to the extreme darks and brights. Logarithmic color profiles are used to record more information on a camera sensor. In Premiere, linear color is referred to as 8-bit color and logarithmic color is referred to as floating point color, or float. And color that goes beyond 8-bits is referred to as HDR, or High Dynamic Range color.

Color Grading and Image Quality

When it comes to quality in digital video, you can't improve compressed video by "bumping it up" to an uncompressed codec. But having the full color spectrum available does help when color grading. For that reason, most films get exported to an uncompressed format before the final color grading occurs, that is if they're not already uncompressed. The most common uncompressed codecs used in filmmaking are the Apple Animation codec (RGB 444 16-bit), Apple ProRes 444 (RGB or YCbCr 16-bit), JPEG 2000 (RGB 444 24-bit), and Avid DNxHR RGB 444 10-bit (the name says it all). When you see a fourth channel, i.e. 4:4:4:4, that means a transparency or alpha channel is included in the file and is also uncompressed. In addition to your color grading needs, you'll also find that distributors, such as streaming services, theaters, and broadcasters, will have very specific color specifications for the final digital master file of your film. For example, at the time of this writing high-end streaming (4K, UHD) and films that will get projected in theaters use the RGB 444 24-bit JPEG 2000 codec, which conforms to the IMF (Interoperable Master Format) and DCP (Digital Cinema Package) formats. Broadcast television is HD 422 YCbCr with 8-bit color. Your final color grade will need to conform to these specifications.

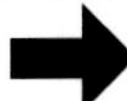

Understanding Digital Color

We just raced through a lot of big concepts regarding color because we want to focus on Premiere Pro. So if you need a deeper explanation of how color works in digital video, you'll find it in Chapter 3, Digital Video Primer, and Chapter 16, Color Grading, of *The Digital Filmmaking Handbook*. It's also worth reading the section on color temperature in Chapter 6, Lighting.

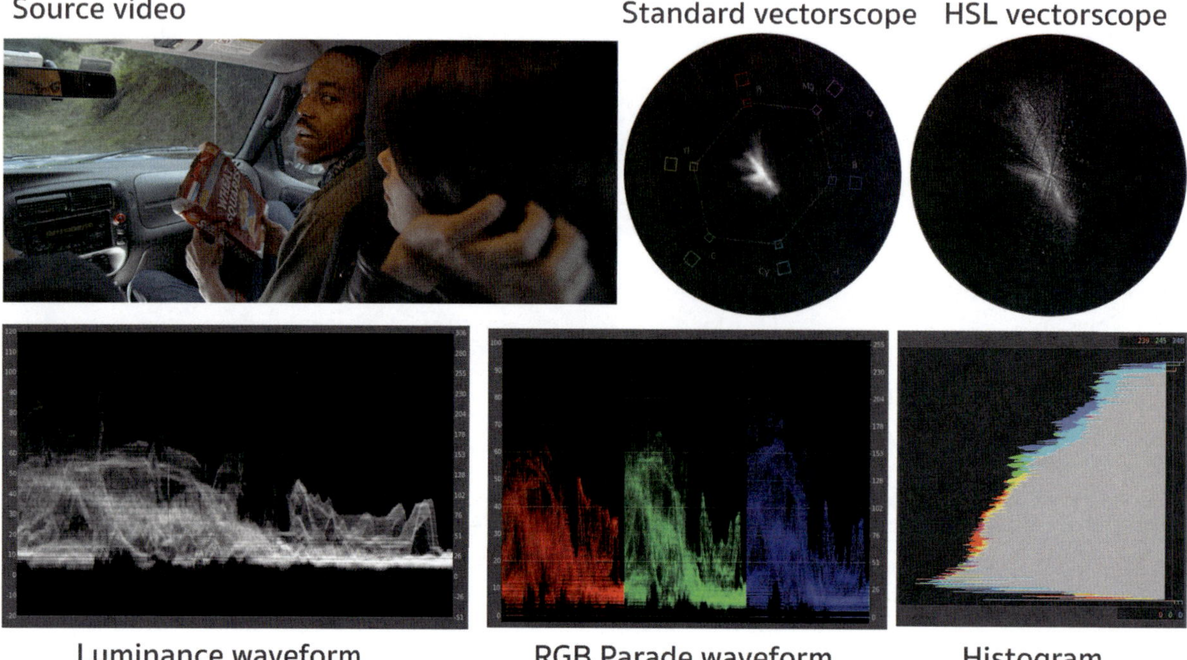

Figure 13.8 A selection of monitors from the Lumetri Scopes panel in Premiere all showing the same thing, with a standard video source image for reference (upper left). Each display shows you a different way to view the brightness and color of your video.

When to Color Grade?

We're talking a lot about how films finish and that's because color grading is one of the last things you do before you finish a film. So how does color grading fit in with visual effects, graphics, and other post-production processes? The normal process is that you lock picture on your film first, then finish the visual effects, then you color it. Most feature films and episodic series hire a colorist to do the color grading for their project and they'll do that work while the sound is sent to a professional mixer. But the reality today is that post is more fluid. You can mix as you go, color as you go, and so on and some of that might be of value for the finish—in fact, if you're going DIY it will definitely be of value to work on color as you go. Only you know what your film needs and which process and budget level is right for you.

If you decide to use a professional colorist, they will usually ask for a clean version of the film to work with. That could be an export of the film in an uncompressed codec, the untreated camera-original media, or both. For the uncompressed export, you'll remove all graphics and titles, along with all temporary color. Effects that do not affect color, such as resizing and image stabilization are usually left intact and your colorist will tell you whether or not to leave the camera LUTs in place. When the color work is completed, the new final video will get edited back together with the mixed audio and you'll create your masters from that, all of which is covered in the next chapter.

If your film is short, or low-budget, or it's early in your career as filmmaker, you may want to do the final color grading yourself. If so, it's up to you how the workflow goes but many choose to follow the typical professional workflow, as described above. It means there's less chance that you'll have to doubleback and re-color a scene because you changed it. That said, the main reason that not a lot of time is devoted to color during the rough cut phase of filmmaking is that it takes a lot of time and will eventually get tossed out. But if your DIYing it, you can spend as much time as you like, knowing you'll use it in the end.

Tools for Working with Color

Working with color gets easier when you have the right tools. If you're planning to hire a colorist to do the color grade for your film, you won't need these tools but many of them are built into Premiere, so they're there if you need them or just want to play around and see how it all works.

Monitoring Color

The most important tool for working with color is one that allows you to see it—the monitor. If you're working in 4K, you'll need a 4K monitor to see it and if you're working in 10-bit color, you'll need a monitor that can display over a billion colors. Colorists invest a lot of money into their monitors and they also spend a lot of effort in calibrating them so that the colors are accurate. In addition to your computer monitor, you may also find it useful to have a video monitor or TV hooked up to your system, especially if you plan to finish your film in the YUV/YCbCr color space. Your computer monitor is RGB so you can't see YUV color unless you add a YUV monitor.

In addition to hardware monitors, there are also special software-based monitors that are crucial for judging color accurately—in Premiere these are found in Settings menu at the bottom right corner of the Lumetri Scopes panel. There are several different types of monitors and you can select more than one at a time—just highlight it in the menu and a check mark will appear next to it indicating that it's active (Figures 13.8 and 13.9).

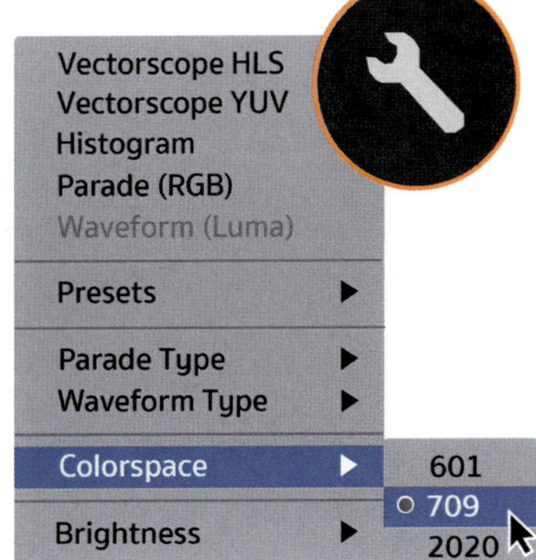

Figure 13.9

Use the Lumetri Scopes Settings menu to choose the right color space for your media, based on ITU video standards.

Waveforms display the values of your video in a wave shape, similar to audio waveforms. Waveform monitors are especially useful for judging luminance, or the range from black (0) to white (100). If your whites go too high you'll see clipping or overexposure, if your blacks go too low they'll get "crushed" or posterized. Premiere has several types of waveforms available and they differ based on the color space and bit-depth of your video.

Histograms also display the luminance values of your video similar to waveforms but in Premiere the range is shown vertically instead of horizontally.

Parade view shows a waveform for each of the three channels in your video—one each for RGB (Red, Green, and Blue) or YUV (one luminance and two chroma channels).

Vectorscopes display the colors of your video as a graph so that you can see when colors are oversaturated. Each of the primary and secondary colors has a box that indicates optimal saturation and the ring that connects these boxes indicates the safe area for the colors in your video.

? Video Standards

HD video destined for broadcast and streaming services must follow a set of specifications outlined by the International Telecommunications Union (ITU) known as Rec. 709. The standard for SD video is Rec. 601 and the standard for UHD is Rec. 2020. In Premiere, choose the color space you want to work in (based on the ITU recommendation) using the Lumetri Scopes Settings menu (Figure 13.9). Most indie features choose to comply with Rec. 709 at the time of this writing.

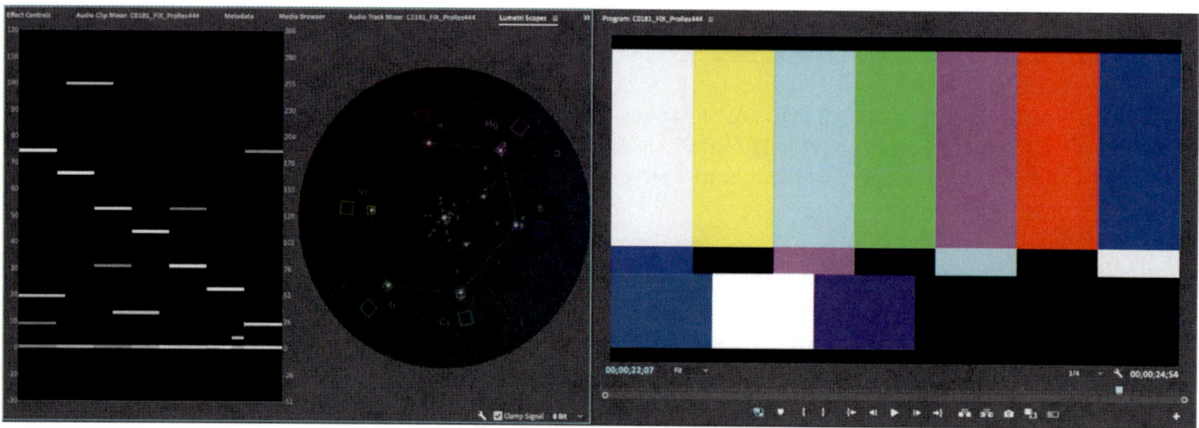

Figure 13.10

Color bars are a test pattern designed to help you calibrate the color of a video file or display. To the left are the Luma Waveform and Vectorscope, which should always look the same when displaying color bars.

Color Charts and Test Patterns

A quick way to judge the color in your video is to embed a color reference in the video itself. Color charts are used during the shoot and when the video comes back to post, you can adjust white balance, white levels, and black levels in a flash (Figure 13.1). The rest of the colors tend to fall into place after that, but you can use the colors in the chart to really dial it in. Test patterns are added to the head of a film, before the countdown, so that anyone who needs to can set up the color for it on any type of display (Figure 13.10). They are primarily used for broadcast video but are functional for any type of display. When a test pattern is played, you'll see a distinctive pattern in the waveform and vectorscope.

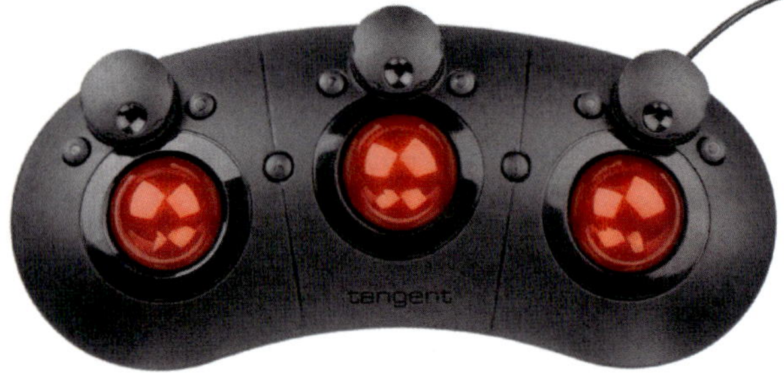

Figure 13.11

Hardware-based controllers like this one from Tangent allow for a finer degree of control when color grading.

Hardware Controllers

If you've ever played around with the color controls in any editing application, you probably noticed that the changes you made weren't that subtle—suddenly everything was green. To get that slow, subtle gradation of color, it's easier if you use hardware controllers with roller balls like the pros (Figure 13.11). If you've ever used a roller ball mouse, it's the same except there's three balls—one for each channel of video.

Identifying Colors

Color is inherently subjective. What you might call blue, someone else might call violet. Traditional names of colors work fine if you have a limited palette, but when you're talking about millions or billions of colors, the method for identifying individual colors needs to be more specific.

You're probably already family with the Color Picker (Figure 13.12). It's available for certain effects in the Effect Controls panel, like the Type effect. You can use the mouse to select any color in the gradient but to get a precise color, it's better to use the text entry fields to the right, where you have a choice of five different ways to identify a color in Premiere. You can enter the value of each RGB channel, which range from 0 to 255. For example, the magenta hue in Figure 13.12 is R240, G10, B220. You can also enter the value of each YUV channel, in this case Y104, U58, V86. And you can use HSB and HSL values (Hue, Saturation, Brightness or Lightness) or the six-character, hexadecimal code for that color, in this case F00ADC, which is used in programming and web design. This degree of specificity is very useful when you're making graphics. For example, when you want all your lower third titles to be the exact same shade of blue, knowing the RGB values or hex code gets rid of any guessing. And just to be clear, you can use any of the five sets of values in the Color Picker—they are five different ways of identifying the same color.

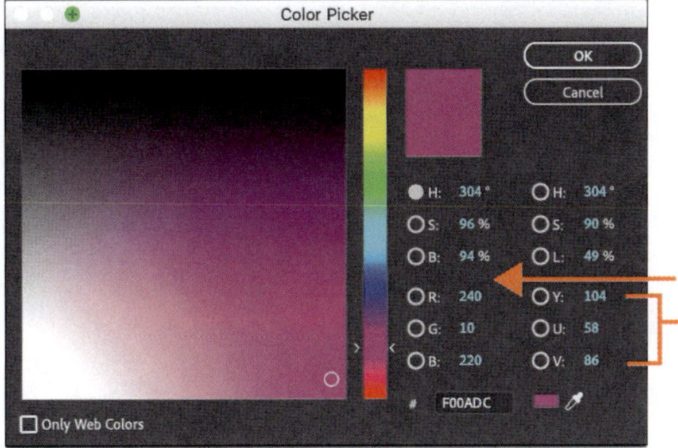

Figure 13.12

The Color Picker in Premiere shows five different ways of defining a single color.

Creative Color Grading

This chapter has been highly technical, and yet color grading is one of the most artistic processes in filmmaking. Every film has different needs when it comes to color, but they all share five basic goals:

Highlight the actors The subject of most films is people and so there is a priority in color grading towards skin tones. It's cool if you make your scene dark, but not if your actors disappear into the background. That said, it's a creative call—if your scene is set in a spaceship or a nightclub, you may not care about naturalistic skin color.

Enhance the story Color has a unique ability to set a mood, guide the eye, and tell us how to feel about what's happening in a film. Whatever type of film you're making, you'll want color that suits the tone. The eye is drawn to bright spots and vibrant colors, so you can use them to enhance or diminish parts of the image in order to focus attention where you want it.

Fix any problems Shooting is always a challenge and sometimes there are issues that come from the field. Poor exposure, incorrect white balance, unavoidable hot spots, cameras that don't match, and changes you want to make to the time of day—all of these items can be fixed or at least improved with color grading.

Keep it legal Color for broadcast television has to conform to FCC regulations—that's right, there are actual laws governing it. But today most films follow the rules laid down by the International Telecommunication Union, or ITU—specifically their recommendation for color specs known as Rec. 709. Luckily, the Lumetri Color effect in Premiere is designed to work within the Rec. 709 specifications and as always, if you push the whites, blacks, and saturation too far, your film will not pass the quality control checks that are performed by all distributors.

Avoid making it worse Color adjustments are capable of degrading your image by introducing noise, posterization, and clipping. So as much as you may want to push the color in your media, you don't want to go too far. Waveforms and vectorscopes are there for that reason, so that you can easily see any problems that you might introduce. We'll show you how to use them in the next section.

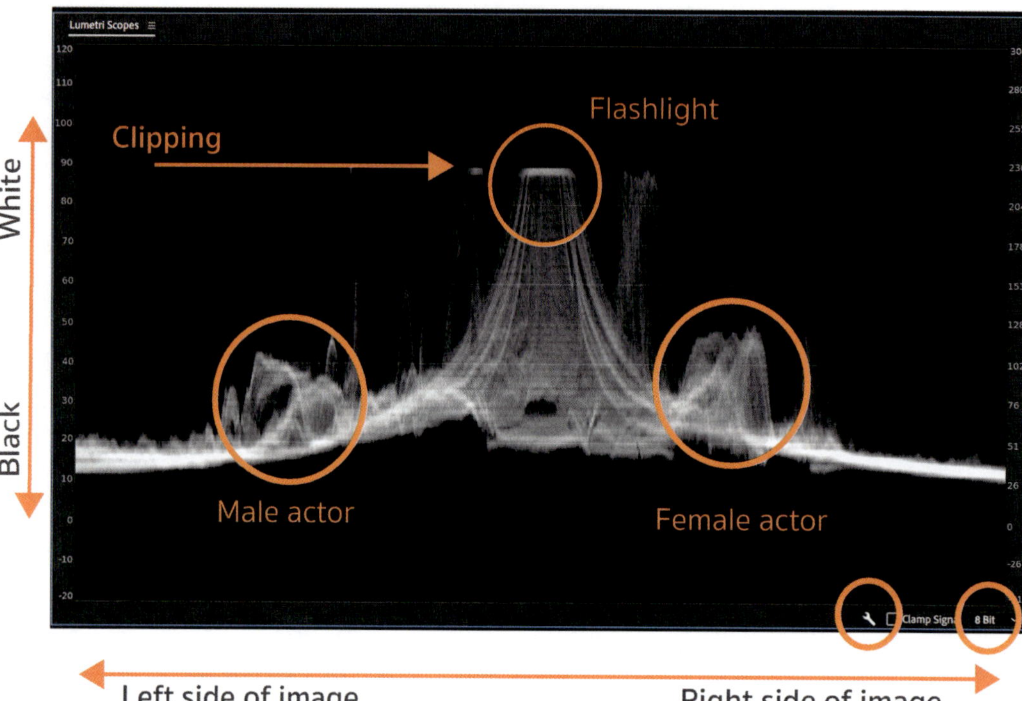

Figure 13.13

The Luma Waveform view in the Lumetri Scopes panel shows the range from white to black for the image in Figure 13.15. Here, you can easily pick out the bright flashlight and the two actors. Note the two small circled menus in the lower right corner, the Lumetri Scopes Settings menu and a menu for selecting bit depth.

Figure 13.14

The Luma Waveform is found in the Lumetri Scopes settings menu.

To LUT or Not?

Depending on your skill level and self-confidence, you can start with a LUT or start from scratch. This is entirely your call. A lot of colorists prefer to start over but then again, if you did a lot of work with the temporary color why throw it all out? If you do keep the LUTs, remember that they serve a technical purpose—to bring logarithmic color into a range that suits the human eye and meets the specifications set by Rec. 709. That said, LUTs do not fix problems—if the white balance in your footage was set wrong in the field, it will stay that way unless you fix it. But if your footage was shot well, the amount of improvement to the image they add can be impressive, and that might be all you need.

Setting Black and White Levels

The first step in color grading is to define the darkest black and whitest white for your media and to do that, you'll need to use the Luma Waveform (Figure 13.13), found in the Lumetri Scopes Settings wrench menu (Figure 13.14). There are other types of waveforms—RGB and YUV—but for setting black and white levels they just add some potentially confusing information that you don't need right now. Figure 13.13 shows the luminance waveform of the image in Figure 13.15—they are basically two ways to view the same shot. The waveform view reflects your image from left to right, but from top to bottom it shows the range from black to white. If you look at Figures 13.13 and 13.15, you can compare the position of the two actors and the bright flashlight and you can also see how bright or dark they are relative to each other. It might sound counter intuitive to start out working with luminance values, after all there is no color involved. But you'll often find that setting the black and white levels is all you need to do to get the color right.

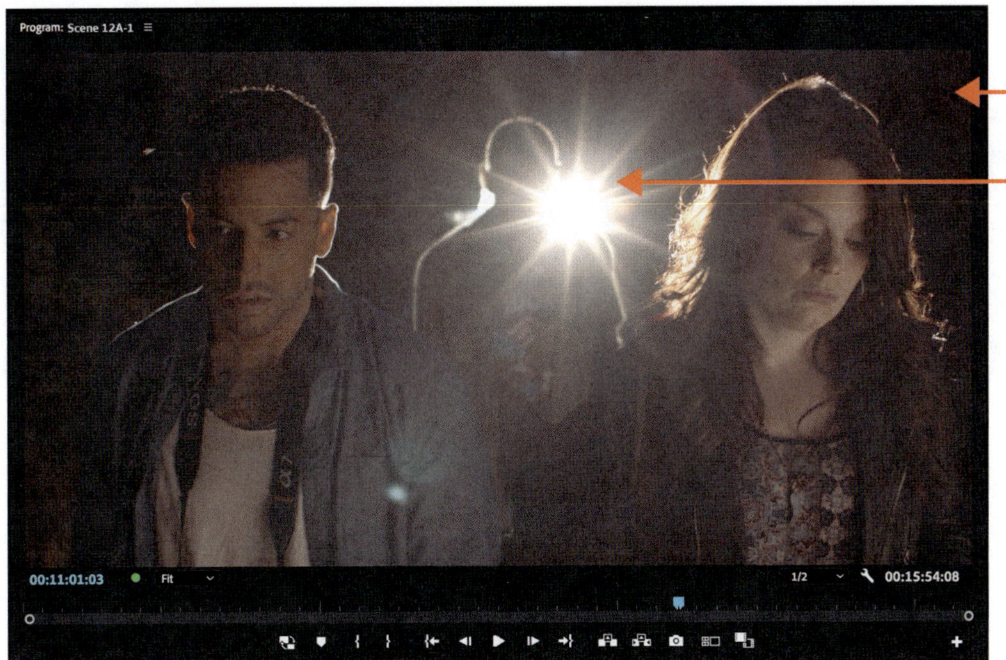

Figure 13.15

The Program monitor in this image and the Luma Waveform monitor in 13.13 show the same frame in different ways.

In Premiere, use the black and white sliders in the Basic Correction section of the Lumetri Color panel (Figure 13.16) and to make sure your black and white levels are good, watch the Lumetri Scopes panel to view your changes as you make them. Along the left side of the luminance waveform is a scale the ranges from -20 to 120 IRE. This is to help you keep the brights and darks within the legal limits. When you set the blacks, they should never go below 0 and the whites should never go above 100. For most films, you'll want as full a range as possible between black and white. In the case of the untreated image in Figure 13.13 and 13.15, the blacks are not that black and the whites are not that white, so the first thing to do is use the Blacks slider in the Basic Correction area of the Lumetri Color panel to get the blacks as close to 0 as possible, then use the Whites slider to pull up the whites closer to 100.

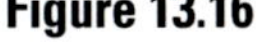

Figure 13.16

Basic Correction sliders are used to set black and white levels.

Along the right side of the luminance waveform is another scale that ranges from -51 to 306. This is the range from black to white for 8-bit color, which is used to confirm that your black and white levels are acceptable for Rec. 709. There are 256 colors in 8-bit video where 0 is black and 256 is white. For Rec. 709 this range is narrowed: blacks are set to 16 and whites are set to 235. If you're not working with 8-bit color, you'll select floating point or HDR color from the small menu in the lower right corner of the Lumetri Scopes panel and the scales on the waveform will change to reflect your choice.

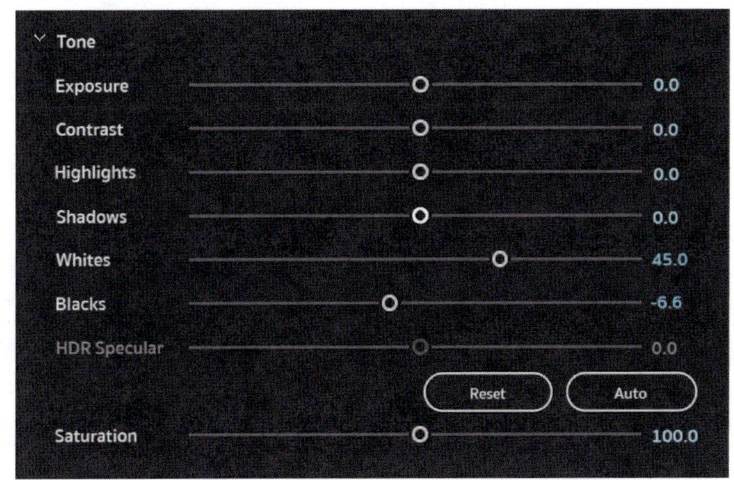

In the shot in Figure 13.15, the white light from the flashlight is overexposed, so there's clipping which you can clearly see in the waveform—instead of the top of the wave continuing in a natural curve, it is truncated into a flat line. That's because the white of the flash light was brighter than what the camera

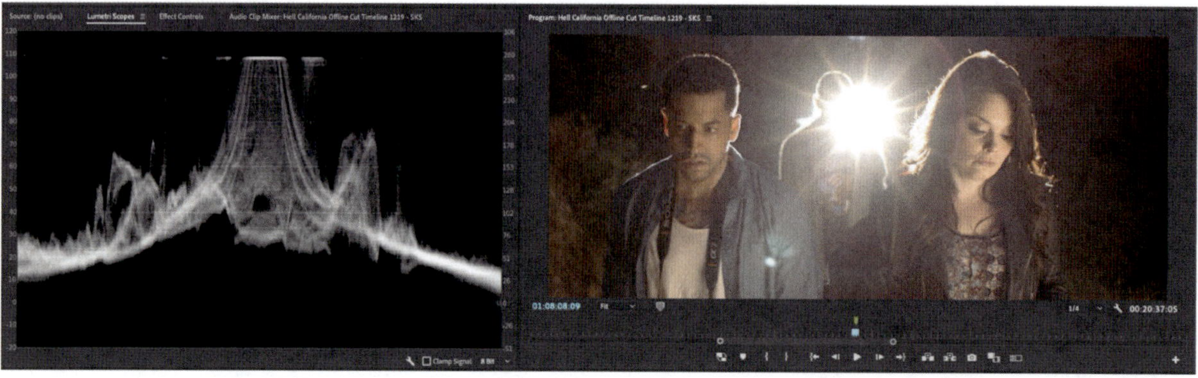

Figure 13.17

Even if you pull the whites up as high as they'll go with the slider, the luminance for the faces of the two actors remain well below 100. This results in a stylized look. Note how much bigger the glare of the flashlight appears now.

sensor could handle. And there's nothing you can do to remove this clipping. As you can see in Figure 13.13, the white levels are well below 100, so lowering them further will not help.

But the interesting thing about this particular shot, it that the clipping is not a mistake on the part of the camera crew. The director wanted a blown out look, so the flashlight is intentionally bright. This is a great example of how stylistic choices can bend the rules. With a shot like this, you can pull the whites all the way up to 100 and you'll have a perfectly good range of luminance in the rest of the image. In fact, you can pull them even higher. Why? They're already clipped, so if they get clipped more it's not going to degrade that part of the image. In fact, by pulling them much higher—say up to 110 or even 120—you'll end up with a stronger look where the image has more glare and the flashlight feels more intrusive which might work better for the story (Figure 13.17). And that, in a nutshell, is why color grading is an art form. Even something as simple as setting white levels can make a big difference in the tone of your film.

By the way, you might be wondering why we are using the Luma Waveform instead of the Y No Chroma Waveform—they both show only luminance. But the Luma Waveform shows the areas above 100 and below 0, known as overbrights and crushed blacks. Personally, I like to see the whole range, so I prefer the Luma Waveform. And speaking of seeing the whole waveform, you should also deselect the checkbox next to Clamp Signal at the bottom of the Lumetri Scopes panel—Clamp Signal limits the range of the waveform in the display but not the actual video, so it's potentially misleading.

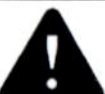 Lumetri Scopes are RAM Hogs

Having the Lumetri Scopes panel active uses a lot of RAM, since you're basically playing multiple streams of video at the same time. If things are sluggish, close the Lumetri Scopes until you need them or simply click on another tab in the Source monitor panel to hide them temporarily.

Adjusting Midtones

Now that you have defined the darkest blacks and brightest whites, where do you want all the shades in between to fall? This is where you get creative, but we're still just talking about the range from black to white, not color. In films, most of the important imagery falls into the range known as the midtones, and not surprisingly, this is the area where the human eye is most sensitive. There are several ways to adjust the midtones, but the easiest is to use the color wheel sliders, found in the Color Wheels & Match area of the Lumetri Color panel (Figure 13.18).

The shot in Figure 13.19 is almost all midtones. On the right, you can see the footage before they have been adjusted—black and white levels are set but it looks kind of blah. In this case, it's a horror movie—it's meant to be a dimly lit, scary room. We pushed the midtones down using the slider next to the midtones color wheel (Figure 13.18). The sliders next to the color wheels shift the three ranges—shadows, midtones, and highlights—from dark (down) to bright (up) without changing the color. If you're familiar with Levels in Photoshop, this is a very similar tool. If you push the midtones way down like we did, the shadows and highlights will get darker too, so you'll have to compensate by pulling up the highlights. That in turn will pull up the shadows so to get a higher contrast image with dark shadows and midtones but bright highlights, you'll have to pull the Shadows slider down as well. As you make adjustments like this you should always be checking your black and white levels in the Luma Waveform view. In Figure 13.19, you can see the results of the changes in the image on the right.

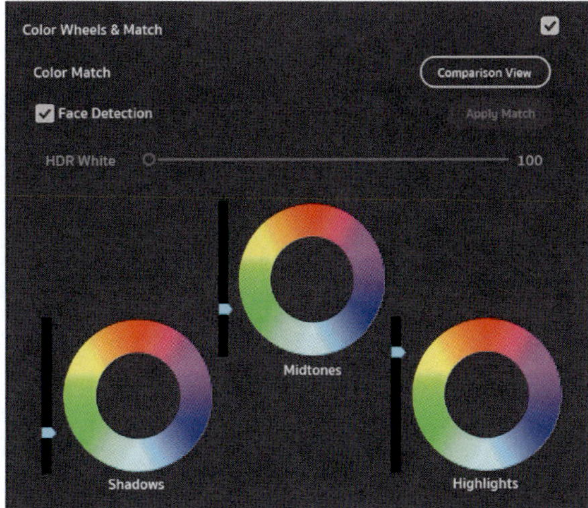

Figure 13.18

Use the sliders to the left of each color wheel to adjust the luminance of the shadows, midtones, and highlights.

☑ Comparison View

You can switch the Program monitor to Comparison View by selecting it from the Program monitor Settings menu (wrench). In Comparison View, you have a choice of side-by-side (Figure 13.19), vertical split, or horizontal split. You can also choose to compare two different shots or the before and after of a single frame, which is shown here. Drag the playhead on the left to select a reference shot in Shot comparison mode. Comparison View stores the reference frame as the clip appears when you launch it, so if you want to see untouched footage as a reference, you'll need to activate Comparison View before you make any changes to it in the Lumetri Color panel. It's very useful for matching the color in different shots and checking the changes you make against the original video.

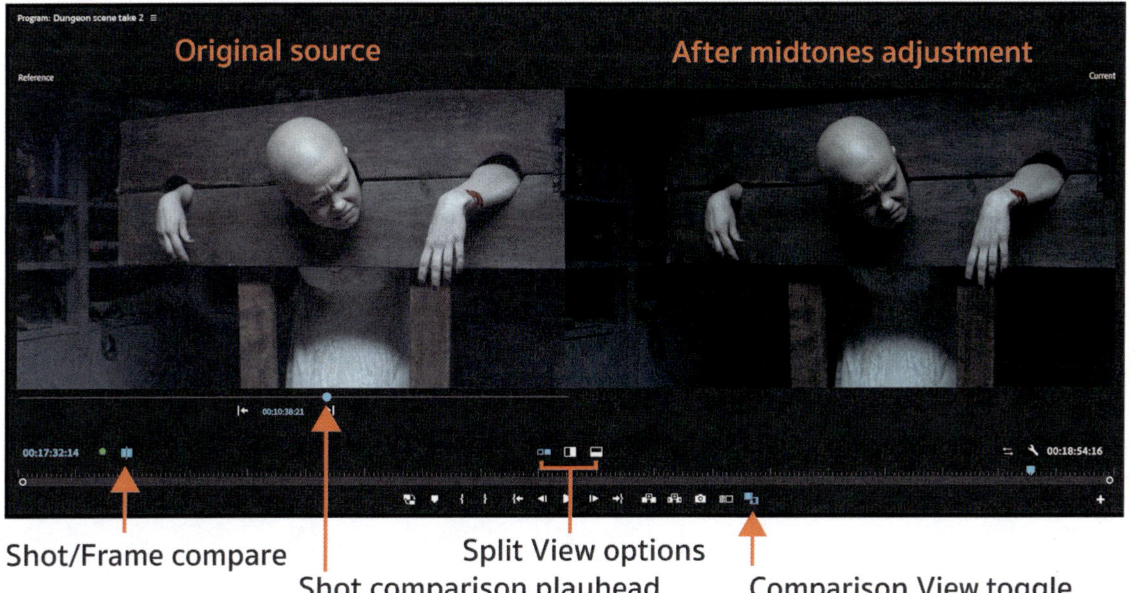

Figure 13.19

Comparison view lets you see how much your image has changed as you make color adjustments.

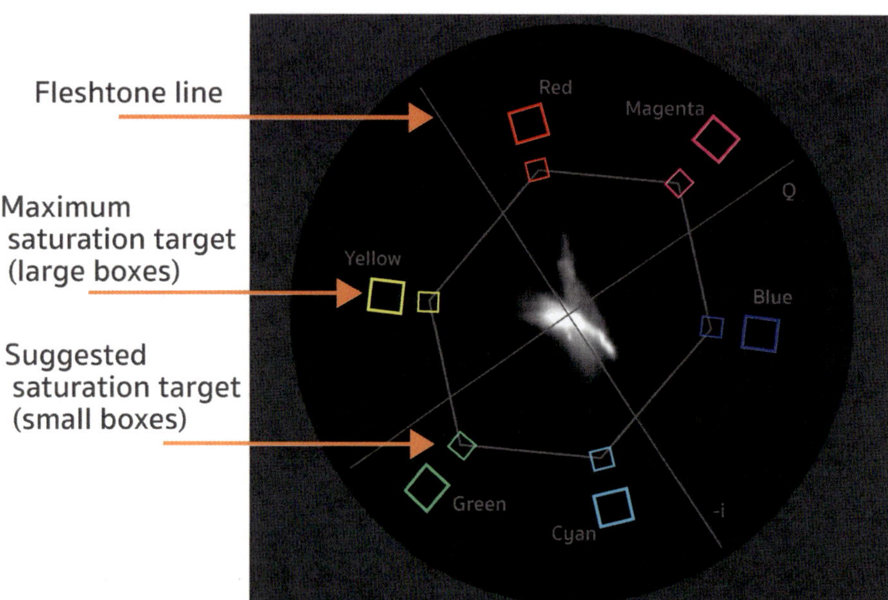

Figure 13.20

Vectorscopes resemble a color wheel and show the intensity of color in a video clip. The white area in the center is the color signal, or chroma, and here it shows that the shot of the truck (Figure 13.21) is heavily balanced towards the blue and yellow part of the spectrum.

Increase Saturation (Usually)

Once you have blacks, whites, and midtones in place, you have a solid base on which to add color. In fact, you might not need to do much to the color at all. Nevertheless it's worth playing with the Saturation slider in the Basic Correction section of the Lumetri Color panel—this slider will increase the saturation for all of the colors in a shot equally. There's almost always room for a little boost in saturation.

To make sure that your colors don't get out of control, switch the Lumetri Scopes panel to Vectorscope RGB/YUV (Figure 13.20) using the Settings menu. (Premiere will determine whether to offer you the RGB or YUV vectorscope based on the color space of your footage.) The vectorscope displays the chroma in an image and it's a lot like a color wheel made up of the additive primary and secondary colors: red, green, blue, cyan, yellow, and magenta. Each color has two target boxes—a small one that suggests a healthy level of saturation and a large on that suggests the maximum. A line that links the smaller targets together gives you the suggested limit for the color in your image, it's not recommended to go beyond this line. The ghostly white blob in the center is the color signal from the media. It will shift as your video plays and the color in the frame changes. The vectorscope on this page shows the color levels for the footage of the truck in Figure 13.21. Most footage will hover around the center of the vectorscope—it would take a lot of color manipulation to push it beyond the suggested saturation limits.

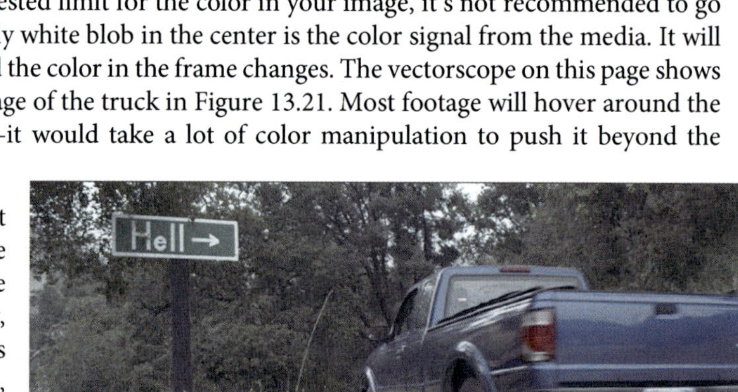

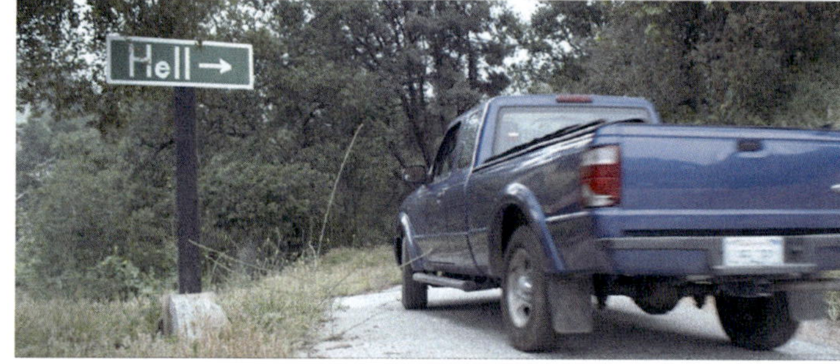

Figure 13.21

Almost all video can do with a little saturation boost. In this comparison, increasing the overall saturation pushes the color further into the blue and yellow areas. Red is boosted too, as you can see in the brake light and also in Figure 13.20, but there's just not much red in this image.

You might also notice that the vectorscope in Figure 13.20 shows a heavy balance towards blue and yellow, with a spike of red. That's basically the truck (blue), the landscape (yellow), and the brake light (red). Why is the landscape yellow and not green? The true shades of the colors in a light-based, additive system, like digital video color, are not identical to the shades of the primary colors in a subtractive system, like paints or crayons. In an additive system, blue is almost violet, rather than a bright "true" blue and you can see in the vectorscope that the colors are not evenly spaced around the circle as a result. The opposite of blue is yellow and it's found directly across the circle. Because the blue is closer to violet, the yellow must be closer to green, so it's actually a greenish-yellow. Add to that the dry desert tones of a California landscape and you have a "green" that is enhanced by boosting the yellows.

As you adjust saturation, it can be tempting to park your playhead on an exemplary frame and shift the color while your video is paused, but to see if it's really working you have to watch the footage in motion. The fact is that increasing saturation can result in compression artifacts such as posterization or banding. These problems are much more noticeable when video is playing compared to static shots. If your footage is dark, you might find that you can really push the saturation and it's also easier to push the color in shots like this one of the truck, where you don't have to worry about skin tones.

☑ Try Stacking Effects

You can apply more than one Lumetri Color effect to your media simply by dragging it onto your shot multiple times. Sometimes it helps to split out different color grading tasks to separate instances of the Lumetri Color effect—say one for getting the luminance right, one for overall color, and another for dialing in special effects. It also makes it easier if you want to reset part of your color work and start over without removing the other elements that you're happy with. The latest version of Premiere lets you add as many Lumetri Color effects as you like, so take advantage.

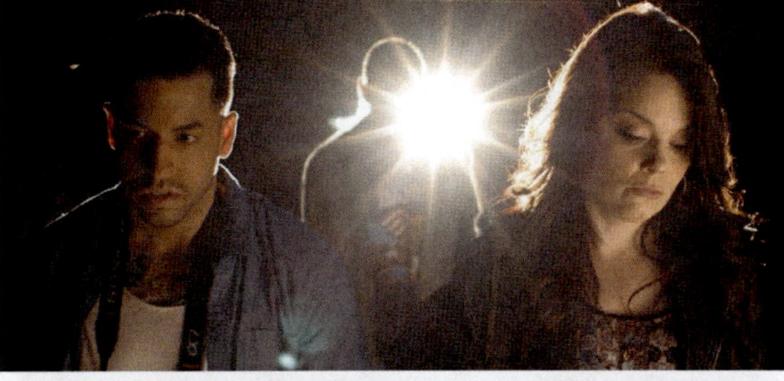

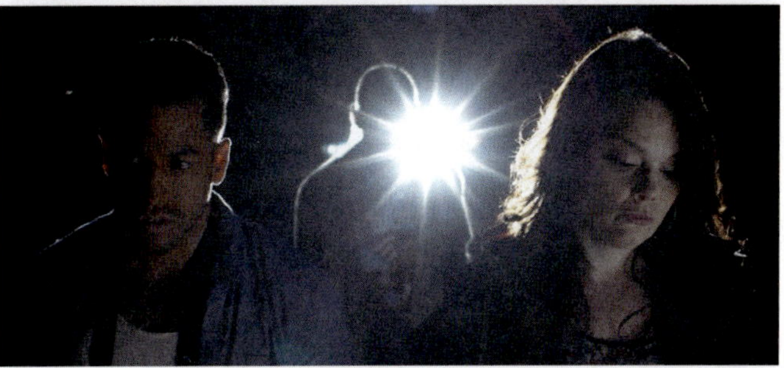

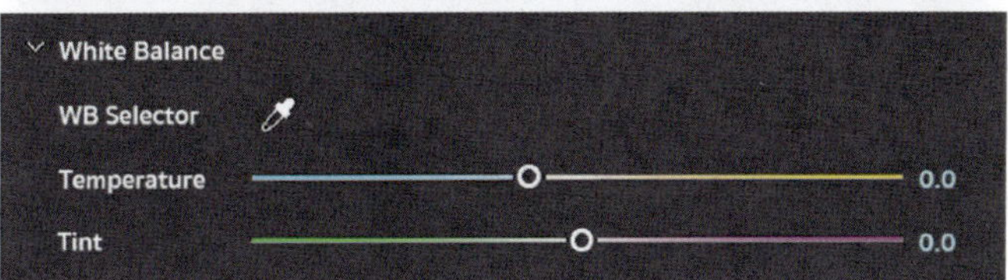

Figure 13.22

By simply dragging the Temperature slider in the Basic Correction area of the Lumetri Scopes panel towards the blue end, we were able to create a more dramatic nighttime look for this shot.

Adjust the Overall Color Balance

There's one last overall element to adjust—the balance of color. Did you shoot at noon but want it to look like sunset? Or maybe someone forgot to set the white balance on the camera and everything looks blue. Whatever the reason, this is usually a quick fix. Use the temperature slider in Basic Correction to shift the color temperature along the blue to orange spectrum that comprises daylight (Figure 13.22). If you want to adjust colors along the green to magenta spectrum, use the Tint slider. As always, a little goes a long way with color.

? What About White Balance and Exposure?

Premiere has an automated tool to help you adjust exposure and correct for bad white balance, the WB Selector eyedropper in the Basic Correction area of the Lumetri Color panel (Figure 13.22). Simply activate it and select a white area in your frame (hold Control/Command to draw a sample from a 5-pixel area). But the truth is you probably won't need it. Getting the blacks, whites, and midtones right in terms of luminance should fix any issues with exposure and by adjusting temperature and tint, you'll have corrected the white balance.

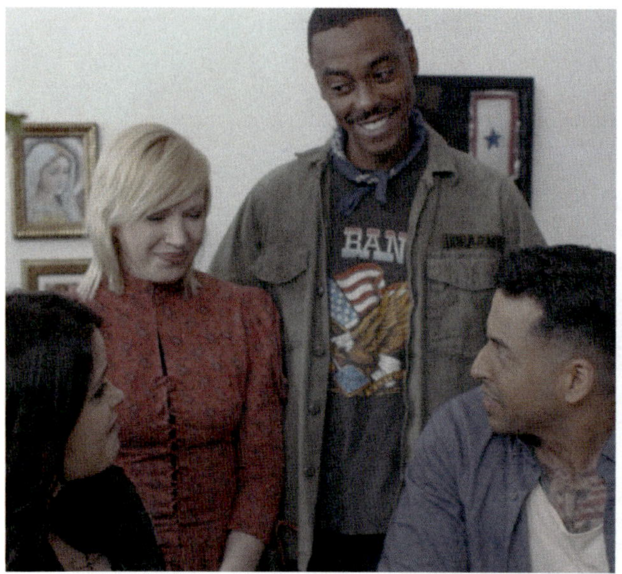

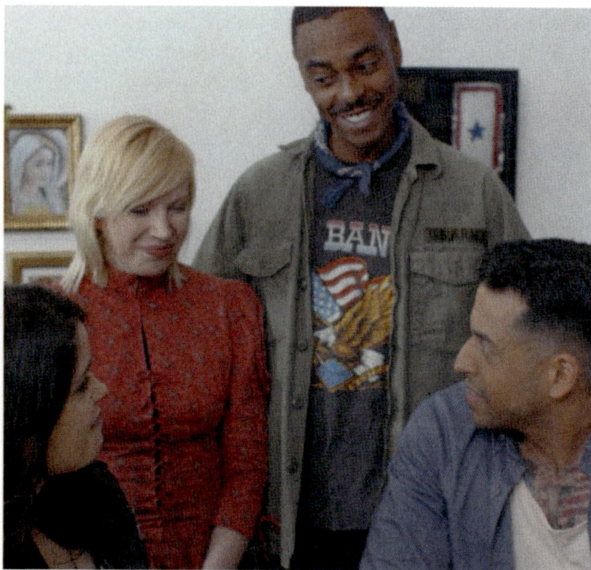

Figure 13.23

Everyone looks good with a red-yellow boost.

Getting Skin Tones Right

We mentioned it earlier, but humans are the subject of most films and so one of the main goals of color grading is to make humans look, well, human. All skin tones, however light or dark, fall somewhere in the area between red and yellow in the color spectrum. In fact, every vectorscope has a diagonal line between red and yellow known as the Flesh Tone Line or FTL for short (Figure 13.20). Of course there are going to be plenty of other colors in your image, but to get skin to look naturalistic, you'll need a healthy amount of saturation along the FTL (Figure 13.23). If you've worked your way through all the adjustments listed above and your actors still look wan, you're going to need to dive deeper into color. You can use the Basic Correction sliders or Color Wheels to adjust skin tones, but there are two major areas of the Lumetri Color panel that we have yet to explore—Curves and HSL Secondary—that are great tools for adjusting very specific colors.

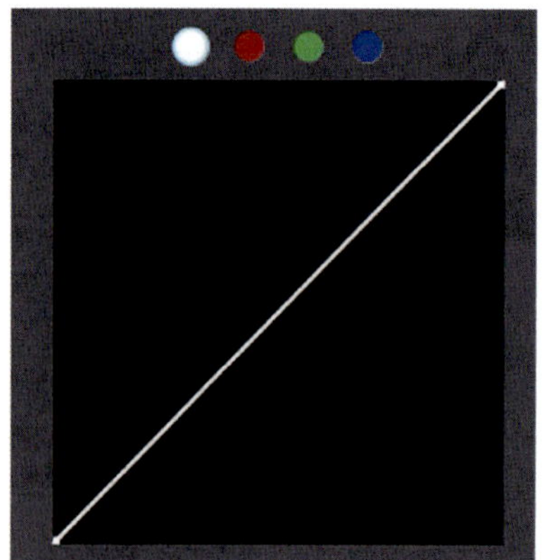

Figure 13.24

(Lower left image) The Curves section of the Lumetri Color panel. Each curve starts out as a straight line.

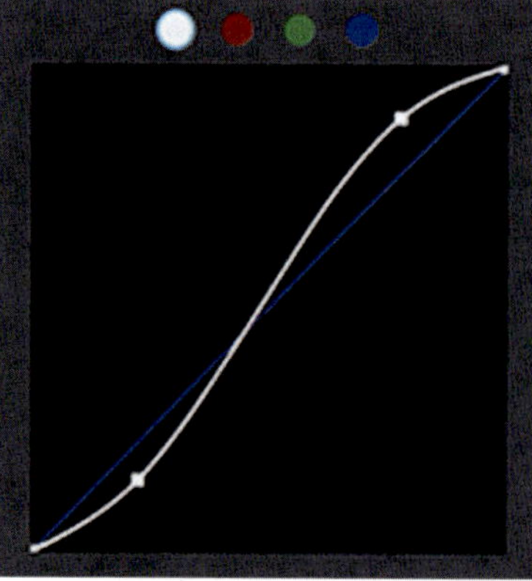

Figure 13.25

(Lower right image) Added anchor points yield an S-curve.

Working with Curves

One of the more advanced methods for adjusting color is the RGB Curves tool found in the Curves section of the Lumetri Color panel (Figure 13.24). You can use curves to do everything we've described so far in terms of color grading. The RGB Curves tool is an intensity graph that starts out with color values mapped to a straight line. You can choose between four values to adjust: luma (white) and each of the three RGB channels (red, green, and blue).

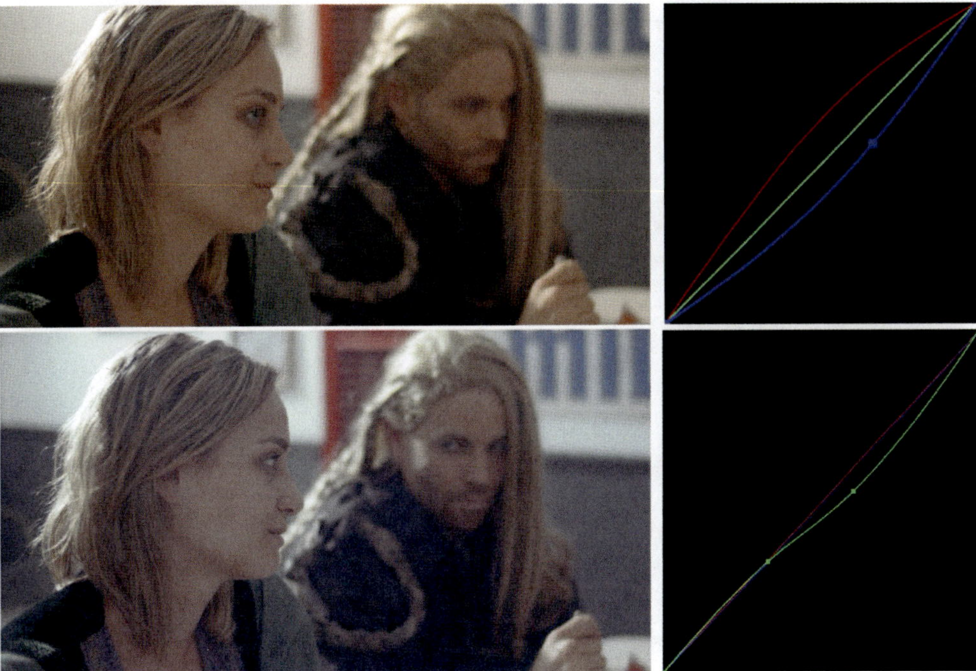

Figure 13.26

Increasing the red midtones and diminishing the blues results in more saturated skin tones (top). But wait, they're zombies! Do they really need that healthy red-yellow glow? Usually the green channel isn't that useful for skin tones but in this case a nice magenta cast balances the greens of her jacket without destroying the reds, whites, and blues of the background and keeps their sickly pallor intact (bottom).

The upper right corner is the most intense value, in the case of luma it's white, and the lower left corner is the least intense value, or black. By changing the line into a curve, you can adjust the values in a very customized way. To create a curve, click on any point on the line (the cursor will switch to the Pen tool) and you'll see an anchor point added. Drag the anchor away from the diagonal line to create a curve. S-curves are a classic technique to create a higher-contrast image (Figure 13.25). Simply add two anchors, one in the bright area and another in the dark area and drag them in opposite directions. You can also adjust the upper and lower end points of the line, which is an alternate way of setting black and white levels. You can add as many anchor points as you wish, which means you can create a very specific curve that's exactly suited to your needs.

By now you may have noticed that changes in color are relative—darken the shadows and you'll pull down the highlights as well, shift the color temperature towards orange and the blues will diminish, shift the tint towards magenta and the greens will fade. Nowhere is this more apparent than when using the RGB Curves.

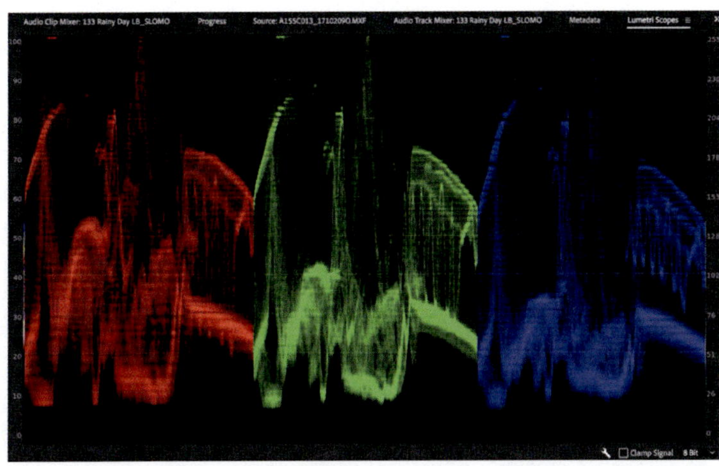

Figure 13.27

RGB Parade view shows a waveform of each of the three-color channels in an RGB video file. This view in the Lumetri Scopes works hand-in-hand with the RGB Curves tool in the Lumetri Color panel. Shown here is the RGB Parade view of the upper image in Figure 13.26.

To manipulate skin tones, you'll need to adjust individual colors in the RGB curves. There are only three colors available to change but each color also affects its opposite, or complementary, color. That means the blue channel also controls yellow, the green controls magenta, and the red controls cyan. In the luma curve the values that shift are from bright to dark. In the separate RGB curves, the values that shift are from saturated (top) to desaturated (bottom) and from primary color (left) to complementary color (right). So an S-curve identical to the one in Figure 13.25 but situated in the blue channel would result in yellow shadows and blue highlights. To increase saturation in the red-yellow Flesh Tone Line, you'll need to increase the saturation of the red channel in the midtones (literally, the middle of the diagonal line) and decrease saturation of the blue midtones, thereby increasing the saturation of the yellow midtones. Your curves might look like the ones in the top of Figure 13.26.

As you work with RGB Curves, you should be looking at the RGB Parade view in the Lumetri Scopes panel (Figure 13.27). Here you'll see each of the three color channels represented as a waveform, which are exactly the same as the luminance waveform we talked about earlier. You'll be able to see the intensity of each color on the same 0 to 100 scale on the left and 0 to 256 scale on the right (if you're working with 8-bit color). Once again, you'll want to make sure nothing goes above 100 or below 0. And of course, looking at a vectorscope is also a good idea.

RGB Curves take a little getting used to and a light touch really helps—it's rare that the curves stray far from the diagonal line. Remember that hardware controller we showed you earlier, in Figure 13.10? That's a tool that really comes in handy if you're working with curves. Why? Because the smallest adjustment can turn your whole image red, and who wants that? In theory, I love what RGB curves do, in practice I only use them rarely. They make me feel like a Prius driver in a Ferrari due in a large part to the fact that I don't have the special hardware. I wish that Adobe and other software purveyors would offer a "subtle adjustment" mode for curves and color wheels alike. I also don't like the fact that there's no reset button on the curves. Once they go wrong, adding more anchor points often just makes a mess—I'd like the ability to set them back to a straight line without have to reset the entire Lumetri Color effect.

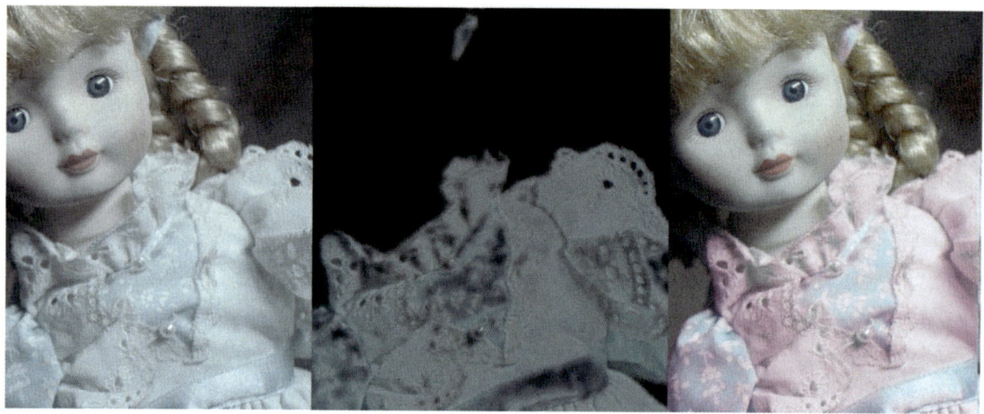

Figure 13.28

Secondary color mattes let you isolate a range of colors and grade them separately. In this case, we were able to easy pull a matte (center) from the white dress of the scary doll and change the color to pink.

Secondary Color Mattes

Another advanced tool is Secondary Color masking, which is found in the HSL Secondary section of the Lumetri Color panel. If your image has areas that you can isolate based on color, you can use this tool to create a mask and make color adjustments that are constrained to the area limited by the mask. For example, if you wanted to recreate the famous *Schindler's List* effect of the girl in the red coat against the monochrome backdrop, this would be one way to do that. Bar none, this is the coolest color grading tool in Premiere in my opinion. It lets you do things like make the color cast of a scene green or blue but keep the skin tones intact or completely change the color of a prop (Figure 13.28). By the way, don't let the name confuse you—secondary refers to a second color grade, not secondary (complementary) colors.

To create a mask, use the eyedropper tool on the left and select the color in your image that you want to change (Figure 13.29). The eyedropper will select the color of a single pixel, which is usually not going to be representative of your color choice, so hold the Command/Control key to get a selection based on five pixels. After you've selected a color, the HSL (Hue, Saturation, and Lightness) sliders will change to show a range of values based on your selection. You can also select one of the colored dots above the HSL sliders if you want to constrain your selection within a certain range of hues—only blues, for example. You can adjust the range of each value by dragging the ends of it. The triangles at the end of each range shift the ramp that softens the edges of your selection. You can also drag these to make them shorter (more abrupt) or longer (softer). Of course the key here is finding a color in your image that you can isolate. It would be nice if you could also see a swatch of the color you picked, but alas you'll have to go by the HSL values.

After you've selected a color, check the box next to the unintuitively named Color/Grey menu. This will show your mask, like in the center of Figure 13.28. You can choose between a grey or black background against the color of the image, or a black and white mask. You can also invert the mask if needed, by clicking the button to the right of the menu. Depending on the contents of your image, you'll find that one of these mask views will make it easier to see your work. Next, use the Refine sliders to clean up the matte by removing noise (spots) and blurring the edges. Once you have a good matte, you can use tools in the Correction area to grade the color for just the matted part of your image. In the scary doll, we boosted saturation and shifted the tint and temperature to the warmer areas to turn the dress pink. If the sliders aren't enough, you can use the overall color wheel or switch to the three-way color wheels.

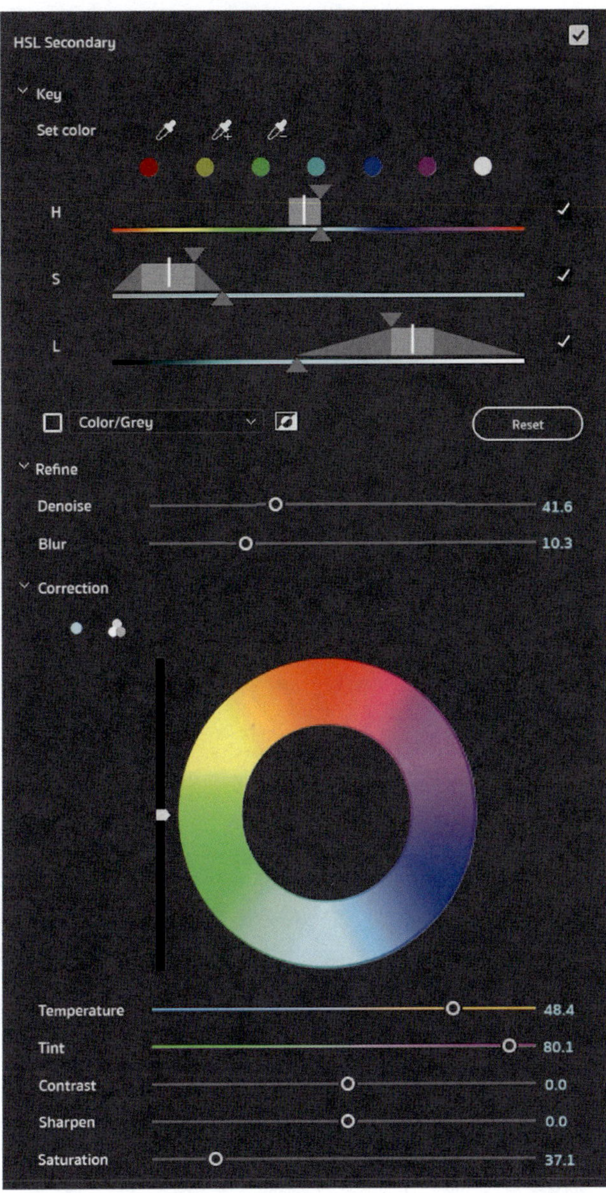

Figure 13.29

The HSL Secondary area of the Lumetri Scopes panel lets you pull a matte based on selected colors and perform a second color grade on just the matted part of your shot.

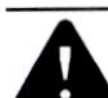 Lumetri Color Works From the Top Down

The order from top to bottom of the Lumetri Color panel is the order in which each adjustment is applied. That means LUTs come first, then Basic Correction, then Creative/Looks, then Curves, then Color Wheels & Match, then HSL Secondary, and finally, Vignette. Knowing this is important because it means you should work from top to bottom. So for example, if you tint your image green in Basic Correction, you won't be able to select the original red tones for your secondary color matte. For this reason, you might find that in addition to working from top to bottom, you may also want to stack multiple versions of the Lumetri Color Effect on your clip, as suggested earlier, or even treat multiple copies of your clip and composite them together after you've finished the color. That said, there's a lot of duplicity between the sections of the Lumetri Color panel and you aren't likely to need all of them.

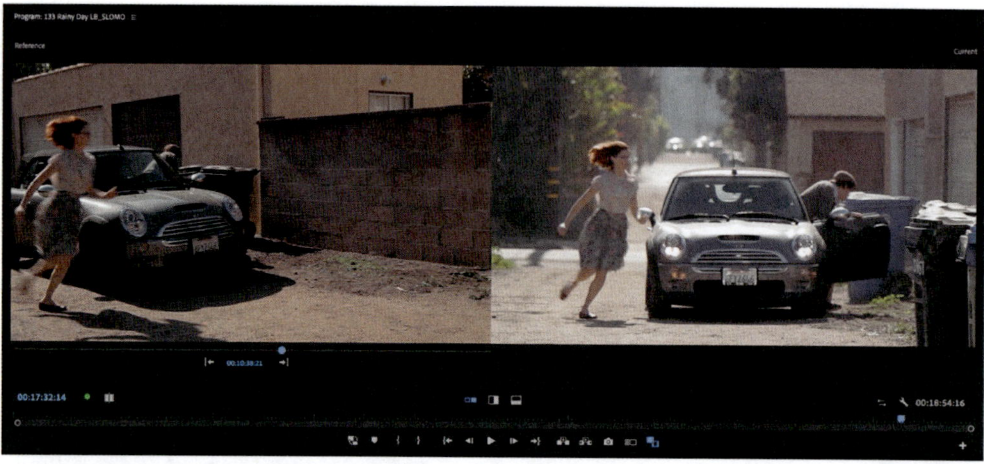

Figure 13.30

The camera angle on the left, shown here in shot Comparison View, has a very different look than the camera on the right.

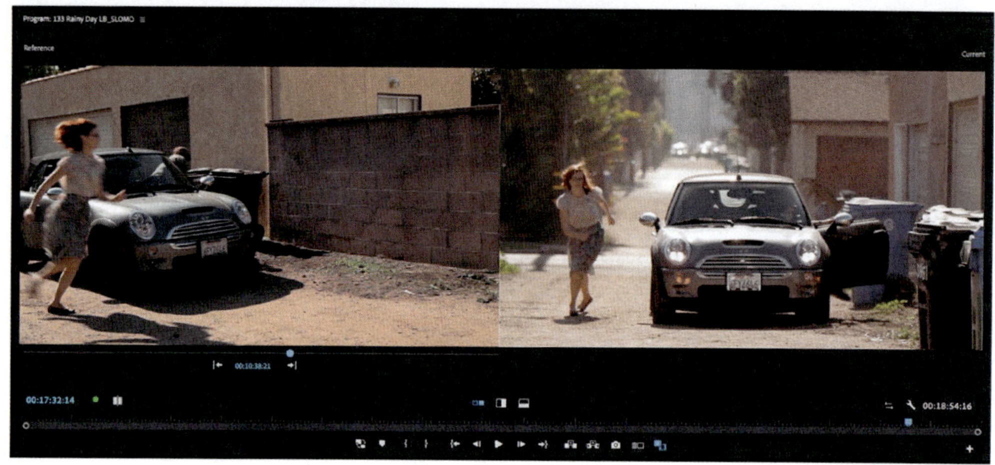

Figure 13.31

The automated Apply Match feature, found in the Color Wheels & Match area of the Lumetri Color panel, did a pretty good job matching these two camera angles.

Matching Shots

One of the more prosaic color grading tasks is matching footage that was shot with different cameras, on different days, or under different lighting conditions (Figures 13.30 and 13.31). Premiere offers automated color matching, found in the Color Wheels & Match area of the Lumetri Color panel (Figure 13.32). Here you'll find two buttons, Comparison View and Apply Match. Comparison View opens in the Program monitor when you select the button and the view will automatically be set to Shot comparison. (We covered Frame comparison earlier in this chapter.) In Shot Comparison View, you'll see the shot you're working on to the right and a reference shot to the left. The reference shot has a time ruler under it and you can use it to drag through your entire sequence until you find the shot you want to match. Once you've got the shots lined up, just hit the Apply Match button and an automated match will be applied. (Be aware that Apply Match will reset any Lumetri Color Effect settings you added to the shot previously.) You'll see the sliders and color wheels change, in the lower portion of the Color Wheels & Match area of the Lumetri Control panel (Figure 13.32). To use the color wheels, you should

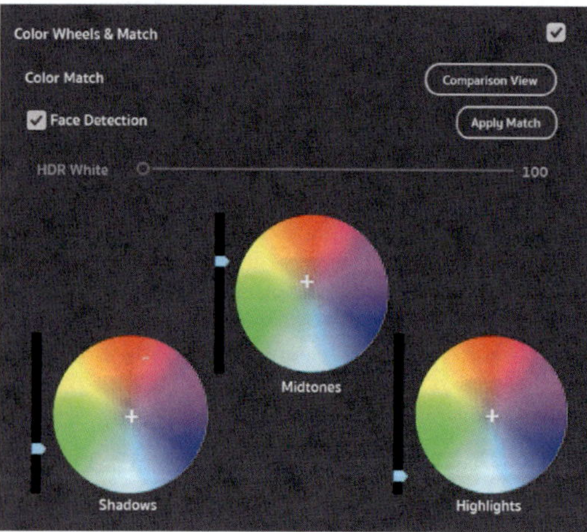

Figure 13.32

The Color Wheels & Match area of the Lumetri Control panel, showing here the results of the automated color matching applied to the shots above.

know that the center of each color wheel is neutral, so when you want to shift the color cast of any of three wheels, just click on that color area away from the center with your mouse. As usual, you don't have to shift the center much to see results. Also, when color wheels are untouched, they have a hollow center (Figure 13.18) and after they've been adjusted they appear filled in with a plus sign that indicates where you've targeted the color cast. In Figure 13.32 you can see the adjustments made by the automated color match—they're quite subtle and remain close to the center but the sliders to the left of each color wheel, which control luminance, have been adjusted more dramatically. If you think the automated match is not quite perfect, you can use any of the tools described in this chapter to improve it. One last thing, there's a checkbox for Face Detection in the auto match settings—this will prioritize matching skin tones. If there aren't any people in your shot, you can turn it off.

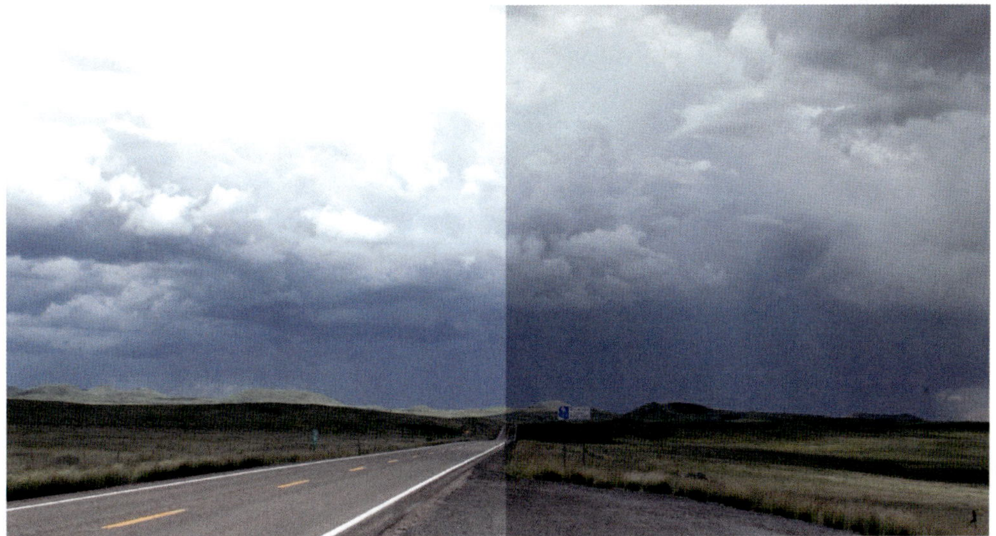

Figure 13.33

HDR video (right) gives you a much larger range from black to white compared to standard video (left). The biggest differences are seen in the bright whites, such as the sky shown here, and the shadows.

HDR Color

If you've been making films, you're probably used to seeing blown out skies in your daytime footage and night shots where the stars and clouds disappear in darkness (Figure 13.33). Most cameras cannot capture the large dynamic range that the human eye can see. Enter High Dynamic Range video, or HDR, which has many more shades of grey between white and black than regular video and also a larger number of colors. At present, HDR video has not been widely adopted in filmmaking, in part because audiences need HDR monitors in order to view it. But there are a number of cameras that can shoot HDR video so it's growing in popularity. Premiere offers some tools within the Lumetri Color effect to work with it.

The first step in color grading HDR video is to activate High Dynamic Range from the Lumetri Color panel menu on the tab—this opens up access to the HDR tools. What changes? HDR video ranges from 0 (black) to 10,000 (white) measured in nits (a digital upgrade to IRE that is roughly equivalent, 100 nits are the same as 100 IRE)—that's a big difference from the standard dynamic range of 0 to 100 IRE—and the color depth is 10-bit. You'll need to select HDR from the menu at the bottom right corner of the Lumetri Scopes and change the color space to 2020 in the Settings (wrench) menu. You'll see the scales on the sides of the Waveform change and the circle of acceptable color saturation will be larger in the Vectorscope. You'll also need a hardware HDR monitor to properly view your work as you color grade.

In the Lumetri Color panel, you'll now find added controls in Basic Correction—an HDR White slider and an HDR Specular slider. You'll also get a fourth color wheel, HDR Specular, added to Color Wheels & Match and a slider for HDR Range added to the Curves. What does all this do? It accounts for the massively increased range from black to white. The HDR White and the HDR Range sliders allow you to define the value of white—just because it can be set at 10000 doesn't mean you'll need that value. And the HDR Specular controls are kind of like highlights over your highlights—since you have so many more values between standard dynamic range white and HDR white, you get another slider and color wheel to adjust them.

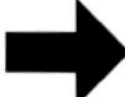

More Color Grading Techniques

More detailed information on to how to use waveforms and vectorscopes are found in *The Digital Filmmaking Handbook*, Chapter 16 Color Grading, and also more examples for fixing problems like bad white balance, mismatched time of day, and overexposure.

Save Custom LUT Presets

Once you have the colors set for a scene, it's a good idea to save them as a preset so that you can easily reuse them as needed. In addition to saving a standard effects preset, you can export your color settings as a custom LUT or Look. Use the menu on the tab at the top of the Lumetri Color panel (not the Lumetri Color menu—confusing, I know) and choose Export .look. An alternate format for LUTs, Export .cube, is also available from this menu.

What About Vignettes?

The last section of the Lumetri Color panel is dedicated to a special type of masking known as vignetting. Certain lenses create dark shadows around the edge of the frame and sometimes this effect is desirable and gets recreated in post. Vignettes serve to draw the eye away from the edge of the frame. As you can see in Figure 13.34, the normal image looks pretty good but with a vignette added (bottom) the eye is focused on the woman in the nun's habit near the center. And thanks to the darkness of the shot, the vignette feels quite natural and subtle—you could easily be convinced the shot was actually lit this way. Unfortunately, at the time of this writing, the Vignette area of the Lumetri Color panel is very limited—it can only create a vignette that is centered in the frame. To create an off-center vignette, you'll have to use any of a variety of masking techniques.

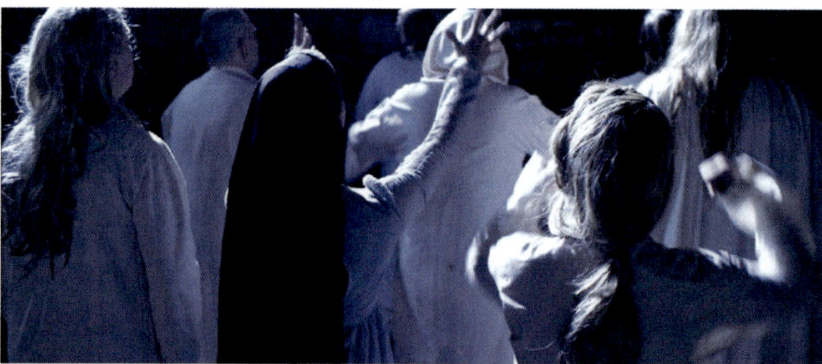

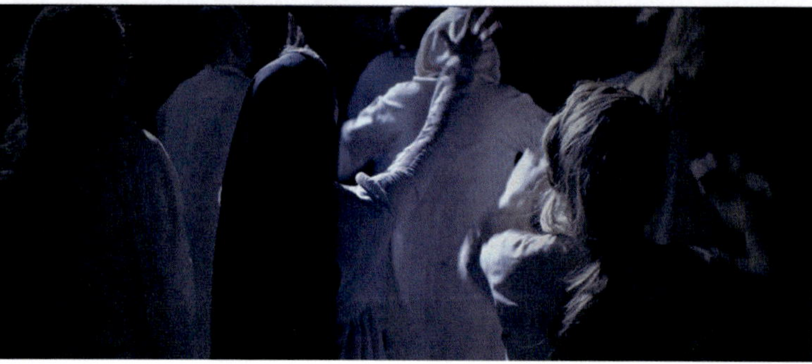

Figure 13.34

Vignetting is a popular technique for drawing the eye to the center of the frame. Shown here, the dramatic lighting in the original shot (top) is enhanced by a subtle, dark vignette (bottom).

TUTORIAL: Creative Color for Horror

Remember the guy in the stockades from *Hell CA*? Well he's not alone in there. In this tutorial, we're going to color grade another shot from the same scene, featuring two other actors (Figure 13.35). This scene is meant to be scary and we really want to make it look unique—after all, it's a horror film and there's a lot of room for creative color. We don't need to worry as much about things looking naturalistic, so there's room to have a little fun with it. We've already added a LUT to the footage so that we can jump straight to the good stuff, knowing that we have a decent base of black and white levels and saturation to build on. This footage is h.264 so make sure your color space is set to 709 in the Lumetri Scopes Settings menu (wrench) and that the color is set to 8-bit in the small menu next to the Settings. Grab the shot called Hell_CA_color.mp4 from the Hell CA Media folder and import it into a new Premiere project.

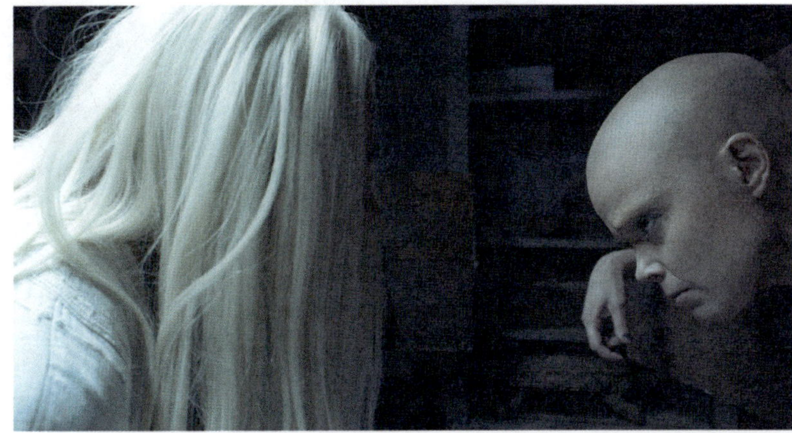

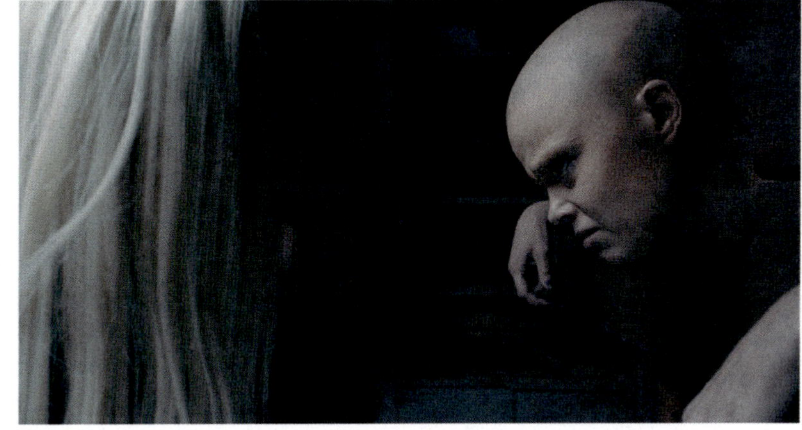

Figure 13.35

In this tutorial, we'll work on color grading this shot from *Hell CA* (top). It already has a basic technical LUT applied, so our job is to make it work for the story. By working with a secondary color mask, we'll show you how to adjust the color of the background separately from the color of the actor's face (bottom).

STEP 1: Adjust the Color Temperature

Keeping in mind that Premiere will apply the effects at the top of the Lumetri Color panel first and work its way down, we're gonna do the same thing and start at the top. There's already a LUT on it so we'll skip that but the clip has a greenish cast, so we're gonna use the White Balance sliders to make the skin tones better.

If you want to use Comparison View as you work, which I highly recommend, activate it now. Comparison View stores the reference frame as the clip appears at launch, so if you want to see your untouched footage as a reference, you'll need to activate Comparison View before you make any changes. Select Shot comparison and either Horizontal Split or Side by Side view. Horizontal split gives you a pretty good indication of how your color changes will affect both actors and doesn't take up too much screen space but Side by Side view gives you a clear waveform of both images in the Lumetri Scopes. If Comparison View is too fussy, you can just use Match Frame (M) to bring up the raw video in the Source monitor.

Move the Temperature slider towards the orange end until the bald woman looks better. She's one of the good guys, so there's no value in making her look like the undead. The guy's white hair looks like he's been swimming chlorine, so let's make it more neutral. Move the Tint slider a little way towards magenta. I ended up with 28 orange and 17 magenta—you can type these

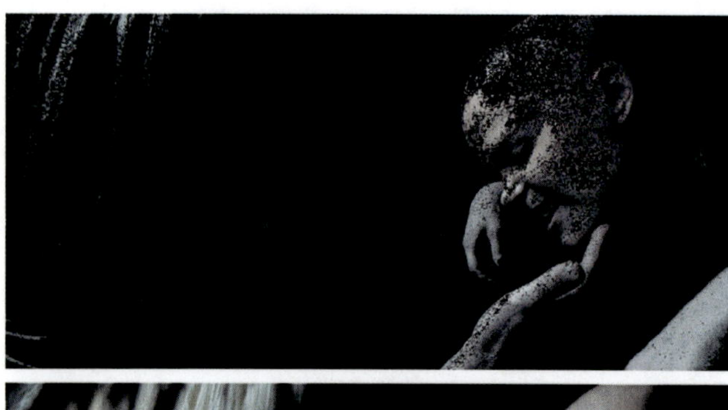

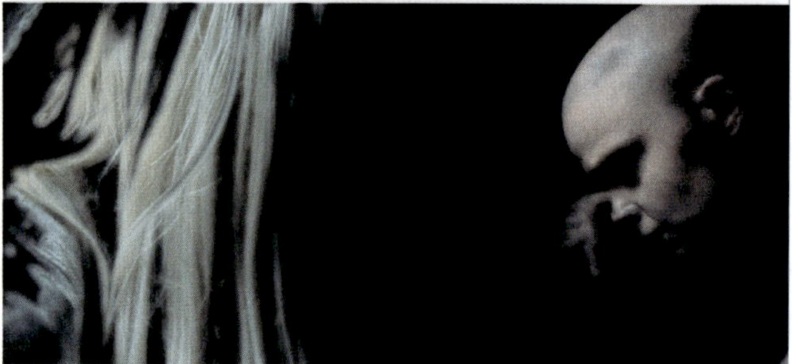

numbers in, by the way. Now we have a nice healthy, neutral shot—perhaps a bit too normal for our film though.

STEP 2: Separate the Actor from the Background

One of the most popular color looks that you see in films all the time—especially dramatic films—is orange highlights with cyan shadows. There's a good reason for this. We already know that skin tones are enhanced by a boost along the red-yellow Flesh Tone Line and what is red-yellow? Orange, of course. And so any color opposite orange is likely to provide a nice contrast to the skin tones of the actors—that can be any color from dark green to violet but cyan is very effective. The result is a color cast that enhances skin tones but keeps the environment dramatic and perhaps even unfriendly. And that's exactly what we want for this shot.

Figure 13.36

Create a mask of the actor's face using the HSL Secondary area of the Lumetri Color panel. By using the eyedropper, you can select the colors for the mask (top), then use the Denoise and Blur sliders to smooth the edges of the mask (bottom).

We'll use HSL Secondary to make a mask of the woman's face because that's the main area that we want to stay in the orange part of the color spectrum. Use the eyedropper on the left to select part of her face that's well lit—the forehead or cheek bone. Check the box next to Color/Gray and select Color/Black from the Mask View Options menu. Now you can see how much of her face has been masked out (Figure 13.36). Use the eyedropper with the plus sign to add more colors to the mask and the eyedropper with the minus sign to remove colors until you feel like her face and head looks pretty good in the mask. The guy's white hair is going to end up in it as well, but that's okay. Play around with the Denoise and Blur sliders to smooth out your mask.

STEP 3: Color the Shadows

Now for the tricky part. We don't want to change her face, it's already safely in the orange flesh tone range. What we want to do is shift the color of the shadows towards the blue-green spectrum. So we're gonna invert the mask so that our color changes are applied to the background. Click on the Invert Mask button next to the Mask View Options menu—when it's blue it's inverted—this will switch the mask from the actor's face to the background (Figure 13.37). Next, use the controls in the Correction section in the lower half of the HSL Secondary area to change the colors.

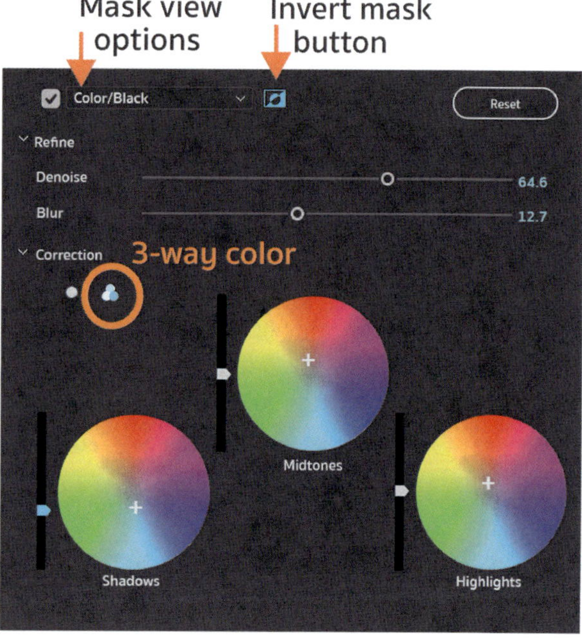

Figure 13.37

Control how you view your mask as you work using the Mask View Options. In Figure 13.36, it's set to Color/Black which means you'll see the selected portion of the mask in full color against a black background. Use the invert mask buttons to toggle the mask from the actor's face to the black background. Then use the 3-way color wheels to adjust the colors and brightness for the background.

Select the three-dot icon to switch to three-way color wheels and click in the cyan area of the Shadows color wheel. You'll have to stay pretty close to the center or else your whole image will turn blue. I also darkened the shadows by lowering the slider next to the Shadows color wheel. Then to compensate, I increased the Highlights slider and shifted the color of both the Highlights and the Midtones along the Flesh Tone Line. There's no FTL in the color wheels but it falls on the same diagonal as in the vectorscope. If you want to see our version, it's called Hell_CA_color_graded.mp4 in the Hell CA cuts folder.

☑ Go Crazy With Color (For Now)

It's rare that you have to make major color adjustments for film media—usually it's just a process of setting the luminance values, the saturation, and maybe a little tonal shift to adjust time of day or white balance. So go ahead and play around with all the color bells and whistles in the Lumetri Control panel. Get it out of your system and at the same time, get to know the tools as hand.

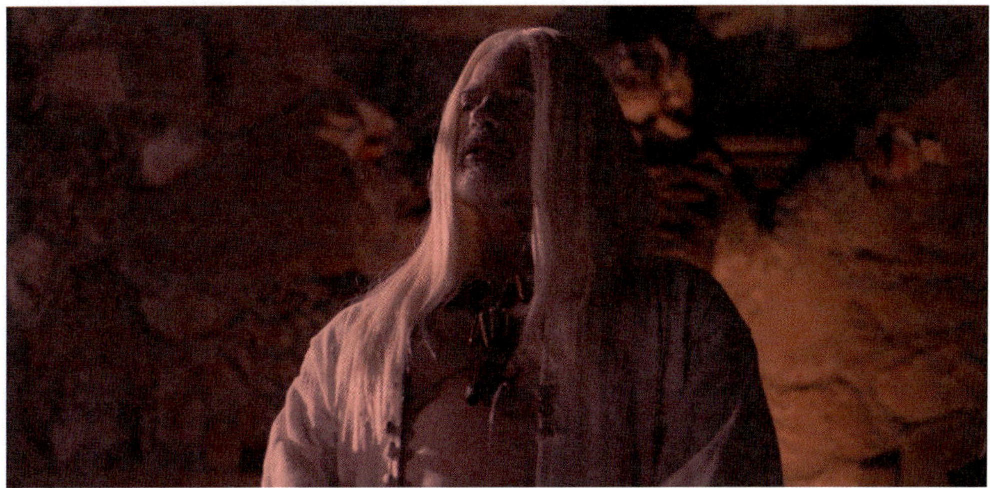

Figure 13.38

Although technically not a color effect, using Opacity blending modes can result in big changes in color. Shown here, a red overlay layer was blended with video using Multiply. You can see in the area to the right of the figure that it's not just a monochrome image. The yellows of the lighting are coming through.

Other Color Effects

Earlier we said that the Lumetri Color effect is one-stop shopping, and it is for color grading. But there are other color effects, you know, special effects for color.

32-bit effects Some of the effects available in Premiere can work with a bit-depth of 32 per channel—that's trillions of colors. If your source video has a high bit-depth, you'll want to stick with these effects. You can easily identify them by selecting the 32-bit Color button at the top of the Effects panel. To get the best results, you'll want to turn on Maximum Bit Depth rendering in your sequence settings (Sequence > Sequence Settings). As you might suspect, the effects that utilize 32-bit color tend to be color effects.

YUV effects are native to the YUV color space. That means your video doesn't go through the extra step of processing in the RGB color space and converting back to YUV. (Premiere does all this in the background.) So if you have YUV source video and plan to export a YUV final project, stick to the YUV effects whenever possible. They are easily found by selecting the YUV button at the top of the Effects panel.

Stylize effects All the classic color effects—posterize, solarize, mosaic, etc.—are found in the Style subfolder in the Effects panel.

Keying effects often involve color since mattes are traditionally pulled from colors, such as green screen backgrounds. The more color available in your source footage, the better luck you'll have with creating clean mattes.

Blending modes let you choose how layers of video combine together (Figure 13.38). While not specifically a color effect, certain blending modes can really affect color. They're found as an option in the fixed Opacity effect. To use blending modes, you'll need video on two or more tracks. Select the video on the higher track and open the Effect Controls panel. Under Opacity, you'll see a menu for Blend Mode, which is by default set to Normal, or dissolve. Open the menu and you'll see a huge list of alternative blending modes. If you're a Photoshop user, they'll be very familiar to you. To get a quick understanding of how they work, use the Shape tool (found under the Pen tool in the Tools panel) to draw a rectangle that covers the screen and fill it with a bright color like red. Then in Opacity, select some different blending modes to see what happens—try Darken, Lighten, Multiply and Overlay. Use the Opacity slider to shift the intensity of the blend mode and let the original video show through more.

Color for VR projects There are a few color-oriented effects available in the Immersive Video folder that are just for VR media. To get the most out of your 360-degree media, we recommend using plugins, such as Mocha VR from Boris FX.

What to Watch: *Annihilation*

The beautiful, pastel-colored shimmer in Alex Garland's *Annihilation* is worth checking out if you are interested in color effects that go beyond grading and defy stereotypes.

Colorful Problems to Solve

As you work on the color for your movie, it's important to keep in mind your final goals, after all, color is one of the last steps in a traditional post-production workflow. Here are some things to consider:

Will your film get projected? Projectors can emit a brighter range of lights and darks than monitors, and it's important to make sure that plenty of light comes through so films that will get theatrically released often push the brightness.

How much does your audience care about high image quality? Big budget costume drama and Marvel movie fans care a lot about image quality—the visuals are a huge element of what's fun about those films—and they're likely to watch the film in theaters or own high-end home video equipment to make sure they can see them at their best. If your audience is more likely to stream via YouTube over a mobile phone, you might not need HDR or uncompressed color.

14

Finishing

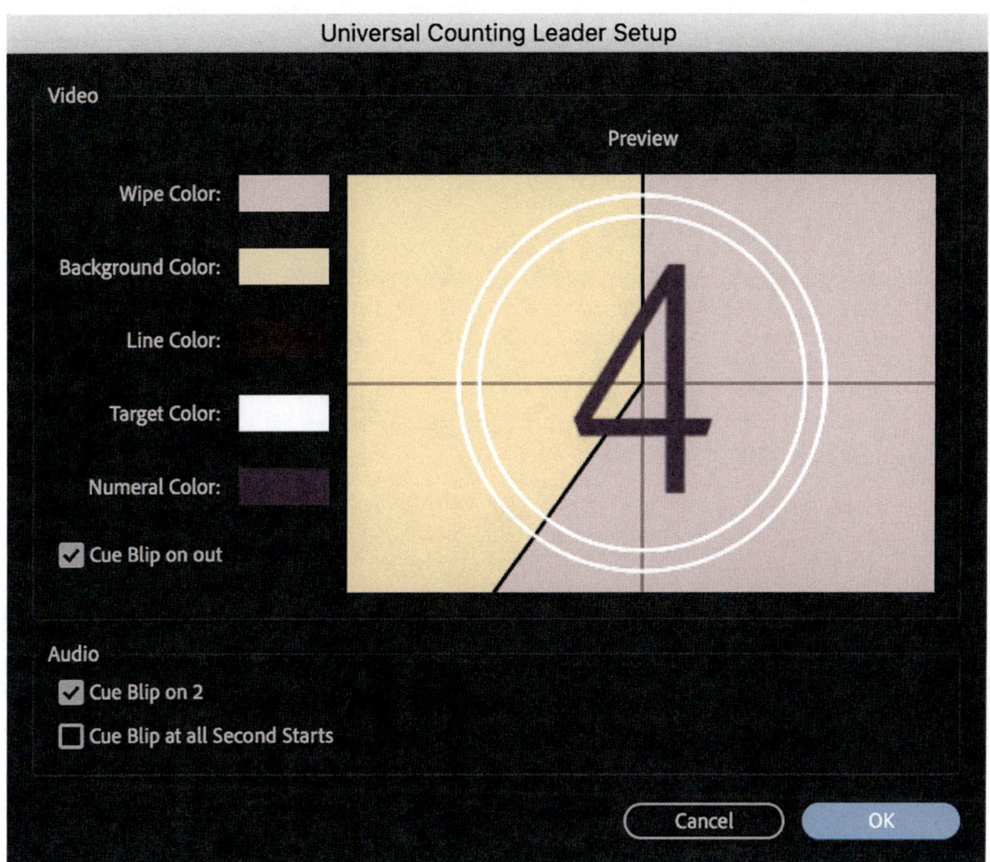

Figure 14.1

Universal countdown leader is used in post for feature films. Premiere lets you pick custom colors—who knew?

How Will You Show Your Film?

FINALLY, YOU'RE READY TO EXPORT YOUR FILM. And no matter how big or small your movie is, you'll have to consider these possibilities:

> **Theatrical** The dream for most filmmakers is to get their film into theaters—projected on the big screen (Figure 14.1). Doing the festival circuit is another form of theatrical screening. For these, you'll need a DCP, which is the file format used to deliver digital files to theaters for projection. DCPs tend to be 2K or 4K, which share the 1.85 aspect ratio. Some festivals will accept easier-to-DIY formats like MOV (QuickTime) and MP4, which tend to be HD (1920 x 1080), with the 1.78 aspect.

Streaming At this point, you can assume that your film will stream and that is the way that most people will see it. Streaming services tend to use UHD and HD formats, which share the 1.78 aspect ratio.

Broadcast and cable If you're lucky enough to sell your film or series to a broadcast or cable network, rest assured that they will provide you with a giant, detailed list of everything they need from you, aka the deliverables. And if that's the case, you'll also have the budget to get some help creating all the master files and mixes they require.

Work-in-progress screenings Not every export is the big finish, you might need to send a copy to a potential collaborator or screen a rough cut for some trusted friends. Work-in-progress exports use the same process as the final finish but obviously you won't go to the same degree of perfectionism to get there. And of course, they are a great learning tool to prepare you for the real finish when you do get to that point.

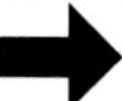

The Big Picture

Chapter 18, Screening and Finishing in *The Digital Filmmaking Handbook* is a must read for understanding the process of finishing a film discussed in this chapter, from locking picture to mixing to color grading to distribution and the film festival circuit, it's all in there.

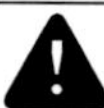

Locking Picture

A locked film means it's complete, the creative part of editing is finished, and the overall timing will not change in any way. All of the processes described in this chapter rely on a film that is locked. Sure, you can always make changes and "unlock" your film, but that tends to create a lot of extra work and confusion. The best practice is to work on the rough cut until it is perfect, then formally lock it, and commit to that locked picture going forward.

Mixing Audio in Premiere

Before you start any export, you'll need an audio mix. Mixing simply means adjusting the way that all of the audio sources in your film play together. Do you want the music to be loud and dominant or to serve as a background element under dialogue? Do you want the dialogue to stand out over all the other sounds, as is common with narration, or do you want it to sound more like the way people speak in real life—lower volume if they are farther away, etc. These are creative decisions and they will vary from one project to another.

While you were editing your film, you were also creating a temp mix—that is, you set the levels for each piece of audio in your movie and made adjustments for different types of audio media. And because all computer systems, headphones, and most video monitors use stereo speakers, you most likely made a stereo temp mix.

For some projects, that's all you'll need. But because there are many pieces to the film distribution food chain, the reality is that most filmmakers create more than one mix.

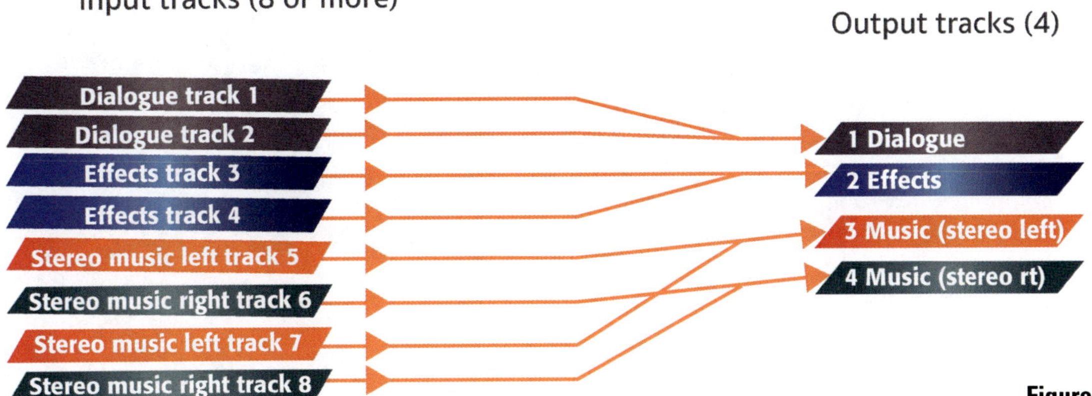

Figure 14.2

A DM&E mix is commonly part of the deliverables list for a film. Primarily it's used to dub films into other languages. It's just one of several types of final mixes that you may need.

Types of Final Mixes

When it comes to playing your film in theaters, offices, houses, or on the web, you'll have to choose between different types of final audio mixes. And in fact, many film projects opt for more than one of these choices.

Stereo mixes are the most common choice. Consisting of two channels of right and left sound, stereo mixes work everywhere. The two channels in a stereo mix are not simply two copies of the same track. Instead, each track is panned slightly left and right to mimic the experience of hearing sound with your ears in the real world. This mostly affects how the music and certain sound effects sound, such as car-bys.

Surround sound If your film is acquired by a distributor, they may require a surround sound mix, especially if your film will play in theaters. Unless the content of your movie has specialized sound design (think *Star Wars*), the addition of surround sound won't change your film much. But if your sound design was built for a surround mix, you'll probably choose to work with a dedicated sound mixer to create a true surround sound environment. In Premiere, surround sound is limited to 5.1 channels.

Split-track mixes are a hack where you take a standard stereo sequence and pan all the music to the right and everything else to the left. (You'll need to organize the audio tracks in your sequence to make this possible.) This means that you and other people on your team can turn the music on and off as needed. This is particularly useful when creating guide exports for composers and sound editors. When creating split-track mixes, you'll use a stereo mix sequence and shift the panners in the Audio Track Mixer.

DM&E Films that get international distribution are required to have a DM&E mix—short for Dialogue, Music, and Effects (Figure 14.2). Each track in a mix like this is known as a stem, because together they add up to the full mix for the movie. DM&E mixes have four channels: one channel of dialogue-only, one channel of effects and ambiences, and two (stereo left and stereo right) channels of music. DM&E mixes allow distributors to turn off the dialogue and replace it with dialogue dubbed in another language. When creating a DM&E mix, you'll use a four-track multichannel sequence.

Mono or single-channel mixes are rarely used today—they are made by mixing all the audio in a film down to a single track.

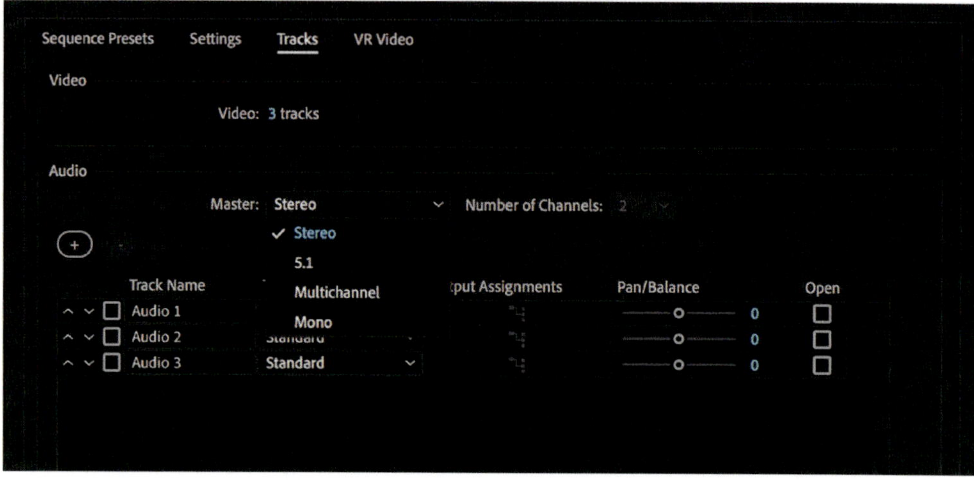

Figure 14.3

A master track configuration, or mix, is assigned to each sequence as you create it in the Tracks tab of the New Sequence window. You have a choice of stereo, surround, multichannel, and mono.

Choosing a Mix in Premiere

What most of us call the mix is referred to as Master Tracks in Premiere. When you create a sequence in Premiere, you can choose between four different master track configurations: stereo, 5.1 surround sound, multichannel, and mono (Figure 14.3). The master track configuration defines how audio is output from Premiere. No matter what the destination is—simply playing through speakers or exporting to a digital file—the master track mix is something you set up in the New Sequence settings. You can have unlimited tracks in a sequence for editing but they ultimately get mixed down, or bussed, to fit the master track configuration you chose when you created your sequence. We've recommended throughout the book to work

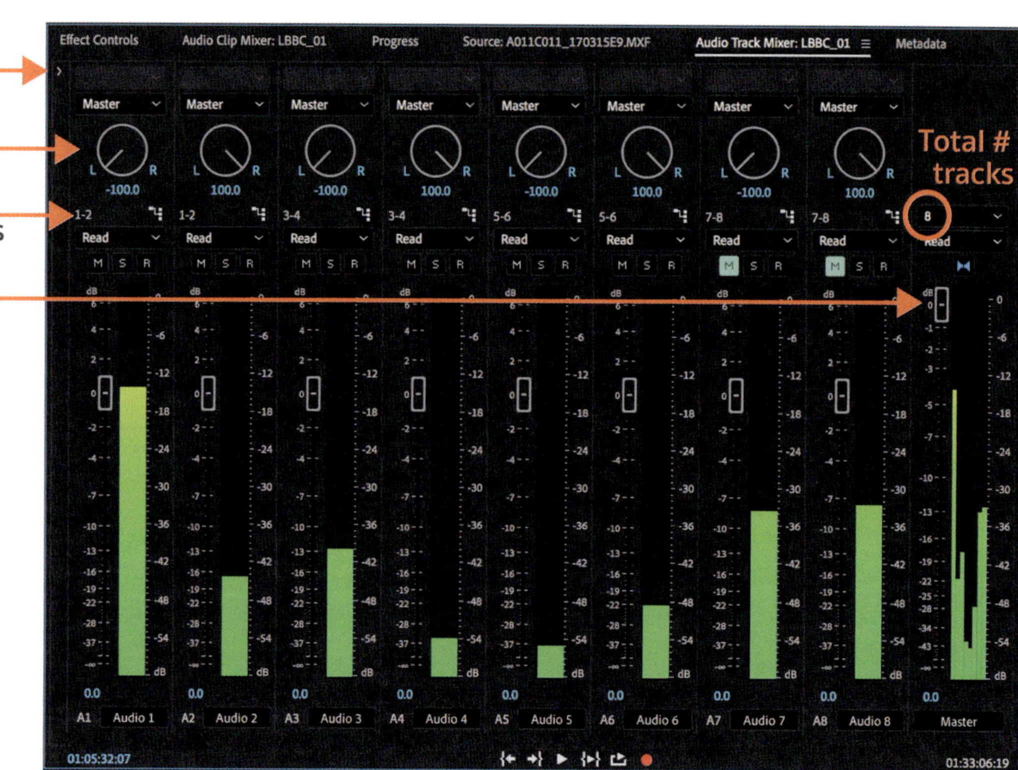

Figure 14.4

The Audio Track Mixer is used for global adjustments across an entire sequence and to create special track arrangements for exports. If you have a lot of tracks, the Audio Track Mixer gets pretty big. You might have to enlarge the panel to see all the tracks, especially the Master track on the far right.

in stereo and in fact, stereo is the default setting for the master track configuration in Premiere. But to create the various types of final mixes we talked about in the previous section, you'll need to create new sequences that have the right master track configuration—master tracks are one of the few sequence settings that you cannot change after the fact. But no worries, it's easy to create a new sequence with the new master track configuration and then use Copy and Paste to copy your film into it.

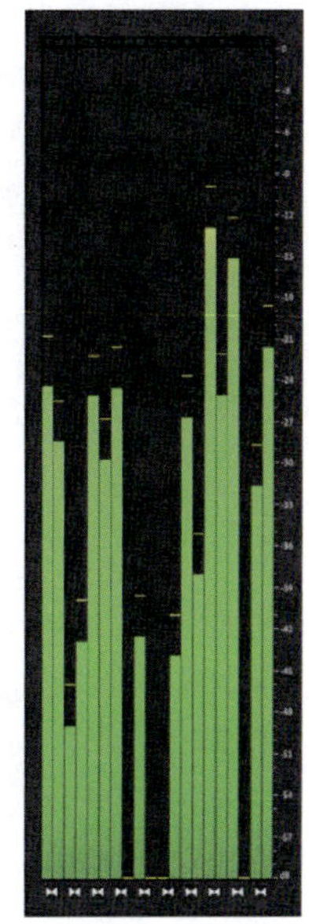

Figure 14.5

The Audio Meters panel changes to reflect the number of output channels assigned to your sequence.

Audio Track Assignments

If you have a lot of audio tracks, you can rely on Premiere to automatically mix them down into your master track configuration or you can use the Audio Track Mixer (Window > Audio Track Mixer) to create sub-mixes by sending each track to the output track of your choice (Figure 14.4). For example, if you have twelve tracks of dialogue, you can send them all to channel 1. Your sequence will look the same in the Timeline but when you output it, the dialogue will be constrained to a single channel, track, or speaker. This would be useful if you are building a multichannel sequence with a four-channel master track configuration in order to create a DM&E mix.

To re-route tracks in Premiere, you'll need a multichannel sequence. Multichannel sequences are the most flexible type of audio track configuration in Premiere but you'll also have to do the most work to set them up in the way that you want. If you've been working with a stereo sequence, you'll need to create a new sequence, setup the Master Tracks configuration as Multichannel, and Copy and Paste your film into it in the Timeline. You can set the panning, re-routing, and number of input and output tracks when you create your new sequence or after the fact in the Audio Track Mixer. Even though you can't change the Master Tracks configuration after the fact, you can change everything else and you'll see your output track choices reflected in the Audio Meters panel (Figure 14.5).

Multichannel sequences default to two-channel output routing, even if they have more than two input channels—you'll see that the Track Output Assignments in the Audio Track Mixer are all set to tracks 1-2. To re-route the tracks, open the Audio Track Mixer (Figure 14.5) and select the Audio Track Assignment button on each track (Figure 14.5) to choose an output track destination in the Track Output Channel Assignments window. Figure 14.6 shows an 8-track multichannel sequence with eight output channels. It's not the best interface because you have to go back to the Audio Track Mixer and select the Audio Track Assignment button for every track. Premiere has an added quirk: to isolate a single channel in the Audio Track Mixer, you'll need to pan the track to the left (-100) for odd-numbered channels and to the right (100) for even-numbered channels. If tracks are panned to the center (0), they'll get mixed across the pair of tracks they are assigned to—track 1 will be sent to both track 1 and 2, as will track 2, etc. It's awkward and unnecessary, but that's the way it is in Premiere at the moment—hopefully they'll change it in future upgrades of the software. To quickly pan all the way in either direction, click on the blue L (left) or R (right) next to the pan knob.

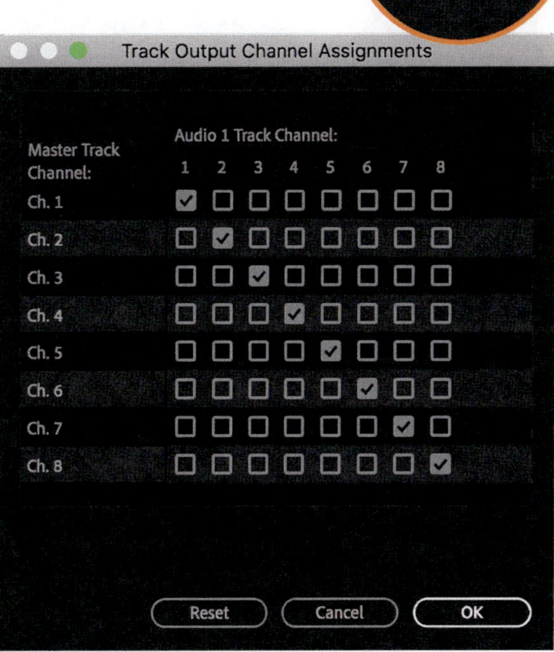

Figure 14.6

This button is found in the Audio Track Mixer and also in the Tracks tab of the New Sequence window. It brings up the Track Output Channel Assignments window, where you designate the audio track assignments for each track.

☑ A Word About Music

Music cues always consist of two stereo tracks. And as recently as a couple years ago, they would take up two tracks in your sequence when editing. But now, they only take up a single track, just like all the other sound in your film. However they still have two tracks, it's just that editing software has gotten smarter in how it handles them in a sequence. That's great because they used to take up a lot screen real estate and a lot of tracks in your sequence as well. That said, you may still need to split them up for exports, like if your sound mixer requests it. If so, you'll select the clip you want to change in the bin, then choose Modify > Audio Channels from the right-click menu. In the Modify Audio Channels window, change the number of clips to 2 and send Clip 1 to the Left and Clip 2 to the right. And unfortunately, you'll have to re-edit that audio back into your sequence—anything that's already in a sequence will not automatically change.

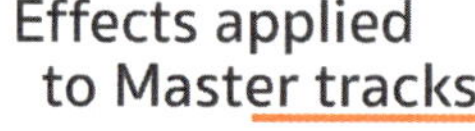

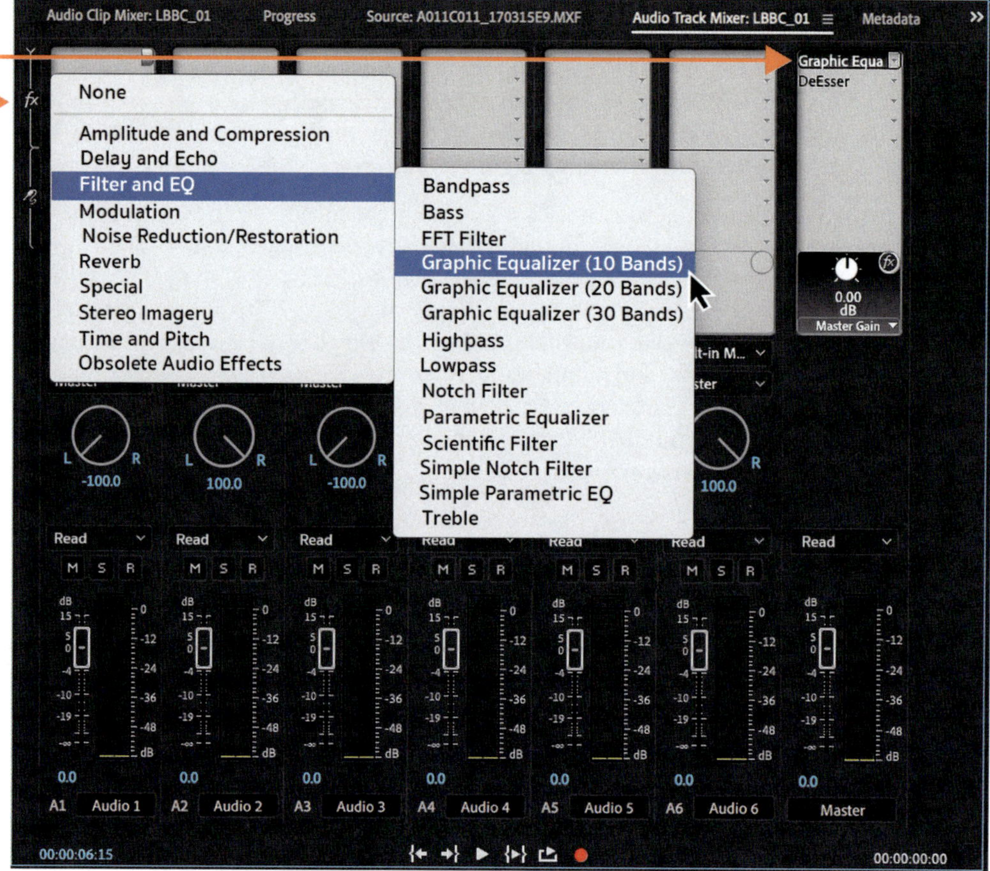

Figure 14.7

You can add effects to an entire track in the Effects Rack of the Audio Track Mixer. When the Effects Rack is open, the FX menu lets you select audio filters to apply to a whole track or all of your tracks together by adding effects to your master tracks.

Global Audio Changes

We went over setting levels on each piece of media in a sequence using the Audio Clip Mixer or in the Timeline with rubber bands and keyframes in Chapter 10. But sometimes as you finalize the sound for your film, you may find that you want to change the levels on a whole track, or all the tracks. To do that, you can adjust the levels for each track using the sliders in the Audio Track Mixer. For example, if you think your music tracks might be a hair too loud, you can lower them by 1-2 dB. Or you can raise the levels on every single track if you like how they overall mix works but think it's a bit too low. Just be aware that every single piece of audio on that track in your sequence will change, so this only works well if the mix across the track is consistent. Generally, using the Audio Track Mixer to adjust levels is best avoided.

Similarly, you may wish to adjust equalization across an entire track, especially if your tracks are broken down into distinct sets of sounds. For example, a track that is all music or all voice-over narration. Each track in the Audio Track Mixer has an area where you can add effects, called the Effects Rack (Figure 14.7). You'll find it by spinning down the triangle at the top right of the mixer and see a light grey window open above the pan controls for each track. Here, you can click on the menu at the upper left and select effects that you want applied to the entire track from the menu. Double-click on each effect to change the parameters. You can also apply effects to the master tracks channel, which means they'll get applied to all the tracks across the film.

Upgrading Media in Premiere

Finishing your film means that you can discard any temporary media that you were using during the editing process and replace it with the final full-quality media. These instructions assume you are outputting at the highest-quality possible. All of the following should all be upgraded to match the resolution of the final output:

Remove proxies You can simply turn off proxy media by using the Toggle Proxies button, but it's better to choose Reconnect Full Resolution Media from the clip right-click menu. Anecdotal evidence says that sometimes Premiere has trouble "forgetting" the proxies—if that's the case, you might want to move them to a different drive and then remove the drive from your system to force-relink your full-res media.

Remove splices If you have an` splices in continuous media, aka "through-edits," you should go through your cut and delete them to restore each shot to a single piece of media in the timeline. You'll need to choose Sequence > Show Through-Edits to make the bow tie icon visible so that you can quickly identify them. Remove them by selecting the splice in the Timeline and hitting Delete.

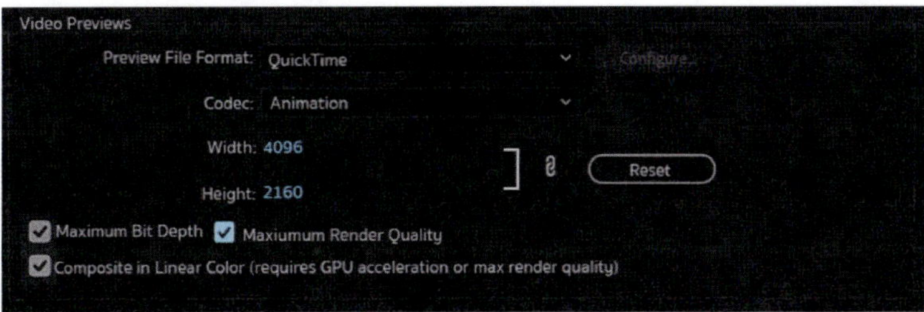

Figure 14.8

Use an uncompressed codec for video previews (aka renders) if you are exporting at the highest possible resolution.

Discard old renders If you've been rendering your sequence as you edit, it's a best practice to discard those old renders and re-build them. If you don't know where they are, you can find them by looking at your scratch disk settings (File > Project Settings > Scratch Disks) for the location of the Video Preview and Audio Preview files. Navigate to those folders on your hard disk and simply drag the contents to the trash. Next, make sure your render settings are high resolution, in fact, "uncompressed" is probably the best choice for most. Render settings are found in your sequence settings (Sequence > Sequence Settings) under the Video Previews (Figure 14.8) and Audio Previews sections. Audio previews are most likely already set to 48 kHz (48000 Hz), which will work for most projects. Video previews should be set to uncompressed, which is any 444 codec, and pixel dimensions should match your sequence. You'll want to check all the boxes at the bottom for highest-quality rendering.

Flatten multicam and nested sequences If your project uses multicam or other nested sequences, it's considered a good idea to flatten them when you finish your film. Flattening simply means that every clip in your sequence will now reference the original master clip and links to the intermediary, nested/multicam sequence will be removed (Figure 14.9). You'll no longer be able to match frame to the nested sequence or switch cameras if it's multicam. But hey, you locked picture, so you don't need them anymore. To flatten the clips in a sequence, make sure Linked Selection is on, then highlight the clips you want to flatten in the Timeline and go to Clip > Multi-Camera > Flatten. Be aware, if you've been editing with multicam sequences and have sections where you only have the audio in the Timeline, you won't be able to flatten them. For some reason, you can only flatten media that has video attached. There's a workaround

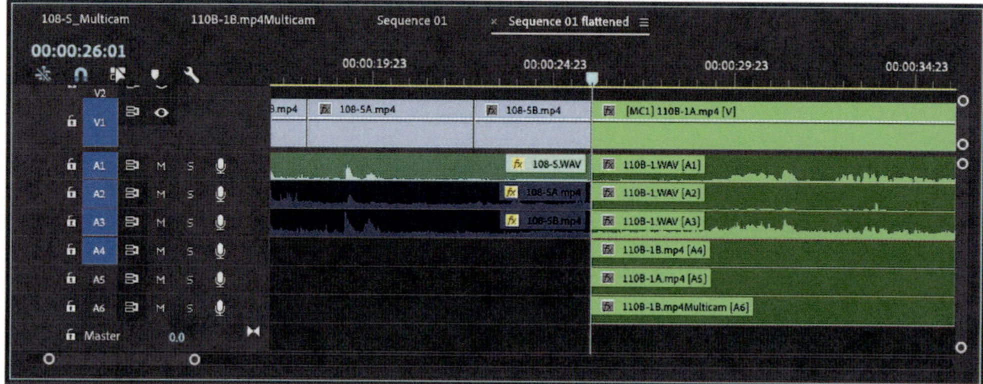

Figure 14.9

Flattening multicam and other nested sequences in the Timeline replaces any nested sequence with master clips. Shown here, the clips from a nested multicam sequence to the left of the playhead have been flattened.

however, you can simply Link the audio to any piece of video and flatten it, then delete the extra video.

Finalize Dynamic Link media If you're been using media from a partnered After Effects composition, thanks to Adobe Dynamic Link, now is the time to replace it with the real thing. Render your composition in After Effects which automatically exports with an uncompressed codec that matches the pixel dimensions of your Premiere Pro sequence. Bring it into Premiere and replace the Dynamic Link media with it. (There is a more automated way to do this using Clip > Render and Replace in Premiere Pro, but you'll have to build an uncompressed encoding preset in Media Encoder first—more on that later in this chapter.)

Adding black media When you're used to working in a simple, digital space—editing projects that you then upload yourself to the internet, for example—the idea of adding pieces of black media to your film is bizarre. But if you think about old movies shot on film, the black frames were not an absence of film. They were actual pieces of film exposed to look black. Without them, the film would have fallen apart in the projector. Today, you have no need for a physical piece of black media, but you do want to make sure that everyone who works on your film in post understands when blacks are intentional—that it's not a mistaken gap in the Timeline. And the easiest way to do that is to fill every black space with a piece of black media. You can use Premiere to generate a piece of black media (File > New > Black Video) and then drop it into your cut anywhere that you have cuts or fades to black. You will need to replace any dissolves so that they engage with the Black Video.

Updating fonts If you have last minute font changes to your on-screen text created with Adobe TypeKit fonts in Premiere, you can change them globally using the Graphics > Replace Fonts in Projects command.

Final color-graded media If you worked with a colorist, you'll need to add that final color-graded video to your sequence. They will most likely provide you with a video file that is either uncompressed or matches your final delivery codec. You'll need to bring it into Premiere and add it to a new empty track in your sequence. (It's a good idea to keep your original clips on other tracks for reference, but you can turn them off with the eye button.) You'll want to make sure you have disabled any Ingest Settings that might transcode your uncompressed color file before you import it.

Final mixed audio If you worked with a sound mixer, you'll need to bring the final mixed tracks back into your project and add them to your sequence. If you made your mix in Adobe Audition, you can either export your mix as separate tracks, known as stems, or as a mixdown that matches the mix format you require (stereo, surround sound, and so on). As with video, it's a good idea to keep your original source audio in the sequence but Mute those tracks.

Exporting a Final Master

You've got your color graded video, your final mixed audio, and everything is upgraded—so now you're ready to export your film to a digital film format. Which codec should you use? There are really only four options, based on what your goals are:

JPEG 2000 If your film is headed for theaters, including certain festival screens, you'll need to use the JPEG 2000 codec in order for your film to meet the criteria for a DCP (Digital Cinema Package), as defined by the DCI (Digital Cinema Initiative). Typically, you'll export a JPEG 2000 master file of your film and then either use a professional service or another software application to create the DCP from that file. Similarly, if your film is headed for high-resolution streaming (4K or UHD), you'll need to use the JPEG 2000 codec in order to meet the specifications for IMF (Interoperable Master Format). IMF is a new(ish) standard set by SMPTE (Society of Motion Picture and Television Engineers) to make digital file delivery more streamlined. It hasn't been universally adopted but its usage is growing.

Apple ProRes 422 For almost everything else, Apple ProRes 422 is the most common codec for exporting.

H.264 For lean and mean streaming, h.264 offers high quality and small(er) file sizes. We used it for all the tutorials in this book for that reason. Most high-end distributors (Netflix, Amazon, etc.) won't accept films in this format, but it's ideal if you're self-distributing via Vimeo, YouTube, etc.

Uncompressed Of course, you may find you need all of them. If so, it's a good idea to make an uncompressed master of your film and use it as a source going forward for any other format that you find you need. You don't need to do this—you can just export different masters from your project and sequence as needed. But there's less margin for error if you do it this way. As you'll see later in this chapter, there are a lot of boxes to check as you export your film and it's really easy to miss one of them.

Preparing a Sequence in Premiere

For many projects, you don't just export your sequence as is—you need to add information about your film so that when it goes out into the world and you're not there with it, others can screen it properly. Be aware that different distributors have different requirements. Festival submissions will have very detailed information about what needs to go at the head of your film, as will traditional broadcasters. Streaming services, on the other hand, usually do not want anything besides the film in the file. So do your homework before proceeding.

Here are the most common things you'll need to add to your film to prepare it for output:

Slates It's common to add a title card before the start of the film that has the title of the film, the length or TRT (Total Run Time), the date of the export (if it's not the final master), and the audio configuration. Film festivals will tell you exactly what information they require on the head slate, as will most distributors. Often production company contact info is included as well or added after the end of the film as a tail slate.

Universal leader Everyone's seen the classic film ten-second countdown, like the image on the first page of this chapter. It's called universal countdown leader and you can generate a version of it in Premiere (File > New > Universal Counting Leader). Countdowns always start ten seconds before the first frame of the film, so that the sync pop on the 2 lands two seconds before the film starts. This sync pop, or 2-pop, is there to give you a nice warm, fuzzy feeling that your film is in sync when you watch it.

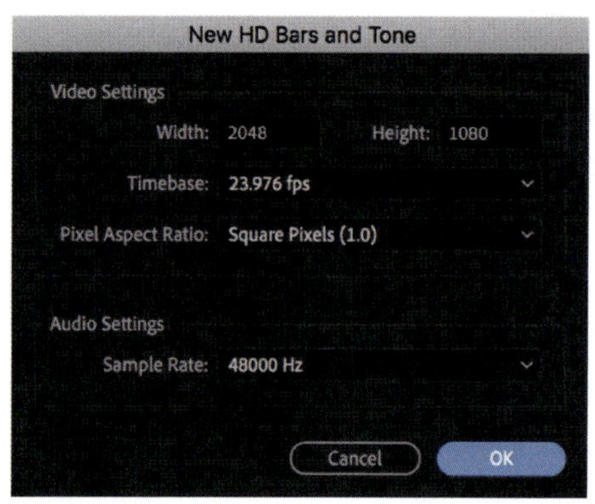

Figure 14.10 Premiere can generate several types of media including bars and tone, film leader, and black media.

Bars and Tone Many films and series add a familiar test pattern, known as Bars and Tone, to the head of their films. We talked about color bars a bit in Chapter 13—they're a test pattern that's used to calibrate monitors so that your film is displayed properly. That's the "bars," the "tone" is a 60 Hz audio tone that is calibrated to fall at 0 or -12 on the audio level meters (depending on the type you are using). Bars and Tone can be generated within Premiere (Figure 14.10) by selecting Bars and Tone or HD Bars and Tone from the File > New menu. Typically they're left up for a minute or more, so as to give the engineer or projectionist time to adjust the color and audio without having to rewind.

Setting the start time before "hour one." All films and television series start at a very specific timecode, hour one or 01:00:00:00. Everything that comes before the first frame of the movie must come before 01:00:00:00. Typically there's two minutes of material before the start of a film—the slate, the countdown leader, test patterns, and so on—so your sequence timecode will start at 00:58:00:00. To change the start time of a sequence in Premiere, go to the Timeline panel menu on the tab next to the name of your sequence and select Start Time. A window will appear that lets you enter the new timecode for the start of your film.

Ending on an even second It's considered good form to end on an even second, with no frames. So if your film ended up with a TRT of 01:32:15:07, you should trim off those extra 7 frames so that it ends at 01:32:15:00. Extra frames are like pennies—no one likes them apparently. When a film or series is broken into smaller pieces, such as acts or reels, these are also supposed to end on an even second.

Metadata is information about the production company, copyright ownership, keywords, and so on, that's embedded in the exported film file itself. It's usually added on export, so more on this later.

Bugs, watermarks, and other global graphics If you're working for a network, you may need to add some sort of on-screen logo, or "bug" in the corner of your film. Alternately, you may wish to add a watermark to protect work-in-progress copies of your film from piracy. These sorts of global graphics can be added to your sequence in the Timeline or as you export your film, via the Effects menu in the Export Settings window.

Captions and subtitles If your delivery requirements include closed-captioning, you can either use a specialized application to create them and import them into Premiere (File > Import) or you can create them yourself directly in Premiere (File > New > Captions). Either way, you'll want to choose Closed Caption Display > Enable from the Program monitor Settings menu (wrench icon) in order to view them. Close-caption files get edited into tracks in the Timeline like any other piece of video. You can change the text, font, timing, and other variables in the Captions window (Window > Captions). Most distributors have very specific requirements when it comes to closed captions, so be sure to check with them. Subtitles are usually created by the foreign distributor, but if you have a small number of subtitles, such as a single scene in another language, they are commonly added as standard title graphics. Alternately, they can be created as open captions, which are just like closed captions except they are always visible. To create an open caption, use File > New > Captions and then right-click on the caption file and select Modify > Captions and use the Standard menu in the Target Stream Format area to switch from closed to open.

The Export Settings Window

There are many options to wade through as you export a film from Premiere. Luckily, most filmmakers can ignore a lot of them. That's because the Export window in Premiere has two functions—it can add elements to your film (titles, timecode, LUTs, captions, metadata, etc.) and it can export a file. If you've followed traditional filmmaking workflow for sound and color, you probably won't need any of the added elements. In fact, if you're film is headed to Amazon, Netflix, and other major streaming services, they'll have very strict guidelines that you'll follow and as a rule, extras like captions or subtitles are delivered as separate files.

That said, if you're still at the work-in-progress stage, you might find these add-ons very useful. Exporting a file with a timecode window for review purposes is a classic example. Or if you haven't been doing any color work on your film but don't want to export it with dull, log color you can add a global LUT here that makes your export look better.

We'll talk about all those extras but first, let's go over the basics of actually exporting a video file from Premiere.

To export a film from Premiere, you'll need to have the sequence loaded in the Timeline or selected in a bin. Go to File > Export > Media and the Export Settings window will open up. It's a big window with a lot of options (Figure 14.11). On the left, you'll see a monitor that displays your sequence with a time ruler below it and to the right you'll see the options for exporting that is divided into three areas: export settings, a menu bar with several sub-sections (Effects, Video, Audio, Captions, and Publish), and a set of checkboxes that control rendering and other options.

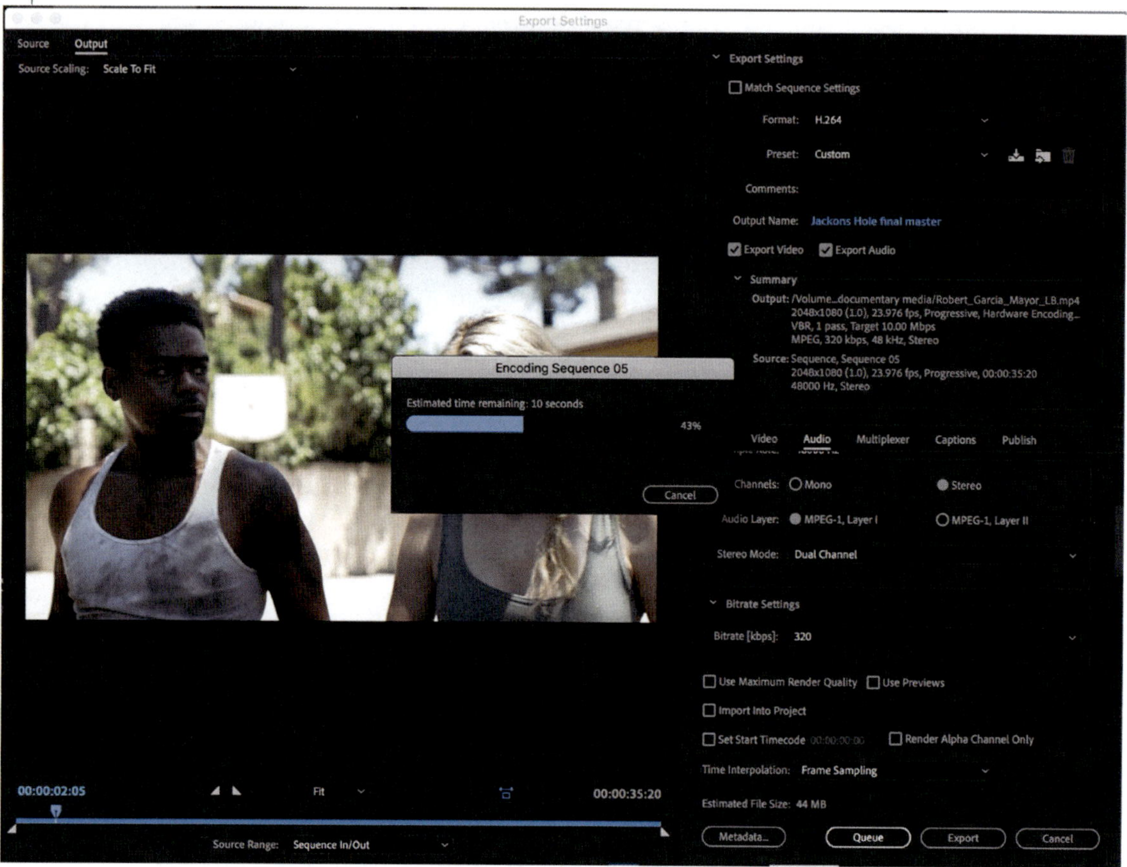

Figure 14.11

The Export Settings window in Premiere lets you choose very specific export options, including titles and other graphic overlays, timecode start time, encoding presets, captions, metadata, resizing, and more.

Export Settings

The Export Settings area is the most important area—it's where you choose a codec and set the name and location for the new file that you are creating. Here you'll also see the Summary that gives you all the specs for your new file. You can refer back to this summary as you make changes to the Export Settings to make sure they are correct. At the very top is the Match Sequence Settings—if you want a file that exactly matches all the specs of your sequence, check this box.

The first menu is Format, which is where you choose a container (or wrapper) file format. This is crucial because whatever you choose here will affect what is available to you in all the other menus in Export Settings window. There are a lot of options in this window but for a final film export, you'll either choose JPEG 2000 MXF OP1a, Apple ProRes MXF OP1a (for ProRes 422 codecs), QuickTime (for uncompressed Animation or ProRes 444 codecs), or h.264. There are other high-resolution codecs available, but these are the most likely choices for finishing. Be aware that the options available to you here will depend on which codecs you have on your system, so if you don't see what you need you may need to install that codec.

Once you pick a format, you'll find a list of options for that format under the Presets menu. You'll have to choose one of them or one will be automatically assigned, but if you don't see an option that suits you, you'll be able to customize it in the Video and Audio menus below. You can also create your own encoding presets in Media Encoder and apply them here.

Encoding Presets

If you know exactly how you want to export your film, it can be very helpful to build a custom encoding preset in Media Encoder and import it into Premiere for all of your future exports. And of course, that preset will also be available in Media Encoder, if you choose to export that way. To create an encoding preset, launch Media Encoder and go to Preset > Create Encoding Preset. The Preset Settings window will open (Figure 14.12) and it's very similar to the right side of the Premiere Pro Export Settings menu. Encoding presets are saved with the extension .EPR in the Adobe documents > Media Encoder > Presets folder on your main hard drive. Back in Premiere, you'll find the new encoding presets you created available in the Export Settings window, under the Preset menu near the top. If you don't see your new codec in the list, use the Import Preset button to the right to add it.

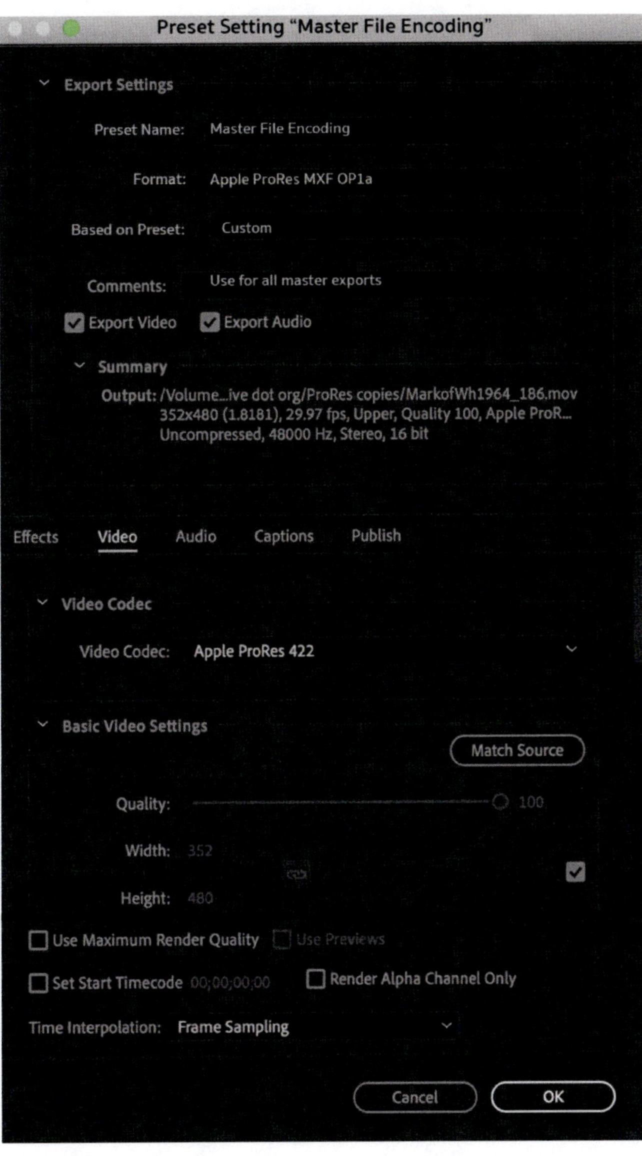

Figure 14.12

Building an encoding preset in Media Encoder and importing it into Premiere can be a big timesaver. Notice that the options here are almost identical to the Premiere Pro Export Settings window in Figure 14.11.

Video Settings

After you choose a container file format and preset, you can customize the Video settings found in the menu bar. Here you'll find the Codec menu, which is where you can choose the codec you want for your export. As we mentioned before, the list of codecs is limited by your choice of container file format in the Export Settings area. If you chose Apple ProRes MXF OP1a, you'll only get a list of ProRes 422 codecs—if you want the full list of ProRes codecs, you'll need to choose QuickTime. That's the only way to get to the Apple Animation or ProRes 444 codecs. But most projects will be looking for an Apple ProRes 422 codec if they're going the ProRes route for final finishing.

Below the Codec menu is Basic Video Settings, where you can choose a frame size, frame rate, and other basics for your video if you don't like the presets. Here, you can use the Match Source button to make these settings identical to your sequence or type in the numbers of your choice. For best quality video, you'll want to check the box next to Render at Maximum Depth. JPEG 2000 offers a range of color profiles under a special Color and Depth menu. If you chose h.264, there are more options beyond Codec and Basic Settings because H.264 is more highly compressed. Similarly, if you chose an uncompressed format like QuickTime with the Apple Animation codec, there will be many more options here because uncompressed formats are not constrained in any way. But most of the options—optimizing stills, adding alpha channels—are not likely to be relevant for final film exports. They're used more for exporting effects and animation clips.

Audio Settings

The audio settings are simpler because most audio is uncompressed with a sampling rate of 48 kHz (48000 Hz). JPEG 2000 and ProRes422 exports can have more up to 32 tracks of audio, while h.264 is constrained to mono (1), stereo (2), or 5.1 surround (6). h.264 also offers two types of audio compression, AAC and MPEG. The most common choice for films that stream is AAC at a high-quality bit rate (320).

Effects

Earlier we mentioned that you can add a lot of things to your export, which is particularly useful for work-in-progress exports. These elements are found under Effects in the menu bar. Here you can choose to globally apply a Lumetri Color Look or LUT preset, add a watermark (Image Overlay), a title over the whole film (Name Overlay), a timecode window (Timecode Overlay). There are also some technical options to keep your video and audio within the legal limits prior to having color graded or mixed your film (SDR Conform, Video Limiter, and Loudness Normalization). And the weirdest option is the Time Tuner which lets you adjust the duration of your film by speeding it up or slowing it down. There aren't a lot of reasons to do this and odds are that it won't have a positive effect on your image quality so it's best to ignore it.

Other Menu Options

The Captions menu lets you choose between saving captions as a separate file (Create Sidecar File), embedding them in the video (Burn Captions Into Video), or not including them in the export (None). The Publish menu lets you export straight to Vimeo, YouTube, Facebook, etc., if you desire. And the Multiplexer menu, which is only available for certain formats such as h.264, lets you choose between two streaming codecs, MP4 and 3GPP.

Render Checkboxes

At the very bottom are some checkboxes that mostly affect rendering. For final finishes, you'll want the best quality possible, so you should select Use Maximum Render Quality. Use Previews results in reduced export times because your sequence render files are used instead of having to re-render the sequence. This is of course assuming that you have a significant amount of your timeline already rendered, which may not be the case if you have a fast computer or your sequence is simple enough to be played back without rendering. And of course, you'll want to make sure your existing renders are of the highest quality. It's considered a best practice to create new renders for a final export, so you should probably deselect this checkbox even if it'll take a little longer.

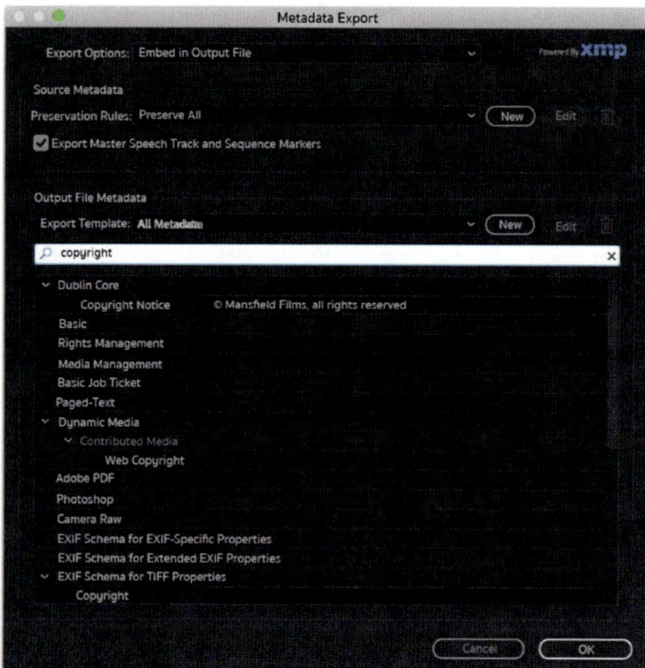

Figure 14.13

The Metadata Export panels lets you add copyright ownership and other information to your file.

Metadata

At the very bottom is the Metadata button, which brings up the Metadata Export window (Figure 14.13). Here you can choose from a huge number of metadata sets. The most important use of metadata at this point is copyright info and, possibly, keywords. You want everyone to know that you own your film. You can use the search field to enter "copyright" or "keywords" and get all the options for entering that data. You may not need them all, of course. The most commonly used metadata sets are Dublin Core (copyright and keywords), Rights Management (more specific copyright and usage info), AS11 (closed captioning), and Dynamic Media (standard film-based info categories). Again, if you're creating a file for a larger distributor, they will have some input on what is allowed and/or required.

Exporting to Media Encoder

At the bottom of the Export Settings window, you have a choice between Export and Queue. Choosing the Export button will create the new file right away, inside Premiere. You'll have to wait as it works, which might be just fine. If not, you can choose the Queue button which will send your export to Media Encoder, which will work in the background. Although Media Encoder will launch automatically, you'll have to go to Media Encoder and choose File > Start Queue to start encoding your export file.

Watch Your Ins and Outs

If you have Ins and Outs set in your sequence, Premiere may constrain your export to just the area between the In and Out points. At the lower left of the Export Setting window, below the time ruler there is a menu where you can choose whether to export Sequence In to Out or Entire Sequence, which will override any Ins and Outs that are set and export the whole thing.

Other Types of Exports

Premiere can export your film in several other formats, which are designed to help share it with other professionals, such as colorists and sound editors. It's getting easier to just share a whole project and hand it off, along with a set of media drives, but that can be cumbersome. Plus they might be working outside the Adobe software family. There are several ways to get your film to another workstation—consolidated Premiere Pro projects, AAFs, XMLs, EDLs, and OMFs. Before you use any of these methods, there are a few key concepts to keep in mind:

Strip down your sequence Each of the most popular film editing applications—Premiere Pro, Avid Media Composer, Apple Final Cut Pro, DaVinci Resolve—has a very different software architecture. So in order to move a sequence and/or project to another system, it needs to get translated into a format the other application can read. That means, the simpler your sequence is, the better that translation will work. Things that will not translate well, or at all, include effects, nested sequences, multicam sequences, proxies, titles, and multiple tracks of video. Basic transitions, aka dissolves, are usually okay. If you have more than one track of video, you can export each track separately, for example if you are sending two layers of media that require compositing to a visual effects artist.

Make a guide export of your film It's always helpful to have a version of the film to check as a reference. Most guide exports are HD, because it works on any system or monitor. For sound editors and composers, guide exports usually have a split audio mix—the dialogue, effects, and ambience are panned to the left and the music is panned to the right so that the music can be turned on and off as needed. Last but not least, guide exports usually have a timecode window so that everyone can be on the same page when discussing the film.

Use handles for consolidated clips To save disk space, it's common to export audio and video as short, or consolidated, clips—basically just the media that's actually in the film, not the whole shot. The idea is to give the colorist or mixer what they need, but not too much more than that. If that's the case, you'll be able designate extra material for the start and end of each consolidated piece of media, aka handles, so that your team isn't overly constrained. Typically 2-5 seconds of handles are enough.

Consolidating with the Project Manager

Sometimes you need to share a project, but maybe not the whole project. If your goal is to move your project to another workstation, whether local or remote, using the Project Manager in Premiere to consolidate a new project might be the best solution. This one works best for those who will work within the Adobe family of software products—effects editors who use After Effects, sound editors who use Audition, and so on. They'll be able to open the new project in Premiere and use Dynamic Link to work with their application of choice.

To consolidate a project, go to File > Project Manager to open the Project Manager window (Figure 14.14). Here you'll have a lot of options to work through, the most important being the choice between moving your source media files in their entirety to a new drive or transcoding

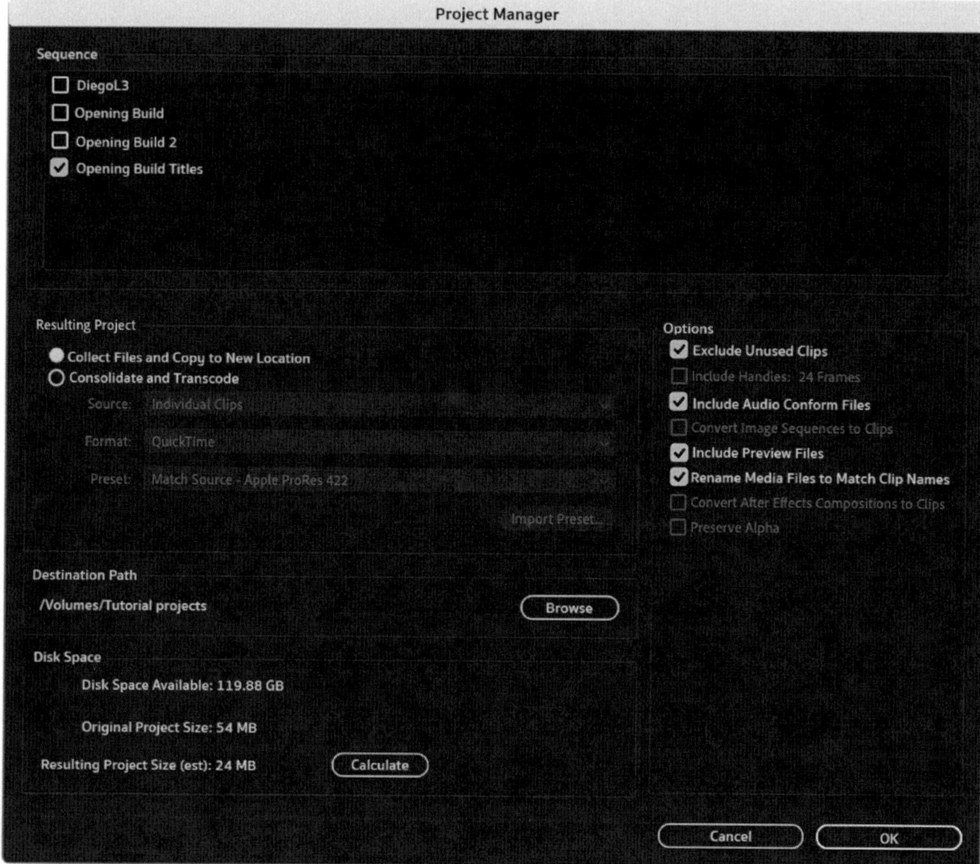

Figure 14.14
The Project Manager is used to create a smaller, streamlined project for sharing with other post-production professionals and archiving your film once it's finished.

them into shorter consolidated clips on the new drive. The former gives more options for the end user but takes up more space. The latter saves space on your transfer drives but risks the introduction of unnecessary compression if you transcode your media to a new format.

At the top of the window, you'll see all the sequences in your current project so that you can select the ones you want to transfer to the new project. To copy source files in their entirety along with the new project, select Collect Files and Copy to New Location. Your original media files will simply get copied and not changed in any way. You'll have some Options to the right, such as only copying source clips that are referenced in the sequence(s) you chose (Exclude Unused Clips), including video and audio renders (Include Audio Conform Files, Include Video Preview Files), and the option to Rename Media to Match Clip Names if the names of your source clips in your project are different than the names of the media files that they reference on your media drives.

Alternately, you can dramatically streamline your project by selecting Consolidate and Transcode. You'll then need to decide whether to have the new clips match your sequence settings, source clip settings, or use a preset. Usually, you'll want to shorten your clips but not change them in terms of codec, aspect ratio, frame rate, image size, and so on. If so, you'll choose Individual Clips from the Source menu. You'll have some additional choices to make from the Options menu to the right. Handles are extra frames at the head and tail of each new, transcoded clip. You probably do want handles and you probably want them to be 2-4 seconds long. Convert Image Sequences to Clips will create a new video clip out of animations and graphics built from sequential still images. Convert After Effects Compositions to Clips will take any AE Dynamic Link media and create a new source clip and break the link to After Effects. Preserve Alpha keeps transparency layers intact, but you'll have to choose a file format that supports alpha channels.

Speaking of file formats, beneath the Source menu on the left, are two submenus, Format and Preset. Format is a list of container file formats you can choose from. Changing the container file, aka re-wrapping your media, does not necessarily change the media itself as long as you don't introduce a new codec. And the list of available presets is determined by your choices in the Source and Format menus. Just like in the main Export Settings menu, you can create your own presets (in Media Encoder) and import them into Premiere so that they are available here. There's an Import Preset button conveniently placed to facilitate that process.

Typically, if you're giving a locked cut of your film to a visual effects editor, colorist, or sound editor, you're going to want to choose Consolidate and Transcode > Source > Individual Clips with handles. That will give them the most streamlined but workable project. If your project is going to someone who will dig deeper—say a film that's still in the rough cut stage that's going to a second editor—you'll want to choose Collect Files and Copy to a New Location, and then select the relevant sequences to use to build the new project and deselect Exclude Unused Clips so that they get all the raw media. If you want to archive a project for storage, you'll probably choose Consolidate and Transcode > Source > Sequence, which means you'll get just the sequence and each clip used in it, usually with handles and transcoded into a format that matches your final film (JPEG 2000, Apple ProRes 422, h.264) or possibly an uncompressed format.

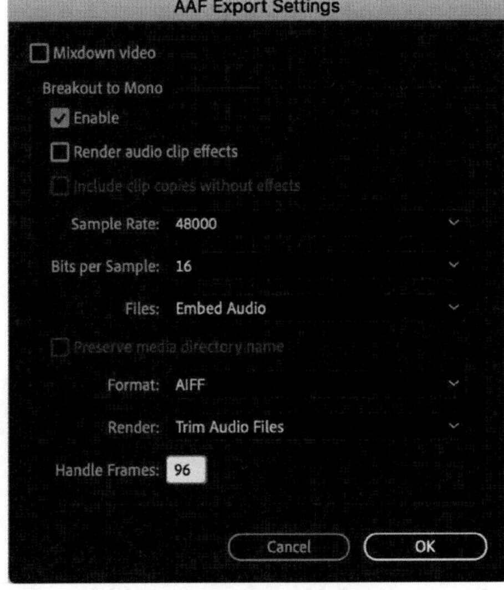

Figure 14.15

AAF exports allow for moving projects from Adobe Premiere to Avid applications like Pro Tools.

AAF and XML Exports

If you want to share your project with someone using another editing application, AAF and XML files are the way to go. Advanced Authoring Format, or AAF, was developed to help make sharing projects and sequences with Avid applications easier—for example, if you want to do your sound design with Avid Pro Tools (Figure 14.15). XML (Extensible Markup Language) exports are used to share projects and sequences with Apple Final Cut Pro. Both are found as File > Export menu options. AAFs and XMLs are a two-way street: if you want to edit in Avid Media Composer or Final Cut Pro and do your sound in Adobe Audition or visual effects in After Effects, they can work in that direction as well.

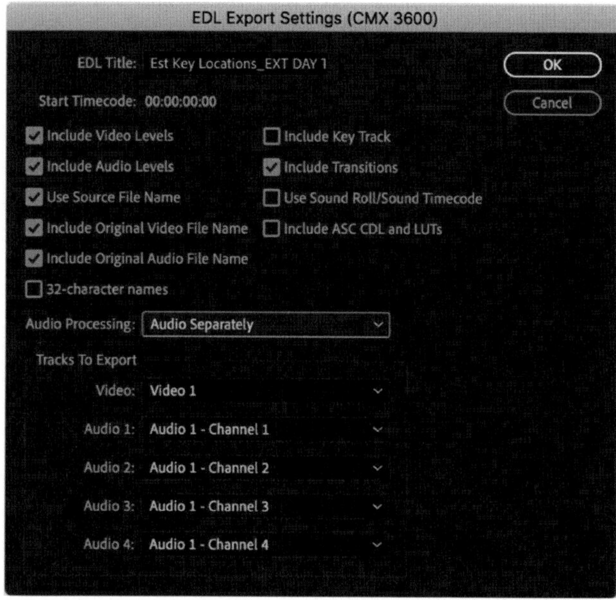

Figure 14.16

EDLs aren't used that much today, but they do have one advantage which is that almost every editing application can use them to rebuild a sequence from raw source media.

EDLs

Edit Decision Lists, or EDLs, are a type of analog code. They use a combination of timecode and source clip IDs to make a list of every edit in your film. Each shot is identified by the name of the source clip and the timecode of the In and Out set in that source clip and every edit is identified by the In and Out of each shot in the sequence. The result is a list of every shot in the film with four columns of timecode. Additional information can be included such as dissolves (transitions) and audio level settings. Once upon a time, a machine called a CMX 3600 could read this list and use it to build a cut from a set of source videotapes onto a master. No one builds cuts from videotape anymore, but the most common format for EDLs is still the CMX 3600 EDL. Premiere, along with other editing apps, can reconstruct a cut from an EDL and a set of source media files.

To export an EDL, you'll need to select a sequence in a bin or in the Timeline, then go to File > Export > EDL. The EDL Export Settings window will come up (Figure 14.16) with a bunch of options. The Audio Processing menu gives you some choices as to how you want your audio information included in the list. Sometimes, audio can be much more complicated than video, so you may wish to add it as a separate list after the video. Be sure to check the box next to 32-Character Names: old school EDLs only allowed for 8-character names and so if your names are longer than that, they'll get cut off. And if they're longer than 32 characters, they'll still get cut off.

Figure 14.17

EDLs are simply a list of every edit in your film with clip names, timecode, and other crucial information.

```
TITLE: test EDL
FCM: NON-DROP FRAME

001  AX       AA/V  C        05:00:58:30 05:02:00:38 00:58:00:00
00:59:02:00
* FROM CLIP NAME: C0181.MP4
* AUDIO LEVEL AT 05:00:58:30 IS -8.86 DB  (REEL AX A1)
* AUDIO LEVEL AT 05:00:58:30 IS -8.86 DB  (REEL AX A2)

002  AX       NONE  C        01:00:00:00 01:04:27:21 00:58:00:00
01:02:27:21
* FROM CLIP NAME: small sails somnambulist.mov
* AUDIO LEVEL AT 01:00:00:00 IS -8.98 DB  (REEL AX A3)
* AUDIO LEVEL AT 01:00:00:00 IS -8.98 DB  (REEL AX A4)
AUD  3    4
```

After you export the EDL, it's a good idea to check it. EDLs are just text files, so even though it has the file extension EDL you should be able to open it in any text editor. You'll see a list of every edit in your film—known as "events"—numbered starting at 001, followed by information about which tracks are affected, four columns of timecode (Source In, Source Out, Sequence In, and Sequence Out), and then the source clip name and any other relevant info depending on how you set up the EDL export (Figure 14.17). You will want to make sure that you see the full list of edits for your sequence, that your file names aren't truncated, and that the file isn't corrupted in any way. Typically when you hand off an EDL and set of media, you'll also include a standard video export of your film as a guide, often with a timecode overlay.

To reconstruct a sequence from an EDL in Premiere, go to File > Import, then navigate to the EDL file and open it. The EDL Information window will open, asking you to confirm the frame rate of your film, usually 24P and then 23.976 from the submenu. After you say Ok, the New Sequence window will open with the name of your EDL already added to the Name field. EDLs do not actually contain information about your media such as aspect ratio, frame size, and so on, so you'll need to set up the new sequence accordingly. After that, a bin will appear in your project containing the new sequence and all the media files referenced in the EDL. They'll be offline so you'll have to select them and use the right-click menu Link Media option to locate the source files on your hard drives.

OMFs

Open Media Framework (OMF) files are used to export audio data from Premiere and other editing applications in a format that sound editors can work with. OMFs are less robust than AAFs and XMLs because they only contain audio, so they're not used as commonly as they were a few years ago. To create an OMF, go to File > Export > OMF. Although the OMF Export Settings window (Figure 14.18) is much simpler than the Project Manager, you'll have some similar decisions to make—whether or not to export your audio source files in their entirety (Render > Copy Complete Audio Files) or to trim them and add handles (Render > Trim Audio Files). Almost all projects will choose a Sample Rate of 48000 Hz, 16 bits per sample, and one of the PCM file formats (WAV, AIFF). The other major decision is whether to save your audio data as part of one large OMF file (Files > Embed Audio) or keep your media files separate from the main OMF file (Files > Separate Audio). Your sound editor will have a strong opinion about all of these options, but OMFs with separate audio sources tend to be less problematic—if one file gets corrupted, you don't have to redo the whole OMF. There's also a 2 GB file size limit for OMFs and it's fairly easy to exceed that with a whole feature film and embedded media. Because there's no video in an OMF, a guide export must accompany the OMF export.

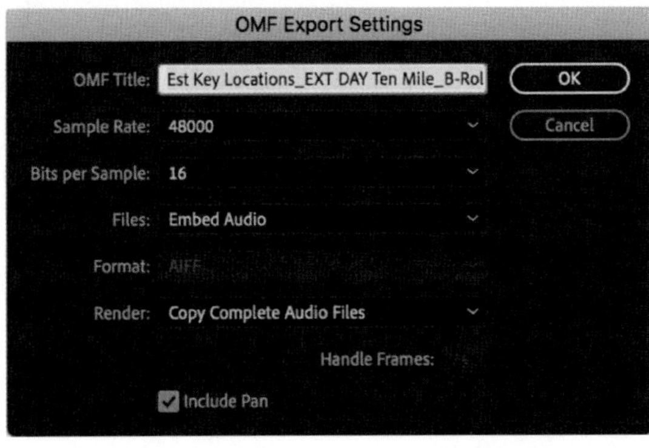

Figure 14.18

OMFs are used to export audio to other applications for sound editing and mixing.

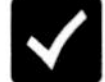

Archiving Your Project

Almost every filmmaker has a closet full of hard drives from past projects, and now you can too! It's kind of a waste but the best way to archive your film is still to just streamline your project with the Premiere Pro Project Manager (File > Project Manager). Use the Project Manager to consolidate your media on a set of drives, then backup it all up on another set of drives. Store one set in your closet (kidding, sort of) and the other at different location. In addition, you should keep versions of your film's master file available in case you need it and it's not a bad idea to export an EDL as well—in a worst-case scenario your film can still be recreated as long as you have your source media. Cloud storage is a great choice for archiving master files and EDLs. And you won't want to risk any piracy if you're handing out professional review copies of your film, so make sure you have a watermarked copy as well or add a title that says something like "Review copy, not intended for distribution."

Distribution Problems to Solve

Your film is finished, at least in terms of editing, but there's a whole new adventure that's beginning—distributing it. And distribution is in the process of huge changes as more and more films and series go to streaming outlets. The festival circuit is one of the major avenues to choose but it's not the only one.

Trailers and teasers Some filmmakers make a trailer early in the editing process, but it's always worth revisiting your trailer after your film is finished. Your understanding of your film and its goals, especially in terms of tone and audience, will be much more clear. Usually, you'll create a couple different versions of your trailer—for a comedy, you might have one that's raunchier and another that shows more emotion. It all depends on the content of your film. In addition, it's common to use a variety of lengths, from as short as ten seconds to as long as three minutes. Any longer, and you'll be making one of those trailers that's like a mini-movie. Whenever I see one of those, I think, "Well, now I don't have to watch that movie." You might feel differently and you might have a good reason for wanting a trailer that's more like a synopsis of your film.

Pull some publicity stills You're going to want a selection of still images from your movie for publicity purposes—good shots of each main cast member, shots that tease the story, etc. You'll want one set that's web resolution (72 ppi) and another set that's high-res for print. If you shot 4K, you're in luck! Still image exports from your film will look great printed at 300 ppi. And if you had an on-set photographer, you're really in luck! If you're film is lower-resolution, you may need to do some image processing in Photoshop.

Pull some publicity clips You'll want a selection of 4-5 short clips to use for publicity purposes. As a rule, you don't want to give away the whole plot but you do want to get people excited to see more. That means pulling clips that include story setups (not payoffs). And you don't have to pull a whole scene, feel free to cut it short to leave people wanting more. Most of your big story setups are going to occur in the first 30 minutes of your film. And of course if you have some amazing footage, money shots, etc. you'll want to include them as well.

Key text documents If you get an unexpected text message from a film reviewer, you're going to want to be ready to give them all the information they need about the movie. That means a press release, a short synopsis, bios of key cast and crewmembers, pull-quotes from the movie, pull-quotes from any reviews, and anything else you have that would be of interest.

Build a website for your film with Adobe Portfolio As an indie filmmaker, I think the Adobe Creative Cloud subscription is kind of expensive, except for one thing that makes it a great deal—they will host your website for free via the Adobe Portfolio web app. (You'll have to pay to register the domain name separately.) Portfolio offers a slim selection of website templates aimed at sites that need to display a lot of visual media. They're all elegant, easy to use, and customizable (to a degree). So put your trailer and publicity clips on Vimeo, use embed codes to add them to your Portfolio site, and use the other items in this list to build out a great website for your film. The only limitation is that Portfolio doesn't have any shopping capabilities. So if you want an online store, you'll have to go elsewhere.

Glossary

1.78 The aspect ratio of HD and UHD video, sometimes expressed as 16:9.

1.85 The aspect ratio of digital cinema video formats (2K, 4K, etc.).

1920 HD High-definition video with a resolution of 1920 × 1080 pixels where each frame consists of a single progressively scanned image. Also referred to as 1080p.

2K A digital cinema video format with a resolution of approximately 2000 pixels, usually 2048 × 1080 pixels. See also **4K**.

2-pop In a traditional eight-second countdown before a film starts, there is a short audio pop that occurs at the first frame of the "2." The "2-pop" makes it easier to confirm that the film is in sync. See also **universal countdown leader**.

23.976 The frame rate of 24 frame per second video adjusted for north American television.

24p A digital video frame rate that consists of 24 progressively scanned frames per second and is akin to the frame rate of 35mm film. Often used as shorthand for 23.976 fps.

32-bit color High-quality color with 32 bits per channel. Many video effects in Premiere Pro work in a 32-bit per channel color mode. See also **bit depth**.

360-degree projection See **equirectangular projection**.

360-degree video A video recording that covers all angles from a given point. The result is a spherical image, similar to a panorama, that can be controlled and rotated by the viewer. See also **virtual reality**.

3D A type of digital media that combines two stereoscopic video streams to create an illusion of enhanced depth perception. See also **virtual reality**.

48 kHz See **audio sampling rate**.

4K A digital cinema video format with a resolution of approximately 4000 pixels. See also **2K** and **UHD**.

6K A digital cinema video format with a resolution of approximately 6000 pixels.

720p High-definition (HD) video with a resolution of 1280 × 270 pixels where each image consists of a single progressively scanned frame.

8-bit color Digital media that has 8 bits of color information per channel, considered the minimum color resolution needed to represent realistic color. 8-bit color has a range of values from 0 (black) to 256 (white) for each of the three color channels.

8K A digital cinema video format with a resolution of approximately 8000 pixels.

AAC (Advanced Audio Coding) An audio file format used for streaming media, generally higher quality than MP3 but not uncompressed like PCM, WAV, or AIFF.

AAF (Advanced Authoring Format) A multimedia file format used to transfer film projects from Premiere to other applications like Avid Pro Tools.

a-side The left side of an edit in a sequence, i.e., the end of the outgoing shot. See also **b-side**.

accelerated effects In Premiere, effects that are designed to work with a computer's GPU to allow for faster previewing.

act See **three-act structure**.

additive color The color mixing system for light and digital video. The primary colors are red, green, and blue. If you mix them, they will yield white.

ADR Automatic Dialogue Replacement. See **looping**.

adjustment layer A special type of clip in Premiere that only contains visual effects. When placed in an upper video track in a sequence, the effects in the adjustment layer are applied to media on the tracks below it, without changing them directly.

AIFF (Audio Interchange File Format) An uncompressed, PCM-based audio file format. See also **WAV**.

alignment When working with text, you have the choice of left alignment, centered, right alignment, justified.

alpha channel An 8-bit color channel that is used to specify the transparency of each pixel in an image. An alpha channel works like a sophisticated stencil and is the digital equivalent of a matte.

ambience An element of sound design used to build the atmosphere of a location in a film.

analog Information represented electronically as a continuous, varying signal. See also **digital**.

analog color space See **YUV**.

anamorphic Video that is saved with a codec that squeezes it horizontally to fit a smaller frame width and unsqueezes it for playback.

Apple Animation compressor A lossless, uncompressed codec.

Apple Final Cut Pro A competitor to Adobe Premiere Pro. See also **Avid Media Composer**, **DaVinci Resolve**.

Apple ProRes A set of codecs designed for use in digital video editing applications. ProRes 422 is a very popular codec in film editing applications.

archival media In documentaries, any media acquired through an outside resource, such as a film archive or footage library, including historical footage, news clips, photographs, and stock media.

AS11 A media specification used for closed-captioning files.

aspect ratio The ratio of the width of an image to its height. Aspect ratios can be expressed as ratios, such as 16:9, or as numbers, such as 1.78.

assembly An early cut of a film, also called a **rough cut**.

Assembly workspace In Premiere, a preset workspace layout designed for building first cuts.

Audio Clip Mixer A panel in Premiere used to set the audio levels in a sequence.

audio effects Digital processing of sounds in a film in order to improve or manipulates it, such as equalization, echo, noise reduction, etc. See also **sound effects**.

audio mixing The process of taking multiple tracks of audio and distilling them down to a limited number, usually two or four, and adjusting levels, panning, and equalization along the way. See also **mix.**

audio sampling rate The number of samples per second that are used to digitize a particular sound. Measured in kilohertz, 44.1 kHz is considered good quality, 48 kHz is considered high quality, and 96 kHz is considered very high-quality. In Premiere, 48 kHz is often written out as 48,000 Hz.

Audio Track Mixer A panel in Premiere used to adjust a mix before export.

audio waveforms See **waveform.**

Audition A professional sound editing application by Adobe, competitor to Avid Pro Tools.

auto-save A setting that saves a Premiere Pro project at pre-specified intervals, usually every 15 minutes.

AVC-Intra A high-definition acquisition codec developed by Panasonic for use with their P2 line of cameras.

Avid DNx codecs A set of HD (DNxHD) and 4K (DNxHR) codecs designed for use in digital video editing applications, particularly Avid Media Composer.

Avid Media Composer A competitor to Adobe Premiere Pro. See also **Apple Final Cut Pro**, **DaVinci Resolve**.

Avid Pro Tools A professional sound editing application.

b-roll Footage acquired for used as cutaways, insert shots, and establishing shots.

b-side The righthand side of an edit in a sequence, i.e., the incoming shot. See also **a-side.**

backtiming (an edit) The process of setting up a three-point edit so that the material is added from the ending position as opposed to start.

banding In color, gradients that are not smooth but instead appears as layers or bands of colors. See also **posterization**.

bandwidth The amount of digital information that can be passed through a connection at a given time. High bandwidth is needed for high-quality media transfer.

bars and tone A combination of color bars and 60Hz audio reference tone, usually added to the start of a video clip. Used for calibrating video and audio levels.

Bezier curves A method of drawing curved lines using anchor points with handles that control the intensity of the curve.

bin A film-editing term that refers to the place where the shots for a scene are stored. In software editing systems, bins can also be referred to as folders, galleries, or libraries.

bit depth The number of bits used to represent the color of a single pixel in a frame of digital media. Bit depth is usually described in bits per channel because each pixel consists of three channels and potentially, a fourth transparency or alpha channel. Bit depth in digital video ranges from 8-bits per channel, the minimum number for realistic color, to 32-bits per channel. See also **alpha channel, color space**.

black level The black level defines how dark a video image is allowed to get. Improperly set black levels can result in dull, grayish blacks. See also **waveform monitor**.

blur An effect to make an image, or part of an image, appear out of focus. Sometimes used to censor unwanted material such as nudity or product logos. See also **bokeh, motion blur**.

bokeh A Japanese term that refers to the parts of an image that are out of focus due to the limitations of a lens and depth-of-field. In post, blur added to the background of an in-focus image for aesthetic reasons or to hide problems. See also **depth of field, motion blur**.

burn-in Titles such as timecode or captions that are rendered into the video track of an exported media file. They can no longer be separated from the video and are considered to be "burned" into the media.

bussing The process of sending audio from one track (or channel) to another. See also **mix**.

CGI (Computer Generated Imagery) Used to refer to any effect that is created digitally, be it a composite or a fully digital image such as a walking dinosaur.

channel Refers to one of two or more elements that combine to create a full video image, still image, or audio mix. The color in an RGB image is divided into channels, one each for the red (R), green (G), and blue (B) information in the image, when these channels are combined, a full-color image results. In audio, a left channel and a right channel add up to a stereo mix. See also **track.**

captions In video, on-screen text that adds information, such as translation of dialogue into another language, transcription of difficult to understand dialogue, or for the hearing impaired (closed-captioning).

capturing The process of taking an analog source, such as a voice recording or footage from videotape, and converting it to digital media.

checkerboard A way to arrange each piece of sound across a group of audio tracks so that no piece of sound is directly "touching" any other piece of sound, resulting in a checkerboard-like appearance.

checksum A number that is generated to help confirm that data was copied without any errors or corruption. Used when copying media from camera cards to media drives and also when creating backups. See also **MD5 verification**.

china girl An image of a woman next to a color chart used to calibrate film and video in post-production. The reference images in the Lumetri Presets folder in the Premiere Effect panel are a classic example.

chroma The part of the video signal that contains the color information.

chroma key An effect that will render a specific color in a layer transparent. For example, if you shoot someone in front of an evenly lit green screen, you can use a chroma key function to render the green completely transparent, thus revealing underlying video layers. See also **green screen**.

chrominance The saturation and hue of a video signal. Although slightly different in meaning, this term is often used interchangeably with the term *chroma* to refer to color.

clearing frame When the subject of a shot (an actor, a car, etc.) moves past the camera and out of the shot. Often, the moment a subject clears frame is a good place to cut to a new shot.

clips The building blocks of a film, also referred to as shots, footage, or media.

clipping In digital media, an electronic limit that is imposed on the audio and/or video portion of the signal in order to avoid audio that is too loud and video that is too bright, too saturated, or too dark. Clipped blacks are any blacks in an image that are darker than the set black level, usually 0 IRE. Clipped whites are any whites that are brighter than the set white level, or 100 IRE. Clipped audio is any sound that goes into the red area on an audio level meter. Clipped media is indicated by a flat line in a waveform view of the signal.

CMYK color space Used when printing with ink, a subtractive color space consisting of cyan, magenta, yellow, and black. See also **RGB**, **YUV**, and **YCbCr**.

closeup A shot where the subject fills the majority of the frame. If the subject is a person, the shot will consist primarily of the person's head and shoulders.

codec (Compressor/Decompressor) An algorithm for encoding video and audio. Popular codecs for editing in Premiere include Apple ProRes and h.264.

color bars A test pattern used to check whether the color of video system is calibrated correctly. Waveform monitors and vectorscopes are used, in conjunction with color bars, to check the brightness, hue, and saturation.

color channels Digital video has three color channels, plus a fourth transparency, or alpha, channel. The contents of each of the three main color channels depends on the color space of the digital film. See also **RGB**, **YCbCr**.

color correction A post-production process to correct the overall color of a video master in order to get the best quality image, with an emphasis on enhancing skin tones and fixing problems such as bad white balance. See also **color grading**.

color depth The number of colors that a given video system can display. The more bits-per-pixel that are used to store color, the higher the color depth.

color grading The process of adjusting hue, saturation, and contrast to achieve a visually pleasing image. See also **color correction**.

color sampling ratio In digital video, the ratio of the three color channels to each other. 4:4:4 means a full sample of each channel, i.e., uncompressed. 4:2:2 means that for every four samples of luminance (Y), there are two samples of chroma minus blue (Cb) and chroma minus red (Cr). If there is a fourth number in the ratio, it stands for the resolution of the alpha channel.

color space As it pertains to video, a method of organizing digital color that differs for different devices and uses. Light-based devices operate in the RGB or YCbCr color spaces, printers use CMYK.

color spectrum The range of visible light that extends from violet to red.

color temperature Light sources have different color temperatures, which are measured in degrees Kelvin. The color temperature of tungsten light is 3200°K, and the color temperature of daylight is about 5600°K.

compositing The process of layering media to create special effects.

composite video Single-channel (i.e., standard) video, as opposed to multi-channel (i.e., multicam) video.

compression The process of encoding information in a digital format and discarding information to reduce file size.

compression artifacts Distortion as a result of compression in a digital file. Examples include noise, posterization, banding, blockiness, and aliasing.

compressing time In editing, using montage to ellipse time so that the real time required for something to happen is shortened.

conforming The process of re-creating an edit using, usually, higher quality footage.

consolidating The process of streamlining a project or set of media. In Premiere, accomplished with the Project Manager.

container file A type of digital media file that can hold more than one type of data and more than one data stream. For example, a QuickTime movie is a container file that can include video streams, audio streams, an alpha channel, and metadata. Also called a *wrapper*.

contrast The range from light to dark in video. See also **dynamic range**.

copyright The legal right to reproduce a creative work.

coverage The footage needed to properly edit an event or scene.

cropping The process of trimming the edges of an image or video frame to change the aspect ratio or as the result of enlargement.

Curves A method of color correction using a graph, found in the Lumetri Color panel.

cut, copy, paste A simple form of editing.

cutaway In a scene, a shot of something other than the main action or dialogue. Used to build the story and smooth rough edits.

dailies The media that results from a day of shooting. Also used as an organizing principle in post-production.

data rate The amount of data that a particular connection can sustain over time. Usually measured in megabytes per second.

DaVinci Resolve A professional digital color-correction system by Blackmagic Design; also used as an editing application. See also **Apple Final Cut Pro**, **Avid Media Composer**.

dB (decibel) The standard unit for measuring sound. A subjective scale where one unit equals one increment of "loudness."

DCI-compliance Digital media that follows the specifications set by the Digital Cinema Initiatives (DCI).

DCP—See **Digital Cinema Package**.

deliverables Elements of a film that the producers are contractually required to give to the distributor as part of the distribution deal. Can include extraneous elements such as still images, legal documents, etc.

depth of field A measure of how much, and what depth, of the image is in focus.

dialogue Speech between characters, one of the four key types of sound for films.

digital Information recorded electronically as a series of discrete pulses, or samples, usually encoded using a binary system.

digital cinema A phrase used to describe very high-quality digital video that is intended to compete against traditional 35mm film as an acquisition and distribution medium. Digital cinema formats have a resolution of 2K or higher.

Digital Cinema Initiatives (DCI) A group formed by the major film studios to set a standard for digital cinema and projection.

Digital Cinema Package (DCP) A set of digital files used to deliver digital cinema media for digital projection in a theater. DCP video uses the MXF format with the JPEG 200 codec and follows a set of specifications set out by the Digital Cinema Initiatives (DCI).

dissolve A transition in which the first shot is partially or completely replaced by a gradual superimposition of the next shot.

distortion The warping of an image caused by a wide-angle lens or the sound of audio that has been clipped because it's too loud for speakers to handle.

DM&E Dialogue, Music and Effects, a four-channel, split audio mix that allows for easy remixing in case the audio needs to be dubbed in a foreign language.

DNx codecs See **Avid DNx codecs.**

documentary A non-fiction film. Often uses interviews, voice-over, and archival media.

double-system sound A process of recording audio on a device that is separate from the camera and synchronizing it later.

drag-and-drop editing A two-step editing method where the user selects a shot, drags it from one position, then drops it into another position; for example, from a bin to the timeline or from one position in the timeline to another.

dramatic film A film genre that is based on scripted, narrative fiction.

drop zones An overlay that appears when you drag and drop a source clip into the Program monitor. This overlay has several zones, each of which uses a different editing command to add your source media to the sequence in the Timeline.

duplicate media In Premiere, copies of master clips that are automatically created when you copy a sequence from one project to a project on another system.

duration The overall length of a film or edited sequence, usually described as hh:mm:ss:ff. In to Out duration is the length of a marked clip or sequence from the In point to the Out point. See also **TRT**.

DV An early digital video format used in consumer electronics.

Dynamic Link The ability for certain Adobe applications to work seamlessly together, specifically Premiere Pro, After Effects, Audition, and Media Encoder.

dynamic range In video, the range from the darkest shadows to the brightest highlights, also referred to as contrast. In audio, the range from silence (or 0 dB) to the loudest sound that can be heard without distortion.

EDL (Edit Decision List) A text-based list of all the edits and sources in a cut of a film, used to reconstruct the film on another system.

Effects Rack In Premiere, the area above the level sliders for each track in the Audio Track Mixer, used to add audio effects across an entire sequence.

Enable command The ability to turn a clip on (enable) or off (disable) in the Timeline without having to remove it.

encoding The process of creating a digital video or audio file using compression.

Encoding Queue In Adobe Media Encoder, a list of exported files from Premiere Pro, Media Encoder, or After Effects, that are ready to encode.

encoding preset A set of parameters that dictate how a media file is encoded. For Premiere, encoding presets are created in Media Encoder, then added to Premiere via the EPR file format.

EPR A file format for encoding presets created in Adobe Media Encoder that can be imported and used within Premiere.

equalization (EQ) The process of adjusting the volume of individual frequency ranges within a sound. Equalization can be used to correct problems in a sound, or to "sweeten" or enhance the sound to bring out particular qualities.

equirectangular projection A way of dividing a sphere into a grid of rectangles so that it can be mapped on a flat surface. Used in VR and 360-degree video to create a spherical image from multiple rectangular video sources.

establishing shot A shot, often wide or an aerial, that identifies a new location or scene in a film.

exporting The process of rendering a sequence and saving it as a new, self-contained media file.

exposure The amount of light in an image. In color correction, an overall adjustment of the brightness or darkness of an image.

Extend Edit command A command that causes a splice or the end of a shot to jump to the position of the playhead.

external monitor In editing, a display added to a computer workstation that directly shows video in a format that isn't natively displayed by a computer monitor. For example, an HDR monitor.

Extract An editorial command that removes a section of a sequence in the Timeline and automatically closes the resulting gap.

eyedropper A tool used to select a color from a frame of video or still image.

fade out A dissolve from full video to black video or from audio to silence.

fields Each frame of analog video consists of two fields: one field contains the odd-numbered scan lines, and the other field contains the even-numbered scan lines. See also **progressive scan**.

film grain Traditional 35mm film has a visible texture when projected due to the chemical particles that make up the emulsion. Today film grain is one of several video effects that can be used to help digital video mimic the look of film.

filters See **audio effects**.

Final Cut Pro An editing application from Apple that is a competitor to Premiere Pro.

Fit to fill command See **Replace edit**.

fixed effects Effects that are always present on video and audio clips in Premiere but set to neutral unless the user adjusts them. Includes very basic effects such as Motion (including Scale and Position), Opacity, Time Remapping, Panner, and Volume.

flattening A process that removes nested and multicam sequences in a cut and replaces them with the original source clips.

Flesh Tone Line (FTL) In a vectorscope, a line between Red and Yellow that indicates the optimal area of saturation for human skin tones.

float In Premiere, a setting for the Lumetri Scopes panel so that it uses 32 bits (per channel) color, as opposed to 8-bits per channel or HDR.

fps (Frames Per Second) Used to describe the speed at which film and video play. Film plays at 24 fps, digital video usually plays at 23.976 fps, analog PAL video at 25 fps, and NTSC video at 29.97 fps.

frame One complete film or video image. Moving images need at least 18 frames per second to appear as full-motion, and 24 fps to allow for sync sound.

frame blending In Premiere Pro, an optional method of interpolating additional frames when changing the frame rate of a source clip. If new frames need to be created, they are doubled and then blended together for smoother motion. See also **frame sampling**, **Optical Flow**.

frame rate See **fps**.

frame sampling In Premiere Pro, the default method of interpolating missing or additional frames when changing the frame rate of a source clip. If there are too many frames they are removed and if there are too few, the existing ones are doubled. See also **frame blending**, **Optical Flow**.

freeze frame A time-based effect that takes a frame of video and freezes it, so that it plays like a still image clip. In Premiere, freeze frames are called Frame Holds.

frequency An audio signal is made up of different frequencies, or wavelengths, that yield the high (or treble), mid, and low (or bass) tones. The human voice resides mostly in the midtones. Light is also composed of different frequencies, which appear to the human eye as different colors.

FX badge A small label on a clip on a timeline that changes its color depending on the type of effects that are applied to the clip. Right-clicking on it reveals the Clip Effects menu.

gain The strength (or amplitude) of an audio or video signal.

gain boost A method of electronically increasing the strength, or amplitude, of an audio or video signal. In video, the image gets brighter but has more visible noise.

gamma In video, a way to describe the lightness or luminance of a particular camera or device.

gate A special type of audio filter that only allows a specific range of frequencies to pass.

GPU Graphics Processing Unit, the part of your computer that handles video playback and rendering.

GPU acceleration Any process that can be sped up by using your computer's GPU, typically refers to certain types of video effects.

gradient A gradual, continuous shift from one color to another.

graphics In filmmaking, imagery created without a camera, such as illustrations, text on screen, and animation.

green screen A colored backdrop used to separate the subject from the background as an aid in compositing.

green spill Reflected green light that bounces off a green screen onto the subject, making it more difficult to make a clean matte.

growing files Media that can be ingested while still being recorded, common with coverage of live events.

group projects In Premiere, the ability to have multiple users work in the same project file. Options include shared projects and team projects.

guide track An export of a rough cut used as a reference by sound editors and composers. In multicam editing, audio recorded with the camera that is used to synchronize multiple devices.

h.264 A lossy HD codec that is popular as a delivery format for the web.

Hand tool In the Premiere Pro Tools panel, a tool that lets you reposition a sequence in the Timeline by clicking and dragging.

handles Extra footage added to the head and tail of each shot when consolidating or transcoding, in order to give editors and others extra workable material if needed.

hard cut An edit from one shot to another without any type of transition in between, such as a dissolve.

HD High Definition video, a type of digital video defined as having a resolution that is greater than that of Standard Definition (SD) video, or 720 × 480 pixels. HDTV, a subgroup of the digital television broadcast standard, has a 16:9 aspect ratio, a resolution of either 1280 × 720 or 1920 × 1080; a frame rate of 23.96, 24, 29.97, 30, 59.95, or 60fps; and either interlaced or progressive scanning.

HDR Acronym for High Dynamic Range which is a type of video or still imagery with a greater range from black to white that Standard Dynamic Range (SDR) media.

HDR monitor A monitor that has the capacity to display HDR media.

HDV A digital video format that can record HD video on standard DV tapes.

heads The beginning of a film, reel, or shot. See also **tails**.

hexadecimal color code A system of identifying colors used in HTML documents and other forms of web coding.

histogram A graphical representation of the range from light to dark in a frame of video. See also **waveform**.

History panel In Premiere Pro, a window that provides a list of prior editorial commands that you can Undo as needed.

hour one The start time of most TV shows and films, represented in timecode notation as 01:00:00:00.

HSB Just as colors can be defined by specifying RGB (red, green, and blue) values, colors can also be defined by specifying hue, saturation, and brightness. Many color pickers allow you to switch to an HSB mode. For some operations, selecting a color is easier in one mode than in another.

hue The shade of a color.

HSL (Hue, Saturation, Lightness) Similar to HSB, with a different way of describing luminance (lightness).

HSL Secondary A color effect that uses a color-based matte to allow for separate color adjustments to a portion of an image.

I-frame A video compression term. An intermediate frame between two keyframes. I-frames store only the data that has changed from the previous frame.

image stabilization In post, an effect that removes undesirable camera movement.

IMF (Interoperable Master Format) A SMPTE video standard for high-quality digital delivery using the JPEG 2000 codec.

immersive video See **virtual reality**.

Import A command that brings media into Premiere. See also **Media Browser**.

infrared The area beyond red, outside of the visible part of the color spectrum.

In The start of a shot or sequence or the first frame of an edit.

ingest A word used to refer to all the ways of bringing media into a project, whether from an analog source (capturing), digital source (importing), or re-encoding a digital source (transcoding).

ingest settings A set of options that automate how media is brought into a Premiere project.

inbetweening See **interpolation.**

Indeterminate Media Timebase The default frame rate for media that does not have a frame rate that Premiere can automatically discern, such as sequential still-based animation.

Insert command An editing command that adds media to a sequence and pushes anything that's in its way down the Timeline.

insert edit A method of editing in the timeline that allows the placement of a shot between two shots without covering up what's already there. Instead, the second shot (and all the shots following it) are pushed down the timeline to accommodate the new clip. See also **overwrite edit**.

intercutting An editorial technique that involves cutting back and forth between two different scenes or storylines.

interface The controls and windows that you use to operate a program.

interframe compression A sophisticated type of digital video compression algorithm that uses keyframes to reduce file sizes while maintaining image quality. Very efficient but not well-suited to editing.

interpolation The process of calculation that is required to generate all of the frames between two keyframes.

intraframe compression A type of digital video compression algorithm that compresses each frame individually. Better for editing than interframe compression.

IRE A unit used to describe the strength of a standard dynamic range video signal on a scale from 0 (black) to 100 (white). In Premiere, the IRE scale is found on the left side of Lumetri Scopes panel when set to waveform display for 8-bit or float color. See also **nits**.

ITU (International Telecommunications Union) An organization that sets the international rules for each digital video color space. See also **Rec. 709**.

JKL A way of editing using the J, K, and L keys on the computer keyboard. Allows for fast shuttling through clips and sequences.

JPEG 2000 An uncompressed codec used for 4K streaming and digital cinema delivery.

jump cut An edit that is jarring to the viewer. See also **seamless edit**.

kerning For titles and other text-based graphics, a command that adjusts the space between any two letters.

key effect An effect that uses a matte to remove part of an image and replace it with something else. See also **chroma key**, **luma key**.

keyboard shortcuts Pre-programmed or customized key commands that are used to perform common actions in Premiere.

keyframe In animation, keyframes allow you to explicitly define the parameters of each property of each element in the animation (motion, position, transparency, etc.). The computer will automatically calculate the changes that occur between each keyframe. In video compression, a keyframe is a noninterpolated, spatially compressed frame. See also **interpolation**.

keyword A category of metadata that helps when logging a clip or image according to its content.

L-cut See **overlapping edit**.

labels The ability to apply different colors to clips in order to differentiate them at a glance.

lavalier A small, clip-on mic. Usually an omnidirectional, condenser microphone. Often abbreviated to **lav**.

layer See **track**.

leader A countdown placed at the start of a film, used to confirm sync. Today, leaders are only used in post-production, not for film screenings.

leading In type formatting, the vertical distance between two lines of type.

lens flare In post-production, an effect that mimics the artifacts created by light shining directly into the lens of a camera.

letterboxing The process of adding black bars at the top and bottom of the screen to make a wide image fit into a narrower aspect ratio screen or video format. See also **pillarboxing**.

level meters Monitor that show the loudness of sound against a scale measured in decibels.

levels The strength of any component of an audio or video signal. Levels are adjusted in Premiere using the Audio Clip Mixer, the Audio Track Mixer, or the Lumetri Color panel.

Lift An editorial command that removes part of an edited sequence and leaves a gap where the media used to be.

linear color A color profile that is mapped evenly across the available spectrum. See also **log color**.

Link/Unlink A command that removes the link between audio and video files from the same source clip, so that they can be edited separately.

Linked Selection In Premiere Pro, a button that turns on and off the linking of audio and video files from the same source clip in the Timeline.

locking picture The process of formally finalizing the editing of a film for story, so that the sound editors and colorist can start working without have to deal with any changes in timing.

log color A logarithmic color profile that favors the middle of the color spectrum, which accommodates biases in human sight and allows for the recording media with a higher dynamic range in the camera. See also **linear color**, **raw media encoding**.

logging The process of noting the contents of each shot using timecode, shot names, and descriptions. Often the first step in the editing process.

looks A color grading preset often used to mimic a particular camera or film stock.

lookup tables See **LUTs**.

looping The process of re-recording dialog in a studio. Called looping because the actor sometimes watches a continuous loop of the scene that is being re-recorded. Also known as ADR.

lossless Used to denote a form of compression that does not degrade the quality of the image being compressed.

lossy Used to denote a form of compression that degrades the quality of the image being compressed.

lower thirds A title identifying a speaker in a documentary that was traditionally placed in the bottom third of the screen. Today, lower thirds can be place anywhere.

luma key A special matte that uses the luminance values in a layer to determine transparency. For example, a luma key could be set to render the darkest areas of the layer transparent.

Lumetri Color effect A complex color grading interface that includes the application of LUTs and presets.

Lumetri Color panel An interface in Premiere that controls the Lumetri Color effect.

Lumetri Scopes A set of waveform and vectorscope monitors used in tandem with the Lumetri Color effect.

luminance The strength (or amplitude) of the grayscale (or brightness) portion of a video signal.

luminance clamping The process of clamping (or clipping, or scaling) the luminance value in a video signal. In video that has been luma clamped, luminance values over 235 are eliminated, frequently resulting in video with bright areas that look like solid blobs of white.

LUTs (Look Up Tables) A preset for color grading that is often supplied by the camera manufacturer or a technician on the set.

MD5 verification confirms that your copied files are identical to the ones on your camera card, available as an ingest setting in Premiere. See also **checksum**.

M&E See **DM&E**.

Make Offline A reversible command used to remove media from a Premiere project.

markers A method of annotating video and audio clips in Premiere. Used to add comments to a specific frame of video.

master clips In Premiere, the clip that contains the original link between a source file on a hard drive and Premiere.

Master Graphic In Premiere, a title that is converted to a clip, so that it behaves like a piece of media as opposed to a Text effect.

master shot A wide shot that contains all of the action in a particular scene. Used as the basis for building a scene.

Master Text styles In Premiere, a text-oriented formatting preset found in the Essential Graphics editor.

master track configuration See **mix**.

Match Frame A command that brings up the source clip from any frame in the Source or Program monitor.

matching action The editorial process of making movement appear continuous across multiple shots.

matte A stencil-like layer used in compositing to block part of an image.

Media Browser An interface in Premiere used for navigating the contents of hard drives and bringing media into Premiere.

media cache A storage folder that contains media files used by Premiere to enhance playback.

Media Composer See **Avid Media Composer**.

Media Encoder An Adobe application that works with Premiere and After Effects to encode media in the background.

media specifications All of the information used to describe a media file, including but not limited to, dimensions, frame rate, sampling rate, codec, aspect ratio, color sampling ratio, color space, pixel depth, and scanning method.

media scaling A set of media preferences in Premiere that determine how video is scaled when source footage has dimensions that do not match that of a sequence.

Mercury Playback Engine Software-based architecture within Premiere that employs GPU acceleration to enhance playback and performance.

Merge Clips A command in Premiere that takes selected clips and binds them together in a new clip. See also **multicam sequence**.

metadata Text-based information about a file that is stored within the file itself or in an accompanying file.

mix The way that several audio tracks or streams are combined. Stereo mixes are balanced to the right and left, while surround sound mixes are designed to replicate the 3D sound that we hear in real life.

mixdown The process of taking multiple streams of video or audio and combining them into a single stream, usually resulting in a new rendered file.

modifier keys Shift, Control, and Alt on a Windows keyboard. Shift, Command, and Option on a Mac keyboard.

MOGRT (Motion Graphics Template) A file format used to exchange motion graphics settings between Premiere Pro and Adobe After Effects.

monitor The processing of viewing and also a device for viewing. See also **Source monitor**, **Program monitor**, **external monitor**, **waveform monitor**, **vectorscope**, **level meters**.

mono sound A single channel or stream of audio.

monoscopic Video with only a single stream, aka standard video.

montage In editing, the process of putting two shots together to arrive at an effect different from what each shot would achieve on its own.

MOS Film or video footage intentionally shot without audio.

motion effect Any effect that adjust the speed of playback of a clip, such as speed ramps, slow-motion, and freeze frames. In Premiere, Motion is a fixed effect that includes Position and Scale.

motion blur When an object moves quickly, it will look blurrier. Individual frames of video or film show a certain amount of blur around moving objects, so it is often added or enhanced in post-production using visual effects.

motion graphics Text-based animation usually used as titles for film projects.

Motion Graphics Template See **MOGRT**.

MOV format A video and audio container file format created by Apple. See **QuickTime**.

MP3 format A lossy audio format commonly used for streaming delivery.

MP4 format A video and audio container file format that stores video encoded with the MPEG-4 codecs. See also **h.264**.

MPEG A lossy, high-quality family of codecs. MPEG-1 is used for the VCD format, MPEG-2 is used for DVD format video. MPEG-4 comes in two flavors: highly compressed Web video (MPEG-4 part 2) and high-quality HD video (MPEG-4 part 10).

multicam The process of shooting with two or more synchronized cameras, common in television and live events coverage.

multicam sequence A special type of nested sequence that contains multiple streams of synchronized video and behaves like a source clip.

multichannel In Premiere, a flexible audio track configuration that allows for an unlimited number of source tracks that can be routed into any number of output tracks.

mute A button that disables the sound from an audio track.

MXF Material Exchange Format, a type of digital media container file.

nesting The process of embedding a sequence within another sequence.

nits A unit used to measure the strength of a high dynamic range (HDR) video signal ranging from 0 (black) to 10,000 (white). In Premiere, a scale using nits is available in the Lumetri

Scopes panel when set to Waveform display and HDR video. Nits are roughly equivalent to IRE, meaning 100 IRE and 100 nits are about the same.

noise Unwanted data in a video or audio signal, often an artifact of signal processing such as gain boosting or compression. Video noise looks like rapidly moving pixels, or snow, and audio noise sounds like a hiss or hum.

non-linear editing system A digital editing system that uses a software interface and digitized audio and video stored on a hard drive. An NLE allows for random access, non-linearity, and non-destructive editing.

normalize A method of adjusting the gain of an audio clip by setting a target maximum (in decibels). In Premiere, an option found in the Audio Gain panel.

notch A special type of audio filter that can eliminate a specific, defined frequency of sound.

NTSC Analog video standard for North America and Japan, with a frame rate of 29.97fps.

offline Media that is not available when editing. Also may refer to media that is a low-resolution stand-in for higher-resolution media. See also **proxies**.

OMF (Open Media Framework) A format for audio-only exports used by sound editors.

online Media that is available when editing.

Opacity In Premiere, a fixed effect that controls transparency.

operating system The low-level program that controls the communication between all of the subsystems (storage, memory, video, peripherals, etc.) in your computer.

Optical Flow In Premiere Pro, an optional method of interpolating additional frames when changing the frame rate of a source clip. If frames need to be added, a special algorithm is used to create them that is optimized for shots with movement that do not have motion blur. See also **frame sampling**, **frame blending**.

orientation A way to describe the position of a rectangle derived from the tradition of European painting. Landscape orientation means the long side of the rectangle is positioned horizontally. Portrait orientation means that the long side of the rectangle is positioned vertically.

Out A marker that defines the end of a shot or sequence when editing.

out of sync indicators A graphic overlay in the Timeline that highlights any out of sync media with red text displaying the number of frames that it is out of sync.

output tracks Audio tracks that get sent from Premiere to either an exported media file, a set of speakers, headphones, or a device, such as a mixing board. Usually conforms to one of three mix options: stereo, 5.1 surround, or multichannel.

overbrights Bright whites or highlights in a shot that go over the recommended limit for white (usually 100 IRE).

overexposure Refers to video or film that was shot with too much light or the wrong camera settings, resulting in a whitish, washed-out, faded-looking image.

overlapping edit An edit where the picture ends before or after the sound ends. Also called an L-cut or a split-edit.

Overlay command In Premiere, an option for Drag and Drop editing that adds new material to the next available track, so that nothing is overwritten. See also **drop zones**.

oversaturated Color that is too intense for a monitor to display properly.

overscan All video formats scan more image than they need to compensate for the fact that not all monitors and televisions display images at exactly the same size. Overscan is a big problem with older analog monitors but also still a problem, although to a lesser degree, with HD monitors.

over-the-shoulder A medium-close shot of a person that includes the head and shoulders of the person talking to them in the foreground.

overwrite edit An editing command that adds media to a sequence and replaces anything in its path.

P2 card A proprietary solid state storage card used in certain Panasonic cameras.

PAL Analog video standard used in most of Europe and Asia, with a frame rate of 25 fps.

pan The process of shifting the balance of audio from right to left in a stereo mix, or across several channels in a surround sound mix.

panel In Adobe applications, a window.

panel settings menu In Premiere Pro, the menu available for every panel found at the right of the panel name.

parade A waveform view that shows the brightness of each color channel (usually red, green and blue) separately on the same display.

patching tracks The process of reassigning audio or video from one track to another.

PCM (Pulse Code Modulation) A process for encoding lossless digital audio. Used by high-end digital audio file formats such as WAVE and AIFF.

peak amplitude The maximum value of an audio signal. In Premiere, you can view the peak amplitude of an audio clip in the Gain panel.

peak files Media used by Premiere to enhance playback and performance. See also **media cache**.

pick-ups Media from a shoot that occurs after the principal shoot, often to add or improve scenes.

pixel Short for picture element. A single point on your screen.

pixel depth The number of pixels in an inch of screen space, measured in pixels per inch or ppi. Digital video has a pixel depth of 72 ppi and print photographs usually have a pixel depth of 300 ppi.

pillarboxing Black bars found at the sides of the screen to make a narrower image fit into a wider aspect ratio screen or video format. See also **letterboxing**.

pitch shifting An audio effect that raises or lowers the pitch of a sound. Often used to compensate for changes in the speed of an audio clip.

pixel dimensions The size of a digital still image or frame of video, as measured in pixels and described as width × height × depth. Also referred to as "resolution."

playback The ability for a computer to display digital video and audio without skipping frames or pausing.

playhead A blue cursor in the Timeline and other time rulers, that shows your location in a sequence or clip.

plugins Special effects packages that can be added to a host application.

Position In Premiere, a component of the Motion effect that controls placement.

posterization An effect created by using a limited amount of colors in an image. See also **banding**.

post-roll The process of extending video playback several seconds past an edit so that the viewer can take in the effect of the edit in context. See also **pre-roll**.

ppi Short for pixels per inch. See also **pixel depth**.

preferences Options that allow users to customize how an application performs. In Premiere, there are many preferences available.

pre-roll The process of starting video playback at a point several seconds prior to an edit so that the viewer can take in the effect of the edit in context. See also **post-roll**.

preset A saved set of parameters that can be reused as needed.

preview files Media that Premiere creates to help with the playback of certain shots, such as those with lots of effects applied to them. See also **render**.

primary colors The three basic colors in a color system, which can combine to make all other colors.

production sound Audio recorded during a shoot.

Program monitor Part of the Premiere Pro interface, a monitor that displays sequences in the Timeline as they play.

progressive scan A type of video display where each horizontal line is scanned consecutively from top to bottom, resulting in a full frame of video without the need for fields. Often abbreviated with the letter "p," as in "24p."

project The file that contains all the media, bins, and edited sequences for a film.

Project Manager A window in Premiere used to consolidate a project.

Project panel The main directory for a Premiere Pro project.

properties In Premiere, detailed information about a clip or sequence, including all of the media specifications such as frame rate, resolution, codec, and more. Accessed by right-clicking on a clip in a bin.

ProRes See **Apple ProRes**.

proxy A placeholder. Premiere can create a secondary set of low-resolution media and link it to any video clip in a project, so that you have a choice of playing and exporting both low and high-quality video. Used to improve playback for high-resolution video formats, such as 4K.

QuickTime A software architecture created by Apple for displaying and manipulating time-based media (such as video and audio) on a computer.

rack focus A shot where the focus is set on an object in the background, then the focus is pulled, or racked, to an object in the foreground (or vice versa).

radio cut An edit of a scene based on dialogue only, disregarding the video temporarily.

RAID Redundant Array of Independent Discs. A group of hard drives that have been arranged to act like a single, fast storage device.

RAM (Random Access Memory) The electronic memory inside a computer used to hold programs and data when working.

ramp See **interpolation**.

rasterization The process of taking a vector-based graphic or font and turning it into a bitmapped image.

Rate Stretch A tool in Premiere that changes the speed of a shot as you shorten or lengthen it.

raw media encoding A method of capturing media straight from the camera's sensor without image processing. Raw files are technically not actual video files and require post-production processing in order to view and edit them.

reaction A shot of a person reacting to the dialogue or action in a scene.

real-time A function, such as playback or recording, that occurs immediately without the need for rendering.

Rec. 2020 The international specification that defines UHD (ultra-high definition) video.

Rec. 2100 The international specification that defines HDR (high dynamic range) video.

Rec. 601 The international specification that defines SD (standard definition) video.

Rec. 709 The international specification that defines the HD video standard.

reels A way of breaking a feature film into segments of approximately 20 minutes in length. This process originated with analog film, which was limited by the amount of footage that could physically fit on a reel for a projector. Today, reels are still sometimes used for convenience during post-production.

Remove Attributes A command that resets the parameters of fixed effects in Premiere.

render The process of encoding video or audio media, either as a new, self-contained media file stored on a hard drive or as a temporary preview file in order to aid in real-time playback.

renderer The method of GPU acceleration used by Premiere to enhance playback speed and quality. Options available depend on your computer hardware (Open CL, Metal, CUDA, or software-only). See also **Mercury Playback Engine**.

Replace edit Editorial command that exactly replaces any clip in a sequence, matching its duration.

resize An effect that changes the scale of a video clip. In Premiere, resizing is part of the Motion effect.

RGB color space Three-channel color space based on the additive primary colors of red (R), green (G), and blue (B). Used by computer monitors, projectors, and some video codecs.

Ripple A tool in Premiere that adds or removes media from one side of an edit and the resulting changes ripple through the rest of the sequence, shortening or lengthening it accordingly.

Roll A tool in Premiere that lets you push an edit forwards or backwards in time, affecting both sides of the edit and limited by the extent of the media on either side of the edit.

rolling titles Text-based graphics in films that move across the screen, such as end credits.

room tone The sound of the room in which a scene was recorded. During a shoot, the sound recorder will record roughly one minute's worth of the quieted location to create an "empty" sound with the right atmosphere. This sound will be used by the dialogue editor to fill spaces between edits.

rotoscoping The process of painting over existing frames of video or film. Used for everything from painting in special effects to making custom mattes for compositing.

rough cut An early edit of a project, as opposed to a fine cut.

safe margins Area at the edge of a frame of video that is best avoided for titles, graphics, and important action. Usually the outer 10% of the frame.

saturated colors The technical term for bright, bold colors. For example, a pure red is saturated, while pink and maroon are desaturated reds.

saturation The amount of color in the video signal.

Scale In Premiere, a component of the Motion effect that controls the size of a video clip.

scanning method The way that a frame of video is displayed during playback. Can be interlaced (obsolete) or progressive. See also **fields**.

scratch disks Space on a hard drive used for temporary storage during the operation of software like Adobe Premiere and Photoshop.

scrubbing The process of dragging a mouse through an audio or video clip to monitor the media at a variable speed.

SD video (Standard Definition) Digital video with a resolution of 720 × 480 pixels or less.

seamless edit A style of editing where the edits appear natural and do not call attention to themselves. A traditional Hollywood movie dialogue scene is usually seamlessly edited.

secondary color correction The process of using a color mask to separate part of the video image and color grade it separately.

Selection tool The main cursor in Premiere Pro, displayed as an arrow or pointer.

sequence An assembly of shots edited together.

sequential stills Animation and graphics that are stored in folders of consecutive images, as opposed to single video clips.

shared projects Local network-based project sharing in Premiere. See also **team projects**.

sharpening An effect used to reduce blurriness or softness in an image.

shooting ratio The ratio of the length of footage shot to the length of the final film. For example, a project with a 5:1 ratio would have shot five hours of footage for a one-hour long final project.

signal Electronic information (video or audio) that is passed from one device to another.

signal clamping In Premiere, a checkbox at the bottom of the Lumetri Scopes panel that limits the display in waveform view to show only values from 0 to 100 IRE.

single A shot that shows only one person, often a closeup.

slating When recording the sound separately from the video or film, the process of clapping a slate in front of the camera to provide a sync point for post-production.

Slide A tool used in trimming to move a shot backwards or forwards in a sequence without changing the overall duration of the sequence.

Slip A tool used in trimming to adjust the contents of a shot without changing anything else in the sequence.

slow-motion A shot that plays at a slower speed than full-motion film or video. Usually described as a percentage of full motion. True slow-motion footage is acquired in the camera with a high frame rate, such as 60 fps, which results in high-quality motion as opposed to slow motion created by slowing down 24 fps video in post-production.

smart folders In Premiere, specialized search bins that automatically update as new media is added to the project.

SMPTE The Society of Motion Picture and Television Engineers, an organization that has developed many of the technical standards for film and video in the United States, including the IMF (Interoperable Media Format) specifications for 4K and UHD streaming delivery.

Snapping Mode that causes the cursor to stick to edits as you drag in the Timeline.

solo A button in the Timeline, Audio Clip Mixer, and Audio Track Mixer that tells Premiere to play only the audio from a single designated track in a sequence or clip.

sound design The process of building a sound track for a movie, by manipulating dialogue, sound effects, ambience, and music.

sound effects Audio clips added to a film to convey the sound of a specific element, such as explosions, door slams, horn honks, etc. See also **audio effects**.

Source monitor The monitor or window that displays unedited source footage, as opposed to the destination, or Program monitor, which plays the edited sequence.

spanned clip A clip that starts on one camera card and jumps continuously to the next card, only available with certain cameras. Spanned clips need to be correctly interpreted for Premiere by using the Media Browser to bring them into a project.

specular highlights Bright areas in video that result from reflections on shiny surfaces. HDR video allows for additional control over specular highlights when color grading.

speed ramp A motion effect that speeds up or slows down over time.

splice Any edit, but often specifically an edit added to a continuous piece of video, used to cut it in two.

split-track mix A hack that uses a stereo mix and pans the music to the right and all the other audio to the left so that the film can be viewed without the music. Used for guide exports given to composers, sound editors, etc. See also **stems**.

spotting Screening a locked-picture edit of a movie with the intent of identifying all of the sound effects and music cues that will be needed.

subtitles On-screen graphics used to translate dialogue from one language to another or to clarify hard to hear dialogue.

stems A set of sub-mixed tracks that add up to the full mix. For example, a music cue might have stems for vocals, different instruments, etc. See also **DM&E**.

stereo Audio with two channels or streams, balanced to the right and left to mimic the way that humans hear sound in real life.

storyboard The process of arranging shots or images in order of a story. A tool to help build early cuts of films.

straight cut A cut across all tracks in a clip or sequence.

streaming video Video that is downloaded, on-demand and in real time, to the viewer's computer.

subtractive color A color system used by ink and paint where the more colors you mix together, the darker they get until you get black. The primary colors of paint are red, yellow, and blue. The primary colors of modern printing inks are cyan, yellow, and magenta.

surround sound 5.1 or 7.1 channel audio that mimics the sound of a three-dimensional environment.

sweetening The process of polishing the audio on a project by adding effects, equalizing, and fine-tuning edits.

switching In multicam editing, the process of jumping from one camera to another.

synchronizing The process of aligning audio and video media so that they play in tandem.

sync pop See **2-pop**.

tails The end of a film, reel, or shot. For example, a tail slate is a slate clap at the end of a take. See also **heads**.

team projects Internet-based project sharing for Premiere that uses Adobe Creative Cloud media storage. Requires an extra subscription, Adobe Creative Cloud for Teams.

temp mix The mix created during the rough cut stage of editing a movie, before it is handed over to the sound editor. See also **mix**.

test pattern See **bars and tone**.

Text effect In Premiere, text created with the Type tool is considered an effect, rather than a clip, and is edited in the Effect Controls panel or the Essential Graphics panel.

textless master A master file of a film that has no titles or any other text in it. Used for foreign language versions.

three-act structure A type of story structure based on the idea that each story has a beginning, middle, and end.

three-point editing A way of editing that uses three markers to define the start and end of a source clip and where it will be added to a sequence. See also **In**, **Out.**

three-way color wheels A trio of color controls that allow for the adjustment of shadows, midtones, and highlights. In Premiere, found in the Lumetri Color panel.

through-edits See **splice**.

thumbnails Small images used to identify each shot in a bin or the Timeline, usually the first frame of the shot or the frame where an In point is set.

time base See **fps**.

timecode A numbering system that measures time in a media clip. Timecode notation uses the format hh:mm:ss:ff, where h = hours, m = minutes, s = seconds, and f = frames.

timecode generator A device used during a shoot to set the timecode for all the devices that are recording.

timeline A chronological display of an edited sequence in a non-linear editing system.

Timeline panel The primary editing window in Premiere that contains the edited sequence.

time remapping In Premiere, a fixed effect that allows for the manipulation of time in a shot.

time ruler An interface for scrolling through a shot or sequence, found in many panels in Premiere.

titles Text-based on-screen graphics that provide an additional layer of information about a film, such as who worked on it, its name, key locations, and so on.

title safe A guide to make sure titles are not cropped. To ensure that your titles are visible on any monitor, always make certain that they fall within the title-safe area, which usually means avoiding the outer 10% of the frame.

toggle Buttons in Premiere that turn various functions on and off. See also **Linked Selection, Snapping.**

tone Sixty-cycle tone, or 60Hz tone, is used as an audio reference to calibrate the audio levels on editing equipment and speakers. Typically, the 60Hz tone should fall at 0dB on a VU meter. See also **bars and tone**.

Tools panel A window in Premiere that contains a selection of editorial tools such as Ripple, Roll, Slip, and Slide.

tool tips Text labels for various elements in the Premiere Pro interface that appear when you hover over them with the mouse. Must be turned on in the General Preferences panel.

top and tail A method of ripple trimming based on the keyboard shortcuts W and Q.

track A single, chronological stream of audio or video. Also, single stream components of the Timeline panel in Premiere. See also **channel**.

track locks Buttons in the Timeline header for each track that prohibit changes to that track when activated.

Track Select Forward A tool in Premiere that will select all of the media going forward from any point in the Timeline.

track selectors Buttons in the Timeline header for each track, used to define the destination for audio and video tracks as they are edited from a source clip into a sequence. See also **patching tracks**.

transcoding The process of taking a digital media file and re-encoding it with a different codec.

transition In film, any segue from scene to scene or shot to shot. In Premiere Pro, an effect that spans the edit from one clip to another in a sequence. See also **dissolve**.

transfer mode A calculation used to determine how layers in a digital image will combine together.

transparency See **alpha channel.**

transparency grid In Adobe applications, a view that shows the transparent background of graphics and media with alpha channels as a grey and white checkerboard pattern.

traveling matte In digital video, a stencil that changes to track the motion of a subject over time.

trim mode A special interface for adjusting, or fine-tuning, an existing edit in Premiere

trimming The process of whittling down a rough cut. In Premiere, trim tools include Trim, Ripple, Roll, Slip, Slide, and Trim mode.

TRT Short for Total Run Time. Often listed on the head slate of a film. See also **duration**.

TV pilot The first installment of a series, often used to sell the series to a distributor.

two-shot A shot that shows two people in the frame.

Type tool In Premiere, a tool used to create text-based graphics.

Ultra High Definition (UHD) A designation for video that has a resolution greater than that of HD. Often used to refer specifically to video with the dimensions of 3840 x 2160 pixels.

uncompressed Video or audio that has not had any compression applied to it or that is encoded with an uncompressed codec.

undo Command to remove the last action performed. In Premiere, you can remove up to 100 actions.

unique identifier A number assigned to a file by the operating system or an application to distinguish it from other files.

universal countdown leader The classic 8-second film countdown used to help insure that a film is in sync.

Unlink See **Link/Unlink**.

unscripted Any project that is created without a script, such as documentaries, reality television, and improvisation.

vector graphics Line or shape-based graphics and illustrations valued for their small file sizes and infinite scalability.

vectorscope A special display used to calibrate the hue and saturation in a video signal.

verité A style of shooting, often handheld, where the camera follows the action in a scene or event without stopping and starting. Originated as a documentary technique but often used in narrative filmmaking as well.

video previews In Premiere, files used to improve playback during editing. In earlier versions of Premiere, video and audio previews were called renders.

vignetting An effect that darkens the edges of a frame of video.

virtual memory A process by which disk space can be used as a substitute for RAM.

virtual reality (VR) In digital video, a spherical video that the viewer can rotate and spin to look in all directions. See also **360-degree video**.

visual effects Video imagery that is manipulated or created in post-production.

voice-over Narration that is audio-only (as opposed to audio from interviews or on-camera hosts).

VR See **virtual reality**.

walla Audio of a group of people talking, used as ambience in films.

Warp Stabilizer An effect in Premiere that uses distortion to stabilize media.

watermark A transparent graphic overlay. Often used to identify the copyright owner of a film in order to protect it from piracy.

WAV An uncompressed, PCM-based audio file format. See also **AIFF**.

waveform A visual display for sound or components of a digital video signal (luminance, color channels).

waveform monitor A display for calibrating the brightness, or luminance, of a video signal. Waveform monitors are used to define the proper white and black levels.

white balance The process of defining what is white in a shot or scene, either on the set or in post-production via color correction software such as Premiere's Lumetri Color effect.

white level The peak level of the luminance (or grayscale) of the video signal; in other words, the brightest part of the image, usually set at 100 IRE.

widescreen Footage that's shot with a 16:9 aspect ratio (or wider). Most film features are shot in a widescreen aspect ratio.

wide shot A shot that shows the full geography of a scene, whether interior or exterior.

wild lines Dialogue recorded as audio-only, without accompanying video.

Windows Media Video (WMV) A video container file format and set of codecs developed by Microsoft for use in the Windows operating system.

workspace A group of interface layout presets in Premiere dedicated to various tasks such as editing, audio, graphics, and so on.

XML (Extensible Markup Language) A format used to share multimedia files between different applications. Often used to share projects between Premiere Pro and Apple Final Cut Pro.

XMP (Extensible Media Platform) A digital file format created by Adobe to save text-based metadata. XMP metadata can be added to a digital video file or saved in a separate XMP sidecar file.

XMP ID A unique number that identifies a file and can be saved in metadata so that Premiere can recognize that file going forward. See also **unique identifier**.

YCbCr The color space for some digital video codecs, abbreviated in Premiere and elsewhere as YUV. In YCbCr, the three channels that make up the video image are divided into luminance (Y) and two color difference channels (Cb and Cr).

YUV Three-channel analog color space consisting of luma (Y) and two color difference channels (U and V). See also **YCbCr**.

YUV effects A class of visual effects in Premiere that work within the YCbCr color space.

zoom bar At the bottom of the Timeline, a slider that adjusts the magnification of view. Also available in the keyframe mapping area of the Effect Controls panel, and at the bottom of the Source and Program monitors.

Zoom A tool in Premiere that increases or decreases the magnification of the view in the Timeline.

Index

B

D

E

F

G

H

I

J

K

L

M

N

O

P

Q

R

S

T

U

V

W

X

Y

Z

Made in the USA
Middletown, DE
10 December 2020